RAY G. JONES, JR.
DEAN DUDLEY

Appalachian State University

Finance

Prentice-Hall, Inc., Englewood Cliffs, New Jersey 07632

Library of Congress Cataloging in Publication Data

Jones, Ray G
   Essentials of finance.

   Includes index.
   1. Finance. 2. Corporations—Finance. 3. Business
enterprises—Finance. I. Dudley, Dean A., joint author.
II. Title.
HG153.J66   658.1'5   77-7898
ISBN 0-13-286088-0

Essentials of Finance

RAY G. JONES, JR. / DEAN DUDLEY

Printed in the United States of America

10 9 8 7 6 5 4 3 2

Prentice-Hall International, Inc., *London*
Prentice-Hall of Australia Pty. Limited, *Sydney*
Prentice-Hall of Canada, Ltd., *Toronto*
Prentice-Hall of India Private Limited, *New Delhi*
Prentice-Hall of Japan, Inc., *Tokyo*
Prentice-Hall of Southeast Asia Pte. Ltd., *Singapore*
Whitehall Books Limited, *Wellington, New Zealand*

Contents

THE VALUE OF MONEY   33

THE IMPACT OF RISK   58

THE IMPACT OF CYCLES   80

Financial Management   95

FUNCTIONS OF FINANCIAL MANAGEMENT   97

TOOLS OF FINANCIAL MANAGEMENT   110

THE MANAGEMENT OF
CASH AND MARKETABLE SECURITIES   138

THE MANAGEMENT OF
RECEIVABLES AND INVENTORIES   160

SHORT-TERM FINANCING   179

Financial Markets 389

AN OVERVIEW OF FINANCIAL MARKETS 391

What Is a Market? *392* The Savings-Investment Process *393*
Claims on Capital Accumulations *397*
Financial Intermediaries: A Special Case *400*
Legal Characteristics of Financial Claims *402*
Maturity Characteristics of Financial Claims *404*
Financial Markets and Economic Efficiency *405* Summary *409*

PROBLEMS 409

PRICES IN FINANCIAL MARKETS 410

Indexes of Satisfied Demand *411* Prices in Financial Markets *413*
Prices of Individual Securities *417*
Rates of Return on Individual Securities *422*
The Term Structure of Interest Rates *427* Summary *431*

APPENDIX TO CHAPTER 20:
Asset Pricing under CAPM 431

PROBLEMS 433

FINANCIAL MARKETS: MONEY MARKETS (SHORT-TERM OBLIGATIONS) 435

The Need for the Money Market *436* Money-Market Transactions *436*
Money-Market Instruments *439* The Structure of Money-Market Ratios *447*
The Role of the Federal Reserve in Money Markets *449*
The Role of the U.S. Treasury in Money Markets *451* Summary *451*

PROBLEMS 452

FINANCIAL MARKETS: CAPITAL MARKETS (LONG-TERM OBLIGATIONS) 454

The Savings-Investment Relationship *455*
The Ground Rules for Capital Markets: The Two Basic Acts *456*
The Primary Market *457* The Secondary Market *462*
The Issue of Efficient Markets *471* Summary *472*

PROBLEMS 472

Preface

Finance is the study of the issuance, distribution, and purchase of financial claims. The *raison d'etre* for ESSENTIALS OF FINANCE is to provide a book that integrates the field under the broad topics of financial management, financial markets, and financial investments. Traditionally, the first course in finance dealt exclusively with financial management, or corporation finance. We recognize that corporation finance is the cornerstone, and as the cornerstone it is covered in chapters 2, 3, 4, 6–13, 16, 17, 20, 21, and 22. This book provides an alternative for those who prefer a broader scope in the first course.

Topics that are essential to an understanding of the field of finance (taxes, time value of money, risk and cycles) are introduced early in the text. These topics cut across all the areas of finance and are woven into the treatment of financial management, financial markets, and financial investments. The application of sound financial decisions rules in all fields of finance is found throughout the book. The consideration of risk in specific decisions is presented consistent with the most recent developments in capital market theory.

DISTINGUISHING FEATURES

The title, ESSENTIALS OF FINANCE, is an accurate representation of the book's contents in that the essentials of each field of finance have been included to allow the instructor to choose the areas of finance best suited to his needs and his course. This treatment of the essentials provides a foundation for additional study.

We have found that allowing the student to view the entire field of finance has created an interest in it that we have never seen. We have observed students returning to take additional course work in finance as a direct result of having had their intellectual appetites whetted through the use of this approach.

This book "demystifies" finance. The discipline has much intuitive appeal and contains great internal beauty and symmetry. For some years, we have felt that these characteristics have not been apparent in the textual literature. This book fills the void.

PEDAGOGICAL COMMENTS

We follow financial investments with financial markets. However, the market chapters may precede either the investment chapters or the financial management chapters. The book has been written so that the user may proceed according to his preferences.

The manuscript has been class tested. Not all of the material can be covered in one semester. We recommend that the instructor select pertinent portions from financial management, investments, and markets in the one-semester course. We have found this to be a good way of stimulating student interest and response.

The problems have been carefully class tested. We recommend that all problems be used. They are closely keyed to chapter material.

Finance has been slow to adopt new terms. We have endeavored to use current terminology throughout. For example, we use statement of financial position (position statement), statement of earnings (earnings statement), and owners' equity in place of the older terms balance sheet, income statement, and net worth. The Accounting Principles Board Statement Number 4 suggests that the current terminology mentioned above is more descriptive than that previously used.

ACKNOWLEDGMENTS

We are grateful to a number of colleagues who have made specific comments on the text. Their detailed reviews and suggestions have improved the quality of the book. In particular, we are grateful to Professors Sheldon Balbirer, University of North Carolina at Greensboro; Ronald Charvonia, Glendale Community College; David T. Crary, Louisiana State University; Eugene F.

Drzycimski, University of Wisconsin at Oshkosh; George B. Flanigan, University of North Carolina at Greensboro; J. R. Longstreet, University of South Florida at Tampa; Thomas J. McKenna, Fresno City College; David F. Scott, Jr., Texas Tech University; Sol Shalit, University of Wisconsin at Milwaukee; Thomas E. Stitzel, Boise State University; and Larry Trussell, University of Nebraska.

We owe special thanks to Professor Charles A. D'Ambrosio of the University of Washington (another Prentice-Hall author) for his comments and encouragement in the early stages of the preparation of this book. In view of his international reputation as a scholar in finance, we are deeply indebted to him.

We are indebted to the Prentice-Hall staff—specifically to Susan Anderson and Paul McKenney—for their efforts on our behalf. Susan encouraged us from the inception of our idea for the book and guided us in the preparation of the manuscript. Paul editorially supervised the turning of the manuscript into the bound volume. We are grateful to both of them.

We wish to express appreciation to our wives, Anneliese Jones and Lenore Dudley. They have first claim on our lives, but unfortunately for 18 months they have not had first claim on our time. We appreciate their understanding and encouragement.

RAY G. JONES, JR.
DEAN DUDLEY

Essentials
of Finance

The Environment of Finance

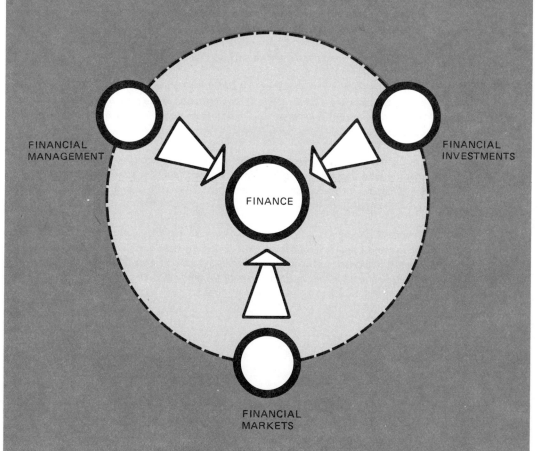

FINANCIAL
MANAGEMENT

FINANCIAL
INVESTMENTS

FINANCE

FINANCIAL
MARKETS

This part of the book introduces the topics that are common to the entire field of finance. The topics included in this section have an impact on all financial decisions. The financial manager, the financial investor, and the dealer in financial markets are all concerned with taxes, the value of money, risk, and economic cycles of good times and bad times. Thus, the title of Part I, "The Environment of Finance."

Although no specific chapter on asset pricing is included in this section, it is recognized as a unifying theme of finance. The capital asset pricing model is first discussed in Chapter 1. It is used in the later sections of the book to show how assets are valued by the financial manager (Part II), how portfolios are constructed by the financial investor (Part III), and how prices are determined in the financial markets (Part IV).

We turn now to the specific chapters in this section of the book. Chapter 1 treats early the rules the student of finance will need throughout the course. The relationship between finance and other disciplines is shown graphically. In addition, some principles of finance are introduced in this chapter that are applicable to the entire field of finance.

In Chapter 2, the impact of taxes on financial decisions is examined. Emphasis is placed on delaying both the taxable event and the payment of the tax. Any legal delay in payment of a tax is an interest-free loan by the government to the taxpayer. If the delay extends for a period of years, the interest savings is substantial.

Chapter 3 discusses the value of money. Both the time value of money and the purchasing power of money are examined. Finally, an illustration of the combined effects of "time is money" and of the "value of money" helps internalize the distinction between the two concepts.

The impact of risk is covered in Chapter 4. It has been said (good-naturedly, we hope) that the most important word in finance ends with a K. The chapter attempts to explain the difference between risk and uncertainty. Standard deviation is used as a general measure of risk.

Chapter 5 introduces a review of economic cycles and their application to decision making in the major areas of finance. Most financial practitioners and academicians appreciate the importance of cycle theory and its impact on financial decisions, and therefore the discipline of finance must incorporate the study of cycles.

The Focus of Finance

The purpose of this book is to present clearly and accurately the essentials of finance—those principles that will be of lasting value not only to finance students but to all students.

Much activity exists today in finance in determining the proper approach to the subject. Most texts still cling to the traditional approach, which is corporation finance. Some texts are approaching finance from the viewpoint of capital markets. It is our contention that a more diversified approach is best. We identify the main areas of finance as financial management, financial investments, and financial markets, and we believe strongly that an introductory course in finance should delineate the three fields.

To understand what is causing a proliferation of approaches to basic finance, we turn first to the evolution of finance. We believe that a historical perspective aids in understanding the current controversy as to what is the best approach to the first course of study in finance.

The study of finance is applied microeconomic theory and thus a subdivision of economics. As a separate discipline, it is of fairly recent origin. It was during the 1890s that finance first emerged as a separate field of study. At first, it emphasized investment banking, merger and consolidation, and various types of corporate securities. The critical problem facing business firms in the early 1900s was that of obtaining capital. Thus, the traditional approach to finance was concerned primarily with the acquisition of funds. The first text in finance was Greene's *Corporation Finance*.* Probably the most scholarly treatment of the traditional concept of finance is found in Dewing's *Financial Policy of Corporations*.†

The focus of finance shifted from the perspective of the outsider to that of the insider beginning in the 1920s. This concept is known as the managerial approach. It is concerned with not only the acquisition but the application and conservation of funds. The managerial approach was slow to gain acceptance. Probably Hunt and Williams's *Case Problems in Finance* helped establish the managerial approach.‡

In the late 1950s, emphasis began to shift from the descriptive to the quantitative. The decision-making approach was reinforced with the advent of the computer. The analytical trend continues with various quantitative models developed that give a range of optimal solutions to financial problems.

During the 1960s and 1970s, the decision-making approach to business finance prevailed. Less emphasis was placed on the descriptive approach and more emphasis was given to the analytical approach in the area of financial markets and financial investment. The latter two were studied within the context of corporate financial decisions.

---

*Thomas L. Greene, *Corporation Finance* (New York: Putnam's, 1897).

†Arthur S. Dewing, *The Financial Policy of Corporations* (New York: Ronald Press, 1920).

‡Pearson Hunt and Charles M. Williams, *Case Problems in Finance* (Homewood, Ill.: Richard D. Irwin, 1940).

4

DEFINITION OF FINANCE

The word "finance" comes indirectly from the Latin word *finis*. Under Roman law, a contract was not completed until there was a binding agreement for monetary or credit arrangements. Finance is defined as the issuance of, the distribution of, and the purchase of liability and equity claims issued for the purpose of generating revenue-producing assets. These claims are commonly referred to as financial claims.

The suppliers of financial claims are business firms and government units. It is incumbent upon these suppliers to use the funds efficiently in order to render a fair return to the holders of the claims. Implicit in this is the administration and conservation of funds by financial management.

Financial investors are the demanders of financial claims. They supply the funds to firms and government units in exchange for financial claims, in the expectation of receiving the going rate of return on their investments.

Financial claims are traded in financial markets. Such markets consist of both money and capital markets. In the former, short-term credit investments are bought and sold. In the latter, long-term credit and equity claims are bought and sold.

RELATIONSHIP BETWEEN FINANCE AND OTHER DISCIPLINES

Finance is often viewed as having inputs from four disciplines. The relationship is depicted in Figure 1.1. First, finance is considered the brightest jewel in the crown of *economics*. It is grounded in the economic theory of optimality and the microeconomic theory of the firm. Economics, then, provides the theoretical framework for finance and, thus, many of the decision rules.

Finance is concerned with *management* because of the managing of financial resources and the behavioral ramifications of financial decisions. The financial manager manages the assets of the firm; the financial investor manages his portfolio of securities; and the allocation process takes place through financial markets. Behavioral aspects of financial decisions are manifest in all areas of finance. For example, the psychology of mass emotions in the marketplace affects and governs financial decisions by all the market participants.

Finance has relied greatly upon *accounting* for years. Without good financial reporting, financial analysis is difficult. Conversely, good financial reporting is necessary for both the financial manager and the financial inves-

FIGURE 1.1 Relationship between Finance and Other Disciplines.

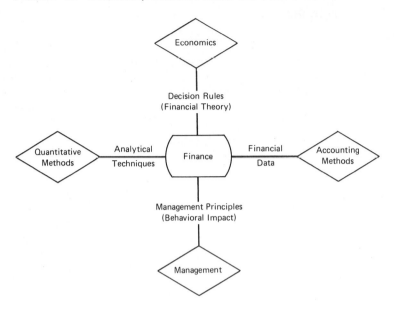

tor. Accounting provides the sources of data for financial decisions. It is the basis for good financial analysis.

In recent years, finance has drawn heavily upon *quantitative methods*. Various models and analytical techniques have been developed for financial management, financial investments, and financial markets. For example, statistical and mathematical programming models have been developed for the three areas of finance. Finance has always been concerned with numbers. Thus, quantitative analysis has become rather commonplace in the field of finance as an analytical tool for financial decisions.

SOME PRINCIPLES OF FINANCE

Although finance has three distinct subdivisions, there are some principles that are common to all the fields. In this section we will review a number of these principles. The list is not meant to be exhaustive; however, it is representative. It shows that all the principles apply equally to participants in financial management, financial investments, and financial markets.

Risk Return Tradeoff　　The first of these principles is known as the *risk–return tradeoff*. It says that in any financial decision, the risk (the variability of returns) must be commensurate with the expected return (the average return). For example, the financial manager is always concerned with whether the return on assets is worth the risk of acquiring them. The securities dealer attempts to balance risk with return. Likewise, the financial investor chooses securities based on their risk–return relationship. Thus, the world of finance is one of a tradeoff between risk and expected return. This principle is used as the frame of reference throughout this book. It is depicted in Figure 1.2.

FIGURE 1.2 Risk–Return Tradeoff.

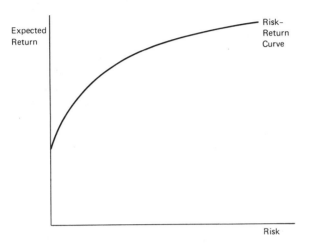

It should be noted here that most financial decisions are made under conditions of risk and uncertainty, because business conditions are such that the future cannot be known. Thus, the financial manger, the financial investor, and the financial-market dealers must make decisions based on risk and uncertainty.

Time Value of Money   The principle of the *time value of money* is central to finance and applies to all the major fields. Financial decisions are based on discounted cash-flow values. That is, a stream of future cash flows is reduced by an interest factor in order to determine the present value of the cash flows.

Maximization of Wealth   The *maximization of wealth* means that the financial manager operates the firm in such a way as to maximize the stockholders' wealth; the financial investor makes decisions that maximize his wealth in the selection of financial claims; and the financial dealer maximizes his wealth by making a market for financial claims. Basically, wealth is maximized by the process of buying low and selling high.

Suitability   The principle known as *suitability* involves financing short-term assets with short-term funds and long-term assets with long-term funds. This is because the assets in which funds are invested should not have a longer life than the financial claims that were issued for the funds. For example, financial managers and financial investors who use short-term money for long-term investments are violating the principle of suitability. In the event that cash is not generated by the investment before the short-term borrowing matures, one must seek to either renew the loan or locate alternate sources of funds. Whenever refinancing of short-term liabilities is not possible, the borrower may be forced to liquidate assets. See the E.T. Barwick case in Chapter 6 for an illustration of the principle of suitability.*

Liquidity vs.   A fifth principle of finance is *liquidity versus profitability*. Profitability is
Profitability   how much one hopes to make. It is the opposite of liquidity, which is how readily one can convert assets back to cash. This principle holds true whether the decision concerns the firm's assets, the investor's portfolio of securities, or the securities dealer's inventory of stocks and bonds. Refer to the case on Coca-Cola in Chapter 6 for an illustration of this principle.

Financial Cycles   *Financial cycles* are business fluctuations that affect everyone. Thus, financial decisions made by all participants should include the effects of the business cycle on their decisions. For example, the yield curve used in financial markets is a graph of expectations about the future. The shape of the curve is affected by the business cycle.

Magnifying Effect   Another principle is that financial *leverage magnifies profits as well as*
of Leverage   *losses*. Again, this holds true for all participants—the financial manager who uses debt to finance assets, the investor who uses debt to finance the purchase of securities, and the securities dealer who uses debt to finance his inventory of stocks. The use of financial leverage is like a double-edged sword; that is, it can cut two ways. It can magnify profits if things go as planned, or magnify losses if adversity occurs.

Efficient   The principle *efficient diversification* holds that bundles of assets should
Diversification   be combined to mitigate unsystematic risk. Too much or too little of any one asset can be detrimental. In other words, there is a middle course (an efficient portfolio) for which the prudent decision maker strives. For example, the financial manager is faced with such problems as the proper mix

---

*It should be noted that financial intermediaries must violate this principle. The reason is that most firms and individuals prefer to borrow for long periods and lend for short periods. Thus, the necessity for the process of financial intermediation (lending—investing—long and borrowing short).

of assets and of claims on assets. The financial investor is faced with the question of what securities to select and in what proportion in order to reduce risk for the same return. And the financial dealer is confronted with the pricing of assets in financial markets.

CAPITAL-MARKET THEORY

During the past few years, the development of portfolio theory has decompartmentalized the field of finance. Although it has always been desirable, it is now possible to use portfolio theory to examine asset expansion decisions, the expected return on bundles of assets (portfolios), and the pricing of assets. All are variations of market equilibrium models under risk. Thus, such models measure the value of assets for financial management, investment returns for financial investments, and prices in financial markets. All this stems from portfolio theory, which constitutes the theoretical underpinning of finance.

The last principle is a form of the capital asset pricing model, which is discussed and applied in each of the sections on financial management, financial investments, and financial markets. The basic premise involves getting the highest expected return for a given level of risk, or getting a given expected return at the least possible risk. Thus, if markets are efficient, the rates of return on assets are proportionate to risks taken.

The important thing to realize at this point is that the market is seen in the capital asset pricing model (CAPM) as the ultimate limit of efficient diversification. Such diversification can be obtained in a portfolio of risky investments. The market is, in a sense, the optimal risky portfolio, and therefore, market risk cannot be further reduced through additional diversification. CAPM is concerned with asset choice, the factors that must be considered in selecting assets, and the riskiness of such assets. Thus, capital asset pricing is a unifying theme of finance that integrates financial management, financial investments, and financial markets.

ORGANIZATION OF THE BOOK

Finance is a viable, changing discipline. As a result of the changes taking place, financial textbooks are constantly being restructured. Here, we depart from the traditional texts in a number of ways. Such departures are purposeful and we consider them to be significant. The primary reason for this text is to present the three broad areas of finance (financial management, financial investment, and financial markets) in a lucid and interesting fashion. This is a major departure from the traditional textbook in finance, but we have found that such an approach gives the reader a much better understanding and appreciation of the fields of finance.

The organization of this book reflects our own experience as well as that of others who have guided our efforts. The book is organized into five parts:

    I. The Environment of Finance

   II. Financial Management

 III. Financial Investments

 IV. Financial Markets

  V. Emerging Areas in Finance

Part I:
The Environment
of Finance

Part I consists of five chapters. Some principles of finance are presented in Chapter 1. Chapters 2, 3, 4, and 5 deal with subjects that permeate the entire field of finance: the impact of taxes, the value of money, the the impact of risk, and the impact of cycles on financial decisions. Organizationally, these subjects are treated early because of their importance to the three fields of finance—a significant change. More important, cycles are treated in a separate chapter. We feel that finance must address itself eventually to the role that cycles play (or should play) in financial decisions.

Part II: Financial
Management

Eight chapters are devoted to the basics of financial management. These include the function of the financial manager, tools of analysis, cash and working-capital management, decisions involving long-term assets, the cost of capital, and financial structure and valuation. A section in Chapter 13 presents the capital asset pricing model, with practical applications for the businessman. The customary sources and forms of long-term corporate financing are deferred until Part III, and the marketing of financial claims until Part IV.

Part III: Financial
Investments

Part III consists of five chapters covering the basics of investing. Types of accounts, margin trading, and investor information are presented in Chapter 14. Chapters 15 through 17 cover the spectrum of marketable securities on the risk–return curve. Chapter 18 discusses the approaches to investing, both traditional and modern. An appendix at the end of Chapter 18 illustrates the use of the beta estimate and how it is derived.

Part IV: Financial
Markets

The financial-markets section consists of five chapters. Here the basic aspects of financial claims are examined. Topics covered are the money market and its instruments, the capital market and its instruments, and the federal regulations in financial markets. In addition, the transactors in financial markets are identified and discussed in some detail. The importance of the savings–investment process and the corollary of efficient markets are presented.

Part V: Emerging Areas in Finance   This part consists of five chapters. Chapter 24 discusses small-business finance, which is beginning to appear in finance curricula. Likewise, another latecomer in the discipline is the area of international finance, the subject of Chapter 25. Chapter 26 integrates the three fields of finance. Then, in the last chapter, we examine some future trends in finance that are on the horizon—some already in the making, others perhaps more remote from the viewpoint of today. Most of the topics in Part V are emerging as significant areas in finance.

2

The Impact of Taxes on Financial Decisions

It has been suggested that the federal government has a stake in every business firm in the country. The stake is federal taxes, primarily income taxes. Given the advent of relatively heavy taxation at the federal level as well as at state and local levels, taxes have become an important consideration in financial decision making. For that reason, the purpose of this chapter is not to turn you into a tax expert but rather to acquaint you with major provisions of individual and corporate income tax requirements at the federal level. Since income taxes are the major source of tax revenues, we shall focus on them.

A BRIEF HISTORY OF FEDERAL INCOME TAXES

The first income tax at the federal level was legislated in July 1862 to assist in financing the Civil War. The law provided for the progressive taxation of incomes and the withholding of taxes. It also created the agency that preceded the Internal Revenue Service. The prosperity of the 1870s permitted the repeal of the war-born income tax.

The need for increased federal revenues in the 1890s brought about attempts to reinstate the federal income tax. These were met with constitutional challenges. The Supreme Court twice overturned income tax legislation that violated the constitutional provision against direct taxation without direct apportionment among the states. The Sixteenth Amendment, passed by Congress in 1909 to permit federal income taxes, was finally ratified in 1913 by three-fourths of the states. The first income tax, in 1913, was 1 percent of net income up to $50,000, scaled upward to a maximum of 6 percent of net incomes of $500,000 or more. Rates have been repeatedly raised, of course, since then.

IMPORTANCE OF INCOME TAXES

The largest single source of tax revenue for the federal government is the income tax. Of all income taxes collected, about three quarters come from individuals and one quarter from corporations. Table 2.1 bears this out,

TABLE 2.1 Net Individual and Net Corporate Income Tax Collections, Fiscal Years 1970–75 (dollars in millions)

FISCAL YEAR	NET INDIVIDUAL INCOME TAX	% OF TOTAL	NET CORPORATE INCOME TAX	% OF TOTAL	TOTAL
1970	$ 90,142	73	$32,879	27	$123,021
1971	86,230	76	26,785	24	113,015
1972	94,737	75	31,536	25	126,273
1973	103,246	74	36,152	26	139,398
1974	118,952	75	38,619	25	157,571
1975	122,386	75	40,622	25	163,008

Source: *Federal Reserve Bulletin.*

showing the six fiscal years* from 1970 through 1975. Thus, individuals are the most important source of income taxes, and income taxes are the most important source of tax revenues.

INDIVIDUAL INCOME TAXES

Individual income taxes are levied upon the incomes of human beings, as opposed to corporations. Although they are frequently referred to as personal income taxes, they are more correctly designated as individual income taxes, as in the official literature of the Internal Revenue Service.

Taxable Income   Generally, all income received in the form of wages, salaries, and other cash inflows is reportable as income for tax purposes. Specifically included are directors' fees, jury-duty fees, executor fees, alimony payments, commissions, tips, and gambling winnings.† If a taxpayer is in doubt about the reportability of an inflow, he should consult the Internal Revenue Service.

Calculation of Tax   The basic method of calculating one's income tax is not complex. The method involves summing income from all sources, and adjusting this gross income with such items as employee business expense and individual contributions to qualified retirement funds. The result is adjusted gross income. To arrive at taxable income, deductions and personal exemptions are subtracted from adjusted gross income. Taxable income is then used as the base for calculating tax liability. From the tax liability, a personal tax credit is deducted—in 1977, $35 a person, or 2 percent of the first $9,000 of taxable income, whichever is greater.

These relationships are shown in Figure 2.1, the tax schematic for individual income taxes.

Deductions   Many expenses incurred by the taxpayer are deductible from adjusted gross income to reduce his tax base. Categories of deductible items are medical expenses, taxes, interest, contributions, casualty or theft loss(es) and miscellaneous. All these are subject to limitations, but in years in which taxpayers sustain heavy expenses in the permissible areas, they may substantially reduce their tax liability by itemizing deductions.

---

*The fiscal year of the federal government runs from October 1 to the following September 30. It is designated by the calendar year in which it ends.

†Gambling losses may be deducted, but only up to the amount of net winnings.

FIGURE 2.1 The Tax Schematic. (*Source: Prentice-Hall Tax Service.*)

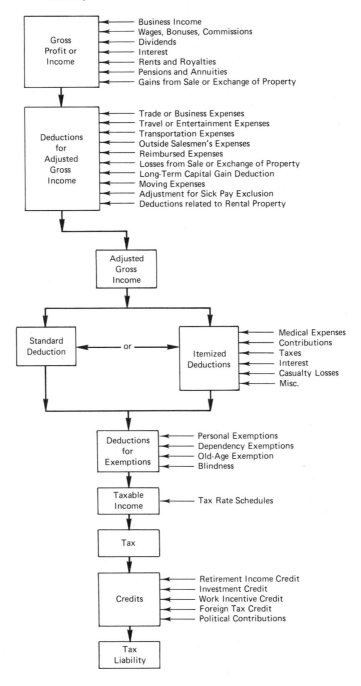

For the taxpayer who does not desire to itemize deductions, the standard deduction may be taken. The standard deduction is equal to 16 percent of adjusted gross income, not to exceed $2400 for a single person, or $2800 for a married couple filing a joint return. The standard or itemized deduction is the first amount to be subtracted from adjusted gross income; the second and final reduction of adjusted gross income is the personal exemption.

Personal Exemptions The individual taxpayer may reduce his adjusted gross income by $750 for each dependent in his household, including himself. Blind taxpayers and those 65 or older are permitted to take two exemptions—that is, $1,500.

After the standard or itemized deduction and personal exemptions are subtracted from adjusted gross income, the result is the taxable income. The next step is the calculation of the tax liability.

Bases of Tax Rates There are five categories into which tax returns are divided, each with its own tax-rate schedule. Taxpayers with adjusted gross incomes of less than $15,000 who elect to take the standard deduction form one group. The others are single taxpayers, married taxpayers filing joint returns, married taxpayers filing separate returns, and unmarried taxpayers who qualify as heads of households. Those falling into these latter four categories may itemize deductions.

The 1977 tax rate schedules and the first page of Tax Tables A, B, C, and D are reproduced in Figure 2.2. Note that the schedules portray a *graduated* or *progressive tax*, one whose rate increases more rapidly than its base.

Capital Gains Capital gains and losses result from the sale of assets held for investment, or for personal purposes. A long-term capital gain is one sustained on an asset held for more than twelve months. Short-term capital gains result from the sale of assets held for twelve months or less.* Net capital gains are calculated in the following way:

1. Long-term gains are netted against long-term losses, then

2. Short-term gains are netted against short-term losses, then

3. Short-term losses are netted against long-term gains.

If net long-term gains result from this process, they may be reported as ordinary income, or they may be used to calculate the alternate tax. The alternate tax is calculated by deducting the net capital gain from ordinary

---

*The holding period required for long-term gains or losses was lengthened to 9 months in tax year 1977, and to 1 year thereafter by the Tax Reform Act of 1976.

FIGURE 2.2 1977 Tax Rate Schedules and 1977 Tax Table. (*Source: Internal Revenue Service.*)

1977 Tax Table A—SINGLE (Box 1)

(For single persons with tax table income of $20,000 or less who claim fewer than 4 exemptions)

To find your tax: Read down the left income column until you find your income as shown on line 34 of Form 1040. Read across to the column headed by the total number of exemptions claimed on line 7 of Form 1040. The amount shown at the point where the two lines meet is your tax. Enter on Form 1040, line 35.

The $2,200 zero bracket amount, your deduction for exemptions and the general tax credit have been taken into account in figuring the tax shown in this table. Do **not** take a separate deduction for them.

Caution: If you can be claimed as a dependent on your parent's return AND you have unearned income (interest, dividends, etc.) of $750 or more AND your earned income is less than $2,200, you must first use Schedule TC (Form 1040), Part II.

If line 34, Form 1040 is— Over	But not over	1	2	3	If line 34, Form 1040 is— Over	But not over	1	2	3	If line 34, Form 1040 is— Over	But not over	1	2	3
If $3,200 or less your tax is 0					5,800	5,850	419	264	100	8,400	8,450	890	748	580
					5,850	5,900	427	273	108	8,450	8,500	900	757	590
3,200	3,250	4	0	0	5,900	5,950	436	283	116	8,500	8,550	909	767	601
3,250	3,300	11	0	0	5,950	6,000	444	292	124	8,550	8,600	919	776	611
3,300	3,350	18	0	0	6,000	6,050	453	302	133	8,600	8,650	928	786	622
3,350	3,400	25	0	0	6,050	6,100	461	311	141	8,650	8,700	938	795	632
3,400	3,450	32	0	0	6,100	6,150	470	321	150	8,700	8,750	947	805	643
3,450	3,500	39	0	0	6,150	6,200	478	330	158	8,750	8,800	957	814	653
3,500	3,550	46	0	0	6,200	6,250	487	340	167	8,800	8,850	966	824	664
3,550	3,600	54	0	0	6,250	6,300	495	349	175	8,850	8,900	976	833	674
3,600	3,650	61	0	0	6,300	6,350	504	359	184	8,900	8,950	985	843	685
3,650	3,700	69	0	0	6,350	6,400	512	368	192	8,950	9,000	996	852	695
3,700	3,750	76	0	0	6,400	6,450	521	378	201	9,000	9,050	1,007	862	706
3,750	3,800	84	0	0	6,450	6,500	529	387	210	9,050	9,100	1,018	871	716
3,800	3,850	91	0	0	6,500	6,550	538	397	219	9,100	9,150	1,029	881	727
3,850	3,900	99	0	0	6,550	6,600	546	406	229	9,150	9,200	1,040	890	737
3,900	3,950	106	0	0	6,600	6,650	555	416	238	9,200	9,250	1,051	900	748
3,950	4,000	114	0	0	6,650	6,700	563	425	248	9,250	9,300	1,062	909	758
4,000	4,050	122	0	0	6,700	6,750	572	435	257	9,300	9,350	1,073	919	769
4,050	4,100	130	0	0	6,750	6,800	580	444	267	9,350	9,400	1,084	928	779
4,100	4,150	138	0	0	6,800	6,850	589	454	276	9,400	9,450	1,095	938	790
4,150	4,200	146	0	0	6,850	6,900	597	463	286	9,450	9,500	1,106	947	800
4,200	4,250	154	4	0	6,900	6,950	606	473	295	9,500	9,550	1,117	957	811
4,250	4,300	162	11	0	6,950	7,000	615	482	305	9,550	9,600	1,128	966	821
4,300	4,350	170	19	0	7,000	7,050	624	492	314	9,600	9,650	1,139	976	832
4,350	4,400	178	26	0	7,050	7,100	634	501	324	9,650	9,700	1,150	985	842
4,400	4,450	186	34	0	7,100	7,150	643	511	333	9,700	9,750	1,161	996	852
4,450	4,500	194	41	0	7,150	7,200	653	520	343	9,750	9,800	1,172	1,007	862
4,500	4,550	203	49	0	7,200	7,250	662	529	352	9,800	9,850	1,183	1,018	871
4,550	4,600	211	56	0	7,250	7,300	672	538	362	9,850	9,900	1,194	1,029	881
4,600	4,650	220	64	0	7,300	7,350	681	546	371	9,900	9,950	1,205	1,040	890
4,650	4,700	228	71	0	7,350	7,400	691	555	381	9,950	10,000	1,216	1,051	900
4,700	4,750	236	79	0	7,400	7,450	700	563	390	10,000	10,050	1,227	1,062	909
4,750	4,800	244	87	0	7,450	7,500	710	572	400	10,050	10,100	1,238	1,073	919
4,800	4,850	251	95	0	7,500	7,550	719	580	409	10,100	10,150	1,249	1,084	928
4,850	4,900	259	103	0	7,550	7,600	729	589	419	10,150	10,200	1,260	1,095	938
4,900	4,950	266	111	0	7,600	7,650	738	597	428	10,200	10,250	1,271	1,106	947
4,950	5,000	274	119	0	7,650	7,700	748	606	438	10,250	10,300	1,282	1,117	957
5,000	5,050	283	127	0	7,700	7,750	757	615	447	10,300	10,350	1,293	1,128	966
5,050	5,100	291	135	0	7,750	7,800	767	624	457	10,350	10,400	1,304	1,139	976
5,100	5,150	300	143	0	7,800	7,850	776	634	466	10,400	10,450	1,315	1,150	985
5,150	5,200	308	151	0	7,850	7,900	786	643	476	10,450	10,500	1,326	1,161	996
5,200	5,250	317	159	6	7,900	7,950	795	653	485	10,500	10,550	1,337	1,172	1,007
5,250	5,300	325	168	14	7,950	8,000	805	662	495	10,550	10,600	1,348	1,183	1,018
5,300	5,350	334	176	21	8,000	8,050	814	672	504	10,600	10,650	1,359	1,194	1,029
5,350	5,400	342	185	29	8,050	8,100	824	681	514	10,650	10,700	1,370	1,205	1,040
5,400	5,450	351	193	36	8,100	8,150	833	691	523	10,700	10,750	1,381	1,216	1,051
5,450	5,500	359	202	44	8,150	8,200	843	700	533	10,750	10,800	1,392	1,227	1,062
5,500	5,550	368	210	52	8,200	8,250	852	710	542	10,800	10,850	1,403	1,238	1,073
5,550	5,600	376	219	60	8,250	8,300	862	719	552	10,850	10,900	1,414	1,249	1,084
5,600	5,650	385	227	68	8,300	8,350	871	729	561	10,900	10,950	1,425	1,260	1,095
5,650	5,700	393	236	76	8,350	8,400	881	738	571	10,950	11,000	1,436	1,271	1,106
5,700	5,750	402	245	84										
5,750	5,800	410	254	92										
Continued next column					Continued next column					Continued on next page				

Page 19

FIGURE 2.2 (Cont.)

1977 Tax Table B—MARRIED FILING JOINTLY (Box 2) and QUALIFYING WIDOW(ER)S (Box 5)

◄(For married persons filing joint returns or qualifying widow(er)s with tax table income of $40,000 or less who claim fewer than 10 exemptions)

To find your tax: Read down the left income column until you find your income as shown on line 34 of Form 1040. Read across to the column headed by the total number of exemptions claimed on line 7 of Form 1040. The amount shown at the point where the two lines meet is your tax. Enter on Form 1040, line 35.

The $3,200 zero bracket amount, your deduction for exemptions and the general tax credit have been taken into account in figuring the tax shown in this table. Do not take a separate deduction for them.

If line 34, Form 1040 is— Over	But not over	And the total number of exemptions claimed on line 7 is—							
		2	3	4	5	6	7	8	9
		Your tax is—							
If $5,200 or less your tax is 0									
5,200	5,250	4	0	0	0	0	0	0	0
5,250	5,300	11	0	0	0	0	0	0	0
5,300	5,350	18	0	0	0	0	0	0	0
5,350	5,400	25	0	0	0	0	0	0	0
5,400	5,450	32	0	0	0	0	0	0	0
5,450	5,500	39	0	0	0	0	0	0	0
5,500	5,550	46	0	0	0	0	0	0	0
5,550	5,600	53	0	0	0	0	0	0	0
5,600	5,650	60	0	0	0	0	0	0	0
5,650	5,700	67	0	0	0	0	0	0	0
5,700	5,750	74	0	0	0	0	0	0	0
5,750	5,800	81	0	0	0	0	0	0	0
5,800	5,850	89	0	0	0	0	0	0	0
5,850	5,900	96	0	0	0	0	0	0	0
5,900	5,950	104	0	0	0	0	0	0	0
5,950	6,000	111	0	0	0	0	0	0	0
6,000	6,050	119	0	0	0	0	0	0	0
6,050	6,100	126	0	0	0	0	0	0	0
6,100	6,150	134	0	0	0	0	0	0	0
6,150	6,200	141	0	0	0	0	0	0	0
6,200	6,250	149	4	0	0	0	0	0	0
6,250	6,300	156	11	0	0	0	0	0	0
6,300	6,350	164	18	0	0	0	0	0	0
6,350	6,400	171	25	0	0	0	0	0	0
6,400	6,450	179	32	0	0	0	0	0	0
6,450	6,500	186	39	0	0	0	0	0	0
6,500	6,550	194	46	0	0	0	0	0	0
6,550	6,600	201	54	0	0	0	0	0	0
6,600	6,650	209	61	0	0	0	0	0	0
6,650	6,700	216	69	0	0	0	0	0	0
6,700	6,750	224	76	0	0	0	0	0	0
6,750	6,800	232	84	0	0	0	0	0	0
6,800	6,850	240	91	0	0	0	0	0	0
6,850	6,900	248	99	0	0	0	0	0	0
6,900	6,950	256	106	0	0	0	0	0	0
6,950	7,000	264	114	0	0	0	0	0	0
7,000	7,050	272	121	0	0	0	0	0	0
7,050	7,100	280	129	0	0	0	0	0	0
7,100	7,150	288	136	0	0	0	0	0	0
7,150	7,200	296	144	0	0	0	0	0	0
7,200	7,250	304	151	4	0	0	0	0	0
7,250	7,300	312	159	11	0	0	0	0	0
7,300	7,350	320	166	19	0	0	0	0	0
7,350	7,400	328	174	26	0	0	0	0	0
7,400	7,450	336	181	34	0	0	0	0	0
7,450	7,500	344	189	41	0	0	0	0	0
7,500	7,550	352	197	49	0	0	0	0	0
7,550	7,600	360	205	56	0	0	0	0	0
7,600	7,650	368	213	64	0	0	0	0	0
7,650	7,700	376	221	71	0	0	0	0	0
7,700	7,750	384	229	79	0	0	0	0	0
7,750	7,800	393	237	86	0	0	0	0	0
7,800	7,850	401	245	94	0	0	0	0	0
7,850	7,900	410	253	101	0	0	0	0	0
7,900	7,950	418	261	109	0	0	0	0	0
7,950	8,000	427	269	116	0	0	0	0	0
8,000	8,050	435	277	124	0	0	0	0	0
8,050	8,100	444	285	131	0	0	0	0	0
8,100	8,150	452	293	139	0	0	0	0	0
8,150	8,200	461	301	146	0	0	0	0	0
8,200	8,250	469	309	154	6	0	0	0	0
8,250	8,300	476	317	162	14	0	0	0	0
8,300	8,350	484	325	170	21	0	0	0	0
8,350	8,400	491	333	178	29	0	0	0	0

Continued next column

If line 34, Form 1040 is— Over	But not over	And the total number of exemptions claimed on line 7 is—							
		2	3	4	5	6	7	8	9
		Your tax is—							
8,400	8,450	499	341	186	36	0	0	0	0
8,450	8,500	506	349	194	44	0	0	0	0
8,500	8,550	514	358	202	51	0	0	0	0
8,550	8,600	521	366	210	59	0	0	0	0
8,600	8,650	529	375	218	66	0	0	0	0
8,650	8,700	536	383	226	74	0	0	0	0
8,700	8,750	544	392	234	81	0	0	0	0
8,750	8,800	553	400	242	89	0	0	0	0
8,800	8,850	561	409	250	96	0	0	0	0
8,850	8,900	570	417	258	104	0	0	0	0
8,900	8,950	578	426	266	111	0	0	0	0
8,950	9,000	587	434	274	119	0	0	0	0
9,000	9,050	595	443	282	127	0	0	0	0
9,050	9,100	604	451	290	135	0	0	0	0
9,100	9,150	612	460	298	143	0	0	0	0
9,150	9,200	621	468	305	151	1	0	0	0
9,200	9,250	629	477	314	159	9	0	0	0
9,250	9,300	638	485	323	167	16	0	0	0
9,300	9,350	646	494	331	175	24	0	0	0
9,350	9,400	655	502	340	183	31	0	0	0
9,400	9,450	663	511	348	191	39	0	0	0
9,450	9,500	672	520	357	199	46	0	0	0
9,500	9,550	680	529	365	207	54	0	0	0
9,550	9,600	689	539	374	215	61	0	0	0
9,600	9,650	697	548	382	223	69	0	0	0
9,650	9,700	706	558	391	231	76	0	0	0
9,700	9,750	714	567	399	239	84	0	0	0
9,750	9,800	723	577	408	247	92	0	0	0
9,800	9,850	731	586	416	255	100	0	0	0
9,850	9,900	740	596	425	263	108	0	0	0
9,900	9,950	748	605	433	271	116	0	0	0
9,950	10,000	757	615	442	279	124	0	0	0
10,000	10,050	765	624	450	288	132	0	0	0
10,050	10,100	774	634	459	296	140	0	0	0
10,100	10,150	782	643	467	305	148	0	0	0
10,150	10,200	791	653	476	313	156	4	0	0
10,200	10,250	799	662	485	322	164	11	0	0
10,250	10,300	808	672	494	330	172	19	0	0
10,300	10,350	816	681	504	339	180	26	0	0
10,350	10,400	825	691	513	347	188	34	0	0
10,400	10,450	833	700	523	356	196	41	0	0
10,450	10,500	842	710	532	364	204	49	0	0
10,500	10,550	850	719	542	373	212	57	0	0
10,550	10,600	859	729	551	381	220	65	0	0
10,600	10,650	867	738	561	390	228	73	0	0
10,650	10,700	876	748	570	398	236	81	0	0
10,700	10,750	884	757	580	407	244	89	0	0
10,750	10,800	893	765	589	415	253	97	0	0
10,800	10,850	901	774	599	424	261	105	0	0
10,850	10,900	910	782	608	432	270	113	0	0
10,900	10,950	918	791	618	441	278	121	0	0
10,950	11,000	927	799	627	450	287	129	0	0
11,000	11,050	935	808	637	459	295	137	0	0
11,050	11,100	944	816	646	469	304	145	0	0
11,100	11,150	952	825	656	478	312	153	0	0
11,150	11,200	961	833	665	488	321	161	6	0
11,200	11,250	969	842	675	497	329	169	14	0
11,250	11,300	978	850	684	507	338	177	22	0
11,300	11,350	986	859	694	516	346	185	30	0
11,350	11,400	995	867	703	526	355	193	38	0
11,400	11,450	1,003	876	713	535	363	201	46	0
11,450	11,500	1,012	884	722	545	372	209	54	0
11,500	11,550	1,020	893	732	554	380	218	62	0
11,550	11,600	1,029	901	741	564	389	226	70	0

Continued on next page

FIGURE 2.2 (Cont.)

1977 Tax Table C—MARRIED FILING SEPARATELY (Box 3)

(For married persons filing separate returns with tax table income of $20,000 or less who claim fewer than 4 exemptions)

To find your tax: Read down the left income column until you find your income as shown on line 34 of Form 1040. Read across to the column headed by the total number of exemptions claimed on line 7 of Form 1040. The amount shown at the point where the two lines meet is your tax. Enter on Form 1040, line 35.

The $1,600 zero bracket amount, your deduction for exemptions and the general tax credit have been taken into account in figuring the tax shown in this table. Do not take a separate deduction for them.

Caution: If you or your spouse itemize deductions, or if you can be claimed as a dependent on your parent's return AND you have unearned income (interests, dividends, etc.) of $750 or more AND your earned income is less than $1,600 you must first use Schedule TC (Form 1040), Part II.

If line 34, Form 1040 is— Over	But not over	1	2	3
		Your tax is—		
If $2,600 or less your tax is 0				
2,600	2,625	2	0	0
2,625	2,650	5	0	0
2,650	2,675	9	0	0
2,675	2,700	12	0	0
2,700	2,725	16	0	0
2,725	2,750	19	0	0
2,750	2,775	23	0	0
2,775	2,800	26	0	0
2,800	2,825	30	0	0
2,825	2,850	33	0	0
2,850	2,875	37	0	0
2,875	2,900	41	0	0
2,900	2,925	44	0	0
2,925	2,950	48	0	0
2,950	2,975	52	0	0
2,975	3,000	56	0	0
3,000	3,050	61	0	0
3,050	3,100	69	0	0
3,100	3,150	76	0	0
3,150	3,200	84	0	0
3,200	3,250	91	0	0
3,250	3,300	99	0	0
3,300	3,350	106	0	0
3,350	3,400	114	0	0
3,400	3,450	121	0	0
3,450	3,500	130	0	0
3,500	3,550	138	0	0
3,550	3,600	146	0	0
3,600	3,650	154	4	0
3,650	3,700	162	11	0
3,700	3,750	170	19	0
3,750	3,800	178	26	0
3,800	3,850	186	34	0
3,850	3,900	194	41	0
3,900	3,950	203	49	0
3,950	4,000	211	56	0
4,000	4,050	220	64	0
4,050	4,100	228	71	0
4,100	4,150	237	79	0
4,150	4,200	245	87	0
4,200	4,250	254	95	0
4,250	4,300	262	103	0
4,300	4,350	271	111	0
4,350	4,400	280	119	0
4,400	4,450	289	127	0
4,450	4,500	299	135	0
4,500	4,550	308	143	0
4,550	4,600	318	151	0
4,600	4,650	327	159	6
4,650	4,700	337	168	14
4,700	4,750	346	176	21
4,750	4,800	356	185	29
4,800	4,850	365	193	36
4,850	4,900	375	202	44
4,900	4,950	384	210	52
4,950	5,000	394	219	60

Continued next column

If line 34, Form 1040 is— Over	But not over	1	2	3
		Your tax is—		
5,000	5,050	403	227	68
5,050	5,100	413	236	76
5,100	5,150	422	245	84
5,150	5,200	432	254	92
5,200	5,250	441	264	100
5,250	5,300	451	273	108
5,300	5,350	460	283	116
5,350	5,400	470	292	124
5,400	5,450	479	302	133
5,450	5,500	489	311	141
5,500	5,550	498	321	150
5,550	5,600	508	330	158
5,600	5,650	517	340	167
5,650	5,700	527	349	175
5,700	5,750	536	359	184
5,750	5,800	546	368	192
5,800	5,850	555	378	201
5,850	5,900	565	387	210
5,900	5,950	574	397	219
5,950	6,000	584	406	229
6,000	6,050	593	416	238
6,050	6,100	603	425	248
6,100	6,150	612	435	257
6,150	6,200	622	444	267
6,200	6,250	631	454	276
6,250	6,300	641	463	286
6,300	6,350	650	473	295
6,350	6,400	661	482	305
6,400	6,450	672	492	314
6,450	6,500	683	501	324
6,500	6,550	694	511	333
6,550	6,600	705	520	343
6,600	6,650	716	530	352
6,650	6,700	727	539	362
6,700	6,750	738	549	371
6,750	6,800	749	558	381
6,800	6,850	760	568	390
6,850	6,900	771	577	400
6,900	6,950	782	587	409
6,950	7,000	793	596	419
7,000	7,050	804	606	428
7,050	7,100	815	615	438
7,100	7,150	826	626	447
7,150	7,200	837	637	457
7,200	7,250	848	648	466
7,250	7,300	859	659	476
7,300	7,350	870	670	485
7,350	7,400	881	681	495
7,400	7,450	892	692	504
7,450	7,500	903	703	514
7,500	7,550	914	714	523
7,550	7,600	925	725	533
7,600	7,650	936	736	542
7,650	7,700	947	747	552
7,700	7,750	958	758	561
7,750	7,800	969	769	571

Continued next column

If line 34, Form 1040 is— Over	But not over	1	2	3
		Your tax is—		
7,800	7,850	980	780	580
7,850	7,900	991	791	591
7,900	7,950	1,002	802	602
7,950	8,000	1,013	813	613
8,000	8,050	1,024	824	624
8,050	8,100	1,035	835	635
8,100	8,150	1,046	846	646
8,150	8,200	1,057	857	657
8,200	8,250	1,068	868	668
8,250	8,300	1,079	879	679
8,300	8,350	1,090	890	690
8,350	8,400	1,101	901	701
8,400	8,450	1,114	912	712
8,450	8,500	1,126	923	723
8,500	8,550	1,139	934	734
8,550	8,600	1,151	945	745
8,600	8,650	1,164	956	756
8,650	8,700	1,176	967	767
8,700	8,750	1,189	978	778
8,750	8,800	1,201	989	789
8,800	8,850	1,214	1,000	800
8,850	8,900	1,226	1,011	811
8,900	8,950	1,239	1,022	822
8,950	9,000	1,251	1,033	833
9,000	9,050	1,264	1,044	844
9,050	9,100	1,276	1,055	855
9,100	9,150	1,289	1,066	866
9,150	9,200	1,301	1,079	877
9,200	9,250	1,314	1,091	888
9,250	9,300	1,326	1,104	899
9,300	9,350	1,339	1,116	910
9,350	9,400	1,351	1,129	921
9,400	9,450	1,364	1,141	932
9,450	9,500	1,376	1,154	943
9,500	9,550	1,389	1,166	954
9,550	9,600	1,401	1,179	965
9,600	9,650	1,414	1,191	976
9,650	9,700	1,426	1,204	987
9,700	9,750	1,439	1,216	998
9,750	9,800	1,451	1,229	1,009
9,800	9,850	1,464	1,241	1,020
9,850	9,900	1,476	1,254	1,031
9,900	9,950	1,489	1,266	1,044
9,950	10,000	1,501	1,279	1,056
10,000	10,050	1,514	1,291	1,069
10,050	10,100	1,526	1,304	1,081
10,100	10,150	1,539	1,316	1,094
10,150	10,200	1,551	1,329	1,106
10,200	10,250	1,564	1,341	1,119
10,250	10,300	1,576	1,354	1,131
10,300	10,350	1,589	1,366	1,144
10,350	10,400	1,602	1,379	1,156
10,400	10,450	1,616	1,391	1,169
10,450	10,500	1,630	1,404	1,181
10,500	10,550	1,644	1,416	1,194
10,550	10,600	1,658	1,429	1,206

Continued on next page

FIGURE 2.2 (Cont.)

1977 Tax Rate Schedules

If you cannot use one of the Tax Tables, figure your tax on the amount on Schedule TC, Part I, line 3, by using the appropriate Tax Rate Schedule on this page. Enter tax on Schedule TC, Part I, line 4.
Note: Your zero bracket amount has been built into these Tax Rate Schedules.

SCHEDULE X—Single Taxpayers Not Qualifying for Rates in Schedule Y or Z

Use this schedule if you checked **Box 1** on Form 1040—

If the amount on Schedule TC, Part I, line 3, is:

Over—	But not over—	Enter on Schedule TC, Part I, line 4:	of the amount over—
Not over $2,200 ----			
$2,200	$2,700	14%	$2,200
$2,700	$3,200	$70+15%	$2,700
$3,200	$3,700	$145+16%	$3,200
$3,700	$4,200	$225+17%	$3,700
$4,200	$6,200	$310+19%	$4,200
$6,200	$8,200	$690+21%	$6,200
$8,200	$10,200	$1,110+24%	$8,200
$10,200	$12,200	$1,590+25%	$10,200
$12,200	$14,200	$2,090+27%	$12,200
$14,200	$16,200	$2,630+29%	$14,200
$16,200	$18,200	$3,210+31%	$16,200
$18,200	$20,200	$3,830+34%	$18,200
$20,200	$22,200	$4,510+36%	$20,200
$22,200	$24,200	$5,230+38%	$22,200
$24,200	$28,200	$5,990+40%	$24,200
$28,200	$34,200	$7,590+45%	$28,200
$34,200	$40,200	$10,290+50%	$34,200
$40,200	$46,200	$13,290+55%	$40,200
$46,200	$52,200	$16,590+60%	$46,200
$52,200	$62,200	$20,190+62%	$52,200
$62,200	$72,200	$26,390+64%	$62,200
$72,200	$82,200	$32,790+66%	$72,200
$82,200	$92,200	$39,390+68%	$82,200
$92,200	$102,200	$46,190+69%	$92,200
$102,200	----	$53,090+70%	$102,200

SCHEDULE Y—Married Taxpayers and Qualifying Widows and Widowers

If you are a married person living apart from your spouse, see page 7 of the instructions to see if you can be considered to be "unmarried" for purposes of using Schedule X or Z.

Married Filing Joint Returns and Qualifying Widows and Widowers

Use this schedule if you checked **Box 2 or Box 5** on Form 1040—

Over—	But not over—	Enter on Schedule TC, Part I, line 4:	of the amount over—
Not over $3,200 ----			
$3,200	$4,200	14%	$3,200
$4,200	$5,200	$140+15%	$4,200
$5,200	$6,200	$290+16%	$5,200
$6,200	$7,200	$450+17%	$6,200
$7,200	$11,200	$620+19%	$7,200
$11,200	$15,200	$1,380+22%	$11,200
$15,200	$19,200	$2,260+25%	$15,200
$19,200	$23,200	$3,260+28%	$19,200
$23,200	$27,200	$4,380+32%	$23,200
$27,200	$31,200	$5,660+36%	$27,200
$31,200	$35,200	$7,100+39%	$31,200
$35,200	$39,200	$8,660+42%	$35,200
$39,200	$43,200	$10,340+45%	$39,200
$43,200	$47,200	$12,140+48%	$43,200
$47,200	$55,200	$14,060+50%	$47,200
$55,200	$67,200	$18,060+53%	$55,200
$67,200	$79,200	$24,420+55%	$67,200
$79,200	$91,200	$31,020+58%	$79,200
$91,200	$103,200	$37,980+60%	$91,200
$103,200	$123,200	$45,180+62%	$103,200
$123,200	$143,200	$57,580+64%	$123,200
$143,200	$163,200	$70,380+66%	$143,200
$163,200	$183,200	$83,580+68%	$163,200
$183,200	$203,200	$97,180+69%	$183,200
$203,200	----	$110,980+70%	$203,200

Married Filing Separate Returns

Use this schedule if you checked **Box 3** on Form 1040—

Over—	But not over—	Enter on Schedule TC, Part I, line 4:	of the amount over—
Not over $1,600 ----			
$1,600	$2,100	14%	$1,600
$2,100	$2,600	$70+15%	$2,100
$2,600	$3,100	$145+16%	$2,600
$3,100	$3,600	$225+17%	$3,100
$3,600	$5,600	$310+19%	$3,600
$5,600	$7,600	$690+22%	$5,600
$7,600	$9,600	$1,130+25%	$7,600
$9,600	$11,600	$1,630+28%	$9,600
$11,600	$13,600	$2,190+32%	$11,600
$13,600	$15,600	$2,830+36%	$13,600
$15,600	$17,600	$3,550+39%	$15,600
$17,600	$19,600	$4,330+42%	$17,600
$19,600	$21,600	$5,170+45%	$19,600
$21,600	$23,600	$6,070+48%	$21,600
$23,600	$27,600	$7,030+50%	$23,600
$27,600	$33,600	$9,030+53%	$27,600
$33,600	$39,600	$12,210+55%	$33,600
$39,600	$45,600	$15,510+58%	$39,600
$45,600	$51,600	$18,990+60%	$45,600
$51,600	$61,600	$22,590+62%	$51,600
$61,600	$71,600	$28,790+64%	$61,600
$71,600	$81,600	$35,190+66%	$71,600
$81,600	$91,600	$41,790+68%	$81,600
$91,600	$101,600	$48,590+69%	$91,600
$101,600	----	$55,490+70%	$101,600

SCHEDULE Z—Unmarried or legally separated taxpayers Who Qualify as Heads of Household

Use this schedule if you checked **Box 4** on Form 1040—

Over—	But not over—	Enter on Schedule TC, Part I, line 4:	of the amount over—
Not over $2,200 ----			
$2,200	$3,200	14%	$2,200
$3,200	$4,200	$140+16%	$3,200
$4,200	$6,200	$300+18%	$4,200
$6,200	$8,200	$660+19%	$6,200
$8,200	$10,200	$1,040+22%	$8,200
$10,200	$12,200	$1,480+23%	$10,200
$12,200	$14,200	$1,940+25%	$12,200
$14,200	$16,200	$2,440+27%	$14,200
$16,200	$18,200	$2,980+28%	$16,200
$18,200	$20,200	$3,540+31%	$18,200
$20,200	$22,200	$4,160+32%	$20,200
$22,200	$24,200	$4,800+35%	$22,200
$24,200	$26,200	$5,500+36%	$24,200
$26,200	$28,200	$6,220+38%	$26,200
$28,200	$30,200	$6,980+41%	$28,200
$30,200	$34,200	$7,800+42%	$30,200
$34,200	$38,200	$9,480+45%	$34,200
$38,200	$40,200	$11,280+48%	$38,200
$40,200	$42,200	$12,240+51%	$40,200
$42,200	$46,200	$13,260+52%	$42,200
$46,200	$52,200	$15,340+55%	$46,200
$52,200	$54,200	$18,640+58%	$52,200
$54,200	$66,200	$19,800+60%	$54,200
$66,200	$72,200	$27,000+61%	$66,200
$72,200	$78,200	$30,660+63%	$72,200
$78,200	$82,200	$34,440+64%	$78,200
$82,200	$90,200	$37,000+66%	$82,200
$90,200	$102,200	$42,280+67%	$90,200
$102,200	$122,200	$50,320+68%	$102,200
$122,200	$142,200	$63,920+69%	$122,200
$142,200	$162,200	$77,720+69%	$142,200
$162,200	$182,200	$91,520+70%	$162,200
$182,200	----	$103,120+70%	$182,200

Page 31

income, calculating the ordinary income tax on this base, and adding back in 50 percent of the capital gain. When the taxpayer sustains a capital gain,* he should calculate his tax using the alternate tax method and the ordinary income method and elect the lower resulting tax.

Assume that a married taxpayer filing a joint return has a $3,000 net capital gain, and taxable income of $40,000. Using the alternate method, his tax liability would be calculated as follows:

$ 40,000	ordinary income
−3,000	capital gains
$ 37,000	
$ 10,790	tax on $37,000
+1,500	50% of capital gains
$ 12,290	total tax

Had the alternate capital gains tax not been used, the capital gains would be taxed as ordinary income in the following way:

$ 40,000	ordinary income
+3,000	capital gains
$ 43,000	total income
$ 12,620	tax on $43,000

In this case, the taxpayer should opt for the alternative tax method.

Dividend Income   The first $100 of dividend income is excludable; that is, it need not be reported as income. For tax purposes, married couples filing joint returns may "pool" their exclusions if both own the dividend-producing security. In some community-property states, stock in one spouse's name is considered jointly owned and so are the stock's dividends, and thus the dividends on this stock can be utilized by either party in calculating the $100 exclusion.

Maximum Taxable Income   The Tax Reform Act of 1975 placed a maximum tax rate of 50 percent on *earned* income.† The maximum rate applies only to income that is earned in exchange for personal services, or from pensions and annuities. It does not apply to income from dividends, interest, and so on. The maximum tax may be elected by single taxpayers and heads of households

---

*The maximum amount of net *capital loss* that can be deducted against ordinary income in a year was increased from $1,000 to $2,000 in tax year 1977 and $3,000 thereafter.

†The Tax Reform Act of 1976 did not change these provisions.

having earned taxable income in excess of $38,000, and married taxpayers filing jointly with earned taxable income in excess of $52,000.

Conclusion   This section has outlined individual tax requirements. Knowledge of both individual and corporate tax requirements is an important input in the financial decision-making process. We turn now to a discussion on corporate tax considerations.

CORPORATE INCOME TAXES

Introduction   Since the corporation is a legal being separate and apart from its owners, it has legal rights and responsibilities separate from those of its owners. One of the responsibilities is the payment of taxes. In this section we shall view the basis upon which income taxes are levied against the corporation. The discussion of corporate taxes is divided into three parts: the corporate tax rate, adjustments to gross revenue to arrive at the tax base, and adjustments to the tax once it is calculated.

Corporate Tax Rate   The corporate rate is relatively uncomplicated. It is applied to the tax base. The corporate tax rate is:

1st 25000 17% 4250.
2nd 25 000 20% 5000
3rd 25000 30% 7500
4th 25000 40% 10,000
7 100,000 46%

20 percent of first $25,000

22 percent on all over $25,000

26 percent surtax on all over $50,000

Since there is a 22 percent tax rate on all taxable income over $50,000, and a 26 percent surtax on the same base, this adds to 48 percent on all taxable income over $50,000. Therefore, the corporate tax-rate structure can be rewritten:

20 percent on first $25,000

22 percent on second $25,000

48 percent on all over $50,000

It must be remembered that these rates are applied to the *tax base*, or taxable income of the corporation.

Calculating the Tax Base   The basic method of determining the corporation's tax base is to subtract from its gross revenue a series of costs of doing business that are recognized as deductible for tax purposes. The basic deductible expenses are the cost of goods sold and salaries and administrative expenses. Other legitimate deductions from gross revenue, such as interest and depreciation, are within the purview of the financial manager and are discussed below.

Interest Payments Interest paid on debts of the corporation that are incurred in producing its product or service is deductible from gross income. The deductibility of interest for tax purposes has important implications for selecting financing sources. Tax deductibility of debt effectively reduces the cost of debt below its nominal rate.

Since dividends are a part of the residue of revenue after all expenses have been deducted, they are not considered a cost of doing business for tax purposes and are therefore not deductible.

Depreciation Depreciation is an expense designed to match up the cost of capital equipment used in the production of a product with the revenue produced from the sale of the product.

In a world of perfect knowledge, the exact market value of the amount of the capital equipment incorporated into the product would be known; therefore, its cost would be as certain as the cost of the other raw materials going into the product. But there is no world of perfect knowledge, and the amount of capital consumption—depreciation—must be approximated. The three methods of approximating depreciation allowed by the Internal Revenue Service are straight line, declining balance, and sum of the years' digits.

Straight Line. The straight-line method is the simplest. The salvage value is deducted from the cash outlay, and the resulting value—the depreciable base—is divided by the useful life of the asset. That is:

$$D = \frac{CO - S}{L}$$

where:

$D =$ annual depreciation in dollars

$CO =$ cash outlay of the asset

$S =$ salvage value of the asset

$L =$ useful life of the asset in years

Thus, if an asset costing $110,000, with a 10-year life and a $10,000 salvage value, were being depreciated under the straight-line method, substituting into the formulation above would produce:

$$D = \frac{\$110{,}000 - \$10{,}000}{10}$$

$$= \$10{,}000$$

The straight-line method results in a depreciation figure that is the same for all years. The two other methods produce depreciation figures that are different for each year, and therefore more closely approximate the actual rate of depreciation.

Double Declining Balance. In the double-declining-balance method, the same percentage is applied to each year's base, and thus to a declining base. Although the IRS does not permit the depreciation of salvage value, initially the percentage can be applied against the full purchase price of the asset, not cost less depreciation. Under most conditions, an annual rate twice the straight-line annual rate is permitted. In the previous example, the straight-line annual rate was 10 percent, so the annual rate for double declining balance would be 20 percent. Using the example above of the purchase of a $110,000 asset, and applying the declining-balance method, it would appear:

YEAR	RATE	DEPRECIABLE BASE	DEPRECIATION
1	.20	$110,000	$22,000
2	.20	88,000	17,600
3	.20	70,400	14,080
4	.20	56,320	11,624
5	.20	44,696	11,624
6	.20	35,757	8,939
7	.20	28,606	7,151
8	.20	22,885	5,721
9	.20	18,308	4,577
10	.20	14,646	3,662
			2,929

The declining-balance method recognizes the fact that the value of an asset diminishes more in its early years than in its later years. As shown above, the use of the double-declining balance method will not fully depreciate the asset. Thus, the IRS permits a firm to switch to the straight-line method at any time. In practice, the firm changes depreciation methods when the amount of depreciation using the straight-line method exceeds the amount of depreciation using the double-declining balance method.

Sum of the Years' Digits. The sum-of-the-years'-digits method also allows for greater depreciation in the earlier years. In this method, the individual years of the asset's life are summed to determine the denominator of the fraction applied to the base. The numerator of the fraction is the number of years of useful life left in the asset. When this method is used, salvage value is deducted, and the remaining value forms the base of the depreciation. In the example above, the following steps would be performed:

Step 1. Calculate sum of the years' digits:

$$1 + 2 + 3 + 4 + 5 + 6 + 7 + 8 + 9 + 10 = 55$$

or use the formulation:

$$D = \tfrac{1}{2}(N)(N) + \tfrac{1}{2}(N)$$

where:

D = sum of the years' digits

N = the number of years in the life of the project

Substituting:

$$= \tfrac{1}{2}(10)(10) + \tfrac{1}{2}(10)$$
$$= 5(10) + 5$$
$$= 55$$

Applying to sum of the years' digits:

YEAR	FRACTION	DEPRECIABLE BASE[a]	DEPRECIATION[b]
1	10/55	$100,000	$18,182
2	9/55	100,000	16,364
3	8/55	100,000	14,545
4	7/55	100,000	12,727
5	6/55	100,000	10,909
6	5/55	100,000	9,091
7	4/55	100,000	7,273
8	3/55	100,000	5,455
9	2/55	100,000	3,636
10	1/55	100,000	1,818
			$100,000

[a]$110,000 cash outlay minus $10,000.
[b]Depreciation balance is rounded to nearest whole dollar.

To sum up, the three methods of depreciation recognized by the IRS are straight line, declining balance, and sum of the years' digits. The first results in equal-amount depreciation charges, and the latter two result in greater depreciation charges in the earlier than in the later years.

Capital Gains The corporation must report all income from operations and from capital gains. Capital gains are defined as the positive difference between the purchase price of a capital asset and its sale price. All assets of a corporation are capital assets except those destined for sale to customers, depreciable assets, and real property. In general, capital gains result from the sale of financial claims owned by the firm.

Long-term capital gains or losses are those that result from the sale of assets held for more than twelve months.* Short-term gains or losses result from the sale of assets owned for twelve months or less.

The calculation of the capital gains liable for taxes appears complicated, but really is not. First, long-term capital losses are subtracted from long-term capital gains. Second, short-term capital losses are subtracted from short-term capital gains. Last, short-term capital losses are subtracted from long-term capital gains. The result, net long-term capital gains, is reportable for tax purposes. In tabular form, the calculation of net capital gains is:

Long-term capital gain
Long-term capital loss
                Long-term capital gain

Short-term capital gain
Short-term capital loss
                Short-term capital loss
                Net long-term capital gain

Net capital gains may be added to and taxed as ordinary income. Thus, if a corporation had $100,000 of ordinary income and $50,000 of net capital gains, its tax would be calculated:

Total taxable income   = $150,000
20% of first $25,000   = $ 5,000
22% of second $25,000   =   5,500
48% of remaining $100,000 =   48,000
       Total tax   = $ 58,500

But under the capital gains alternative, the firm may elect to pay a maximum of 30 percent on capital gains. Using this alternative, with ordinary income of $100,000 and capital gains of $50,000, the tax calculation would be:

Ordinary income tax:
  20% of first $25,000   = $ 5,000
  22% of next $25,000   =   5,500
  48% of remaining $50,000 = 24,000
      Total income tax $39,500
Capital gains tax:
  30% of $50,000   15,000
      Total tax $54,500

*See footnote, p. 16.

It would pay this corporation to take the capital gains tax alternative, since the incremental capital gains are taxed at 30 percent instead of 48 percent. Because of the corporate tax structure, it usually pays a corporation with $50,000 or more taxable income to elect the capital gains alternative. Under $50,000 taxable income, the marginal corporate rate is only 22 percent.

Before we leave the subject of capital gains, it should be noted that *net* short-term capital gains are declarable and taxed as ordinary income.

Adjustments to Taxable Income   In the preceding section we were concerned with provisions of the tax code that alter revenue before the determination of taxable income. In this section, we view two provisions of the revenue code that permit reduction of the taxable-income figure once it is calculated. These two provisions are carry-back, carry-over and the investment tax credit.

Carry-Back, Carry-Over.   The purpose of the carry-back, carry-over provision of the tax code is to permit corporations to net out losses against taxable income, and therefore reduce tax liabilities. The carry-back, carry-over provision permits a corporate taxpayer to reduce *taxable income* by the amount of net operating losses, subject to one constraint. A current net operating loss *must* be applied according to the following pattern: 3 years back, 7 years forward.* In other words, a net operating loss must be used to reduce *taxable income* in the third year previous to it, then to the second previous year, then the preceding year, then, after the current year, to each succeeding year till the seventh, or until the loss is consumed by offsetting taxable income.

Suppose that a corporation had taxable incomes as listed in Table 2.2. Note that in 1972, this firm sustained an $800,000 loss, which could be carried

TABLE 2.2   Carry-Back, Carry-Over

	TAXABLE INCOME	NET TAXABLE INCOME AFTER CB, CO	AMOUNT OF CB, CO
1969	$200,000	0	$200,000
1970	150,000	0	150,000
1971	50,000	0	50,000
1972	(800,000)		
1973	100,000	0	100,000
1974	150,000	0	150,000
1975	200,000	$ 50,000	150,000
1976	250,000	950,000	
1977	400,000	400,000	
1978	350,000	350,000	
1979	400,000	400,000	

*The Tax Reform Act of 1976 changed the carry-back, carry-over period from the previous 3 years back, 5 years forward.

back to the three previous years and forward to the seven succeeding tax years. Note that the carry-back, carry-over provision permits this corporation to wipe out its tax liability from 1969 through 1974 inclusive and to reduce the 1975 tax base by $50,000. In this case, the corporation would file amended tax returns for the previous years to reclaim taxes no longer owed because of the carry-back, carry-over provision.

The Investment Tax Credit. The first investment tax credit was passed by Congress in 1961 as an inducement to businessmen to acquire capital goods, thus stimulating economic activity through purchases of capital equipment. The Tax Reduction Act of 1975 increased the investment tax credit to 10 percent of the purchase price of the capital asset.* This amount serves as a direct reduction of the tax liability.

Certain qualifications are necessary for a capital asset to be eligible for the investment tax credit:

1. The asset must be depreciable.

2. The asset must have a useful life of at least three years.

3. The asset must be a tangible asset used in the production of the firm's good or service. Buildings do not qualify.

Assume that the Bowles Corporation, with taxable income of $200,000, purchased a truck costing $20,000. The income tax and tax credit would be calculated as follows:

20% of first $25,000	=	$ 5,000
22% of next $25,000	=	5,500
48% of next $150,000	=	72,000
Tax		$82,500
Investment tax credit*a*		−2,000
		$80,500

*a*Investment tax credit calculation:
.10 × $20,000 = $2,000.

The investment tax credit in this case has reduced the tax liability by $2,000.

Subchapter S. The carry-back, carry-over provision and the investment tax credit both permit adjustment to the tax liability of a corporation. Subchapter S changes the tax liability but in a different way. It permits qualifying corporations to elect not to be subject to the corporate income tax. If a qualifying corporation so elects, its earnings before taxes may be proportionally allocated among its shareholders for tax purposes. The shareholders then include the apportioned corporate income as personal income and calculate income taxes accordingly. The earnings of the corporation need not

---

*The Tax Reform Act of 1976 extended the 10 percent investment tax credit to 1980. The Carter Administration has discussed raising this to 15 percent.

be paid out as dividends in order to qualify for Subchapter S treatment. Thus, the earnings of a Subchapter S corporation escape double taxation— that is, escape being taxed as corporate income and again as personal income to the shareholders.

In order to qualify to elect not to be taxed as a corporation, the Subchapter S corporation must:

1. Be chartered in the United States.
2. Not be a member of a holding-company affiliated group.
3. Have only one class of common stock.
4. Have not more than 15 common shareholders.

If a corporation meets these conditions, it may elect not to pay corporate income taxes. The decision to elect Subchapter S status depends, of course, upon the tax bracket of shareholders of the corporation. If all shareholders are in the 70 percent marginal bracket, it would pay them not to elect Subchapter S status, but to pay the corporate income tax on earnings. If, on the other hand, shareholders were in lower than 48 percent marginal brackets, it would be wiser to elect Subchapter S status and pay personal income taxes on the corporation's earnings.

SUMMARY

Knowledge of tax provisions permits the financial manager discretion in attempting to legally minimize the firm's income tax liability. Reducing the firm's tax base and its tax liability is a continuing responsibility of the financial manager, the investor, and the dealer in financial markets.

PROBLEMS

1. The Gentleman Phred Corporation, a renter of men's evening clothes, qualifies as a Subchapter S corporation. Its most recent earnings statement appears below:

Sales	$600,000
Cost of goods sold	−250,000
Gross earnings	$350,000
Operating expense	−200,000
EBIT	$150,000
Interest	−25,000
EBT	$125,000

Each of its 15 shareholders *earns* $50,000 taxable income before return on his investment in the corporation is calculated. Each files a joint return with his spouse, and each owns 1/15 of the common stock of the corporation.

    a. Calculate the Internal Revenue Service's total "tax take" if the corporation elects Subchapter S status.

    b. Calculate the Internal Revenue Service's total "tax take" if the corporation does not elect Subchapter S status.

2. The Winona Bologna Corporation had taxable income as follows:

1970	$ 300,000
1971	200,000
1972	100,000
1973	(1,300,000)
1974	200,000
1975	300,000
1976	200,000
1977	400,000
1978	900,000
1979	11,000,000
1980	200,000

    a. Without applying the carry-back, carry-over provision, calculate the corporation's income tax liability for each year. (Assume that the current tax-rate schedule applied in all years.)

    b. Now apply the carry-back, carry-over provision and recalculate the income tax liability for each year. What is the difference between the total tax liabilities under the two conditions?

3. The Rancho Cordova *Republican*, a California corporation, is the local newspaper for Rancho Cordova, California. The newspaper is purchasing a new printing press, the details of which follow:

Cash outlay	$65,000
Scrap value	$15,000
Useful life	5 years

[handwritten: 50,000 over 5yr]

The earnings statement of the *Republican* is:

Sales	$200,000
Cost of goods sold	−50,000
Gross earnings	$150,000
Operating expense*a*	−45,000
Earnings before depreciation & taxes	$105,000

*a*Does not include depreciation on new printing
    press.

    a. Generate the depreciation schedules for the new printing press under the straight-line method, the declining-balance method, and the sum-of-the-years'-digits method.

b. Calculate the *Republican*'s income tax liability under each depreciation method. To get the taxable income in each case, subtract the first year's depreciation from $105,000.

4. The Wendy Scott Corporation, a manufacturer of swimming pools and pool equipment, had taxable ordinary income of $55,000 and a net capital gain of $5,000 for the most recent income period. Calculate the corporation's tax liability under the ordinary-income method and the capital gains alternative. Which option should the Wendy Scott Corporation adopt? Why?

5. The Halapeenyo Food Company owns and operates eight taco stands. It prepares daily a variety of Mexican foods in a central kitchen and delivers them to its eight retail outlets. Up to this point, the food has been delivered daily by RTX, Inc., a firm with a fleet of refrigerated trucks.

The owner and president of the corporation, José Ortega, has read of the investment tax credit, and wonders if the company's purchase of its own truck would be warranted. In the coming year, it is anticipated that taxable income will be $350,000. A refrigerated truck would cost $40,000 and would qualify for the investment tax credit. What would be the corporation's tax liability if it purchased the truck?

6. Susan Anderson is single. Her taxable income, all of which results from earnings, is $11,000. What is her tax liability? What is her average tax rate?

7. George and Lucille Dooley have a combined taxable income of $10,200. They also receive dividends as follows:

$120 from stock in the name of George Dooley

$60 from stock in the name of Lucille Dooley

The state they live in is not a community-property state. What is their tax liability?

8. Grace and Michael Beaudreaux have a net long-term capital gain of $5,000 from the sale of stock. Their taxable ordinary income is $62,000. They file a joint return. Calculate their tax liability using the ordinary-income method and the alternate tax method. Which produces the smallest tax liability? Why?

9. A corporation had a $6,620 tax bill this year. What were its taxable earnings?

hand in

10. The taxable income of XYZ Corporation is as follows (losses in parenthesis):

1975	0
1976	$75,000	*calculate tax*
1977	$350,000	" "
1978	($200,000)	*what is refund*

2,750 on 100,000
+ 46% on 25,000

What is XYZ's tax payment (or refund) *each* year?

1978 - 55,000 refund

200,000
1976   25,000   16,750
77   125,000   38,250
*   55000*

The Value of Money

The purpose of this chapter is to introduce the value of money early in the text and in a forceful manner. An understanding of the concepts presented will provide a foundation for the entire field of finance. Failure to learn the material in this chapter will greatly impede one's mastery of the discipline.

Although the calculations are not difficult, practice is necessary to comprehend the value of money concepts. We strongly suggest that the calculations be made with pencil and paper as you proceed through the chapter. Do not rely upon your intuition!

We have all heard the expressions "Time is money," and "the value of a dollar." But what do these sayings mean? What do we mean when we say that time is money? Are we referring to the fact that over a period of time, money increases in value, or to the fact that it may decrease in value?

The concept underlying each expression is separate and distinct. There are two forces that cause money to change in value. Oftentimes the two are confused or, even worse, substituted for each other. "Time is money" refers to the fact that money will earn interest; therefore, it has the power to grow in value over time. Of course, money in a shoe box or mattress would not earn interest over a period of time, and therefore would not increase in value based on the "time is money" concept.

"The value of a dollar" refers to how much a dollar will buy. This is known as the *purchasing power* of money.* In periods of inflation, prices rise and money depreciates (declines in value). Conversely, money appreciates (rises in value) and prices fall in periods of deflation. Based on the value of a dollar, let's look at what happens to the money in the shoe box. During periods of rising prices, the money is worth less and less, because its buying power is declining. In times of falling prices, the value of money in the shoe box is rising. Thus, the value of a dollar is related to economic activity; in other words, there is a tendency for money to buy more during recessions and depressions and to buy less during periods of prosperity and rising prices.

In the next section of this chapter, we will consider the time value of money; that is, how money increases in value when it is invested or saved at a given rate of growth or interest. In the following section, we will examine changes in the purchasing power of money based upon periods of rising and falling prices.

THE INFLUENCE OF TIME ON THE VALUE OF MONEY

It is a tenet of finance—whether you are a corporate financial manager, a financial investor in the marketplace, or a dealer in financial markets—that a dollar today is worth more than a dollar tomorrow. This is true because a

*It is sometimes called *inflation risk*.

dollar received today can be invested now, but investment of a dollar received later must be deferred until that dollar is received. Therefore, the dollar received today is growing in value, since it is earning interest; but the dollar received tomorrow (or next month, next year, or five years hence) is not growing, because it is not yours to invest until it is received by you.

A basic model of finance centers around the time value of money. It is $(1 + i)^n$; where 1 is a dollar invested or saved, i is the interest rate per year (or period), and n is the number of years (or periods) interest is earned. The expression $(1 + i)^n$ is at the very heart of finance. It is the interest factor used in bond tables, valuation of common stock, and capital budgeting decisions. In fact, virtually all financial decisions are based upon the time value of money.

How is this relationship derived? It is simply a statement that principal plus interest increases over time. The model is derived in the following manner: Principal + (Principal × Interest) is the same as Principal × $(1 + i)$. To make the statement general so that any number of years may be computed, the exponent n is added; that is, Principal × $(1 + i)^n$. This means that the quantity inside the parentheses is raised to the nth power. As we shall see soon, this quantity can be found by consulting a table of values in which all factors have been raised to the appropriate power.

The Compounding Process The time value of money is concerned basically with determining a future value from a value today (present value), growing at a given rate of interest. The growth in value is achieved because subsequent interest payments are added to the principal to form the base for future interest calculations. This process is called compounding. Of course, we can compound one lump sum or we can compound an even series of sums. Thus, $1 (a single payment) can be placed in a savings account to earn interest over a number of years; or $1 a year for a number of years (equal payments, or annuity) can be placed in savings to earn interest. In both cases, we are compounding a sum or sums of money at a rate of interest.

Examples of Compounding. In order to show the difference between compounding a single sum and a series of equal payments, let us use an illustration of each. For example, how much will $1 today (present value) be worth in five years (future value) if money earns 10 percent per year? This process is shown by longhand calculations as follows:

YEAR	COMPOUNDED VALUE (YEAR t − 1) ×	COMPOUND FACTOR (1.10) =	COMPOUNDED VALUE (YEAR t)
0	–	–	$1.00
1	$1.00	1.10	1.10
2	1.10	1.10	1.21
3	1.21	1.10	1.331
4	1.331	1.10	1.464
5	1.464	1.10	1.611

Thus we see that $1 grows to $1.611 in five years at 10 percent. Now refer to the "Future Value of $1" in Table A-1 in the appendix at the back of the book. There you will see the interest factor (IF) 1.611 at the intersection of the year 5 row and the 10 percent column.

Both future-value and present-value tables are constructed on the basis of $1. However, the tables can accommodate any sum of dollars. Simply multiply the factor in the table by the dollar amount involved. For example, the illustration above could have asked us to find the value of a single payment of $100, $500, or $1,000 in five years at a growth rate of 10 percent per year. To find the answer, multiply the respective amounts by the interest factor (IF) of 1.611 and you get $161.10, $805.50, and $1,611.00.

In the compounding of an annuity, equal payments are made into the annuity fund at periodic intervals (usually yearly). For example, $1 a year for five years reaches a value of $6.105 (future value) if money earns 10 percent interest per year. This process is shown by longhand calculations below:

YEAR	VALUE AT END OF PRIOR YEAR	×	COMPOUND FACTOR	=	PRINCIPAL WITH INTEREST	+	ANNUITY PAYMENT, END OF YEAR	=	VALUE AT END OF YEAR
1	–		–		–		$1.00		$1.00
2	$1.00	×	1.10		$1.10		1.00		2.10
3	2.10	×	1.10		2.31		1.00		3.31
4	3.31	×	1.10		3.641		1.00		4.641
5	4.641	×	1.10		5.105		1.00		6.105

Notice that the annuity payment is made at the end of each year. By convention, the "Future Value of Annuity of $1" table does not compound the last payment. Such a process is known as a *regular annuity* or a *deferred annuity*.

To summarize, we are compounding when we find the *future value* of a single sum or the *future value* of an even series of sums. Even series of sums are commonly called annuities.

The Discounting Process   The reverse of compounding is a process called discounting. Now we are attempting to determine the present value (value today) from a future value that will be discounted at a given rate of interest. Discounting is the process of finding the value today of a sum (single payment) in the future or of a series of sums (equal payments) in the future. For example, $1 received five years hence (future value) is worth only 62 cents today (present value) if money earns 10 percent per annum.* If $1 is received in each

---

*To reverse the process and compound, 62 cents invested now (today) at 10 percent interest per year would grow to $1 in five years (tomorrow).

of the next five years (future value), that even series of $1 each period is worth $3.79 today (present value), if money is discounted at 10 percent per year. Remember that we are discounting—the reverse of compounding—when we are looking for the *present value* of a sum in the future or the *present value* of an even series of sums in the future.

Examples of Discounting. First, a single payment in the future is discounted using the example above. This process is shown by longhand calculations as follows:

YEAR	DISCOUNTED VALUE (YEAR t + 1)	×	DISCOUNT FACTOR (1/1.10)	=	DISCOUNTED VALUE (YEAR t)
5	–		–		$1.00
4	$1.00		.909		.909
3	.909		.909		.826
2	.826		.909		.750
1	.750		.909		.682
0	.682		.909		.620

Note that the value in year 0 is 62 cents. Year 0 is always described as today, now, or the present. The value in year 0 is commonly called *present value*. Now refer to the "Present Value of $1" table. The interest factor for the present value of a single payment made five years from today and discounted at 10 percent per annum is *.620*.

To discount an annuity, equal payments must be received from (paid out of) the annuity fund at periodic intervals (usually yearly). Using the example above, $1 received in each of the next five years is worth $3.79 today if money is discounted at 10 percent per annum. Again, the process is shown by longhand calculation:

YEAR	TOTAL VALUE (YEAR t + 1)	×	DISCOUNT FACTOR (1/1.10)	=	DISCOUNTED VALUE (END OF YEAR)	+	ANNUAL RECEIPT (END OF YEAR)	=	TOTAL VALUE (END OF YEAR)
5	–		–		–		$1.00		$1.00
4	$1.00		.909		$ .909		1.00		1.909
3	1.909		.909		1.735		1.00		2.735
2	2.735		.909		2.486		1.00		3.486
1	3.486		.909		3.169		1.00		4.169
0	4.169		.909		3.790		0		3.790

Notice that the annuity receipt is received at the end of each year. By convention, the "Present Value of an Annuity of $1" table is constructed so that payment is made from the annuity at the end of each year.

Another View of Discounting Annuities. Since many people have difficulty understanding the concept of the present value of an annuity of $1, the last example is presented below in a different fashion. Originally we discounted a series of future sums received from year 5 descending to year 0 to determine the *present value* of the annuity. Since we now know the present value of the annuity, let's go from year 1 to year 5 to see how the process actually works.

Remember that money earned 10 percent per annum in the last example. Thus, we will compound the present value of the annuity and deduct the $1 receipt at the end of each year. *Year 0 is never compounded.* So we begin with year 1. Notice that the concept of the present value of an annuity of $1 is actually a combination of compounding a single sum and simultaneously reducing the value by the amount of the annual series of receipts. Thus, the present value of an annuity of $1 is simply a variation of the future value of $1. We begin with $3.791 (present value of annuity of $1) and end year 5 with *zero dollars*. The process shown below is exactly how a mortgage is reduced from the amount borrowed (present value of annuity) to *zero dollars* (ending value).

YEAR	COMPOUND VALUE (YEAR $t-1$)	×	COMPOUND FACTOR	=	COMPOUND VALUE (END OF YEAR)	−	ANNUITY RECEIPT (END OF YEAR)	=	TOTAL VALUE (END OF YFAR)
0	–		–		–		–		$3.791
1	$3.791		1.10		$4.170		$1.00		3.170
2	3.170		1.10		3.487		1.00		2.487
3	2.487		1.10		2.736		1.00		1.736
4	1.736		1.10		1.909		1.00		.909
5	.909		1.10		1.000		1.00		0

Thus, the present value of an annuity of $1 can be viewed as a compounding process with periodic withdrawals or receipts.

Now let's examine in detail each of the four variations of the time value of money introduced above. They are (1) the future value of $1, (2) the present value of $1, (3) the future value of an annuity of $1, and (4) the present value of an annuity of $1.

The Future Value of $1

As you have learned, money has a time value. One dollar today is worth more than one dollar tomorrow. This is a central tenet of finance. The future value of $1 is defined as the value today (principal) adjusted for two things—the rate of interest paid and the number of years (or periods) interest is paid. In other words, future value is the amount to which a sum will grow by the end of n periods when it is invested at i percent per year (or period) and compounded. Compounding is the computation of interest on the sum of the principal and on the accumulated interest that has accrued at regular intervals.

The future value of $1 is based upon the concept and formulation shown in Table 3.1. The time line, introduced to aid in visualizing the process of compounding, represents the passage of time running from left to right. It is important to place values in their respective places on the time line. This helps to ascertain the perspective of the concept.

TABLE 3.1 Future Value

	TODAY		TOMORROW
Concept:	Present Value	Compounded at $i\%$ over n Periods $\longrightarrow$	Future Value
Time line:	$1		?
	t_0		t_n

Formulation: Present Value plus (Present Value times Interest) equals Future Value, or Principal plus (Principal times Interest) equals Future Value

Symbolically:	$P + P(i)$	$=$	V	
Factor out P:	$P(1 + i)$	$=$	V	

Generalizing for Value and number of years (or periods)

$$V_0(1 + i)^n = V_n \qquad (1)$$

or

$$PV(IF) = FV \qquad (1a)$$

(where IF is the interest factor from the appropriate table—"Future Value of $1," here)

To illustrate, $1,000 invested at a rate of 6 percent for 10 years is (using the preceding formulation):

$$\$1,000(1 + .06)^{10} = V_{10}$$
$$\$1,000(1.06)^{10} = V_{10}$$
$$\$1,000(1.791) = V_{10}$$
$$\$1,791 = V_{10}$$

This means that the amount of $1,791 is the value to which $1,000 grows in 10 years at 6 percent interest compounded annually (but *only*, of course, if the interest is reinvested each year). The expression $(1 + i)^n$, or $(1.06)^{10}$ in the example, can be computed by raising the value 1.06 to the tenth power or by locating the interest factor (IF) in Table A-1, "Future Value of $1," in the Appendix.* To use the table, find the value at the intersection of the 6 percent column and the 10-year row. We strongly recommend the use of the table for the interest factor for a number of reasons. Among them is the fact that use of the table is quicker and easier, and results in fewer mistakes than other calculations do.

The Present Value of $1   We have just seen that $1 today is worth more than $1 tomorrow. Obviously it follows that $1 in the future (tomorrow) is worth less than $1 now (today). This is what present value is all about. It is the value today of a sum in the future. If we ask you, "Which do you prefer, $1,000 now or $5,000 in two years?" the answer is $5,000 two years from now. The reason for such an answer is based on the time value of money—specifically, in this case, the present value of $1. The concept and formulation for present value are introduced in Table 3.2.

Armed with this knowledge of present value (the value today), let's do the problem of $1,000 now (today) or $5,000 in two years (tomorrow), and assume that money is worth 10 percent to you. This problem can be worked from either Table 3.1 or Table 3.2. If Table 3.1 is used, the value for $(1 + i)^n$, or $(1.10)^2$ in this case, is either calculated or found in Table A-1 in the Appendix by going down the 10 percent column to row 2 (year 2). At this intersection in Table A-1 we find that the interest factor is 1.210. Now divide the factor, 1.210, into the future value of $5,000. The result is $4,132.23.

If Table 3.2 is used, the value for $1/(1 + i)^n$ is either calculated or found in Table A-2 in the Appendix. Notice that the values in Table A-2 are simply reciprocals of the values in Table A-1. In other words, if you divide a value in Table A-1 into 1, you obtain the value in Table A-2 for the same interest rate and number of years. For example, in the preceding paragraph, we found a value of 1.210 for an interest rate of 10 percent and two years. Now divide this value into 1 and you get .826. The resulting value (the reciprocal of 1.210) is the interest factor found in Table A-2 for 10 percent at two years. Now multiply the future value of $5,000 by the interest factor of .826. The

---

*Functions of the form $f(x) = c \cdot a^{i(n)}$ are called exponential functions and have many applications in financial analysis. One use is to model the growth of capital under compound interest. Since compound interest is an exponential growth function, geometric means can be determined by $(1 + i)^n$. For example, the problem above can also be solved with logarithms, as follows:

$$\text{natural log } 1.06 = .058269$$
$$.058269 \times 10 = .58269$$
$$\text{antilog } .58269 = 1.7908$$

1.7908 is the factor by which $1 grew during the 10-year period, compounded annually. Note that it is the value in the 10-year row, 6 percent column of the "Future Value of $1" table.

TABLE 3.2 Present Value

	TODAY		TOMORROW
Concept:	Present Value ◀	Discounted at $i\%$ over n Years	Future Value

Time line:	?		$1

t_0 ————————————————— t_n

Formulation: Present Value equals Future Value discounted at a rate of interest, or Principal is equal to the Future Value discounted

$$P \quad = \quad V/(1+i)$$

Generalizing for Value and number of years:

$$V_0 \quad = \quad V_n\left[\frac{1}{(1+i)^n}\right] \qquad (2)$$

$$\text{or} \quad PV \quad = \quad FV\,(IF) \qquad (2a)$$

(where IF is the interest factor from the appropriate table—"Present Value of $1," in this case)

answer is $4,130. (The slight difference in the two figures, $4,130 and $4,132.23, is due to rounding.) Be sure that you follow the reasoning above with both your calculator and the tables.

Thus, the solution to present-value (or future-value) problems that involve a single payment can be found by using either formula 1 or formula 2. This is possible because the interest factor for the future value of $1 is the reciprocal of the interest factor for the present value of $1. The formulas are restated (in general form) with the alternatives of $1,000 today or $5,000 two years hence if money is worth 10 percent to you:

Future value of $1:
$$V_n = V_0(1+i)^n \qquad (1)$$
$$\$5,000 = V_0(1.210)$$
$$\$4,132.32 = V_0$$

Present value of $1:
$$V_0 = V_n\left[\frac{1}{(1+i)^n}\right] \qquad (2)$$
$$= \$5,000(.826)$$
$$= \$4,130$$

NOTE: Rounding errors in the interest tables cause the difference of $2.32.

Let's look at another application of present value. Suppose that your father says he will give you $100,000 in 25 years. Further assume that money is worth 10 percent to him. That is, he can earn 10 percent on his investments or savings. Now the question is, how much does your father need to set aside now in order to give you $100,000 in 25 years? The answer is $9,200; that is, $100,000 × .092. Money does have a time value. It will work for you, and the sooner you put it to work, the more you will have.

Future Value of an Annuity of $1   So far, we have calculated the present and future values of only one payment. But much of finance is concerned with equal periodic payments.

Consider, for example, the periodic interest payments payable to a bondholder, or the periodic payments due the owner of a home mortgage. We shall now look at the basic methods of calculating the present value and future values of *periodic payments*. In finance, obligations involving periodic payments are known as *annuities*.

An annuity is defined as an even series of payments (equal receipts) over a fixed period. By convention, each payment occurs at the end of the year. This means that the last year's payment does not earn interest. Remember that the annuity tables are based on this fact. Therefore, do not make an adjustment for the last year. If payments are made at the beginning of the year, one must shift each receipt backward into the prior year to reflect the fact that the last payment occurred at the end of the year.

An example of future value of an annuity of $1 is making equal annual payments into a savings account every year. The future value of an annuity of $1 is based upon the concept and formulation shown in Table 3.3, using

TABLE 3.3   Future Value of Annuity

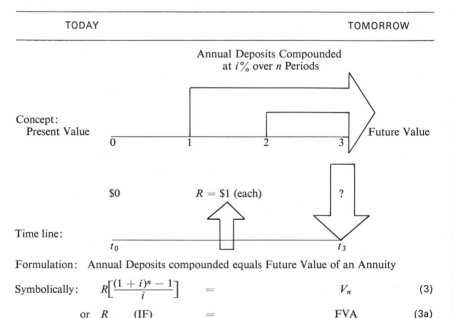

TODAY		TOMORROW

Annual Deposits Compounded at $i\%$ over n Periods

Concept: Present Value — Future Value

$0 \qquad R = \$1 \text{ (each)} \qquad ?$

Time line: $t_0 \qquad\qquad t_3$

Formulation: Annual Deposits compounded equals Future Value of an Annuity

Symbolically: $R\left[\dfrac{(1 + i)^n - 1}{i}\right] \quad = \quad V_n$ (3)

or R (IF) $= \quad$ FVA   (3a)

again the time-line device. In the use of the time line to illustrate annuities, the periodic payment is represented by upward-pointing or downward-pointing arrows. Arrows pointing upward indicate payments *into* an annuity fund. Arrows pointing down indicate payments *from* an annuity fund.

Let's assume that $1,000 per year for three years is paid into a savings account that yields 6 percent interest. The problem can be worked using Table A-1, Table A-3, or formula 3. Remember that Table A-1 is the basic table. It contains $(1 + i)^n$ values. So let's use that table to do the calculation the long way first, as follows:

YEAR	CALCULATION		FUTURE VALUE
1	$1,000 (1.124)	=	$1,124
2	1,000 (1.060)	=	1,060
3	1,000 (1.000)	=	1,000
	$1,000 (3.184)	=	$3,184

Using the time-line helper, the preceding problem, with R made at the end of the year, is:

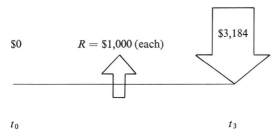

$0 $R = \$1,000$ (each)

t_0 t_3

Using formula 3a:

$$FVA = R(IF)$$
$$= \$1,000(3.183)$$
$$= \$3,183$$

Notice that the interest factors from Table A-1, when added, equal the interest factor from Table A-3 at the intersection of the 6 percent column and the 3-year row.

A good application of the future value of an annuity is in determining the value of a pension. Assume that you want to know how much you will have at retirement if you contribute $1,519.81 a year for 30 years, and money is worth 10 percent. Using the time-line helping device, a graph of the problem appears as follows on page 44:

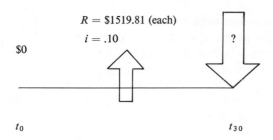

We want to know what the future value of an annuity is, so we turn to Table A-3, "Future Value of an Annuity of $1," in the Appendix. Using the interest factor there in the following expression gives:

$$V_{30} = (R)(\text{IF})$$
$$= 1519.81 \times 164.494$$
$$= \$249,999.62 \cong 250,000$$
$$= 250,000$$

Again, the slight error is due to rounding of the interest factor.

This says that if you contribute $1,519.81 a year for 30 years at 10 percent, you can draw out a quarter-million dollars. But 30 years times $1,519.81 is only $45,594.30. Where does the rest of the $250,000 come from? It comes from the compounding effect. Your first annual payment of $1,519.81 is invested for 29 years at 10 percent compounded, your second payment for 28 years, your third for 27, and so on. The compound growth effect accounts for the dramatic growth of your annual contribution.

Present Value of an Annuity of $1 In the future value of an annuity, we saw that the beginning value was zero and the value of the annuity increased with each payment. Now, under the present value of an annuity, the annuity value is large at the beginning, decreases as each payment is made, and has an ending value of zero. It is essential that you grasp this difference—the future value of an annuity increases as time passes, whereas the present value of an annuity decreases with the passage of time (to zero at the end of the very last period). The concept and formulation of the present value of an annuity of $1 is as shown in Table 3.4.

Assume that $1,000 per year for three years is withdrawn from a savings account that yields 6 percent interest. How much money must be in the account in order to make the withdrawals? Stated differently, what is the present value of this annuity? The problem can be worked using Table A-2, Table A-4, or formula 4.

TABLE 3.4 Present Value of Annuity

TODAY	TOMORROW

Annual Receipts Discounted
at $i\%$, over n Years

Concept:
Present Value

Future Value
\$0 at End of Annuity

Time line:

t_0 t_3

$R = \$1$ (each)

Formulation: Present Value of an Annuity equals Annual Paid-out Receipts discounted

Symbolically: V_0 $=$ $R\left[\dfrac{1 - \dfrac{1}{(1 + i)^n}}{i}\right]$ (4)

   or   PVA $=$ $R\,(IF)$ (4a)

Remember that Table A-2 values are reciprocals of the values in Table A-1—the basic table. Table A-2 contains the $1/(1 + i)^n$ values. Use Table A-2 to make the calculation the long way first, as follows:

YEAR	CALCULATION		PRESENT VALUE
1	\$1,000 (.943)	=	\$ 943
2	\$1,000 (.890)	=	890
3	\$1,000 (.840)	=	840
	\$1,000 (2.673)	=	\$2,673

Using the time-line helper, the problem above is as follows on page 46:

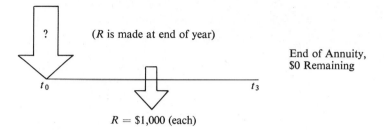

(R is made at end of year)

End of Annuity,
$0 Remaining

$R = \$1,000$ (each)

Using formula 4, the problem above is solved as follows:

$$V_0 = R(\text{IF})$$
$$= \$1,000(2.673)$$
$$= \$2,673$$

Notice in the long calculation above that the values in Table A-4, "Present Value of an Annuity of $1," in the Appendix are simply summations of the values in Table A-2, "Present Value of $1." (That is, sum the values for a specific interest rate over a specific number of years in Table A-2 and you have the *value* at the intersection in Table A-4 for the same interest rate and period.)

To illustrate the concept of present value of an annuity of $1, consider the following proposition: Would you rather have $10,000 today or receive $1,519.81 a year for 30 years? Assume that money is still worth 10 percent to you. Using the time-line helper again, the problem would appear:

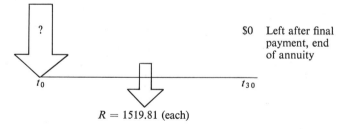

$0   Left after final
payment, end
of annuity

$R = 1519.81$ (each)

We must find out what $1,519.81 a year for 30 years at 10 percent is worth now (t_0), so we can compare it with the $10,000. Using Table A-4, we get the interest factor to use in the following expression:

$$V_0 = (\$1,519.81) \times (\text{IF})$$
$$= (\$1,519.81)(9.427)$$
$$= \$14,327.25$$

The present value of the annuity—that is, the value right now of the equal payments—is $4,327.25 ($14,327.25 minus $10,000) greater than $10,000. Rationally, we would take the annuity.

The Value of the Periodic Payment. An additional dimension of the time value of money arises when we deal with annuities. We frequently have to determine the value of the periodic payment. For example, assume that a firm must pay off $100,000 in debt in five years. How much does it have to set aside annually if money is worth 8 percent? Using our time-line helper, the problem would appear:

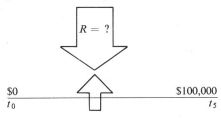

This problem is one we have already solved, with a minor twist to it. We know the future value of an annuity of $100,000. Let's assume that it is that kind of problem. Then:

$$V_s = (R)(IF)$$

Substituting those values we know:

$$\$100,000 = (R)(5.867)$$

However, we don't know R, the equal payment. It is, in fact, what we are seeking. But we can find it by simple algebra. If:

$$(5.867)(R) = \$100,000 \; (\textit{transposing from above})$$

then:

$$R = \frac{\$100,000}{5.867}$$

$$= \$17,044.49$$

The firm must set aside $17,044.49 a year to retire a debt of $100,000 in five years. This simple problem has given us a new dimension on annuities. To find the equal payment (R) for either the present or the future value of an annuity, divide the annuity value by the interest factor.

Special Use of the Interest Tables To extend years beyond the length of Tables A-1 and A-2 in the Appendix, multiply interest factors together. For example, if you have $4,000 today, how long will it take at 8 percent for the sum to grow to $1 million? The problem is solved in the following manner:

$$PV(IF) = FV$$

$$\$4,000(IF) = \$1,000,000$$

$$IF = 250$$

At 30 years, for 8 percent, the IF is 10.063. Multiply the IF by itself and you get a factor of 100 for 60 years. At 12 years, the factor is 2.5, which, multiplied by 100, is 250, or 72 years. So the rule is that when years are added in Table A-1 or A-2, the interest factors are multiplied.

To extend years beyond the length of Appendix Tables A-3 and A-4, use formula 3 or 4 and substitute the value for $(1 + i)^n$ that comes from Appendix Table A-1.

The *Rule of 72* is helpful in determining when a principal will double, based on interest rate or on number of years. In one case, the interest rate is divided into 72 to determine the number of years it takes for a sum to double. In the other, the number of years is divided into 72 to determine the interest rate required to double a sum of money.

Multiperiod compounding is accomplished by dividing the yearly interest rate by the number of periods in the year and increasing the periods of the payment accordingly. For example, a semiannual interest payment over five years is:

$$V_n = P\left(1 + \frac{i}{2}\right)^{5(2)}$$

In general:

$$V_n = P\left(1 + \frac{i}{m}\right)^{mn}$$

where m is the number of times a sum is compounded in a year.

Refer to the appendix to this chapter for additional material on continuous compounding.

Summary   The value of money changes with time. This is true primarily because of the compounding effect. We have viewed the calculations of the present and future values of a single payment, and the present and future values of periodic payments of an annuity. We strongly recommend the use of the time line for the definition of the problem. It helps classify the problem into its two components: (1) the present or future value, and (2) single or equal payments.

Another aid is the use of the matrix in Table 3.5. You must at a minimum learn the four simple formulas. Then always set up a problem using one of the formulations. This ensures that the correct concept is chosen and, therefore, the appropriate Appendix table is used.

The concepts of the time value of money learned in this chapter will be used frequently throughout the book. Time value of money is one of the most important and most used principles of finance.

TABLE 3.5

	SINGLE PAYMENT OR SERIES OF UNEQUAL PAYMENTS	SERIES OF EQUAL PAYMENTS
Future value	FV = PV (IF)	FVA = R (IF)
Present value	PV = FV (IF)	PVA = R (IF)

THE IMPACT OF PRICE CHANGES ON THE VALUE OF MONEY

Separate from the fact that money earns interest are the effects of inflation and deflation on the value of a dollar. If money earns 5 percent interest and the purchasing power of money declines 10 percent, then a dollar invested will lose 5 percent. The dollar in a shoe box will lose the full 10 percent.*

Periods of Rising Prices Changes in the value of money are often associated with cyclical changes in business and employment. Financial managers seem to find it easier to make a profit during periods of rising, rather than falling, prices. To a large extent, this is due to the fact that profits are a residual element—that is, profits are what is left after all expenses have been met—and many business costs tend to be relatively stable in the short run. Certainly the interest cost on bonded debt incurred in the past does not increase during periods of rising prices. Other items, such as rents, utilities, and wages, are not subject to month-to-month changes. If enough business costs are of this nature—lagging behind the general advance in prices—the financial manager finds that sales at advancing prices result in gratifying profits. Profits may be stimulated further by accounting practices, particularly in regard to inventory and depreciation. Some of the profits may be more apparent than real, but to the extent that the financial manager is influenced by them, he will expand production, employ more workers, purchase more from other firms, and maybe add to his existing plant and equipment. All this leads to

*If inflation rates remain constant over time, compound interest and annuity tables can be used to calculate the impact of inflation on present and future values.

increased sales for other firms. In short, nearly everyone finds business to be good.

Periods of Falling Prices When the value of money is rising (prices are falling), however, almost all businesses, households, and governments find it more difficult to show a profit or to save income. Just as we saw above, many of their costs are relatively stable even though prices in general are falling now. Interest, rent, wages, and some other costs are not immediately reversed when there is a drop in price levels. Some businesses can lay off workers in order to reduce costs. Others, burdened with fixed costs, find profits sharply curtailed.

This is the way the business cycle works: Excessive debt and deflation are two factors associated with the recurrence of downturns in the business cycle. And these two causes tend to produce and reinforce each other. Falling prices make debt repayment difficult, and overindebtedness leads to the need to reduce the amount of debt. Since debt (private and public) is the basis of the money supply, shrinkage in total debt reduces the supply of money. And this, in turn, reduces prices still further.

We are not concerned with the causes of price changes here, but rather with the effects of price changes on the value of money. During price rises, creditors are paid in cheaper, less valuable money than was borrowed. For example, during the rampant German inflation of 1922–24, those who had borrowed heavily and bought property at the beginning of the inflation found little trouble in paying their debts. Sometimes mortgages on land were paid with as little as a dozen eggs. On the other hand, those who owned the mortgages suffered great financial loss. In 1924, 100,000,000,000 marks were needed to purchase the same amount of goods that one mark bought in 1921.

During periods of declining prices, debtors must repay creditors in money that is much dearer—much harder to get. Now the tide has turned and the creditors (or owners of the debt) are the ones who benefit. During the 1930s' depression in the United States, many of those who had bought land and stocks on credit in the booming 1920s were wiped out financially. Some have facetiously said that the function of a recession or depression is to restore property to its rightful owner.

How are changes in price levels measured? There are a number of ways. However, we will examine the one most familiar to you—the Consumer Price Index.

Consumer Price Index (CPI) The Consumer Price Index (CPI) is a measure of changes in the prices of goods and services. Although it is often called the cost-of-living index, its official name is the Consumer Price Index for Urban Wage Earners and Clerical Workers. The index is based on approximately 400 items selected as representative of the thousands of commodities and services generally purchased. It is a weighted index and gives a fairly accurate measurement of price levels. The CPI for the years since 1967 are shown in Table 3.6.

TABLE 3.6 The Consumer Price Index and the Value of Money (1967 = 100)

YEAR	CONSUMER PRICES	PURCHASING POWER OF MONEY
1967	100.0	100.0 %
1968	104.2	96.0
1969	109.8	91.1
1970	116.3	86.0
1971	121.3	82.4
1972	125.3	79.8
1973	133.1	75.1
1974	147.7	67.7
1975	161.2	62.0
1976	170.5	58.6
1977	181.6	55.1

Source: *Federal Reserve Bulletin.*

In order to determine the price level for any given year (P_n) relative to a prior year (P_0), divide the current year by the base year:

$$\text{Price level} = \frac{\text{Current year}}{\text{Base year}} = \frac{P_n}{P_0}$$

From 1967 to 1976, prices rose from 100 to 170.5 (170.5/100 = 1.7). Price levels are usually quoted without the decimal, such as 170 instead of 1.7.

There is no direct way to measure the value of money. But we can compare its purchasing power in one period with that in another period. Even this measure is made indirectly. That is, the price levels in one period are compared with those in another. We do know that the value of money falls when price levels rise. Therefore, we can say that they are reciprocals of each other.

$$\text{Purchasing power of money} = \frac{P_0}{P_n} = \frac{\text{Base year}}{\text{Current year}}$$

Based on 1967 price levels, the dollar in 1976 bought only 58.6 percent as much as it did in 1967 (100/170.5 = 58.6).

SUMMARY

In this chapter we have examined the influence of time on the value of money, and the impact of price changes on the purchasing power of money. These two forces are important from the viewpoint of the financial manager because anything that changes the value of money will probably change financial decisions. They are important for the financial investor because anything that changes the value of money could change investment decisions. And last, they are important because of their impact upon supply and demand of securities traded in financial markets.

APPENDIX TO CHAPTER 3: CONTINUOUS COMPOUNDING AND GEOMETRIC PROGRESSIONS

CONTINUOUS COMPOUNDING

If the number of periods, m, within a fixed time interval, x (usually years), grows unlimited, it is as if we were compounding continuously. Banks frequently refer to this as compounding "daily." So, if $x = n$ is fixed at one year and the number of compounding periods, m, is allowed to vary, we have:

$$f(x) = \lim_{m \to \infty} P\left(1 + \frac{i}{m}\right)^{mn} = P\left[\lim_{m \to \infty} \left(1 + \frac{1}{m/i}\right)^{m/i}\right]^{in}$$

The limit within the brackets on the right appears so frequently in mathematics and its applications that it has been given a special name, e. The limit does exist and is a number between 2 and 3. It cannot be written as a fraction or a finite decimal. Therefore, its value is approximated:

$$e = \lim_{m \to \infty} \left(1 + \frac{1}{m}\right)^{m} = 2.7182818284\ldots$$

The continuous compounding function can be written:

$$A(x) = Pe^{i(n)}$$

where:

P = principal

i = annual interest rate

n = number of years

For example, $1,000 compounded annually at 12 percent for one year is $1,120. If it is compounded semiannually for one year:

$$V_1 = P\left(1 + \frac{i}{m}\right)^{mn}$$

$$= \$1,000\left(1 + \frac{.12}{2}\right)^{2\,(1)}$$

$$= \$1,000(1.06)^2 = \$1,124$$

If compounded quarterly for one year:

$$V_1 = P\left(1 + \frac{i}{m}\right)^{mn}$$

$$= \$1,000\left(1 + \frac{.12}{4}\right)^{4\,(1)}$$

$$= \$1,000(1.03)^4 = \$1,126$$

If compounded monthly for one year:

$$V_1 = P\left(1 + \frac{i}{m}\right)^{mn}$$

$$= \$1,000\left(1 + \frac{.12}{12}\right)^{12\,(1)}$$

$$= \$1,000(1.01)^{12} = \$1,127$$

If compounded continuously, $1,000 compounded at 12 percent finally reaches a limit of:

$$V_1 = Pe^{i(n)}$$

where:

i = annual interest rate

n = number of years

$$= \$1,000e^{(.12)(1)}$$

$$= \$1,000(1.1275) = \$1,127.50$$

(refer to Table B in Appendix for e values)

To compound continuously for periods greater than one year, multiply the interest factor by the number of years. For example, we want to know the value of $1,000 compounded continuously at 12 percent for 20 years. The solution is as follows:

$$V_{20} = Pe^{i(n)}$$

$$= \$1,000e^{(.12)(20)}$$

$$= \$1,000(11.023) = \$11,023$$

(refer to Table B in Appendix for e values)

GEOMETRIC PROGRESSION

A geometric progression is a sequence of numbers in which each term following the first one is obtained by multiplying the preceding term by a constant factor, called the *common ratio*. Thus, 1, 2, 4, 8, 16 is a geometric progression with a common ratio of 2. And 1, 1.1, 1.21, 1.331, 1.4641, 1.6105 is a geometric progression with a common ratio of 1.10. (We saw the latter example in the early part of Chapter 3.)

The geometric mean is one way to determine the common ratio in a progression. The geometric mean is calculated by:

$$gr - \sqrt[n]{(1 + r_1)(1 + r_2) \cdots (1 + r_n)} - 1$$

where $(1 + r)$ is the period, or incremental, relative.

For example, $100 increases by 50 percent in the first period to $150, which increases by 75 percent in the second period to $262.50, and finally the amount increases by 100 percent in the third period to $525. The geometric mean is:

$$gr = \sqrt[3]{(1.5)(1.75)(2)} - 1 = \sqrt[3]{5.25} - 1 = 1.738 - 1 = .738$$

1 is subtracted to reduce the answer to the percentage of increase—73.8 percent per annum.

Since compound interest is an exponential growth function, geometric means can be determined by the expression $(1 + i)$. In the example above, simply divide the ending sum of 525 by the beginning sum of 100 to get 5.25. Then refer to Table A-1, "Future Value of $1," in the Appendix to find the factor 5.25 in row 3 between the 70 and 80 percent columns (approximately 74 percent).

Some electronic calculators now handle some geometric means by finding the log of the product of the relative, then dividing by n, and find the antilog of the result.

In any case, it should be recognized that Table A-1, "Future Value of $1," is a geometric-progression table.

PROBLEMS

1. At an annual growth rate of 6%, how long will it take to double a sum of money? *annual compounding* *use rule 72*

2. You bought 100 shares of a non-dividend-paying stock in 1967 for $20 per share, and the stock sold for $40 in 1976. *doubled in 9 years* *A.1 9 yr → look for 2*

    a. At what rate of annual interest did your capital grow?

    b. What was the value of your total 1976 stock holdings based on the 1967 dollars paid for the stock?

3.   a. At age 20, how much should one invest each year, assuming a 15% annual growth rate, in order to have $1,000,000 at age 50? *future value of an annuity*

    b. At age 20, how much should one invest in one lump sum in order to have $1,000,000 at age 50? Assume 15% annual growth rate. *FV*

4.   a. At age 35, how much should one invest each year in order to have $1,000,000 at age 50? Assume 15% annual growth rate.

    b. At age 35, what lump-sum investment can one make that will equal $1,000,000 at age 50 at a rate of 15% per annum?

5. Your 65-year-old aunt is expected to live only another eight years. You have placed her life savings of $120,000 in a savings and loan account earning 7% annually. How much can she withdraw each year to leave exactly zero in the account at the end of the eighth year? *present value of an annuity*

$$\left(1 + \frac{i}{m}\right)^{nm} - 1$$

6. A mutual savings bank advertises a 7% rate of interest compounded semi-annually. What effective rate of interest is the bank paying? *3½% every 6 months*

7. What amount would an investor be willing to pay for a $1,000, ten-year bond that pays $35 interest semiannually ($70 a year) and is sold to yield 8%?

8. If a person deposits $1,000 into an account that pays him 5% for the first five years and 8% for the following ten years, what is the annual compound rate of interest for the 15-year period? *table 1*

9. Big Brother Corp. is establishing a sinking fund to retire a $200,000 mortgage that matures on December 31, 1984. The company plans to put a fixed amount into the fund each year for eight years. The first payment will be made on December 31, 1977, the last on December 31, 1984. The company

future value of an annuity $FVA = R(IF)$

$FVA = R(IF)$

$200,000 = R(9.549)$

$R = 20,944.60$

anticipates that the fund will earn 5% a year. What annual contributions must be made to accumulate the $200,000 as of December 31, 1984?

10.   a. Assume that you plan to retire at age 40 with $100,000. How much income per year will the $100,000 provide, ignoring taxes, if it grows at 8% per annum, and if you completely deplete your $100,000 at age 80?

PVA

b. Assume you retire at age 40 with $100,000 and live off the interest for the next 40 years. If the money is invested at 8% per annum, how much per year can you withdraw from age 40 to 80 and leave the principal unchanged? (Ignore taxes.)

11. Between January 1, 1969, and December 31, 1975, the number of finance majors in a university tripled. What is the annual average compound growth rate?

12. You buy a house for $50,000 and put $10,000 down on it. You finance the balance at 12% for 20 years with equal annual installments on the loan. How much are the annual installments? *R=a periodic payment*

$$PVA = (R)(IF)$$

13. The Barracuda Bank pays 8% and compounds interest *quarterly.* If you put $500 initially into a savings account, how much will it have grown to be in 9½ years? *FV =*

14. The Brotherhood Loan Company compounds interest *monthly* on the loans it makes. If you have to repay $300 a month for the first seven months, and $500 a month for each of the next five months, how much did you borrow? The company charges 20% interest compounded *monthly* on its loans.

15. You can buy an old bond that pays $40 interest semiannually ($80 a year). The bond matures in 7½ years. Its face value is $1,000. You can also buy a newly issued bond that pays 6% interest. How much would you pay for the old bond?

16. Your rich uncle Bert has promised to give you $350,000 in cash on your thirtieth birthday. Today is your twenty-first birthday. Uncle Bert wants to know two things:

FVA a. If he decides to make annual payments into a fund, how much will each have to be if the fund pays 7%? *R(11.978) = 350,000*

present value of $1 b. If he decides to invest a lump sum in the account now and let it compound annually, how much will the lump sum be? *PV = FV(IF)   PV = 350,000(.544)   PV = 190,400*

17. It is estimated that in 15 years, the student population of ASU will be 19,200. If the annual compound growth rate is 6%, what is the student population today? *FV*

PVA = R (IF)

18. Which would you rather have, (a) an annuity of $5,000 per year for 30 years, or (b) an annuity of $10,000 a year for 20 years, or (c) $50,000 in cash right now? In each case, money is worth 12%. *find & compare present values of annuties to $50,000 cash today*

homework 19. Calculate the future sum if $3,000 is deposited for ten years at a stated 12% annual rate and compounded:

   a. Annually

   b. Semiannually

   $V_n = P \left(1 + \dfrac{i}{m}\right)^{mn}$

   c. Quarterly

   d. Monthly

   e. "Daily"

20. Calculate the value of each of the following bonds, all of which pay interest semiannually:

BOND	PAR VALUE	COUPON RATE	MATURITY	MARKET RATE
A	$1,000	10%	20 years	12%
B	1,000	8	10 years	10
C	1,000	6	15 years	6
D	1,000	10	30 years	8
E	1,000	12	6 years	12

PVA 21. You would like to have a fixed annual income, and you have determined that an annuity is your best bet. An insurance agent has offered you three possible annuities. If you could earn 7% on your money elsewhere, which of the following annuities, if any, would you prefer? Why?

   Annuity 1: Pay $40,000 in order to receive $7,000 per year for the next 10 years.

   Annuity 2: Pay $70,000 in order to receive $7,000 per year for the next 20 years.

   Annuity 3: Pay $60,000 in order to receive $7,500 per year for the next 15 years.

Convert i from qtr to mo

22. You deposit $7,500 in an account paying 8% interest per annum compounded quarterly, and you withdraw $100 per month. *.66% per month*

   a. How long will the money last? *103.86 mos   8.65 yrs*

   b. How many dollars will you receive?

The Impact of Risk

Determination of the proper treatment of risk is a major problem in the field of finance. Prior to the early 1950s, risk was either assumed away or treated qualitatively by finance writers. It was rarely included explicitly in financial management models or financial investment models. In 1952, Harry Markowitz suggested a way of measuring portfolio risk and using it for investment decisions. Since then, the measurement of risk has played an increasingly important role in the field of finance.

Probably no other area of finance has received as much attention and enthusiasm in the past two decades as that of risk. As a result, current financial management models dealing with valuation, capital budgeting, and current assets include the measurement of risk. In addition, financial investment models dealing with security analysis and portfolio management also include risk measures. Finally, risk is used in the determination of prices in financial markets.

The purpose of this chapter is to answer such questions as, What is risk? How does it differ from uncertainty? How can risk be measured? and, finally, What is the impact of risk on financial decisions?

A distinction can be made between information on future events in which we have complete foreknowledge or certainty, and information that diverges from perfect knowledge. The opposite extreme from sure knowledge of the future is no knowledge. The latter state is called uncertainty. Between these extremes of certainty and uncertainty lies a range that is known as chance process, or stochastic knowledge. The stochastic process is more commonly referred to as *risk* situations. Thus, decisions may be made in situations of certainty, uncertainty, or risk. These states will be referred to collectively as the continuum of decision-making situations. Table 4.1 illustrates the three states.

TABLE 4.1 Continuum of Decision-Making Situations

	STATES IN DECISION MAKING				
	OUTCOME KNOWN	OUTCOME ALMOST KNOWN	OUTCOME PARTIALLY KNOWN	OUTCOME ALMOST UNKNOWN	OUTCOME UNKNOWN
Information on future events	Complete or perfect knowledge	Partial knowledge of future			Ignorance of future
States of nature	Certainty	Risk situations			Uncertainty
Probabilities	100% known	Known probabilities of outcomes			100% unknown
Subjective vs. objective probabilities	Objective probabilities	Mixture of objective and subjective probabilities			Subjective probabilities only

The Nature of Certainty We encounter *certainty* if each action is known to lead invariably to a specific outcome. For example, a firm purchases a $100,000, 90-day U.S. government Treasury bill, which is expected to yield 6 percent. We can accurately forecast the return on this commitment of funds and do so with certainty. This is so because we assume the U.S. government to be one of the most stable forces in this country. Therefore, decisions made in situations of certainty do not relate to statistical decision theory. That is, the outcome is known to have a probability of 1. Since we know how things are or will be, the decision strategy is *deterministic*; we simply evaluate alternative actions and select the best one.

The Nature of Risk   We have *risk* if each action leads to one of a set of possible specific outcomes. Each outcome must, however, occur with a known probability. If, for example, the firm invests in more inventory instead of the $100,000 in Treasury bills, we cannot precisely estimate the future return from the investment. Although the specific outcome of the inventory investment cannot be predicted, the expected value of the action based on past experiences can be determined. The expected value will never be realized as a result of any single specific action. This is because of the *stochastic* process (chance process) where events are not identical nor individually predictable with certainty. In such a case, whether a given decision will turn out to be the best decision is not known until after it has been implemented. Purely by chance, the outcome of an alternative decision might have turned out to be the best.

Risk, then, is the appropriate term when the probability distribution of the outcome is known to the decision maker. Certainty, in contrast, was the case in which the probability assigned to one state was known to be 1 and the probability assigned to the other states was 0.

The Nature of Uncertainty   A situation concealed in *uncertainty* is related to decision theory but not to the statistical variety. If a situation is uncertain, we can list the possible ways things might turn out. However, we have no knowledge about how often to expect each (that is, no knowledge about the probabilities of the possible outcomes). Thus, we encounter uncertainty if the probabilities of the outcomes of each course of action are completely unknown or are not even meaningful. It follows that if the probabilities are completely unknown, the expected value of any decision cannot be determined.

For example, instead of investing in Treasury bills or inventory, the firm invests in a project so new that there is insufficient information from which to derive any objective quantitative measure of risk. Lacking such probabilities to weigh the consequences, modern decision theorists (game theorists) have invented ways to select the "best" from among all the alternative actions available. For example, a firm might adopt a rule that minimizes its maximum loss. Operation under this rule assumes that the worst things that can happen will happen. See the appendix at the end of this chapter for a discussion of decisions where probabilities are undefined.

Ambiguity of Terms   Some financial writers, unfortunately, have come to look upon risk not only as the state when the probability distribution of the outcomes is known to the decision-maker (which it is) but as the state when uncertainty exists (which it is not). Rather than adopting some of the strategies designed to handle uncertainty (see the appendix at end of this chapter), these writers artificially translate uncertainty into risk. To force a problem of uncertainty into one involving risk is considered to be tentative at best. We think the distinction between risk and uncertainty should be maintained. Therefore, the two terms will not be used synonymously in this book. Risk will refer to a state in which probability distributions are known or assumed to be known. Uncertainty will refer to a state in which probabilities are completely unknown or are not even meaningful.

It should be noted that there is a great degree of risk in uncertainty. That is, even though one has no knowledge of the future, the outcome may range from a very large loss to a very large gain. However, there is no way to know all the possible outcomes or to assess the probability of each occurrence. Conversely, there is a degree of uncertainty in risk. That is, the outcome can not be predicted with certainty. Confusion is further caused by the use of the terms. "Risk" is ordinarily used to refer to an unfavorable contingency, whereas "uncertainty" refers to a favorable outcome. For example, we speak of the "risk" of a loss and the "uncertainty" of a gain. Aware of this, we will preserve the distinction between *measurable uncertainty* and *unmeasurable uncertainty* as "risk" and "uncertainty" respectively.*

WHAT IS RISK?

In common parlance, the word *risk* is used in many different ways, variously referring to general uncertainty, doubt, an insured object, or chance of loss. Likewise, *risk* has been assigned various meanings in finance. Some writers define risk as the probability of a loss. They consider that a loss has occurred when the return falls below some predetermined level. Such a level is usually the expected return; in other words, risk causes the actual return to be less than the expected return. Other writers define risk as the probability that a return will be less than some target level. The target level is usually zero; that is, risk causes the actual return to be less than zero.

We reject both these definitions of risk in finance. Unfortunately, risk is not, as some authors suggest, only the left portion of the probability distribution. That is, risk is not just the possibility that actual future returns will be below expected returns. This restricts risk to an outcome that is worse than expected. To extend such thinking, the term riskier would mean that the return will not be above average but rather that it can only be below average —and by a large amount, if one is unlucky. In general, such authors attempt to define risk as the possibility of realizing returns less than the expected return. Although such views are rather prevalent in financial literature, we

---

*Frank H. Knight, *Risk, Uncertainty and Profit* (Chicago: University of Chicago Press, 1971), p. 233.

categorically believe that such a view is shortsighted, unwarranted, and in error.

Sometimes risk is considered by some financial managers a proxy for opportunity loss. However, risk is not the measure of that opportunity loss. It is the measure of an independent factor that contributes to the opportunity loss.

Risk is defined as an independent variable that is proportionately related to the variability of a dependent variable. The definition above holds true for any risk situation, whether it be future returns, inventory production, lotteries, or target practice. Loosely defined, risk is not knowing what the outcome will be—that is, the chance of doing better or worse than expected. In other words, the variability of the entire probability distribution is viewed as risk. Using the risk–return tradeoff (refer to Chapter 15), risk is the possibility of exceeding or failing to attain the expected return. For example, in Figure 4.1, both investments A and B may do better or worse than expected. Yet B is riskier than A.

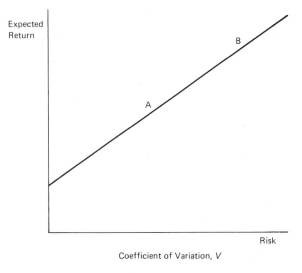

FIGURE 4.1 Risk–Return Tradeoff.

Even though one is happy to exceed the expected return, certain problems may ensue. For example, the firm that grows from $2 million in sales to $10 million in three years will have problems if such growth was not planned. Because of risk, the firm that fails to plan for large returns will have financial problems related to liquidity. In fact, it may have to curtail growth until risks can be properly assessed. Otherwise, such a firm may be forced into liquidation owing to the risk of growing too fast.

When the future course of events is perfectly predictable (100 percent known), there is no risk. If we know for sure that something will happen or that it will not happen, there is no uncertainty and hence no risk. It is the inability to predict with perfect knowledge the course of future events that introduces risk. As events become more predictable, risk is reduced. Conversely, as events become less predictable, risk is increased.

THE MEASUREMENT OF RISK

So far, the term *risk* has been used in a qualitative way to refer to a state of knowledge about outcomes in the future—that is, a situation where probabilities can be assigned to possible future occurrences. In finance, risk is used to describe a situation that deviates from certainty. Thus, the degree of deviation is referred to as the degree of risk. A risky proposition in business is presumed to be one with a wide range of possible returns. This concept of risk as degree or range of possible deviation can be quantified. The most common way of doing this is to define risk in the same way that the statistician defines variability. In any probability distribution it is possible to identify some central tendency or average of possible outcomes. *Variability* refers to the degree to which possible outcomes deviate from this central tendency.

The most common measure of central tendency is a weighted arithmetic mean. The mean is often referred to as the *expected value*. This value is constructed by multiplying each possible outcome by its associated probability and summing the products. For example, the probability distribution .3($100), .4($200), and .3($300) has a mean of $200. The most common measure of the variability of this distribution is the *standard deviation*.* To calculate the standard deviation, the following steps are used:

1. Calculate the mean or expected value of the distribution:

$$\text{Expected value} = \bar{R} = \sum_{i=1}^{n} (R_i, p_i)$$

where

R_i = the return associated with each outcome

p_i = the probability of occurrence of each outcome

$\bar{R}$ = the expected value

2. Calculate the deviation from each possible outcome:

$$\text{Deviation} = R_i - \bar{R}$$

3. Square each deviation.

4. Multiply the squared deviations by the probability of occurrence for its related outcome.

---

*One standard deviation (σ) equals 68 percent of distribution of possible outcomes, 2σ equals 95 percent, and 3σ equals 99 percent.

5. Sum all the products. This is called the variance.

$$\text{Variance} = \sigma^2 = \sum_{i=1}^{n} (R_i - \bar{R})^2 p_i$$

6. The standard deviation is found by taking the square root of the variance:

$$\text{Standard deviation} = \sigma = \sqrt{\sum_{i=1}^{n} (R_i - \bar{R})^2 p_i}$$

For the probability distribution introduced in the preceding example, with an expected value of $200, the standard deviation is calculated as shown in Table 4.2.

TABLE 4.2 Calculation of Expected Return, Variance, and Standard Deviation

PROBA-BILITY p_i	OUT-COME R_i	RETURN $p(R_i)$	DEVIATION $(R_i - \bar{R})$	SQUARED DEVIATION $(R_i - \bar{R})^2$	PROBABILITY X SQUARED DEVIA-TION $p_i(R_i - \bar{R})^2$
.3	100	30	−100	10,000	10,000(.3) = 3,000
.4	200	80	0	0	0(.4) = —
.3	300	90	+100	10,000	10,000(.3) = 3,000
	$E(\bar{R}) = 200$				Variance $= \sigma^2 = 6,000$

Standard deviation $= \sigma = \sqrt{\sigma^2} = \sqrt{6,000} = 77.46$

The use of the standard deviation is sometimes criticized when taken by itself as a risk measure because it measures absolute variability of returns and ignores the relative size of an asset's expected return. A measured deviation is important for business firms only when compared with central tendency. For example, the possibility of a year's return varying by $100,000 is critically significant to a very small business. However, a large business would gladly accept a deviation of only $100,000. This has prompted the use of the *coefficient of variation*, which is a "normalized" standard deviation. It measures the relative variability of returns. Research has shown that the coefficient of variation captures facets of risk different from those captured by other risk measures.*

---

*Other measures of risk with close substitutability for the standard deviation are range, semi-interquartile deviation, mean absolute deviation, semivariance, and lower confidence limit. Coefficient of variation and coefficient of quartile variation have very low correlations with other measures and thus identify a different characteristic of the probability distribution. Higher moments of distribution such as skewness and kurtosis describe still different aspects of risk. Finally, beta does not group with the other risk measures, which indicates that it captures an additional dimension of risk.

The coefficient of variation is easily determined. Simply divide the standard deviation of a probability distribution by its central tendency (expected value):

$$\text{Coefficient of variation} = V = \frac{\sigma}{\bar{R}} = \frac{77.46}{200} = .39$$

The quotient obtained, called the *coefficient of variation*, is the most commonly used basic quantitative specification of risk as applied to business firms.

If the distribution has equal probability for each outcome, the computation is greatly simplified. For example, assume that the outcomes in Table 4.2 are equally likely (that is, 1/3, 1/3, and 1/3). The calculation of the expected return, variance, and standard deviation for three possible outcomes with each outcome equally likely is shown in Table 4.3. Column 2 lists the

TABLE 4.3 Calculation of Expected Return, Variance, and Standard Deviation (equally likely states)

STATE OF NATURE	RETURN (R)	(RETURN)^2 (R^2)
1	33.33	1110.89
2	66.67	4444.89
3	100.00	10,000.00
Sum	200.00	15,555.78

$$E(R) = \sum R/n = 200/3 = 66.67$$

$$E(R)^2 = \sum (R^2)/n = 15{,}555.78/3 = 5185.26$$

$$\begin{aligned}\text{Variance} &= E(R^2) - [E(R)]^2 \\ &= 5185.26 - (66.67)^2 \\ &= 740.37\end{aligned}$$

$$\text{Standard Deviation } (\sigma) = \sqrt{740.37} = 27.21$$

returns (R) and column 3 shows the squared values of each return (R^2). Taking averages of each column results in an expected return of 66.67, a variance of 740.37, and a standard deviation of 27.21.

The standard deviation is a good measure of risk for single-security portfolios.* It is a measure of the variability of past common-stock yields, or returns. It is not necessary to "normalize" the variability in this case. The reason is that the absolute deviation is as good a measure as the relative deviation when the expected return is in a stable range.

---

*The determination of the beta estimate, an index of nondiversifiable risk, is illustrated in the appendix to Chapter 18.

To illustrate this, assume that a growth stock* provided the investor with the following average annual yields over the past five-year period.

PERIOD	RETURNS	R^2
1971	19.00	361
1972	9.00	81
1973	− 4.00	16
1974	20.00	400
1975	11.00	121
	55.00	979

$E(R) = 55/5 = 11.00$ mean

$E(R^2) = 979/5 = 195.8$

$\text{Var} = E(R^2) - [E(R)]^2$

$= 195.8 - 121$

$= 74.8$ average annual yield

- most risky

std dev 8.65

Thus, the mean is 11, the standard deviation is 8.65 ($\sqrt{74.8}$), and the coefficient of variation is .79 (8.65/11).

To determine if such a variation is large or not, let's compare the results with an investment in an income stock.† The following is the five-year historical yield for the same period for an income stock.

PERIOD	RETURNS	R^2
1971	10	100
1972	9	81
1973	8	64
1974	11	121
1975	12	144
	50	510

$E(R) = 50/5 = 10$

$E(R^2) = 510/5 = 102$

$\text{Var} = E(R^2) - [E(R)]^2$

$= 102 - 10^2$

$= 2$

std dev 1.414

In this case, the mean is 10, the standard deviation is 1.414 ($\sqrt{2}$), and the coefficient of variation is .1414 (1.414/10).

The income stock is less risky than the growth stock. That is, the standard deviation is 1.41 for the income stock and 8.65 for the growth stock. The standard deviation expressed as a percentage of the mean (the coefficient of

*See Chapter 17 for the definitions of growth and income stocks.
†See Chapter 17 for the definitions of growth and income stocks.

variation) is 14 percent for the income stock and 79 percent for the growth stock.

Risk with Respect to Time   A good indication of this risk is the function of interest rates over time. *Ceteris paribus*, the businessman or investor will demand a higher risk premium in the form of interest on instruments that mature in the future.

The same rationale holds true for any stream of cash flows into the future. Although the expected return may be the same dollar amount for each year, the variability of returns is larger for the more distant years. Therefore, risk increases over time.

TYPES OF RISK

There are two basic types of risk that are commonly referred to in finance literature. They are diversifiable risk and nondiversifiable risk.* Every asset possesses these risks. They are just as real for the assets of the business firm as they are for the securities of individual investors. *Diversifiable risk* is defined as the unique factors of an asset that influence its value. Such a risk is also known as the residual risk or unsystematic risk. *Nondiversifiable risk* is defined as the systematic influence of the market in which the asset is traded. This risk is sometimes called systematic risk.

Diversifiable Risks   There are two risks that are peculiar to an asset and can be moderated or lessened by diversification. They are the business risk and the financial risk. The distinction is useful when one considers the distribution of risk to various financial participants in a business. The firm holds a stock of assets. The returns on such assets have a risk dimension that is called *business risk*. These returns from the firm's assets are all subject to financial claims. Portions are assigned to creditors and other debtors, with the remaining amount for the owners. The returns to individual claimants on returns have a risk dimension that is called *financial risk*.

The *business risk* is defined as the variability of the earnings of a firm. A decline in company sales that causes earnings to drop would have a dramatic adverse effect on the market price of the common stock. Conversely, an increase in company sales that causes earnings to rise would generally be accompanied by a rise in market price of the common stock. In general, all firms are susceptible to the risk of a change in earnings, stemming from the

---

*The concepts of diversifiable risk and nondiversifiable risk are usually presented within a portfolio context. This we do in Chapter 18. They are introduced here because the financial manager, the financial investor, and the dealer in financial markets must recognize these risks and make decisions that involve them.

inherent nature of the business. Diversification usually reduces the fluctuation of earnings and hence the risk involved. For example, American Home Products (AHP) is a well-diversified company. Its major areas are drugs, foods, and household products. Consequently, AHP enjoys an upward earnings trend (that is, its earnings are not erratic).

Financial risk is defined as the variability of returns to investors resulting from the way a firm finances its assets. Firms may be financed entirely with equity or with a combination of debt and equity. If a firm is financed wholly by equity, earnings accrue solely to the owners. If a firm is financed by debt and equity, the interest payable to debt holders has a claim on earnings prior to that of the owners. Such prior claims are usually fixed and therefore influence the size and variability of earnings available to the owners of the firm.

Consider a firm with the probability distribution of earnings of .3($2) and .7($4). During the next time period, it is obligated to pay $3 to creditors. If the best return possible occurs, creditors get $3 and owners are left with $1. If the worst return occurs, creditors get $2 and owners receive $0. These returns are presented first in matrix form below and then in graphic form in Figure 4.2.

	FIRM	=	CREDITORS	+	OWNERS
Best (.7)	.7(4) = 2.80		.7(3) = 2.10		.7(1) = .70
Worst (.3)	.3(2) = .60		.3(2) = .60		.3(0) = 0
Expected returns	3.40		2.70		.70

FIGURE 4.2 Probability Distribution of Returns.

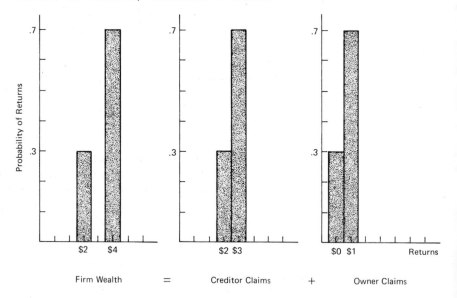

Table 4.4 portrays the mean, variance, standard deviation, and coefficient of variation for the firm, the creditors, and the owners. Notice that the wealth distribution of the firm has a mean of \$3.40, a standard deviation of .9165, and a coefficient of variation of .27. The wealth distribution of the

TABLE 4.4 Mean ($\bar{R}$), Variance (σ^2), Standard Deviation (σ), and Coefficient of Variation (V) of the Wealth Distribution

			FIRM		
PROBABILITY	OUTCOME R_i	RETURN $p(R)$	DEV. $R_i - \bar{R}$	DEVIATION SQD. $(R_i - \bar{R})^2$	SQD. DEV. × PROB.
.3	2	.60	−1.40	1.96	1.96(.3) = .588
.7	4	2.80	.60	.36	.36(.7) = .252
		$E(\bar{R}) = 3.40$			$\sigma^2 = .840$

$$\sigma = \sqrt{.840} = .9165$$

$$V = \frac{\sigma}{\bar{R}} = \frac{.9165}{3.40} = .2695$$

			CREDITORS		
PROBABILITY	OUTCOME R_i	RETURN $p(R)$	DEV. $R_i - \bar{R}$	DEVIATION SQD. $(R_i - \bar{R})^2$	SQD. DEV. × PROB.
.3	2	.60	− .70	.49	.40(.3) = .147
.7	3	2.10	.30	.09	.09(.7) = .063
		$E(\bar{R}) = 2.70$			$\sigma^2 = .210$

$$\sigma = \sqrt{.210} = .45825$$

$$V = \frac{\sigma}{\bar{R}} = \frac{.45825}{2.70} = .1697$$

			OWNERS		
PROBABILITY	OUTCOME R_i	RETURN $p(R)$	DEV. $R_i - \bar{R}$	DEVIATION SQD. $(R_i - \bar{R})^2$	SQD. DEV. × PROB.
.3	0	0	− .70	.49	.49(.3) = .147
.7	1	.70	.30	.09	.09(.7) = .063
		$E(\bar{R}) = .70$			$\sigma^2 = .210$

$$\sigma = \sqrt{.210} = .45825$$

$$V = \frac{\sigma}{\bar{R}} = \frac{.45825}{.70} = .6547$$

creditors has a mean of $2.70, standard deviation of .45825, and coefficient of variation of .17. Similarly, the wealth distribution of the stockholders has a mean of $.70, standard deviation of .45825, and coefficient of variation of .65.

The results show some important relationships. One is that *the mean wealth of the firm is equal to the mean wealth of all claimants against the firm's assets.* It is important to see that this is a restatement of the traditional accounting equation (Assets = Liabilities plus Owners' equity). Furthermore, *the summation of the standard deviation of the claimants equals the standard deviation of the firm.* That is, the risk borne by the firm must be absorbed by those who have claims upon its assets. We can now conclude, based on the last relationship, the following very important generalization: *Total financial risk is normally equal to the business risk.*

Nondiversifiable Risks   We have just seen how firms may exercise control over business and financial risks. This is done by diversifying the fields of endeavor, the product produced, and the financing of assets. Some factors, however, firms have little control over. Likewise, investors have little or no control over these factors. The factors are *purchasing-power risk* and *market risk*. They are influenced by forces outside the firm, such as technology, demographics, consumer tastes, government regulation, and natural forces (cycles).

The *purchasing-power risk* is defined as the variability of returns arising from changes in the purchasing power of the dollar. It is sometimes called inflation risk. However, the latter term implies only one aspect of changes in the prices of goods and services—that is, that prices will always rise. If the past is any guide (and it should be), we know that prices also fall. Rising prices benefit debtors, who may repay in cheaper dollars. Falling prices benefit creditors, who are repaid in dearer dollars than were loaned. Both aspects of purchasing power—rising as well as falling prices—must be considered.

For example, if prices are rising, one may want to hedge against inflation with the purchase of common stock, art objects, real estate, and so on. Such action preserves the buying power of the dollar. But when prices are falling, one now hedges against deflation by converting investments into the more liquid assets of the money market, or gold and its surrogate, gold stocks, in capital markets. Since the buying power of the dollar is now rising relative to the prices of goods and services, it makes sense to hold dollars (and earn the nominal return) instead of holding assets (securities, plants, homes, and the like), which are falling in value.

The *market risk* is the variability of returns arising from changes in the market price of assets. Such changes occur because of changes in the market price of all assets. That is, the risk caused by changes in market price is unrelated to the unique value of the company itself. Both the firm and the investor must be prepared for the market price of assets to fluctuate. This is considered normal. In fact, there are short-term fluctuations and long-term fluctuations that occur with somewhat fixed periodicity. The former fluctuations are caused by the business cycle, the latter by the long waves of economic activity.

THE IMPLICATIONS OF RISK
(HOW RISK IS HANDLED)

Most businessmen and investors are averse to risk. That is, they prefer little or no risk situations if possible. However, almost all business and investment decisions have some risk inherent in them.

For example the, following set of return and risk situations are given:

Situation 1. Expected return of A $<$ B
Risk of A $\quad\quad = $ B

Situation 2. Expected return of A $=$ C
Risk of A $\quad\quad < $ C

Situation 3. Expected return of A $<$ D
Risk of A $\quad\quad < $ D

These are shown graphically in Figure 4.3.

The graphs in Figure 4.3 illustrate how risk is handled:

1. Given two situations (A and B) with similar measures of risk, one would always prefer the situation with the higher expected return (B).

FIGURE 4.3a Expected Return and Risk of Investments A, B, C, and D.

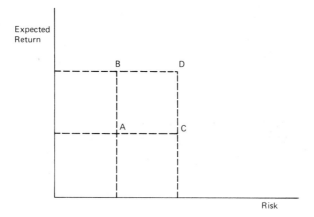

FIGURE 4.3b Probability Distribution of Returns.

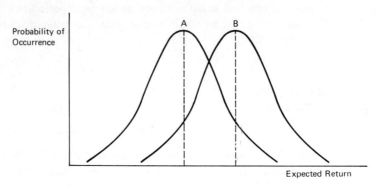

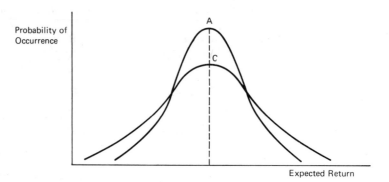

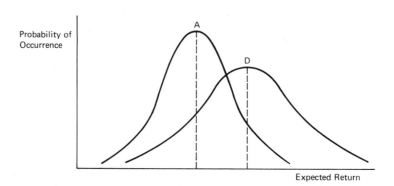

2. Given two situations (A and C) that are similar with respect to expected returns but that differ with respect to risk, one would always prefer the less risky situation (A).

3. Given two situations (A and D) such that A's return is less than D's and A's risk is also less than D's, one is perhaps not sure of the choice between A and D.

What alternatives are there for handling risk? They may be grouped together under the three following headings:

1. Assume the risk and minimize probable deviations.
2. Combine the assets subject to risk into a large, diversifiable portfolio of assets.
3. Transfer or shift the risk to another party.

That is, ensure against variability of returns. Some insurance companies provide mutual funds that insure the investor against loss. He may not have a gain, but at least he has no loss. Similar insurance policies are available to business firms to reduce or eliminate the chance of loss in the firm.

SUMMARY

Two things are certain about risk.* One is that most businessmen are averse to risk. The second is that some risk is inherent in almost every financial management or financial investment situation. Although the business and financial risks can be diversified away, one has little control over systematic risk. Diversifiable risk can be measured by the standard deviation. Standard deviation is an approximate measure of risk for investors and businessmen who hold single-security (asset) portfolios.

The beta estimate (see appendix to Chapter 18) is an index of nondiversifiable risk. Although standard deviation may be used for a single security, investors (and businessmen) can be efficient diversifiers. Thus, the beta should be used, since unsystematic risk may be diversified away.

omit

APPENDIX TO CHAPTER 4:
DECISIONS WHERE PROBABILITIES ARE UNDEFINED

Game theorists have developed five decision rules to be followed in situations of uncertainty. Probabilities are assumed to be known in order to assess each event. The decision rules are (1) EMV, or Expected Monetary Value; (2)

---

*A third thing, which has not yet been proved satisfactorily, can be said about risk. That is, corporations that invest in more risky packages of real assets will not actually obtain observably higher-than-average returns. One plausible explanation is that any risk premiums that do exist are apt to be small and thereby difficult to detect in view of the dynamic change that characterizes the business world.

Minimax; (3) Most Likely; (4) Equally Likely; and (5) Maximax. Each is discussed briefly.

1. EMV—Mathematical expectation for each event.

DECISION POINT	EVENT	STATE	PROBABILITY	OUTCOME	EXPECTED VALUE
		Normal	$p = .5$	+ 500	250
	Project A	Boom	$p = .3$	+ 600	180
		Recession	$p = .2$	− 200	− 40
				EV =	390
		Normal	$p = .5$	+ 600	300
	Project B	Boom	$p = .3$	+1,000	300
		Recession	$p = .2$	−1,000	−200
				EV =	400
		Normal	$p = .5$	+ 200	100
	Project C	Boom	$p = .3$	+ 100	30
		Recession	$p = .2$	− 100	− 20
				EV =	110

2. Minimax—Minimize the maximum damage that could occur. Label worst that can happen on each set of events. The decision maker should select that alternative with the least of the maximum regrets possible.

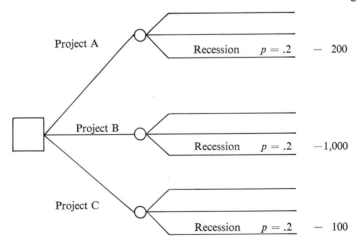

3. Most Likely—Used more in business than any other! Assumes that the event that is most likely, based on probabilities or preferences, will happen.

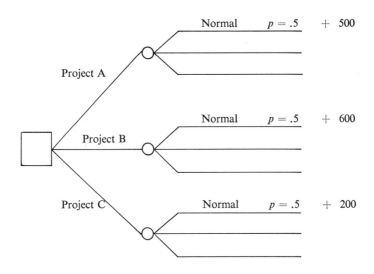

4. Equally Likely—Rather naive approach. Assumes every event is just as likely to happen. So just add up the totals.

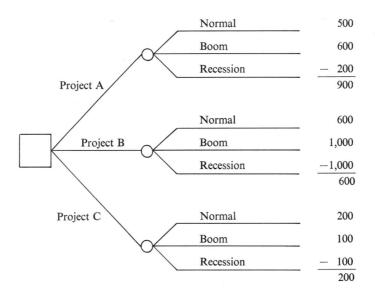

5. Maximax—Trying to maximize best thing that can happen to you. Pick alternative that gives best possible return, *ignoring the damage that could occur.*

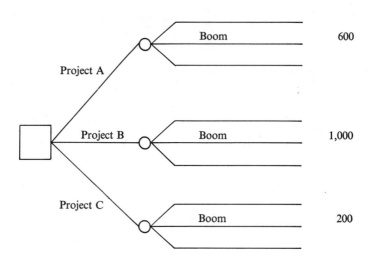

FIVE DECISION RULES (SAME PROBLEM, TWO FORMATS)

Format I: Payoff Table

BEST ACT			EVENTS	A	B	C
Minimax	C		Normal	500	600	200
Maximax	B		Boom	600	1,000	100
Equally			Recession	−200	−1,000	−100
Likely	A					
Most			Max. Loss	−200	−1,000	−100
Likely	B					
EMV	B		Max. Gain	600	1,000	200
			(Total)	900	600	200
			Most Likely	500	600	200
			EMV	390	400	110

Format II:
Decision Tree

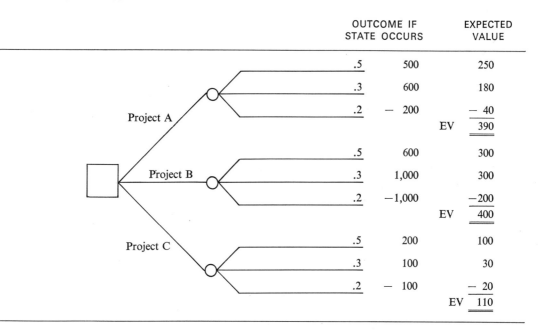

		OUTCOME IF STATE OCCURS	EXPECTED VALUE
Project A	.5	500	250
	.3	600	180
	.2	− 200	− 40
		EV	390
Project B	.5	600	300
	.3	1,000	300
	.2	−1,000	−200
		EV	400
Project C	.5	200	100
	.3	100	30
	.2	− 100	− 20
		EV	110

The *decision tree* has advantages in complex problems. The *payoff table* is for elementary problems.

PROBLEMS

1. Given the following sets of probabilities and returns for each outcome:

FIRM A

PROBABILITY	RETURN
.3	$1,200
.4	3,600
.3	6,000

FIRM B

PROBABILITY	RETURN
.3	$ 2
.7	100

a. Compute the mean, standard deviation, and coefficient of variation for firms A and B.

b. Which measure of variability (i.e., σ or V) is better for comparing the risks of the two distributions? Why? *break it down to a percentage*

Homework

2. You are considering two mutually exclusive investment proposals. The proposals cost the same and have similar characteristics. The probability and return on each are shown below:

	PROBABILITY	RETURN
Proposal A	.2	$2,400
	.6	3,000
	.2	3,600
Proposal B	.2	200
	.6	1,000
	.2	1,800

a. Compute the mean and standard deviation of each proposal.

b. Which proposal is riskier? Why?

3. Name the risk indicated by the following:

a. Price of GM goes to $25 per share. *market risk*

b. GM's Monte Carlo goes to $20,000. *purchasing power risk*

c. GM announces a decline in earnings. *business risk*

4. A firm is faced with two expansion choices: to build a large plant or a small plant. The probabilities for high, medium, and low growth of sales over the next few years are shown in column 1. Column 2 shows the expected return for each outcome in millions of dollars.

	PROBABILITIES (1)	RETURN (2)
Large Plant:	.3	6
	.5	0
	.2	(3)
Small Plant:	.3	2
	.5	1
	.2	0

a. Compute the risk-to-return ratio for each plant. (*Hint:* Use coefficient of variation.)

b. Which plant should be built?

5. Rates of returns on securities A and B are projected for the four years listed below. Each state has an equal probability of occurrence.

RATE OF RETURN

STATE OF NATURE	CO. A	CO. B
1978	18%	27%
1979	11	5
1980	− 7	34
1981	14	−20

a. Calculate the expected return of each security.

b. Calculate the variance and standard deviation of each.

c. Calculate the coefficient of variation.

d. Which security is more risky? Why?

5

The Impact of Cycles

Consideration of cycles of economic activity is a logical extension of the study of risk. In fact, we saw in Chapter 4 that one of the major risks to be considered in finance is the impact of market fluctuations on financial decisions. This impact is felt by both the financial manager and the financial investor and manifests itself in the financial markets.

In order to understand the present and to plan for the future with any degree of certainty, it is necessary to study the past. History tends to repeat itself, but never in the same detail. Each period has new factors at work that lead to a somewhat different course of events than what would have been predicted from a study of past events alone.

To be able to analyze business fluctuations, then, it is necessary to measure past changes as well as current changes in economic indicators. A true and complete picture of a cycle could be obtained only by examining the data for all kinds of business activity, but it is difficult to comprehend simultaneously the large number of indexes involved (800 or more). The key to the problem lies in the fact that the business cycle is a movement of business in general. For practical purposes, a first approximation to the problem can be obtained by using a single index that is widely inclusive, such as the index of industrial production.

If business activity continued at a steady pace, rising gradually as population dictated and technology allowed, many economic problems would disappear. But one of the most obvious facts of economic life is that all is not smooth. Business fluctuates. This can be seen from an examination of almost any statistical time series describing the course of business—changes would be noted in national income, production, prices, sales, employment, bankruptcies, profits, inventories, investments, money supply, and a host of other areas.

An examination of a large number of time series (a set of economic data over a period of time) shows that the vast majority fluctuate with the business cycle.* That is, most of the economic indicators tend to move in the same direction. However, they are not uniform in their fluctuations. Some indicators, such as money supply and department-store sales, move more closely with the trend of aggregate business activity than do others, such as electrical output and construction contracts awarded. Some series move earlier in the cycle, such as orders for capital goods, while others lag behind the cycle, such as short-term interest rates. The early movers are called *leading indicators* and the late movers are called *lagging indicators*. A third series of economic data tend to move almost in precision with the overall economy. These are called *coincident indicators*.

A list of leading, lagging, and coincident economic indicators that are the most consistent has been established by the National Bureau of Economic Research (NBER). The list contains twelve leading, eight coincident, and six lagging indicators. The leading indicators have predicted every turn in general economic activity. Table 5.1 depicts each of the indicators, along with the median lead (−) or lag (+) expressed in months; for example, −5 represents a five-month lead time, whereas +5 is a five-month lag time. *Business Conditions Digest*, a monthly publication of the U.S. Department of Commerce, publishes data on the 26 indicators mentioned above, plus many others.

In spite of the general movement of economic indicators, there are differences in movement clearly discernible within the general pattern. For

*One exception is unemployment, which for obvious reasons moves inversely to the trend.

example, wholesale prices tend to move faster and further than retail prices. Moreover, the prices of primary commodities (basic raw materials) are even more volatile. Such differences among price movements persist over the years and seem to be part of a general pattern in business cycles.

Many economists question even the use of the term "cycles," maintaining that it implies more regularity than actually exists. Some either doubt the

TABLE 5.1 Economic Indicators

CLASSFICATION AND SERIES TITLE	MEDIAN LEAD (−) OR LAG (+) IN MONTHS
Leading indicators (12 series):	
Average workweek, production workers, manufacturing	−5
Average weekly initial claims, state unemployment insurance, thousands (inv.)[a]	−8[b]
Index of net business formation	−7
New orders, durable goods industries	−4
Contracts and orders, plant & equipment	−6
New building permits, private housing units	−6
Change in book value, manufacturing and trade inventories	−8
Industrial materials prices	−2
Stock price, 500 common stocks	−4
Corporate profits after taxes, Q^c	−2
Ratio, price to unit labor cost, mfg.	−3
Change in consumer installment debt	−10
Roughly coincident indicators (8 series):	
Employees in nonagricultural establishments	0
Unemployment rate, total (inv.)[a]	0
GNP in current dollars, Q^c	−1
GNP in constant dollars, expenditure estimate, Q^c	−2
Industrial production	0
Personal income	−1
Manufacturing and trade sales	0
Sales of retail stores	0
Lagging indicators (6 series):	
Unemployment rate, persons unemployed 15+ weeks (inv.)[a]	+2
Business expenditures, plant and equipment, Q^c	+1
Book value, manufacturing and trade inventories	+2
Labor cost per unit of output, mfg.	+8
Commercial and industrial loans outstanding	+2
Bank rate, short-term business loans, Q^c	+5

[a] Inverted.
[b] This series has had a lead of 10 to 22 months and an average lead of 15 months at the peak, but is almost coincident at the trough.
[c] Quarterly series.

Source: *Adapted from Geoffrey H. Moore and Julius Shiskin*, Indicators of Business Expansions and Contractions, *National Bureau of Economic Research, Inc. (New York, 1967), p. 68.*

existence of cycles in business activity or believe they can be legislatively controlled. However, there is no adequate ground, as yet, for believing that business cycles do not exist or that they will soon disappear by legislative edict. It seems apparent that the government will not resist inflation with as much tenacity as it does depression.* It is also unwise to believe that deep but brief contractions in business, such as occurred in 1920–21 and 1937–38, will never take place again.

Limited experience with contracyclical policy does not provide strong support for the belief, so often expressed by theoretical writers, that government is capable of adjusting its spending, taxing, and regulatory policies with the fine precision and promptness needed to assure full employment and a virtually stable price level at all times.

TYPES OF CYCLES

In studying time series, one finds three types of movements all occurring simultaneously. They are:

1. Seasonal variations—movements in specific indexes that recur regularly at the same period each year. Such movements are due to changes in the weather, to customs related to the seasons of the year, and to the unequal number of days in the months.

2. Secular trend—a long-term, persistent movement in one direction or another. This trend is the persistent underlying movement that has taken place in a series of data over a period of time that covers several business cycles. It is the inherent basic growth or decline that would occur even if there were no business cycles.

3. Cyclical fluctuations—more or less regularly recurring fluctuations around the long-term trend. A cycle is characterized chiefly by the fact that it seems to affect simultaneously most parts of the economy, and particularly the economic aggregates, such as prices, production, employment, and income. By convention, such a movement is not called a cycle unless it runs more than a year from peak to peak (or trough to trough).

There appear to be a number of rather well-defined cycles that jointly influence the cyclical behavior of business as a whole. There is a 3-to-4-year cycle, another cycle of 7 to 11 years, and perhaps yet another of 47 to 60 years. The movement of each is not completely periodic. That is, there is neither a

---

*Note the federal deficit spending year after year. Refer to Chapter 23 for budget deficits since 1960.

uniform length for each type of cycle nor uniform periods of contraction and expansion. Even if each cycle were perfectly regular, the pattern resulting from their joint effect would be far from simple. When some are falling while others are rising, there may be little effect on business activity. However, when all are falling or rising, their combined effect on business tends to be pronounced.

The Kitchin Cycle
(3 to 4 Years)

The short cycle, the Kitchin cycle, is generally identified with accumulation and depletion of inventories. An Englishman, Joseph Kitchin, discovered the 40-month cycle. It is more commonly known as the business cycle.

The business cycle is defined as a general movement of aggregate business activity up and down around the secular trend. The typical business cycle, or Kitchin cycle, is divided into four periods or phases: depression, recovery, prosperity, and recession.* See Figure 5.1.

FIGURE 5.1 The Business Cycle.

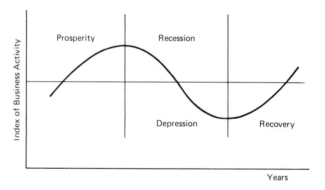

The business cycle averages 3 1/3 years (40 months) in length, with individual cycles usually running between three and four years. Forty months fits the timing of the average cycle pattern reasonably well, except during the long depressions of the 1870s and the 1930s, and during major wars (the Civil War, World War I, World War II, and the Vietnam War). The 40-month business cycle has been seen in the American economy for over 100 years.

The Juglar Cycle
(7 to 11 Years)

The Juglar cycle is an intermediate cycle of from seven to eleven years. These cycles, also known as trade cycles, consist of two to three business cycles.

---

*Sometimes the four phases of the cycle are referred to as lower turning point, upswing, upper turning point, and downswing.

The trade cycle is defined as an aggregate fluctuation of two or more business cycles. It averages about nine years in length. Such cycles are more dramatic and have more serious results than the business cycle. Trade cycles are often characterized by panic or crisis and by the fact that they are of greater amplitude than business cycles, which occur more frequently.

Clement Juglar, a Frenchman, discovered the 7-to-11-year trade cycle in the late 1800s. Juglar divided the trade cycle into three periods: prosperity, crisis, and liquidation.* Juglar observed that epochs of activity, prosperity, and high prices always end in crises, and these are then followed by some years of depressed activity and low prices.

The Kondratieff Long Waves (47 to 60 Years)   In the 1920s, Nikolai D. Kondratieff, a Russian economist and statistician, discovered the existence of long waves in capitalistic economies by the analysis of time series.† Each wave, or cycle, averages almost 54 years in duration. A number of series of data were tested from Great Britain, France, Germany, and the United States. The tested series of data included price levels, interest rates, bank deposits, wages, foreign trade, and production of selected products.

The following characteristics of long waves established by Kondratieff are summarized as follows:

1. The long waves are a part of the same complex dynamic process of the capitalist economy in which intermediate cycles (7 to 11 years) and short cycles (about $3\frac{1}{2}$ years in length) also occur. During the upswing of the long cycle, years of prosperity are more numerous. During the downswing, years of depression tend to dominate.

2. During the downswing of the long wave, agriculture goes into a long depression. This happened after the Napoleonic Wars (circa 1815). It happened again from the 1870s onward, and again after the World War I period.

3. During the downswing of the long wave, important inventions and discoveries in transportation and communication are made, which are usually applied on a large scale at the beginning of the next long upswing. See Table 5.2 for inventions in transportation and communication.

---

*Sometimes the three periods are referred to as good times, panic, and hard times.

†Kondratieff was sentenced to solitary confinement, became mentally ill, and died in a Russian labor camp. See Aleksandr I. Solzhenitsyn, *The Gulag Archipelago* (New York: Harper & Row, 1973), pp. 50, 331, 626.

TABLE 5.2 Inventions in Transportation and Communication

1814–1849 (DOWNSWING)	1849–1873 (UPSWING)	1873–1896 (DOWNSWING)	1896–1920 (UPSWING)	1920–1949 (DOWNSWING)	1949–1974 (UPSWING)
1823—Calculating Machine	1868—Typewriter	1876—Telephone	1896—Wireless	1920—Microphone Condenser	1960—Laser
1827—Differential Gear		1878—Cathode Ray Tube		1922—Radar	
1839—Photography		1885—Differential Gear for Automobile		1927—Electronic TV	
1841—Rotary Printing Press		1887—Gasoline Automobile		1929—Coaxial Cable	
		1895—Diesel Engine		1929—Rocket Engine	
		1896—Experimental Airplane		1939—Automatic Sequence Computer	
				1939—Jet Engine	

Source: *Ray G. Jones, Jr., "The Reinforcing Effect of the Long Waves on the Business Cycle,"* Appalachian Business Review, *Fall-Winter, 1976.*

4. At the beginning of the upswing, gold production increases and the world market for goods is enlarged through the absorption of new and colonial countries into the mainstream of civilization.

5. During the upswing period of the long wave, the most disastrous wars and revolutions (internal wars) occur.

6. Wars of expansion usually occur about midway on the downswing.

Turning-point dates for the Kondratieff long waves, along with price movements in the United States and the United Kingdom, are shown in Table 5.3.

TABLE 5.3 Turning-Point Dates for Kondratieff Long Waves and Price Movements in U.S. and U.K.

TURNING POINT	KONDRATIEFF LONG WAVES	PRICE MOVEMENTS	
		U.S.	GR. BRITAIN
Trough	1785–1795	1789	1789
Peak	1810–1817	1814	1813
Trough	1844–1851	1843	1849
Peak	1870–1875	1864	1873
Trough	1890–1896	1896–1897	1896
Peak	1914–1920	1920	1920
Trough		1932	1933

Source: *A. F. Burns and W. C. Mitchell,* Measuring Business Cycles *(New York: National Bureau of Economic Research, 1947).*

THE NATURAL LAW OF CYCLES

A theory of business fluctuations proposed in the late nineteenth century was based on sunspot cycles. It held that the disturbances on the surface of the sun (sunspots) exhibited a close correlation with agricultural cycles. The reasoning was that sunspots must affect the weather, the weather in turn influences agricultural crops, and the crops affect business conditions. For a number of years when we were an agrarian society, economics used sunspot cycles to predict business cycles. However, the method has now been discarded, since the extremely high correlation was thought to be the result of accidental rather than causal factors.

Cycles are found throughout our natural system. Some cycles in nature occur with a fixed periodicity, such as the four seasons of the year. Others occur with somewhat more erratic periods, such as the sunspot cycles; however, these cycles do tend to exhibit recurring series, such as eleven years, then nine years, then seven years, and back to eleven again.

Adam Smith, the father of economics, suggested that business fluctuations are as natural a phenomenon as are the orbits of the earth or the cycles of the moon, even though the latter are fixed, whereas business fluctuations appear to be erratic. However, the business cycle does operate on approximately a $3\frac{1}{2}$-year period. Of course, exceptions are made for unusual occurrences such as wars and depressions. Thus it appears that the business cycle can be influenced by government action.

THE IMPLICATION OF CYCLES FOR FINANCIAL MANAGERS AND INVESTORS

Since cycles do exist, it follows that financial managers and investors should plan for them accordingly. This holds true for both short cycles and the long waves of economic activity. How to plan for the cycles and what to do when they occur are discussed below.

Business Cycle In our capitalistic system, most production is done for the market. As a result, businessmen cannot wait until the orders come in and then produce precisely the amount that is needed. So managers try to estimate what the future demand will be and try to have a supply of goods ready to meet the hoped-for demand. The possibility of error is great. Both revenue and cost forecasts can be wrong, so that undesired inventory accumulation or depletion or dramatic price changes may occur. Uncertainty as to the outcome may cause managers to further alter plans, and this will affect the economy. The problem arises because production takes time. If output could be created instantaneously, no inventories would be maintained, and no possibility of error in expected outcome would exist.

Figure 5.2 shows the occurrence of business fluctuations since 1920. With exceptions made for wars and depressions, the business cycle always

FIGURE 5.2 Business Fluctuations.

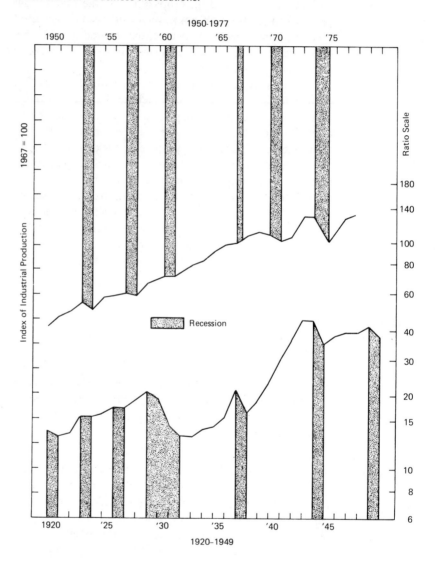

ranges between three and four years.* In order to eliminate over- or under-production of inventories, the manager should be aware of and plan for business expansions and recessions. Financial managers should think for themselves and not be tempted to follow the crowd. For example, most firms built inventories in the first half of 1974 because everyone was doing it. However, massive inventory liquidations occurred in late 1974 and early 1975 as the recession unfolded and took its toll.

Maybe another factor is that most economists tend to be optimistic. Therefore, if the manager is influenced by the overoptimistic forecasts of private and government economists, he is subject to serious error. And it's a fact of life that businessmen themselves prefer to be optimistic. However, there is a time for everything—a time to be optimistic and a time to be realistic.

Figure 5.2 indicates seven recessions since World War II. This has much relevance to the investor, because each time a recession has occurred, the stock market has declined. Some authorities believe in a four-year election cycle, in which the market rises when the incumbent party retains the presidency. However, this is not necessarily borne out, and the business cycle is the reason. Notice in Table 5.4 that the stock market declined in 1948 and 1960. Both these years represented the beginning of a recession. The market rose in the other postwar election years, because the business cycle was in its expansion phase. Based on the presidential-election-year cycle, the market should have fallen in 1952, 1968, and 1976 because the incumbent party lost. Of course, this did not occur, because these were boom years.

The fact that stock prices are a good indicator of business activity is borne out by the 1967 study conducted by the National Bureau of Economic Research. The NBER study found stock prices to be the most reliable leading economic indicator out of 36 such indicators widely used by business analysts since 1873.

It is suggested that a shortened business cycle is often largely compensated for by a lengthened one following it. Therefore, the knowledge of the average cycle length and cycle variations is a valuable aid in forecasting.

Recessions can now be rather precisely measured by coincident indicators. The Department of Commerce has developed a composite index of four coincident indicators. They are (1) employees on all nonfarm payrolls, (2) the Federal Reserve's index of industrial production, (3) personal income less "transfers" (non-wage-salary income like Social Security), and (4) all manufacturing and trade sales. The dollar figures for income and sales are adjusted to eliminate inflation.

The index has been empirically tested over a number of years. The

---

*The business cycle is measured from either trough to trough or peak to peak.

TABLE 5.4 Presidential-Election-Year Cycle

			DOW JONES INDUSTRIAL AVERAGE			
			YEAR BEFORE	ELECTION YEAR		PATTERNS: ✓ CONFIRMED × NOT CONFIRMED
CANDIDATES	(% VOTE)	ELECTED (PARTY); TOTAL VOTE (THOUSANDS)	YEAR-END	YEAR-END	YEAR'S CHANGE	
1976: Jimmy Carter	(50.6%)	Carter (Dem.)	852	1004	+152	×
Gerald Ford	(48.4%)	79,605				
1972: Richard Nixon	(60.7%)	Nixon (Rep.)	890	1020	+130	✓
George McGovern	(37.5%)	77,719				
1968: Richard Nixon	(43.4%)	Nixon (Rep.)	905	943	+38	×
Hubert Humphrey	(42.7%)	73,212				
1964: Lyndon Johnson	(61.1%)	Johnson (Dem.)	762	874	+112	✓
Barry Goldwater	(38.5%)	70,645				
1960: John Kennedy	(49.7%)	Kennedy (Dem.)	679	615	−64	✓
Richard Nixon	(49.5%)	68,838				
1956: Dwight Eisenhower	(57.4%)	Eisenhower (Rep.)	488	499	+11	✓
Adlai Stevenson	(42.0%)	62,027				
1952: Dwight Eisenhower	(55.1%)	Eisenhower (Rep.)	269	291	+22	×
Adlai Stevenson	(44.4%)	61,551				
1948: Harry Truman	(49.6%)	Truman (Dem.)	181	177	−4	×
Thomas Dewey	(45.1%)	48,794				

Source: The World Almanac *and* Barron's.

results coincide remarkably with both the beginnings and ends of recessions. The record covering the 1973–75 recession shows that the peak occurred in November 1973 and the trough occurred in March 1975. The month-by-month readings are shown in Table 5.5.

TABLE 5.5 1973–75 Recession

MONTH	INDEX	MONTH	INDEX
Nov. 1973	178.2	Aug. 1974	171.9
Dec.	175.6	Sept.	171.0
Jan. 1974	173.7	Oct.	169.0
Feb.	172.6	Nov.	162.8
Mar.	172.2	Dec.	156.4
Apr.	171.8	Jan. 1975	152.5
May	172.5	Feb.	149.7
June	171.6	Mar.	147.0
July	172.4		

Source: *"The Outlook,"* Wall Street Journal, *January 12, 1976, p. 1.*

Knowing when a recession starts and ends can be of value to the financial manager and investor. Although that recessionary feeling can linger for quite a while after the expansion begins, the composite coincident indicator along with leading indicators helps alleviate such feelings.

A typical cycle portraying interest rates and security data in different phases of the business cycle is shown in Figure 5.3. Note that interest rates peak during a recession and bottom out after a recession is over. Securities prices tend to peak prior to a recession and hit bottom during a recession.* Observe that security prices and dividend yield are mirror images of each other. The implications for the financial manager and the financial investor are explicitly indicated by the relationships in Figure 5.3. For example, the financial manager should plan to liquidate inventories and have excess cash as recessions begin and interest rates peak. The financial investor should be fully invested as securities prices hit bottom during recessions and should be heavy in cash or money-market instruments as securities prices peak prior to recessions.

FIGURE 5.3 A Typical Cycle.

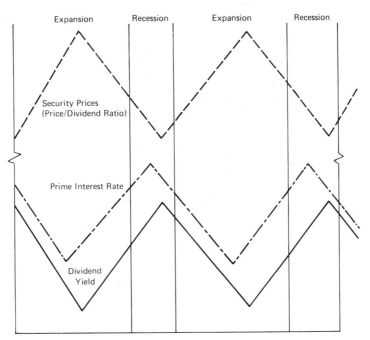

Long Waves Possibly more important is the reinforcing effect of the long waves on the business cycle. For example, the year 1920 witnessed the end of a long

---

*If recessions are mild, a la 1967, interest rates peak prior to the beginning of the recession and securities prices both peak and bottom prior to the beginning of the recession. See Figure 5.2.

trend in one direction (upward, in most factors) and the commencement of another long but largely opposite trend. As a result, factors that had strongly advanced from 1896 to 1920 (such as prices, incomes, wages, interest, banking, and stock quotations) could be expected to greatly modify their upward movement, while other factors that had advanced moderately might move downward.

During the last upswing of the long wave (1949 to 1974), total U.S. debt grew from $400 billion to $2.5 trillion.* The later figure is composed of $1 trillion in corporate debt, $600 billion in mortgage debt, $500 billion in U.S. government debt, $200 billion in state and local government debt, and $200 billion in consumer debt.

These figures may help explain some of the current economic situations. For example, many of our major cities are in financial trouble (difficulty in servicing outstanding debt) for the first time since the 1920–30 period. Almost half the states have budget deficits, some even bordering on default of their bond issues. And the U.S. government has had a series of deficits, with the one for the 1976 fiscal year estimated at between $60 and $75 billion. Many corporations have experienced financial trouble—some fatally—as evidenced by Penn Central Railroad, Lockheed Corp., Chrysler Corp., Pan Am World Airways, and W.T. Grant. Now add deflation to the weight of the mountain of debt. The consequences are foreboding. Excessive debt plus deflation may result in another depression.

Note the four Kondratieff cycles in Figure 5.4. Just as 1920 signified a peak in the long-term uptrend, it appears that 1974–75 may also mark the

FIGURE 5.4 Four Kondratieff Cycles. (*Source: Adapted and extended from The Review of Economic Statistics, Vol. XVII, No. 6, November 1935, pp. 105–15.*)

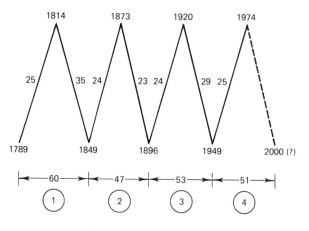

*"The Debt Economy," *Business Week*, October 12, 1974, p. 45.

end of a long-term uptrend. This has significance for both the financial manager and the investor. Long waves should not be ignored, even though most economists find one reason or another to fault Kondratieff's work.

Some interesting observations can be made concerning the application of long waves to the U.S. economy. Today, we have four long waves to view instead of the three established by Kondratieff in the 1920s (see Figure 5.4). Price-level movements have been shown to correlate closely with the peaks and troughs of the long-wave cycle. Prior to the peak of each of the first three long waves, the United States had just fought a war—the War of 1812, the Civil War, and World War I. Approximately ten to twelve years after each of these wars, a great depression, or washout, occurred—the depressions of 1822, 1877, and 1931. This cycle has operated with eerie precision on three occasions, with the depressions, or washouts, occurring approximately every 54 years.

The sobering aspect of long-wave cycles in the United States is that a major war (Vietnam) ended in 1973, just prior to the peak of the fourth cycle. Proponents of the long wave expect the next few years to be very bullish for the stock market (as in the 1920s). The next "great crash" will not come until the mid 1980s. And ten to twelve years after the Vietnam War will mark the beginning of the next washout, or depression, on the downswing of the fourth Kondratieff long wave.

Patterns of long waves can be demonstrated only over four cycles. Possibly this is not enough evidence to confirm the fact that such long waves exist and reinforce the business cycle. However, history does tend to repeat itself, even if never in the same detail. If we are in the downswing of the fourth Kondratieff cycle, as the figures suggest, one can look for the next three to four business cycles to be adversely affected by the existence of long waves. That is, upswings in the business cycle will be shorter and less pronounced, while downswings will be longer and more severe than is the case under upswings in the Kondratieff long waves. This scenario has policy implications as well. Monetary and fiscal policies may have to be more rigorously pursued in order to combat the consequences of a soft or unhealthy economy —high unemployment rates, low rates of production, and ultimately an economic depression. Certainly, Kondratieff cycles should be seriously considered in exercising economic policy as well as financial decisions. But because of the lack of incontrovertible evidence, caution should also be exercised.

SUMMARY

Three types of cycles have been distinguished, each of whose length depends on the disturbances that brought it about. The short cycle, known as the Kitchin or business cycle, is identified with inventory accumulation and depletion lasting between three and four years. Thus, labor hiring and termination policies principally underlie the business cycle. Interest rates tend to peak during recessions and bottom during periods of prosperity. Securities prices peak near the end of periods of prosperity and hit bottom during recessions.

The intermediate cycle, known as the Juglar or trade cycle, relates to individual innovations, such as new textile machines, dynamos, electric motors, and refrigerators. Such cycles last between seven and eleven years.

Finally, the long wave, named for Kondratieff, is marked by the appearance of major inventions in transportation and communication, which cannot be carried through in one Juglar cycle. Thus, long-run trends become part of the cyclical phenomena and, indeed, can be understood as the result of shorter-run changes. Fixed capital investment and debt policies are primarily involved in the generation of long waves of economic activity.

PROBLEMS

1. Describe the timing relationships that exist among business cycles, stock and bond prices, and interest rates.

2. What are leading, coincident, and lagging indicators? When is each group of indicators used?

3. Given that the business cycle occurs with relative fixed periodicity (except during wartime and depression), when should a recession follow the 1973–75 recession? Did the recession actually occur at that time? If so, why? If not, why not?

4. Given that washouts, periods of severe depression, occur in accordance with the long waves, when should the next washout occur? How will one know that the event is imminent? What can one do to prepare for such an event?

5. Why do businessmen and government economists not utilize the impact of cycles more in their planning?

Financial
Management

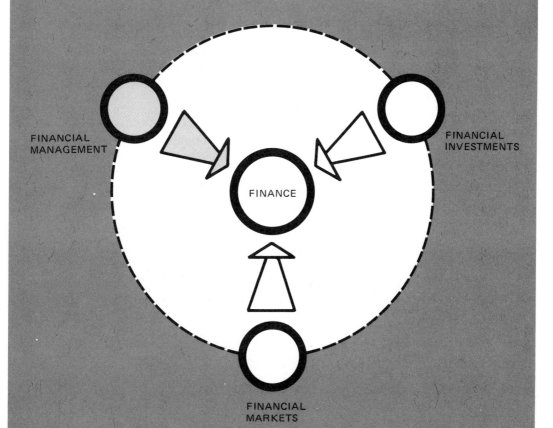

In Part I we examined some easily applied decision rules that involved taxes, present value, risk, and cycles. In Part II we apply these decision rules to financial management.

It is important that the decision maker understand all aspects of the financial decision. Thus we weave in the relationship of financial investments and financial markets to financial management. All participants in the finance arena are trying to maximize wealth. Normally, there is a correlation between the price of a security in the marketplace and the decisions made by the financial management of the firm.

A business decision maker could possibly despair of ever finding an easily applied rational approach to financial decisions. We have attempted to present the material in lucid form with an operational tone. Short case studies are added to give more insight into the complexities of financial management. We hope that a knowledge of these complexities will lead to more reasonable procedures.

Part II contains eight chapters covering what we consider to be the fundamentals of financial management. Chapter 6 examines the functions of financial management. The The earnings-cycle model is presented, along with standardized terminology. Short case studies conclude the chapter.

Chapter 7 presents the tools of financial analysis. Various ratios are presented and discussed. A unique feature of this chapter is the inclusion of the investibility ratios. This we find to be the unifying theme between financial management and financial investment in this chapter.

The next three chapters (8, 9, and 10) examine in some detail working-capital management. Chapter 8 covers the management of cash and marketable securities. Chapter 9 covers accounts receivable and inventory management. Finally, short-term financing is examined in Chapter 10. The theme in these chapters on current accounts is that risk in current-asset management can be greatly reduced.

The last three chapters of Part II are concerned with determining the optimal financial structure for a firm. Chapter 11 discusses arrangement and ranking of data and risk considerations in the capital budgeting process. The cost of capital and its components are outlined in Chapter 12. Also, leverage and debt are related to their effects on the cost of capital. In Chapter 13, a look is taken at capital structure and valuation. Valuation of individual securities and of the firm is undertaken in this chapter. Finally, asset expansion under the parameters of the capital asset pricing model is presented.

6

Functions of
Financial
Management

We could manage this matter to a T.

Laurence Sterne,
Tristram Shandy, *bk. II, 1760*

Since financial management is a subdivision of general management, it must share the goals of general management. A broad goal of management is success for the firm and its continued life. But what are the manifestations of success and long life?

We shall assume that the maximization of the common shareholders' wealth position is the major goal of management. This means that management must take all actions that increase the value of the common stock, and take no actions that will decrease the value of the common stock. One of the actions that will increase the market value of the common stock is the maximization of earnings after taxes. Other things equal, the greater the earnings after taxes, the greater the value of the firm, and the greater the value of the firm, the better off is the common shareholder.

Some studies have suggested that the management of large corporations does not respond to the needs of the shareholder, but rather tries to maximize dimensions of the firm other than earnings or shareholder wealth. Other variables mentioned include sales, asset size, and executive compensation. We shall circumvent these motivations and, for the purpose of analysis, assume that the managers of firms are motivated to maximize earnings after taxes and shareholder wealth. We feel this is a legitimate course, since we are out to test the efficacy of financial decisions, and their impact can be traced directly to the profitability of a firm as measured by earnings after taxes. The impact of financial decisions upon the other variables is not so easily measured, and for this reason, they are rejected as goals of management.

DEFINITION OF FINANCIAL MANAGEMENT

A General Definition   *Management* is frequently defined as the planning, organizing, directing, and controlling of the firm's resources.* Cast in these terms, *financial management* is the planning, organizing, directing, and controlling of the firm's financial resources. It is concerned primarily with efficiently executing the financial functions of the firm.

A second area of responsibility of the financial manager involves assisting in general management functions that impinge upon, or have feedback effects upon, the financial health of the firm. One area, for example, that has a great impact upon the firm's finances, yet is not *primarily* the financial manager's responsibility, is asset management. Yet the financial manager should, and does, get involved in assisting and advising on asset-management matters. Consider, for example, the contents of Chapters 7, 8, and 9, which follow. These chapters all deal with the management of assets, a skill crucial to efficient financial management.

Before we use this information to derive a specific definition of financial management, we shall take a look at the earnings-cycle model. The purpose of the earnings-cycle model is to give an overview of the finance function in the firm.

An Overview of the   Figure 6.1 presents an overview of the finance function in the firm. The
Finance Function: model is titled "The Earnings-Cycle Model" because a major function
The Earnings-Cycle   of financial management is to see that funds attracted to the firm are
Model   converted to earnings after taxes, and this cyclical process is demonstrated in the diagram.

Beginning at the extreme right-hand side of the diagram, note that funds are attracted to the firm in exchange for debt and equity claims. Funds attracted by these claims are used to purchase assets whose primary function is to generate revenue. Assets, and only assets, produce revenue. The debt and equity (owner) claims represent proportional claims upon the structure of assets and the revenue they produce. The listing of debt and equity claims and the asset structure constitute the firm's position statement.

---

*See, for example, Henry L. Sisk, *Management and Organization*, 2nd ed. (Cincinnati, O.: South-Western Publishing, 1973), p. 8.

FIGURE 6.1 The Earnings-Cycle Model.

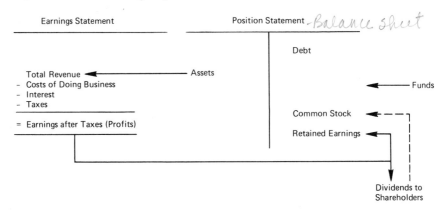

Revenue that accrues to assets is accounted for on the earnings statement. The earnings statement shows that after the costs of doing business—such as wages, fuel costs, rent, and so forth—are deducted from revenue along with interest and taxes, the residue is earnings after taxes. Earnings after taxes is the *raison d'être* of the firm. It is the return on investment and efforts for which the owners assume the risk of the enterprise.

The firm has two options for use of earnings after taxes. It can turn over all the earnings to the owners of the corporation in the form of dividends. Or the firm can retain the earnings and use them to purchase new assets. Retaining earnings is a major source of growth of the firm. When the firm retains earnings, it starts the cycle again. That is, retained earnings are used to purchase new assets that generate revenue, and this in turn results in additional earnings after taxes. These can be distributed to the owners or retained further by the firm.

One part of the diagram bears elaboration: the dotted line running from "Dividends to Shareholders" to "Common Stock." The management of the corporation would hope that the corporation continues to be financially healthy and an attractive investment. Given this, it would be hoped that, after dividends are paid, they would be used to purchase additional common stock in the corporation.

This view of the earnings cycle in the firm has given an integrated view of how funds attracted to the firm are converted into ultimate earnings for the shareholders. The model is useful in viewing the responsibilities of financial management.

A Specific Definition and Functions of Financial Management

The earnings-cycle model of the financial function in the firm, outlined in the preceding section, is an extremely important—and valuable—diagram of the critical relationships among the financial variables in the firm.

The model is useful in delimiting the basic and specific responsibilities that will be discussed in this section. The earnings-cycle model isolates and identifies the critical points in the earnings cycle. These critical points provide a readily identifiable set of specific definitions of the functions of the financial manager. Breaking into the earnings cycle on the liability-capital side of the balance sheet, each critical point in the cycle will be identified as a function of financial management and discussed in detail.

Funds Acquisition. As suggested previously, a major function of the financial manager is the acquisition of funds at the lowest possible cost to the firm.* This involves the issuance of debt and equity claims upon the asset structure and revenue of the firm. Knowing the mood and condition of capital markets, in order to issue the "right" security—claim—at the "right" time in order to minimize its cost, is also a function of the financial manager. He must constantly monitor and have knowledge of the receptivity of investors to the spectrums of both debt and equity claims.

Another responsibility of the financial manager is generating funds on the right-hand side of the position statement. Managing the *structure* of claims management of the capital structure involves constantly assessing the cost interrelationships among funds sources. The financial manager stresses the substitution of low-cost sources for the high-cost ones. (Capital structure and its management are discussed in detail in Chapter 13.)

Asset Acquisition and Management. The next sequential step is the acquisition of assets. The financial manager is heavily involved in measuring and evaluating revenues that accrue to potential assets. He is also responsible for measuring the cost of funds that are used for the purchase of assets. The process of measuring cost and return on funds used for the acquisition of long-term assets is the topic of Chapter 11.

The management of individual assets, as well as the structure of all assets, is not a primary responsibility of the financial manager. But the financial manager can, and frequently does, become involved in assisting in asset management, for two reasons. First, it is for assets that debt and equity claims are issued, and the financial manager learns a great deal about assets and their utilization in arranging for their financing. A second reason involves the maximization of earnings for the firm. It is possible for a firm to exploit the market for its product exhaustively, generate massive revenues, and still fail because of sloppy management of assets. The business history of the United States is studded with examples of firms with brilliant production histories coupled with financial failure.† The management of cash, of receivables and

---

*Some financial experts would argue that this is the *only* responsibility of the financial manager.

†Some of these are discussed later in this chapter.

inventories, and of long-term assets are all examples of asset management that have crucial financial implications. These topics are discussed in Chapters 8, 9, and 11, respectively.

Revenue and Expense Control. One of the goals of asset management is the maximization of revenues, which takes us to the next critical point of the earnings-cycle model, the earnings statement. The earnings statement is the statement of the firm's revenues, its expenses, and their difference, earnings after taxes (EAT). Since the maximization of earnings after taxes is a major goal of the firm, it follows that the financial manager has a hand in maximizing revenues—basically, efficient asset management—and the minimization of expenses. It is by constant monitoring of the firm's financial condition through the use of ratios, discussed in the following chapter, that expense control is effected. Maximizing profitability—earnings after taxes— plays a large part in making the firm attractive to potential investors.

Summary. We have come full circle in the earnings-cycle model. Profitability is an attractive characteristic of a firm, and makes both its debt claims and its equity claims attractive to the investing public. Without the confidence and support of the investing public, the firm's funds sources dry up, the cycle is broken, and, at best, growth is curtailed. At worst, the firm is forced to "dry up" and eventually cease operations.

The basic responsibilities of financial management are defined in terms of the critical points in the movement of funds in the earnings-cycle model. The crucial points in the cycle, and therefore the basic responsibilities of financial management, are:

1. Funds acquisition through the issuance of debt and equity claims.

2. Asset acquisition and asset management. This involves minimizing asset cost at acquisition, and maximizing revenues once the asset is acquired.

3. Revenue and expense control. Maximizing revenues and minimizing expenses on the earnings statement leads to the maximization of earnings after taxes.

4. Maintaining the "investability" of the firm, by generating earnings after taxes and striking the necessary balance between earnings retention and dividend payments.

SHORT CASE STUDIES

In this section, four short case studies are presented. The purpose of relating these cases is to illustrate the crucial responsibilities of financial management, the penalties that are paid when financial function is not discharged responsibly, and the rewards reaped from astute financial management. The cases of E.T. Barwick Industries, Inc., and W.T. Grant Company illustrate the financial penalties, whereas the cases of McDonald's Corporation and the Coca-Cola Company illustrate the financial rewards. In each case, the backdrop will be presented, and the genesis of financial success or failure will be discussed.

Barwick Industries:
Lack of Expense
Control

E.T. Barwick Industries, Incorporated, was founded by Mr. E.T. Barwick in 1949.* Mr. Barwick was a pioneer in the development of tufted carpeting, a much lower-cost process than weaving. Using the tufted manufacturing process, the Barwick Corporation grew very rapidly. Mr. Barwick was also instrumental in gaining market acceptance for carpeting in areas of the home not usually carpeted, such as the kitchen and the patio. This also aided greatly in making the firm one of the major producers in the carpeting industry.

But there was trouble on the horizon. To assist in the rapid growth of the firm, Mr. Barwick employed a great deal of leverage; that is, debt was used to a large extent in financing the purchase of required assets. Not only was leverage used heavily, but much of the debt was short term, and expensive factoring† agreements were also relied upon to provide funds for asset expansion. These financing schemes were to create fairly serious problems.

In addition to the financing of growth with expensive short-term funds, expense control was lax. For example, only recently has the firm installed a computerized cost-accounting system in order to determine and keep track of unit costs of production. To further reduce costs, an expensive jet airplane was sold.

Asset acquisition also presented problems. One executive of the firm reported that it has the physical capacity to produce $300 million worth of carpets a year. Yet the biggest year the company ever had was $192 million. The same executive reported that a $450,000 carpet-dyeing machine purchased in 1967 had yet (as of 1975) to be uncrated.

In terms of the crucial points in the earnings-cycle model of financial management, it appears that E.T. Barwick Industries made three errors in financial management:

1. In the area of funds acquisition, it used expensive short-term funds for long-term expansion. This is a violation of the principle of suitability.

---

*The discussion of Barwick Industries draws heavily from the article, "A Financial Expert for Beleaguered Barwick," *Business Week*, May 19, 1975, pp. 58, 60.

†See Chapter 9. Factoring is the process of selling accounts receivable, usually to a financial intermediary.

2. In the area of asset management, it did not have a program for rationally evaluating asset needs and asset acquisitions. This is a failure to use capital budgeting techniques and effective forecasting.

3. In the area of expense control, it failed to systematically monitor expenses. This is a violation of a most fundamental management responsibility.

These errors might not have proved critical had it not been for the worst recession since the 1930s, which resulted in the following problems for Barwick in 1974 and 1975:

1. Short-term interest rates rose dramatically.

2. Demand for carpeting dropped off.

3. Synthetic fiber, raw material to the company, rose sharply in price.

These three developments combined to create losses for the firm. For its last three fiscal years, the firm has posted losses. The losses, of course, were charged to the shareholders, whose equity in the company dropped from $42 million in April 1974 to $19 million in January 1975.

One result of these developments is that the founder of the firm, Mr. E.T. Barwick, stepped aside as chief executive officer under pressure from the firm's creditors.* He was replaced as chief executive officer by Charles E. Selecman, a former president of U.S. Industries. Mr. Selecman has no expertise in carpets but has instituted financial controls. Under Mr. Selecman, losses of $27.9 million in fiscal year 1975 were reduced to $8.8 million in fiscal year 1976. Cost cutting was accomplished primarily by the sale of unprofitable manufacturing facilities and office space. Even the company's corporate headquarters building is up for sale, and the headquarters staff will be moved to a smaller, leased building.†

W. T. Grant: On October 2, 1975, the W.T. Grant Company, a large retailing chain,
Unbridled Growth filed a petition for arrangements under Chapter XI of the Bankruptcy Act.‡ This action signaled clearly the massive financial problems experi-

---

*Mr. Barwick remained "chairman of the company"—basically an honorary title.

†"The Bizarre Power Struggle at Barwick," *Business Week*, November 29, 1976, pp. 81, 82. This article details the conflict between Mr. Barwick and Mr. Selecman.

‡This discussion of W.T. Grant Company's financial problems draws upon the following articles in the *Wall Street Journal:* "Hard-Nosed Salesman Shuts Stores, Cuts Jobs to Save W.T. Grant," December 4, 1975, pp. 1, 28; "Grant Creditors to Ask Ruling of Bankruptcy," February 11, 1976, p. 5.

enced by that company. The chain of events leading to the filing for bankruptcy by Grant revealed weaknesses in the general management of the firm, and specifically in its financial management.

As in the previous case, basic weaknesses in financial management are related to the crucial parts of the earnings-cycle model.

The basic problem of Grant started with rapid expansion of the number of stores. The number of stores grew to more than 1,000 nationally. Many of the stores were not located in high-volume locations. In order to generate the revenue required to support the many new stores, Grant entered into selling "big-ticket" items, major household appliances and furniture. The sale of these product lines required the extension of credit to its retail customers. And the extension of credit was not carefully supervised.*

Consider the precarious condition of Grant: overextension of store locations, with attendant inventory problems, and massive amounts of new credit on its books, much of it marginal. These would be precarious conditions in the best of times, but with a downturn in the nation's economy, they could be the worst of conditions, and the nation's economy did turn down. The sudden downturn in the economy was translated into a downturn in sales and an increase in bad debts.

The inevitable happened. The slowdown in sales and the increase in bad debts drove down the value of the firm's assets, which fell precariously. In the attempt to stave off bankruptcy, the number of stores was slashed from 1,069 in May 1975 to 493 in December 1975. The remaining stores were located mostly in the Northeast. Additionally, the payroll was cut in half, from 62,000 employees to 30,000. These measures were not successful, of course, in staving off bankruptcy. In March 1976, W.T. Grant was liquidated.†

The problems of W.T. Grant Company arose primarily from an ill-conceived expansion program, which in turn created follow-up problems of asset management. In order to utilize the newly acquired fixed assets (that is, stores), inventory had to be expanded rapidly, and to sell the expanded inventory, marginal credit was extended to move the inventory. These are problems of asset management, and they reduced this once national retail chain to a regional chain within three months, to a bankruptcy case within another month, and finally completely out of business within a very short period of time.

---

*The president of W.T. Grant Company, Robert H. Anderson, said of the company's credit practices, "Anyone whose breath could be seen on a mirror was granted credit." *Wall Street Journal*, December 5, 1975, p. 28.

†For one view of the human tragedy of W.T. Grant, see Rosh Loving, Jr., "W.T. Grant's Last Days—As Seen from Stock 1192," *Fortune*, April 1976, pp. 108 –114.

The Success of McDonald's. McDonald's Corporation has been a leader in the fast-food industry. Starting in 1954 as a nationally franchised chain of hamburger restaurants, it grew rapidly. This growth is documented by the figures in Table 6.1, which shows three important dimen-

TABLE 6.1 Number of Restaurants, Total Revenues, and Earnings Per Share, McDonald's Corporation, 1970–75

YEAR	NUMBER OF RESTAURANTS	TOTAL REVENUES ($000)	EARNINGS PER SHARE
1970	1,592	$200,300	$ .49
1971	1,904	290,630	.69
1972	2,272	422,490	.94
1973	2,717	592,211	1.31
1974	3,222	729,040	1.70
1975	3,550	941,060	2.17
Growth factor	2.23	4.70	4.43

Source: McDonald's Corporation Annual Reports.

sions of the firm: number of units (restaurants), total revenues, and earnings per share. Over the five-year period covered by the table, the number of restaurants grew by a factor of 2.23, total revenues grew 4.7 times, and earnings per share increased 4.43 times. Because of good management and a new idea in retailing prepared food, McDonald's has been a very successful corporation. But the success of McDonald's probably would have not been manifested had it not been for some creative financing used relatively early in the corporation's history, and it is this creative financing that the following thumbnail sketch attempts to highlight.

A Successful Idea. Two brothers, Richard and Maurice McDonald, moved from New England to San Bernardino, California, at the end of World War II and started a successful drive-in restaurant.* But labor problems plagued them. It was difficult to keep reliable waiters, waitresses, dishwashers, and other help. In order to solve this problem, they hit upon the idea of a limited menu served on paper plates. The idea was efficiency of operations and high volume. McDonald's was one of the first, if not *the* first, firm in the soon-to-grow-rapidly fast-food industry. Thus, the McDonald's restaurant was prospering when it was discovered by Ray Kroc.

---

*The material in this and the following sections draws heavily from the article, "For Ray Kroc Life Began at 50, or Was It 60?" *Forbes*, Vol. III, No. 2 (January 15, 1973), 24–30.

Ray Kroc: Expansion. In 1954, Ray Kroc, a promoter and milkshake-machine salesman, happened upon McDonald's. He knew a winner when he saw one. He talked the McDonald brothers into allowing him to franchise the restaurants around the country. With little working capital,* Kroc set about to build McDonald's.

By 1954, Kroc had taken in a partner, who was made responsible for financing McDonald's operations. In 1960, it occurred to Mr. Sonneborn, the new partner, that a great deal more money could be made by buying land, building the restaurant on it, and then enjoying two sources of revenue: the franchise fee, and the rent from the land and restaurant building.

But this required a massive new infusion of funds into McDonald's. Kroc managed to get an appointment with a senior officer of a New England insurance company. Said the officer:

> We looked hard, and saw there was more than a chain of hamburger stands. They had operations under *tight financial controls.*†

The insurance companies lent McDonald's Corporation $1.5 million and, as a premium, took 20 percent of the common stock. One of the insurance companies later sold its McDonald's stock for $7 million—all profit, since the equity premium was in addition to the loan.

Kroc now began a program of building McDonald's. One of his first acts was to buy the McDonald brothers out in 1961. The brothers wanted $2.7 million for their interest in the corporation. Sonneborn raised money again, this time by arranging a five-year loan. The lender demanded an equity participation, but Kroc refused to part with any more stock. In lieu of giving stock, Kroc agreed to assign the .5 percent royalty the McDonald brothers had been receiving.‡

Kroc, now in complete control, began aggressively to build McDonald's. During the following years, McDonald's grew rapidly and became the nation's largest fast-food retailer. Because it was so well managed, it weathered the recessions in the fast-food industry that destroyed lesser firms. Today, McDonald's is still growing, and now it is extending into foreign markets.

But had it not been for recognition that a major source of revenues would be the leasing of land and buildings to franchisees, and the creative financing used to bring about the real estate operation, the Golden Arches of McDonald's might still be unknown.

---

*One of Kroc's early secretaries took her salary in stock. In 1973, it was estimated that she owned 1,000,000 shares.

†"For Ray Kroc," p. 25. (Emphasis supplied.)

‡By 1973, the royalty added up to $14 million.

Coca-Cola: Cash for Acquisition   The Coca-Cola Company was organized in 1885. It is generally agreed that the soft drink, Coca-Cola, is one of the most successfully marketed products of all time. Today Coca-Cola ("Coke") is sold in more than 155 countries.

A simplified ratio analysis gleaned from the company's 1975 annual report is presented in Table 6.2. Several tentative conclusions about the management of the Coca-Cola Company can be drawn from analysis of the ratios presented.

TABLE 6.2   Selected Ratios, the Coca-Cola Company, 1975

Liquidity:	
Current ratio	2.05 ×
Quick ratio	1.99 ×
Cash/total assets	4.80%
Current assets/total assets	52.6%
Leverage:	
Total debt/total assets	28.0%
Asset management:	
Inventory turnover	9.4 ×
Fixed-asset turnover	1.7 ×
Return:	
Return on total assets	14.0%
Return on equity	24.0%
Common-stock data:	
Earnings per share	$4.00
Dividends per share	$2.30
Payout ratio	57.5%
Price range	$69.87 to $89.75

Source: *Calculated from* Annual Report 1975, *the Coca-Cola Company.*

A Contradiction: Liquidity and Profitability.   Analyses of the ratios will reveal that the company has three characteristics: It is well managed, it trends to be liquid, and it is profitable.

The well-managed characteristic is attested to by the asset-management ratios. They indicate that the company incorporated its inventories into its products 9.4 times during 1975, and that it "turned over" or incorporated its fixed assets into its products 1.7 times on the average.

The profitability of the Coca-Cola Company is attested to by the return ratios. The return on total assets was 14 percent and the return to owners' equity was a whopping 24 percent. It should be noted that the return to owners' equity was dramatically high despite a lack of employment of leverage. The leverage factor, at 28 percent, was relatively low.

The ratios tell the story of the company's great liquidity. The current ratio at 2.05 is high. But perhaps more astounding is the quick ratio, which was almost 2 times also (1.99). This means that the Coca-Cola Company could pay off its current liabilities twice over, recognizing that it could not count upon prepaid items as a source of cash. This is liquidity.

A question arises. How can a corporation so liquid be so profitable? It is a tenet of finance that liquidity and profitability are mutually exclusive. That is, riskless cash earns no return, and risky assets are not liquid. The question that arises is, How can the Coca-Cola Company defy the basic tenet and simultaneously be liquid and profitable at the same time?

The answer, like many things in finance, is so simple that it is deceptive! The answer is simply that the company uses its liquidity to purchase "bargain" companies, which, under Coca-Cola management, become profitable. Consider, for example, the following list of Coca-Cola acquisitions:

YEAR	ACQUISITION
1960	Minute Maid
1964	Duncan Foods
1970	Aqua-Chem, Inc.
1975	Thomas Companies
1977	Taylor Wine Company

These wholly owned subsidiaries produce some of the nation's best-known brand-name products within the "Coke family" of companies. For example:

Minute Maid	Frozen juices
Snow Crop	Frozen juices
Hi-C	Fruit drink
Maryland Club	Coffee and tea
Butternut	Coffee and tea
Admiration	Coffee and tea
Thomas J. Webb	Coffee
Huggins	Coffee

In addition, the company has used cash and stock to acquire, or merge with, Coca-Cola bottling operations. For example, in 1975, the Coca-Cola Company acquired the Thomas companies, three franchised bottling companies. These acquisitions allow the company to have greater control over the production and distribution of Coca-Cola products.

The description of these acquisitions is not to take away from the activities of the prime thrust of the company, the production and distribution of Coca-Cola and other soft-drink products. But the ability of the Coca-Cola Company to acquire promising subsidiaries for good prices is partially related to its policy of conservativeness and liquidity. And thus Coca-Cola can be, to a degree, both liquid and profitable.

SUMMARY AND CONCLUSIONS

This chapter has attempted to place financial management in perspective with overall general management of the firm. It was seen that financial management is a special case of the responsibilities of the general management of the firm.

The earnings-cycle model is an attempt to "photograph" the cycle of responsibilities of the financial manager. The earnings-cycle model depicts the flow of financial activities from the acquisition of funds, by issuance of financial claims, to their employment in asset acquisitions, to the effective measurement of their productivity in the earnings statement, and, to complete the cycle, to the disposition of earnings in dividends to the firm's owners or to retained earnings, reinvestment in the firm by its owners.

Four very short case studies were presented to show the importance of financial management to the fortunes of the firm. The four short cases and their central themes are replicated below:

E.T. Barwick: Lack of expense control

W.T. Grant: Difficulty with rapid expansion

McDonald's Corporation: Creative financing

Coca-Cola Company: Making liquidity pay off

These short cases point up the importance of effective financial management to the health of the firm.

7

Tools of Financial Management

In the previous chapter, the broad functions and responsibilities of financial management were presented. Capital asset pricing was introduced to show its relationship to the concept of wealth maximization. Failure and success in financial management were highlighted in case studies.

This chapter presents some techniques, including ratio analysis, by which financial management monitors the condition of the firm. Proficiency in the art of ratio analysis permits the financial manager both to discharge the broad responsibilities of financial management and to deal with such specific topics as management of cash, receivables, and inventories; capital budgeting; and management of the firm's cost of capital.

A successful physician must both analyze the physical conditions of his patients and prescribe those medicines and actions which will help them maintain, or recover, good health. A firm's financial manager has similar responsibilities; he must monitor the financial health of the firm and prescribe actions to maintain it.

Although the principles of accounting and financial analysis are relatively standardized, terminology is not. This chapter presents a standardized terminology of financial analysis that will be used throughout. Terms used in the chapter will suggest their financial functions, and are used for this reason. A summary of the major principles of accounting is attached in the appendix to this chapter.

110

The two basic accounting statements are the Statement of Financial Position (the position statement) and the Statement of Earnings (the earnings statement). They contain the major sources of information guiding the actions of the financial manager.

The Position The position statement (see the example in Table 7.1) is defined as the
Statement listing of the firm's assets and the claims of the creditors and owners against those assets. There are several characteristics of the position statement that are important.

TABLE 7.1 Statement of Financial Position, the Blue Ridge Corporation, December 31, 197–

Current assets:			Current liabilities:		
Cash	$ 500,000		Accounts payable, 7%	$ 500,000	
Accounts receivable	700,000		Notes payable	1,500,000	
Inventory	1,500,000		Total current liabilities	$2,000,000	
Prepaid expense	300,000				
Total current assets		$3,000,000	Long-term liabilities:		
			5% bonds	4,000,000	
Fixed assets:			Total liabilities		$6,000,000
Plant, equipment	$9,000,000				
Minus depreciation	2,000,000		Owners' equity:		
Total fixed assets		7,000,000	Contributed capital, common stock (par value $5)	$2,000,000	
			Retained earnings	2,000,000	
			Total owners' equity		4,000,000
			Total liabilities and owners' equity		$10,000,000
Total assets		$10,000,000			

Time Element. It is important to recognize that the position statement is a stock concept; that is, the values it represents exist at one point in time. In this regard, the position statement is frequently compared to a snap-shot. A snapshot portrays a series of objects and their interrelationships at an instant of time. This characteristic is also true of the position statement. The position statement is in effect a snapshot at an instant of time of the recorded values of the firm's assets and the value of the claims against the assets.

Balancing. Another characteristic of the position statement is the fact that assets equal claims on assets. The reason that the values on the asset side are equal to the values on the liability-and-owners' equity side is perhaps not as obvious as the observation that they do balance. An understanding of why both sides of the position statement are equal is important.

As liability claims are issued by the corporation, they are recorded at face value—that is, the amount of promised repayment. Again, assets are purchased with the funds thus generated, and the assets are recorded at their cost.*

Common stock is recorded on the right-hand side of the position statement at its par value, an arbitrary bench-mark figure assigned at the time of the sale of the stock.† The book value of the owners' interest in the firm is illustrated by the basic identity:

$$\text{Assets} = \text{Liabilities} + \text{Owners' equity}$$

The relationship can be transposed, however, to highlight the residual, unfixed nature of the owners' claims on the asset structure. Rearranging terms:

$$\text{Owners' equity} = \text{Assets} - \text{Liabilities}$$

Stated this way, the relationship takes on new meaning. It says symbolically that if, for any reason at all, the market value of the assets falls, it is the owners who absorb the loss. The residual nature of the owners' claims not only is illustrated on the position statement, but is also a key to the construction of the earnings statement as well. More on this later.

The position statement "balances" because of the way it is defined. Given the fixed nature of the firm's debts, it follows that any changes in the market value of the assets must be immediately reflected in the value of the owners' claims.

---

*This practice leads sometimes to a wide divergence between "book" value and current market value of the asset. This is especially true if the price of the asset fluctuates violently after the asset is purchased.

†The surplus, if any, of the stock's par value over its sale price is recorded in a "paid-in surplus" account in the owners'-equity section of the position statement. Common stock plus paid-in surplus is increasingly termed "contributed capital" on position statements. This has more significance than the traditional method.

Order of Listing. Another important characteristic of the position statement is the order of listing of the accounts. It is a basic principle that asset accounts as well as liability accounts are listed in order of liquidity.* On the asset side, this means that cash is listed first, because it is, by definition, the most liquid of all assets. Accounts receivable are usually listed after cash. As their name suggests, they are short-term debts that are due—that is, receivable—by the firm. They normally arise from the sale of the firm's products to its customers on credit.

Listed next in order is inventories. For a merchandising firm—a retailer or wholesaler—the merchandise in the storerooms that will be soon turned into cash is the inventory. In a manufacturing firm, inventories can be raw materials awaiting the production process, and can also be finished goods awaiting shipment to customers.

Prepaid expenses can be the next asset listed in order of liquidity. Prepaid expenses are expenses that the firm has paid prior to their due date. A firm might, for example, prepay a bill to take advantage of a large discount. In this case, the prepayment represents a piece of valuable property, and is listed as such on the position statement.

Fixed assets are usually defined as assets with a life greater than one year. Machinery, trucks, equipment, buildings, and real estate are all assets that fall in this category. Normally, the firm will have charged earnings for the expense of physical depreciation of the plant and equipment. The sum of these charges constitutes the depreciation account. This sum is subtracted from the plant-and-equipment account to get the "residue" of value in the plant and equipment.

On the liability side, accounts payable are usually the shortest-term debts. These accounts are the result of trade credit extended *to* the firm by its suppliers. The next shortest-term debt is usually notes payable. These are debts resulting from short-term borrowing, such as from commercial banks. These loans are usually for 90, 180, or 270 days.

Bonds represent long-term debt,† and are usually listed last in the liability section. Long-term notes issued, along with real estate mortgages, are similar to bonds, and are so treated.

After all debts—liabilities—are listed, the owners'-equity section appears.‡ The owners'-equity section usually consists of two accounts: con-

---

*Liquidity is simply defined as "closeness" to cash—i.e., the ability of an asset to be converted to cash without loss.

†Bonds that have less than one year to maturity are, of course, short-term liabilities.

‡The term "owners' equity" is to be differentiated from net worth. Owners' equity is used to refer to the total position-statement values of the owners' claims. Net worth, on the other hand, denotes the market value of owners' claims—i.e., the market value of one share of stock times the number of shares outstanding—plus the value of accumulated earnings.

tributed capital and accumulated earnings. The common-stock portion of contributed capital records the par value of the common-stock issue. If the par value of each share of stock is $10 and if 100,000 shares were sold, the common-stock account would have a balance of $1,000,000.

If, however, the investing public paid $20 for each share of stock, the common-stock account balance would not accurately reflect the amount of equity claims. To record and account for the $10 above par value ($20 — $10) that each of the investors paid for the stock, an account entitled, "Paid-in Surplus" is created, with a balance of $1,000,000, the total amount above par value that the shareholders paid for the issue—that is, ($20 — $10) × 100,000 shares.

Funds that the firm has accumulated out of previous earnings are accounted for in the accumulated-earnings account. These are earnings, after taxes, that were not paid to shareholders as dividends. As stated previously, earnings represent the largest single source of capital funds for U.S. corporations. In the case of our position-statement example in Table 7.1, the accumulated-earnings account has a balance of $2,000,000. It is not uncommon, however, to find the accumulated-earnings account exceeding the common-stock account, indicating that capital funds accumulated from earnings exceed the original investment in the corporation by the shareholders.

Position-Statement Summary. Thus we have a total picture of the position statement. It is important to remember these characteristics of the position statement:

1. It exists at a point in time.

2. It records the purchase price of all the firm's assets, minus their depreciation.

3. It records the claims against the firm's assets owned by creditors and owners.

4. Creditor claims are fixed in value, and when their value is subtracted from assets, the residual value is owners' equity.

The Earnings Statement   The earnings statement is a listing of the firm's revenues and expenses and their difference, earnings after taxes. In this section, the major characteristics of the earnings statement will be discussed, along with its major function—to isolate the funds available to the common shareholders.

The earnings statement has other titles: the profit and loss statement, income statement, and statement of operations, among others. The term "earnings statement" is preferred here because it emphasizes the function of this important financial statement: to isolate the earnings available to the common shareholders after all expenses, including tax liabilities, have been met.

Table 7.2 gives the earnings statement for a mythical firm. It contains, however, all the characteristics of the earnings statement that are important and that will be isolated and discussed.

TABLE 7.2 Earnings Statement, the Blue Ridge Corporation, January 1, 197– to December 31, 197–

Sales	$12,000,000
Less: Cost of goods sold	3,076,923
Gross earnings	8,923,077
Less: Operating expense	1,000,000
Earnings before interest and taxes (EBIT)	7,923,077
Less: Interest charges	305,000
Earnings before taxes (EBT)	7,618,077
Less: Taxes (48%) 48%	3,656,677
Earnings after taxes (EAT)	3,961,400

Memorandum:		
	Number of shares outstanding	= 400,000
	Earnings per share (EPS)	= $9.90
	Payout ratio	= 50%
	Price-earnings ratio	= 10×

First, note that the earnings statement in Table 7.2 is for a year. This characteristic immediately differentiates the earnings statement from the position statement. Whereas the position statement is a listing of values at a *point in time*, the earnings statement is a listing of values generated over a *period of time*. Whereas the position statement has been compared to a snapshot because of its stock values, the earnings statement has been likened to a motion picture because of its time-flow nature. More specifically, the earnings statement is defined as a listing of all a firm's revenues and expenses over a period of time, generated for the purpose of isolating and determining the firm's earnings after taxes for the period.

The first figure on the earnings statement is the total amount of sales for the period. This is the gross revenue of the firm. From this figure is deducted the cost to the firm of the goods themselves that were sold. If it is a merchandising firm, the cost-of-goods-sold account reflects the purchase price to the firm of the goods that it acquired and sold during the period of the statement. If the firm is a manufacturing corporation, the cost of goods sold represents the acquisition cost of raw materials, as well as all costs incurred to convert the raw materials into the finished product.

After the cost of goods sold is deducted, the remainder is gross earnings, from which operating expense is next deducted. Operating expenses are the various costs incurred to sell the firm's product. Chief among these are advertising and sales expenses, as well as various overhead expenses incurred in the production and marketing of the firm's products. The figure obtained after operating expenses are deducted is earnings before interest and taxes (EBIT). EBIT is isolated and highlighted because both interest and taxes are expenses that the financial manager can attempt to influence in order to minimize.

Interest payments on both long- and short-term debt are deducted next. Usually, but not always, the major interest expense item will be interest on bond issues, the long-term debt of the firm.

The figure that results from deducting interest is earnings before taxes (EBT), the tax base. This is the figure upon which the corporate income tax liability is calculated. At the current time, the corporate tax rate is 22 percent on the first $25,000 of income, 25 percent on the next $25,000 to $50,000, and 48 percent on everything over $50,000.

After the corporate tax liability is calculated and deducted, the result is earnings after taxes (EAT). This residual income belongs to the common shareholders.* The corporation has the option of paying out the earnings to shareholders in cash, or reinvesting the earnings in the corporation for the benefit of the shareholders.

The earnings statement is an important financial record, for it reveals two very important dimensions of the firm: how successful its sales efforts are, and how successfully it controls expenses. Both sets of activities are very important, for success in both can increase the all-important residual account, earnings after taxes, the amount that belongs to the common shareholders.

Summary The position statement and the earnings statement are the two most important accounting statements generated in the firm. The position statement shows us how funds for assets are acquired and how assets are employed to earn revenues. The earnings statement reveals the level of earnings and how they are allocated to expenses, taxes, and the shareholders. Taken individually and in tandem, the position statement and the earnings statement are the sources of information for the financial analysis of the firm.

A BASIC TOOL OF FINANCIAL MANAGEMENT: RATIO ANALYSIS

Ratio analysis is a powerful tool of the financial manager. In the following section, the concept of the ratio will be examined, and this concept will then be applied to financial variables.

---

*We are assuming that the corporation has no preferred stock outstanding. If it did, preferred-stock dividends would be paid out of EAT, and the residual from this would then belong to the common shareholders.

What Is a Ratio? The English word *ratio* comes directly from Latin. The Latin word has many derivatives in the English language; among them are reason, ration, rational, and rationale. *Ratio* is defined formally as "the indicated quotient of two mathematical expressions"—and indeed, a ratio does result from the division of one number into another—and as "the relationship . . . between two or more things."*

An operational definition of a financial ratio is the *relationship* between two financial values. The word "relationship" implies that a financial ratio is the result of comparing mathematically two values. And this numerical comparison is important, for these ratios are used as indexes, and as indexes, they are used to make qualitative judgments about the financial health of the firm.

View total-asset turnover (TAT), for example. A firm's total-asset turnover is calculated by dividing the firm's total-asset value into its sales figure. Note first that this ratio is a *relationship*. It is the quantified relationship between sales and total assets. The figure is also an index. It tells us, on the average, how many times the value of total assets was incorporated into the firm's products. The total-asset turnover is an index that permits qualitative judgment to be made about the efficiency of the management of the firm's assets. Other things equal, the higher this ratio, the more efficiently the firm's assets are being managed, up to a limit. If a firm's total-asset turnover is significantly more than the average for its industry, it is possible that the firm is trying to produce its product without an adequate asset base. The point is, however, that this ratio permits quantification of an important relationship, which in turn permits a qualitative judgment to be made; and such is the case with all financial ratios.

The raw material of financial ratios comes from the two important financial statements already discussed, the position statement and the earnings statement. One distinct benefit of ratio analysis is that it permits analysis and cross-fertilization of data contained in each of the statements. For example, the total-asset turnover (TAT) ratio discussed above is one such ratio. It quantifies the relationship between an earnings-statement account, sales, and a position statement variable, total assets.

TYPES OF RATIOS

Financial ratios are categorized according to the financial activity or function to be measured. In the discussion that follows, five categories are presented

---

*Webster's New Collegiate Dictionary, 8th ed. (Springfield, Mass.: G. & C. Merriam, 1975), p. 958. "By permission. From Webster's New Collegiate Dictionary © 1977 by G. & C. Merriam Co., Publishers of the Merriam-Webster Dictionaries."

and discussed. These categories are:

1. Ratios that measure ability to meet current obligations (liquidity ratios)
2. Ratios that measure degree of debt employment (leverage ratios)
3. Ratios that measure efficiency of asset management (activity ratios)
4. Ratios that measure earnings success (profitability ratios)
5. Ratios that measure the benefit/cost effect on the existing (or potential) shareholder return (investibility ratios)

Each of these categories and their ratios will be discussed. The financial statements of the Blue Ridge Corporation—the position statement, Table 7.1, and the earnings statement, Table 7.2—will be used to generate and exemplify the various ratios.

Ratios Which Measure Ability to Meet Current Obligations (Liquidity Ratios)   It is extremely important for a firm to be able to pay its many bills as they come due. It is also important that the firm strike a balance between being able to meet its obligations and having too much of its asset structure in highly liquid assets.

The penalty to a firm for not being liquid enough to meet its bills is, at best, great embarrassment; at worst, cessation of its activities because of lawsuits, bad credit ratings, and destruction of confidence in the firm to conduct its affairs in an acceptable manner.

There is a penalty levied for being too liquid also. Cash and its substitutes earn very little or no return. Funds sitting in checking accounts and safes earn no revenue for the firm.

It is necessary to strike a balance between liquidity and lack of liquidity. The ratios discussed in this section are indexes of liquidity or lack of it, and assist the financial manager in striking the vital balance.

The Current Ratio.   The current ratio is calculated by dividing current assets by current liabilities. Symbolically, the current ratio is written:

$$\text{Current ratio} = CA/CL$$

where:

CA = current assets

CL = current liabilities

For Blue Ridge,

$$\text{current ratio} = \frac{\$3,000,000}{\$2,000,000} = 1.5\times$$

Current assets are cash and other assets that can be converted to cash within a short period, usually a year. Assets convertible into cash are accounts receivable and inventories. Prepaid expenses, discussed earlier in the chapter, are also current assets because they represent payments the firm *will not* have to make in the near future. Current liabilities are all obligations that will mature in one year or less. These can include accounts payable, bank loans and notes payable, and estimated federal income tax liabilities.

Translated into dollar terms, the current ratio stipulates the number of dollars of current assets the firm has to meet each dollar's worth of current liabilities. A ratio of greater than 1 indicates that the firm has more dollars of current assets than liability claims on the current assets.

The current ratio is a good "rough-and-ready" estimate of a firm's liquidity. A more precise measure of liquidity is available, however. It is the quick ratio, sometimes called the acid test.

The Quick Ratio. The quick ratio answers the question, For each dollar of current liabilities, how many dollars of current assets are there that can be converted into cash *immediately*? The quick ratio is a measure of the firm's liquidity under the worst possible conditions. Usually, only cash, accounts receivable, and marketable securities are counted as current assets in the quick ratio. This excludes inventories, prepaid expenses, and other assets that cannot be converted to cash immediately. Symbolically:

$$\text{Quick ratio} = \frac{\text{Current assets} - \text{Noncash assets}}{\text{Current liabilities}}$$

For Blue Ridge,

$$\text{Quick ratio} = \frac{\$1,200,000}{\$2,000,000} = .6\times$$

Thus, if Blue Ridge had to meet all its current obligations immediately, it could pay only 60 cents on the dollar. The possibility of Blue Ridge's having to pay all its current liabilities immediately is probably slim. But the quick ratio is an index of the firm's liquidity, nevertheless.

These indexes of liquidity, the current ratio and the quick ratio, provide important liquidity bench marks that can be used for comparison with industry averages, and with each other in "spread sheet" or time series analysis in which the trend in liquidity is charted.

Ratios Which Measure Degree of Debt Employment (Leverage Ratios)   It was suggested on a previous page of this chapter that the liability-and-net-worth side of the position statement reflects the financing of the firm's assets by these two funds sources. Leverage ratios are designed to measure the degree of employment of debt funds in the firm's assets.

The Debt Ratio. The debt ratio is defined as total debt, including both short- and long-term debt, divided by total assets. Symbolically:

$$\text{Debt ratio} = \text{TD/TA}$$

where:

TD = total debt

TA = total assets

For Blue Ridge,

$$\text{Debt ratio} = \frac{\$6,000,000}{\$10,000,000} = .6$$

The debt ratio is important because it assists the financial manager in making sure that fixed charges—contractual interest payments—do not get to be too large. The employment of *relatively* low-cost debt is beneficial as long as sales are increasing. But if debt is employed heavily and sales decline dramatically, such as during a downturn in the business cycle, the burden of interest payments on debt becomes onerous. The debt ratio, TD/TA, is an index of the degree of employment of debt.

Time Interest Earned (TIE). Another measure of the employment of debt is the times-interest-earned ratio. This measure gives an indication of the firm's ability to meet its fixed interest charges after all expenses except interest and taxes have been taken out. Symbolically:

$$\text{Times interest earned} = \text{EBIT/I}$$

where:

EBIT = earnings before interest and taxes

I = interest charges

For Blue Ridge,

$$\text{Times interest earned} = \$7,923,077/\$305,000$$
$$= 25.98\times$$

The perceptive reader may notice that this ratio comes entirely from the earnings statement, whereas ratios previously discussed came from the position statement.

The larger the TIE figure, the greater is the firm's ability to pay its interest charges. The TIE figure taken in conjunction with the debt ratio gives an indication of the degree and efficiency of debt employment by the firm. Again, these ratios can and should be compared to industry averages, as well as plotted on a time-series basis in order to monitor the trend in the employment of debt.

Ratios Which Measure Efficiency of Asset Management (Activity Ratios)

It was stated earlier that revenues accrue to assets, for it is assets that produce the goods and/or services that result in sales. The degree of efficiency of use of assets is a major determinant of the profitability of the firm. The firm that can efficiently utilize its assets without waste or duplication is the firm that will probably be successful.

There are four basic ratios that assist in gauging the efficiency of asset management. All are turnover ratios. The four ratios are accounts-receivable turnover, inventory turnover, fixed-asset turnover, and total-asset turnover.

Accounts-Receivable Turnover (ART). The firm frequently has to extend credit to its customers for competitive reasons. That is, it must ship products on the promise of later payment. This practice results in the generation of the accounts-receivable account in the short-term-asset section of the balance sheet.

As in the management of all assets, a happy balance must be struck in the creation of accounts receivable. If a firm grants too little credit, it may lose sales as a result. On the other hand, if the firm is too generous in the extension of credit, it will soon have much of its short-term assets tied up in slow or uncollectable accounts.

The accounts-receivable turnover (ART) is a measure of the number of times on the average that receivables turn over each year. Symbolically:

$$\text{Accounts-receivable turnover} = \frac{\text{Sales}}{\text{Accounts receivable}} - average \left(\frac{month\text{-}end}{balances} \div 12 \right)$$

For Blue Ridge,

$$\text{Accounts-receivable turnover} = \frac{\$12,000,000}{\$700,000}$$

$$= 17.14\times$$

To calculate the accounts-receivable turnover, divide the net sales by accounts receivable.* As is the case with all turnover ratios, the greater its value, *ceteris paribus*, the more efficient is the management of the asset.

---

*Traditional finance texts calculate the average collection period. This can be done by dividing the ART into 360 days. Thus Blue Ridge's average collection period is 21 days (360/17.14).

As in all ratios, the accounts-receivable turnover is not to be taken by itself. It must be compared with the industry average, and with itself over time to determine its trend value. Again, this kind of comparison is necessary in order to interpret the significance of the accounts-receivable turnover.

Inventory Turnover (IT). The more units of its product the firm can sell, the greater will be its revenues, other things equal. The inventory-turnover ratio (IT) indicates the number of times, on the average, its inventory moved through the organization, as was suggested in the discussion dealing with the balance sheet. The inventory of a merchandising firm—wholesaler or retailer—is the goods on the shelf that the firm has purchased for resale. In the manufacturing firm, inventory can be raw materials, goods in process, or finished product, or some combination of the three. At any rate, the more times the inventory, regardless of its nature, can be moved through the organization—"turned over"—the greater the revenue of the firm.

Inventory turnover is defined as net sales divided by inventory.* Symbolically:

$$\text{Inventory turnover} = \text{Sales/} \sout{\text{Inventories}} \; \textit{Cost of goods sold}$$

For Blue Ridge,

$$\text{Inventory turnover} = \frac{\$12,000,000}{\$1,500,000} = 8\times$$

This means that, on the average, the firm's inventories are moved through the organization 8 times in one year. Taken by itself, this figure tells very little. Again, the figure must be compared to industry averages, and the trend in the figure should be determined by plotting it over time.

Fixed-Asset Turnover (FAT). As discussed earlier, fixed assets are all assets with an economic life greater than one year. They normally include such assets as machinery, trucks, equipment, buildings, and real estate. Normally, it can be expected that, because of their fixed and long-term nature, the turnover of fixed assets will be smaller than the turnover of inventories.

Fixed-asset turnover is defined as sales divided by the dollar volume of fixed assets. Symbolically:

$$\text{Fixed-asset turnover} = \text{Sales/Fixed assets}$$

---

*An average inventory figure from quarterly statements is usually used in order to "smooth out" fluctuations in cyclical inventories. The *accounting* definition of inventory turnover is cost of goods sold divided by *average* inventory— (Beginning plus ending inventory)/2. Accountants do this because it is consistent with the accounting convention of consistency (i.e., cost-vs.-cost comparison).

For Blue Ridge,

$$\text{Fixed-asset turnover} = \frac{\$12,000,000}{\$7,000,000} = 1.71 \times$$

This means that, on the average, the firm's assets are incorporated into the firm's products 1.71 times.

As with all ratios, this figure must be "bench-marked" by comparing it to the industry average, and by plotting it against time to determine the trend in the figure. By itself, it means very little.

Total-Asset Turnover (*TAT*). Again, it is suggested that the basic function of assets is to produce revenue. The greater the volume of sales per dollar of assets, the more efficient is the utilization of assets.

Total-asset turnover is defined as sales divided by total assets. Symbolically:

$$\text{Total-asset turnover} = \text{Sales/Total assets}$$

For Blue Ridge,

$$\text{Total-asset turnover} = \frac{\$12,000,000}{\$10,000,000} = 1.2 \times$$

As before, this means that on the average, the firm incorporates its total assets into its product 1.2 times each year. As in the case of all other ratios, this one is useless by itself. It must be used in conjunction with industry averages and a plot of time-series data showing the trend of the ratio.

All the ratios discussed above—accounts-receivable turnover, inventory turnover, fixed-asset turnover, and total-asset turnover—are measures of asset activity. Because of this, they are sometimes called activity ratios.

Ratios Which Measure Earnings Success (Profitability Ratios) It has been suggested that a major reason—if not *the* reason—for the existence of the firm is to generate a return on the investment of the owners. The purpose of profitability ratios is to measure the various dimensions of earnings after taxes, the net revenue after all costs of doing business, including taxes, have been deducted from the firm's revenues. Comparing earnings after taxes to several variables in the firm can assist in measuring the success of the firm's profit-seeking activities. Because the function of these ratios is to measure profitability, the earnings-after-taxes (EAT) figure from the earnings statement will in each case constitute the numerator of the ratio.

Return on Sales (*ROS*). This ratio is basically a measurement of the firm's ability to control its expenses. In order to confirm this observation, look at the earnings statement of the Blue Ridge Corporation (Table 7.2). Note that it begins with the sales figure, the gross revenue of the firm. And further note that it ends with earnings after taxes (EAT). In between these two figures are listed all the expenses of the firm. If earnings after taxes constitute a large proportion of sales, then the firm must be successful in its attempts to control its expenses.

The return-on-sales ratio is calculated by dividing earnings after taxes by sales. Symbolically:

$$\text{Return on sales} = \text{EAT/Sales}$$

where:

EAT = earnings after taxes

For Blue Ridge,

$$\frac{\text{EAT}}{\text{Sales}} = \frac{\$3,961,400}{\$12,000,000} = .33$$

The return on sales of the Blue Ridge Corporation is 33 percent.

The return on sales is a key figure in the financial analysis of the firm. It takes on importance as a component part of the DuPont analysis, which will be discussed later in the chapter.

Return on Assets (ROA). Since the function of assets is to generate revenues, it is appropriate to measure the efficiency of asset management by relating earnings after taxes to them, and that is what this ratio does. The return on total assets is calculated by dividing earnings after taxes by the total-asset figure. Symbolically:

$$\text{Return on assets} = \text{EAT/TA}$$

where:

EAT = earnings after taxes
TA = total assets

$$\text{ROA} = \frac{\text{EAT}}{\text{TA}} = \frac{\$3,961,400}{\$10,000,000} = .3961$$

The return on assets of the Blue Ridge Corporation is 39.61 percent.

This figure should be taken in conjunction with the industry ratios and the time-series analysis. Again, as with all ratios, it is recommended that these comparisons be made in order to clearly understand the significance of the firm's return on total assets.

Return on Equity (ROE). As was mentioned in the discussion of the balance sheet, equity represents the owners' interest in the firm. Although not all the earnings after taxes may be paid to the shareholder—some may be retained—the earnings-after-taxes figure does represent the return to the shareholder in the form of either cash dividends or reinvestment in the firm. It is therefore appropriate that earnings after taxes be used to measure the return to the shareholders' investment in the firm.

Return on equity* is calculated by dividing earnings after taxes by the summation of all owners'-equity accounts. Symbolically:

$$\text{Return on equity} = \text{EAT/OE}$$

where:

EAT = earnings after taxes

OE = owners' equity

For Blue Ridge,

$$\text{Return on equity} = \frac{\$3,961,400}{\$4,000,000} = .99$$

Although 99 percent may sound like a high figure, it may not be so in comparison with the industry average, and the trend in the figure must be considered. So once more, it is suggested that the industry average be used for comparative purposes along with the trend of the figure. These should be considered in conjunction with the return-on-equity figure.

Ratios Which Measure the Potential of the Firm as an Investment (Investibility Ratios)

Those who are considering the purchase of the firm's common stock must undertake an analysis of the firm and its potential as an investment possibility; it will pay the financial manager to make the same analysis in order to know the "investibility" of his firm. The ratios presented in this section measure various dimensions of the firm's investment potential.

Earnings per Share (EPS). This ratio is calculated by dividing the earnings after taxes (EAT) by the total number of shares outstanding. It reveals, in effect, the amount of the period's earnings after taxes that accrues to each share of common stock. It is an important index because it indicates whether the wealth of each shareholder on a per-share basis has changed over

---

*Other finance texts still refer to ROE as return on net worth. Such a practice is misleading, because owners' equity refers to the position-statement value, whereas net worth refers to the *market* value of the owners' interest.

the period. This important ratio takes into account changes in the number of shares outstanding as well as changes in the earnings after taxes.

$$\text{Earnings per share} = \frac{\text{EAT} - \text{Preferred dividends (if any)}}{\text{No. of shares of common stock outstanding}}$$

For Blue Ridge,

$$\text{Earnings per share} = \frac{\$3,961,400}{400,000} = \$9.90$$

This figure does not, of course, take into account whether the $9.90 per share is paid as dividends, or held as retained earnings, or some combination of these. It does, however, show the profitability—efficiency in managing assets and expenses—of the firm on a per-share basis. For this reason, it is a valuable and widely used ratio.

Price per Share.   The price per share is defined simply as the *market price* of each share of the firm's common stock.* It is the valuation of the firm's earning ability. The price per share is an extremely important variable. It is used as the basis of comparing earnings and dividends, and thus in determining the investor's return on his investment. Blue Ridge's common is trading for $99.00

Dividend Yield.   The ratio of the dividend paid per share to the market price per share of the firm's outstanding stock measures the percent of return to the investor from dividends. This is expressed:

$$\text{Dividend yield} = \text{DPS/PPS}$$

where:

DPS = dividends per share

PPS = price per share

For Blue Ridge,

$$\text{Dividend yield} = \frac{\$4.95}{99.00} = 5 \text{ percent}$$

The Price–Earnings Ratio.   The ratio of the market price per share of a firm's stock to the earnings per share measures the number of times its earnings that a share of stock sells for. The ratio is the number of dollars necessary to buy one dollar of earnings.

---

*The market price is different from the par value. A stock's par value is an arbitrary value assigned for accounting purposes at the inception of the corporation. Blue Ridge common stock's market value is $99.00; its par value is $5.00.

$$\text{Price–earnings ratio} = \text{PPS/EPS}$$

where:

PPS = price per share

EPS = earnings per share

For Blue Ridge,

$$\text{Price–earnings ratio} = \frac{\text{PPS}}{\text{EPS}} = \frac{\$99.00}{\$9.90} = 10 \times$$

The price–earnings ratio is always greater than zero,* and for this reason, it is sometimes called the price–earnings multiple.

The price–earnings multiple is a useful ratio in the securities industry. The price–earnings ratio is reported, for example, in the *Wall Street Journal*.

The Payout Ratio. The ratio of dividends per share to earnings per share measures the percentage of earnings paid out to investors in the form of dividends. That is:

$$\text{Dividend payout ratio} = \text{DPS/EPS}$$

where:

DPS = dividends per share

EPS = earnings per share

For Blue Ridge,

$$\text{Dividend payout ratio} = \frac{\$4.95}{\$9.90} = .50$$

An alternate method of calculation is:

Payout ratio = Price–earnings ratio × Dividend yield (10 × .05 = .50)

The payout ratio for Blue Ridge is 50 percent. That is, the company pays one-half its earnings in the form of dividends to the stockholders.

New and growth firms tend to have a low payout ratio, because the majority of their earnings are "plowed back" into the business. Mature and stable firms tend to have payout ratios ranging from 50 to 70 percent.

All the ratios above were designed to reveal important perspectives on the investibility of the corporation. Although the ratios were designed for

---

*If a firm has deficit earnings (i.e., loss), a P/E ratio is not meaningful, and so it is not calculated.

use by investors, the financial manager should, and does, have equal interest in them, since one of his responsibilities is to maintain his firm as an attractive investment.

The DuPont System:
Capstone Analysis

A system of analysis has been designed that presents a summary overview of the financial dimensions of the firm. This system is the DuPont system of analysis. It is extremely useful because of its two major characteristics, analytical power and simplicity.

The DuPont analysis is stated:

$$\text{Return on investment (ROI)} = \frac{\text{Sales}}{\text{TA}} \times \frac{\text{EAT}}{\text{Sales}}$$

The DuPont return on investment (ROI) for the Blue Ridge Corporation is calculated as follows:

$$\text{ROI} = \frac{\$12,000,000}{\$10,000,000} \times \frac{\$3,961,400}{\$12,000,000}$$

$$= 1.2 \times .33 = .396$$

The analysis is predicated upon the assumption that the profitability of the firm is directly related to the ability of management to manage assets efficiently and to control expenses effectively. The DuPont analysis measures both.

The first term of the equation above is the total-asset turnover. As suggested previously, the total-asset turnover is a measure of efficiency of asset management. Other things equal, the greater the index, the more efficiently assets are being managed.

The second term of the DuPont analysis is the return-on-sales ratio. It is a measure of efficiency of expense control. Since the difference between sales and EAT is the expenses and taxes of the firm, the smaller these expenses, the larger will be the ratio of EAT to sales. In other words, the larger the return on sales, the greater the success in controlling expenses. So the second term of the DuPont analysis is an index of expense control.

The power of the DuPont analysis should now be apparent. If the index of asset-management efficiency is multiplied by the index of expense control, the result is a magnified index of the firm's financial well-being. Again, as with other ratios, the ROI must be taken in conjunction with industry averages, and with the time spread of the firm's own ROI.

The DuPont ROI does assist in pinpointing basic financial problems in the firm. A weakness in asset-management efficiency can be compensated for by a more-than-average control of expenses, and vice versa. But if the firm's ROI is below the industry average, the DuPont analysis helps to pinpoint the problem as one of deficiency in asset management, or in expense control, or both.

SUMMARY

This chapter has presented the need for ratio analysis in financial management. One should recognize the fact that a ratio is a mathematical quantification of a *relationship* between two financial variables. As such, financial ratios are important indexes of financial conditions in the firm.

There are five categories of financial ratios:

1. Ratios that measure ability to meet obligations (liquidity ratios)
2. Ratios that measure degree of debt employment (leverage ratios)
3. Ratios that measure efficiency of asset management (activity ratios)
4. Ratios that measure earnings success (profitability ratios)
5. Ratios that measure investment potential in the firm (investibility ratios)

Finally, and importantly, the DuPont system is presented as a very powerful tool of financial analysis.

APPENDIX TO CHAPTER 7: GENERALLY ACCEPTED ACCOUNTING PRINCIPLES

Although there is no official list of generally accepted accounting principles, the following concepts* are almost always followed in the preparation of financial statements:

Separate entity assumption. The resources of a business are accounted for separately from the resources of the owners.

Continuity assumption. The accounting entity is presumed to have an indefinite life for accounting purposes. This does not imply that accountancy assumes permanent continuance; rather, there is a presumption of stability and continuity for a period of time sufficient to carry out contemplated operations, contracts, and commitments. This concept establishes the scope of accounting on a *nonliquidation basis* and thus establishes the basis for many of the valuations and allocations in accounting.

Unit-of-measure assumption. Money is the unit of measurement for financial-statement purposes. The purchasing power of money is assumed to

---

*Compiled by Dr. Dale L. Flesher.

be stable or constant. This means that 1940 and 1980 dollars are assumed to have equivalent purchasing power.

Time-period assumption. The results of operations of a specific business enterprise cannot be known precisely until its final liquidation. However, because the various users of financial statements are interested in periodic reports on performance and financial status in order to make decisions, the life of a business is customarily divided into arbitrary time periods, usually one year in length.

Cost principle. The amount of cash, or its equivalent, paid to acquire an asset is the dollar amount to be accounted for.

Revenue principle. The revenue principle holds that revenue should be recognized *when realized*. The problem of determining when revenue should be considered as realized is a critical one. Commonly used bases for recognition of revenue are (1) sales basis, (2) cash basis, and (3) production basis.

Matching principle. Revenue realized during an accounting period should be matched with the costs (consumed) during the period. Application of the matching principle often requires the accountant to deal with estimates.

Objectivity principle. As far as possible, financial statements are based on bargained transactions in which the money amounts represent prices determined in the marketplace and not amounts based on opinions.

Consistency principle. In order to provide comparability in financial statements, it is necessary to analyze and record transactions the same way from one accounting period to the next. This permits a meaningful analysis of the financial statements of one company over several time periods.

Full-disclosure principle. All material facts that might influence the decisions a statement user might make should be disclosed either in the body of the statement or as footnotes to it. The degree of disclosure should be such that the financial statements will not be misleading.

Materiality. The principle of materiality holds that strict adherence to any accounting principle is not required if the cost to adhere is proportionately great and the lack of adherence will not materially affect reported net income.

Conservatism. Where alternatives for an accounting determination are available, each having some reasonable support, the alternative having the least favorable immediate influence on owners' equity should be selected. This means that the accountant should generally report the *lowest* of several possible values for assets and revenues and the *highest* of several possible values for liabilities and expenses. However, if carried too far, this could result in a complete distortion of accounting data.

Industry peculiarities. In view of the concern of accounting for usefulness, feasibility, and appropriateness, the peculiarities of an industry (not an individual company) warrant certain exceptions to accounting principles and practices.

PROBLEMS

1. The following are the financial statements of the RAMCO Corporation:

STATEMENT OF FINANCIAL POSITION
DECEMBER 31, 1977

Cash		$ 57,000
Accounts receivable		232,000
Inventories		172,000
Property & equipment	$595,000	
Less allowance for depreciation	186,000	409,000
		$870,000
Accounts & notes payable—trade		$ 94,000
Notes payable—bank		22,000
Accrued liabilities		16,000
Estimated federal income tax liability		21,000
First mortgage, 4% bonds, due in 1978 *current liab*		150,000
Second mortgage, 4% bonds, due in 1982		50,000
Common stock—$5 par value, 50,000		
shares issued & outstanding		250,000
Contributed capital		26,000
Reserved for plant expansion		65,000
Retained earnings		176,000
		$870,000

Note: P/E is 10, and yield on common is 6%.

STATEMENT OF EARNINGS, YEAR ENDED
DECEMBER 31, 1977

Net sales	$972,000
Cost of goods sold	671,000
Gross earnings	$301,000
Operating expense	233,000
EBIT	$ 68,000
Interest	11,000
EBT	$ 57,000
Federal income tax (estimated)	27,000
EAT	$ 30,000

From the Ramco Corporation's financial statements, compute the following:

a. Current ratio

b. Return on sales

c. Accounts-receivable turnover

    d. Inventory turnover

    e. Return on equity

    f. Number of times interest was earned (before taxes)

    g. Earnings per share of common stock

    h. Price per share of common stock

    i. Payout ratio

2. You have just completed the training program of the Abacus National Bank, and have been made loan officer. You are assigned a series of loans to handle. One of these is a loan made to the Ace Auto Parts Company, a sole proprietorship and a retailer of auto parts. James McCormack started Ace twenty years ago, and has made a comfortable living from it. About a year ago, he was elected chairman of his local school board. This position, although personally rewarding and satisfying to Mr. McCormack, takes a great deal of his time.

Ace's loan for $200,000 is up for renewal, and it is the first loan upon which you must make a decision. To help you make your decision, you have been provided with the following statements of position and earnings statements for the past three years.

You must make a decision whether or not to renew the loan of Ace Auto Parts Company.

STATEMENT OF FINANCIAL POSITION
DECEMBER 31, 1977

Cash	$ 100,000	Accounts payable	$ 50,000
Accounts receivable	200,000	Bank loan (7%)	200,000
Inventory	1,000,000	Owners' equity	1,100,000
Fixed assets	50,000		
	$1,350,000		$1,350,000

STATEMENT OF EARNINGS
JANUARY 1, 1977—DECEMBER 31, 1977

Sales	$270,000
Cost of goods sold	120,000
Gross earnings	$150,000
Operating expense	60,000
Earnings before interest, taxes	$ 90,000
Interest	14,000
Earnings before taxes	$ 76,000
Tax (40%)	30,400
Earnings after taxes	$ 45,600

STATEMENT OF FINANCIAL POSITION
DECEMBER 31, 1978

Cash	$ 50,000	Accounts payable	$ 300,000
Accounts receivable	300,000	Bank loan (7%)	200,000
Inventories	1,200,000	Owners' equity	1,100,000
Fixed assets	50,000		
	$1,600,000		$1,600,000

STATEMENT OF EARNINGS
JANUARY 1, 1978—DECEMBER 31, 1978

Sales	$280,000
Cost of goods sold	140,000
Gross earnings	$140,000
Operating expense	70,000
Earnings before interest, taxes	$ 70,000
Interest	14,000
Earnings before taxes	$ 56,000
Tax (40%)	22,400
Earnings after taxes	$ 33,600

STATEMENT OF FINANCIAL POSITION
DECEMBER 31, 1979

Cash	$ 30,000	Accounts payable	$ 480,000
Accounts receivable	400,000	Bank loan (7%)	200,000
Inventories	1,300,000	Owners' equity	1,100,000
Fixed assets	50,000		
	$1,780,000		$1,780,000

STATEMENT OF EARNINGS
JANUARY 1, 1979—DECEMBER 31, 1979

Sales	$300,000
Cost of goods sold	150,000
Gross earnings	$150,000
Operating expense	75,000
Earnings before interest, taxes	$ 75,000
Interest	14,000
Earnings before taxes	$ 61,000
Tax (40%)	24,400
Earnings after taxes	$ 36,600

RATIO MATRIX

	1977	1978	1979
LIQUIDITY			
Current			
Quick			
LEVERAGE			
Debt ratio			
TIE			
TURNOVER			
Inventory			
Fixed assets			
Total assets			
PROFITABILITY			
Return on assets			
Return on sales			
Return on equity			
DuPont ROI			

a. Calculate the proper ratios, and use them to fill in the ratio matrix provided.

b. Use the ratios to build an analytical profile of changes in Ace's financial position.

c. Write a letter to the president of your bank detailing your decision.

3. Assume there are two corporations, Alpha and Omega, which have the following financial characteristics:

	ALPHA	OMEGA
Sales	$100,000	$400,000
Total assets	300,000	2,000,000
Earnings after taxes	21,000	35,000
DuPont ROI		

a. Calculate the DuPont return on investment for both corporations.

b. Explain how the figures are similar and how they are different.

4. The Rhoda Dendron Company, a sole proprietorship, is an old-line women's fashion house. Mrs. Helen Carter started the business to fill the hours while her lawyer husband was in court. After his death, she became totally involved in the business. Mrs. Carter is a well-known designer of women's clothes, and has enjoyed a degree of personal success and notoriety in the fashion industry.

But she now wants to make sure that the firm is returning all it can to her as sole owner of the common stock. She has hired your financial consulting firm to analyze the financial health of Rhoda Dendron. Your contract with her specifies that you will analyze the firm, report deficiencies, and make suggestions for improvement. You are presented with the following financial statements and industry information.

THE RHODA DENDRON COMPANY
STATEMENT OF FINANCIAL POSITION
DECEMBER 31, 197–

Current assets:			Current liabilities:		
Cash	$ 60,000		Accounts pay.	$ 50,000	
Accounts rec.	150,000		Bank loan (8%)	100,000	
Inventory	300,000				
Prepaid exp.	40,000				
		$550,000			$150,000
Fixed assets:					
Store fixtures					
& limousine	$30,000				
Minus depr.	4,000		Owners' equity		
		26,000			426,000
Total assets		$576,000			$576,000

THE RHODA DENDRON COMPANY
STATEMENT OF EARNINGS
JANUARY 1, 197—DECEMBER 31, 197–

Sales	$115,000
Cost of goods sold	50,000
Gross earnings	$ 65,000
Operating expense	30,000
Earnings before interest, taxes	$ 35,000
Interest	8,000
Earnings before taxes (EBT)	$ 27,000
Tax (33%)	9,000
Earnings after taxes (EAT)	$ 18,000

WOMEN'S FASHION INDUSTRY
RATIO AVERAGES

Liquidity:	
Current	3.00
Quick	1.00
Leverage:	
Debt ratio	.50
Times interest earned	2.50
Turnover:	
Inventory turnover	.75
Fixed-asset turnover	1.00
Total-asset turnover	.50
Profitability:	
Return on assets	.15
Return on sales	.16
Return on equity	.20

a. Analyze the Rhoda Dendron Company relative to the fashion industry.

b. Write a letter to Mrs. Carter reporting your conclusions and your recommendations.

c. What are your suggestions to her as a result of your using the Du-Pont analysis?

5. Assume that a firm in the machine-tool industry has an owners' equity of $40,000. The median financial ratios for the machine-tool industry are:

Current debt	.40
Total debt/owners equity	.60
Fixed assets/OE	.40
TAT	2.00×
Inventory turnover	8.86×

Complete the following statement of condition, given the information above.

Assets:	Liabilities & owners' equity:
Cash	Current debt
Inventory	LT debt
Total current assets	Total debt
Fixed assets	Owners' equity
Total assets	Total liability & owners' equity

6. Below are the statements of condition and earnings of the Carolina Conveyor Corporation for the years 1972 to 1976 inclusive. During this period, the corporation undertook a major expansion program. The shareholders are interested in the results of the expansion program and its impact upon their position.

CAROLINA CONVEYOR CORPORATION
STATEMENTS OF FINANCIAL POSITION

	1972	1973	1974	1975	1976
Assets:					
Cash	$100,000	$100,000	$100,000	$100,000	$100,000
Accts. rec.	100,000	100,000	100,000	100,000	100,000
Inventory	800,000	1,300,000	1,800,000	2,300,000	2,800,000
Fixed assets	2,000,000	3,000,000	4,000,000	5,000,000	6,000,000
Total assets	$3,000,000	$4,500,000	$6,000,000	$7,500,000	$9,000,000
Liability & owners' equity:					
Accts. pay.	$ 50,000	$ 50,000	$ 50,000	$ 50,000	$ 50,000
Bonds	500,000	2,000,000	3,500,000	5,000,000	6,500,000
Common stock	2,000,000	2,000,000	2,000,000	2,000,000	2,000,000
Retained earnings	450,000	450,000	450,000	450,000	450,000
Total L & OE	$3,000,000	$4,500,000	$6,000,000	$7,500,000	$9,000,000

CAROLINA CONVEYOR CORPORATION
STATEMENTS OF EARNINGS

	1972	1973	1974	1975	1976
Sales	$600,000	$900,000	$1,200,000	$1,500,000	$1,800,000
Cost of goods sold	200,000	300,000	400,000	500,000	600,000
Gross earnings	$400,000	$600,000	$800,000	$1,000,000	$1,200,000
Operating expense	50,000	100,000	200,000	300,000	400,000
EBIT	$350,000	$500,000	$600,000	$700,000	$800,000
Interest	30,000	135,000	255,000	390,000	540,000
EBT	$320,000	$365,000	$345,000	$310,000	$260,000
Tax	135,100	150,700	147,100	130,300	106,200
EAT	$184,900	$214,300	$197,900	$179,700	$153,800
No. shares	10,000	10,000	10,000	10,000	10,000
PPS/EPS	12×	12×	10×	8×	8×

RATIO MATRIX

	1972	1973	1974	1975	1976
1. Current					
2. Quick					
3. Debt					
4. TIE					
5. ART					
6. FAT					
7. TAT					
8. ROA					
9. RO sales					
10. RO equity					
11. DuPont analysis					
12. EPS					
13. PPS					

a. Complete the ratio matrix by calculating the respective ratios for each of the six years.

b. Write a short paragraph detailing the development of the financial health of the firm, with particular attention paid to the position of the common shareholder.

The Management
of Cash and
Marketable Securities

In Chapters 6 and 7, we learned that the prime responsibility of the financial manager is the efficient acquisition, application, and conservation of the funds of the firm. Now we turn our attention to one of the more critical aspects of financial management—the management of cash.

Cash is sometimes described as the lubricant that provides for the smooth and efficient operation of a business. Too little cash can cause problems for the firm in both the short and the long run. Short-run problems range from the inability to pay some bills on time (financial embarrassment) to the dissipation of assets (financial attrition). The ultimate long-run problem, of course, is financial insolvency, which may lead to bankruptcy. (Technically, insolvency occurs when a firm is unable to pay its maturing current obligations. Legally, insolvency occurs when the liabilities of a firm exceed the market value of its assets.)

In this chapter, the timing and magnitude of cash flows (receipts and expenditures), cash balances, and short-term investments are considered. The objective of cash management is defined broadly as keeping the amount of cash and of near-cash items (U.S. government and other marketable securities that are expected to be converted into cash within a year) at a level that is sufficient to operate the firm. This means that the timing of cash flows and the amount of cash balances must be closely monitored.

The topics of this and the next chapter will be discussed in order of liquidity—that is, from the most liquid current asset to the most nonliquid current asset. In this chapter, we will deal with the cash aspect (the most liquid current asset) of current-asset management.

IMPORTANCE OF CASH MANAGEMENT

Cash is defined as funds* that are immediately available for disbursement without any restriction. The bulk of such funds is usually on deposit in checking accounts in commercial banks. The remainder is coins, currency, and checks in cash registers or other temporary storage facilities of the firm. Cash management is defined as the management of cash flows into the firm, cash flows out of the firm, and cash flows within the firm (intrafirm cash flows), as well as cash balances held by the firm.

The importance of cash management is emphasized by comparing the proportion of management time required for it with the size of the current assets. It is reliably estimated that the financial manager spends between 80 and 90 percent of his time in day-to-day financial decisions involving short-term assets and liabilities. Although current assets vary from industry to industry, they constitute between 50 and 60 percent of the total assets of manufacturing concerns. A comparison between asset composition and management time is shown in Table 8.1. We can see that the amount of the financial manager's time consumed by the current accounts is not in proportion to asset composition.

TABLE 8.1 Asset Composition vs. Management Time Spent on Each Group

ASSET GROUP	PERCENT OF TOTAL ASSETS	PERCENT OF MANAGEMENT TIME
Current assets	55%	87.5%
Fixed assets	45	12.5
Total	100%	100%

*Funds are usually defined as working capital.

Current assets are defined as any item on the position statement that will be converted into cash within one year, or during the operating cycle if more than one year. The spectrum of short-term or current assets ranges from the most liquid to the most illiquid. This is reflected on the position statement, where the list of current assets always begins with *cash* (the most liquid asset) and ends with *prepaid expenses* (the least liquid current asset). The five customary subdivisions of current assets, in order of liquidity, are:

Cash

Marketable securities (near-cash)

Notes and accounts receivable

Inventories

Prepaid expenses

The current assets of all nonfinancial corporations shown in Table 8.2 are approaching $1 trillion. The three largest current-asset items, in descending order, are (1) notes and accounts receivable, (2) inventories, and (3) cash and U.S. government securities. Actually, receivables, inventories, and cash and government securities represent 41, 39, and 12 percent, respectively, of total current assets.* Of all the assets of the firm, cash constitutes one of the smaller items. *Yet more time is usually devoted to the management of cash than to that of any other asset of the firm.*

TABLE 8.2 Total Current Assets of Non-Financial Corporations, 1967–76 (in billions of dollars)

END OF PERIOD	CASH	MARKETABLE SECURITIES	ACCOUNTS RECEIVABLE	INVENTORIES	OTHER	TOTAL
1967	56.4	7.2	219.7	152.3	27.6	463.1
1968	53.0	6.7	173.9	166.0	26.9	426.5
1969	51.1	7.4	197.0	186.4	31.6	473.3
1970	50.2	7.7	206.1	193.3	35.0	492.3
1971	53.3	11.0	221.1	200.4	43.8	529.6
1972	57.5	10.2	243.4	215.2	48.1	574.4
1973	61.6	11.0	269.6	246.7	54.4	643.2
1974	62.7	11.7	293.2	288.0	56.6	712.2
1975	68.1	19.4	298.2	285.8	60.0	731.6
1976	76.0	20.0	328.0	312.0	64.0	800.0
Percent of 1976 total	9.5%	2.5%	41%	39%	8%	100%
Annual Increase	3.0%	10.8%	4.5%	7.5%	8.8%	5.6%

Source: Federal Reserve Bulletin.

Federal Reserve Bulletin.

Cash is both the most important and the least productive asset a firm possesses. It is important because bills must be paid with cash. However, cash is sterile. It is not directly productive. It does not, per se, produce goods for sale or induce customers to buy, as do fixed assets, inventories, and accounts receivable. Because of this, the goals in cash management should be to maintain enough for the firm to remain comfortably liquid and to put any excess cash to work in a productive way.

STRATEGIES OF CASH MANAGEMENT

A firm has two basic cash flows—the collection of cash and the payment of cash. Generally, the financial manager cannot time the cash inflows to coincide with the required cash outflows. Thus, during some periods, more cash will be flowing out than in, because of such items as tax payments, dividend payments, and seasonal inventory buildups. At other times, more cash will flow into the firm than out, because accounts receivable will be collected in large sums, sometimes over several months, after a heavy period of selling.

If cash inflows and cash outflows were perfectly synchronized and could be forecast with certainty, a firm would need no cash balance. Since such an ideal situation does not exist, a firm must develop some strategies for cash management. The basic strategies that should be employed by the firm are fourfold: *First*, the cash surplus or deficit for each period of the planning horizon should be projected. The cash budget is used for planning cash inflows and outflows for the future. *Second*, the firm must decide how much cash resources to hold, considering (1) the probabilistic nature of the projection, (2) the opportunity cost of excess liquidity, and (3) the penalty for cash deficiency. *Third*, a firm should develop a strategy for economizing by accelerating cash inflows or decelerating cash outflows. *Last*, the division between bank balances and marketable securities must be determined.

FORECASTING CASH NEEDS

All companies, whether large or small, receive and disburse certain amounts of cash in transacting business. Increased competition, higher costs, and greater taxation permit a firm to retain only a small percentage of total revenue from sales. Even though the earnings statement continues to show adequate profits, a company may be "cash poor," because cash is required for increases in receivables, inventories, and fixed assets in order to maintain the sales growth. For example, if the return on total assets is 6 percent while total assets increase at a rate of 12 percent, the firm must finance at least half the asset increase. Forecasting cash needs is a means of correcting a cash-flow problem before its actual occurrence.

Cash forecasts protect the financial condition of a firm by developing a projected position statement from a forecast of expected cash receipts and expenditures for a given period. This is true whether the forecast simply reflects the course of present operations or attempts to project future profits as a result of new products, investments, or policy changes. Forecasts guide management in formulating plans and measuring the results.

Cash forecasts can be made on a daily, weekly, and monthly basis. The size of the firm generally dictates the period and frequency of the cash forecast. Large corporations require divisions to submit daily cash forecasts based on daily and weekly periods. Medium-sized firms usually require cash forecasts weekly and monthly. Small firms generally do not prepare formal cash projections, because the owners possess neither the information nor the time to do so. When small firms do prepare cash projections, it is usually on a monthly basis. In general, medium to large corporations prepare one or more cash projections for planning periods of different lengths. And as firms grow larger and more complex, cash planning is essential to continuing success.

Cash Budgeting   Financial forecasts usually stem from budgets. Budgets are used for many purposes. One purpose is to forecast the future position of the firm. The most generally used budget for financial forecasts is the cash budget.

The cash budget is merely a summary of projections of all the estimated uses of cash (disbursements) and all the sources of cash (revenues) which may include additional financing. If cash expenditures exceed cash revenues, the resulting figure is the amount that must be obtained by borrowing or from other sources if the planned program is to be carried out. If it is believed that this amount cannot be raised, the indication is that the estimated uses of cash must be cut back.

A cash budget is essential to financial management in examining short-run cash projections. A cash-flow statement is analogous to a cash budget. The only difference is that the former records on a yearly, monthly, or weekly basis what actually happened in the past (see Table 8.3), whereas a cash budget is used to anticipate changes in the future.

A common approach is to prepare a cash budget by months for the next six months to a year. The normal starting point for such a budget is a sales forecast by months. From the sales forecast it is possible to estimate collections of accounts receivable, payments for inventory, and other cash payments. The cash budget deals only with cash. It does *not* consider noncash expense items such as depreciation, amortization, and depletion allowances.

We shall study the cash budget of the Meeks Toy Store, a retailer of children's toys, for the period August 1 through January 31. Because of the nature of the business, Meeks's sales vary seasonally. Sales are the highest

TABLE 8.3 Meeks Toy Store, Cash-Flow Statement for the Year 197–

USES (HOW SPENT)		SOURCES (HOW FINANCED)	
Increased:		Decreased cash	$ 2,000
Accounts receivable	$10,500	Sold portion of	
Inventories	10,000	ownership	20,000
Acquired new fixed assets	45,000	Borrowed:	
Salaries paid	13,000	Accts. payable	7,000
		Bank loan	4,500
		Mortgage	20,000
		Funds from operation:	
		Net income 23,560	
		Depreciation 1,440	
			25,000
	$78,500		$78,500

during the Christmas season. Management wishes to arrange for adequate financing, supported by good projections that will make the terms of the loan more favorable. Thus, the manager begins with the position statement of July 31, as shown in Table 8.4 and prepares a cash budget. Table 8.5 forecasts the monthly breakdown of sales revenue for the next seven months. Table 8.6 shows the estimated salary costs for the same period.

TABLE 8.4 Meeks Toy Store, Position Statement, July 31

ASSETS			LIABILITIES & OWNERS' EQUITY	
Cash		$14,080	Accrued wages	$ 500
Accts. receivable		7,000	Other liabilities	1,800
Inventory[a]		20,500	Contributed capital	52,880
Equipment	$16,000			
Depreciation	2,400			
		13,600		
		$55,180		$55,180

[a]Composed of $10,000 minimum inventory plus $10,500 of inventory scheduled to be sold next month.

TABLE 8.5 Sales Forecast

August	$14,000	November	$38,000
September	26,000	December	48,000
October	22,000	January	18,000
		February	16,000

TABLE 8.6 Salary-Expense Budget

August	$1,600	November	$1,600
September	1,600	December	1,600
October	1,600	January	1,600

Given the information in these tables, certain additional assumptions or estimates must be made in order to prepare a cash budget. In estimating the seasonal cash requirements, the store is expected to operate in the following way:

1. Sales (scheduled in Table 8.5) are 30 percent cash and 70 percent credit. The credit sales are collected in the following month and no bad debts are expected.

2. Sales for July were $10,000.

3. Gross profit margin on sales averages 25 percent. *75% of sales = purchase*

4. All inventory purchases are paid for during the month in which they are made.

5. A basic inventory of $10,000 (at cost) is constantly maintained. The store will follow a policy of purchasing enough additional inventory each month to cover the following month's sales.

6. A minimum cash balance of $4,000 will be maintained at all times.

7. Accrued salaries and other liabilities will remain unchanged.

8. Other monthly expenses of the store are:

Rent	$400
Depreciation	$120
Other expenses	1 percent of sales

9. This is a partnership.

10. Any borrowing (or repayments) will be in multiples of $1,000.

11. A 12 percent interest charge on borrowed money is paid at the first of the month on the preceding month's loan balance.

The cash budget in Table 8.7 was prepared from the information above. The information is organized according to the direction of the cash flow (that is, whether cash receipts or cash disbursements). The difference between cash inflow and outflow plus borrowings (minus loan repayments) is the *cash balance*. An advantage of this method is that the net cash flow in the cash-balance schedule shows the actual monthly results from operations. The cash

TABLE 8.7 Cash Budget

	JULY	AUG.	SEPT.	OCT.	NOV.	DEC.	JAN.	FEB.
			SCHEDULE 1: CASH RECEIPTS					
Total sales	10,000	14,000	26,000	22,000	38,000	48,000	18,000	16,000
Cash inflows:								
Cash		30% 4,200	7,800	6,600	11,400	14,400	5,400	
Collection of receivables		70% 7,000	9,800	18,200	15,400	26,600	33,600	
Total receipts		11,200	17,600	24,800	26,800	41,000	39,000	

	AUG.	SEPT.	OCT.	NOV.	DEC.	JAN.
	SCHEDULE 2: CASH DISBURSEMENTS					
Cash outflows:						
Purchases	75% of Sept sales 19,500	16,500	28,500	36,000	13,500	12,000
Salaries	1,600	1,600	1,600	1,600	1,600	1,600
Rent	400	400	400	400	400	400
Other expenses	140	260	220	380	480	180
Total disbursement	21,640	18,760	30,720	38,380	15,980	14,180

	AUG.	SEPT.	OCT.	NOV.	DEC.	JAN.
	SCHEDULE 3: CASH BALANCE					
Total receipts	11,200	17,600	24,800	26,800	41,000	39,000
Total disbursements	21,640	18,760	30,720	38,380	15,980	14,180
Net cash flow	(10,440)	(1,160)	(5,920)	(11,580)	25,020	24,820
Cash balance, BOM[a]	14,080	4,640	4,470	4,530	4,870	29,690
Monthly borrowing, repayment BOM[a]	1,000	1,000	6,000	12,000	–	(20,000)
Interest charges	0	(10)	(20)	(80)	(200)	(200)
Cash balance	4,640	4,470	4,530	4,870	29,690	34,310
Cumulative borrowing, BOM[a]	1,000	2,000	8,000	20,000	20,000	0

[a]BOM = Beginning of month

balance shows the final results (operating transactions and financial transactions combined).

Cash-Budget Model In order to forecast cash flow changes for any month, the criteria for cash decisions for Meeks's Toy Store can be set out unambiguously and compactly in the following model. It is exactly the same as in the cash budget. The model reveals the net cash flow for any month.

$$\text{Net cash flow} = (.30S_t + .70S_{t-1}) - (.75S_{t+1} + F + .01V_t)$$

where:

$S = $ sales

$t = $ forecast month

$F = $ fixed expenses

$V = $ variable expenses

For the month of December, the net cash flow for Meeks Toy Store is:

$$= [.3(48,000) + .7(38,000)] - [.75(18,000) + 2,000 + .01(48,000)]$$
$$= 41,000 - 15,980$$
$$= \$25,020$$

Notice in Table 8.7 that $25,020 is the "Net cash flow" figure for the month of December.

By use of the model, the impact of possible changes in the sales figure can be evaluated through sensitivity analysis. This is done, but on a percentage basis, through use of the following formula:

$$C = S\left(\frac{V}{V + F}\right)$$

where:

$C = $ percentage change in cash requirement

$S = $ percentage change in sales

$V = $ variable net cash flows (receipts minus disbursements)

$F = $ fixed expense

For example, a 25 percent increase in sales for December for Meeks Toy Store causes a 27 percent change (increase) in cash.

$$C = .25\left[\frac{41,000 - 13,500 - 480}{(41,000 - 13,500 - 480) + (-2000)}\right]$$
$$= .25(1.0799)$$
$$= 27\%$$

The change is not in direct proportion. In fact, the greater the fixed expenses, the more disproportionate the change will be. Sales and cash requirements would vary by the same percentage if all cash receipts and disbursements were constant proportions of sales.

Pro Forma Statements After the cash budget is prepared, pro forma statements are developed, using data from the initial financial statements and the cash-budget results. The pro forma earnings statement is developed first, to project the profitability of the store for the cash-budget period. This is shown in Table 8.8. Then the pro forma position statement, as shown in Table 8.9, is prepared as of the end of the projected period. Notice that the balancing figure is the projected earnings. Thus, the firm, knowing its financial position at the end of the last accounting period, can project receipts and expenses ahead to a future period. Financial statements (pro forma) are developed before the actual operation of the firm takes place in the future. They are like road maps without which the company's financial destination is in doubt. Pro forma

TABLE 8.8 Meeks Toy Store, Pro Forma Earnings Statement, August 1–January 31

			PERCENT OF SALES
Sales		$166,000	(100%)
Cost of goods sold:			
Beginning inventory	$ 20,500		
Purchases	126,000		
Total	$146,500		
Ending inventory	22,000	124,500	(75%)
Gross margin		$ 41,500	(25%)
Operating expenses:			
Salaries	$ 9,600		
Rent	2,400		
Depreciation	720		
Interest on loan	510		
Other expense	1,660		
		14,890	
Net earnings		$ 26,610	

TABLE 8.9 Meeks Toy Store, Pro Forma Position Statement, January 31

ASSETS		LIABILITIES & OWNERS' EQUITY		
Cash	$34,310	Accrued salaries		$ 500
Accounts receivable	12,600	Other liabilities		1,800
Inventory	22,000	Contributed capital	$52,880	
Equipment $16,000			26,610	
Depreciation 3,120				79,490
	12,880			
Total assets	$81,790	Total liabilities		
		& owners' equity		$81,790

70% of Jan total Sales (18000) [handwritten annotation next to Accounts receivable]

statements formalize management decisions and indicate whether cash will be plentiful, adequate, or short.

Accounting Equation The accounting equation may assist one in preparing the pro forma position statement:

$$\text{Assets} = \text{Liabilities} + \text{Owners' equity}$$
$$\$81,790 = \$2,300 + \$79,490 \qquad \text{(Meeks Toy Store)}$$

The equation can be expanded to include the pro forma earnings statement, by:

$$A = L + OE + (R - E)$$

where:

$A = $ assets

$L = $ liabilities

$OE = $ owners' equity

$R = $ total revenues

$E = $ total expenses

For the Meeks Toy Store:

$$81,790 = 2,300 + 52,880 + (166,000 - 139,390)$$

CASH BALANCES NEEDED

The maintenance of sufficient liquidity of current assets so that current liabilities can be settled at the proper time is a basic responsibility of the financial manager. This goes beyond the traditional problem of "meeting the payroll" to include *all* demands upon the enterprise for cash. Repayment of bank loans, remittances to suppliers, dividend payments to stockholders, payment of federal income taxes, and compliance with payment requests for countless other legitimate purposes must all be honored. The liquidity test, in short, is a *cash* test of the ability of the firm to pay its debts when due.

Determining the level of cash balances involves fundamental decisions with respect to the firm's liquidity and its cash payables. Such decisions are influenced by a tradeoff between risk and profitability. Thus, the decision variable to examine on the asset side of the balance sheet is the liquidity of assets; in other words, how rapidly are such assets turned into cash? For example, the financial manager needs to know the number of inventory turns, the average collection period of receivables, and the maturity dates of marketable securities. Such decisions affecting asset liquidity include (1) the management and control of cash and U.S. government securities, (2) the management and control of accounts receivable, (3) inventory management and control, and (4) the administration of fixed assets.

With respect to current assets, the lower the proportion of liquid assets to total assets, the greater can be a firm's return on total investment. In general, the lower the cash balance of a firm relative to its assets, the higher can be the rate of return. However, realistic lower cash balances can be attained only if more time is given to the management of cash. Therefore, the cost of attaining a lower cash balance must be weighed against the opportunity cost of maintaining higher cash balances. Opportunity cost is the highest return that would be earned if funds were invested in an alternative project. In other words, the firm must give up the opportunity of using the cash in the business in order to hold the higher cash balances. The return on holding cash is generally considered to be less than the return on other assets of the firm.

Cash balances can be determined from industry averages and from good cash-flow projections. Since many small companies do not make formal projections of cash, their cash balances are determined in a "hand-to-mouth" fashion. This is also true of some large corporations. Such a haphazard way of determining cash balances is a sure route to trouble, because of the cash-stockout problem.* As noted at the beginning of this chapter, cash shortage extends over a wide spectrum of problems, ranging from financial embarrassment to financial attrition to financial insolvency.†

So a minimum planned cash balance is what the firm is striving to achieve. The optimal cash balance for a firm depends upon three major factors. They are (1) the compensating balance required by banks, (2) the amount of cash that is needed for daily transactions, and (3) the amount of cash needed for unexpected contingencies.

FINE-TUNING CASH MANAGEMENT

Once cash-flow projections are made and appropriate cash balances established, the financial manager can take additional steps toward more aggressive cash-management activities. These fall into the categories of external and internal controls. External controls discussed here include mainly banking relationships.

---

*Sometimes referred to as "shortening of the bankroll."

†Technical insolvency occurs when a firm is unable to pay its maturing current liabilities. Legal insolvency occurs when the liabilities of a firm exceed the market value of assets.

Acceleration of Firms use banks to accelerate cash inflows. This is done mainly by con-
Cash Inflows centration banking, control banking, and lockbox banking. A small
firm may deal with only one bank, located in its home community.
However, a large national firm may have several hundred accounts in as many
banks.

Concentration Banking. Every morning, the corporate cash manager
is confronted with major unknowns about where his cash is, what to do with
it, and how to place it where it will pay the most. The larger companies have
on-line computer information about the cash position of their own subsidiaries; yet they do not have instantaneous data from their banks. General
Motors, for example, records telephoned information each morning from its
50 largest banks about its multibillion-dollar cash flow. One bank in each
area is selected to service the needs of one or several of the firm's branches.
Funds are maintained there up to a certain point. When the balance rises
above the limit (generally through the collection of receivables), the excess
is transferred to a concentration bank in a large city.

Control Banking. The concentration banks are in turn linked to a
central bank in Detroit, GM's home office. The central bank works closely
with GM in meeting its liquidity requirements, in investing its temporary
idle balances, and in maintaining control of GM's entire banking network.
Thus the firm is using the services of a control bank to reduce the financial
manager's administrative burden.

Compensating Balances. An extension of the technique above is to
maintain compensating balances with your major bank (or banks) only. Do
not maintain balances with minor banks. In fact, some financial managers
withdraw balances as fast as possible from less important banks and pay the
resulting service charges. Of course, the firm should also use one balance for
both credit and banking activity. Thus, checks are written on the bank with
the compensating balance, which is good cash management.

Lockbox Banking. Firms can speed the cash inflow from accounts-
receivable collections by lockbox banking. The firm rents a postal box in
each area where it has a large number of customers, or in each city where the
firm has a servicing bank. In either case, arrangements are made with a bank
to collect the mail daily, deposit the checks, and send the firm the deposit-
slip listing. Such a procedure can be further sophisticated by having the bank
telegraphic transfer the balance each day to its central bank. The purpose of
lockbox banking is to reduce the float (both postal and banking). Thus, the
process gets cash to the control bank a few days sooner.

Internal Controls Internal control refers in part to some of the cash-management procedures of the firm from within. They include the following:

1. Take away from lower or divisional levels all decision-making control relating to balance levels and cash movement. Reduce cash management at these levels to a routine basis. A centralized control of cash is important in order to reduce the amount of cash necessary for operations. Personnel in places distant from the main office will not send in excess cash unless forced to do so. Their rationale is that they may need it in two or three weeks. Therefore, centralized control reduces cost of operations, because cash is in the treasury (or bank) instead of being idle somewhere in the system. It is important to realize that idle cash is often the most nonproductive asset a firm possesses. For example, a firm has $100,000 of idle cash that could earn $8,000 if invested. With a return on sales of 5 percent, it would take sales of $160,000 annually to generate the $8,000 cash ($8,000/.05 = $160,000).

2. Use zero-balance accounts for aggressive cash management. A company should check its cash balance with its bank balance. It is possible to have a near-zero balance on the books of the company, especially if checks written by the firm are slow in clearing. The firm's cash on its books relative to cash in the bank should be closely monitored in order to determine proper cash levels for the company to maintain on its books. Conversely, excess cash in a checking account in the bank is also idle cash—quite often the most nonproductive of all assets.

EXCESS CASH LEVELS

The cash assets of some firms are large enough to warrant vigorous and thoughtful management, involving much more than keeping excess cash fully invested. Even if surplus funds are invested continuously, the net after-tax return from even the less conservative money-market instruments is modest. Cost of capital to the firm is usually above this return. Therefore, the carrying of unnecessarily large money assets may tend to dilute the firm's overall rate of return.

When cash or bank balances reach some predetermined level, further increases in cash can be applied to reduce short-term borrowings or to "invest" in the current accounts. The following alternatives are suggested for excess cash:

1. "Invest" it in higher-level accounts receivable.

2. "Invest" it in inventory.

3. "Invest" it in highly liquid short-term items, for a return in the form of interest. The latter is suggested as a means for investing temporary idle-cash balances. One must remember that this is not the primary reason a firm is in business. Studies indicate that the use of investment in marketable securities on other than a temporary basis is not a

common practice. Many firms seldom use marketable securities as a substitute for cash. Such businessmen prefer to let their banks maintain the liquid reserves, and then borrow to meet temporary cash shortages.

Marketable Securities   When the cash balances of a firm exceed the balances desired in the short run, a firm should consider investing the temporary idle-cash balances in highly liquid marketable securities.* Highly liquid securities with little or no market-price risk and small transaction costs are the primary goal for temporary idle cash. This is true because the firm may need to sell the short-term securities on very short notice. Thus, excess funds invested as a cash reserve have a relatively low return at a relatively low risk.

The division between bank balances and marketable securities has been formulated in various inventory models.† The cost of holding cash (that is, being liquid) can be represented by averaging the cash balance over the cash-cycle period and multiplying by the annual interest rate. Thus, the total cost of holding cash is:

$$\text{Holding costs} = i\left(\frac{C}{2}\right)$$

where:

i = annual interest rate

C = cash quantity

If there is no investment of idle cash, the cost each period is figured as follows:

$$\text{Holding costs} = i\left(\frac{C}{2}\right)\left(\frac{D}{360}\right)$$

where:

D = days in period

For example, if the interest rate is 12 percent, and the firm has a $100,000 cash balance over 60 days, the holding cost is:

$$\text{Holding costs} = .12\left(\frac{100,000}{2}\right)\left(\frac{60}{360}\right)$$

$$= .12(50,000)(1/6)$$

$$= \$1,000$$

---

*The types of marketable securities are discussed in Chapter 21.

†See William J. Baumol, "The Transactions Demand for Cash: An Inventory Theoretic Approach," *Quarterly Journal of Economics*, November 1952, pp. 545–56.

The cost of not being liquid (that is, having to sell short-term securities) is represented by the brokerage costs, b, times the number of transactions (the selling of securities). The cost of having to sell securities for needed cash is:

$$\text{Selling costs} = b\left(\frac{T}{C}\right)$$

where:

b = fixed brokerage costs

T = estimated cash need over period

C = cash quantity (or withdrawal lot)

The cost of the combined expressions (holding costs and investment costs) is the total cost associated with cash maintenance:

$$\text{TC} = b\left(\frac{T}{C}\right) + i\left(\frac{C}{2}\right)$$

To determine the optimum amount of short-term investment and the best pattern of cash withdrawals from the marketable securities, we differentiate the expression with respect to C. Then we set the derivation equal to zero in order to find the minimum point in the total-cost function, shown in Figure 8.1.

FIGURE 8.1 Liquidity Costs and Economic Order Quantity.

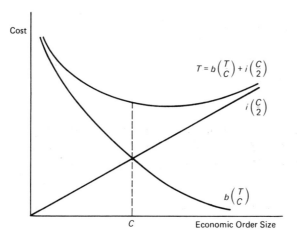

Differentiating and setting the result equal to zero gives:*

$$C = \sqrt{\frac{2BT}{k}}$$ *economic order quantity*

where:

to calculate amt of disinvestment over pd

C = optimal cash quantity (or withdrawal lot)

$$k = i\left(\frac{D}{360}\right)$$

B = fixed transaction costs

T = total cash

For example, assume that the firm needs $100,000 over the next 60 days, that the interest rate is 12 percent, fixed transaction costs are $5, and broker's commission is .5 percent of the total order. Then:

$$k = i\left(\frac{D}{360}\right) = .12\left(\frac{1}{6}\right) = .02$$

$$C = \sqrt{\frac{(2)(B)(T)}{k}} = \sqrt{\frac{(2)(5)(100,000)}{.02}} = \sqrt{50,000,000}$$

$$= \$7,071$$

To determine how much of the $100,000 receipts ($R$) should be held ($R - I$) and how much invested (I), the following formulation is used:

$$R - I = C + R\left[\frac{(2)(b)}{k}\right]$$

where:

b = broker's commission

$$= 7,071 + 100,000\left[\frac{(2)(.005)}{.02}\right]$$

$$= \$57,071$$

Thus, the firm should invest $42,929 in marketable securities and hold the difference ($R - I$) of $57,071 as cash balance. Each $7,071 increment will last 4.24 days (60 days ÷ 100,000/7,071). The initial cash held will last 34.2

---

*The differentiation process is shown in Chapter 9.

days (that is, 57,071/7,071 times 4.24 days). After 34.2 days, $7,071 should be withdrawn every 4.2 days until a new cycle begins.

WORKING-CAPITAL MANAGEMENT

The discussion up to this point has been concerned only with cash flows and cash balances. Now we take a brief look at a broader concept, funds flow. *Funds* are defined as any value in the firm that can be converted into cash in a short period of time. Funds flow usually refers to the flow of working capital. (The next chapter deals with the area of funds instead of cash.)

Closely tied to cash management is the management of working capital. And a major concern of the financial manager is the financing of a firm's working-capital needs and the management of the working-capital position. These financial considerations are important for new ventures, going concerns, and expanding businesses. Because each particular industry has unique factors determining allocation of current assets, the working-capital positions may vary among different types of industries.

The computation of a firm's working-capital position is made by referring to current assets (cash and those assets that will be converted to cash within one year) and current liabilities (all debts that are scheduled for payment within one year). *Working capital* is defined in this text as the excess of current assets over current liabilities.

For a better understanding of working capital, it can be described as the portion of the current assets furnished by permanent financing. That is, a portion of the current assets is offset by current liabilities, and the owners and bond holders must furnish the remainder of the current-asset financing, which is called working capital.

Occasionally, working capital is said to be the total current assets of a firm. Such a statement is true only if the firm has *no* current liabilities. When current liabilities exist (as is the usual case) on the position statement, the term *current assets* is the correct way to express the short-term assets of the firm. It is confusing and unnecessary to coin another term for a perfectly good one like *total current assets*. So working capital can be defined as the investment the firm makes in short-term assets if current liabilities are nil. In order to avoid confusion, some use the term *net working capital* to mean the difference between current assets and current liabilities.

A firm's working capital can be increased by any of the following procedures:

1. Noncurrent assets can be sold and converted into cash, marketable securities, or other current assets.

2. Long-term debt can be increased to provide ready funds to increase current assets or reduce current liabilities.

3. Additional equity capital can be invested in the firm.

4. Retained earnings generated from operations can be plowed back into the current accounts.

Any one of these major financial transactions will improve the firm's working-capital position by either increasing current assets or decreasing current liabilities. All these measures that increase working capital will ease the pressure on cash-management decisions.

The business cycle (3-4 year cycle) has an effect on short-term-asset management. The effects of the long waves of the Kondratieff cycle on short-term asset decisions are especially important. These were discussed in Chapter 5. In general, it is the opinion of the authors that the long waves have an influence on the priority of business decisions and postimplementation of the decisions. That is, during the upswing of the long waves, managers are more concerned with the acquisition and management of long-term assets. However, during downswings of the long waves, the pendulum swings more to an impetus on decision making for day-to-day management of the business (that is, short-term asset management). Thus, the firm is forced to be more efficient.

There is a logical reason for this shift in priorities. After many capital acquisitions, as well as the use of relatively inexpensive debt financing during the upswing of the long wave, many firms (as well as governments) are debt-ridden and must of necessity turn their attention to survival. Therefore, the importance of working-capital management during the downswing of the long wave emerges.

This is demonstrated by the fact that for the past 25 years, banks have not asked for cash budgets. That is, banks have not insisted on them before and during the period of a loan. However, we believe that the next 25 years will see much more emphasis placed on the cash budget, owing to excessive debt and accompanying liquidity problems.

SUMMARY

Basically, cash management is concerned with cash flows and cash balances. There are two possible extremes in cash management. One is to keep too little cash on hand to conduct the affairs of the business. This will manifest itself in the inability to take cash discounts and pay bills on time. The more serious the cash shortage, the more overdue the accounts and notes payable become. The other extreme is to keep too much cash on hand. Excess cash is much more difficult to detect. Financial managers probably prefer to err on the side of excessive liquidity.

PROBLEMS

1. A company has an outstanding bank loan of $200,000 at an interest rate of 8%. The company is required to maintain a 20% compensating balance in its checking account. What is the effective interest cost of the loan, assuming that the company would not normally maintain this average amount?

2. The ABC Company has a cash policy of maintaining a $400,000 minimum balance. A need has arisen for $5 million in short-term funds. NBNC has offered the company a $5 million loan at 8%, on the condition that a 20% minimum balance is maintained, with the interest and principal payable together at the end of the year. NBFSH has offered the same size loan, discounted at 6%, and payable in monthly installments, with no minimum balance required.

8% w/ compensating balance is better deal

a. What is the effective cost of NBNC's loan?

b. What is the effective cost of NBFSH's loan?

c. Which offer is the more attractive, assuming the company would have no trouble meeting the monthly installments?

3. A firm is currently handling all its credit customers from New York City. Annual credit sales are $90 million. The firm is analyzing the desirability of establishing a lockbox system in strategic geographical areas to reduce the amount of float. Studies suggest that the float could be reduced by four days.

a. How much extra cash will be generated by the lockbox system?

b. If the company can earn 10% on its money, and the charge for the lockbox system is $80,000 a year, what will be the net gain (or loss) from the lockbox system?

c. Will the increase in cash be reflected as an increase in assets?

4. Handleman Corporation estimates a need for $4,000 over the next year from near-cash items. Transaction costs on short-term investments are $20 each, and the yield on such securities is 4%.

a. Compute the optimal amount that should be withdrawn from the portfolio periodically.

b. If transactions costs were reduced to $5, what would the optimal amount be?

c. If the interest were increased to 10%, and transactions costs were $18, what would the optimal amount be?

5. The Eden Company cash cycle is 90 days, with a cash inflow of $900,000 at the first of the period and cash outflows of $10,000 per day. The firm has a policy of investing in marketable securities, with each transaction costing $2 in addition to a commission of 1/2 of 1 percent on the amount of funds invested. The annual interest rate is 18 percent.

a. How much of the $900,000 should the company invest?

b. How often should the investments be liquidated?

c. How much should be disinvested each time?

6. Given the following information about Kaufhof Klothiers, Inc.:

POSITION STATEMENT
DECEMBER 31

update to June 30

june credit Sales

ASSETS			LIABILITIES & OWNERS' EQUITY	
beg Cash *balance*		$100,000	Accruals	$ 12,750
beginning Accounts receivable		427,500	Second mortgage	50,000
Inventory		120,000	Bonds, 6s, 2003	500,000
+ purchases Plant & eqpt.	$480,000		Contrib. capital	500,000
Less depr.	24,000		Retained earnings	40,750
less ending inventory		456,000		
		$1,103,500		$1,103,500

(1) All prices and costs remain constant.

(2) Sales are 75% for credit and 25% for cash.

(3) For credit sales, 60% are collected in the month after the sale, 30% in the second month, and 10% in the third month after the sale. Bad-debt losses are insignificant.

(4) Sales, actual and estimated, are:

75% of 300,000 = 225,000

10% of 225000 = 3rd mo after sale figures in Jan cr. sales

Oct. 1974	$300,000	Mar. 1975	$200,000
Nov. 1974	350,000	Apr. 1975	300,000
Dec. 1974	400,000	May 1975	250,000
Jan. 1975	150,000	June 1975	200,000
Feb. 1975	200,000	July 1975	300,000

(5) The store has a gross margin of 20% and purchases and pays for each month's anticipated sales in the preceding month.

in Jan purchases are for Feb
80% of 200,000 (feb) are purchases in Jan

(6) Wages and salaries are:

Jan.	$30,000	Apr.	$50,000
Feb.	40,000	May	40,000
Mar.	50,000	June	35,000

(7) Rent is $2,000 per month.

(8) Interest on 6% bonds is due at the end of each calendar quarter. *6% of*
500,000
for 1 qtr
÷ 4

(9) Retirement of second mortgage is due in April.

(10) $30,000 is planned to expand facilities in June.

(11) $100,000 is the minimum desired level for cash.

(12) Straight-line depreciation is recorded at $1,000/month. *doesn't require*
pymt of cash

(13) Assume accruals remain unchanged.

(14) Interest-bearing loans can be obtained in multiples of $5,000 on a monthly basis at 12% per annum. Interest is payable monthly and is not accrued.

    a. Prepare a cash budget for January through June.

Homework   b. Prepare pro forma earnings and position statements. *June 30*
inc depreciation

    c. How long has this company been operating, based on the data given? *2 yrs   depr $1000/mon   total dep 24,000*

7. Given the following assumptions about a company:

    (1) Sales:

January	$ 75,000
February	85,000
March	90,000
April	83,000
May	100,000

    (2) The company collects 50% of sales in cash and 50% the following month.

    (3) Purchases are 60% of the month's sales.

    (4) Fixed costs are $150,000.

    (5) Variable costs (labor and variable overhead) are 31% of sales.

        a. What is the net cash flow for April?

        b. What is the percent change in net cash flow for April, if sales increase 10 percent?

The Management
of Receivables
and Inventories

The level of inventories [and receivables] that a business will normally desire to hold will depend . . . on a balance between costs of holding and benefits from doing so.

Carl A. Dauten and
Lloyd M. Valentine,
Business Cycles
and Forecasting, *1975*

In Chapter 8 we were concerned with the liquid position of the firm. An in-depth analysis of cash management was made, including profitability and risk. And near the end of the preceding chapter a cursory look was taken at a larger concept—working-capital management.

In this chapter, we analyze the two main uses of working capital—receivables and inventories. The purpose of this chapter is to determine the role of receivables and inventories in maximizing return on investment.

The two current assets of receivables and inventories are the major components of working capital. Recall that working capital is defined in Chapter 8 as that portion of a firm's current assets financed with long-term funds. In keeping with the principle of suitability, current liabilities (short-term funds) finance the most liquid current assets. Thus, inventories and receivables tend to be financed by long-term funds furnished by the bond- and stockholders of the firm. The more conservatively managed firm tends to finance all current assets with long-term funds, whereas the aggressively managed firm tends to finance all current assets with short-term funds.

Accounts receivable and inventories combined total over $500 billion of the assets of U.S. nonfinancial corporations. See Table 8-2. The financial manager's dilemma between liquidity and profitability is brought into sharp focus by the management of these assets. Although every financial decision made in a business involves a compromise between liquidity and profitability, investments in inventories are considered less liquid than investments in receivables. Receivables are converted rather quickly into cash by collecting amounts owed to the firm, whereas inventories are more difficult to convert to cash. On the other hand, inventories tend to be more profitable than receivables.

Levels of receivables and inventories are dictated to some extent by the business operation. Almost all buyers of the firm's products expect the firm to have inventory to sell on demand. Furthermore, the firm is expected to finance the purchases via credit sales, a process that results in accounts receivable.

On the other hand, the selling firm expects similar treatment. Thus, inventories (that is, raw materials for finished inventories) are financed to a large degree by trade credit. This creates accounts receivable for the supplier of trade credit and accounts payable for the user of trade credit.

Thus, most firms use trade credit as well as extend trade credit. Generally, large firms tend to be net suppliers of trade credit (so that their accounts receivable are greater than accounts payable), and small firms tend to be net users of trade credit (their accounts payable tend to exceed accounts receivable).

ACCOUNTS-RECEIVABLE MANAGEMENT

Since the end of World War II, trade credit in nonfinancial corporations has grown at a more rapid rate than have sales. A number of reasons explain this phenomenon. *First*, during most of the postwar period, credit has been readily available at attractive rates. Easy money has contributed to the expansion of industry and profits. *Second*, in order to maintain profits and utilize plant capacity, sales levels have been emphasized during a period of rising competition and customer accommodation via more lenient trade-credit terms. *Finally*, the 25-year upswing of the Kondratieff long wave has reinforced the actions of businessmen.

Lenient vs. Stringent Credit Policy   Accounts-receivable management strives to maximize the return on investment. Policies that stress short credit terms, stringent credit standards, and highly aggressive policing of collections tend to minimize bad-debt losses and the amount of funds tied up in receivables. But such policies may restrict sales and profit margins. In spite of a low receivables investment, rate of return on total investment of the firm may be lower than that attainable with higher levels of sales, profits, and receivables. Conversely, extremely lenient credit extensions may well inflate receivables and bad debts without compensating increases in sales and profits. The objective of receivables management, then, is the achievement of a balance that, in the particular circumstances of the firm, results in the combination of asset turnover and profit margins that maximizes the overall return on investment of the firm.

Limited financial resources of a firm may force a stricter credit policy than would be ideal from the viewpoint of investment return. If the availability of funds is restricted, their use in inventory, equipment, or other assets offering even higher return may dictate severe restraints on credit administration.

Gauging Benefits, Costs, and Risk of Credit Policy   There are a number of ways to gauge credit policy. We shall examine four indexes, which range from the operational aspects of credit policy to returns on new accounts. The four indexes are (1) acceptance index, (2) marginal-return index, (3) past-due index, and (4) bad-debt-loss index.

Acceptance Index. The acceptance index is an indication of credit attitude. The line of business and the stage of the business cycle are both conditioning influences. The index is formulated as follows:

$$\text{Acceptance index} = \frac{\text{Applications accepted}}{\text{Applications submitted}}$$

A perfect ratio of 100 indicates a credit policy that is too lax. An example of this was W.T. Grant's policy to solicit aggressively and approve all credit applicants.* The actual acceptance index is a result of a number of factors that may be peculiar to the individual firm or industry. The cost factor reflected in this index is an opportunity cost of lost sales owing to over-restrictive credit policies or normal credit and collections costs in financing receivables.

Marginal-Return Index. This index measures the benefits gained from trade credit. Under this approach, the firm estimates the differences in sales volumes when no trade credit is extended, when limited amounts of credit sales are approved, and when liberal credit terms and financing are supplied to its customers. Next, the firm estimates the increase in profits from the additional sales gained through more liberal credit policies. Finally, the firm must estimate the additional investment required in accounts receivable. The index is:

$$\text{Marginal-return index} = \frac{\text{Increase in earnings (before taxes)}}{\text{Increase in receivables}}$$

Assume that a firm has reliable estimates of a 10 percent increase in current sales of \$15 million if trade-credit terms are liberalized, a doubling of accounts receivable from \$2 million to \$4 million, and an increase in earnings before taxes of \$350,000. The increased return to the firm is:

$$\text{Marginal-return index} = \frac{\$350,000}{\$2,000,000} = 17.5\%$$

The most obvious costs in providing trade-credit financing are the carrying costs involved. The funds invested in accounts receivable entail an interest cost to the firm, and the longer the average collection period, the greater the interest costs will be. These are included in the example above, since costs are deducted from sales to get the earnings-before-taxes figure.

Another element in the cost of receivables is an opportunity cost. In the example above, it was estimated that the firm could earn a 17.5 percent return on \$2 million invested in additional accounts-receivable financing. However, if the firm could earn 20 percent on the same funds if they were invested in inventory, then the difference of 2.5 percent would have to be considered as a part of the added cost of the new accounts receivable.

Past-Due Index. The past-due index is a gauge of trend in poor payment or improper collection procedures. The index is a measure of how the firm is meeting established objectives in the credit and collection area. It

---

*Refer to the case study of W.T. Grant in Chapter 6.

is formulated as follows:

$$\text{Past-due index} = \frac{\text{Delinquent accounts}}{\text{Credit customers}}$$

The index can be based on the number of delinquent accounts to number of credit customers, or the dollar value of delinquent accounts to the dollar value of credit sales. Either way, the firm is striving for a low index. The cost factor reflected by this index is the additional costs (or lack of them) that result when customers are slow in paying their bills.

An increase in the past-due index alerts the collection department that more accounts are slow and may become delinquent. In Chapter 7, the average collection period was discussed as a measure of the appropriateness and efficiency of the credit and collection department. Yet an overall figure such as that produced by accounts-receivable turnover (ART) or average collection period (360/ART) tends to conceal troublesome accounts. Hence, many firms use the past-due index to alert them to shifts in customer paying practices, and an aging schedule, if necessary, to identify specific collection problems. The aging schedule simply indicates what proportions of accounts receivable are due within various time periods. For example:

0 – 30 days	$100,000	50%
31 – 60 days	80,000	40%
61 – 90 days	14,000	7%
Over 90 days	6,000	3%
	$200,000	100%

Bad-Debt Loss Index. The bad-debt loss index is a measure of the efficiency of the credit and collection departments. Bad debts are related to the sales that created them. Some factors that determine an acceptable index are (1) profit margin, (2) production capacity, and (3) business conditions. The index is calculated as follows:

$$\text{Bad-debt loss index} = \frac{\text{Bad-debt loss}}{\text{Total credit sales}}$$

A bad-debt loss index of zero indicates that the credit policy of a firm is too stringent. Thus, the firm strives for a low bad-debt loss index, but not an index of zero.

If an account is uncollectible, it should be treated as a bad debt beyond some period of time. It may be written off entirely, or it may be sold to a special collection agency at a substantial discount from its initial value. Thus, delinquent accounts receivable involve a loss in value (as the probability of noncollection rises) as well as greatly increased carrying and administrative costs.

Accounts-Receivable Investment

The level of the investment in accounts receivable is dependent upon (1) the volume of credit sales, (2) the time required to collect the credit sales and (3) the financial resources of the firm. The collection time between sale and payment is dependent upon external factors such as general swings in the business cycle, and internal factors such as the credit policy of the firm. Although external factors are not controllable, the firm's credit policy consists of several controllable variables.

Analysis of accounts-receivable management begins with consideration of the controllable factors that influence the level of receivables. There are several major determinants for the size of investments in receivables. Of particular importance are the following variables of credit policy: (1) determination of credit standards, (2) determination of credit terms, (3) gathering of credit information, (4) credit-granting decision, and (5) collection of receivables.

Credit Standards. One of the major decisions a firm has to make is the amount of trade credit it will extend to its customers. Oftentimes, industry competition establishes or determines credit standards. In general, a firm should liberalize credit standards to the point where the profitability generated from the additional sales is equal to the additional cost incurred in accepting the additional accounts receivable. The costs of accepting more accounts receivable are (1) the increased cost of the credit administration, (2) the increased potential of bad debts, and (3) the opportunity cost of the increased investment in accounts receivable.

In sum, an optimal credit-extension policy involves a tradeoff between the additional profitability and the additional cost resulting from changes in credit standards. At a minimum, the optimal tradeoff involves (1) the change in sales that results from a change in credit policy, and (2) the change in costs as a result of changes in the average collection period and changes in bad-debt losses.

Terms of Credit. The "terms of credit" refers to the period of time over which credit is extended and the discount that may be given for early payment. Cash discounts are usually offered by a firm to speed up its receivables collections and thereby reduce its average investment in receivables. The credit period is lengthened in order to increase sales and, ultimately, gross profits. Again, there is a tradeoff between a speedup in collections and the cost of increasing the allowable discount.

Typical credit terms are 2/10, net 30. This means that a 2 percent discount is allowed if payment is made within ten days of invoice date, and full payment is due within 30 days. What is the effective price to a customer when goods are offered on terms of 2/10, net 30? If each unit of the product is priced at $1.00, then the customer may pay 98 cents in cash per unit within ten days from the invoice date. This assumes that the customer takes full advantage of the discount and pays on the tenth day. Furthermore, if money carries an annual return of 12 percent for the customer, the ten days of free credit have an implicit value of about 1/3 cent per unit (.98 × .12 × 10/360). Subtracting the implicit value from 98 cents gives an effective price of 97.67 cents, which is equivalent to a 2.3 percent reduction in cash price. The effective price is formulated as follows:

$$
\begin{aligned}
\text{Effective price} \atop \text{(discount taken)} &= P - Pd - P(1-d)\frac{kt}{360} \\
&= 1.00 - 1(.02) - 1(1-.02)\frac{.12(10)}{360} \\
&= 1.00 - .02 - .98(.00305) \\
&= 97.67 \text{ cents}
\end{aligned}
$$

where P is the invoice price, d the cash discount, k the value of money to the customer, and t the discount period. Thus, the effective price to the customer equals the invoice price less the cash discount less the value of free credit during the discount period.

That formulation above assumes that the customer takes the cash discount. This is usually the case because trade credit is so expensive that few firms find its use justifiable. More about this aspect of trade credit is considered when we study the sources of short-term financing in Chapter 10.

If the customer does not take the discount, the effective price (assuming payment is made on the last day) is calculated as follows:

$$
\begin{aligned}
\text{Effective price} \atop \text{(discount missed)} &= P - \frac{kt}{360} \\
&= 1.00 - \frac{.12(30)}{360} \\
&= 99 \text{ cents}
\end{aligned}
$$

where t is the number of days until payment.

Thus, we can evaluate credit terms by converting credit policy into an effective price with or without the discount. This is a reliable method by which both the seller and the buyer can determine the cost and stimulative effects of trade credit. Effective prices per $1 for the customer are shown in Table 9.1 for various credit terms and annual returns (the value of money to the customer) of 12 and 18 percent. For a given return, it is easy to determine whether cash discounts should be taken or missed. The firm should be indifferent between taking or missing the cash discount if the effective price is the same for either option. We know that credit terms of 2/20, n/60 imply an 18 percent cost (.02 × 360/40) if the discount is missed and the invoice is paid on the last day. Thus, Table 9.1 shows that a firm with an annual return of 18 percent is indifferent between taking and missing a cash discount if the terms are 2/20, n/60.

TABLE 9.1 Effective Price Factors (with and without discount)

CREDIT TERMS	ANNUAL RETURN (VALUE OF MONEY TO THE CUSTOMER)			
	$k = .12$		$k = .18$	
	DISCOUNT TAKEN	DISCOUNT MISSED	DISCOUNT TAKEN	DISCOUNT MISSED
2/10, n/30	.9767	.99	.975	.985
2/10, n/60	.9767	.98	.975	.97
2/10, n/90	.9767	.97	.975	.955
2/20, n/30	.9733	.99	.97	.985
2/20, n/60	.9733	.98	.97	.97
2/20, n/90	.9733	.97	.97	.955

Credit Information. A firm generally requires the customer desiring credit to fill out a credit application, which consists of various forms requesting financial and credit information and credit references. Working from the credit application, the firm then obtains additional credit information about the customer from other sources. The major external sources of credit information are (1) financial statements, (2) Dun & Bradstreet, (3) the National Credit Interchange System, and (4) the applicant's bank.

The Tradeoff Between Stringent and Lax Credit Policies The basic tradeoff between stringent and lax credit policies is one of expected profits versus bad-debt losses. Credit losses are regrettable but unavoidable. No one has yet found a way to forecast accurately which customers will produce them. As for the other customers, some slowness is almost a universal characteristic of business. One alternative to consider in lieu of a tougher credit policy is to raise prices by a fixed percentage, then offer new credit terms of "X percent discount if paid in 10 days; net paid at 60 days."

Possibly the best approach to extension of credit is the marginal-return index, which was discussed earlier in the chapter. A direct comparison of increased profits to increased receivables is a sound method of evaluating a credit policy.

INVENTORY MANAGEMENT

Some would argue that only the current assets of cash, marketable securities, and receivables are decisions for the financial manager. They contend that inventories are production or physical-distribution decisions. However, because of the close relationship among accounts receivable, inventories, and accounts payable, plus the financial administration of all assets by the financial manager, we strongly believe inventories as well as receivables are areas that merit the attention of the financial manager.

The management of inventories is possibly the most critical item in the current account. This is true because inventories are necessary for business operations, and yet excessive amounts of inventories are in many cases difficult to sell. Thus, the timing of additions to and reductions of inventories is crucial in the success of the firm. If too many units of finished inventory are produced, the financial manager must use funds to finance their production, storage and handling, and possible obsolescence. On the other hand, if production is insufficient to meet demand, the sales division will be unable to fill orders on a timely basis, and profits will suffer owing to loss of sales and cancellations of orders by customers.

Efficient Diversification Basically, the "too little, too much" principle is especially applicable to inventories. The reason is that inventories are relatively illiquid in nature. (That is, they are not readily convertible into cash, since it takes time to sell finished goods.) Thus, excessive inventory may have to be sold at less margin (a smaller markup).

The automotive industry, for example, refused to believe that the coming recession of 1973–75 would be very severe. Thus, production of autos continued at near-normal levels until the industry had a 100-day supply—about 3 million cars. Automotive plants were closed down in desperation in late 1974, and auto workers were laid off. This action further aggravated the downturn in business activity, because fewer people were gainfully employed. Of course, the effect rippled throughout the economy because of the many auto-related industries. As a result of excessive inventories in the economy, unemployment climbed to almost 10 percent in 1975. During that year, massive inventory liquidations occurred in most industries. This action was necessary because inventories in excess of normal operating needs must be financed, which ties up a scarce resource—capital. Therefore, periods of recession with accompanying high unemployment rates compound the problem of excessive inventories.

The subsequent effect of excessive inventories is inadequate and out-of-stock inventory conditions. This occurs because during severe recessions, firms continue to cut inventories until they are dangerously low. Thus, business is unable to make sales on certain items near the end of the recession. This happened in late 1975 and early 1976 because of out-of-stock inventory items.*

---

*In January 1976, a businessman (shoe retailer) told the authors that he had reduced his inventories during 1974–75. Thus, his inventory-turnover ratio increased from four to eight times a year. But he confessed that he had lost sales in late 1975 and was planning to increase inventories to retain his customers. This reinforces the action of the "too little, too much" principle.

Inventory Levels What are the consequences of over- and understocks of inventories? It is logical that firms lose money via finance, storage, and insurance charges if inventories are piling up in the face of declining sales. And if such excess inventories are sold at a reduction in price (as with the auto rebates of 1975), the firm loses some of its anticipated profits as well. Conversely, if inventory is out of stock, the firm cannot fill some orders and loses potential, or would-be, profits.

A number of things can be learned from the "too little, too much" episode of inventories. First, the business cycle adversely affects inventories at the turning points of the cycle. That is, the businessman continues to produce at normal rates even after a recession is underway.* Then many businesses, being on shaky financial ground owing to a loss of sales and revenues caused by the recessions, cut back inventories drastically in order to survive. Many of the cutbacks last well into the upswing of the four-phase business cycle.

Second, inventory levels are affected by management decisions. That is, management attempts to carry sufficient but not excessive inventories. Firms have established production- and inventory-control departments to aid in keeping predetermined amounts of inventories. This is generally done by taking the first derivative (or rate of change) of the cost function (or curve) of total inventory costs. Two methods of computing inventory amounts are shown in the "Inventory Management Techniques" section of this chapter.†

Third, inventory levels are affected by changing market conditions. That is, there is a strong demand for a product for a while, but suddenly the demand dries up. Many firms that have large supplies (or inventories) of faddish items are in serious trouble when the demand diminishes. Therefore, merchants and manufacturers who plan poorly are caught with thousands of items such as Twiggy dresses, hula hoops, and narrow ties for men. Such businesses experienced severely lower profits when the public no longer wanted their products.

Fourth, management must be ready to respond to innovations and new ideas with adequate inventories. Competition forces management to do so. For example, textile firms that failed to gear up for doubleknit fabric in the late 1960s were no match for the competition that resulted in the early 1970s. Such firms were left behind, and many went out of business as a result of their failure to be ready with adequate inventories of doubleknits.

Fifth, the reluctance of wholesale and retailing firms to build inventories causes the manufacturer to have to stock more inventory. This is a big factor

---

*The 1973–75 recession began in November 1973. Auto production was not shut down until December 1974.

†At one time, line managers largely performed this function with a black book kept in the hip pocket. They ordered raw materials and made finished goods according to past experience and "pressures" from various members of management.

for the manufacturer. If the economy turns down, the producer incurs the greatest consequences. It is often necessary to cut back immediately on production. Many manufacturers are left with inventories that cannot be liquidated in the near future. Again, the solution lies in the "too little, too much" principle. That is, have enough inventories, but don't have too much. To accomplish this requires a constant monitoring of inventory levels, business conditions, and consumer demand.

The last factor is the valuation of inventories. The Internal Revenue Service allows for inventory valuation based on a "first-in, first-out" (FIFO) basis or a "last-in, first-out" (LIFO) basis. If prices are rising, FIFO will relatively overstate inventory values on the position statement, and understate the cost of goods sold on the earnings statement. LIFO has the opposite effect; it understates inventory on the position statement and overstates cost of goods sold on the earnings statement. If prices are falling, FIFO and LIFO's effects on inventory valuation, goods sold, and earnings are reversed from that of rising prices. In general, LIFO is used during periods of rising prices and FIFO during periods of falling prices.* The reason for the use of LIFO or FIFO is to decrease the tax bill of the firm. See Table 9.2.

TABLE 9.2 Inventory Valuation

	DURING PERIODS OF RISING PRICES	
	FIFO RESULTS IN:	LIFO RESULTS IN:
Sales	$12,000	$12,000
Cost of goods sold	8,000	12,000
Gross earnings	$ 4,000	0
	DURING PERIODS OF FALLING PRICES	
	GROSS MARGIN UNDER FIFO	GROSS MARGIN UNDER LIFO
Sales	$12,000	$12,000
Cost of goods sold	8,000	6,000
Gross earnings	$ 4,000	$ 6,000

Costs and Risks of Inventory Management The amount of inventory carried by a corporation determines to a large extent the carrying costs involved. These costs include insurance, interest, taxes, storage space, and obsolescence. A management decision must be made to determine what inventory level should be maintained

---

*Firms are allowed to switch from FIFO to LIFO. However, the Internal Revenue Service requires justification when a firm switches from LIFO to FIFO. There is usually a penalty for changing from LIFO to FIFO.

for manufacturing efficiency and customer service. Increasing inventory levels becomes unprofitable when the additional investment can no longer be justified. Additional inventories can be justified if production requirements increase, or if initial production-run costs increase relative to the product's unit cost. However, storage costs and other overhead expenses must be considered when increasing inventory.

Inventory policy should blend several factors for consideration into a wise procurement program. Among these factors are a minimum inventory necessary for uninterrupted operations and stable employment, economical size of purchase orders and production runs, advance purchases to gain several discounts, and anticipation of price changes and supply shortages.

Inventory absorbs capital. The cash spent for finished goods, work in process, and raw materials is not available for other uses as long as these stocks remain on hand. Consequently, financial policy dealing with the allocation of capital to competing uses frequently places a ceiling on the size of inventories.

A common way to limit inventory is to budget the total dollar value every month. Each time the budget is revised, the use of capital for inventory is weighed against other needs. This establishes a procedure for seeking the optimum use of capital throughout the company. Naturally, since inventory serves as a buffer between sales, production, and purchasing, the actual inventory may deviate from the budgeted amount.

Inventory Control   There are a number of traditional measures that are used to control inventories. One is the inventory turnover ratio. For example, a manufacturer may aim for an inventory in relation to sales of 12.5 percent, or eight turns per year.* Such a turnover standard creates pressure to dispose of slow-moving, obsolete stock since accumulation of such stock is likely to lead to future losses. Also, inventory that is high in proportion to sales increases a company's exposure to price fluctuations. Since inventory turnover is often taken into consideration by outside credit analysts, a company's credit standing can be improved by inventory turnover faster than industry averages.

It is useful to indicate desirable or undesirable conditions in the aggregate, but one ratio cannot ensure that inventory imbalances do not exist for specific items. Separate turnover ratios for raw materials and for finished goods, broken down by product, are more useful than is a total composite figure. The turnover can be stated in months of supply, to avoid controversy about values to be used. The importance of this kind of control is to encourage managers to decide which stock is worth holding and to eliminate items of small turnover.

---

*An inventory turnover ratio which uses sales rather than cost of goods sold is not an actual measure of the physical rate of turnover. However, if used consistently, it is a good relative measure of inventory turnover.

A common way to limit inventory is the inventory budget. A budget is usually more sensitive to short-term control requirements than the turnover ratio is, because it is based on sales forecasts and production schedules that cover short periods, such as a quarter or a month. Expressed in total dollars, the inventory budget may not disclose inventory-item imbalances. However, refinements can be made in the inventory budget to reflect product lines in order to disclose imbalances. Budgetary control of inventories is particularly well suited to companies that have seasonal fluctuations. For example, the accumulation and disposition of agricultural supplies and Christmas merchandise call for planned short-run adjustments.

A more sophisticated inventory-control system usually specifies minimum and maximum inventory levels. Many factors must be considered in order to determine proper inventory levels. The care with which such factors are used to establish and maintain minimum and maximum levels of inventory will determine the effectiveness of the control.

Anticipated demand is the first factor. This demand may be based on historical records or on a sales forecast. Probably a sales forecast is a better basis. Such a forecast must frequently be modified because of fluctuations.

Another factor is the lead time—both vendor and production lead time. Since lead times are not exactly predictable, a common practice is to establish a six-week average inventory for each item. Then a one- to two-week deviation is allowed from the average.

A third factor is the value of the item. High-value items are controlled more closely than low-value items. Therefore, companies tend to stratify their inventories into groups of relative values.

Other factors for controlling inventories are storage space and the cost of carrying the inventories. The availability of space, or lack of it, is an important factor. Carrying costs need to be determined and used. Both these factors influence inventory levels.

The following are proven inventory-management principles:

1. Sales of large manufacturing firms correlate closely with the gross national product (GNP). Therefore, GNP should be considered in inventory and production decisions.

2. Formulas (or models) exist to aid in the management of inventory and production levels.

3. Management needs to assess the risk factor of over- or understocking inventories. Also, the risk of each product stocked needs to be determined and evaluations made on a periodic basis.

Inventory-Management Techniques   There are a number of basic methods for managing inventory. We will examine two of the techniques—the ABC system and the economic order quantity.

The ABC System. A large manufacturer may carry an inventory of more than 1,000 different items. Those unfamiliar with inventory control may be surprised to learn that as little as 20 percent of the firm's inventory accounts for 90 percent of the firm's inventory investment. Thus, 80 percent of the inventory items account for only 10 percent of the firm's investment in inventories. In order to deal with this phenomenon, the ABC system was developed.

This distribution of the dollar value of inventory and the percentage of items are shown in Table 9.3. The A group should receive the greatest attention, since it represents the largest amount of dollars invested in inventory. The B and C groups merit little attention unless there are essential items in these groupings that require special attention.

TABLE 9.3 Percentage Distribution of Items Relative to Dollar Investment in Inventory

GROUP	PERCENTAGE OF ITEMS	PERCENTAGE OF DOLLAR INVESTMENT
A	20	90
B	30	8
C	50	2
Total	100	100

The ABC system is used to control all inventory or as a first step in inventory control. Either way, the method forces management to specify priorities. Some firms use a variation of the ABC system by simply selecting the most important production department (dollarwise) to control. For example, a tufted-textile manufacturer has sales of $25 million in wall-to-wall carpets, of $2 million in area rugs, and of $500,000 in bath rugs. The logical inventory items to control are the wall-to-wall carpets. In fact, the firm's carpet inventory consists of 24 styles, in 12- and 15-foot widths, all in twelve colors each. Thus, the firm is faced with 600 items of finished inventory that averages about $10 million in value.

ABC analysis may be used in terms of the percentage of inventory items relative either to the percentage of sales dollars or to the percentage of inventory dollars. The ABC method ensures that tight inventory control is maintained for A items. Somewhat less control is used for B items, and least control, but not absence of control, is needed for C items. Studies show that a substantial number of firms use ABC classifications for inventory control and also for production control.

The Economic Order Quantity (EOQ). A basic function of all types of inventories is to provide for efficient production and management between successive stages in the operating cycle. The cycle extends from the initial purchase of raw materials through the ultimate sale of the finished product. Inventories over the cycle range from raw materials to work in process to finished goods.

The scheduling of production and the management of inventories (in other words, production control and inventory control) provided an early application of quantitative methods to business decisions. The EOQ model was one of the first models to be used by businessmen. Today there are some extremely sophisticated analytical techniques for the management of inventory. Since these are generally covered in quantitative and management courses, we will introduce the basic EOQ model.

The EOQ model. Total inventory cost consists of three items. They are (1) order costs, (2) purchase costs, and (3) carrying costs. The total dollar cost per order (other than ordering and carrying) is bQ, where Q is the number of items ordered at one time and b the unit purchase price. If F is the fixed cost per order, the total purchasing and ordering costs for a year are the sum of $F + bQ$, times the number of orders placed per year, S/Q, where S is the annual demand (or sales) in units. *Convince yourself that the number of orders per year will be total annual sales or demand (in units) divided by the number of units per order.* Thus, total inventory purchasing and ordering costs per year are:

$Q = $ # of items ordered at one time

$b = $ unit purchase price

$F = $ fixed cost per order

$S = $ annual demand in units

$$(F + bQ)\frac{S}{Q} = \text{total inventory purchasing + ordering costs}$$

The total carrying cost is the carrying cost per item times the average inventory carried during the year. If k equals the carrying cost per item and Q the number of units per order, the average inventory carried during the year is $Q/2$ (assuming constant usage), and the inventory carrying costs are:

$$k\left(\frac{Q}{2}\right) = \text{carrying cost}$$

Thus, the total inventory costs are the carrying costs, the fixed ordering costs, and the purchase price of the items. This is represented by the following:

Total inventory costs = Carrying costs + Fixed ordering costs

+ Purchase-price costs

$$\text{TIC} = k\left(\frac{Q}{2}\right) + F\left(\frac{S}{Q}\right) + bS$$

To determine the economic order quantity, we find the lowest total cost (the point of zero slope on the total-cost curve). To locate the minimum total cost, we differentiate TIC with respect to Q and set the first derivative equal to zero. Notice that only two of the costs determine the lowest point on the total-

FIGURE 9.1 Graphic Determination of Economic Order Quantity.

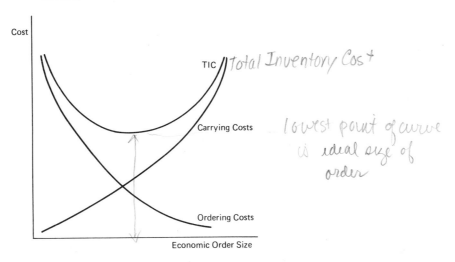

cost curve. This is shown in Figure 9.1 and in the differentiation process below.

$$\frac{d(\text{TIC})}{dQ} = \frac{d}{dQ}\left(\frac{kQ}{2} + \frac{FS}{Q} + bS\right)$$

Then:

$$= \frac{k}{2} - \frac{FS}{Q^2} = 0$$

$$\frac{FS}{Q^2} = \frac{k}{2}$$

$$Q^2 = \frac{2FS}{k}$$

and:

$$Q = \sqrt{\frac{2FS}{k}}$$

The last expression is the economic order quantity (EOQ). Now let's see how the EOQ resolves the inventory problem. Assume that we know that the annual demand for XYZ's product is 5,000 units. Further assume that we can determine the cost figures from the firm's records, as follows:

$$F = \$100$$
$$b = \$5 \text{ per unit}$$
$$k = \$1$$

First, the total inventory costs are shown in Table 9.4 for ordering one, two, five, ten, and twenty times each year. We see that the minimum cost is $26,000. This represents ordering five times per year, with an order size of 1,000 units.

TABLE 9.4 EOQ Determination for XYZ Company

NUMBER OF ORDERS PER YEAR S/Q	ORDER SIZE Q	FIXED COST $F\left(\frac{S}{Q}\right)$	+	PURCHASE COST bS	+	CARRYING COST $k\left(\frac{Q}{2}\right)$	=	TOTAL INVENTORY COST $F\left(\frac{S}{Q}\right) + bS + k\left(\frac{Q}{2}\right)$
1	5,000	$ 100		$25,000		$2,500		$27,600
2	2,500	200		25,000		1,250		26,450
5	1,000	500		25,000		500		26,000←
10	500	1,000		25,000		250		26,250
20	250	2,000		25,000		125		27,125

Now, using the EOQ formula, which centers only on fixed order costs and carrying costs, the following results are obtained:

$$EOQ = \sqrt{\frac{2FS}{k}}$$

$$= \sqrt{\frac{(2)(100)(5000)}{1}}$$

$$= \sqrt{\frac{1,000,000}{1}}$$

$$= \sqrt{1,000,000}$$

$$= 1,000 \text{ units}$$

Thus, the same result is obtained with the EOQ formulation as with the TIC curve. Either result locates the economic order quantity that results in the lowest calculation of ordering and carrying costs.

A number of different calculations can be made at this point. We will examine number of orders per period, average inventory, and the reorder point. Allowance for risk can be built into the reorder point by the use of a safety stock allowing delivery time. We use 500 units safety stock and three weeks delivery time for XYZ Company. The three formulations are given below, with examples from the XYZ Company:

$$\text{Number of orders per period} = \frac{S}{EOQ}$$

$$N = \frac{5,000}{1,000} = \underline{\underline{5 \text{ orders}}}$$

$$\text{Average inventory} = \frac{S/2}{N} \text{ or } \frac{\text{EOQ}}{2}$$

$$= \frac{5,000/2}{5} \text{ or } \frac{1,000}{2} = \underline{\underline{500 \text{ units}}}$$

$$\text{Reorder point} = \text{Safety stock} +$$

$$\text{Delivery time}\left(\frac{\text{Annual demand}}{\text{Weeks per year}}\right)$$

$$= 500 + 3\left(\frac{5,000}{50}\right)$$

$$= \underline{\underline{800 \text{ units}}}$$

SUMMARY

Effective accounts-receivable and inventory management is essential if a company is to maximize its profit-making opportunities. Because of the imposition of uncontrollable external factors, both these assets require a closely monitored system, maintained on a continuing basis.

Trade credit as a stimulant for increasing sales has grown tremendously since World War II. The effect of liberalized trade-credit terms on sales can be measured on the basis of average or marginal returns; the latter approach is analytically more sound. However, expanded trade credit may lower the turnover of accounts receivable (increase the average collection period) and result in greater bad-debt losses. The main expense in customer trade credit is the carrying cost, which consists of interest, opportunity costs, and administrative and collection costs.

Trade credit may take several different forms, but most of it is extended in open accounts. The management of trade credit is usually referred to as credit and collection activities. The former function involves the analysis of the debtor's credit standing or position. The latter entails the firm's routine work in handling cash payments as well as any extra efforts to collect slow or delinquent accounts.

The many variables that must be considered in making inventory decisions require the use of objective methods in order to obtain reliable results. Such methods are available through the use of such mathematical calculations as the economic order quantity. For large operations, the computer can be utilized. Inventory is managed best when the total of the various costs involved is minimized.

The management of inventory entails decisions about the timing and size of purchases of items. Thus, the right inventory level is a tradeoff between conflicting goals. That is, the less often a firm purchases inventory, the lower the fixed ordering costs. However, the more often a firm purchases inventory, the lower the carrying costs. This conflict is easily resolved by the EOQ model.

PROBLEMS

1. MTU produces ball bearings at a constant rate, and uses 800 tons of steel a year. Ordering costs are $1,000 per order, carrying costs are $10 per ton per year, and variable costs are $100 per ton. *purchase cost*

   a. Compute the minimum point on the total-cost curve via the first derivative of the cost function.

   b. Draw an approximate graph of the function and the optimal point.

2. A college bookstore is attempting to determine the economic order quantity for a popular finance text. The store sells 3,000 copies of this book a year at a retail price of $15.00. The publisher allows the store a 20% discount from this price. The store figures that it costs $1 per year to carry a book in inventory and $50 to prepare an order for new books.

   a. Determine the total costs associated with ordering one, two, five, ten, and twenty times a year.

   b. Determine the economic order quantity.

3. Imagine that you are a customer of each of the following industries, which sell their products on terms indicated. Calculate the effective cost of credit for each set of terms:

   a. Carpets—5/10, net 60

   b. Luggage—2/10, net 30

   c. Automotive supplies—4/15, net 45

4. A firm has bad-debt losses of $2,000 and total credit sales of $100,000. It is estimated that a doubling of credit sales will result in an increase in earnings of $15,000 and an increase of bad-debt losses to $5,000. If the firm's cost of doing business is 15%, should credit sales be expanded?

5. The ZF Corp. estimates cash payments of $6 million for a one-month period, and payments are to be made at a steady rate over the period. The fixed transaction cost is $100 and the interest rate on marketable securities is 6 percent per annum, or 0.5 percent for the one-month period.

   a. What is the optimal transaction size?

   b. How many marketable securities-to-cash transactions will the firm make during the month?

10

Short-Term Financing

In the long-run, we are all dead.
attributed to
John Maynard Keynes

In Chapter 8, the management of cash and marketable securities was examined, and in Chapter 9, the management of accounts receivable and inventories. This chapter completes the series of chapters on working-capital management.

BASIC DEFINITION AND PRINCIPLE

Short-term financing is defined as any source of funds with a maturity of less than one year. Such funds are usually considered to be temporary in nature. One of the more important principles of short-term financing was referred to in Chapters 1 and 6—the principle of suitability. This principle stipulates that short-term needs (that is, temporary needs) should be financed by short-term borrowings (temporary sources), and that long-life assets (permanent needs) should be financed by long-term borrowings or equity (permanent sources). A firm that adheres to this principle should rarely be paying for unneeded funds. Likewise, the firm should have funds available to meet maturing obligations.

There are instances when short-term funds are used to meet long-term needs. However, the use of short-term funds to finance long-term needs is a violation of the suitability principle and entails more risk. The theoretical view of short-term credit is that it is to be used to meet temporary "working-capital" needs. Such needs are based on seasonal peak demands for funds, coupled with the usual delays in the receipt of proceeds from sales relative to the incidence of expenditures.

COMPOSITION OF SHORT-TERM LIABILITIES

Current liabilities are defined as obligations whose liquidation is reasonably expected to require the use of current assets or the creation of other short-term liabilities. Current liabilities become due in the near future, usually within one year from the date of the position statement. The spectrum of short-term or current liabilities ranges from the shortest to the longest average maturity. Thus, current liabilities begin with *trade accounts payable* (shortest maturity) and end with *estimated federal income tax liability* (longest average maturity). Current liabilities are not as firmly structured as current assets. The four customary subdivisions of current liabilities in order of maturity are:

Trade accounts payable

Notes payable

Accruals

Estimated federal income tax liability

Sometimes these are simply listed as:

Accounts payable

Bank loans

Other accounts

Current liabilities for non-financial corporations for the past ten years are depicted in Table 10.1. Over the past decades current liabilities have almost doubled, reaching a total of nearly half a billion dollars in 1976. The largest category is notes and accounts payable, which represents 61.6 percent of total current liabilities. Payables grew at an annual rate of five percent. The fastest growing item was accruals, which almost tripled in size. Accruals accounted for 33.8 percent of current liabilities and grew at an annual rate of 12 percent.

TABLE 10.1 Total Current Liabilities of Non-Financial Corporations, 1967–1976 (in billions of dollars)

END OF PERIOD	NOTES AND ACCOUNTS PAYABLE	ESTIMATED FEDERAL INCOME TAXES	ACCRUALS	TOTAL
1967	196.4	14.1	60.8	271.4
1968	216.2	16.4	69.1	301.8
1969	245.4	16.6	80.6	342.7
1970	211.3	10.0	83.6	304.9
1971	220.5	13.1	92.4	326.0
1972	234.4	15.1	102.6	352.2
1973	265.9	18.1	117.0	401.0
1974	292.7	23.2	134.8	450.6
1975	288.0	20.7	148.8	457.5
1976	302.0	22.5	166.0	490.0
Percent of 1976 total	61.6%	4.6%	33.8%	100%
Annual increase	5%	5%	12%	7%

Source: Federal Reserve Bulletin.

The smallest category is estimated federal income taxes, which accounts for 4.6 percent of current liabilities. This category grew at 5 percent per annum. Thus, it is not surprising that accruals and estimated federal income taxes comprised a larger percent of current liabilities in 1976 than 1967. These represent funds which have *no cost* to the firms. Notes and accounts payable, which have an implicit as well as explicit cost, are growing at a more moderate rate.

NONINSTITUTIONAL SOURCES OF SHORT-TERM FUNDS

The majority of short-term financing used by business firms in the United States is noninstitutional in origin—that is, it is not supplied by financial institutions. Such sources are referred to as spontaneous credit. They consist mainly of trade credit and accruals. They appear on the position statement as accounts payable and accrued expenses.

Trade Credit   More than two-fifths of all short-term financing is via trade credit. The seller-producer at one stage of production temporarily finances the purchaser-producer at the succeeding stage by permitting him to delay payment. Thus, trade credit is similar to a loan of goods instead of money. The principal advantages of trade credit are its ready availability and flexibility. The financing is unsecured and informal. The principal disadvantages of trade credit are its cost and its potential undependability during downturns in the business cycle.

Credit Terms.   The firm's credit terms state the credit period, the size of the cash discount, the cash-discount period, and the date the credit period begins. The selling terms "2/10, net 30," for example, mean that the buyer gets a cash discount of 2 percent if he pays cash by the tenth day after the date of the invoice. Otherwise, the full amount is due 30 days after the date of the invoice. The free credit during the ten-day period is referred to as spontaneous credit because its value rises and falls with the volume of the firm's purchases from its suppliers. The buyer should always use this free credit to full advantage by paying on the last day of the discount period.

Cost of Trade Credit.   Although no explicit cost is charged the recipient of trade credit, the firm extending the credit does incur a cost, since its money is tied up in the interim. Extending credit to customers requires the investment of funds that could be used elsewhere. To compensate for this, the firm that extends trade credit passes the cost on to the recipient of trade credit in the form of higher prices on its merchandise.

An additional cost is incurred by the recipient of trade credit if the cash discount is missed (or foregone). For example, if purchases are made on terms of 2/10, net 30 and the customer fails to take the discount, the cost is calculated as follows. Assuming that the firm waits until the thirtieth day to pay, the cost is 2 percent of the purchase price. Since the extra 20 days of credit are one-eighteenth of a year, the cost on a per annum basis is 36 percent (18 times 2 percent). The formulation is:*

$$\text{Approximate interest cost} = \text{Cash discount} \times \frac{360}{\text{Credit period} - \text{Discount period}}$$

The trade-credit process is shown in Figure 10.1 for credit terms of 2/10, net 30. Trade credit can be viewed as a discount (or free credit) if payment is

FIGURE 10.1 Trade Credit—Discount vs. Penalty.

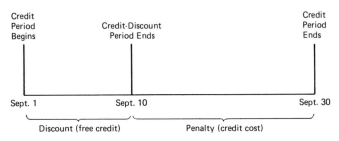

made before the discount period ends. It can be viewed as a penalty (cost of credit) if payment is made after the discount period ends. The penalty or cost is based on the difference between the date payment is made and the discount date. If a firm misses the discount on the tenth day of the month and pays on the eleventh day, the cost is:

$$\text{Approximate interest cost} = 2\% \times \frac{360}{11 - 10}$$

$$= .02\left(\frac{360}{1}\right) = 720\%$$

---

*The calculation above is accurate enough for most purposes. However, figuring the cost precisely results in a slightly higher value. This is so because there are 365 days in a year and the actual base price is price net of discount. Thus the actual cost is:

$$\text{Interest cost} = \frac{\text{Percent discount}}{1 - \text{Percent discount}}\left(\frac{365 \text{ days}}{\text{Credit period} - \text{Discount period}}\right)$$

$$= \frac{.02}{.98}\left(\frac{365}{20}\right)$$

$$= 37.24 \text{ percent}$$

If a firm pays on the twentieth day, the calculation of cost is:

$$\text{Approximate interest cost} = 2\% \times \frac{360}{20 - 10}$$

$$= .02\left(\frac{360}{10}\right)$$

$$= 72\%$$

We saw previously that payment on the thirtieth day results in a cost of 36 percent. Thus, if a firm misses the cash discount, payment should not be made until the end of the credit period (assuming optimality). As a general rule, the high cost of trade credit means that a firm should take the cash discount whenever possible. There are exceptions, of course; see the discussion in the preceding chapter on the effective price of accounts receivable.

Accruals The second noninstitutional source of short-term credit for the firm is accruals. Accruals are liabilities for services received for which payment has not been made. Various accrued expenses account for about a fifth of all short-term credit. The most common accruals are wages and taxes. Accruals are a free source of financing, because the firm has use of the funds for wages and taxes until they are paid to employees and the government respectively.

A firm can use accruals to increase its financing. One method is to pay employees monthly instead of weekly or semimonthly. Such use of accruals as an interest-free source of financing is acceptable and consistent with paying bills as late as possible. This rule holds as long as the firm does not damage its credit rating. In the case of accrued wages, the firm must be sure that delayed payment does not lower employee morale. In general, accruals should be used as often and for as long as possible.

INSTITUTIONAL SOURCES OF SHORT-TERM FUNDS

The three principal sources of short-term credit from financial institutions are commercial bank credit (about a fifth of all short-term financing), finance-company loans (about 10 percent), and commercial paper (about 10 percent).* Although institutional credit does not dominate short-term financing, it does provide a substantial amount of credit, particularly to larger corporations.

Commerical Bank Loans Commercial banks have specialized in short-term business credit to a much greater extent than have all the other financial institutions combined. Since commercial banks are the largest and most important

---

*Commercial paper is discussed in Chapter 21.

source of short-term loans to business, our discussion of institutional sources will primarily deal with bank credit, which appears on the position statement as notes payable.

Short-term loans can be divided into two categories—unsecured and secured loans. Unsecured bank credit is usually made (1) under a one-time line of credit, (2) under a revolving credit agreement, or (3) on a transaction basis. Prior credit arrangements help to reduce the element of uncertainty in cash management. Secured loans are generally required for firms of questionable credit risk.

Methods of Computing the Interest Rate. The cost of commercial bank loans can be controlled to some extent by the firm. When a firm borrows money, the interest on the loan may be paid when the loan is repaid or may be deducted from the proceeds at the time the loan is made. The first type of loan is called a simple-interest loan. The second is known as a discounted-interest loan. In either instance, the determination of the effective rate of interest is:

$$\text{Effective rate} = \frac{\text{Annual dollar interest}}{\text{Loan proceeds}}$$

Interest-bearing loan. Interest is paid on an interest-bearing loan when the loan matures. In other words, the interest is paid at the time the loan is either repaid or renewed. When interest is paid as a loan matures, the stated rate of interest is also the effective rate of interest. For example, interest of $120 is charged for a $1,200 one-year loan at 10 percent.

$$\text{Effective rate} = \frac{\text{Annual dollar interest}}{\text{Loan proceeds}} = \frac{\$120}{\$1,200} = 10\%$$

Discounted-interest loan. When interest is deducted from the original amount of the loan, the loan is said to be discounted. That is, the proceeds received from the loan are less than the amount of the loan, because interest has been deducted in advance. The same one-year $1,200 loan at 10 percent with interest deducted in advance results in a higher effective rate than the stated rate of 10 percent because the borrower paid to use $1,200, but received only $1,080.

$$\text{Effective rate} = \frac{\text{Annual dollar interest}}{\text{Loan proceeds}} = \frac{\$120}{\$1,080} = 11.1\%$$

Installment loan. If the loan is to be repaid on a monthly basis and interest is calculated on the original balance, the effective rate of interest is higher than for the discounted loan. The reason is that the borrower has paid to use the money for a full year, but gets full use of only the last month's payment amount. Thus, he has paid interest to use the first month's payment amount a whole year, but only gets one month's use of the money. The second month's payment amount he gets to use for only two months, and so on. Therefore, the effective rate will be almost double the stated rate of 10 percent. Although the effective-rate calculation is rather complex for a monthly installment loan, the following formulation gives a good approximation:

$$\text{Effective rate on discounted installment loan} = \frac{2PC}{A(n+1)}$$
$$= \frac{2(12)(120)}{1,200(13)}$$
$$= 18.5\%$$

where:

P = number of payments in a year

C = dollar interest costs

A = amount borrowed

n = total number of payments

Financing Accounts Receivable Accounts receivable can be converted into cash before maturing in two ways. They can be sold outright, without recourse, to a "factor," or they can be used as collateral for advances from a finance company or a bank. Either method accomplishes the same purpose, and both forms are used. Accounts-receivable financing permits undercapitalized firms to obtain funds on a continuing basis. This money remains available for as long as a firm is able to sell goods to customers whose financial standing is sufficiently strong. Ordinary bank loans also are often employed on a fairly permanent basis, if the lender is willing constantly to renew the credit.

Factoring companies concentrate more upon the financial position of their client's customers, as distinguished from the net worth and solvency of the client himself. This is because the factor approves the credit before shipment is made and accepts full risk of loss on the receivables that result. Such approval, however, is often advantageous to the firm. For example, factoring companies would not approve sales to W.T. Grant as early as one year prior to Grant's bankruptcy. Protection such as this is of vital importance to the firm. Factoring charges usually run between 2 and 4 percent, depending upon such things as credit standing of the firm's customers, total volume of business, average size of invoice, and the average maturity of the receivables. An additional charge of 2 to 3 points above the prime rate is made on funds advanced before the calculated "average due date" on the receivables acquired.

Factoring accounts receivable is often an ideal solution to the credit problem of small firms. It not only provides funds, but also relieves management of much of its concern over credit and collection problems. This allows management to concentrate on sales and production.

Commercial banks have made loans on accounts receivable since the turn of the century. But it was not until the 1930s that banks began making loans on receivables in large numbers. A few banks have specially trained personnel to handle such financing. Their method of operation is similar to that of the finance companies. The cost of this type of credit, therefore, is usually higher than for other bank loans. The effective rate may reflect a service charge similar to a factoring commission.

In states where usury laws apply to both corporate and noncorporate business, lending on accounts receivable is not done. In such cases, finance companies may resort to outright purchase of the receivables, called factoring, a process not subject to usury laws.

Accounts-receivable financing may enable a firm to increase its profits by generating a larger volume of sales on its capital investment. These additional earnings can be added to the owners' equity. Eventually, such an enterprise may qualify for unsecured bank credit. Finance companies expect to lose their more successful clients to the banks in the course of time. Banks that initiate a customer relationship on the security of receivables look forward to the time when the firm's financial position will justify the extension of unsecured credit.

THE IMPACT OF PROFIT ON SHORT-TERM CREDIT

The use of short-term debt as opposed to long-term debt is likely to result in higher profits, because such debt will be paid off on a seasonal basis during periods when it is not needed. In other words, profitability with respect to current liabilities relates to the difference in costs between various methods of financing and to the use of financing during periods when it is not needed. In general, the greater the proportion of short-term debt to total debt, the higher can be the profitability of the firm. Many of the successful growth companies, such as American Home Products, Coca-Cola Company, and Digital Equipment Corporation, adhere to this principle. Such companies have very little or no long-term debt. Yet their return on owners' equity is between 20 and 30 percent annually, and earnings growth ranges from 12 to 40 percent annually.

Higher profitability results in such cases because (1) short-term interest costs are generally less expensive than long-term interest costs, and (2) short-term financing is used only when needed, as opposed to long-term financing, which spans a number of years, even decades. Both its lower cost and flexibility make short-term financing more attractive to the firm. Of course, risks are involved, and carrying this idea too far can jeopardize repayment of current liabilities. In addition, firms may be unable to refund short-term debt because of unforeseen problems, such as strikes, competition, and recessions.

REDUCING THE RISK IN CASH MANAGEMENT
THROUGH SHORT-TERM-DEBT MANAGEMENT

Up to this point we have been treating cash-management decisions as if little or no risk existed. Of course, the lack of certainty of cash needs and cash balances is a real problem. Such a risk, however, can be greatly reduced if not eliminated through the intelligent use of credit. Loans from commercial banks and finance companies are readily available during periods when it might otherwise be difficult to obtain loans. Such credit is like having a cash-management insurance policy.

A business firm's relationship with its bank has an important influence on the size of deposit balances maintained. In return for making loans, most banks prefer to be partially compensated in the form of demand deposits. This is an important factor to many business firms, for two reasons. First, banks are particularly interested in meeting the credit needs of customers who have maintained large deposit accounts. Second, banks provide a wide range of valuable services to active customers.

The terms of the loan are important to the financial manager. First of all, a loan with the best interest rate possible lowers the cost to the firm. Second, whether the loan is interest-bearing or discounted makes a difference. Finally, installment loans generally carry the highest rate of interest. So the firm should maintain a high credit rating in order to get as favorable terms as possible. Of course, economic conditions have an effect on loan interest. For example, during the tight money (high-interest) days of the second half of 1974, many banks were extending loans only if they were discounted and paid on an installment basis. The effect, of course, was a higher cost to the business-man.

The financial manager of a firm should always advise the creditors of the company's financial conditions. Changes that may occur, especially adverse ones, should be brought to the attention of the creditors (such as banks, insurance company, suppliers, and so on) as soon as the possibility of occurrence is known to the firm. The reason for apprising creditors of adverse situations is to avoid last-minute financial crises. Creditors don't like surprises. So the rule should be *no surprises* for the creditors. Even ask suppliers if you can pay just once on a 60-day basis instead of a 30-day basis, for example. This is simply a good principle of business communication.

SUMMARY

Short-term credit is defined as any source of funds with a maturity of less than one year. This chapter has discussed the two major sources of short-term funds—noninstitutional sources and institutional sources.

The largest category of short-term financing is noninstitutional debt. This consists mainly of trade credit and accruals. Trade credit, represented by accounts payable, is the largest single item of short-term credit. Trade credit is generally easy to obtain because it arises from ordinary business transactions. However, the financial manager needs to be aware of the implied costs of trade credit when discounts are offered for prompt payment (for example, 2/10, net 30).

Accruals are liabilities for services received for which payment has not been made. Various accrued expenses account for almost 20 percent of all short-term credit. The most common accruals are wages and taxes. Accruals are a *free* source of financing because the firm has use of funds owed for wages and taxes until such funds are actually paid to employees and the government respectively.

The other category of short-term financing, institutional sources, consists mainly of commercial bank credit, finance-company loans, and commercial paper. Of the three, bank credit is the largest. Commercial banks have specialized in short-term business loans to a much greater extent than have all the other financial institutions combined.

APPENDIX TO CHAPTER 10: INSTALLMENT LOANS— FINANCE CHARGES UNDER ADD-ON INTEREST, ANNUAL PERCENTAGE RATE (APR), AND THE "RULE OF 78"

In the discussion of installment loans in Chapter 10, it was indicated that the effective interest rates calculated there were only approximations. Here we will discuss installment loans in more detail.

Add-on Interest Interest on installment loans is generally calculated by the "add-on" method. To illustrate the calculation, assume that someone borrows $1,132.08 from a bank on a one-year installment loan calling for a 6 percent add-on rate. The funds received from the bank total $1,132.08, and the interest on the loan is calculated as follows:

$$\text{Interest} = (\$1,132.08)(.06) = \$67.92$$

This interest charge is added on to the funds received, and the borrower signs a note for $1,200 to be repaid at the rate of $100 per month for twelve months.

Annual Percentage Rate (APR) Prior to the passage of the truth-in-lending law, most lenders simply quoted the add-on rate, 6 percent in our example, and did not go on to explain that the actual effective rate on an installment loan was really much higher. Now, however, banks and other lenders are required by law to state on the face of all installment loans the true effective rate, called the *annual percentage rate*, or APR. The APR is calculated by solving the first equation following for i to get the monthly rate, then multiplying i by 12 to convert to an annual rate:

$$\text{Amount borrower receives} = \sum_{t=1}^{n} \frac{\text{monthly payment}}{(1+i)^t}$$

$$\text{APR} = 12i$$

The first equation is laborious to solve without a computer. However, virtually all banks have computerized loan records, and both equations are solved almost instantaneously to determine the APR for each loan written or even discussed. If a very complete set of financial tables, such as the 884-page *Compound Interest and Annuity Tables* published by Financial Publishing Company, is available, the APR can be estimated by linear interpolation; we calculated 10.9 percent per annum by this method as follows:

$$\$1,132.08 = \sum_{t=1}^{12} \frac{\$100}{(1+i)^t}$$

$$\text{PVA}_{\text{IF}} = 11.321$$

This PVA_{IF} lies between the 11.344 for twelve months at $10\frac{1}{2}$ percent and the 11.300 for twelve months at $11\frac{1}{4}$ percent. By interpolation, we find the APR to be 10.9 percent. This can be checked with a hand calculator. 10.9 percent per annum is 0.9083 percent per month. Using

$$\left[\frac{1-(1+i)^{-n}}{i} \right]$$

gives

$$\left[\frac{1-(1.009083)^{-12}}{.009083} \right] \text{ or } 11.321.$$

Rule of 78—Payoff Computation This is a method by which refunds of finance charges are computed when an account is paid out early. It is also a method by which unearned interest charges are taken into income by the bank. As a given amount of unearned interest is taken into income, that amount is then not available as a refund. Virtually all banks, and most other installment lenders, use a "sum-of-the-months'-digits" method, commonly known as the *Rule of 78*, to determine the interest refund. Under the method, there are 78 earning units in a twelve-month loan. Hence the name *Rule of 78*.

The sum of the months' digits is figured by the following formula:

$$(1/2N \times N) + 1/2N = \text{Sum of months' digits}$$

where N is the number of payments.

For a twelve-month period:

$$[1/2(12) \times 12] + 1/2(12) = 78 \text{ earning units}$$

or, to show this graphically:

First month has	12 units
Second month has	11 units
Third month has	10 units
Fourth month has	9 units
Fifth month has	8 units
Sixth month has	7 units
Seventh month has	6 units
Eighth month has	5 units
Ninth month has	4 units
Tenth month has	3 units
Eleventh month has	2 units
Twelfth month has	1 unit
Total units	78

Longer-term loans are computed the same way, with more earning units involved:

$$18\text{-month loan} = (9 \times 18) + 9 \quad = 171 \text{ earnings units}$$
$$24\text{-month loan} = (12 \times 24) + 12 = 300 \text{ earning units}$$
$$36\text{-month loan} = (18 \times 36) + 18 = 666 \text{ earning units}$$

An alternative formula of $N(N + 1)/2$ may be used to compute the number of earning units.

Consider the following example:

$$\$1,000 \text{ loan @ } 6\% \text{ add-on} = \$60 \text{ interest}$$
$$\$60 \div 78 \text{ units} = .7692 \text{ per unit}$$

In the chart below, the value per unit is multiplied by the number of units earned in each installment to give earned interest.

MONTH	UNITS EARNED	×	VALUE PER UNIT	=	EARNED INTEREST	UNEARNED INTEREST
1	12		.7692		$9.23	$50.77
2	11		.7692		8.46	42.31
3	10		.7692		7.69	34.62
4	9		.7692		6.92	27.70
5	8		.7692		6.15	21.55
6	7		.7692		5.38	16.17
7	6		.7692		4.62	11.55
8	5		.7692		3.85	7.70
9	4		.7692		3.08	4.62
10	3		.7692		2.31	2.31
11	2		.7692		1.57	.77
12	1		.7692		.77	.00
					$60.00	$ –

The *unearned interest* is the earned interest subtracted from the total interest of $60.00. After six months, earned interest adds up to $43.83. Thus, $60.00 (total) − $43.83 (earned) = $16.17 (unearned interest). Alternatively, total units in the remaining months times the value per unit equals unearned interest (21 units × .7692 = $16.15 unearned interest). In this example, the *refund ratio* during or at the end of six months is $16.17 ÷ $60.00 = .2695. The *refund ratio* at any point in the contract is:

$$\frac{\text{Sum of remaining units}}{\text{Total units in contract}} = \text{Refund ratio}$$

The refund ratio times total finance charges equals the interest refund. For example, .2695 × $60.00 = $16.17.

Subtract the finance-charge refund from the balance on the loan to arrive at the payoff. For example, $530.00 (balance) minus $16.20 (refund) equals $513.80 (payoff).

The computer figures all this and prints out the payoff in the trial balance. However, from a professional standpoint, you should know how to compute a payoff manually.

Payoff Computation for Other Payment Periods. Even though the number 78 is applicable only for twelve payments, banks generally follow the same procedures for loans of 18, 24, and 36 months and other monthly periods. For example, the total units in a 36-month loan are:

$$(1/2N \times N) + 1/2N, \text{ or } (18 \times 36) + 18 = 666 \text{ units}$$

The refund ratio for prepayment during or at the end of the first month is:

$$\text{Refund ratio} = \frac{666 - 36}{666} = .9459 = 94.59\%$$

During or at the end of the second month:

$$\text{Refund ratio} = \frac{666 - (36 + 35)}{666} = 89.34\%$$

This process continues until prepayment in the 36th month is:

$$\text{Refund ratio} = \frac{1}{666} = .0015 = .15\%$$

For a three-year, or 36-month, installment loan of $5,000 at a 6 percent add-on rate, total interest charges would be $3 \times .06 \times \$5,000 = \$900$. The monthly payments would be $\$163.89 = (\$900 + \$5,000) \div 36$. If the loan were paid off after six payments had been made, the payoff would be $4,288.32, calculated as follows:

Balance: $163.89 × 30 =	$4,916.70
Less interest refund:	
(1) $666 - \dfrac{(36 + 35 + 34 + 33 + 32 + 31)}{666} = .6982$	
(2) .6982 × $900 =	628.38
Payoff:	$4,288.32

PROBLEMS

---

1. A firm plans to increase its inventory, but doesn't have the cash to do so. If trade-credit terms are 1/10, n/60 and the bank rate is 9 percent, should the firm take the discount? $\dfrac{.01}{1-.01} \times \dfrac{360}{60-10}$ $\dfrac{.01}{.99} \times \dfrac{360}{50} \cong 7.3\%$

NO

2. Compute the approximate cost of interest on the following terms of sale:

   a. 3/15, n/90 /05

   b. 4/10, 2/30, n/60

3. Recompute Problem 2 assuming a 15-day grace period after the final due date.

4. You borrow $1,000 at 10 percent for one year. What is the effective interest rate if the loan is:

    a. Discounted and payable in one lump sum

    b. Interest-bearing, payable in one lump sum

    c. A simple-interest loan payable in monthly installments

5. The Spinoff Corporation needs $500,000 in cash to make an out-of-court settlement in a legal suit against the company. Compute the implicit or effective rate of interest on each of the alternatives:

    a. Forego cash discounts on terms of 2/10, net 50.

    b. Borrow from a bank at an 8% rate of interest, with monthly installment repayments for a one-year period.

    c. Borrow at 12% discounted, to be repaid in one year.

6. You obtain a $10,000 property-improvement loan from your bank. The loan is to be repaid in monthly installments over a five-year period. The total interest cost is $3,600. What is the effective rate of interest?

7. Assume that the loan in Problem 6 is a Rule-of-78 loan:

    a. What are the total units in the contract?

    b. If the loan is paid off at the end of the second year, what is the amount of the refund (in dollars)?

8. You obtain a $4,000 property-improvement loan from your bank. The loan is to be repaid in monthly installments over a seven-year period. The total interest cost is $1,600. What is the effective rate of interest?

9. Assume that the loan in Problem 8 is a Rule-of-78 loan:

    a. What are the total units in the contract?

    b. If the loan is paid off at the end of the sixth year, what is the amount of the refund (in dollars)?

10. A firm can factor its receivables for 3%. The firm sells $250,000 per month to open accounts with n/30 terms. The operations of the credit department have a fixed cost of $3,000 per month and a variable cost of 2% of receivables.

    a. What is the cost of factoring?

    b. What is the cost of the firm's credit department?

    c. Should the firm use the factor?

Measuring
the Desirability of
Long-Term Assets

The critical factor in future business success is today's investment decision.

Richard E. Ball and
Z. Lew Melnyk,
Theory of Managerial
Finance: Selected
Readings, *1967*

Thus far, Part II has been concerned with financial functions, tools, and planning in financial management, as well as the management of assets. In the latter category, the management of the short-term assets—cash, receivables, and inventories—has been treated. In the present chapter, the analytical framework designed for decisions in the acquisition of *long-term* assets is treated. The entire area of analysis of decisions involving the acquisition of long-term assets and measuring their desirability is known as *capital budgeting*.

The objective of this chapter is to introduce the importance and techniques of capital budgeting, and to bring the reader to the level of sophistication required to work problems in capital budgeting.

The commitment of funds to long-term assets is a major decision within the firm, and it must be made carefully. This chapter will view the long-term asset acquisition decision, capital budgeting, by viewing its component parts:

1. Analysis of cash inflows
2. Analysis of cash outlays
3. Analysis of the relationship between cash inflows and cash outlays, the capital budgeting decision

After these basic principles of capital budgeting have been examined and illustrated, several "real-world" nuances will be presented. Among these are the analysis of projects with uneven receipts, the analysis of the purchase of new assets versus replacement assets, and the introduction of risk analysis in the capital budgeting decision.

A capital expenditure is one that is expected to benefit the firm for a period of time longer than a year—usually, much longer. Two usual characteristics of capital expenditures are that (1) a considerable commitment of funds is involved, and (2) decisions involving capital outlays cannot be reversed easily. In fact, a firm is usually stuck with a capital expenditure decision. It is much easier to reverse decisions in inventories, accounts receivable, and cash than decisions to invest in fixed assets.

The economic problem is the allocation of scarce resources (funds of the firm) among competing alternatives, known as capital expenditure proposals. Firms do not have unlimited funds. Therefore, the best (or a few best) selections among the alternatives must be made in order to maximize the wealth of the common stockholders.

The decision-making process is the conscious selection of one policy or course of action from among numerous options. Capital budgeting is basically a decision-making process. An evaluation is made to determine which capital proposals in fixed assets would be profitable for the firm. Then the most profitable is selected, provided its rate of return exceeds the cost of capital of the firm. Capital budgeting is the process of evaluation and selection of capital expenditures that increase the wealth of the owners of the firm.

The significance of capital budgeting is manifold. First, the fact that the results of the decision continue over a long period of time reduces the flexibility of the manager. The decision maker is bound by the decision, whether it is good or bad. He has committed the funds of the firm and is at the mercy of future developments.

Second, the fact that capital expenditures usually involve large sums of money necessitates a careful job of planning and evaluation. This fact is just as important as the first one. If a firm buys expensive capital assets, the decision to do so had better be a good one. Otherwise, the firm will suffer financially in time to come in two ways: the funds of the firm may have been exhausted, and the return from the expenditure will not be rewarding.

Last, the fact that expenditures for capital assets are not easily reversed is the most significant aspect of capital budgeting. Once the asset is purchased, there is difficulty in changing the decision even if management would prefer to do so. In fact, it is much easier to buy assets than it is to sell them, just as it is easier to build a brick wall and a roof than it is to disassemble them.

Investment Proposals   Capital budgeting proposals fall into two categories. One involves the replacement of existing assets. The other involves the addition of new assets and/or product lines. Probably, the easier decision to make is the one involving replacement of assets. Since the firm has a benefit/cost record of the old asset that can be compared against benefit/cost estimates of a replacement asset, the decision can be made with more certainty.

The addition of new assets or product lines is a more complex decision for the firm. Such decisions are made under more uncertainty. The firm is allocating capital for addition of plant capacity and for other needs. In such cases, the firm is entering a new phase of operations (expanding or new product lines). Many of the figures used in the decision-making process will be nothing more than educated guesses. Therefore, the firm should exercise great care in making such decisions.

Properties of Capital   Capital budgeting has four basic properties that must be considered.
Budgeting   They are (1) the time value of money, (2) cash flows, (3) the firm's required rate of return, and (4) risk and/or uncertainty.

The underlying concept of capital budgeting is that money has a time value; that is, a dollar received today is worth more than a dollar received in the future. This means that we can invest a dollar received now, but we have to defer investment on a dollar received later. Based on the time value of money, it would be more desirable for purposes of maximizing the rate of return to realize the higher receipts in the earlier years and the lower receipts in the later years. In other words, there is a preference for an early receipt of money over a later one.

All problems in capital budgeting must be set up and formulated in terms of cash flows. Two sets of cash flows are used, cash outflows and cash inflows. Cash flows out of a firm are a result of a capital investment. Cash flows into a firm are a result of implementing a capital proposal.

The matter of the firm's required return will be discussed at length in Chapter 12, and the properties of risk and uncertainty are ones that run throughout this text, having been introduced in Chapter 4.

ARRANGING DATA

Since capital budgeting is concerned primarily with comparing the present value of cash flows of a project with the present value of the project's cash outlay, it is important that inflows and outflows be correctly adjusted for the influence of *depreciation* and *taxes*.

Project Inflows   The inflows to a project used in capital budgeting are always the project's cash inflows. Net cash inflows are equal to the "after-tax earnings, plus depreciation" figure for the project's inflows. To calculate a project's cash flow, perform the following steps for each year of the project's life:

1. Sum all cash inflows that accrue to the project.

2. Deduct annual operating expenses and depreciation of the project. The result is earnings before taxes of the project.

3. Subtract taxes from earnings before taxes. The result is the after-tax earnings of the project.

4. To the after-tax earnings of the project, *add back* the annual depreciation.

This process is illustrated in Table 11.1. It is necessary to understand how taxes and depreciation adjust the cash flow of a project in order to completely understand the capital budgeting process.

First, the tax liability of the project is calculated, because it represents a direct charge to the project. If the project is not added to the firm's assets, then no tax liability is incurred from the project. For this reason, the tax liability must be charged directly to the project, and it therefore reduces the project's worth.

Note carefully that the tax liability represents a *cash* outflow from the project. A check must be written to the Internal Revenue Service for the income tax liability accruing to the project. Such is *not* the case with the depreciation chargeable to the project. Depreciation is indeed an expense of the project. It is an earmarking of income to recognize the incorporation of capital goods into the firm's products. But depreciation *is not a cash outflow* from the firm. No check is written to pay depreciation expense in the same way taxes are paid. Depreciation is subtracted from the project's gross cash

TABLE 11.1 New Asset, Even Annual Receipts

Cost of new printing press	$32,000
Salvage value	$6,000
Economic life	4 yrs.
Tax rate	50%
Cost of capital	12%
Annual benefits	$12,000
Depreciation (Straight line)	$6,500

Calculations:

1. Initial outflow and annual reductions

$32,000	cash outlay
−6,000	salvage value
$26,000	depreciation base
÷4	years
$ 6,500	annual depreciation

	BOOK ACCOUNT	CASH-FLOW ACCOUNT
2. Annual benefits		
Δ Sales	$15,000	$15,000
Less: Δ operating expenses	3,000	3,000
Less: Δ depreciation	6,500 *— not cash outlay*	
Δ Earnings before taxes	$ 5,500	
Less: Δ income taxes (50%)	2,750	2,750
Δ Earnings after taxes	$ 2,750	
Δ Cash flow		9,250

[handwritten annotations: "amt generates by project"; "depreciation — even tho does not effect cash flow reduces taxes"]

3. Alternate method of figuring cash flow
   Cash flow = earnings after taxes + depreciation
   = $2,750 + $6,500
   = $9,250

flow in order to calculate the tax liability of the project, for indeed depreciation is a cost of doing business, and therefore is a tax-deductible expense. But since *cash* does not leave the firm in payment of depreciation, depreciation is added back to the after-tax earnings figure of the project. It should be clear why the cash flow accruing to a project is always calculated as the "after-tax earnings, plus depreciation" income figure.

Project Outflows In almost all cases, project outflows are the sum of cash payments that must be made to acquire the project—that is, the cash cost of the project.* Thus, cash outflows are not discounted if they all occur in year zero—the year the project is implemented. That is, the present value factor of the outflows above is 1.000.

---

*In some cases where a replacement decision results in a tax loss because of the replaced asset, the tax loss is subtracted from the cash price of the new project.

INDEXES OF WORTH: PROJECT-RANKING METHODS

There are many methods of evaluating the relationship between a project's cash inflows and outflows. Four of the most generally used and accepted will be defined and discussed in this section. The data in Table 11.1 will be used to illustrate each of the four project-ranking methods. The four methods are the average rate of return (ARR), the payback period (PBP), the net present value (NPV), and the internal rate of return (IRR). A comparative analysis of the four methods will conclude this section.

Average Rate of Return (ARR) This method, sometimes called the accounting rate of return, measures the relationship between the project's *average* earnings after taxes and the project's cash outflow.
Symbolically:

$$ARR = \frac{\bar{X} \text{ EAT}}{CO}$$

where:

$\bar{X}$ EAT = the project's mean earnings after taxes

CO = cash outlay

The average-rate-of-return method has several strengths. Among these are the facts that it uses accounting income, not cash flow, and that it is easy to calculate; and for these reasons, the method is frequently used. Among the shortcomings of the ARR method is the fact that it ignores cash flows, the cost of capital, and the time value of money in its calculation.

In the project contained in Table 11.1, the average rate of return is 8.6 percent. That is:

$$ARR = \frac{\bar{X} \text{ EAT}}{CO}$$

$$= \frac{2,750}{32,000}$$

$$= 8.6\%$$

The Payback Period (PBP) The payback period is defined as the *period of time* required for a firm to recover its cash outlay. The cash flow (after tax, plus depreciation figure) is used in calculating the payback period.
Symbolically:

$$PBP \text{ (years)} = \frac{CO}{CF}$$

where:

CO = cash outflow of the project

CF = cash flow

In the example in Table 11.1, the payback period is 3.4 years. That is:

$$\text{PBP (years)} = \frac{CO}{ACF}$$

$$= \frac{\$32,000}{\$9,250}$$

$$= 3.4 \text{ years}$$

The payback-period method has been severely criticized in recent years because it, like the average-rate-of-return method, does not take into account the cost of the firm's capital and the principle of time value of money. In spite of these shortcomings, the payback period does have characteristics to recommend it. If business decision makers are as concerned as they should be with the phenomenon of risk, then using the payback period assists them in minimizing it, for the emphasis of the payback period is on minimizing the period of time that the cash outlay is exposed to risk. The authors do agree, however, that the payback period should be used in conjunction with the internal-rate-of-return or the net-present-value methods.

The reciprocal of the payback period has received increased attention as a useful tool provided that (1) cash flows are an annuity and (2) twice the payback period is less than the project life. The reciprocal—the payback period divided into 1—is an annual percentage figure. In the example above, the reciprocal of the payback figure is .29, that is, 1/3.4. This figure says that the firm recovers 29 percent of its investment per year.

Furthermore, the internal rate of return on a project will be closely approximated by the payback reciprocal. In fact, a project with an infinite life would have a rate of return exactly equal to the payback reciprocal. In practice, the payback reciprocal is useful in estimating the true rate of return if the project life is at least twice the payback period.

Net Present Value (NPV) The net present value of a project is defined as the difference between the present values of all cash outflows and the present values of the expected cash inflows when discounted at a rate of return consistent with the level of risk associated with the project.

Historically, the net present value has been calculated using the weighted-average cost of capital of the firm as the discount rate. But recent additions to the body of financial theory suggest that the discount rate should be a surrogate for the riskiness of the project under examination. Some projects, for example, are inherently riskier than others, and for this reason, intuition suggests a higher discount factor to compensate for higher risk. This subject is discussed at the close of Chapter 13. Symbolically, the net-present-value (NPV) method appears:

$$NPV = PV_{ci} - PV_{co}$$

where:

PV_{ci} = present value of cash inflows, discounted at the relevant discount factor chosen to account for risk.

PV_{co} = present value of cash outlays, using the same discount rate as above

The calculation of the net present value is somewhat more complicated than the previous methods, and for that reason, perhaps an example is in order.

The example used appears in Table 11.2. This example is that of a project whose cash inflows (AT, PD) are all equal for each of four years. This makes the problem one of an annuity, and we shall proceed to calculate the NPV on the basis of an annuity. (It does not have to be an annuity, however, to calculate the NPV. Table 11.3, later in this chapter, contains an example

TABLE 11.2 Calculating Net Present Value and the
Internal Rate of Return

A. If 8%, 4 years:
　　3.312 × $9,250 = $30,636 *PV of future cash flows*
　　.735 × 6,000 = 4,410 *salvage value*
　　　　　　　　　35,046 *PV of all future cash flows*
　　　− Cash outlay 32,000
　　　　　　　　　3,046 = Net present value

B. If 16%, 4 years:
　　2.798 × $9,250 = $25,881
　　.552 × 6,000   3,312
　　　　　　　　　29,193   *negative PV − < 32,000*

C. If 12%, 4 years:
　　3.037 × $9,250 = $28,092
　　.636 × 6,000 =   3,816
　　　　　　　　　31,908 ≅ $32,000

Recapitulation:
　　　Cash outlay = $32,000
　　　PV at 12% ≅ 32,000
　　　　　NPV =   0
Therefore, the internal rate of return must be 12%.

---

of the calculation of NPV for a project whose income streams are unequal—that is, do not form an annuity.)

Assume in Table 11.2 that the risk factor associated with the project outlined is equal to the cost of capital, 8 percent. (Keep in mind that this is a simplifying assumption, and that the discount factor need not be equal to the cost of capital.) In the table, the cash flows (AT, PD) are calculated to be $9,250 a year for four years. This forms an annuity, the present value of which we must determine. We must also determine the present value of the $6,000 salvage value of the new project, which is payable once and only once at the end of the project; therefore, this value is not of an annuity.

Drawing on the time-line technique outlined in Chapter 3, the present value of the cash flows would appear:

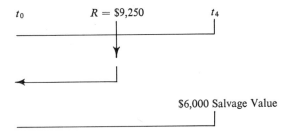

First, the determination of the present value of the equal cash flows (annuity) for four years is in-order. Table A.4 in the Appendix gives the correct interest factor:

$$PVA = IF(R)$$
$$= 3.312 \times \$9,250$$
$$= \$30,636$$

We must also calculate the present value of the salvage value of the new project, payable once and only once at the end of the fourth year. Table A-2 gives the correct interest factor:

$$PV = FV(IF)$$
$$= \$6,000 \times .735$$
$$= \$4,410$$

The sum of the present value of the periodic income streams and the present value of the salvage gives the present value of the investment at 8%:

$$PV = \$30,636 + \$4,410$$
$$= \$35,046$$

Recalling the fact that NPV is equal to the present value of the project's income minus the cash outlay, we have:

$$NPV = PV_{ci} - PV_{co}$$
$$= \$35,046 - \$32,000$$
$$= \$3,046$$

The net present value of the project in Table 11.2 is $3,046.00. It is important for the reader to grasp the significance of this figure. The figure means that the value of the firm will rise by $3,046.00 *immediately* if this project is purchased. It means that the project will increase the value of the firm *right now* if it is purchased. It should be understood also, that a *negative* net present value represents a *decrease* in the value of the firm if the project is purchased.

The net-present-value method has much to recommend it. It does not have the shortcomings of the ARR and PBP. The NPV does use the cost of capital and/or a discount factor that represents risk. And the NPV obviously does recognize the time value of money in its calculations.

Internal Rate of Return (IRR)   The internal rate of return is that *rate of discount* that equates the present value of the income streams of the project to the value of the cash outlay.

In other words, the internal rate of return is the rate of discount that sets the net present value equal to zero. The net present value has to be zero if the present value of the project's income streams is equal to the present value of the project's cash outlay.

The internal rate of return is directly comparable with the firm's cost of capital, or with the project's discount rate reflecting its risk class. The mechanics of the calculation of the internal rate of return are more involved but not more difficult than the calculation of net present value, or indeed any of the other methods.

The first step in calculating the internal rate of return is to calculate the net present value of the project, using the firm's cost of capital as the discount factor as done in step A in Table 11.2.

Consider the project that is the subject of Table 11.2. The net present value was calculated to be $3,046.00 when using the cost of capital, 8 percent, as the discount factor. Since the net present value is greater than zero, the IRR must be greater than the cost of capital. Said differently, a discount rate greater than 8 percent is required to drive down the present value of the income streams to the value of the cash outlay. Calculating the net present value first establishes (1) how close the cost of capital is to the internal rate of return, and (2) given that they are not equal, the direction of the discount factor must be changed in order to move the net present value toward zero.

Since a 8 percent discount rate resulted in a positive NPV in our example project, it is clear that the IRR is greater than 8 percent. Calculating the present value of the income streams at a discount rate of 16 percent results in an NPV of −$2,807 ($29,193 − $32,000). Since a discount rate of 8% is too small, and a discount rate of 16% is too large, the internal rate of return must be between them.

Using 12% as a discount factor, the net present value is very close to 0, as shown in step C of Table 11.2. The method of calculating the internal rate of return is one of successive approximations, beginning with the cost of capital, or imputed risk factor, which is used as the initial discount factor, and using incremental discount factors until the one is found which results in a net present value very close to $0.

The internal-rate-of-return technique is useful and has many positive points. Among them are the facts that it does recognize the time value of money, and that it does make a comparison with the cost of capital.

There are some shortcomings to the use of the internal-rate-of-return method. If any of the income streams are negative (losses) or if any of the income streams are zero, multiple answers are possible, and this greatly limits the usefulness of the internal-rate-of-return method.

EVEN VS. UNEVEN CASH INFLOWS

Genesis of the Problem Up till this point, it has been assumed that all cash inflows, except for salvage value, are equal. This is the condition for an annuity, and for this reason, the calculation of the net present value and the internal rate of return are relatively easy. But there are frequently encountered cases in the "real world" that do not have equal cash inflows. In this case, the assumptions of an annuity are violated. The purpose of this section is to introduce and describe the techniques of calculating net present values and internal rates of return under conditions of equal and unequal cash inflows to a project.

Even Cash Inflows: The Annuity In the case where all cash inflows are equal, the technique of calculating the present value of an annuity is used. The example in Table 11.2 portrays an annuity-type problem. At the cost of capital, 12 percent, the net present value is $2,945.25. This indicates that the internal rate of return is greater than 12 percent. Using approximation, it can be seen that a discount rate of 16 percent reduces the present value of the project's cash inflows and its salvage value to $31,991.50, for a negligible NPV of $8.50.

To summarize, when cash inflows are equal, they are treated as an annuity in calculating their NPV and IRR.

TABLE 11.3 New Asset, Uneven Annual Receipts

Cost of new printing press $34,000
Salvage value $0
Economic life 4 yrs.
Tax rate 50%
Cost of capital 10%

Annual benefits:

YEAR	BENEFITS
1	$12,000
2	14,000
3	16,000
4	18,000

Depreciation: Straight line

Calculations:

1. Annual depreciation:

$34,000 cash outlay
-0 salvage value
$\overline{\$34,000}$ depreciable value
$\div 4$ years
$\overline{\$8,500}$ annual depreciation

2. Annual cash flows:

	YEAR			
	1	2	3	4
Benefits	$12,000	$14,000	$16,000	$18,000
− Depreciation	8,500	8,500	8,500	8,500
= Tax base	$ 3,500	$ 5,500	$ 7,500	$ 9,500
× Tax rate	.50	.50	.50	.50
= After-tax income	$ 1,750	$ 2,750	$ 3,750	$ 4,750
+ Depreciation	8,500	8,500	8,500	8,500
= AT, PD	$10,250	$11,250	$12,250	$13,250

3. Calculation of net present value.

YEAR	IF 10%	AT, PD	PV
1	.909	$10,250	$9,317.25
2	.826	11,250	9,292.50
3	.751	12,250	9,199.75
4	.683	13,250	9,049.75
			36,859.25

PV = $36,859.25
− Cash outlay = 34,000.00
NPV = 2,859.25

A.

YEAR	IF 12%	AT, PD	PV
1	.893	$10,250	$9,153.25
2	.797	11,250	8,966.25
3	.712	12,250	8,722.00
4	.636	13,250	8,427.00
			35,268.50

B.

YEAR	IF 14%	AT, PD	PV
1	.877	$10,250	8,989.25
2	.769	11,250	8,651.25
3	.675	12,250	8,268.75
4	.592	13,250	7,844.00
			33,753.25

NPV ≅ 13%

Uneven Cash Inflows   Uneven cash inflows cannot be treated as an annuity. In the calculation of the present value of a series of uneven receipts, the interest factor (IF) for each period must be secured from Table A-2 and each year's receipts multiplied by its interest factor.

Table 11.3 shows the calculation of the net present value and internal rate of return of a project with uneven receipts. Discounted at the cost of capital, 10 percent, the (uneven) cash inflows reveal an NPV of $2,859.25, which means that the IRR is greater than 10 percent. Using 12 percent as an approximation, and multiplying each year's cash flows by its interest factor, it is seen that the present value of the income streams is $35,268.50, and the NPV is $1,268.50. Using the same process with a discount factor of 14 percent gives a negative net present value. The internal rate of return is therefore approximately 13 percent.

To summarize, when cash flows are unequal, they *cannot* be treated as an annuity, and the present value of each year's cash inflow must be calculated.

ANALYSIS OF REPLACEMENT DECISIONS

What Are Replacement   Up to the present discussion, only the acquisition of new assets has
Decisions?   been discussed. But perhaps more realistic is the replacement decision—that is, the decision to replace an existing capital asset with a new one. This decision is more complex than the new-asset acquisition, since the replacement decision involves the replacement not only of the new asset but also of depreciation schedules, and other considerations.

A Typical Example   The matrix for analysis of replacement decisions is presented in Table 11.4. Outflows are arrayed first, followed by inflows. The data in the table are derived from the following transaction of the Pilot Printing Company:

NEW PRINTING PRESS

Cost	$35,000
Salvage value	$10,000
Life	8 years
Increased benefits	$4,000

OLD PRINTING PRESS

Cost	$30,000
Salvage value	$4,000
Life	10 years (as of 2 years ago)
Can be sold for	$10,800

TABLE 11.4 Replacement Decision, Pilot Printing Company

	BEFORE TAX	AFTER TAX	IF	PV
Outflows:				
New printing press	$35,000	$35,000	—	$35,000
Sale of old press	(10,800)	(10,800)	—	(10,800)
Tax loss	(10,000)	(5,000)	—	(5,000)
Total cash outlay				$19,200
Inflows:				
Increased sales	$4,000	$2,000	5.335	$10,670
Depreciation, new	5,000	2,500	5.335	$13,337
Depreciation, old	(2,600)	(1,300)	5.335	(6,935)
Salvage, new	10,000	10,000	.467	4,670
Present value of inflows				$21,742

NET PRESENT VALUE

PV inflows	$21,742
PV outflows	19,200
Net present value	$ 2,542

The cost of capital of Pilot Printing is 10 percent. Each line of Table 11.4 will be discussed in order to make clear how cash outflows and inflows are netted out, and how the replacement decision is made.

Outflows   Note that the present values of all the outflows are at the beginning of the life of the project. This means that their present value is the same as the cash outflows.

New Printing Press.   The press cost $35,000, so this expenditure shows up as a $35,000 cash outflow.

Sale of Old Press.   This is the cash inflow, $10,800, from the sale of the old press. Since Pilot Printing receives this payment only once (not periodically), it is treated as a reduction in the purchase price of the new machine, in much the same way that payment for a used car being traded in is considered a reduction in the price of the new car.

Tax Loss.   The difference between what the records say an asset is worth and its realized price represents a loss or gain to the firm, depending upon its value. In the case outlined in Table 11.4, the difference between the book value and the market value of the *old* press is calculated as follows:

1.	Total value being depreciated ($30,000 price minus $4,000 salvage)	$26,000
2.	Depreciation used in past 2 years (2 × $2,600)	5,200
3.	Book value now of machine ($30,000–$5,200)	$24,800
4.	Minus current market value of machine	10,800
5.	Difference between book value and market value	$14,000

What this tabulation reveals is that there is a $14,000 difference between what the books say the old machine is worth and what it is actually worth. This difference, a minus number, is a deductible loss for tax purposes. With a tax rate of 50 percent, the loss is reduced to $7,000. The $7,000 is a *reduction* in the purchase price of the new machine, because it represents a one-time-only *reduction* in tax cash outflow.

Inflows   *Sales.*   The increased sales are the reason for considering the purchase of the new machine. At a tax rate of 50 percent, the $4,000 increased sales becomes an annuity of $2,000 for the four-year life of the machine. The $2,000 is multiplied by the IF 5.335 to get the present value, at 10 percent, of the 8-year cash flow.

Depreciation New.   The depreciation on the new machine represents a funds flow that must be accounted for. The after-tax annual depreciation, $2,500, forms an annuity of 8 years, and discounted at 10 percent, its present value is $13,337.

Depreciation Old.   If the old machine is sold, its depreciation must be taken off the books, and the firm loses a funds source. It is for this reason that the old depreciation figures are negative in Table 11.4 on an after-tax basis. The present value of lost annual depreciation is $6,935.

Salvage of New Machine.   The last value to be accounted for is the salvage value of the new machine. Unlike the other inflows, the salvage value of the new machine is not an annuity but appears only once, at the end of the eighth year. The present value of this single amount is $4,670, and it is added to the present value of all other inflows.

Calculating the Net Present Value.   As in previous examples, the present value of the cash outflows is subtracted from the present value of the cash inflows to determine the net present value.

In the example in Table 11.4, the net present value is $2,542, indicating that there is an increase in the value of the firm if the new printing press is purchased.

CAPITAL BUDGETING UNDER CONDITIONS OF RISK

**The Need for
Considering Risk** Up to this point in the discussion of capital budgeting, we have assumed that future cash flows are known with certainty. This condition, the condition of perfect knowledge into the future, rarely exists in the real world. As in other areas of financial decision making, however, risk can be anticipated and its impact made less destabilizing through the use of probability analysis in attempting to anticipate the impact of varying income streams in the future.

The use of probability analysis in capital budgeting is straightforward and relatively easy to understand. Consider the two examples in Table 11.5. Assume that a home-heating-oil dealer is considering whether or not to build a new storage area. Hanging heavily over his head is the possibility of another Arab oil boycott. If there is another boycott, fuel supplies will be interrupted and revenues will be decreased. It would not be sensible for the oil dealer to ignore the possibility of another boycott. But how to account for it in his decision to accept or reject a new storage facility baffles him.

TABLE 11.5 Introducing Risk into the Capital Budgeting Decision

CONDITION	(1) PROBABILITY OF OCCURRENCE	(2) CASH FLOW	(3) EXPECTED CASH FLOW (1 × 2)
No probabilities considered	1.0	$28,000	$28,000
Arabs will boycott	.70	$20,000	$14,000
Arabs will not boycott	.30	$30,000	$ 9,000
Expected cash flow			$23,000

This is an instance in which probability analysis assists in making better capital budgeting decisions. In Table 11.5, when probability analysis is not used, it is determined that the cash flow (after tax, plus depreciation) will be $28,000 to the storage project. This figure is used without considering the possibility of interruption of fuel oil supply from another boycott.

But in the second part of the table, more information has been brought to bear. First, the possibility of an Arab boycott is recognized. This recognition permits a more sophisticated—and therefore more likely to be accurate—analysis of the decision.

Note that the oil dealer has estimated his revenues under conditions of boycott and no boycott, $20,000 per year and $30,000 per year, respectively. He has also considered the probabilities of a boycott or no boycott, 70 percent and 30 percent, respectively. Multiplying each cash flow by its probability gives its expected value (E), and summing the expected cash flows leads to the total expected cash flow to the project, considering all contingencies and their probabilities of occurrence. Referring to Table 11.5, it makes much more sense to use $23,000 than $28,000 as the cash-flow figure because:

1. It considers different possible outcomes.

2. It considers the probabilities of the possible outcomes.

The reliability of the expected cash flows is conditional upon the confidence in the probability coefficients as well as in the anticipated cash flows under different conditions. But given the accuracy of these variables, *it is always better to account for risk than not to.*

SUMMARY

Capital budgeting is an important part of the financial manager's responsibility. The ability to evaluate the usefulness of long-term assets under conditions of certainty, risk, and uncertainty, and with respect to depreciation and tax effects, is a skill needed to maintain the financial health of the firm, and therefore assist in maximizing the shareholders' wealth position.

The problem involved in capital budgeting is the allocation of scarce funds among competing alternatives, that is, capital projects. Therefore, capital budgeting is a decision-making process. It is the process of rationally analyzing various capital asset acquisitions available to the firm, and selecting the one(s) which will maximize shareholder wealth.

The capital budgeting techniques are summarized in the following matrix:

	UTILIZES TIME VALUE OF MONEY	UTILIZES CASH FLOW	GIVES RESULTS IN
1. Internal rate of return	✓	✓	% return
2. Present value	✓	✓	$ return
a. Net PV	✓	✓	Net $ return
b. Profitability index	✓	✓	±1
3. Payback period		✓	Years
Payback reciprocal		✓	% return
4. Average rate of return			% return

PROBLEMS

1. Assume that you are considering the purchase of a five-year bond with a coupon rate of 8%. If the face value of the bond is $1,000 and the market rate for similar bonds is 6%, what is the present value of the bond to you as an investor?

2. Assume the same situation as Problem 1, but the coupon rate is 4% and the market rate for similar bonds is 6%. What is the present value of the bond to you as an investor?

3. Two conflicting proposals of equal risk have been made for the purchase of new equipment. The data on each are given below:

	A	B
Net cash outlay	$8,400	$6,000
Salvage value	0	0
Estimated life	6 years	6 years
NET CASH BENEFITS BEFORE DEPRECIATION AND TAXES		
1–3 years	$2,600	$1,600
4–6 years	2,000	1,600

Assume straight-line depreciation and a corporate tax rate of 40%. Cost of capital is assumed to be 8%. a. What is the net present value of each proposal? b. Which project should be accepted? Why?

4. Assume that you are evaluating a machine with an initial investment of $75,000. You are trying to determine the internal rate of return. You are given the following data:

Annual cash flow, first five years	$14,000
Annual cash flow, second five years	10,000
Terminal salvage value	10,000
Tax rate	50%

Obviously, the machine has a ten-year economic or service life. Interpolate!

5. The Apple-Atchian Corporation is engaged in growing and marketing apples in western North Carolina. It is an old, well-established, and well-known corporation.

The corporation has the opportunity to secure one of three investment opportunities. The board of directors has specified that only one of the following three projects be accepted:

PROJECT A:
Cash outlay: $3 million
Annual income stream: $488,202 for 10 years*

PROJECT B:
Cash outlay: $3 million
Annual income stream: $699,627 for 7 years*

PROJECT C:
Cash outlay: $3 million
Annual income stream: $480,231 for 9 years*

The corporation's cost of capital is 10%.

*These annual income streams are cash benefits after
    depreciation and taxes; i.e., they are cash flows.

    a. Calculate:
        (1) The payback period for each project
        (2) The net present value of each project
        (3) The internal rate of return for each project

    b. Which project should be accepted? Justify your answer.

6. Sonny Scruggs is a cattle rancher in South Dakota. He is considering
building a new cattle feeder for next year's growing season. Below are the
data on the proposed cattle feeder:

Cash outlay $100,000
Salvage value   0
Life of feeder   10 years
Cost of capital   10%

Sonny uses straight-line depreciation and his corporate ranch is in the 50%
tax bracket.

Sonny knows that the weather will influence his decision to build the feeder.
If it is too dry or too wet, the revenues accruing to the feeder will be decreased.
Below are his estimates of income *before taxes and depreciation* associated
with each type of weather:

WEATHER CONDITION	PROBABILITY OF OCCURRENCE	INCOME[a]
Too wet	.15	$20,000
Just right	.70	30,000
Too dry	.15	20,000

[a] Before taxes and depreciation.

    a. Calculate the cash flows after taxes and depreciation for growth
incomes of $20,000 and $30,000.

    b. Calculate the expected return (*E*), given the weather probabilities.

c. From the expected return, calculate the average rate of return, the payback period, the net present value, and the internal rate of return.

d. Should Sonny build the feeder? Why, or why not?

7. Calculate the net present value and internal rate of return of your education. Is it worth it? Why, or why not?

8. You have a chance to purchase one of the following investments. Find the present value of each of the series of cash flows. The interest rate is 12%. Which investment would you rather have? Why?

ICE CREAM PARLOR		HOT DOG STAND	
YEAR		YEAR	
1	$ 600	1	$1,200
2	800	2	1,000
3	1,000	3	800
4	1,200	4	600

Measuring the Firm's Required Rate of Return

In Chapter 6, it was shown that one of the many responsibilities of the financial manager is to seek funds with which to purchase profitable assets. In this process, funds move from right to left across the position statement; that is, funds from the sale of claims on assets are used to purchase revenue-generating assets. Chapter 11 examined what is called capital budgeting, where the objective is to determine the asset (or assets) that optimize stockholder wealth.

In this chapter, the methods of analyzing the cost of funds used to purchase assets are examined.

Basic Definitions   In order to enhance your knowledge in this chapter, the meanings of some broad concepts are given here. *Financial structure* refers to the way the firm's assets are financed. The term includes the entire claims-on-assets section of the position statement. *Capital structure* refers to the permanent financing of the firm. The term includes long-term debt, preferred stock, and common equity. Thus, capital structure includes all accounts in the claims-on-assets section of the balance sheet *except* current liabilities. *Common equity* is used to refer to common stock, contributed capital, and retained earnings (accumulated earnings).*

The key concept used in this chapter is the capital structure of the firm. Based upon the various components of the capital structure (bonds, preferred stock, and capital equity), the cost of capital of the firm is determined. The *cost of capital* is the rate of return that is necessary to maintain the value of the firm.

Relevance in the   The cost of capital has relevance in the business world. Consider the
Business World   following statement by the financial manager of one of the country's large oil companies:

> We [Sohio] have been using a cost of capital concept in our financial planning and administration for more than fifteen years. . . . Generally speaking, our attempt has been to arrive at a figure which measures a nondilution cost of capital—that is, the cost of capital which will maintain a rate of earnings without dilution of the stockholders' equity.†

Supply–Demand   Because of the imagery it evokes, supply-and-demand analysis has been
Aspects   compared to the blades of a pair of scissors. Each blade by itself is useless, yet in tandem the blades become a powerful cutting tool. The

---

*Note that preferred stock is excluded from common equity. As a hybrid security, preferred has some of the characteristics of bonded debt and some of the characteristics of common stock. This will be discussed more fully later in the chapter.

†Jerome B. Cohen and Sidney M. Robbins, *The Financial Manager* (New York: Harper & Row, 1966), p. 735.

same is true of supply-and-demand analysis of capital funds, and we shall witness their combined power.

If we plot the cost of capital and the return on the capital assets, the resulting curves would appear as they do in Figure 12.1. Portrayed there are the supply and demand curves for capital assets. The cost curve is positively sloped (cost rises as units of capital acquired increase) because increments to the capital base involve decreasingly efficient capital sources. The demand curve for capital is negative (the return on capital assets decreases as capital size increases) because of the principle of diminishing marginal productivity.

FIGURE 12.1

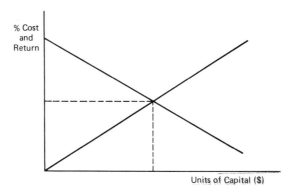

Units of Capital ($)

Required Rate of Return
In theory, the required rate of return for a firm is the rate that leaves unchanged the market price of the stock. *Required rate of return* (*RRR*) is defined as the rate of return that suppliers of capital (the financial markets) expect to receive for the use of their funds. Conversely, the cost of capital is the rate of return which the firm must pay to suppliers of capital (the financial markets) for use of their funds. In general, cost of capital is the minimum acceptable rate of return on investments made by the firm. It is the return specified by a market-determined rate (a market-equilibrium relationship).

The required return is established in financial markets by the collective actions of investors competing against each other. The required return ensures that stockholders will be no worse off if the firm does nothing—that is, rejects a proposal to purchase capital assets. Thus, cost of capital of a firm may be viewed as a rate of return on a firm's assets below which the value of the firm will fall, and above which the value of the firm will rise.

Risk and Claims on Assets
In our private lives, there are basically two sources of capital—saving out of current income, and borrowing. The same is true for the corporation, with one important difference. In addition to saving out of current income and borrowing, a corporation can sell claims on future income

streams as well. Claims on future income streams are offered through the sale of stock (both common and preferred). Thus, the sale of stock, the sale of debt, and saving out of current income constitute the sources of a firm's capital.

The priority of the claims on the firm's assets with respect to income is determined by the risk associated with each claim. The risk–return tradeoff curve specifies that rates of return are proportional to risk. Thus, the priority of claims gives rise to the risk element as well as to the cost. Strictly speaking, however, it is the risk involved that gives rise to the cost.

Because of relatively low risk, debt has the first claim on earnings. In exchange for this priority, the creditor generally accepts a lower return for his funds. Common stock represents the ownership of the corporation. As with all owners, common shareholders exercise control over the firm through election of the directors. And also like other firm owners, common shareholders can claim the residue of the firm's income after all others have been paid. The possibility of great return is present; so is the possibility of great loss. Recalling the risk–return tradeoff principle advanced in Chapter 1, we can see why common shareholders usually receive the highest return on their investment in the firm.

Somewhere between the debt of a corporation and its common stock is preferred stock. Preferred stock is a hybrid; it has characteristics of both debt and equity. It has a fixed return, but it is payable only if there are earnings available. Preferred stock is considered a part of the equity base, although preferred shareholders normally do not vote for the board of directors. Thus, three claims—debt, preferred stock, and common stock—constitute the external sources of capital available to the corporation.

There is an additional source of capital—retained earnings. This is the corporate equivalent of savings out of current income. Retained earnings are income net of all previous claims not paid to the shareholder. The corporation in effect says to its shareholders that it will hold earnings in trust and invest them in assets for the benefit of the shareholder. The shareholder is usually compensated for these funds by growth in the market value of the stock.

These are the claims on the assets of the corporation: debt, preferred stock, common stock, and retained earnings. By now, the perceptive reader has probably recognized that these are also the permanent sources of capital of the firm.

Relative Importance of Capital Sources   Table 12.1 gives the values for three important capital sources for the seven-year period, 1970 to 1976. We have attempted to show the relative importance of retained earnings as a source of capital. Roughly one-third to one-half of all capital represented in the table was in the form of retained earnings, corporate saving. It would be foolish and unwise to fool ourselves into believing that retained earnings is a costless source of funds, especially in view of its relatively large contribution to the capital base of the corporation. The fact is that retained earnings is one of the costlier sources of capital.

TABLE 12.1 Dollar Value of External Equity, Bonds, and Retained Earnings Raised by Corporations, 1970 to 1976

($ million)

YEAR	PREFERRED	COMMON	BONDS & NOTES	RETAINED EARNINGS	TOTAL	RETAINED EARNINGS AS % OF TOTAL
1970	$1,390	$ 7,240	$29,495	$14,100	$52,225	27
1971	3,670	9,291	31,917	21,300	66,178	32
1972	3,370	10,725	26,132	30,000	70,227	43
1973	3,337	7,642	21,049	40,900	72,928	56
1974	2,253	3,994	32,066	44,400	82,713	56
1975	3,458	7,405	42,756	33,200	86,819	42
1976	2,789	8,305	42,262	48,300	101,656	49

Source: Federal Reserve Bulletin.

The Impact of Taxes on the Cost of Capital Since stockholders are concerned with earnings after taxes, the appropriate measure of cost of capital is the after-tax cost. This is also true because dividends on preferred and common stock are residual in nature. This means that they are not considered costs of doing business. Therefore, the amount of dividends paid by the firm is not a tax deduction. Thus, the costs of preferred stock and of the common equity (common stock and retained earnings) are *always* formulated on an after-tax cost basis.

A *tax adjustment* is required to determine the after-tax cost of debt. This is so because interest expense is tax-deductible. That is, interest payments are deducted from earnings before taxes are paid. Thus, the higher a firm's interest-expense payments, the lower the firm's tax bill. As is the case for any tax deduction, the federal government pays part of the deduction. To the extent to which the government pays, the firm's tax liability is reduced. Thus, interest payments result in a reduced tax liability that actually lowers the firm's cost of debt capital.

The after-tax cost of debt capital is calculated as follows:

$$\text{After-tax cost of debt} = \text{Before-tax cost} \times (1 - \text{Tax rate})$$

For example, assume the firm pays 10 percent to borrow funds and has a tax rate of 40 percent. The after-tax cost of debt is:

$$ATC_i = .10 \times (1 - .40) = .10 \times .60 = 6\%$$

Had the firm's tax rate been 48 percent, the after-tax cost of debt would have been 52 percent of 10 percent (the interest rate), or 5.2 percent. In the event of a net loss for the firm, there would be zero taxes. Thus, the after-tax cost of debt would be equal to the interest rate.

Flotation Costs Flotation costs are defined as the cost of marketing new securities. They include all costs involved in moving new securities from the issuer to the ultimate investor. They include legal fees, printing expenses, sales commissions, and profit to the underwriting syndicate, among other things. Flotation costs are so called because they are incurred in "floating" new securities. They are also sometimes called underwriting costs or issuance costs.

We are concerned here with flotation costs because they raise the cost of a firm's capital when they are incurred. Notice that flotation costs reduce the cash proceeds from the sale of a security. For example, a firm issues $20 million of new common stock. If flotation costs are 10 percent, the issuing firm will receive only $18 million.

The reduction of proceeds when flotation costs are incurred is not accompanied by a reduction in the return to the capital suppliers, however. Consider the following example. Assume that a corporation issues a $1,000 bond that promises a 9.5 percent return. Thus, the issuer promises to pay $95 interest each year. That is:

$$.095 \times \$1,000 = \$95$$

Without flotation costs, the issuer need earn only 9.5 percent before taxes on his assets to pay the bondholder, other things equal. But when flotation costs are introduced, the picture changes. Assume that it costs $50 to market each bond. This means that the firm gets proceeds of only $950 ($1,000 − $50) with which to work on the asset side of its position statement. But the bondholders are still expecting a $95 return for each bond they hold. Thus, in order to earn $95 for each bond, the $950 must earn 10 percent, not 9.5 percent ignoring the tax effects momentarily. That is:

$$\frac{\$95}{\$950} = 10\%$$

Flotation costs can be included in the cost of capital by adjusting the market return rate. The cost of capital including flotation costs is figured as:

$$\text{Cost of capital} = \frac{\text{Market rate of return}}{1 - \text{Flotation cost percentage}}$$

In the example above, the market rate of return was 9.5 percent and flotation costs were 5 percent. Using the formula above gives:

$$\text{Before-tax cost of debt} = \frac{.095}{1 - .05} = \frac{.095}{.95} = 10\%$$

Flotation costs represent a financial market distortion which increase the cost of new issues. This is especially true for the cost of new equity issues.

Of course, k_i will be reduced by $(1 - \text{tax rate})$ to account for the reduced effect of taxes on the cost of debt.

COMPONENTS OF THE COST OF CAPITAL

In the following sections, the cost of debt, preferred stock, common stock, and retained earnings will be discussed. Bear in mind that cost of capital is a forward-looking concept. That is, we are concerned with the cost of *new* capital, and not *old* capital obtained in the past. The reason for this is that cost of capital is used in a decision-making process. The decision is whether to obtain capital for new investment projects.

The Cost of Debt   The cost of debt is the required rate of return that must be paid to suppliers of debt capital when a firm undertakes investment projects. Stated differently, the cost of debt is the interest rate that must be paid to attract new debt capital to the firm.

The annual cost of debt is stated as a percentage of the par value of the bond. The par value is usually $1,000. Thus, as in the previous example, if the borrowing firm agrees to pay $95 a year in order to use $1,000, the cost of debt is 9.5 percent. That is:

$$\text{Cost of debt} = \frac{\text{Interest}}{\text{Principal}} = \frac{\$95}{\$1,000} = 9.5\%$$

The after-tax cost of debt if the firm's tax rate is 48 percent is:

$$k_i = .0995 \times .52 = 5.2\%$$

Corporations can approximate the cost of debt generally by consulting several sources. One source is the interest rate paid by similar corporations in the same risk class. If a corporation is anticipating a new bond issue, it can gather interest-rate information from corporations similar to itself that recently issued bonds, or it can calculate the rate on existing bonds of such corporations.

A second source of interest rate information is consultation with an investment banker,* in an investment banking house. Investment bankers are experts in capital-market conditions, and can give expert advice on current interest-rate requirements in the market.

It must be kept in mind, as discussed in the preceding section, that interest, as a cost of doing business, is tax deductible. This means that the cost of debt as calculated above is reduced even further by the amount of the effective tax bracket.

Flotation costs for new issues of debt drive the cost up, as discussed previously. The greater the flotation cost, other things equal, the higher is the cost of debt.

The following formulation accounts for the incidence of flotation costs and tax effects:

$$k_i = \frac{r(1-t)}{(1-f)}$$

where:

$r =$ internal rate of return or yield

$t =$ the marginal tax rate

$f =$ flotation cost percentage

Cost of debt adjusted for flotation costs of $50 per bond and adjusted for 25 years to maturity of bond is approximated by:

$$\text{Cost of debt} = \frac{I + \left(\dfrac{PV - NP}{\text{Years to maturity}} \right)}{\dfrac{PV + NP}{2}}$$

where:

$I =$ interest in dollars

$PV =$ par value of bond

$NP =$ net proceeds from bond

$$= \frac{95 + \left(\dfrac{1,000 - 950}{25} \right)}{\dfrac{1,000 + 950}{2}}$$

$$= \frac{95 + 2}{975} = 9.95\%$$

---

*See Chapter 22 for a broad view of all activities of the investment banker.

The Cost of Preferred Stock   The cost of preferred is defined as that rate of return that must be paid to suppliers of preferred equity capital when a firm undertakes investment projects. This is discussed in Chapter 16. Preferred stock is a stated percentage claim on the income stream of the firm, usually into perpetuity. The cost of preferred stock is the return to the preferred investor.

The cost (return) on preferred stock is usually stated as a percentage of its par value which is 100 generally. If a preferred stock issue pays $6 per share per year, and the par value is $100, the cost to the firm is 6 percent. That is:

$$\text{Cost of preferred stock} = \frac{\$6}{\$100} = 6\%$$

As with debt, the cost of preferred stock can be determined from consulting the preferred issues of firms of like risk class, or by consultation with an investment banker.

The before-tax and after-tax cost of preferred stock are the same, for the preferred dividend is *not* a tax-deductible expense.

As is the case with the issuance of debt, the incidence of flotation costs increases the firm's cost of preferred. Flotation costs in the cost of preferred stock can be accounted for in the following formulation:

$$k_p = \frac{D}{P_0(1-f)}$$

where:

D = stated annual dividend

P_0 = market value of preferred

f = flotation cost percentage

The Cost of Common Stock   In the cases of both debt and preferred stock, the investor is promised a specific dollar return in exchange for his funds. This is not true of common equity because of its residual nature. The purchase of a share of common stock brings with it no contractual obligation of a specific rate of return. This complicates the determination of the cost of common stock.

There are two dimensions to the return (cost) of common stock. The common shareholder may accept his return in the form of a cash dividend, in the form of an increase in the market value of the stock, or through a combination of the two. In other words, the cost of common stock must be related to its cash dividend and the increase in market value, capital gain.

The increase in the market value of the stock is closely related to the corporation's growth rate. The more, generally, that a corporation grows, the greater is the market value of its stock.

A cost-of-capital formulation for common stock that accounts for both dividends and the corporation's growth rate, assuming a constant growth rate, is:

$$\text{cost of common stock} = \frac{D_1}{P_0} + g$$

where:

D_1 = dividend per share expected at the end of the current period

P_0 = market value of the stock at beginning of the current period

g = the average annual growth rate of earnings

The formulation, in words, states simply that the cost of common stock is equal to the rate of return on the firm's dividends, added to the firm's growth rate.

If a corporation pays a $3 dividend per share on stock that has a market value per share of $50, and has an annual growth rate in earnings of 6 percent, the cost of its equity capital is 12 percent. It is calculated as follows:

$$\text{Cost of common stock} = \frac{\$3}{\$50} + .06$$

$$= .06 + .06$$

$$= .12$$

The formulation above is useful because it accounts for both the firm's cash dividend and its retained earnings. The growth factor, g, is a surrogate for retained earnings, because the corporation's growth is usually (not always) related to the retention of earnings.

As is the case with other forms of capital claims, the incidence of flotation costs increases the cost of common stock. Flotation costs are accounted for by subtracting them from the market value of the common stock. The formulation then becomes:

$$\text{Cost of common stock} = \frac{D_1}{P_0(1 - FC)} + g$$

If flotation costs were $5 per share, the cost of common stock would rise from 12 percent to 12.6 percent. Thus:

$$\text{Cost of common stock} = \frac{\$3}{\$50 - \$5} + .06$$

$$= .066 + .06$$

$$= .126$$

The cost of common stock is usually the highest in the capital structure, because common stock has the highest risk associated with it.

The Cost of Retained Earnings

Retained earnings represent corporate saving out of income. Determining the cost of retained earnings presents a problem, for retained earnings do not have a market-determined price, as is the case with the other three kinds of capital discussed.

Conceptually, retained earnings belong to the common shareholders, because retained earnings are shareholder funds that were not paid out. For this reason, the cost of common stock is imputed to retained earnings. Therefore, we consider the cost of retained earnings to be the same as the cost of common stock.

No flotation costs are incurred with the use of retained earnings. Thus, retained earnings is a less expensive form of financing than new issues of common stock.

An Index of the Cost of Capital

The costs of individual prices of capital discussed above may be consolidated into an index cost figure of the entire capital structure. This is done through calculating the weighted-average cost of capital. The weighted-average cost of capital (WACC) is a device giving a summary figure that takes into account the relative importance of each capital source.

Calculating the Weights. Table 12.2 shows an example of the calculation of the weighted-average cost of capital. Column 1 lists the types of capital—bonds, preferred stock, common stock, and retained earnings. Column 2 contains the book value of each capital source. These figures will be used to determine the relative importance of each capital source. The values in column 3 are calculated by dividing the amount of each type of capital by the total capital figure. For example, bonds contribute 30 percent of the capital—$30,000,000/$100,000,000 = .30. Since the percentage of the *total* capital base is being calculated, the weights must sum to unity, 1.0.

TABLE 12.2 Calculating the Weighted-Average Cost of Capital
(Book-Value Weights)

(1) CAPITAL COMPONENT	(2) BOOK VALUE	(3) BOOK-VALUE WEIGHT (2) ÷ 100,000,000	(4) BEFORE-TAX COST	(5) AFTER-TAX COST[a]	(6) WEIGHTED COST OF CAPITAL (3 × 5)
Bonds	$ 30,000,000	.30	.096	.048	.01440
Preferred stock	5,000,000	.05	.105	.105	.00525
Common stock	50,000,000	.50	.120	.120	.0600
Retained earnings	15,000,000	.15	.120	.120	.0180
Total	$100,000,000	1.00			WACC=.09765

[a]Tax rate = 50%.

Calculating the After-Tax Cost. Column 4 contains the before-tax cost of each type of capital. This figure is generated as previously outlined in this chapter. Column 5 contains the after-tax cost of each type of capital. This figure is calculated by applying the tax rate to the before-tax cost. The only type of capital in Table 12.2 whose cost is tax-deductible is debt. Applying the 50 percent rate to the before-tax rate on debt of .096 leaves an after-tax cost of .048. That is:

$$.50 \times .096 = .048$$

Recalling from a previous discussion that the costs of preferred, common, and retained earnings are not tax-deductible, we see that their after-tax cost is the same as their before-tax cost.

Calculating the Cost of Capital and WACC. Column 6 is a very important one. Column 6 contains the weighted cost of each type of capital source. It is calculated by multiplying the capital source's weight (column 3) by its after-tax cost (column 5). This process of weighting each component of the structure accounts for the relative importance of each. For example, the cost of debt accounts for 30 percent of the total, the cost of preferred accounts for 5 percent of the total, and so forth. Summing column 6 gives the weighted-average cost of capital (WACC) for the firm. It is an index figure, an average, that summarizes the entire capital structure. It says that, taking into account the relative importance of each capital source, the average cost of capital is 9.77 percent.

Importance of WACC. The weighted-average cost-of-capital figure is an important one. It summarizes the after-tax cost of the entire capital structure. It is used as the discount rate in calculating the net present value of investment proposals. It is used as the cutoff rate when arraying proposed projects by their internal rates of return. That is, no projects with internal rates of return less than the weighted-average cost of capital are accepted.*

Book-Value Weights Versus Market-Value Weights. Table 12.2 is constructed using book-value weights. That is, the values for the various kinds of capital are values listed on the position statement, and come from the accounting records ("books") of the firm. Some argue that this is inaccurate, since the book value of capital is not necessarily its current value. These people argue that the cost of capital is used in future-oriented decisions, and to use historical book costs is inaccurate. They suggest that book-value weights be replaced by market-value weights.

---

*For an application of the WACC as used in capital budgeting, see Chapter 11.

TABLE 12.3 Calculating the Weighted-Average Cost of Capital (Market-Value Weights)

(1) CAPITAL COMPONENT	(2) MARKET VALUE	(3) MARKET-VALUE WEIGHT (2) ÷ 111,000,000	(4) BEFORE- TAX COST	(5) AFTER- TAX COSTa	(6) WEIGHTED COST OF CAPITAL (3 × 5)
Bonds	$ 28,500,000	.26	.096	.048	.0125
Preferred stock	4,500,000	.04	.105	.105	.0042
Common stock	60,000,000	.54	.120	.120	.0648
Retained earnings	18,000,000	.16	.120	.120	.0192
Total	$111,000,000	1.00			.1007

aTax rate = 50%.

Table 12.3 is based upon market-value weights. Column 2 contains the market value of the firm's capital rather than its book value.

The market value of bonds is calculated by multiplying the number of bonds outstanding by each one's current market value. In Table 12.3, each of the company's bonds sells for $950, and there are 30,000 bonds outstanding, for a total market value of bonds of $28,500,000. There are 50,000 shares of preferred outstanding, each with a market value of $90, for a total value of $4,500,000. Likewise, there are 1 million shares of common stock outstanding, each with a market value of $60, for a total of $60,000,000. By definition, retained earnings have no explicit market value, but again, the key to their valuation is taken from common stock. Since common stock is selling for 20 percent more than its book value ($60,000,000/$50,000,000), we *impute* the same increased value to retained earnings, and increase their value by 20 percent, from $15,000,000 to $18,000,000. Thus, we now have *market-value weights* instead of book-value weights.

The remainder of Table 12.3 has been left the same as Table 12.2 in order to trace out only the impact of changed weights. Note that when market-value weights are used, higher-cost common stock and retained earnings assume a greater role, and lower-cost debt and preferred assume a smaller role. This has to result in a higher WACC, and so it does, 10 percent as opposed to 9.77 percent.

Using market-value weights in lieu of book-value weights is dependent upon the availability of current and reliable market prices for the firm's securities. If such market prices are available, market-value weights may be used.

A Weakness of WACC The WACC concept is valid to use if all existing projects and proposals of the firm are homogeneous with respect to risk. When this is not the case, the use of the firm's WACC may result in erroneous decisions.

When the firm's existing investment projects and proposals differ with respect to risk, reject-or-accept decision criteria must be formulated for each project. The capital asset pricing model (CAPM) provides a means for evaluation. CAPM changes some aspects of the traditional WACC measurement by introducing and quantifying risk. Risk is defined in CAPM as the standard deviation of expected return. In the case of a proposed investment project, the relationship between the expected return for the project and the return for the market portfolio of such projects is used. This process is shown in Chapter 13.

DEBT, LEVERAGE, AND THE COST OF CAPITAL

Under normal capital-market conditions, the cost of debt is less than the cost of preferred and common equity, especially when the tax advantage of debt is considered. This factor leads to the practice of substituting relatively low-cost debt for more expensive equity. This practice is called *leverage* and is sometimes referred to as *trading on the equity*.

Limits on Leverage   The practice of leverage will normally lower the firm's cost of capital. Indeed, that is why it is practiced. But there are limits on the use of leverage. As debt grows, relative to a fixed equity base, more preferential claims on the income stream of the firm are added. *Risk* of nonpayment, first to equity owners and later to bondholders, grows as debt grows, and new bondholders require a greater return. Thus, the cost of capital rises. If leverage continues, the price of the common stock falls,* and the cost of common equity rises. (Put a lower P_0 figure in the cost of common-stock formulation and see what happens to the cost of equity.)

Figure 12.2 portrays these relationships. The graph in the figure assumes that the amount of equity in the firm's capital structure remains constant, and only debt is added.

First the weighted-average cost of capital falls, because cheaper debt is being substituted for expensive equity, until it falls to its lowest point, $WACC_E$. At this point, bondholders begin to perceive increased risk, and require a higher rate of return. Equity owners also begin to perceive new risk, and require a higher rate of return. As these two forces combine, the weighted-average cost of capital begins to rise very fast. The growth of the firm's capital stock must now await new equity additions, either from the sale of new common stock or through additional retained earnings.

---

*Why?

FIGURE 12.2 The Cost of Capital and Leverage.

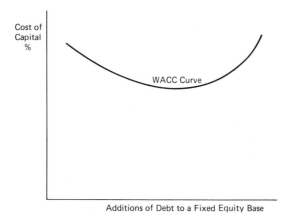

Additions of Debt to a Fixed Equity Base

SUMMARY

A firm's cost of capital, commonly expressed as an annual percentage rate, is simply the rate of return that its assets must produce in order to justify raising funds to acquire such assets. Cost of capital is defined as the rate of return that is necessary to maintain the value of the firm. This is based on the notion that the objective of business enterprises is to increase the value of shareholders' wealth over time. In order at least to maintain the value of the enterprise, a rate of return required by the market for this level of risk must be present. This is the cost of capital.

Cost of capital is a forward-looking concept. That is, the primary concern with the cost of capital is its application to new units of capital (new debt, new preferred, or new common equity). The importance of the cost of capital is for use in a decision-making process of whether to obtain capital for new investments. The fact that the firm obtained capital at high or low rates in the past is not relevant to the current decision.

PROBLEMS

1. The right side of the position statement of a firm shows $250,000 debt and $750,000 equity. Interest paid on the debt is 8%; common stock is selling for $30 per share; and $1 in dividends per share is paid to the common stockholders. If the firm is in the 40% tax bracket and its growth rate is 12%, what is the weighted-average cost of capital?

2. Given a tax rate of 40% and the following cost estimates of the various financial-structure possibilities of debt to equity:

FINANCIAL STRUCTURE	COST OF DEBT	COST OF EQUITY
0/100	–	20%
20/80	6.0%	20%
40/60	8.0%	23%
60/40	14.4%	32%

    a. Graph the weighted-average cost of capital.

    b. Of the structures given:

        (1) Which is the optimum capital structure?

        (2) Which results in the minimum cost of capital?

3. Given the following data for OMIRA Company:

    (1)

POSITION STATEMENT
12/31/78

Current assets	$30,000	Current liabilities	$10,000
Land	10,000	7-yr. bank notes, 10%	5,000
Plant	40,000	Bonds, 6's, '94	10,000
Equipment	20,000	8% preferred stock,	
		50 shares, $100 par	5,000
		Common stock, 4,500 shares,	
		$10 par	45,000
		Retained earnings	25,000
Total assets	$100,000	Total liab. & net worth	$100,000

    (2) Bonds are quoted at 80, preferred stock at 75, and common stock at 50.

    (3) Earnings per share for common were $1.00, Dec. 31, 1973, and $1.90, Dec. 31, 1978. *growth rate* *common* *1.90* *13.7%*

    (4) Dividends per share for 1978 are $1.50.

    (5) Tax rate is 48%.

Compute the weighted-average cost of capital.

4. The OMIRA Company is planning to raise $20,000 additional capital for 1979. The following assumptions are made:

    (1) Optimum capital structure is as stated in Problem 3.

    (2) Bonds will be sold at a coupon rate of 10% to the public through an underwriter at $1,010 each. Underwriting costs and bond-issuance expense amount to $50 per bond. Bonds mature in ten years.

(3) 7-year bank notes cost 12%.

(4) New preferred stock costs 10% (ignore flotation costs).

(5) The equity portion will be provided from internal funds.

Compute the WACC.

5. The treasurer of a new venture, Start-Up Scientific, Inc., is trying to determine how to raise $6 million of long-term capital. His investment advisor has devised the alternative capital structures shown below:

ALTERNATIVE A		ALTERNATIVE B	
$2,000,000	9% debt	$4,000,000	12% debt
$4,000,000	Equity	$2,000,000	Equity

If alternative A is chosen, the firm would sell 200,000 shares of common stock to net $20 per share. Stockholders would expect an initial dividend of $1.00 per share and a dividend growth rate of 7%.

Under alternative B, the firm would sell 100,000 shares of common stock to net $20 per share. The expected initial dividend would be $0.90 per share, and the anticipated dividend growth rate is 12%.

Assume that the firm earns a profit under either capital structure and that the effective tax rate is 50%.

a. What is the cost of capital to the firm under each of the suggested capital structures? Explain your result.

b. Explain the logic of the anticipated higher interest rate on debt associated with alternative B.

c. Is it logical for shareholders to expect a higher dividend growth rate under alternative B? Explain your answer.

6. You are the financial manager of the A-Shoe Corporation. Two investment projects have become available to the firm in the last few days, and the Executive Committee is interested in their financial feasibility. Below are the relevant data pertaining to the two projects:

Project A:
Cash outlay: $20,000,000
Income: $4,349,522 a year for 8 years. These funds are net of depreciation and taxes, and should be used "as is" in your calculations.

Project B:
Cash outlay: $20,000,000
Income: $4,138,216 a year for 10 years. These funds are net of depreciation and taxes, and should be used "as is" in your calculations.

The following information is available to you as financial manager:

POSITION STATEMENT

Assets		
	6% Bonds	40,000,000
	7% Pfd.	20,000,000
	Common Equity	
	Stock	10,000,000
	Ret. Earn.	30,000,000
100,000,000		100,000,000

Retained earnings are expected to be $6 million this year.

Experience through the years has taught that this capital structure is optimal, and the corporation has a policy that the structure will not be changed.

EARNINGS HISTORY. EARNINGS PER SHARE:

1969	$1.00
1970	1.25
1971	1.30
1972	1.45
1973	1.51
1974	1.56

The current market price of common stock is $50 per share. The expected dividend payable at the end of the current income period is $1.50 per share. New bonds, if needed, can be sold at a cost to the company of 7%. New preferred can be sold for a cost of 9%. New common stock, if needed, can be sold to net the company $42 a share, *after* costs of flotation of $8 a share have been deducted.

The corporation's tax rate is 40 percent.

REQUIREMENTS 1. Calculate the WACC of the incremental $20 million in capital. Round the WACC to the nearest full percentage point if needed in order to use the tables at the end of the book.

2. Calculate the NPV and IRR of Projects A and B.

3. Assume that a shareholders' meeting is scheduled for next month, and the Executive Committee has appointed you to make the analysis and report to the common shareholders at the meeting. Prepare a short script of your remarks, explaining which project should be accepted, and how its acceptance will benefit the common shareholder. Shareholders like numbers, and especially positive ones. They are especially interested in how the value of the firm will change.

Financial Structure and Valuation of the Firm

In previous chapters, we discussed items on the asset portion of the position statement—cash, receivables, inventories, and long-term assets. We then moved to the claims-on-assets portion of the position statement to discuss short- and intermediate-term financing sources, as well as the cost of capital sources to the firm.

We now consider three topics that lace together the asset and liability sides of the position statement. It has been emphasized several times in this book that the liability and equity claims found on the claims-on-assets portion of the position statement represent sources of funds used to purchase income-generating assets. In this chapter we shall view three very important characteristics of these funds sources: (1) financial structure, (2) financial leverage, and (3) valuation of the firm.

The first topic, financial structure, is concerned primarily with the interrelationships of the components on the right-hand side of the position statement, but it does consider the impact of financing sources on revenues to assets. The second topic, financial leverage, treats the relationship between changing debt proportions in the capital structure and resulting changes in income streams that accrue to assets. The final topic, valuation, clearly considers both the asset side and the liability side of the position statement. Valuation is the process of assigning a value to the earnings of the firm. This includes the role of assets as well as the counterclaims on assets, liabilities, and equity.

The Concept of Structure   The term *structure* has been defined as "something made up of interdependent parts in a definite pattern of organization." This definition has all the components required to view the concept of financial structure. We shall define *financial structure* formally as the interrelationships among the funds sources represented by the liability and equity claims on the claims-on-assets portion of the firm's position statement, as well as the overall pattern of organization that results from these relationships.

Perhaps the easiest and clearest way to illustrate the concept of financial structure is to show how the financial structure of a firm develops as the firm's need for assets grows. We shall consider the growth of the firm, and therefore its increasing sophistication of financial structure, from the inception of the firm to its ultimate financial sophistication.

Step 1: New Corporation.   At the firm's inception, its position statement appears thus:

ASSETS	CLAIMS
Assets $100	
	Common Stock $100

The corporation has sold $100 worth of new common stock, and these funds have been allocated into assets. It should be very clear that the sale of common equity is the first source of funds for the firm. These funds provide the "equity base" upon which other claims can be anchored.

Step 2: Growth through Retained Earnings.   As the firm's markets grow and sales increase, the firm will experience a need for increased assets to produce products to serve the growing markets. These assets must be financed with increased funds. The new growth will probably be financed out of savings from its current income—that is, retained earnings. The position statement would appear thus:

ASSETS	CLAIMS	
Assets $110		
	Common Stock	$100
	Retained Earnings	10

Thus, by saving out of current income, the corporation is able to increase its assets by 10 percent, from $100 to $110. But since income is finitely limited, so are the savings out of that income for expansion. Therefore, if a corporation desires to expand beyond the rate specified by its earnings growth rate, it must seek other sources of funds, and in doing so, it adds to and changes the financial structure of the firm.

Step 3: Growth through the Issuance of Bonds. With the equity base now firmly secured, the issuance of bonds, a form of borrowing, may be contemplated by the firm. Assume that a surge in demand for the company's product creates a need for additional assets, and bonds are issued. Again, the issuance of this new form of claim adds to and changes the financial structure of the firm. After the issuance of the bonds, the position statement would appear:

ASSETS		CLAIMS	
		Bonds	$ 40
		Common Stock	100
Total Assets		Retained Earnings	10
	$150		$150

Once more, because the *interrelationships* among capital sources have changed, *financial structure* has changed.

Assume that increased growth of markets calls for increased assets again. Once more, additional capital financing is required. This time, the firm turns to preferred stock as a source of funds.

Step 4: Growth through the Issuance of Preferred Stock. After the issuance of the preferred stock, the position statement may appear as follows:

ASSETS		CLAIMS	
		Bonds	$ 40
		Preferred Stock	20
		Common Stock	100
Total Assets		Retained Earnings	10
	$170		$170

The addition of $20 worth of assets financed by preferred stock completes the cycle of growth for our purpose of illustrating structure. Recalling the two important characteristics of the definition of structure, the interdependence of the parts and the overall pattern of organization of the parts, we are now prepared to put them in perspective with respect to *financial structure*. As each new capital source was added, two things resulted: (1) the relationships among all capital sources changed, and (2) the overall form and pattern of total capital sources changed.

Optimal Capital Structure

Not all capital sources cost the same. Generally, debt costs less than preferred and common equity. As was suggested in the preceding chapter, the costs of the various capital components are controlled by the investing public. The investing public perceives risk associated with incremental claims on the income stream, and adjusts the price of financial claims accordingly.

Initially, the firm may substitute relatively low-cost debt and successfully drive down the cost of capital. Thus, as new debt is added relative to a fixed equity base, the weighted-average cost of capital (WACC) drops. Additional attempts to substitute low-cost debt for relatively high-cost equity cause the WACC to fall more slowly than before. Eventually, it reaches a minimum. Additional attempts to lower it by adding more debt results in raising the WACC. Why?

As more debt is piled upon a fixed equity base, successive units of debt claims represent increased risk of default in interest and principal. This risk is compensated for by increased interest rates, which raise the WACC. As debt owners succeed in receiving higher and higher returns, equity owners perceive additional risk to their residual positions, and they react by demanding a higher return, by means of lowering the price of common stock.* This decrease in the cost of common equity, in conjunction with the increased cost of debt, drives the WACC even higher.

The WACC curve is, under normal circumstances, therefore U-shaped, first falling as debt is piled upon a fixed equity base, then leveling out, and finally turning upward at an increasing rate. There is therefore a combination of debt and equity that results in the lowest WACC, and that combination is found when the curve is at its lowest point. The combination of debt and equity that results in the lowest cost of capital is the optimal capital structure—that is, the capital structure that minimizes the firm's cost of capital.

Importance of Capital-Structure Management

Management of the capital structure is an important responsibility of financial management. Since the various capital sources do not cost the same, and since their costs do not remain fixed through time, the constant monitoring of the firm's financial structure is necessary in order for the manager to detect opportunities to substitute lower-cost forms of capital for higher-cost ones.

---

*Recall that the cost of common stock is:

$$\text{Cost of common stock} = \frac{D_1}{P_0} + g$$

A reduction of P_0 results in a higher cost of common stock.

Another reason that attention to financial structure is required is the opportunity to use the benefits of *leverage*, and if leverage is being used, to ensure that the penalties for the overuse of leverage are not incurred. The judicious use of leverage provides great benefits to the firm, and its injudicious use inflicts great penalties. Because of its importance, we turn now to a major tool in the management of the firm's capital structure, leverage.

FINANCIAL LEVERAGE

Since financial leverage is involved with financing increments of assets with debt instead of equity, leverage is also sometimes called "trading on the equity," because the existence of equity permits the incremental issuance of low-cost debt—that is, low-cost relative to equity.

The object of using leverage is to finance incremental-asset acquisition with relatively cheap debt and thereby *magnify* the returns to the equity owners. This very important financial product of the employment of leverage will be illustrated through the use of position statements, after a brief discussion of the physical principle of leverage; for it is from the physical principle of leverage that the analogous term, *financial leverage*, is taken.

Physical Leverage *Leverage* has been defined as "the action of a lever, and the mechanical advantage gained by it." A *lever* is defined as "a rigid piece that transmits and modifies force or motion where forces are applied at two points and it turns around a third."

The physical principle of the lever is intuitively appealing to most. It is the principle that permits the *magnification* of force when a lever is applied to a fulcrum. The key components of the principle are the result, magnification of a force, and the movement about a fulcrum. This principle permits a person to move an object many times his own weight, for example.

There are direct analogies in financial leverage to physical leverage; hence the borrowing of the name. In physical leverage, the power of the lever is a function of the location of the fulcrum. For example, in the diagram below, as the fulcrum is moved toward point B, the downward force at point A can be lessened, for the leverage factor is increasing; or, stated differently, as the fulcrum moves toward point B, a constant downward pressure at point A will move larger weights at point B. Such is the nature of physical leverage.

B △ A

**Financial-Leverage
Analogies**
The analogies to financial leverage are almost perfect. In the case of financial leverage, the fulcrum is the ratio of total debt to total assets.

The larger this ratio, the greater is the firm's reliance upon debt to finance its assets, and assuming, as we must, that debt is cheaper than equity, as each incremental dollar of assets earns a constant rate of debt, the residual amount for the equity owners increases.

Showing these relationships in terms of leverage, the following diagram results:

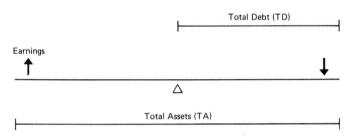

The more the fulcrum shifts to the left—that is, the more the TD/TA ratio increases—the greater is the upward pressure on earnings per share for the equity owner.

So much for the parallels between physical leverage and financial leverage. It remains to be seen now *why* increases in the debt ratio, TD/TA, result in increased earnings per share. A short illustration will show why this is true. Remember that what is being illustrated is that increases in debt financing relative to equity financing result in higher net earnings per share for the shareholders.

Example of Leverage
In the example to be given, the following assumptions are made:

1. Assets always earn 20 percent.

2. Debt costs 5 percent.

3. No preferred stock is used (this assumption does *not* bias the results of the analysis).

4. There are no taxes.

5. Interest is the only cost of doing business.

Given these, assume further that a firm has assets of $100, and that these are financed as in this position statement:

ASSETS		CLAIMS	
Assets	$100	Debt	$ 50
		Equity	50
	$100		$100

I

The earnings statement, following the assumptions above, would appear:

Revenue	$20.00	(.20 × $100)
Interest	2.50	(.05 × $50)
To shareholders	$17.50	

Now assume that this firm has the opportunity to add $100 in assets, and that the new assets will be financed entirely with debt. Given these and the assumptions above, the position statement would appear as follows:

ASSETS	CLAIMS	
Total Assets	Debt	$150
	Equity	50
$200		$200

Again, using all assumptions, the earnings statement would appear:

Revenue	$40.00	(.20 × $200)
Interest	7.50	(.05 × $150)
To shareholders	$32.50	

Let's stop here and find out why the shareholders' return increased by $15 ($32.50 — $17.50) when they made *no new investment* in the business.

It's true that the incremental investment of $100 was made entirely by the creditors—the bondholders. Let's calculate how that incremental $100 investment fared in the business. Remember that the following earnings statement applies only to the *incremental* investment by the bondholders.

Revenue	$20.00	(.20 × $100)
Interest	5.00	(.05 × $100)
	$15.00	

Of the $20 earnings, the debt-financed assets earned $5 that went to the suppliers of the funds, and $15 that went to the firm's owners, the shareholders. Did the shareholders enjoy a "free ride," in view of the fact that they contributed nothing *directly* to the incremental $100 investment? No, of course not. The shareholders, as residual claimants, must be willing to accept the increased risk associated with the incremental investment, and the $15 incremental return compensates them for the additional risk.

Of course, in our example, there is no risk, for we have stipulated that the incremental investment will *always* earn 20 percent. But to plant a seed of things to come, we ask the following question: What would be the position of the common shareholders if the incremental investment of $100 had earned *nothing*?

To continue the example, and to increase leverage, let's assume that another $100 worth of assets is added, and that these assets are financed by the issuance of additional debt. The position statement under these conditions would appear:

ASSETS		CLAIMS	
Total Assets		Debt	$250
		Equity	50
	$300		$300

Again, assets have increased by $100, and again debt has increased by $100 because the increase in assets has been entirely financed by debt.

The earnings statement would appear:

Revenue	$60.00	(.20 × $300)
Interest	12.50	(.05 × $250)
To shareholders	$47.50	

Again, even though they have made no *explicit* additional investment in the firm, their return increased. Why? Because the leverage factor TD/TA increased, and the shareholders were being compensated for additional risk.

The fulcrum of financial leverage is the TD/TA ratio. The value of this ratio is a surrogate for the degree of leverage. That is, the larger the TD/TA ratio, the greater the volume of assets financed with debt, and therefore the greater the financial leverage being applied. We can summarize, in tabular form, the results of the increasing leverage factor by tracing the relationship between the leverage factor, TD/TA, and earnings available to shareholders. Table 13.1 presents the figures from the previous examples of increasing leverage.

TABLE 13.1 Summary Figures

TOTAL DEBT	TOTAL ASSETS	TD/TA	TO SHAREHOLDERS
$ 50	$100	.50	$17.50
150	200	.75	32.50
250	300	.83	47.50

Analysis of the data in the table leads to the conclusion that there is a positive and close relationship between earnings available to shareholders and leverage factors *when total revenue increases along with leverage ratios*. This is an important qualification. For leverage to have a positive and desirable result for shareholders' return to assets, total revenue must increase parallel to the leverage ratio.

Risk in Leverage   What happens when this condition is violated? What happens when the leverage factor *increases* when total revenues *decrease*? It was suggested previously that leverage is asymmetrical, that its impact is different when revenue is increasing and when revenue is decreasing. We have already seen that when revenue is increasing, increased leverage results in increased earnings for the shareholders. But what happens when leverage is increased, or held constant, in the face of declining revenues? Intuition suggests that shareholders suffer losses.

We shall set out to illustrate how *increasing* leverage and *constant* revenues can result in losses to the shareholders. We shall do so by using each of the previous cases, but this time, regardless of the leverage factor, revenue will be held constant at $20, and it will be shown that shareholders experience a *decline* in earnings.

The first example is as before; that is, total assets are $100, and they are financed half by debt and half by equity. That is:

ASSETS		CLAIMS	
Total Assets		Debt	$ 50
		Common Stock	50
	$100		$100

The earnings statement, too, is as before:

Revenue	$20.00
Interest	2.50
To shareholders	$17.50

We shall hold revenue constant, and increase the leverage factor by adding new assets financed by debt. We add, as before, $100 in new assets financed by debt. The position statement appears thus:

ASSETS		CLAIMS	
Total Assets		Debt	$150
		Common Stock	50
	$200		$200

and the earnings statement:

Revenue	$20.00	(constant)
Interest	7.50	(.05 × $150)
To shareholders	$12.50	

The earnings available to shareholders decreased by $5, from $17.50 to $12.50.

Now consider what happens when assets are increased once more by $100, and revenue remains constant at $20. The position statement is:

ASSETS		CLAIMS	
Total Assets		Debt	$250
		Common Stock	$ 50
	$300		$300

The earnings statement would be:

Revenue	$20.00	(Constant)
Interest	12.50	(.05 × $250)
To shareholders	$ 7.50	

Again, the residual amount available to shareholders decreased.

Now consider the impact upon earnings available to shareholders under both conditions—that is, when earnings increases keep pace with increases in debt, and when they do not. For purposes of contrast, the earnings available to shareholders, derived from our calculations, are analyzed in Table 13.2.

TABLE 13.2 The Effect of Leverage on Earnings Available to Shareholders, When Revenue Increases and When Revenue Remains Constant

ASSET SIZE	SHAREHOLDER EARNINGS, REVENUE INCREASES	SHAREHOLDER EARNINGS, REVENUE REMAINS CONSTANT
$100	$17.50	$17.50
200	32.50	12.50
300	47.50	7.50

This table illustrates the effect of leverage when revenues do not increase as fast as leverage ratios. It can be said another way. Leverage can exert a powerful and positive influence on earnings available to the shareholders as long as revenues justify leverage factors. But if revenues do not justify the leverage factor being used, or, more frequently, if revenues fall while a firm is so highly levered, leverage *can cut into residual earnings for shareholders and even turn them negative.* As a matter of fact, many firms headed into the recession of 1973–75 with highly levered positions, and when the recession reduced their revenues, they were left with large volumes of unserviceable debt. This development contributed to many business failures in that economic downturn.

Indexes of Leverage   There are two key indexes of comparative leverage in the firm. Both were discussed in Chapter 7, but both bear repeating here.

The first index is the TD/TA ratio referred to previously in this chapter. It measures the degree of debt financing of assets and is frequently referred to as the *leverage ratio* or the *leverage factor.* Naturally, the higher the ratio, the more the asset structure is financed with debt, and therefore the greater is the leverage factor.

The leverage factor is a position-statement phenomenon, because the two terms in the ratio are debt and assets. But the second of the two indexes is an earnings-statement phenomenon, because both its terms come from the earnings statement.

The second leverage index is the times-interest-earned figure, frequently abbreviated as TIE. Times interest earned is determined by adding earnings before taxes (EBT) to the interest charge (I), and then dividing the sum by the interest change (I). Symbolically,

$$TIE = \frac{EBT + I}{I}$$

The times-interest-earned figure measures the capacity of the firm to meet the accrued interest on its debt structure. This means it is an inverse measure of debt employment by the firm, and therefore it is an inverse measure of leverage. The measure is inverse because the greater the TIE figure, the greater is the ability of the firm to meet interest payments and, by inference, the smaller is the debt burden.

Summary   The purpose of leverage is to employ relatively low-cost debt to finance assets, and thereby magnify the residual returns to the equity owners.

Leverage is a two-edged blade: As long as revenues are increasing, leverage does magnify the residual returns to equity owners. But if revenues fall, and fall far and fast enough, then the effect of leverage is to magnify the deficit in earnings that accrue to the shareholders. If the firm is highly levered, the results are losses to the equity owners.

VALUATION

Introduction The process of valuation is the process of assigning a dollar value to an asset, or to a "bundle of net assets," the firm. Valuation is an important part of the field of finance. Whether trying to determine the value of a security for one's own portfolio or to determine the value of an entire firm involved in a merger, the principles of valuation are important and useful, and they form cornerstones in finance.

Keep in mind during all of the following discussion that the basic purpose of valuation is to assign a money value to an asset or a group of assets.

Some Basic Concepts There are three component parts of an asset to which we are trying to assign a value. These three parts are:

1. The market value of the asset at the present time. Assume for a moment that we know what the value is.

2. The value of the income streams that will accrue to the asset in the future. All assets have promise of future income, either in monetary income or in utility. We are concerned in finance with monetary income, but consider your purchase of a new hand-held calculator. When you purchase the machine, you must consider that the future *utility* will be greater than the current cost, or you would not purchase the calculator. So the future income need not be in cash flows.

3. The "rate of return" or the "discount" rate that sets the current market value equal to the present value of income streams.*

The relationships among these three variables is as below:

where:

MV = current market value of the asset

PV = present value of the future income streams discounted at the relevent rate

---

*The perceptive reader will note that this principle is a variation of a capital budgeting technique described in Chapter 11, under "Internal Rate of Return (IRR)."

$R_1, R_2 \ldots$ = values of periodic income accruing to the asset

r = the discount rate, or the asset purchaser's demanded rate of return

In the valuation process, we are attempting to discover the market value by applying the rate of return and the periodic returns to the asset.

The market value of an asset, or of a bundle of net assets, is systematically and predictably related to the asset's earning ability. It is intuitively appealing, and empirically demonstrable, that the larger and longer an asset's earnings, the greater is its current market value. The process of systematically relating an asset's revenue to its market value by use of a discount rate is called "capitalizing the income streams."

This simple observation means that the process of valuation is the process of determining the relevant rate of return and the value of the future income streams, for when these are accurately determined, the current market value is therefore determined.

Some Concepts of Valuation   There are two concepts of valuation of assets that bear examination in a discussion of valuation. These are the concepts of book value of the asset and the going-concern value of the firm. Although neither provides an *operational* method of assigning a value to the firm, both offer powerful insights into the valuation process, and are discussed for that reason.

Book Value.   *Book value* is defined as the value of the firm's assets, liabilities, and equity that is carried on the firm's position statement ("books"). This value may or may not reflect the current market value or earning power. Asset values are an accumulation of *historical* costs, and may or may not reflect current market values. To the extent that book values of assets represent historical costs that are different from current costs, book value is *not* a useful valuation device.

Since owners' equity is derived by subtracting liabilities from asset values, and to the extent that book values misstate asset values, equity positions are therefore misstated. Book value as a technique of valuation is therefore not highly reliable; that is, it cannot be relied upon to give a current value of the firm or of an asset. Book value does serve the function of establishing a bench-mark figure in valuation, however. For this reason, it is sometimes reported.

Going-Concern Value.   Consider individually all the assets that go to make up an auto-parts supplier. Were we to add up the current market value of the inventory, equipment, and so forth, there is a good chance that the current market value of the firm would exceed the market value of the assets. Why? Because of intangible assets that give the business momentum and direction. Call it reputation, call it goodwill,* call it synergy, but it is true that a bundle of assets organized into a dynamic and income-generating firm are worth more than the summation of the market value of the assets individually. The *going-concern* concept also suggests that it is the *earning power* of assets that generate their ultimate value.

Valuation of Individual Assets   In this section, we discuss the valuation of three financial assets: bonds, common stock, and preferred stock. But you are asked to bear in mind that all assets are evaluated in a comparable manner.

Bond Valuation.   Suppose you are considering the purchase today of of a $1,000-par-value bond issued 20 years ago by the Perpendicular Pump Company. The *coupon rate* is 6 percent, the interest is payable semiannually, and the bond has ten years to run. How much would you pay for the bond if you could get 8 percent on your money today by buying new bonds of similar risk? This is a classical problem in asset valuation, the determination of the relationship between income flows and a specified rate of return.

Here is how we go about the valuation of the bond in the problem above. First we specify all the component parts of the problem:

Coupon rate $= 6\%$

$.06 \times \$1,000 = \$60$ annual interest

$\$60$ annual interest$/2 = \$30$ semiannual interest

10 years to maturity $\times 2 = 20$ semiannual interest periods

Borrower promises to repay $1,000 at the end of 10 years

Current interest rate (market rate) $= 8\%$ (or 4% semiannually)

Translated into the time-line concept, the problem appears:

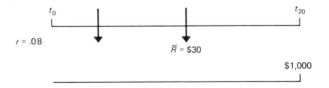

In other words, the interest payable on the bond forms an annuity of $30 per period for 20 periods (6 percent semiannually for ten years). The issuer of the bond has promised to repay $1,000 at the end of the twentieth semiannual period. The sum of the present values at 8 percent of the $30

---

*Some economists have suggested that goodwill value is nothing more than the firm's monopoly power.

annuity and the repayment of the $1,000 principal represents the current value of the bond.

Then we calculate the present value of the annuity formed by the semi-annual interest payments discounted at 4 percent, the *current* interest rate on bonds. The interest factor (IF) for present value of an annuity for 20 periods at 4 percent is 13.590. Therefore, the present value of the interest payments is:

$$13.590 \times \$30 = \$407.70$$

Next, we figure the present value of the principal, which will be paid once at the end of the twentieth period. The IF for the present value of a single payment to be made at the end of the twentieth period is .456. Therefore, the present value of the principal is:

$$.456 \times \$1,000 = \$456$$

Summing:

Present value of interest payments	$407.70
Present value of principle	456.00
	$863.70

The current value, the *valuation* of this bond, is $863.70. If you pay this price for the bond, you will earn an 8 percent return on your investment. If you pay *more* than $863.70, you will earn *less* than 8 percent.

This example has taken you through the valuation of one financial asset, a bond. In it, the income streams and terminal value were discounted at a current demanded rate of return. The result was a *current market value*, the desired result of the valuation process.

Preferred-Stock Valuation. Preferred stock, because of its nature, is relatively easy to assign a value. Remembering that the usual par value of preferred stock is $100, assume that we want to determine the market value of a share of 8 percent preferred stock selling for $80 per share. Since the annual return is based upon a $100 par value, it is therefore:

$$.08 \times \$100 = \$8$$

and since $80 is being spent to get this return, then the return is 10 percent; that is:

$$\frac{\$8 \text{ Annual return}}{\$80 \text{ Market price}} = 10\%$$

Common-Stock Valuation. The process of valuation of a common stock differs from the valuation of a bond or preferred stock issue in several ways. First, a share of common stock has no maturity. It is a claim into perpetuity on the income stream and assets of the issuing corporation. Second, since there is no *promised* rate of return on a share of common stock, the shareholder can take his return in one of two forms: capital gains or dividends. Capital gains refers to the increase in market value of a share of common stock that results from increased earning power of the firm. The firm has the choice between two courses of action with respect to its earnings: It can pay them out in dividends, or it can retain them for further investment in assets, resulting optimally in increased earnings. Conceptually, the shareholder is indifferent between dividends and retained earnings. If earnings are paid in dividends, the shareholder has his return. If earnings are retained, they are invested in new assets and the value of the firm rises; and therefore, theoretically, the value of its stock rises by an amount equal to what the dividend would have been. If the shareholder in the latter case wants cash, he need only sell his share to get his dividend.*

Therefore, in valuation, we must assign a current value to the share of common stock, regardless of the form in which shareholders take their income.

The following expression accounts for the valuation of a share of common stock:

$$P_0 = \frac{D_1}{r - g}$$

where:

P_0 = current value of the stock

D_1 = cash dividend at the *end* of the current income period

r = demanded rate of return by shareholders

g = expected growth rate in the firm's earnings

To give life to the equation, let's assume the following: The cash dividend at the end of the current income period will be $1 ($D_1$ = \$1.00$), the shareholders' rate of return is 10 percent (r = .10), and the shareholders expect a 5 percent growth rate (g = .05). Under these conditions, what is the current value of the stock?

Solving:

$$P_0 = \frac{\$1}{.10 - .05}$$

$$= \frac{\$1}{.05}$$

$$= \$20$$

---

*There are different tax effects, of course. The dividend as income is taxed at a rate different from the capital gain. See Chapter 2.

The *current value*, the result of the valuation process, is $20. At this value, the shareholders are receiving their demanded rate of return of 10 percent, and this market value is justified by a 5 percent annual growth rate in the firm.

Valuation of the Firm   It happens frequently that there is need to assign a value to an entire firm as an operating entity—that is, as a going concern. The occasion of the sale of a firm, the occasion of its merger with another firm, and the case of levying inheritance taxes by value are examples of times when we need to assign value to an entire firm. Various methods of valuation are available, including the book-value method, the replacement-value method, and the capitalization-of-income method. Each of these will be discussed in turn.

Book-Value Method. The book-value method was described briefly earlier in the chapter as the value of the firm on the "books"—the accounting records of the firm. It is not a highly reliable method of valuation of the firm, since the asset values and liability values are probably not current. This is because they result from a series of historical values placed on the books. But, as stated previously, book value may be useful in establishing a "ballpark" figure.

Replacement-Value Method. The replacement-value method suggests that the current market value of all assets be summed. The result is the value of the firm, minus any liability claims, at current market. The replacement-value method may not result in a suitable value for the firm, since it does not include the "going-concern" value of the firm. The going-concern value of a firm is the value above and beyond the replacement value. It is value added to the firm's assets because the assets are combined in a *successful* way to create an income stream. The difference between the replacement value of a firm's assets and its going-concern value is sometimes called "goodwill." Goodwill may include such things as good location, a quality reputation, and monopoly power, such as being the only supplier of a good or service in a remote market. Regardless of the dimensions of goodwill, it adds value to the firm above and beyond the replacement asset value.*

Capitalization-of-Income Method. The capitalization of income, as discussed earlier, involves converting an income stream into perpetuity into a capital value as of this moment. The generalized formulation of the capitalization-of-income method is:

$$P_0 = \frac{R}{r}$$

---

*According to accounting convention, goodwill is not recognized as an asset unless it is purchased.

where:

P_0 = market value at t_0

R = value of each income stream into perpetuity

r = demanded rate of return

As an example, if a firm has earnings after taxes of $40,000 per year, and an investor requires an 8 percent return on his money, how much will he pay for this firm?

Substituting into the general formulation:

$$P_0 = \frac{\$40,000}{.08}$$

$$= \$500,000$$

The answer of $500,000 says that the investor will receive an 8 percent return on his investment if he pays $500,000 for the firm. Since a firm is considered to be a "bundle" of net assets that produces an income stream into perpetuity, the capitalization-of-income method is justified.

SUMMARY

The value of the firm, its earning power, and its financial claims are all important considerations for the financial manager and the investor. The assignment of market values to securities in financial markets is the direct result of determining the firm's net earning power through analysis of its financial dimensions.

CAPITAL ASSET PRICING MODEL (CAPM)

Many of the basic ideas underlying the theory of asset prices are simple and intuitively appealing, and have been known and used for a long time. Recent developments in the theory make it possible to restate the old ideas in mathematical terms. Thus, we can now quantify more of the factors that affect the price of a firm's stock and the value of real investments. We will limit our discussion here to the value of real investments. Financial investments are discussed in Part III.

Some basic ideas underlying the theory of asset prices are (1) that businessmen prefer high returns and reduced risk whenever possible, (2) that the standard deviation of the rate of return from a portfolio of assets is a reasonable measure of risk, and (3) that unsystematic risk* can be reduced or eliminated by diversification, while systematic risk is still present in an efficient portfolio of assets. Thus, the basic ideas deal with measuring risk and measuring return.

Portfolio Theory   Portfolio theory has led to the integration of much of the subject matter of finance with the advent of the capital asset pricing model (CAPM). Through the CAPM, the integration of the discipline is possible at a relatively introductory level. The theoretical developments stemming from portfolio theory in financial investments have practical application to financial management as well as financial markets. It is now possible to analyze wealth maximization, asset expansion, valuation, and other financial policies in the broad framework of CAPM. Portfolio theory explains how individuals and firms choose risky securities or assets and how prices are determined in financial markets. Such theories provide a framework for financial investment decisions that financial management must utilize in order to maximize the wealth of the firm (that is, the stockholders' wealth).

Portfolio theory is discussed in Chapter 18.

Required Rate of   The cost of capital was examined in Chapter 12. There we saw that the
Return vs. Cost of   firm's weighted-average cost of capital (WACC) represents its required
Capital   return. When the WACC is used, the common practice is to compare the expected return on a project with the WACC. If the expected return on cost of a project exceeds or is equal to the firm's cost of capital, the traditional practice has been that it is all right to accept the investment proposal. Thus, a proposal is accepted if $E(R) \geq$ WACC.

The capital asset pricing model (CAPM)† generalizes the traditional WACC approach to asset-expansion decisions. Both the WACC and the CAPM establish a boundary between the accept region (on or above the line) and the reject region (below the line). This is shown in Figure 13.1 The WACC is a weighted average of all capital costs. The CAPM is reflected by the market line, which is based on the risk-free interest rate (R_f) plus the market-risk premium (that is, $E[R_m] - R_f$) weighted by β_j,‡ the measure of an

---

*See Chapter 4.

†The capital asset pricing model is developed fully in Chapter 18. It is presented here to introduce the reader to its simplicity and compactness.

‡Beta (β_j) is the regression line of individual project returns to market returns. It can also be expressed as the variance of project period returns times the variance of market period returns normalized by the variance of market returns (that is, covariance (R_j, R_m)/variance (R_m)).

FIGURE 13.1 Required Rate of Return, CAPM vs. WACC.
(*Source: Adapted from Mark E. Rubinstein, "A Mean-Variance Synthesis of Corporate Financial Theory," Journal of Finance, Vol. XXVII, No. 1, March 1973, p. 172.*)

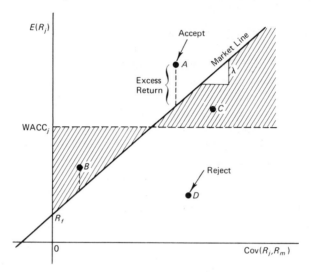

individual project's systematic risk. The formulation is:

$$E(R_j) = R_f + [E(R_m) - R_f]\beta_j$$

where:

$E(R_j)$ = the expected return on an asset, real or financial

R_f = risk-free interest rate

$E(R_m)$ = expected return on a portfolio of real assets

β_j = the variability of the return on the asset relative to the portfolio (i.e., the covariance of returns on asset with portfolio of assets divided by the variance of the portfolio)

Beta Analysis The market is considered the norm. Thus, the market returns always have a beta of 1.0 (that is, variance (R_m)/variance (R_m) = 1.0). Betas for returns on individual securities or projects can range from a value greater than one (riskier than market returns) to a value less than one (not as risky as the market returns). Beta calculations are shown in the appendix to Chapter 18.

Market Line (The Required Rate of Return) A security or project market line is plotted by drawing a line with the property $y = a + bx$ or $y = y\text{-intercept} + \text{slope of market line} \times \text{beta}$. The market line is drawn in Figure 13.1, where

$$R_f = y\text{-intercept}$$

$$x = \text{slope of market line}$$

$$\beta = \text{independent variable or covariance } (R_j, R_m)/\text{variance } R_m$$

For investment proposals A and D, either CAPM or WACC criteria lead to the same decisions. For investment proposals B and C, the decisions differ depending on which criterion is used as the investment hurdle rate (that rate that must be equaled or exceeded). Thus, investment proposals A and C would be accepted using WACC. However, investment C would be rejected by the CAPM approach because its relatively high risk is not commensurate with its return. And investment proposal B would be rejected by the WACC approach, but it is accepted using the CAPM criterion because risk is low.

Thus, the CAPM criterion, as shown in Figure 13.1, is to accept all investment proposals that are on or above the market line (that is, *the required return*) and reject all proposals that are below the market line. Financial managers seek to maximize stockholders' wealth by locating and selecting investment projects, such as A and B, whose returns are in excess of the required return. This is true because the required return as delineated by the market line specifies the market-equilibrium relationship.

When financial managers accept projects that have returns in excess of the required return, the expected return on the firm's common stock will be higher than that required by the market line. Thus, the price of the common will rise until the return drops to the market line, at which point the equilibrium level is reached. That is, buying pressures (demand for stock) cause the stock price to rise until the supply and demand for the firm's stock are in a stable condition. This process is illustrated by the dashed line in Figure 13.1 between project A and the market line. As investors recognize that project A is undervalued, the price of the firm's stock will rise and the return fall. This process will continue until the return required by the market line for projects of such risk is reached.

There are three reasons for the use of the CAPM in financial decisions First, the capital asset pricing model has rendered the traditional weighted-average cost-of-capital approach generally invalid for accept-reject decisions. This is shown in Figure 13.1. Second, the CAPM establishes an economy-wide cutoff value $(\lambda)^*$ for all projects, whereas the WACC must be deter-

---

$$*\lambda = \frac{E(R_m) - R_f}{\text{Var } R_m}$$

mined for each firm individually. Finally, the CAPM is built around the central principle of finance—the risk-return tradeoff.

SUMMARY

This chapter has examined the basic principles of financial structure, financial leverage, and financial valuation.

Financial structure is the interrelationship of all funds sources on the asset-and-liability side of the position statement. Financial structure is important because its careful management results in a lowered cost of capital.

Financial leverage refers to the principle of financing incremental assets with debt rather than equity. This results in increased return to common shareholders because of the fixed return promised to debt owners, and the (increasing) residual amount accruing to the equity owner.

The principle of leverage, however, is symmetrical. It magnifies return to common shareholders when total revenue is on the increase, but when total revenue is decreasing, the common shareholders are liable for losses resulting from the constant claims on the income stream.

Valuation, the process of assigning a market value to an asset, is the process of systematically relating an asset's revenues to its current market value, the relationship being the rate of return. Valuation of debt, common stock, and preferred stock was discussed. It was suggested that the summation of values of all its securities form the total value of the firm.

Finally, we saw that the capital asset pricing model generalizes the traditional WACC approach to asset-expansion decisions by quantifying risk.

APPENDIX TO CHAPTER 13: COMBINING OPERATING LEVERAGE AND FINANCIAL LEVERAGE

We have seen how the use of relatively low-cost debt can magnify the returns to common shareholders—that is, through the use of financial leverage. This is a position-statement phenomenon.

Operating leverage is an earnings-statement phenomenon. Operating leverage is the magnification of operating profits through the employment of relatively high fixed costs. There are many analogies to financial leverage, and these will be discussed later.

Operating leverage can be defined as the relationship (in ratio form) between a percentage change in operating profits resulting from (and therefore associated with) a change in sales.

Symbolically, the degree of operating leverage is:

$$OL = \frac{Q(P - V)}{Q(P - V) - F} \tag{5}$$

where:

OL = operating leverage

Q = units of output (quantity)

P = sales price per unit

V = variable cost per unit

F = total fixed costs

Modifying the expression above by multiplying through and removing the brackets, the expression becomes:

$$OL = \frac{QP - QV}{QP - QV - F} \tag{6}$$

Now, if $QP = S$—that is, if the output times unit sales price is equal to total sales—and if QV, the total output multiplied by each unit's variable cost, equals total variable cost, or V, then substituting gives us:

$$OL = \frac{S - V}{S - V - F} \tag{7}$$

Several observations about equation (7) are in order. The numerator of the fraction is equal to fixed costs plus total profits, for that is all that can be residual if total variable costs are subtracted from total sales revenue (S).

The denominator is equal to total profits, for if total variable costs are subtracted from sales revenue, and if total fixed costs (F) are further subtracted, the result can be only the residual, total profit, or operating profit.

By solving equation 7, the leverage factor can be determined. An example is in order. Assume that a firm produces 20,000 units of a product whose unit price is $10, and whose unit variable costs are $4 each. Further assume that the firm incurs total fixed costs of $80,000. Symbolically:

Q = 20,000 units

P = $10

V = $4

F = $80,000

What is the operating leverage? Substituting into equation (5), the following calculations are made:

$$OL = \frac{20,000(10-4)}{20,000(10-4) - 80,000}$$

$$= \frac{120,000}{120,000 - 80,000}$$

$$= \frac{120,000}{40,000}$$

$$= 300\%, \text{ or 3 times}$$

In other words, the employment of heavy fixed costs relative to revenues has leveraged—magnified—operating profit.

It's important to note that operating leverage magnifies earnings before interest and taxes (EBIT), whereas financial leverage magnifies earnings after taxes (EAT).

When operating leverage is used in conjunction with financial leverage, there results a powerful effect on the earnings of the firm—that is, there is a magnification of the magnification.

If financial leverage, on the income statement, is measured as:

$$FL = \frac{EBIT}{EBIT - I} \tag{8}$$

and recognizing that:

$$EBIT = Q(P - V) - F_1{}^*$$

and substituting this into equation (8), we have:

$$FL = \frac{Q(P - V) - F}{Q(P - V) - F - 1} \tag{9}$$

Equation (9) is financial leverage specified in the same terms as operating leverage. If equation (5), operating leverage, is multiplied by equation (9), financial leverage, the result is combined leverage (CL):

$$CL = \frac{Q(P - V)}{Q(P - V) - F} \times \frac{Q(P - V) - F}{Q(P - V) - F - I} = \frac{Q(P - V)}{Q(P - V) - F - I}$$

---

*This is true because QP is total revenue of the firm—sales—and when QV, total variable costs, and F, total fixed costs, are subtracted from total revenue, the result has to be earnings before interest and taxes.

Combined leverage turns out to be our old friend, operating leverage, with the additional feature that the total interest bill, I, is subtracted from the denominator.

Assume that we want to determine combined leverage (CL) in addition to the operating leverage calculated in the previous example. Assume that the total interest bill (I) is \$5,000. This, in addition to the values already specified, would result in the following list of values used to calculate combined leverage:

$$Q = 20,000 \text{ units}$$
$$P = \$10$$
$$V = \$4$$
$$F = \$80,000$$
$$I = \$5,000$$

Substituting these into the combined-leverage (CL) equation, we have:

$$CL = \frac{20,000(\$10 - \$4)}{20,000(\$10 - \$4) - \$80,000 - \$5,000}$$

$$= \frac{120,000}{120,000 - 80,000 - 5,000}$$

$$= \frac{120,000}{35,000}$$

$$= 343\%, \text{ or } 3.43 \text{ times}$$

If these calculations are correct, they should result in the same answer as would be arrived at by calculating the operating leverage separately and the financial leverage separately, and multiplying the results. We do that now:

$$OL = \frac{Q(P - V)}{Q(P - V) - F}$$

$$= 3\times$$

$$FL = \frac{Q(P - V) - F}{Q(P - V) - F - I}$$

$$= \frac{20,000(\$10 - \$4) - \$80,000}{20,000(\$10 - \$4) - \$80,000 - 5,000}$$

$$= \frac{120,000 - 80,000}{120,000 - 85,000}$$

$$= \frac{40,000}{35,000}$$

$$= 1.142\times$$

Therefore:

$$OL = 3\times$$

$$FL = 1.142\times$$

$$OL \times FL = 3 \times 1.142$$

$$= 3.426, \text{ or } 3.43 \text{ times}$$

And we have thus calculated and demonstrated the value of combined leverage.

PROBLEMS

1. The Rho Delta Corporation manufactures component parts for the space industry. The current position statement and earnings statement are reproduced below. In addition, you are told the following facts about Rho Delta:

(1) Cost of goods sold is always 38% of sales.

(2) Operating expense is always 30% of gross earnings.

(3) Sales are always 50% of total assets.

RHO DELTA CORPORATION
POSITION STATEMENT

Cash	$ 10,000	Accounts payable	$ 50,000
Accounts receivable	50,000	Bank loan (5%)	10,000
Inventory	100,000	Bonds (7%)	100,000
Net fixed assets	50,000	Common equity	50,000
	$210,000		$210,000

RHO DELTA CORPORATION
EARNINGS STATEMENT

Sales	$105,000
Cost of goods sold	40,000
Gross earnings	$65,000
Operating expense	20,000
EBIT	$45,000
Interest	7,500
EBT	$37,500
Tax (40%)	15,000
EAT	$22,500

The corporation, in order to win another government contract, must add $90,000 to its inventory account immediately. Its banker has indicated that the $90,000 can be borrowed at 9% without paying off the existing $10,000 loan, which does not mature for another two years.

    a. Assume the loan is made. Construct a pro forma position statement and earnings statement.

    b. Calculate the following ratios *before* and *after* the loan is made: debt ratio, times interest earned, and return to owners' equity.

    c. Based upon the ratios calculated in question *b* above, write a short statement about the advantages of leverage in this case.

2. After graduation from college, you are employed by a financial consultant specializing in valuation problems. You are given the following case to handle as part of your duties.

The owner of the local franchise of a nationally known bottling company has had an offer to purchase his business. As a result of this offer, he has become a client of your employer. He has been offered $15 million for his franchise and assets of the firm. The purchaser is willing to assume the liabilities of the firm.

Below are the most recent financial statements of the bottling company:

POSITION STATEMENT

Cash	$1,000,000	Accounts payable	$4,000,000
Accounts receivable	2,000,000	Notes payable	6,000,000
Inventory	5,000,000	Common stock	8,000,000
Fixed assets	12,000,000	Retained earnings	2,000,000
	$20,000,000		$20,000,000

EARNINGS STATEMENT

Sales	$10,00,0000
Cost of goods sold	4,000,000
Gross earnings	$6,000,000
Operating expense	2,000,000
EBIT	$4,000,000
Interest	600,000
EBT	$3,400,000
Tax (48%)	1,632,000
EAT	$1,768,000

Mr. C. Cola, the owner of the bottling plant, believes that the prospective purchaser of the plant requires a 9% return on his investment.

Should Mr. Cola accept the offer to purchase his business? Why, or why not?

3. This problem is designed to test your insight into financial structure and the relationships among position-statement and earnings-statement accounts. Based upon the following posited relationships, complete the position statement and the earnings statement.

(1) Current assets are 59.1% of total assets.

(2) Current liabilities (accounts payable and notes payable) are 22.7% of total liabilities and capital.

(3) Cash and accounts receivable are 53.8% of current assets.

(4) Cash is 13.6% of total assets.

(5) Bonds are 18.2% of total liabilities and equity.

(6) Notes payable are 40% of the sum of accounts and notes payable.

(7) Sales are 59.1% of total assets.

(8) Cost of goods sold is 38.5% of sales.

(9) Operating expense is 37.5% of gross earnings.

(10) The tax rate is 48%.

POSITION STATEMENT

Cash		Accounts payable	
Accounts receivable		Notes payable (6%)	
Inventory		Bonds (10%)	
Fixed assets		Equity	
	$22,000,000		

EARNINGS STATEMENT

Sales	
Cost of Goods sold	_____
Gross earnings	
Operating expense	_____
EBIT	
Interest	_____
EBT	
Tax (48%)	_____
EAT	

For Problems 4 and 5, assume that a firm's weighted-average cost of capital (WACC) is 12%, the risk-free return is 5%, and the expected market return is 11%.

4. If the expected return on a project is 13%:

a. What is the required return if the project's beta is 1.5?

b. Draw the market line and plot the WACC and the project's expected return.

c. If the firm implements the project, will it increase or decrease the wealth of the firm?

5. If the expected return on a project is 10%:

a. What is the required return if the project's beta is .5?

b. Plot the values on the market line.

   i. Should the project be accepted based on WACC?

   ii. Should the project be accepted based on the required return as shown by the SML?

Financial Investments

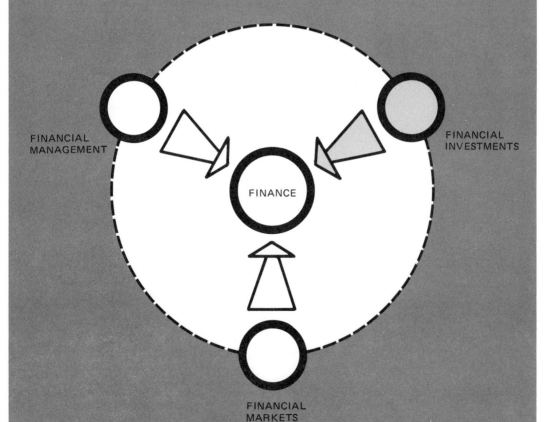

There is a definite link between financial management and financial investments. For example, business firms need dollars to build more plants and equipment. Such firms issue securities in the belief that the dollars obtained can be reinvested to earn more than the cost of using the money. The investor, in turn, depends on the issuer of the securities to deliver on the principal of the investment plus a return on it. So the firm is dependent upon funds from investors, who buy the securities because they expect a return commensurate with the risk involved. Thus, financing and investing decisions are two sides of the same coin.

The interaction between business firms and individuals is generalized by the circular-flow model. Individuals supply resources (land, labor, capital, and managerial skills) to the firm in exchange for payments from the firm. The payments received by individuals is income in the form of rent, wages and salaries, interest, and dividends. Such income creates a demand for the goods and services that have been produced by the firms. The model shown in the figure also depicts savings by individuals (or households) and investments by the firms. If firms desire to invest more than the individuals save, banks may create money for firms in the form of loans.

Circular-Flow Model.

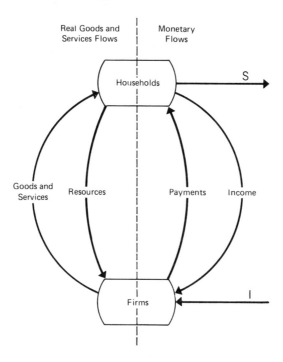

This diagram reinforces the idea that financial management and financial investments are mirror images of each other. As such, the securities section, which is normally treated in traditional finance texts as corporate sources of long-term funds, is presented here from the viewpoint of the individual investor.

Chapter 14 examines the investment process. This involves the need to invest, investment alternatives, the risk-return relationship, and investment procedures. The chapter concludes with a discussion of investment versus speculation and a differentiation of the two processes.

Chapters 15, 16, and 17 are the investment-securities chapters. Both fixed-return and variable-return financial claims are discussed. Emphasis is given to the impact of securities provisions on the investment decision. Finally, the rapid growth of options trading is examined.

In the last chapter of this section, the four approaches to investing are presented. They are the fundamental approach, the technical approach, random selection, and efficient diversification. Portfolio theory is presented at the close of this section on financial investments.

The Financial Investment Function and Process

14

A fool and his money are soon parted.

Benjamin Franklin,
Poor Richard's Almanack

In Chapters 6 through 13, the central theme is the financial manager's need for funds to purchase assets and the efficient utilization of such funds in the administration of assets. The chapters in this section will approach funds from the viewpoint of the individual investor. The rational investor attempts to maximize returns and minimize risks on his investments. In this chapter we examine the investment function, the investment decision, mechanics of investing, and investment versus speculation. The variety of investment securities traded in the marketplace is presented in the chapters immediately following this.

Financial Investment vs. Economic Investment   Our concern in these chapters will be financial investment. To avoid ambiguity, the distinction between financial and economic investment is given here. *Financial investment* is the commitment of funds to claims with the expectation of receiving a going rate of return. This expected rate of return can be in the form of dividend income, interest income, capital appreciation, or a combination of the three. An example of a financial investment is the commitment of funds to shares of common or preferred stocks of corporations. Another example of financial investment is committing funds to Treasury bills and government bonds. In these latter cases, the investor tends to avoid risk that is associated with ownership claims. However, some risks can be encountered on bonds, especially the more speculative ones, such as bonds of corporations or municipalities that may not be able to make the fixed interest payment that the bondholder is entitled to receive.

By contrast, *economic* or *business investment* is the money that businessmen spend on *newly produced* capital goods. Note that without the inclusion of the words "newly produced," one is merely exchanging one asset for another—money (one asset) for used machinery (existing asset). Three things are basically included in business-investment spending by American business firms. These are (1) the purchase of newly produced machinery, equipment, and tools; (2) all construction, which includes commercial structures as well as apartment buildings and residential houses (even though owner-occupied, the residential unit could be rented if the owner so chooses); and (3) inventories that are produced but not sold within the year.

Remember that the key concept in this group of chapters is the process of *financial investment*, not economic investment. If you purchase 100 shares of General Motors common stock, you are making a financial investment. Even if you purchase first-day issues of the common stock of a brand new firm, you are still making a financial investment. The businessmen of the new firm will make economic investments with the funds that you and a host of others supply to the firm.

Savings Allocation   The financial investment function has a dual purpose. First is the allocation of savings to government and business. The users of savings, in turn, provide essential goods and services to the public. For a moment, imagine how it would be if the automotive or telephone industries in this country had to curtail production and services because of a lack of funds to renew plant and equipment. If the situation were permanent, it would mean, at a minimum, driving older cars and making fewer or no phone calls. What if the federal government were unable to borrow money? Certain services would have to be cut or eliminated. Of course, we would all want the other man's service (or check) cut, not ours. As you can see, the ramifications of cutbacks in production and services would stifle the economy. Thus, savings allocation is essential for business as well as government in order to maintain jobs and living standards.

Savings Accumulation   An equally important purpose of the financial investment function is to accumulate savings for issuers of financial claims. The issuers, in turn, reward the suppliers of savings by paying a return on the principal supplied. Thus, individuals invest because of the expectation of a return on the dollars invested. Savings accumulation, which began as the result of saving out of one's own income, is essential to sustain economic growth. In the process, the monetary wealth of the individual investor is enhanced.

THE INVESTMENT DECISION

The investment decision is an activity whereby individuals and institutions obtain and analyze information about various investment opportunities for the purpose of making choices to buy, hold, or sell individual assets with respect to a portfolio of assets. The investment decision involves the problem of wealth, investment choices, risk–return tradeoff, and investment procedures.

The Problem of Wealth   Households must save their nonconsumed income over a period of time in order to plan for large, irregular consumption needs, such as automobiles, houses, college educations, and so on. As money is saved, wealth is being accumulated. The owners of wealth in the form of funds must decide when to invest it, what financial investment to choose, the quantity of funds to be invested, and the period of committing such funds to financial investment. In other words, the accumulation of wealth places upon the owner of such wealth the responsibility for making intelligent decisions in financial investments.

There is an estimated $8 trillion in total personal property and financial assets in the United States. One percent of the population owns approximately 25 percent of all the total wealth—that is, 2 million people own $2 trillion. Five percent (10 million) own 40 percent of the total personal property and financial assets ($3.2 trillion). The relationship is depicted by the Lorenz curve in Figure 14.1.

FIGURE 14.1 The Distribution of Wealth.

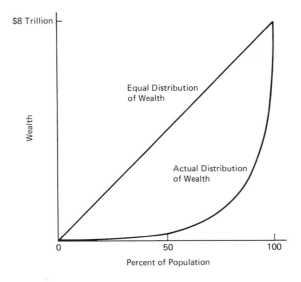

Consider the assets of the top wealth holders in the United States, shown in Table 14.1. The favorite asset of the wealthy, by a wide margin, continues to be common stocks. This is due in part to the passing along of wealth intact from one generation to the next. Other reasons are the need for capital growth as well as marketability.

TABLE 14.1 The Assets of Top Wealth Holders

TYPE OF ASSET	BILLIONS OF DOLLARS	APPROXIMATE PERCENTAGE OF GROUP'S TOTAL WEALTH
Corporate stock	$326	43.3%
Real estate	188	25.0
Cash	71	9.4
Bonds	48	6.4
Notes and mortgages	30	4.0
Insurance equity	16	2.1
Pension-fund reserves, personal trusts	74	9.8
Total wealth	$753	100.0%

Source: "*What the Rich Do with Their Money,*" Business Week, *August 5, 1972, p. 55.*

Choice of Assets Many possibilities exist for financial investments. These range from a simple savings account at a local bank or savings and loan association to such complex investments as real estate, art, coins, antiques, and business ventures. While a savings account in a commercial bank or savings and loan association is relatively liquid and safe, the rate of return is not as attractive as that of some other financial investments. Conversely, investments in real estate, paintings, and business ventures are relatively illiquid and risky. They may produce handsome returns or may be very disappointing. This is the nature of risk. It causes returns to range from losses to large gains.

Choices available to the investor for financial investments are numerous. They are classified below according whether they are choices made by the individual investor or collective choices made by professional investment management:

A. Investment choices of individual investors
  1. Fixed-principal investments:
     a. Cash
     b. Savings accounts *lowest level of earnings*
     c. Marketable certificates of deposit
     d. U.S. government securities *EE bonds 9%*
     e. Municipal bonds *tax free*
     f. Corporate bonds *business debt multiples of $1000* *not insured*
  2. Variable-principal securities:
     a. Convertible securities *bonds converted 11-15% common stock* *preferred converted to comm*
     b. Preferred stocks
     c. Common stocks
     d. Rights
     e. Warrants - *for purchase of common @ specific cost*
     f. Options *w/warrants price is higher, but price of stock will probably go higher than price w/ warrant*
  3. Nonsecurities investments:
     a. Real estate - *tax shelter*
     b. Mortgages
     c. Commodities - *grain, sugar, coffee etc*
     d. Gold, silver, and gems
     e. Art, antiques, coins, and stamps
     f. Business ventures
B. Investment choices by professional investment management
  1. Trust funds - *trustee reinvest funds*
  2. Pension funds - *invest in corp, real estate*
  3. Insurance companies
  4. Investment companies

Rights of common stockholders
right to maintain your share of ownership
rights have value - can be sold
warrant @ market value $50/share
w/warrant $52/share
in 5 yrs stock goes to $55/share

The first group of investments, in category A, consists of investments in which the individual investor makes the final decision to buy, hold, or sell. The responsibility for this decision is the sole province of the individual investor. He can and usually does seek investment help, however. Individuals confronted with investment decisions need to be aware of the main sources of investment information and how to make use of them. These sources are discussed in the next section.

In the latter category, B, are investment decisions made by groups of professionals on behalf of the individual investor. They are claims on "baskets" (or bundles) of assets. In such cases, the individual has no control over the composition of securities in the portfolio. He does have a degree of decision to the extent that he can refuse to enter (or buy) into the portfolio combination and, once in, can leave (or sell) if the investment choices do not appeal to him. Such individual decisions may be somewhat awkward or unpleasant to make, but they are made, as evidenced by the departure en masse of individual investors from mutual-fund portfolios in the 1970s.

On the financial investment continuum between very safe (cash) and very risky (options) is a host of investments that we will be concerned with in this book. These investments, ranging from U.S. government bonds to common stocks, are generally known as *securities*. A security is an instrument, debt or ownership, that has a claim on the assets of the issuing body, is negotiable, and is usually marketable. Securities are by far the most popular form of semiliquid investment because they can be converted rather quickly to cash. Such is not the case with real estate, which may take months or years to sell at your price. In contrast, a security that is traded on one of the major stock exchanges can be sold within minutes.

Risk–Return Tradeoff The investment process involves making a tradeoff between expected returns and the risks associated with the returns. In order to make the necessary tradeoff, the investor should understand the sources that determine the amount and level of risk and return, and be capable of measuring the magnitude of each in some systematic manner. *Such an approach is the essence of investment decision making.*

Measuring Risk and Return. In Chapter 4 we learned that the *variance* and *standard deviation* of expected return are good measures of risk for individual investments. Recall that the standard deviation is the square root of the variance. If the variance is 16, the standard deviation would be 4. Both can be used to measure risk. Whichever one is used, the same decision will result. The standard deviation is an important concept because it permits a rigorous interpretation of the variance. That is, given a normal distribution, approximately 95 percent of the actual returns will fall within a range of plus or minus two standard deviations of the mean. For example, for an expected return of 8 percent and a standard deviation of 4, approximately 95 percent of the actual returns will fall between zero percent and 16 percent, given conditions approaching statistical normality. *The greater the standard deviation or variance, the greater will be the range of possible returns.*

The calculation of the variance and standard deviation of expected return on common stock can be based on a probable distribution of future returns or on past returns. We will base expected future returns on actual returns over the past five years. First, a holding-period return for each of the past five years is calculated, as follows:

$$\text{Holding-period return} = \frac{(P_1 - P_0) + D_1}{P_0}$$

where:

P_1 = the average price for the current period

P_0 = the average price for the preceding period

D_1 = the dividend received for the current period

For example, to calculate the holding-period returns for the common stock of the Coca-Cola Company from 1971 through 1976, the data needed are as shown in Table 14.2. Using the holding-period-return formula, the returns for the years 1971 through 1976 are calculated. The results are shown in Table 14.3. The expected return based on the 1971–1976 returns for Coca-Cola is 7.53 percent. The standard deviation is 24.67. This means that the rate of return may be expected to vary from a negative 17.14 percent to a

TABLE 14.2 Data Needed to Calculate Holding-Period Return for the Common Stock of Coca-Cola Company

PERIOD	PRICE RANGE PER SHARE		DIVIDENDS PER SHARE	DIVIDEND YIELD
	HIGH	LOW		
1970	$ 85	$ 62	—	—
1971	125	82	$1.58	2.14%
1972	150	112	1.64	1.58
1973	150	116	1.80	1.37
1974	128	45	2.08	1.56
1975	94	53	2.30	2.67
1976	95	73	2.65	3.58

TABLE 14.3 Calculation of Expected Return, Variance, and Standard Deviation for the Common Stock of the Coca-Cola Company (1971–1976)

PERIOD	AVERAGE PRICE PER SHARE	RETURN	(RETURN)^2
1970	74	—	—
1971	104	42.68%	1821.58
1972	131	27.54	758.45
1973	133	2.90	8.41
1974	86	−33.77	1140.41
1975	74	−11.28	127.24
1976	84	17.09	292.07
	Sum	45.16%	4148.16

$$E(R) = \Sigma R/n = 45.16/6 = 7.53$$
$$E(R)^2 = \Sigma(R^2)/n = 4148.16/6 = 691.36$$
$$\text{Variance} = E(R)^2 - [E(\overline{R})]^2$$
$$= 691.36 - 56.7 = 634.66$$
$$\text{Standard deviation or } \sigma = \sqrt{\text{Variance}}$$
$$= \sqrt{634.66} = 25.19$$

positive 32.20 percent.* Thus, the risk of owning Coca-Cola common stock appears to be considerable. However, to be more meaningful, the return and risk should be compared to the market risk and return (such as DJIA).

During the same period, the Dow Jones Industrial Average (DJIA) moved form 631 in 1970 to 1,051 in January 1973. From that level, the DJIA moved down to 570 on December 9, 1974, and closed the year 1976 at 1004. The expected return based on the 1971–1976 returns for the DJIA is 10 percent; the risk as measured by the standard deviation is 14.91 as shown in Table 14.4. Thus, the return on the DJIA was higher and the risk lower than the return on Coca-Cola for the 1971–1976 period.

TABLE 14.4 Calculation of Expected Return, Variance and Standard Deviation for the Dow Jones Industrial Average (DJIA), (1971–1976)

PERIOD	RETURN	(RETURN)^2
1971	24	576
1972	13	169
1973	0	0
1974	(15)	225
1975	8	64
1976	30	900
	60	1934

$$E(R) = \Sigma R/n = 60/6 = 10$$
$$E(R)^2 = \Sigma(R^2)/n = 1934/6 = 322.3$$
$$\text{Variance} = E(R)^2 - [E(R)]^2$$
$$= 322.3 - 100 = 222.3$$
$$\text{Standard deviation} = \sqrt{\text{Variance}}$$
$$= \sqrt{222.3}$$
$$= 14.91$$

Alternate Method†

PERIOD	MEAN PRICE DJIA	PRICE CHANGE	DIVIDEND YIELD	R_m	$R_m - E(R_m)$	$[R_m - E(R_m)]^2$
1970	730	—	—	—	—	—
1971	875	.20	.04	.24	.14	.0196
1972	962	.10	.03	.13	.03	.0009
1973	920	(.04)	.04	.00	(.10)	.0100
1974	732	(.20)	.05	(.15)	(.25)	.0625
1975	757	.03	.05	.08	(.02)	.0004
1976	955	.26	.04	.30	.20	.0400
				.60/6		.1334/6
			$E(R) = .10$ or 10%		Variance = .0222 or 222	

†See Chapter 4 for explanation of the alternate method.

*For $\pm 1\sigma$.

Financial Information   It is important for the investor to be well informed about world affairs, economic conditions in the nation, the general level and direction of stock prices, and developments within individual companies.* However, a simple and effective system of gaining information is much more useful to the investor than having a complete knowledge of all sources of information without being able to use any of them. A suggested method of gathering information about financial investment alternatives is to (1) determine the direction of the national economy, (2) choose industries that offer the greatest expectation of profit, and (3) select the most profitable companies of each industry. Unfortunately, this process requires an expenditure of time and money that may be beyond the means of the average investor. However, information on industry and corporations, as well as the economy, is available in libraries or at modest cost. The following sources of financial information are suggested for the implementation of the investment decision.

Information about the National Economy. Information about the national economy can be obtained from many sources, both public and private. One of the most comprehensive federal publications dealing with the national economy is the *Federal Reserve Bulletin*, published monthly by the Board of Governors of the Federal Reserve System, Washington, D.C. Each issue contains a summary of business conditions and over 100 pages of statistical data. The data include statistics on industrial production, employment, construction, retail sales, various types of credit, and consumer prices, plus information about national income, interest rates, sources of corporate funds, business and commercial loans, corporate profits, and other valuable financial data. For the investor who prefers graphic rather than tabular data, the same information is presented on a monthly or annual basis in the *Historical Chart Book*.

The Survey of Current Business, published by the U.S. Department of Commerce, presents data about basic business trends and charts of various economic components: general business indicators, stock price indexes, commodity prices, construction, domestic trade, employment, population, finance, foreign trade, transportation and communications, industry, and other segments of the economy.

Business Conditions Digest, published monthly by the Bureau of the Census, U.S. Department of Commerce, presents valuable information on leading, coincidental, and lagging indicators. An important aspect of the digest is the composite index of leading indicators, which is helpful to the investor in determining expected future movements of the economy and the securities markets.

---

*Details in this section can be skipped without loss of continuity. The material in this section is suggested as reference material for those with an other-than-cursory interest in investments.

A number of good private sources of information on the national economy are available at moderate cost. *Business Week*, a McGraw-Hill publication, contains figures on production, trade, prices, and finance, as well as a business-outlook section that reviews current business and economic developments. The *Monthly Economic Letter*, published by Citibank, N. A., 399 Park Avenue, New York, N.Y., has a lead article on general business conditions in each issue. Forecasts of the U.S. economy based on econometric models by the Wharton School, M.I.T., General Electric, and the U.S. Government are available from time to time in the financial press. Other business periodicals that furnish data on the national economy are *Dun's Review*, *Forbes*, *Fortune*, *Nation's Business*, and *U.S. News & World Report*.

Information on Industries and Individual Companies. In addition to the general economic publications discussed above, a large quantity of information is generated by research agencies and services on specific industries and corporations. Three investment advisory services provide the bulk of information about industries and companies. They are Moody's Investor Service, 99 Church Street, New York, N.Y., owned by Dun & Bradstreet; Standard & Poor's Corporation, 345 Hudson Street, New York, N.Y., owned by McGraw-Hill; and Value Line Investment Survey, 5 East 44th Street, New York, N.Y., owned by Arnold Bernhard & Company. Moody's and Standard & Poor's services include reference volumes called *Moody's Manuals* and Standard & Poor's *Corporation Records*. These volumes contain yearly data and are updated on a periodic basis to include current financial information about thousands of companies classified as industrial, utility, transportation, or finance.

Standard & Poor's also publishes a *Stock Guide* and a *Bond Guide*. Both are published monthly. The *Stock Guide* contains financial information on approximately 5,000 common and preferred stocks. In addition, a mutual-fund summary of about 500 funds is found in the back of the *Guide*. The *Stock Guide* can be purchased from Standard & Poor's or is often available from a stockbroker free of charge. Small investors probably regard the *Guide* as the best source of data for almost all major listed securities in the United States. The *Bond Guide* contains information for all corporate bonds, municipal bonds, and convertible bonds in the United States, and some foreign government bonds.

Moody's and Standard & Poor's both publish detailed reports on individual corporations. The *Handbook* (Moody's) and the *Encyclopedia* (Standard & Poor's) cover about 1,000 or more common stocks. Each is issued quarterly and contains vertical-bar price charts, a history of financial-statement data, an analysis of the firm's background, and recent developments and prospects for the firm. The *Handbook* is published in entirety each quarter. Separate pages of the *Encyclopedia* are issued quarterly and are available through most stockbrokers.

In addition to other publications, Standard & Poor's publishes the *Investors Statistical Laboratory* (*ISL*) and *Compustat*. Both contain elaborate financial data (60 items of position-statement and income-statement data), historical stock prices, and other relevant data. *ISL* is printed data, and *Compustat* is a computer magnetic-tape data file. Both data bases are used for detailed financial analyses.

The Value Line Investment Survey publishes ratings and reports on over 1,600 companies. *The Value Line Survey* is more specific than either Moody's or Standard & Poor's. It covers 60 industries. The service provides betas and statistical financial information, an analysis of new products being designed and marketed, sales outlooks, and recommendations as to quality and potential price movements of the stock. Securities appearing in the *Survey* are rated for appeal on the basis of probable market strength within the next twelve months and within the next three to five years.

In addition to the services listed above, there are numerous investment letters mailed semimonthly or monthly to paid subscribers. The cost of such services ranges from a few dollars a year to over $1,000 a year, depending upon the track record of the publication. *The Investment and Barometer Letter* (Babson's Reports, Inc.) and *Stock Market Survey* (American Investors Corporation) are among leading letters based on securities analysis. Widely respected market-analysis letters are Edson Gould's *Findings and Forecasts* (Anametrics, Inc.) and the *T.J. Holt Investment Advisory* (T.J. Holt & Co.).

Dozens of chart services are available to the investor. Vertical-bar (price-range) charts* are available on a monthly, weekly, or daily basis. Monthly-range charts on over 1,000 companies appear in *Moody's Handbook of Common Stocks*, Standard & Poor's *Stock Market Encyclopedia*, and *The Value Line Investment Survey*. Trendline Corporation publishes monthly-range charts in *Current Market Perspectives*, which also gives an industrial grouping for 972 listed stocks, and daily-range charts in *Daily Basis Stock Charts* on more than 700 stocks. Other chart services include M.C. Horsey Company, Robert Mansfield and Company, and Securities Research Corporation. Point-and-figure charts† are available from Chartcraft, Inc., A.H. Wheelan, and many others. Advertisements for these chart services appear in the *Wall Street Journal* and *Barron's*.

The financial press provides a large amount of information to the investor. One of the largest news services in the United States is Dow Jones & Company. The company publishes the *Wall Street Journal* each business day. It provides a complete list of securities traded on all national, regional, and over-the-counter exchanges. The *Journal* has a special column, "Heard on the Street," which occasionally provides the investor with advice from top

---

*See Chapter 18.
†See Chapter 18.

securities analysts, portfolio managers, and investment advisors. Another publication of Dow Jones is *Barron's National Business and Financial Weekly*, which contains articles on various industries, developments within numerous companies, and news articles on domestic and world situations expected to influence financial decisions. *Barron's* also publishes a substantial amount of information with its weekly stock-price quotations. *Commercial and Financial Chronicle* is a biweekly financial magazine that presents information similar to that carried in *Barron's*. Some of the other financial-press publications include *Financial World*, *The Magazine of Wall Street*, and *The Wall Street Transcript*.

Before subscribing to any of the publications mentioned in this section, the investor should determine if they are available in his public or college library or in his broker's office. Subscriptions are available on a trial basis to almost all the publications.

THE MECHANICS OF INVESTING

Securities Markets Securities markets exist to facilitate the buying and selling of stocks, bonds, and other types of securities. In the United States, there are organized stock exchanges, organized bond exchanges, the over-the-counter market, and the money market. Financial markets (both capital and money markets) are treated in detail in Part IV of this book. Our purpose here, however, is briefly to introduce securities exchanges and markets.

An organized securities exchange (stock or bond) is an association whose members meet face-to-face to buy and sell securities for their customers in a two-sided auction process. Trading is limited to securities that have been formally accepted and listed for trading on the exchange.

The New York Stock Exchange (NYSE) is the best known, largest, and most important securities exchange in the United States. The exchange consists of about 1,400 members who purchase "seats" on the exchange, which have ranged in price from $17,000 to $625,000.* Membership on the exchange is divided into classes based upon the member's activity. For example, the *specialist* has the economic responsibility for maintaining an orderly market and the financial responsibility for keeping a record of each transaction on all stocks assigned to him. Members of the exchange may join together to form member firms. There are about 500 national and regional brokerage firms. Approximately 1,200 companies are listed on the New York Stock Exchange, representing a total of about 1,700 issues. The New York Stock Exchange accounts for about 70 percent of all organized-exchange transac-

*At one time, a "seat" designated the physical place where each member sat. Today the expression has become a figure of speech.

tions and about 80 percent of the dollar market value of all listed shares in the United States.

Another national exchange, of lesser importance, is the American Stock Exchange, which has about 900 listed companies and accounts for about 20 percent of the organized-exchange transactions in the United States. Regional and local exchanges are Boston, Chicago Board Options Exchange, Cincinnati, Detroit, Inter-Mountain, Midwest, Pacific Coast, Philadelphia, and Spokane. These round out the organized exchanges in the United States, with a combined total of only 10 percent of U.S. shares traded on organized exchanges.

The over-the-counter market (OTC) is a network of brokers, traders, and dealers who make a market in individual issues and stand ready to buy or sell to each other and to the public. OTC transactions are handled through a combination of a computer-based quotation system called NASDAQ (pronounced "nazdak") and a communication system utilizing telephone and teletype equipment. NASDAQ furnishes a complete array of the latest bid and asked prices on active issues from the best dealers in the issue. The over-the-counter markets are much more important in dollar volume of securities traded than are all the organized exchanges combined. All publicly held issues that are not listed on a national, regional, or local exchange are traded over-the-counter. They include most bank stocks, most insurance-company stocks, all U.S. government securities, all municipal bonds, most mutual funds, equipment trust certificates issued by railroads and airlines, most corporate bonds, and stocks of a large number of domestic and foreign industrial and public utility companies. About 30,000 issues are in the OTC market, compared to 3,000 on all organized exchanges. There are 2,877 member firms of NASD. Figure 14.2 shows a portion of the over-the-counter market. Your attention is called to Intel Corporation, the company that developed the microcomputer in 1973. This industry (microprocessor) is expected to increase sales from $50 million in 1976 to are over one billion dollars by 1980.

Markets for securities may be broadly divided into primary markets, the channels through which new securities are sold, and secondary markets, the channels through which "used" issues are resold. The primary market is the first sale, or new issue, of a security. Purchases of securities in the primary market are usually made through an investment banker who originates, underwrites, prices, and sells new issues to the investing public. Most transactions in the primary market are OTC trades.

The secondary market is the trading in securities already owned by the public. Secondary trading (or resale of securities) can take place in either the OTC market or on the organized exchanges. The place of sale depends on whether the issue is listed. Issues listed on exchanges are sometimes traded OTC, but OTC issues cannot be traded on the exchanges.

FIGURE 14.2 Selected Over-the-Counter Quotations. (*Source: Wall Street Journal, February 4, 1977, p. 24.*)

Over-the-Counter Markets

4:00 p.m. Eastern Time Prices,

All over the counter prices printed on this page are representative quotations supplied by the National Association of Securities Dealers through NASDAQ, its automated system for reporting quotes. Prices don't include retail markup, markdown or commission. Volume represents shares that changed ownership during the day. Figures include only those transactions effected by NASDAQ market makers but may include some duplication where NASDAQ market makers traded with each other.

Volume, All Issues, 8,273,600

SINCE JANUARY 1

	1977	1976	1975
Total sales	201,570,079	184,155,490	131,930,344

MARKET DIARY

	Thur	Wed	Tues	Mon	Fri
Issues traded	2,528	2,530	2,533	2,553	2,554
Advances	348	464	524	348	379
Declines	429	332	270	481	474
Unchanged	1,751	1,734	1,739	1,704	1,701
xNew highs	81	90	80	57	71
xNew lows	7	7	7	11	13

x-Based on 4 p.m. Eastern time bid quote.

MOST ACTIVE STOCKS

	Volume	4:00 Bid	Chg.
Burmah Oil Co ADR	358,500	1½	....
Applied Digital Data	339,900	13⅞	+ ⅞
Continuous Curve	128,600	11	+ ⅞
Intel Corp	105,200	54½	....
Penn Offshore Gas B	92,900	14⅝	− ¼
Rank Organisatn ADR	88,300	3	....
Dorchester Gas Cp	84,500	1⅞	− ¼
Petroleum Development	77,500	1¼	+ ¼
Daylin Inc	71,700	1½	−1/16
Rocket Research	70,100	9	+ ⅜

Stock & Div.	Sales 100s	Bid	Asked	Net Chg.
--I I--				
IdaFNB 1.28g	30	40½	42½	...
Illini Bf Pckrs	10	4¼	4⅝	− ¼
Immuno Scien	1	9⅛	9⅞	− ⅛
IndBnkshrs 1g	2	23	24½	...
IMS Internatl	123	8¾	9¼	+ ⅛
IndLifeAcc .68	298	13⅞	14¼	...
Ind Mtge Rlty	2	2½	3	...
IndSqlSec 1.68	10	19⅜	19⅞	...
Indiana Gr .60	45	23	23½	− ⅛
Ind Natl Corp	6	9⅝	10⅛	...
IndapWat 1.90	10	23	23½	...
Ind Nucleonic	7	2¾	3⅛	...
IndustFuel .60	8	16¾	17½	...
Indl Vl Bk 1.80	5	24¼	25¼	− ¼
Inforex Incorp	219	6½	6⅞	...
Inform Intl .10	9	12	12½	...
Inform Magne	1	5⅜	5⅞	...
Instrumnt Lab	24	8⅞	9⅜	− ¼
Intercon Engy	43	10¾	11¾	− ¼
Intel Corportn	1052	54½	56	...
IntrfcIInc .32a	25	7⅝	8	...
InmtnGas 1.36	47	17½	18	...
IntBnk Wa .25	48	5⅜	5⅞	+ ½
IntBkWa A .25	31	5⅜	5⅞	+ ¼
Intl Dairy Qn	17	2⅛	2½	+ ⅛
IntlSystems pf	4	13½	15½	...
Intersil Incorp	209	8⅜	8⅞	− ⅛
Inves Annuity	19	2	2⅜	+ ⅛
Iowa So Util 2	20	25⅝	26⅛	− ⅛
IVAC Corp .28	318	26⅞	27⅜	− ⅝
--J J--				
JamesRivr .16	7	15	16	+ ¼
Japan Airlines	8	85¼	86¾	+ 3½
Jamc WaterP	1	4¾	5¼	...
Jamesbury .40	16	15½	16¼	− ¼
JBBigBoy .28d	19	3⅛	3⅝	+ ⅛
JeffsonNat .28	4	11¾	12¼	...
Jensen Indust	22	5	5⅜	+ ⅛
Jerrico In .02d	382	21¼	22	+ ½
Jetero Corptn	z50	3⅝	4	...
JMB Rty 1.60d	2	14	16	...
JoslynM 1.12a	13	15¼	16	...
Justin Indu .60	17	18⅛	18⅝	...
--K K--				

Stock & Div.	Sales 100s	Bid	Asked	Net Chg.
Noble Affil .40	44	27¼	28¼	− ¼
Noland Co .36	9	9¼	9¾	+ ⅛
Nord Resour	22	8½	9¼	− ¼
Nordstrom .28	24	19⅝	20⅛	...
Norin Corprtn	12	7½	8½	...
NCaroNtGas 1	25	13	13⅜	+ ⅛
NothestPet .25	2	13½	14¼	...
NoEuro Oil ut	x3	29¾	30½	+ ½
NoCal SL .50	10	15¾	16¼	− ⅛
No StBncp .40	19	6	6¾	...
Northrup King	1	18⅜	19⅜	...
Nowst NGs .80	146	9⅞	10¼	− ⅛
NwOhBsh 1.70	4	44	46	...
NwstnFcl .30g	22	8½	9	...
Nwst FcIlv .30	5	2⅞	3⅜	...
NwstNatLf .65	89	19½	20	...
NwstPbSv 1.70	15	19⅝	20⅛	− ⅛
NowstEngnr 1	2	13¾	14¾	+ ¼
NwstStsPtlC 1	2	16¾	17¾	− ¼
Nortrust 1.72	15	40¼	41	...
NoxellCorp .56	22	18	18½	...
Nuclear Dyna	39	8¼	8¾	− ⅛
Nucl Expl Dvl	13	3⅜	3⅞	+ ⅛
Nuclr Svc .02b	22	3⅞	4¼	+ ⅛
--O O--				
OakbrkCon .60	4	3¾	4¾	...
OccdntlLf .05b	6	3	3⅜	...
OceanDrill .20	110	25¼	26	− ¼
OceanDrill pf	20	53⅝	54⅝	− ⅛
OceanOil & Gs	1	16¾	17¼	...
Oceangltl .05d	82	7⅛	7⅝	...
Oceanic Explr	41	5	5⅜	...
OdysseyIn .12	6	4⅝	5	...
OffshorLog .28	45	13⅞	14⅜	− ¼
OgilvyMa 1.40	z81	31¼	32	...
Oh CasCp 1.48	50	45	46	− ½
Oh Ferro .80g	28	18½	19½	...
Oilgear Co 1	1	13	15	...
OldNtBcp .84g	11	29½	30¼	...
OldRep Intl 1k	16	22¾	23½	...
Old StoneCp 1	3	16⅛	17⅛	− ⅛
Old Stone Mtg	15	7½	8	+ ¼
OlympBrw .90	51	53¾	54¾	+ ¼
OmahaNat 1½	11	20	22	...
Opticl Coating	24	8½	9½	...

Stock & Div.	Sales 100s	Bid	Asked	Net Chg.
SourCp pf 2.40	13	26⅛	26⅝	− ¼
SoCarolIns .50	40	14	14½	...
So CarNatl .88	7	19½	20½	...
Sothrn Airwys	z50	3⅞	4¼	...
SthnBcpA 1.24	4	30¼	31¼	+ ¼
SoCal Wat 1.18	16	14¼	15	...
SoConnGs 2.20	10	26¼	27	+ ¼
SothrnInd 1.20	12	19¼	20	...
SthrnNtNC .80	z59	17½	18½	...
SoUnPrd .10d	241	40	40¾	− 1¼
SthlandFcl .32	143	11¼	11¾	− ⅛
Soland Pap .64	2	28	29	...
Sowst Factors	z50	1½	1⅞	...
Sowst·GasCp 1	90	11⅜	11¾	+ ⅛
Swstn EIS 1.28	2	16½	17¼	...
SowstnLife .72	96	19½	20	− ⅛
SovergCp .05b	14	4⅛	4½	...
Spectra Phys	136	11¾	12½	− ¼
SpectrlDy .06b	17	7⅛	7⅝	+ ⅛
Spectronic In	9	6½	7	− ⅛
Stanwick Corp	3	4	4½	− ⅛
StaRiteInd .70	30	15	15¾	...
StandyneInc 1	40	24½	25	− ⅜
Std LifeIns .26	1	12	12½	...
Std Microsyst	129	3⅞	4¼	...
Std Regist 1.20	30	18¼	19	...
Standun Incp	72	2⅜	2⅞	− ½
StnlyHmP 1.20	11	17½	18½	...
StaSt Bost 2.40	15	27½	28½	...
StatmGrp .15d	7	3⅞	4¼	...
Steak N Sh .44	9	13⅝	14⅛	...
Stewart Inf .70	z37	14¼	15	− ¼
StewrSndw .15	2	5¼	5¾	...
StewartStv .20	24	12⅜	12⅞	+ ⅛
Stratford ofTx	21	⅜	⅞	...
StrawbC 1.30g	11	26½	28	+ ½
SturmRugr .40	10	18½	20	...
Subar of Am	125	1¾	2⅛	− ¼
SubrBanc 1.20	3	18½	19	...
Sullair Corp	26	13⅛	13⅝	− ⅛
SummerC .32a	6	6½	7¼	...
Summit Engy	162	4⅞	5⅜	+ ⅜
SumitoB Cl .70	1	14	15	...
Summit Propr	21	3	4	...
SunBnkFla .60	104	9¾	10⅛	...

Securities exchanges and markets provide a valuable service to individuals and organizations that wish to buy and sell securities. A far greater benefit, however, is provided to society as a whole, because *the market system for trading in stocks and bonds increases financial investment opportunities available to individual and institutional investors.* This, in turn, expands the total capital resources available to finance economic investments. Capital formation is essential to everyone because it creates jobs; the auction process provides an efficient marketplace that facilitates the process of capital creation and investment. Perfectly free, honest, and liquid securities markets allow for intelligent financial investment decisions by individuals and institutions and provide feedback to financial managers on the effects of their management of the firm (economic investment decisions).

Regulation of Securities Markets A major factor in the efficiency of U.S. securities markets is the regulation of these markets by the federal government. Prior to the stock-market crash of 1929, there were no federal laws requiring that American corporations furnish financial information to their shareholders or to the general public. Although numerous state securities laws existed (Kansas was first in 1911), such laws in most cases were lax and ill-defined. As a result, widespread manipulation in securities trading and wholesale misrepresentation in financial statements abounded. Such questionable, even fraudulent, practices of brokers and corporations, coupled with the excessive speculation of the public, led to the passage of federal laws to strengthen the securities markets.

Major Legislation. The Securities Act of 1933 (the "truth-in-securities law") and the Securities Exchange Act of 1934 (the "exchanges regulation law") provide the basic regulations against fraudulent financial reporting and securities-market manipulation. These acts are discussed in detail in Chapter 22.

Specifically, the 1934 act created the Securities and Exchange Commission (SEC) to administer the federal securities laws. All stock exchanges, member broker firms, and all stocks traded on such exchanges are required to be registered with the SEC. The 1934 act, as amended by the Maloney Act in 1938, requires that associations of securities dealers also be registered with the SEC. As a result, the National Association of Securities Dealers (NASD), consisting of 8,000 broker-dealer members, is registered with the SEC.

There are four other major regulatory acts: (1) The *Public Utility Holding Company Act of 1935* regulates the operations and financial structure of electricity and gas holding companies. The purpose of the act was to free electricity and gas utility companies from the control and abuses of holding companies, and to give the SEC the power to regulate the sale and issuance of securities where the public interest is affected. (2) The *Trust Indenture Act of 1939* requires that corporate debt instruments be issued under an indenture (or contract) that specifies the obligations of the issuer to the lender and that specifies an independent trustee to protect the interests of the lenders. The purpose of this act is to protect the owners of corporate debt. (3) The *Investment Company Act of 1940* regulates the management and disclosure policies of companies that invest in the securities of other firms. The purpose is to protect those of the public who buy shares in closed-end and open-end management companies. (Closed-end companies sell shares and are structured similarly to industrial corporations. Open-end companies are commonly known as mutual funds.) (4) The *Investment Advisors Act of 1940* requires the registration of investment counselors and others who advise the public on investments in securities. All individuals or organizations who act as securities advisors for compensation, either directly or in writing, must register with, and submit semiannual reports to, the SEC. Certain individuals such as bankers, attorneys, teachers, and accountants are exempt from this act.

Margin Trading. There are two types of accounts in brokerage houses —the cash account and the margin account. Margin trading is defined as paying a portion of the transaction expense with cash and the remainder with money borrowed from the brokerage firm. The cash portion is called the margin. Cash accounts and the cash portion of a margin account are known as credit balances; the borrowed portion of margin accounts is called debit balances.

The principal reason for having a margin account is that you control more shares on margin than if you put up the entire transaction price in a cash account. However, before the stock-market crash of 1929, margin requirements were very low—10 percent and less—a fact that was related to much of the speculative excesses in the stock market of the 1920s.

The Securities Exchange Act of 1934 gave the Board of Governors of the Federal Reserve System the power to set initial margin requirements for all stocks and bonds. Regulation T of the Federal Reserve Board states that only securities listed on a major stock exchange (NYSE and ASE) or appearing on a margin-rule list of over-the-counter stocks (now 796 issues) qualify for margin trading. Under Regulation T, transactions in a margin account must provide a cash payment or initial margin equal to a specified percentage of the transaction price. The required percentage is changed periodically as part of the Federal Reserve System's regulation of credit in the economy. Since 1934, initial margin requirements have been allowed as low as 40 percent during the 1937–45 period and as high as 100 percent (no borrowing permitted) in 1946–47. In the first half of the 1970s, initial margin requirements ranged from 80 percent in 1970 to 50 percent effective January 3,

1974. At present (1977), initial margin requirements are 50 percent on margin stocks, 50 percent on convertible bonds, and 50 percent on short sales.*

Under separate margin requirements imposed by the New York Stock Exchange, a balance of $2,000 cash or its equivalent in securities is required to open a margin account. Additionally, a margin maintenance requirement is set by the exchange for both long and short positions.† For a long position, the exchange sets a margin maintenance requirement of 25 percent or $2 per share, whichever is greater in dollar value. For a short position, the exchange sets a margin maintenance requirement of 30 percent or $5 a share, whichever is greater in dollar value.‡ (Some house rules specify a higher margin maintenance requirement. For example, Merrill Lynch requires a 30 percent margin maintenance for long positions.)

Margin requirements are summarized in Table 14.5. The margin requirement that results in the most dollars must be paid to the broker at the time of purchase or short sale. At all times, the customer's margin can be calculated as follows:

$$\text{Percent margin} = \frac{\text{Customer's equity}}{\text{Market value of securities}}$$

where, for a long position, *Customer's equity* is equal to the market value of securities minus the broker's loan to the customer; and for a short position,

TABLE 14.5 Margin Requirements

| POSITION | INITIAL MARGIN REQUIRED | | | MAINTENANCE MARGIN REQUIRED BY NYSE |
	BY FED	BY NYSE		
Long	50%	$2,000	$2/share	If PPS > $2.50; $2.00/share or 25%, whichever is greater If PPS ≤ $2.50; 100% cash
Short	50%	$2,000	$5/share	If PPS ≥ $5.00; $5.00/share or 30%, whichever is greater If PPS < $5.00; $2.50/share or 100%, whichever is greater

*Largest of the three is required.

PPS = Price Per Share

---

*An exception in the Federal Reserve Board margin requirements applies to securities issued by the U.S. government, which can be purchased on 5% margin.

†The term long means that stocks are held in an account. The term short means that stocks which are not yet owned are sold in a margin account.

‡If a stock is long at $2.50 or less, 100% of market value, in cash, is required. If a stock is short at less than $5.00, the greater of $2.50/share or 100% of market value must be maintained.

Customer's equity is equal to the margin plus fictitious credit less the market value of the securities. Thus, if an investor buys 100 shares of McDonald's Corporation at $60 per share on 50 percent margin, and the stock drops to $50 per share, his equity, or percent margin, is now 40 percent ($2,000/$5,000). The formula can be used to determine how much the stock can drop before a margin maintenance call is received from the broker.*

In the case of the McDonald's Corporation long position:

$$\text{Percent margin maintenance required} = \frac{\text{Equity}}{\text{Market value}}$$

$$.25 = \frac{1,000}{4,000}$$

Thus, the stock must drop below $40 per share before the customer will be asked to put more margin in his account. If the price drops to $35 per share, the customer must answer a margin call of $375 or his position in the stock will be closed out by the broker. This is determined as follows:

$$\text{Margin call amount} = \text{Required equity} - \text{Actual equity}$$
$$= .25\ (\$3,500) - \$500$$
$$= \$375$$

Since the customer has $500 left in the account, he must make up the difference between $500 and $875. Thus, he sends $375 to the broker if the margin call is answered.

To illustrate the disastrous effects of the 10 percent initial margin rule in the 1920s, assume that a person paid $1,000 to buy $10,000 worth of securities. As the securities advance in price, the person can purchase more, based on his paper profits in the original investment of $10,000. Assuming paper profits of $1,000 (that is, the securities are now worth $11,000), the person uses this to buy an additional $9,000 worth of stocks. Now he has a $20,000 portfolio of securities on just the initial sum of $1,000. As stocks continue to advance in price, the person continues to add to his portfolio with his paper profits—$9 borrowed for every $1 of paper profits. Suppose further that the portfolio of securities reached $50,000 in value prior to the 1929 crash. His equity, or percent margin, is now 10 percent ($5,000/$50,000). This means that if stock prices fall just 10 percent, this person's equity is wiped out completely. This happened again and again in 1929 as investors were forced to sell their stocks when brokerage houses began to protect their

---

*Various formulas are shown in the appendix to this chapter for calculating the price at which a margin call, for both long and short positions, would be received from the broker.

loans to customers by liquidating their accounts. As more accounts were liquidated, stock prices deteriorated.

Short Selling. Another factor in price deterioration in the 1929 crash was the large amount of uncontrolled short selling. Prior to the crash, there were no rules for shorting stocks, which greatly aggravated the decline in stock prices during the crash.

A short sale occurs when a person sells shares that he does not own, anticipating a price decline in the near future, at which time he buys back ("covers") at the new and lower price. The newly purchased shares are then returned to the lender. Because the buyer in any transaction expects to receive a certificate for the shares he purchases, a short seller must deliver the shares even though he does not own them. This is accomplished for the individual investor through a broker who "borrows" the shares, usually from his own account or from shares he holds in margin accounts. The broker must ensure that the stock certificates can be borrowed at the time of the short sale for delivery (within five days) to the purchaser of the shares sold short. If the broker cannot borrow the shares, a short sale cannot be executed. In practice, short sales are made much more frequently by specialists (who have the responsibility for maintaining an orderly market) and dealers than by individual investors.

Long and Short Positions in Margin Accounts

Examples of long and short positions in a margin account follow. First, the long position.

Assume that you purchase 600 shares of Duke Power Corporation's common stock at $20 a share on 50 percent margin. This means that you must put up $6,000 and your broker will lend you the other $6,000. The total portfolio is worth $12,000 (600 shares × $20). Table 14.6 shows the effects of a $5-per-share increase and a $5-per-share decrease on the long position in Duke Power. If the price rises, the investor has a paper profit. If the price falls, the investor has a paper loss.

TABLE 14.6 Changes in Long Position in Duke Power Corporation (50% Initial Margin Requirement)

SHARES	×	PRICE PER SHARE	=	MARKET VALUE	MARGIN DIVIDED BY MARKET VALUE	=	PERCENT MARGIN	PROFIT (LOSS)
600		$20		$12,000	$6,000/$12,000		50	—
600		25		15,000	9,000/15,000		60	$3,000
600		15		9,000	3,000/9,000		33	(3,000)

A short position is a little more involved. Assume that instead of buying Duke Power (a long position), you sell short 600 shares at $20 per share (a short position) on 50 percent margin. You still must have $6,000 margin. However, there is no loan from the broker, because the proceeds from the sale of the securities will be a fictitious credit to your account. Now assume that the stock rises to $25 per share and then falls to $15 per share. The changes in your short positions are shown in Table 14.7. Notice that your absolute profit and loss are the same, although reversed, as in the long position. However, the percent margin is more volatile in a short position.

TABLE 14.7 Changes in Short Position in Duke Power Corporation (50% Initial Margin Requirement)

SHARES	×	PRICE PER SHARE	=	MARKET VALUE	MARGIN PLUS FICTITIOUS CREDIT	MARGIN DIVIDED BY MARKET VALUE	=	PERCENT MARGIN	PROFIT (LOSS)
600		$20		$12,000	18,000	6,000/ 12,000		50	—
600		25		15,000	18,000	3,000/ 15,000		20	$(3,000)
600		15		9,000	18,000	9,000/ 9,000		100	3,000

The Up-Tick Rule The Securities and Exchange Act of 1934 permitted rules for short selling to be written by the SEC. Several regulations now govern the practice of selling short. The most significant one is the "up-tick" requirement, which precludes a short sale while the price of a stock is declining. For example, if the last transacted price for a stock is $50, then $49\frac{1}{2}$, then $49, no short sale can be made until the stock advances in price. Thus, if the price rises to $49\frac{1}{4}$, a short sale can be executed.

The "up-tick" rule is designed to stabilize the market. One can short a stock only if its price is rising. This helps to curb the advance in the price of a stock. One cannot short a stock if its price is falling. Thus, selling is limited on the downside, which helps to cushion the fall in price. The ideal time to short a stock is at or near the top of a bull market.

Investment Procedures Placing orders to buy or sell securities is the climax of the investment process. To place such orders, an investor must do at least four things: *First,* select a securities firm. One should probably select a firm that is a member of the New York Stock Exchange. The reasons are that the exchange maintains strict standards over member firms, monitors customer practices of member firms, and has an emergency fund that protects the customers of a member firm that goes bankrupt. An additional consideration is that commission brokerage firms of the exchange are also members of the National Association of Securities Dealers, which also monitors the firm's activities and provides the customer access to the over-the-counter market.

Second, choose a registered representative or account executive of that firm to be responsible for handling your transactions. This is best accomplished by getting to know some of the representatives (or brokers) of a firm and deciding which one you believe will serve your needs best. Your broker is just as important to you as your lawyer or physician. A suggested method of choosing a broker is to inform him of the size and type of transactions you will be making, to see if the broker is interested. It all boils down to finding a person with whom you can communicate and enjoy doing business. Of course, the broker selected should give prompt and efficient service and be a person of high integrity.

Third, open an account with your broker. All that is necessary is to fill out a form, giving your occupation, a bank reference, and your investment goals (that is, current income, capital appreciation, or a combination of the two). There are two basic accounts: cash accounts and margin accounts. The simplest type of account is the cash account, which means you agree to purchase stocks for cash and pay for them within five business days of the transaction. If payment is not made within five business days and no extension of payment is requested, the firm is required by law to cancel the trade and restrict the account for 90 days. Trading in a restricted account can be done only if 100 percent cash is deposited before any stock is bought. With a cash account, custody of certificates can be with the investor or with the brokerage firm, depending on the preference of the investor.

The second type of account, the margin account, requires only a portion of the transaction to be paid in cash, while the remaining portion is borrowed from the broker. Short selling can be done only in a margin account. Only securities listed on a major stock exchange or on an approved margin list of over-the-counter stocks can be bought, or sold short, on margin. However, a security that is not approved for margin can be bought in a margin account if 100 percent of the purchase price is deposited in the margin account. (Some house rules permit only margin stocks to be traded in margin accounts.) Opening a margin account requires the signing of a "customers agreement and loan consent" card giving the securities firm the right to retain possession of the certificates, to use them as collateral for loans from banks, or to lend them to customers of the firm or other securities firms for short sales. The cash versus the margin account are contrasted in Table 14.8.

Last, place an order with your broker. Orders are of two basic types: "buy" orders and "sell" orders. Sell orders must be designated "sell long" or

TABLE 14.8 Cash vs. Margin Account

TYPE OF ACCOUNTS	POSITION ALLOWED	PHYSICAL LOCATION OF SECURITIES
Cash	Long position only[a]	Investor or broker[c]
Margin	Long or short position[b]	Broker[c]

[a]Can buy any security.
[b]Restricted to securities on NYSE, ASE, and 795 OTC stocks.
[c]Securities left with the broker are commonly referred to in a "Street Name"—*securities in bearer form.* (Broker cannot lend securities held in a cash account.)

"sell short." Basically, a buy order is entered when the investor has excess funds and/or he anticipates that the price of the stock will rise. Conversely, a sell order (long or short) is entered when the investor needs funds and/or he believes that the price of the stock will decline. Within the basic classification of buy and sell orders, a variety of order types is possible. The three main types of orders used in the auction market of the NYSE are market orders, limit orders, and stop orders.

The order that is simplest and most frequently placed with a broker is the *market order*. It is one to buy or sell a security at the best price available. If a market order is not filled during the day, it is canceled at the end of the trading session.

A *limit order* is one to buy or sell at a specific price or better; on the sell side, the specified price would be above the prevailing market price, and on the buy side, below the prevailing market price. The limit order has a stabilizing effect on the market, since limit buy orders cushion declining stock prices and limit sell orders restrain advancing stock prices.

A *stop order*, sometimes called a "stop-loss" order, specifies a price at which, if the market moves adversely, the customer desires an execution. If the order is on the sell side, it specifies a price below that prevailing; if on the buy side, a price above that prevailing—the reverse of the situation in limit orders. It does not, however, guarantee execution at the specified price, but merely becomes a market order if and when that price is reached. Stop orders tend to have a destabilizing effect on the market. For example, stop buy orders are used to limit the loss of investors who sold short a stock that is rising in price; and stop sell orders are used to limit the loss of investors who have taken a long position in a stock that is declining in price. Table 14.9 shows the relationship of the three orders.

TABLE 14.9 Impact on Market Stability of the Three Basic Types of Orders

MARKET ORDERS	LIMIT ORDERS		STOP ORDERS	
	↓		↑	
	Limit sell orders	49 48	Stop buy orders	49 48
Ask 44¼				
	44–44¼		44–44¼	
Bid 44				
	Limit buy orders	43 42	Stop sell orders	43 42
	↑		↓	
MARKET ORDERS	LIMIT ORDERS		STOP ORDERS	

INVESTMENT VS. SPECULATION

At one time (prior to 1930), common-stock investments were considered very speculative—so speculative, in fact, that endowment portfolios of colleges and universities consisted solely of municipal, rail, and industrial bonds. In 1932, Herbert Hoover, a trustee of Stanford University, prevailed upon the university's board of trustees to change from the bonds-only policy and buy common stock. Today, the largest dollar amount of securities in all college endowment portfolios is in common stocks.

The investment process is usually oriented to long-term analysis and less risky securities investments that yield a satisfactory rate of return consistent with risk. For example, a commitment of funds to high-grade bonds or stocks is viewed as an investment. *Investment is buying securities subject to relatively little risk.*

Speculation is usually thought of as short-term trading for higher profits in the form of price appreciation. A preference for higher profits or yields results in a greater assumption of risk. Greater rewards and greater risks go hand in hand. Thus, *speculation is the taking of large risks in the hope of large returns.* The speculator is primarily interested in short-term price movements. For example, a commitment of funds to securities options is considered very speculative, because the speculator is risking everything in the hope of a very large profit.

The investor also attempts to maximize his return consistent with risk, but is not ready to accept a great deal of risk. Since his risk preference is lower, he must accept lower returns than those obtainable through speculation. The primary difference between an investment and a speculation is the intent of the buyer. For example, a person may buy IBM stock with the intention of holding it for several years. This is considered an investment. The speculator may buy IBM stock if he believes the market price will increase substantially within a short period of time.

SUMMARY

The financial investment function allows savings to be allocated to various assets. For the use of those funds, the investor expects a return in the form of dividends, interest, capital appreciation, or some combination of the three. By this process, both the suppliers of funds (investors) and the demanders of funds (government and industry) benefit.

In the investment process, individuals and institutions obtain and analyze information about various investment opportunities for the purpose of making decisions to buy, sell, or hold individual assets with respect to a portfolio of assets.

There are two basic types of investment accounts—the cash account and the margin account. In the cash account, all purchases are paid in cash. In the margin account, the customer advances a portion of the purchase in cash (the margin) and the broker lends the remaining portion (the debit balance).

Since no single investment security is free from all risks, a commitment of funds into any type of security presents some danger. Margin trading increases the risk as well as the chance for large returns. This is true because margin trading is simply a use of leverage. Of course, with the chance for large returns goes the chance of large losses. However, some securities are more risky than others, as we shall see in the next chapter.

APPENDIX TO CHAPTER 14: MARGIN CALCULATIONS

The term *margin* refers to the amount of *cash* a customer deposits with his broker when purchasing securities on credit. Sometimes, "margin" is used to refer to the ratio between the net amount of the portfolio (customer's equity) and the market value of the portfolio. Equity is calculated by subtracting the broker's loan (debit balance*) from the market value of the portfolio. Margin calculations are shown below for both long and short position.

Long Position The formulas for customer's equity and percent margin for long positions are:

$$\text{Customer's equity} = \text{Market value} - \text{Debit balance} \tag{10}$$

$$\text{Percent margin} = \frac{\text{Market value of securities} - \text{Debit balance}}{\text{Market value of securities}}$$

$$= \frac{\text{Customer's equity}}{\text{Market value of securities}} \tag{10a}$$

where, for a long position, *Customer's equity* is equal to the market value of the securities minus the broker's loan to the customer. For example, an investor has in a margin account 100 shares of McDonald's Corporation common stock whose market price is $60 per share. If the debit balance (loan from the broker) is $3,000, the equity is:

$$\text{Customer's equity} = \$60(100) - \$3,000 = \$6,000 - \$3,000 = \$3,000$$

The margin in the account is:

$$\text{Percent margin} = \frac{\$3,000}{\$6,000} = .50$$

The price below which a margin call would be received from the broker is determined by:

$$\text{Margin call price} = \text{Purchase price} \left(\frac{1 - \text{Initial margin}}{1 - \text{Maintenance margin}} \right)$$

For example, if the initial margin is 50 percent, margin maintenance is 25 percent, and purchase price is $60 per share, a margin call can be expected if McDonald's common-stock price fell below $40. The calculation is as follows:

$$\text{Margin call price} = \$60 \left(\frac{1 - .50}{1 - .25} \right) = \$60 \left(\frac{.5}{.75} \right) = \$40$$

Thus, a margin call (call for more equity) will be issued if the price of the stock drops below $40 per share.

---

*The debit balance is the amount of the customer's loan on the books of the broker. Interest charges are made based on the debit balance.

Short Position Since short positions are considered more risky than long positions, the margin maintenance requirement for short sales is higher.* Thus, when the customer's equity drops below 30 percent of market value of the securities, the short seller can expect a margin call. For a short sale, margin can be calculated by the formula:

$$\text{Customer's equity} = \frac{\text{Initial}}{\text{margin}} - \left(\frac{\text{Market value}}{\text{of securities}} - \frac{\text{Initial value}}{\text{of securities}}\right)$$

$$\text{Percent margin} = \frac{\dfrac{\text{Initial}}{\text{margin}} - \left(\dfrac{\text{Market value}}{\text{of securities}} - \dfrac{\text{Initial value}}{\text{of securities}}\right)}{\text{Market value of securities}}$$

$$= \frac{\text{Customer's equity}}{\text{Market value of securities}}$$

For example, an investor sold short 100 shares of a stock at $100 per share. If the initial margin requirement was 50 percent and the current price is $110 per share, the investor's current margin would be:

$$\text{Percent margin} = \frac{.5\ (\$10,000) - (\$11,000 - \$10,000)}{\$11,000}$$

$$= \frac{\$5,000 - \$1,000}{\$11,000}$$

$$= .36$$

The security price above which a margin call would occur is calculated as follows:

$$\text{Margin call price} = \text{Selling price}\left(\frac{1 + \text{Initial margin}}{1 + \text{Margin maintenance}}\right)$$

Thus, for stock sold short at $100 per share with a 50 percent initial margin and a 30 percent maintenance margin, a margin call would occur at a price above $115.38. The calculation is:

$$\text{Margin call price} = \$100\left(\frac{1 + .50}{1 + .30}\right)$$

$$= \$100(1.1538)$$

$$= \$115.38$$

If the initial margin requirement stems from either the $2,000 minimum or $5 per share, the proceeds involved (margin plus fictitious credit) and margin call price are calculated as follows:

---

*Since the broker does not actually loan any money in a short sale, no interest charges are incurred.

SHORT POSITION			PROCEEDS INVOLVED		STATUS OF ACCOUNT BASED ON MARKET FLUCTUATIONS
NUMBER OF SHARES	× PRICE PER SHARE	= MARKET VALUE	MARGIN +	FICTITIOUS CREDIT	EQUITY/MARKET VALUE
1,000	$ 8	$ 8,000	$5,000	$8,000	$5,000/$8,000
1,000	10	10,000	5,000	8,000	3,000/10,000
1,000	11	11,000	5,000	8,000	2,000/11,000

If the price rises from $8 to $10 per share, no margin call is issued because Equity/Market Value $\geq 30\%$ ($3,000/$10,000 = .30). However, a margin call is issued if price rises to $11 per share because Equity/Market Value must at least equal 30%. (Equity/$11,000 = .30, so Equity required is $3,300.) Since the equity has fallen to $2,000, a margin call of $1,300 is issued (Required Equity − Actual Equity = Margin Call or $3,300 − $2,000 = $1,300).

The initial margin quoted above is established by the Board of Governors of the Federal Reserve System. The minimum maintenance margin is determined by the New York Stock Exchange. The house rules of the individual brokerage firm may require a maintenance margin higher than the NYSE minimum.

PROBLEMS

1. The following rates of return on the securities of a retailing company and a gold mining company are projected for the four states of the business cycle listed below. Each state is given an equal chance of occurrence.

RATE OF RETURN

STATE OF BUSINESS CYCLE	RETAILER	GOLD MINER
Prosperity	18%	27%
Recession	11	5
Depression	−7	34
Recovery	14	−20

Calculate the following from the data given for each security:

  a. Expected return

  b. Variance

    c. Standard deviation

    d. Coefficient of variation

2. From the financial press (i.e., *Wall Street Journal, Barron's, Moody's* etc.) determine the high and low price per share along with the dividend yield for International Business Machines and American Telephone and Telegraph for the years 1970 through 1977.

    a. Calculate holding period returns for IBM and AT&T.

    b. Which stock would you expect to be more risky? Why?

    c. Calculate the expected return, variance, standard deviation, and coefficient of variation for each stock for the 1971–77 period.

    d. What observations can be made about the returns of IBM and AT&T in the year 1978?

3. How much initial margin (amount of cash from customer) is required for the following single transactions in a new margin account:

    a. The purchase of 100 shares of Holiday Inn at $12 per share.

    b. The purchase of 2,000 shares of Ramada Inn at $3.50 per share.

    c. A short sale of 100 shares of GM at $75 per share.

    d. The purchase of 10 shares of IBM at $280 per share.

    e. A short sale of 1,000 shares of Playboy at $8 per share.

    f. The purchase of 10,000 shares of Ramada Inn at $5 per share.

4. You sell short 500 shares of Polaroid at $40 per share. Assuming a 50 percent initial margin requirement, indicate the following:

    a. Amount of customer equity.

    b. Amount of broker loan. *no loan*

    c. Total credit in your account.

    d. Margin call price.

    e. Margin call amount if price of stock rises to $50 per share.

5. Of the various types of orders that can be placed:

    a. Which order is most certain to be completed?

    b. Which order stabilizes the market?

    c. Which order destabilizes the market? *stock*

    d. Which order protects your gain?

    e. Which order cuts your losses?

6. You have a long position of 100 shares each in the common stock of:

YOUR COST PER SHARE
IN 1977

Coca-Cola Company	$36
McDonald's Corporation	37
Intel Corporation	38

You have a short position of 100 shares each in the common stock of:

SHORTED IN 1977 AT

General Motors	$78
UAL	29

a. Determine your positions in the stocks based on current market quotations from the *Wall Street Journal*.

b. Indicate paper profits and losses.

c. What is your equity in the account if all positions taken in 1977 were on 50% margin?

d. What is your overall profit (or loss)?

7. From the financial press determine the high and low price as well as dividend yield for The Dow Jones Industrial Average (DJIA) for the years 1970 through 1977.

a. Calculate the holding period returns.

b. Calculate the expected return, variance, and a standard deviation of returns for the 1971–77 period.

c. How does the return and standard deviation of returns on the DJIA compare with the returns on:

1. IBM (problem 2)

2. AT&T (problem 2)

3. Treasury bills

d. Where should one have invested his or her extra funds during the 1971–77 period?

15

Investment Securities: Government and Municipal Bonds

> *The first public government loan was made on January 20, 1693, and subscriptions were taken by brokers.*
>
> *Bradley D. Nash*, Investment Banking in England, *1924*

This and the next two chapters deal with investment securities. This chapter begins with the spectrum of investment securities on the risk–return curve. Then government and municipal bonds as financial investments are examined.

THE SPECTRUM OF INVESTMENT SECURITIES

Risks Involved   The spectrum of investment securities ranges from short-term securities that possess very little risk to ownership securities in highly speculative ventures. Risks taken in making investments are many and vary according to the specific type of security. However, the risks of investment can be grouped into two types—the credit risk and the market risk.

Credit risk is the risk of repayment. Implicit in this risk is the business risk—a shrinkage in earning power and capacity to pay. U.S. government securities, for example, have little or no credit risk because of the ability of the United States to create money.

Market risk is the risk of loss caused by changes in the market price of a security owing to conditions in money and capital markets. Implicit in this risk is the interest-rate risk. This risk applies to both stocks and bonds. When interest rates are expected to rise, the prices of bonds, and subsequently common stocks, tend to fall. When interest rates are expected to fall, first the prices of bonds and subsequently those of common stocks begin to firm and rise.

FIGURE 15.1   Risk–Return Tradeoff (Marketable Securities).

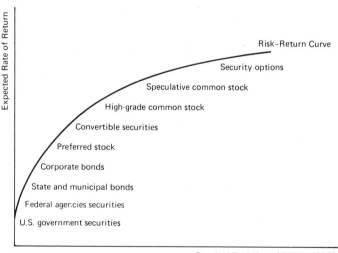

Since investors as a group are averse to risk, the higher the risk of a security, the higher the required rate of return. This tradeoff between risk and return is shown in Figure 15.1. Notice that as we accept more risk, we receive a greater potential return. However, the return does not increase in direct proportion to the risk.

Securities Involved The framework for discussion in this chapter is the risk–return curve. Thus, we begin with the least risky and least rewarding securities and proceed along the curve to those securities possessing the greatest degree of risk and the greatest potential reward. Notice that the risk–return curve *is* the spectrum of financial investment securities.

Both public and private organizations obtain financial backing by issuing securities that are bought and traded by individual and institutional investors. Public securities range from U.S. government bonds to federal-agency bonds to state and municipal bonds.* Private securities range from high-grade corporate bonds to preferred stocks to common stocks. Public securities are considered first because they are located on the lower segment of the risk-return curve.

U.S. GOVERNMENT SECURITIES

The major growth of the United States government debt occurred during World War II. Prior to the war, the debt was only $55 billion. At the end of the war, it had reached $280 billion. Since then, the growth has been more moderate. Yet the trend has been largely upward. The rise in the debt has necessitated a series of increases in the statutory public-debt limit of the United States. The 1976 limit was over $680 billion, and the actual debt was within a few hundred million dollars of the temporary debt ceiling.

Although long-term debt was used extensively during the war, the Treasury has been compelled to rely heavily on issues of five-year or shorter maturity since the late 1950s. Consequently, the average length of publicly held marketable U.S. debt has shortened to less than three years. This is depicted in Figure 15.2. The average length of publicly held nonmarketable U.S. debt is about five years. Total outstanding public debt by type of security is shown in Table 15.1.

---

*All direct domestic obligations of federal, state, and municipal governments in the United States are debentures. That is, they are unsecured bonds protected only by the general promise to pay. In event of default, the debenture holder is merely a general creditor.

FIGURE 15.2 Average Length of the Marketable Debt Privately Held by the Public. (*Source: U.S. Treasury.*)

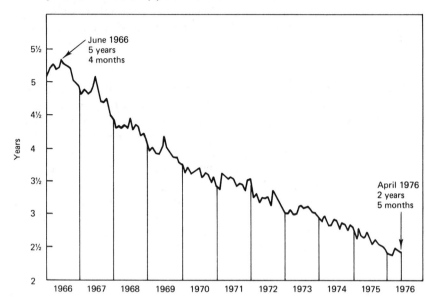

TABLE 15.1 Public Debt of the United States

ISSUE	RATE OF INTEREST (PERCENT)	AMOUNT OUTSTANDING JANUARY 31, 1977 (IN BILLIONS OF DOLLARS)
Treasury bills	Various	161.9
Treasury notes	$1\frac{1}{2}$–$8\frac{3}{8}$	221.0
Treasury bonds	$3\frac{1}{4}$–7	40.7
Total marketable issues		423.6
U.S. Savings bonds:		
Series E	3.66–6.00	66.0
Series H	3.82–6.00	6.6
Certificates and notes:		
Foreign series	6.95–8.40	21.0
Foreign currency series	2.50–8.10	1.5
Other issues		2.3
Total nonmarketable issues		97.4
Total public issues		521.0
Special issues[a]		126.7
Total interest-bearing debt		647.7

[a]Held by U.S. government agencies and trust funds and the federal home loan banks.

Source: Federal Reserve Bulletin.

Marketable Collectively, marketable U.S. government securities are called "govern-
Government Securities ments." These securities are traded freely in the market and are backed
by the full faith and credit of the United States. Marketable securities
include Treasury bills, Treasury notes, and Treasury bonds.

Treasury Bills. Treasury bills are marketable short-term obligations
that provide the Treasury of the United States government with a ready means
of short-term borrowing. Thirteen- and 26-week bills dated on Thursday are
auctioned weekly, usually on the preceding Monday; 52-week bills are auctioned every four weeks, usually on Tuesdays. The bills are issued at discount
in denominations of $10,000 and up. (The $1,000 and $5,000 denominations
previously available were discontinued in March 1970, owing to problems
caused by the increase in the number of small orders.) Bills are in bearer form
only, without stipulated interest.

Treasury bills are money-market instruments. They are purchased by
domestic and foreign investors who desire short-term securities that are highly
marketable and "liquid." Although yields are relatively low, the bills are
considered riskless investments because of the ability and willingness of the
U.S. government to pay. The Federal Reserve System uses Treasury bills
much more frequently than it does any other instrument in its open-market
operations. Sales and purchases are made by the Federal Reserve through
government-security dealers. Individuals buy and sell the bills through commercial banks and other financial institutions that buy and sell "governments."

Income derived from Treasury bills, which are excluded from consideration as capital assets by the Internal Revenue Code, is subject to all federal
taxes. Figure 15.3 shows the quotations of Treasury bills in the "Government
Securities" section of the *Wall Street Journal*. Treasury bills carry no coupon
or interest payment. Instead, they are issued at a discount of par. Because of
this, Treasury bills are quoted on a bank-discount basis. For example, the
price of a 90-day Treasury bill quoted at 8 percent is determined as follows:

$$\text{Quotation Price} = \text{Par} - Y\left(\frac{M}{360}\right)$$
$$= 100 - 8\left(\frac{90}{360}\right)$$
$$= 98$$

where:

$Y =$ quoted yield

$M =$ days to maturity

The answer, 98, means 98 percent of $1,000. Thus, the bill sells for $980.

FIGURE 15.3 U.S. Treasury Bills Quotations. (*Source: Wall Street Journal, February 4, 1977, p. 26.*)

Government, Agency and Miscellaneous Securities

U.S. Treas. Bills					
Mat	Bid	Ask	Mat	Bid	Ask
	Discount			Discount	
2- 8	4.64	4.38	5-31	4.86	4.74
2-10	4.63	4.38	6- 2	4.86	4.76
2-17	4.62	4.38	6- 9	4.88	4.78
2-24	4.62	4.38	6-16	4.90	4.80
3- 3	4.60	4.38	6-23	4.93	4.83
3- 8	4.59	4.39	6-28	4.95	4.83
3-10	4.58	4.38	6-30	4.96	4.86
3-17	4.59	4.39	7- 7	4.98	4.88
3-24	4.59	4.37	7-14	5.01	4.91
3-31	4.60	4.42	7-21	5.02	4.94
4- 5	4.68	4.54	7-26	5.04	4.94
4- 7	4.67	4.53	7-28	5.03	4.95
4-14	4.68	4.56	8- 4	5.01	4.97
4-21	4.72	4.62	8-23	5.11	4.99
4-28	4.74	4.66	9-20	5.16	5.06
5- 3	4.77	4.67	10-18	5.22	5.12
5- 5	4.73	4.69	11-15	5.24	5.14
5-12-	4.79	4.69	12-13	5.28	5.18
5-19-	4.80	4.70	1-10	5.29	5.21
5-26	4.83	4.73			

Refer to the bill at the arrow in Figure 15.3. There you see a Treasury bill maturing "3-3" (March 3, 28 days after this list was published) and quoted at a discount of 4.38. To determine the investor's purchase price of the bill, use the formula:

$$\text{Quotation Price} = 100 - Y\left(\frac{M}{360}\right)$$

$$= 100 - 4.38\left(\frac{28}{360}\right)$$

$$= 99.659$$

The answer, 99.659, means 99.659 percent of $1,000 (maturity value of the Treasury bill). Thus, the dealer sells the bill to the investor for $996.59.

The investor's selling price for the same Treasury bill is the bid of 4.60. Using the formula above, the dealer buys the bill from the investor for 99.616, or $996.16. Note that the bid price is less than the asked price. This is explained more fully in Chapter 20.

Coupon Issues. Certificates, notes, and bonds may be offered to the public for cash subscription or in exchange for outstanding or maturing securities.* Treasury notes are issued with a maturity of not less than one year

---

*A security that the Treasury occasionally resorts to is the certificate of indebtedness with a maturity not exceeding one year. Such securities have not been issued since 1966.

nor more than seven years. The securities trade in the market, responding to changes in interest rates. Yields are generally higher than those for Treasury bills. Notes are owned principally by the Federal Reserve System and commercial banks.

Treasury bonds may be issued with any maturity, but they generally have an original maturity in excess of seven years. There was a time when long-term Treasury bonds were the prime borrowing power of the U.S. government. However, the Treasury has financed its operations recently by notes and bills, because of a 6 percent maximum interest rate on bonds that was imposed by Congress. Treasury bonds appeal to both individual and institutional investors that desire to minimize risks.

Quotations for certificates, notes, and bonds are in the "Government Securities" section of the *Wall Street Journal,* as presented in Figure 15.4.

FIGURE 15.4 U.S. Government Bonds and Notes Quotations. (*Source: Wall Street Journal, February 4, 1977, p. 26.*)

Government, Agency and Miscellaneous Securities

Thursday, February 3, 1977
Over-the-Counter Quotations: Source on request.
Decimals in bid-and-asked and bid changes represent 32nds 101.1 means 101 1-32. a-Plus 1-64. b-Yield to call date. d-Minus 1-64.

Treasury Bonds and Notes

Rate	Mat.	Date	Bid	Asked	Bid Chg.	Yld.
8s,	1977	Feb n	100.2	100.4	.....	2.16
6s,	1977	Feb n	100.1	100.5	.....	3.22
6 1/2s,	1977	Mar n	100.6	100.10	.....	4.20
7 3/8s,	1977	Apr n	100.15	100.19	.....	4.63
6 7/8s,	1977	May n	100.14	100.18	.....	4.67
9s,	1977	May n	101.1	101.5	.....	4.54
6 3/4s,	1977	May n	100.15	100.19	.....	4.75
6 1/2s,	1977	Jun n	100.15	100.19	.....	4.93
7 1/2s,	1977	Jul n	101.2	101.6	.....	4.96
7 3/4s,	1977	Aug n	101.7	101.11	.....	5.11
8 1/4s,	1977	Aug n	101.18	101.22	+ .1	5.15
8 3/8s,	1977	Sep n	101.26	102.30	.....	5.28
7 1/2s,	1977	Oct n	101.12	101.16	− .1	5.40
7 3/4s,	1977	Nov n	101.20	101.24	− .1	5.40
6 5/8s,	1977	Nov n	100.24	100.28	− .1	5.50
7 1/4s,	1977	Dec n	101.11	101.15	.....	5.54
6 3/8s,	1978	Jan n	100.19	100.23	+ .1	5.61
6 1/4s,	1978	Feb n	100.16	100.20	.....	5.62
8s,	1978	Feb n	102.8	102.12	.....	5.66
6 3/4s,	1978	Mar n	100.30	101.2	.....	5.78
6 1/2s,	1978	Apr n	100.20	100.24	.....	5.85
7 1/8s,	1978	May n	101.12	101.16	+ .1	5.88
7 7/8s,	1978	May n	102.8	102.12	.....	5.92
7 1/8s,	1978	May n	101.12	101.16	.....	5.91
6 7/8s,	1978	Jun n	101.2	101.6	+ .1	5.98
6 7/8s,	1978	Jul n	101.3	101.7	+ .1	6.00
7 5/8s,	1978	Aug n	101.3	101.7	+1.27	6.08
8 3/4s,	1978	Aug n	103.22	103.26	+ .2	6.09
6 5/8s,	1978	Aug n	100.23	100.27	+ .3	6.05
6 1/4s,	1978	Sep n	100.4	100.8	+ .2	6.09
5 7/8s,	1978	Oct n	99.16	99.20	+ .3	6.10
6s,	1978	Nov n	99.22	99.26	+ .3	6.11
5 3/4s,	1978	Nov n	99.7	99.9	+ .2	6.13
5 1/4s,	1978	Dec n	98.10	98.12	+ .3	6.17
8 1/8s,	1978	Dec n	103.11	103.15	+ .3	6.16
5 7/8s,	1979	Jan n	99.12	99.14	.....	6.19
7s.	1979	Feb n	102.30	103.6	+1.21	6.34
7 7/8s,	1979	May n	102.30	103.6	.....	6.35
7 3/4s,	1979	Jun n	102.28	103.4	+ .3	6.33
6 1/4s,	1979	Aug n	99.18	99.26	+ .4	6.33
6 7/8s,	1979	Aug n	100.29	101.5	+ .5	6.30
8 1/2s,	1979	Sep n	104.20	104.28	+ .5	6.47
6 1/4s,	1979	Nov n	99.10	99.14	+ .5	6.48
6 5/8s,	1979	Nov n	100.3	100.11	+ .5	6.49
7s,	1979	Nov n	101.2	101.10	+ .4	6.48
7 1/2s,	1979	Dec n	102.12	102.20	+ .6	6.50
4s,	1980	Feb	93.2	93.18	+ .6	6.37
7 1/2s,	1980	Mar n	102.12	102.20	+ .6	6.56
6 7/8s,	1980	May n	100.18	100.26	+ .6	6.60
7 5/8s,	1980	Jun n	102.24	103	+ .12	6.63
9s,	1980	Aug n	106.22	106.30	+ .4	6.75
6 7/8s,	1980	Sep n	100.11	100.19	+ .10	6.69
3 1/2s,	1980	Nov	89.26	90.26	+ .4	6.27
5 7/8s,	1980	Dec n	96.28	97	+ .7	6.76
7s,	1981	Feb n	100.12	100.20	+ .14	6.84
7 3/8s,	1981	Feb n	101.20	101.28	+ .13	6.83
7 3/8s,	1981	May n	101.19	101.27	+ .13	6.88
7 5/8s,	1981	Aug n	102.18	102.26	+ .13	6.89
7s,	1981	Aug	100.3	100.11	+ .1	6.91
7s,	1981	Nov n	100.3	100.11	+ .11	6.91
7 3/4s,	1981	Nov n	102.30	103.6	+ .10	6.99
6 1/8s,	1982	Feb n	96.20	96.22	+ .13	6.93
6 3/8s,	1982	Feb	97.24	98.8	+ .6	6.77
8s,	1982	May n	104.6	104.14	+ .12	6.98
8 1/8s,	1982	Aug n	104.24	105	+ .11	7.03
7 7/8s,	1982	Nov n	103.23	103.31	+ .11	7.03
8s,	1983	Feb n	104.6	104.14	+ .15	7.09
3 1/4s,	1978-83	Jun	81	82	+ .22	6.78
7s,	1983	Nov n	99.2	99.6	+ .10	7.16
6 3/8s,	1984	Aug	96.22	97.22	− .2	6.77
3 1/4s,	1985	May	77	78	+ .26	6.77
4 1/4s,	1975-85	May	82.8	83.8	+ 1	6.95
7 7/8s,	1986	May n	102.26	103.2	+ .6	7.41
8s,	1986	Aug n	103.25	103.29	+ .5	7.42
6 1/8s,	1986	Nov	95.4	96.4	+ .8	6.67
3 1/2s,	1990	Feb	70.16	71.16	+ .6	6.84
8 1/4s,	1990	May	105.28	106.12	+ .10	7.48
4 1/4s,	1987-92	Aug	72.24	73.24	+1.8	7.06
4s,	1988-93	Feb	72	73	+ .18	6.79
6 3/4s,	1993	Feb	94.22	95.22	+ .12	7.21
7 1/2s,	1988-93	Aug	99.24	100.24	+ .10	7.40
4 1/8s,	1989-94	May	71.20	72.20	+ .20	6.85
3s,	1995	Feb	70	71	.....	5.57
7s,	1993-98	May	96.28	97.28	+ .22	7.20
3 1/2s,	1998	Nov	70.8	71.8	− .2	5.85
8 1/2s,	1994-99	May	106.28	107.12	+ .16	7.72
7 7/8s,	1995-00	Feb	101.14	101.22	+ .14	7.70
8 3/8s,	1995-00	Aug	105.30	106.14	+ .16	7.72
8s,	1996-01	Aug	102.18	102.26	+ .12	7.72
8 1/4s,	2000-05	May	105.2	105.18	+ .14	7.73

n– Treasury notes.

These securities are quoted in terms of a percentage of par (usually $1,000). The decimal portion is read in thirty-seconds. For example, a U.S. government bond of 4 percent yield that matures February 1980 (see arrow in Figure 15.4) is quoted at 93.18. The actual price of the bond is figured by one of two methods.

The first method is perhaps the purer of the two, since bonds are in $1,000 denominations. The quoted price of 93.18 is a percentage of $1,000, as follows:

$$\text{Price} = 93\%(\$1{,}000) + \frac{18}{32} \text{ of } 1\%(\$1{,}000)$$
$$= 930 + \$5.625$$
$$= \$935.625$$

Method 2 reverses the procedure. It views the bond as quoted in terms of 1,000 percent:

$$\text{Price} = \$93(1{,}000\%) + \frac{18}{32}(1{,}000\%)$$
$$= \$930 + \$5.625$$
$$= \$935.625$$

Use whichever method appeals to you. Either will give the correct current market price of the bond.

"Flower" Bonds. Income from certificates, notes, and bonds is subject to all federal income taxes. However, there are several U.S. government bonds known as "flower" bonds. The advantage of such Treasury issues is for redemption to pay federal estate taxes. Two main advantages are that (1) payment of capital gains taxes, if any, on the bond is not required, and (2) "flower" bonds bought at a discount can be used at par in the payment of estate taxes. Thus, if the bond was bought at 75 ($750) today and death occurs tomorrow, the bond will be accepted at 100 ($1000) for payment of estate taxes. Since bonds with this provision were last issued in March 1971, the supply is decreasing as bonds are used to pay estate taxes.

Nonmarketable Government Securities Nonmarketable government securities are an important source of financing for the U.S. Treasury. But these securities are not considered investment-type securities, because of their nonmarketability. The largest portion of nonmarketable securities are U.S. savings bonds.

U.S. savings bonds are designed to provide a savings medium for small investors at relatively attractive yields with protection against market fluctuations. There are two series of savings bonds. Series E bonds are sold at a discount (75 percent of face value) in denominations of from $25 to $100,000. If they are held to maturity, five years, the return is 6 percent per annum. The yield is less in case of redemptions prior to maturity. The Series H bonds are similar to Treasury bonds. They are issued and redeemable at par, with interest paid by check semiannually. They sell in denominations of $500 to $10,000 and provide a 6 percent return if held for ten years.

Other nonmarketable (that is, nonsalable) government securities consist mainly of notes or certificates issued to foreign governments and central banks in exchange for surplus dollars.

Securities of Government-Sponsored Enterprises and Federal Agencies   The volume of securities that are not direct obligations of the Treasury, but which in one way or another involve federal sponsorship or guarantee (collectively known as "agencies"), has increased substantially in the past few years. The increased supply has been absorbed readily by the investing public even though the quality of agency securities is slightly lower than that of the direct obligations of the U.S. Treasury. This means, however, that the return is usually higher, and the risk is usually greater, than for U.S. government securities. The outstanding securities of government agencies and sponsored corporations are shown in Table 15.2. Quotations of these securities are listed in the "Government Securities" section of the *Wall Street Journal*, as shown in Figure 15.5. These quotations are also a percentage of $1,000 plus thirty-seconds of 1 percent of $1,000.

TABLE 15.2 Outstanding Securities of Government Agencies and Sponsored Corporations

GOVERNMENT AGENCIES AND SPONSORED CORPORATIONS	AMOUNT OUTSTANDING JANUARY 31, 1977 (IN BILLIONS OF DOLLARS)
Government agencies:	
Export-Import Bank of U.S.	2.2 (est.)
Federal Financing Bank[a]	No issues yet
Federal Housing Administration	.5 (est.)
Government Nat'l Mortgage Assoc.	5.0 (est.)
Tennessee Valley Authority	3.0 (est.)
Government-sponsored enterprises:	
Banks for Cooperatives	4.1
Farmers Home Administration	6.0 (est.)
Federal Home Loan Banks	17.1
Federal Intermediate Credit Banks	10.6
Federal Land Banks	17.2
Federal National Mortgage Assoc.	30.6
Total outstanding securities	96.3

[a]Enacted into law in late 1973 to consolidate the financing of a variety of federal agencies and other borrowers whose obligations are guaranteed by the federal government.

Source: Federal Reserve Bulletin.

FIGURE 15.5 Government-Agency Quotations. (*Source: Wall Street Journal, February 4, 1977.*)

Government, Agency and Miscellaneous Securities

Thursday, February 3, 1977
Over-the-Counter Quotations: Source on request.
Decimals in bid-and-asked and bid changes represent 32nds 101.1 means 101 1-32. a-Plus 1-64. b-Yield to call date. d-Minus 1-64.

Fed. Home Loan Bank

Rate	Mat	Bid	Asked	Yld
7.20	2-77	100.1	100.5	3.94
8.05	2-77	100.3	100.7	3.54
6.95	5-77	100.12	100.20	4.77
7.38	11-83	100.4	100.20	7.25
7.75	5-84	101.12	101.28	7.41
8.75	5-84	106.24	107.24	7.36
7.85	8-84	101.28	102.12	7.43
7.38	11-84	99.16	99.24	7.41
8.10	11-85	102.28	103.12	7.56
7.38	11-93	95.16	96.16	7.75

World Bank Bonds

Rate	Mat	Bid	Asked	Yld
6.40	3-77	99.24	100.4	4.97
8.40	9-77	101.4	101.20	5.58
7.00	3-78	100.4	100.20	6.39
4.25	5-78	96.16	97.8	6.61
6.88	9-78	100	100.16	6.53
4.25	1-79	95.8	96	6.48
8.00	1-80	101.28	102.12	7.07
8.30	7-80	102.20	103.4	7.25
4.75	11-80	92.24	93.16	6.75
8.35	12-80	102.28	103.12	7.32
8.00	7-81	101.28	102.12	7.36
3.25	10-81	95.16	96.16	4.08
4.50	2-82	88.16	89.8	7.10
8.15	1-85	101.16	102	7.80
5.00	2-85	85.8	86	7.34
8.60	7-85	103.20	104.4	7.92
8.85	12-85	105	105.16	7.97
8.38	7-86	102.16	103	7.91
7.80	12-86	99.8	99.24	7.83
4.50	2-90	73	73.24	7.74
5.38	7-91	78.16	79.8	7.80
5.38	4-92	78	78.24	7.79
5.88	9-93	80.16	81.16	7.90
6.50	3-94	85.16	86.8	7.99
6.38	10-94	84.8	85	7.97
8.63	8-95	101.16	102.8	8.38
8.13	8-96	98.16	99	8.23
9.35	12-00	107.8	107.24	8.58
8.85	7-01	103.8	104	8.46
8.38	12-01	99.16	100	8.37

Bank for Co-ops

Rate	Mat	Bid	Asked	Yld
5.65	3-77	100	100.4	3.68
5.60	4-77	100.1	100.5	4.52
7.70	4-77	100.8	100.16	4.40
5.25	5-77	100	100.4	4.65
5.20	6-77	99.31	100.3	4.85
4.75	7-77	99.25	99.29	4.96
5.20	8-77	99.30	100	5.19
8.55	10-78	103.4	103.20	6.20
8.00	10-79	102.24	103.8	6.64
7.75	1-86	100.20	101.4	7.57

Inter-Amer. Devel. Bk.

Rate	Mat	Bid	Asked	Yld
4.25	12-82	88.16	89.16	6.43
4.50	4-84	85	86	7.03
4.50	11-84	84	85	7.05
8.25	1-85	102.4	102.20	7.80
8.00	3-85	100.24	101.8	7.79
8.38	2-86	102.16	103	7.90
5.20	1-92	77	78	7.70
6.50	11-92	86.24	87.24	7.87
6.63	11-93	87.16	88.16	7.87
8.63	10-95	101.16	102.8	8.38
9.00	2-01	103.16	104.16	8.56
8.75	7-01	101.24	102.16	8.50

GNMA Issues

Rate	Mat	Bid	Asked	Yld
6.50	1-00	89.16	90.16	7.76
7.25	1-00	94.16	94.24	7.93
7.50	1-00	96.8	96.16	7.94
8.00	1-00	99.8	99.16	8.02
8.50	1-00	102.12	102.20	8.10
9.00	1-00	105.16	105.24	8.17

Private Expt. Fndg. Corp.

Rate	Mat	Bid	Asked	Yld
8⅜	11-85	102.16	103.16	7.82
7⅞	3-83	101	102	7.45
7.8s	4-86	100	101	7.65

FNMA Issues

Rate	Mat	Bid	Asked	Yld
4.50	2-77	99.29	100.1	0.26
6.30	3-77	100.2	100.6	4.14
7.05	3-77	100.4	100.8	4.19
8.40	12-83	105	106	7.27
6.25	6-84	93.28	94.28	7.16
8.20	7-84	103.20	104.20	7.38
7.95	9-84	102.4	103.4	7.40
6.90	12-84	97.4	98.4	7.21
7.65	3-85	99.28	100.28	7.50
7.90	10-85	101.24	102.8	7.54
7.95	7-86	101.24	102.8	7.61
7.90	9-86	101.8	101.24	7.64
7.30	12-86	97.24	98	7.59
7.80	10-91	99	99.16	7.86
7.00	3-92	94.8	95.8	7.53
7.05	6-92	94.24	95.24	7.52
7.10	12-97	94	95	7.58

Federal Land Bank

Rate	Mat	Bid	Asked	Yld
8.25	4-77	100.16	100.24	4.41
6.25	7-77	100.8	100.16	5.10
7.50	7-77	100.26	101.2	5.08
6.35	10-77	100.8	100.26	5.42
6.60	11-77	100.18	100.26	5.39
6.70	10-77	100.20	100.28	5.40
6.10	1-78	100.6	100.14	5.62

Rate	Mat	Bid	Asked	Yld
8.70	1-78	102.8	102.24	5.71
4.13	2-78	97.12	98.12	5.76
5.13	4-78	98.4	99.4	5.88
7.60	4-78	101.12	101.28	5.95
6.40	7-78	99.16	100.16	6.03
9.15	7-78	103.24	104.8	6.06
7.35	10-78	101.12	101.28	6.16
5.00	1-79	97.16	98	6.10
7.10	1-79	101	101.16	6.27
6.85	4-79	100	101	6.35
8.55	4-79	103.28	104.12	6.39
7.15	7-79	101.4	101.20	6.42
6.80	10-79	99.20	100.20	6.54
6.70	1-80	99	100	6.70
7.35	4-80	101.12	101.28	6.68
7.50	7-80	101.12	102.12	6.72
8.70	10-80	105.12	105.28	6.87
7.10	1-81	99.28	100.12	6.99
6.20	4-81	97.14	97.22	6.84
6.70	4-81	98.24	99.24	6.77
9.10	7-81	107	108	6.98
7.45	10-81	101.4	101.20	7.03
7.80	1-82	102.16	103	7.07
4.90	4-82	99	100	6.90
8.15	4-82	103.28	104.12	7.13
7.30	0-82	99.28	100.28	7.11
8.20	1-83	104	104.16	7.25
7.30	10-83	99.12	100.12	7.22
8.10	7-85	102.28	103.12	7.55
7.95	10-85	101.28	102.12	7.57
8.80	10-85	107.12	107.28	7.55
7.85	1-88	100.28	101.12	7.66
7.95	4-91	101	101.16	7.77
7.95	10-96	100.4	100.20	7.88
7.35	1-97	94.30	95.6	7.83

FIC Bank Debs.

Rate	Mat	Bid	Asked	Yld
6.25	3-77	100.1	100.5	3.74
6.50	4-77	100.6	100.10	4.34
8.70	4-77	100.14	100.22	4.20
6.10	5-77	100.6	100.10	4.62
5.85	6-77	100.5	100.9	4.83
5.80	7-77	100.5	100.9	5.00
5.35	8-77	99.30	100.2	5.14
5.35	9-77	99.30	100.2	5.19
4.90	10-77	99.19	99.23	5.32
5.45	11-77	99.30	100	5.44
7.10	1-78	100.24	101.8	5.66
7.40	1-79	101.12	101.28	6.33
7.40	1-80	101.4	101.20	6.77
7.90	1-81	102.16	103	7.01
7.95	4-86	102	102.16	7.56
6.95	1-87	95.24	96	7.53

Postal Service

Rate	Mat	Bid	Asked	Yld
6⅞	2-97	88.08	89.08	7.95

Quality of Government Securities Despite the great variety of ownership interest in government securities, it is apparent that nearly all investors choose them because of two characteristics: high degree of certainty of payment and a high degree of marketability. Direct obligations of the U.S. Treasury enjoy the lowest credit and business risk and are at the lower end of the risk–return curve. Agency obligations enjoy about the same credit position even though they are not direct obligations of the U.S. government. Consequently, the securities of the U.S. government and federal agencies have received wide acceptance by investors all over the world.

STATE AND MUNICIPAL SECURITIES

State and municipal obligations are known collectively as municipal bonds. As used in the investment field, the word "municipals" refers to the whole range of securities of domestic public agencies below the level of the federal government. The term embraces the bonds of the 50 states, the territories, and their political subdivisions—counties, cities, towns, villages, and school districts. It also includes agencies such as authorities and special districts (fire, water, public power, sewer, hospital, highway, and so on) created by the states, and certain federally sponsored agencies such as local housing authorities.

Municipal bonds, perhaps more than any other class of securities, are bought for investment. The majority of purchasers put them in a vault and give them very little attention except for the periodic clipping of coupons. Although there are some speculators in municipals, the vast majority of buyers are long-term investors. Consequently, the "floating" supply of bonds of any particular issue is usually small. Of the $250 billion of municipal bonds outstanding, approximately 40 percent is held by individuals, 40 percent by commercial banks, and 15 percent by insurance companies.

Why Buy Municipals? The first factor that should occur to you is that the interest income paid to holders of municipal bonds is exempt from federal income taxes. This means that the before-tax return of government and corporate bonds must be greater in order to equal the tax-free return of municipals. For example, a tax-free return of 9 percent is equivalent to an after-tax return of 12 percent if one is in the 25 percent tax bracket ($.09/(1 - .25) = .12$). or 15 percent if one is in the 40 percent tax bracket ($.09/(1 - .40) = .15$). Second, municipal bonds over the long run involve the least risk for the investor of any type of investment with the exception of securities issued by the U.S. government. Third, municipals provide diversification, in that principal and interest are paid from a base of industrial, commercial, banking, and recreational enterprises. Fourth, the majority of issues are scheduled to mature in serial form, so that the investor can diversify by maturity. (Few issues have a single, fixed maturity.) There is also a wide choice between high and low coupon rates, as well as premium and discount bonds, because the larger municipalities borrow periodically whether interest rates are high or low.

Finally, municipals are exempt from margin requirements of the Board of Governors of the Federal Reserve System. Consequently, dealers are willing to lend an investor 80 to 90 percent of the marketable value of the security. There is one proviso: The investor who buys on margin must have a margin account with a minimum deposit of $2,000.

Types of Municipals   There are two basic types of state and municipal bonds: general-obligation bonds and revenue bonds.

General-Obligation Bonds.   General obligations are bonds guaranteed by a political unit that pledges as security its full faith, credit, and taxing power. This implies that these are the ultimate obligations of the state or municipality.* In the case of a state bond, this implies that it is payable from such income sources as franchise taxes, income and personal property taxes, motor vehicle taxes, fees, and all other sources of state revenue that are available. General obligations of a local government are based mainly upon income from property taxes. Some local units also have additional income sources such as sales and income taxes, business taxes, and water, light, and sewer charges not specifically pledged to revenue bonds. If a municipal bond is payable from a single or limited revenue source, it is not a general-obligation bond.

General-obligation bonds are the most widely used means of raising funds for the capital improvements of municipalities. This type of bond is issued by state and local governments to raise money for the construction or improvement of public works, such as schools, streets, roads, public buildings, parks, and forest preserves. A rule of thumb regarding the reasonableness of indebtedness of a community is that the overall debt should not exceed 10 percent of the assessed valuation of its property.

Revenue Bonds.   Revenue bonds are bonds of a political subdivision, or public authority, whose principal and interest are paid solely out of revenues collected from the users of a publicly owned facility or enterprise. State financing for bridges, tunnels, toll highways, and public institutions are known as revenue bonds. The great bulk of the outstanding revenue bonds have been issued by cities, authorities, or commissions such as the Port of New York Authority, Pennsylvania Turnpike Commission, and Municipal Assistance Corporation of New York.†

Between 40 and 50 different uses for revenue bonds have been devised. The most important, with respect to number of issues outstanding and volume

---

*This may not always be enough, as was evidenced by the narrowly-averted potential bankruptcy of New York City in 1975.

†"Big Mac" is backed by revenues from the New York City sales tax and stock transfer tax.

of financing, are (1) utilities—water, light, sewer, and gas; (2) traffic facilities —toll roads and bridges; and (3) municipal transportation systems. Quotations for selected revenue-bond issues are in the "Tax-Exempt Bonds" section of the *Wall Street Journal*. (See Figure 15.6.)

FIGURE 15.6 Tax-Exempts. (*Source: Wall Street Journal, January 4, 1977, p. 25.*)

Tax-Exempts
* * *

New Listings

Fort Worth, Texas, listed $28.4 million of bonds for sale at competitive bidding Jan. 12.

Antelope Valley-East Kern Water Agency, Calif., $18 million of bonds, about Feb. 22.

Tax-Exempt Bonds

Here are current prices of several active tax-exempt revenue bonds issued by toll roads and other public authorities.

Agency	Coupon	Mat	Bid	Asked	Chg.
Bat Park City Auth NY	6⅜s	'14	67	70	.....
Chi Calumet Skyway-f	3⅜s	'95	50½	54½+	½
Chelan Dist	5s	'13	90	92	.....
Chesapeake B Br&Tun-f	5¾s	'00	64	67	.....
Chgo-O'Hare Int Airpt	4¾s	'99	96	98	.....
Dallas-Ft Worth Airpt	6¼s	'02	99	102	+2
Delaware Riv Port Auth	6½s	'11	92	94	+1
Delaware Riv Port Auth	6s	'10	86	88	− ½
Douglas Cnty PU Dist	4s	'18	73	75	+ ½
Florida Turnpike	4¾s	'01	91	93	.....
Gr'ter New Orl Expr	4.9s	'06	84	87	+1
Illinois Toll	3¾s	'95	88	90	.....
Indiana Toll	3½s	'94	87	89	.....
Kentucky Turnpike	6⅛s	'08	98½	100½	.....
Maine Turnpike	4s	'89	100	103	.....
Maryland Br&Tun	5.2s	'08	92½	94½	.....
Massachusetts Turnpike	3.3s	'94	84½	86½	.....
Munic. Assist. Cp. NY	8s	'86	92	95	−1
Munic. Assist. Cp. NY	8s	'91	91½	94½+	½
Munic. Assist. Cp. NY	9s	'85	100	103	.....
Munic. Assist. Cp. NY	9¼s	'90	100	103	.....
Munic. Assist. Cp. NY	10¼s	'93	104½	106½+1	
Munic. Assist. Cp. NY	11s	'83	108	111	+ ½
NJ Turnpike Auth	5.7s	'13	95	97	.....
NJ Turnpike Auth	7s	'09	110	112	.....
NJ Sports & Expos	7½s	'09	98½	101½	.....
NY State Power Auth	5⅜s	'10	93½	96½+	½
NY State Thruway	3.1s	'94	65½	68½+	½
NY Urban Developments	7s	'14	74	77	+1
Ohio Turnpike	3¼s	'92	98½	100½	.....
Penn Turnpike	3.1s	'93	85	88	− ½
Port of NY Auth	8.2s	'11	114	116	+1
Port of NY Auth	5½s	'08	86½	89½+1	
Port of NY Auth	6s	'08	93	96	.....
Richmond-Met Auth	5.6s	'13	92½	95½	.....
West Virginia Turnpike-f	3¾s	'89	79	82	+ ½

f-Trades flat without payment of current interest.

Special types of revenue bonds are dormitory revenue bonds and rental revenue bonds. Dormitory-bond holders are paid generally from student fees. In most cases, there is a stipulation that the state is not liable and that bond indebtedness is taken care of exclusively by income from student fees.

A special category of revenue bonds is known as housing bonds. Pursuant to the Housing Act of 1937, as amended in 1949, all the "New Housing Authority" bonds are issued to provide safe, modern, sanitary housing for the lowest-income groups.* Since the housing program carries social as well as economic implications on a nationwide basis, Congress has provided that such bonds will be backed by federal as well as local resources. The uniqueness of housing bonds is that rentals are not intended to be sufficient to cover operating expenses and debt service. As a result, annual contributions are made, unconditionally, to the local authority by the Housing Assistance Administration (HAA), the federal agency charged with responsibility for fulfilling the obligations of the U.S. government in this housing program.

Municipal Bond Index

The yield on the average index of 20 municipal bonds is shown in Figure 15.7. There is a strong possibility that the near-default of New York City on its bonded debt served as the catalyst that caused municipal yields to peak on September 26, 1975. Oftentimes when the worst news is announced, prices have bottomed and yields, conversely, have peaked. What could be worse than our largest city's being on the brink of default? At any rate, the municipal bond index reached a yield of 7.7 percent (tax-free) in September 1975. Sixteen months later, the yield on the index had fallen 200 basis points (100 basis points = 1 percent).

Quality of State and Municipal Securities

Bonds and notes of cities, states, and local agencies are exempt from federal income taxes, and often those of the issuing state as well. Many municipal bonds are now backed by an irrevocable insurance policy from the Municipal Bond Insurance Association (MBIA), which consists of four of the nation's strongest casualty insurance companies.† In addition, Moody's Investors Service and Standard & Poor's Corporation rate municipals. Moody's ratings range from MIG-1 (highest category) to MIG-4 (lowest category). Standard & Poor's municipal bond ratings are AAA, prime; AA, high grade; A, upper medium grade; BBB, medium grade; BB, lower medium grade; B, low grade; and D, defaults. While ratings provide a

---

*Income groups that would probably live in slums without such housing.

†Members of MBIA and their respective shares of the guaranty are:

The Aetna Casualty and Surety Company (of Aetna Life and Casualty Company)—40%

St. Paul Fire and Marine Insurance Company (of The St. Paul Companies)—30%

Aetna Insurance Company (of Connecticut General Insurance Corporation)—15%

United States Fire Insurance Company (of Crum & Forster Insurance Companies)—15%

FIGURE 15.7 Yields on Selected Securities. (*Source: U.S. Financial Data.*)

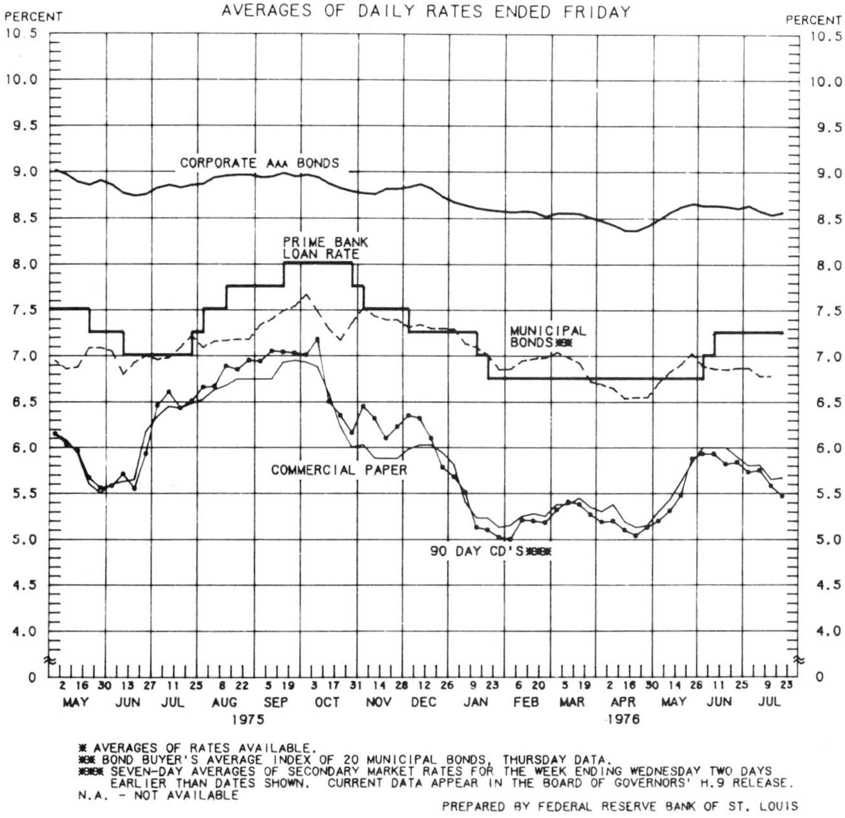

PERCENT
AVERAGES OF DAILY RATES ENDED FRIDAY
PERCENT

CORPORATE AAA BONDS

PRIME BANK
LOAN RATE

MUNICIPAL
BONDS

COMMERCIAL PAPER

90 DAY CD'S

2 16 30 13 27 11 25 8 22 5 19 3 17 31 14 28 12 26 9 23 6 20 5 19 2 16 30 14 26 11 25 9 23
MAY JUN JUL AUG SEP OCT NOV DEC JAN FEB MAR APR MAY JUN JUL
1975 1976

* AVERAGES OF RATES AVAILABLE.
** BOND BUYER'S AVERAGE INDEX OF 20 MUNICIPAL BONDS, THURSDAY DATA.
*** SEVEN-DAY AVERAGES OF SECONDARY MARKET RATES FOR THE WEEK ENDING WEDNESDAY TWO DAYS
EARLIER THAN DATES SHOWN. CURRENT DATA APPEAR IN THE BOARD OF GOVERNORS' H.9 RELEASE.
N.A. - NOT AVAILABLE
PREPARED BY FEDERAL RESERVE BANK OF ST. LOUIS

rough estimate of a bond's safety, they are not a substitute for expert and detailed analysis of the economic, financial, and credit history of municipalities, as well as their prospects for the future.

SUMMARY

Government securities include the broad range of securities issued by the federal government, federal agencies, and state and local governments. The total of government securities outstanding is approximately $1 billion. The quality of "governments" ranges from the relatively risk-free, such as securities of the U.S. government, to municipal bonds, some of which can be speculative. Some highway toll bonds, for example, are in default. These include the Chesapeake Bay Bridge & Tunnel 5 3/4s of 2000 and the West Virginia Turnpike 3 3/4s of 1989 (note the issues coded "f" in Figure 15.6).

State and local securities are called municipals or tax-free bonds. The two main categories are general-obligation bonds and revenue bonds. General-obligation bonds are backed by the taxing power of the issuing unit. Revenue bonds rely upon the revenue produced by specific projects that are financed by the bond proceeds. Municipal bonds are exempt from federal income taxes, which gives a higher effective rate of interest to the investor than does the actual coupon rate of the bond.

In sum, the investor who wants to minimize risk prefers U.S. government bonds. The investor who prefers little risk as well as a tax-exempt yield places his funds in state and municipal bonds.

PROBLEMS

1. Assume that you bought a $1,000 face-value U.S. savings bond, Series E, in January 1969, and held it until maturity in December 1974. The *Treasury Bulletin* gives the selling price and maturity of the Series E bond sold. Consult the *Federal Reserve Bulletin* for consumer prices in January 1969 and in the month the bond matured.

a. What annual rate of interest was earned over the life of the bond?

b. What was the approximate purchasing power of the money at maturity (based on the January 1969 dollar)?

c. How did the buyer of the bond fare?

2. a. Compute the asked prices in dollars for the following bonds, given:

		COUPON	MATURITY	ASKED
(1)	U.S. government	4s	'88–'93	85.22
(2)	Federal Home Loan	6s	'82	101.6
(3)	Municipal Assistance Corp.	11s	'83	$106\frac{1}{2}$
(4)	Florida Turnpike	4 3/4s	'01	$89\frac{1}{4}$

b. Consult a recent issue of the *Wall Street Journal* and determine the current asked prices in dollars for the bonds above.

3. a. Municipal bonds, perhaps more than any other class of security, are bought for investment. Is this statement true? Why?

b. Calculate the return on an after-tax-yield basis of the following, given:

(1) Municipal bond with coupon of 10% and investor's marginal tax rate of 30%

(2) Municipal bond with coupon of 8% and investor's marginal tax rate of 65%

4. You are considering the purchase of $10,000 of 90-day Treasury bills. The bid and asked quotations are 5.23 and 5.15 respectively.

    a. What is the quotation price that you must pay for the bills?

    b. How much will you pay, in dollars, for them?

5. One hundred "flower" bonds are bought at 80 with a coupon of 3% and maturity date of 1994. Assume that the owner lives five years after purchasing the bonds and then dies. Assume also that his marginal tax rate was 50% and the bonds sell at 90 at his death.

Would the person's estate benefit more from his having purchased the "flower" bonds, *or* if he had deposited the money in a savings account at 6% interest for five years?

16

Investment Securities: Corporate Bonds, Preferred Stock, and Convertible Issues

> *It's better to be safe than sorry.*
>
> *Leslie Ford*

In Chapter 15, we examined the characteristics of government and municipal securities, including the advantages and disadvantages of each. As we move from the public securities of federal, state, and local governments to the private securities of corporate enterprises, both risk and return increase. Remember that our frame of reference for the discussion of investment securities is the risk–return tradeoff curve, and that our direction is from the least risky and least rewarding securities to those with the most risk and most potential reward.

In this chapter, the debt and quasi-debt securities of firms (corporate bonds and preferred stock) are discussed. In general, debt has the first claim on the earnings and assets of the firm. Debt claims are followed by the claims of preferred stock, which is so named because of its preference over common-stock claims on both earnings and assets of the firm.

The first group of corporate securities encountered on the risk–return curve is the long-term debt obligations of business firms. Since 1960, corporations have raised about $400 billion by external financing (selling stocks and bonds) as shown in Table 16.1. Of this amount, over $300 billion, or 78 percent, consisted of corporate bonds. High-grade corporate bonds provided investors with relatively safe investments and yields ranging from a low of 4 percent in the 1960s to a high of 10 percent in the 1970s. The yield on AAA corporate bonds in 1977 dipped under 8 percent as shown in Figure 16.3.

Corporate financing sources are bonds, stocks, and internally generated funds. A comparison of these sources of corporate capital for the period 1960 through 1975 is shown in Table 16.1. Internally generated funds represent the largest, most significant source. Such funds averaged approximately

TABLE 16.1 Corporate Sources of Funds, 1960–76 (in billions of dollars)

	EXTERNAL FUNDS			INTERNALLY GENERATED FUNDS	TOTAL
	BONDS	STOCK			
		PREFERRED	COMMON		
1960	8.1	.4	1.7	38.1	48.3
1961	9.4	.4	3.3	39.7	52.8
1962	9.0	.4	1.3	46.1	56.8
1963	10.9	.4	1.0	51.4	63.7
1964	10.9	.4	2.7	54.5	68.5
1965	13.7	.7	1.6	61.9	77.9
1966	15.6	.6	1.9	68.6	86.7
1967	22.0	.9	1.9	68.3	93.1
1968	17.4	.6	4.0	71.0	93.0
1969	18.3	.7	7.7	72.4	99.1
1970	30.3	1.4	7.2	70.6	109.5
1971	32.0	3.7	9.3	81.6	126.6
1972	26.1	3.4	10.7	96.6	136.8
1973	21.0	3.3	7.6	114.5	146.4
1974	32.1	2.3	4.0	129.1	167.5
1975	42.8	3.5	7.4	109.7	163.4
1976	47.4	3.0	11.0	130.4	191.8

Source: Federal Reserve Bulletin.

70 percent of corporate financing. Bond financing averaged 22 percent, preferred financing 3 percent, and common-stock financing 5 percent of total corporate financing for the 1970s. It should be obvious that only external sources will be considered in this section, because no securities are issued for internally generated funds.* Our discussion of corporate securities begins with the least risky external source—corporate bonds.

CORPORATE BONDS

Bond Characteristics   Although corporate bonds vary in the amount and legal characteristics of each issue, they do possess a number of common features. *First,* almost all have definite maturities. *Second,* almost all are issued in denominations of $1,000, although some may be of smaller size and some in multiples of $1,000. *Third,* almost all corporations pay bond interest seminanually. *Fourth,* bonds are issued either in coupon or registered form. To collect the interest on a coupon bond, the owner clips the coupon and mails it to the corporation or other paying agency, such as a commercial bank. On registered bonds, interest is paid by sending a check automatically by mail to the owner of the bond. *Last,* most corporate bonds are callable; that is, the issuer may call or retire the bond issue before maturity.

The terms under which bonds are issued are contained in a legal agreement between the issuing firm and the bondholders, who are represented by a bond trustee. This contract is commonly called the *bond indenture* or *trust agreement*. The indenture normally contains a description of the property pledged by the firm, the coupon rate of the bond, the maturity date of the bond, provisions for early retirement of the issue, and limitation on other debt issues. In general, the indenture spells out the detailed terms and conditions of the loan.

Types of Bonds   Corporate bonds may be either secured (by a pledge of property) or unsecured, or a combination of the two—ranging from first-mortgage bonds (secured) to subordinated debentures (unsecured). Although the security backing a bond is important, it is not the critical element. Earning power, financial condition, and quality of management are the vital factors. Therefore, an unsecured bond of a financially strong firm may have a higher rating than does a secured bond of a financially weak firm. A listing of bond types, with examples of yields, maturity dates, and ratings, is shown in Table 16.2.

---

*Internally generated funds consist of retained earnings and capital consumption allowances (allowances for depreciation). Capital consumption allowances are included in sources of capital because this is a funds-flow measurement. They were not included in the cost of capital in Chapter 12 because there we were concerned with asset measurement.

TABLE 16.2 Bond Types, Yields, Maturity Dates, and Ratings

TYPE OF BOND	COMPANY	CODE	YIELD	MATURITY DATA	QUALITY RATING
Secured Issues:					
First-mortgage bond	Houston Lighting & Power	1st	$5\frac{1}{4}$s	'97	AAA
General mortgage bond[a]	Niagara Mohawk Power	Gen	$6\frac{1}{4}$s	'97	A
Collateral trust certificate	N.Y. Central RR	CT	6s	'90	CCC
Equipment trust certificate	Union Tank Car	Eq Tr	$6\frac{1}{2}$s	'88	A
Unsecured issues:					
Senior debenture	Assoc. Corp. of N.A.	Sr Deb	$9\frac{1}{2}$s	'90	A
Straight debenture	Arvin Indus.	Deb	5.10s	'90	BBB
Sinking-fund debenture	Arvin Indus.	SF Deb	$9\frac{3}{8}$s	'96	BBB
Senior subordinated debenture	Dial Finance	Sr Sub Deb	7s	'86	BBB
Subordinated debenture	General Host	Sub Deb	7s	'94	CCC
Junior subordinated debenture[b]	McCrory Corp.	Jr Sub Deb	5s	'81	CCC
Convertible, income, and warrant issues:					
Convertible subordinated debenture[c]	Aurora Plastics	Cv Sub Deb	$4\frac{5}{8}$s	'80	NR
Subordinated income bond[d]	Missouri-Kan.-Tex. RR	Sub Inc Deb	$5\frac{1}{2}$s	2033	C
Subordinated debenture with warrants					

[a]Also called Second Mortgage, Junior Mortgage, and Consolidated Mortgage Bonds.
[b]Also called Capital Debenture.
[c]Also called Convertible Bond.
[d]Also called Income Bond.

Source: *Standard & Poor's* Bond Guide.

Secured Bonds. When a corporation pledges some or all of its assets as collateral for a bond issue, the bond is said to be secured. That is, in the event the company is unable to pay either interest or maturity value of the bond, the bondholders have claim to the assets of the firm that have been pledged as security. Secured issues consist of mortgage bonds, collateral trust bonds, and equipment trust certificates. Bonds secured by a lien on the real estate (real property) of the issuer are known as *mortgage bonds*. There are two basic types of mortgage bonds: *First-mortgage bonds* have a senior lien on the real property of the corporation. *Second-mortgage bonds* have a junior lien on the real property of the firm. Usually, bonds with junior liens are called "general" or "consolidated" mortgage bonds. Such nomenclature does not clearly label junior issues as such, and the investor should read the indenture to determine the security status of such bonds.

A bond secured by a pledge of specific securities is known as a *collateral trust bond.* These are issued mainly by holding companies, closed-end investment companies, and finance companies. The *equipment trust certificate* is usually used to finance the purchase of rolling stock by railroads. The railroad pays about 20 percent down and the trustee issues a certificate to cover the balance of the purchase price. Since the rolling stock can be moved anywhere in the country, the equipment will be leased or sold to another railroad in the case of default.

Unsecured Bonds. Debentures are the most widely used corporate bond. They are not secured by a pledge of a specific asset. Instead, this type of bond is protected only by the general promise to pay, and by the general credit of the issuing corporation. Unsecured bonds range in type from a senior debenture, the best unsecured bond, to a subordinated income bond, which ranks at the bottom of the debenture list. Debentures of large corporations with good credit, such as Texaco and Exxon, may yield less than secured bonds of more speculative companies, such as Lockheed and Penn Central.

Convertible, Income, and Warrant Bonds. Other types of corporate debt issues are convertible bonds, income bonds, and bonds with warrants attached. All are usually a variety of subordinated debentures. Convertible bonds are a cross between a secured bond and an unsecured bond. They are "secured" by the common stock of the issuing corporation. Such bonds are convertible into common stock and combine the features of bonds with the chance of appreciating in price along with the common stock. Convertibles are discussed in a separate section at the end of this chapter.

Income bonds are also subordinated debentures and rank below the junior subordinated debenture (see Table 16.2). Income bonds are usually used in the reorganization of financially weak firms and as an alternative to preferred stock. They are unique in that interest is not required to be paid unless it is earned. Unearned interest may be cumulative or noncumulative. If cumulative, interest must be paid prior to payment of dividends to lower-ranking securities. Since interest is not assured and the bonds are unsecured, they are normally rated in the C category and carry relatively high yields.

Warrants to buy common stock are usually associated with either preferred stock or bonds. A warrant is defined as a long-term option to purchase a specified number of shares of common stock at a specified price, usually called the "exercise" price. Warrants are attached to bonds to make the issue more attractive to investors. Warrants, which are usually detachable from the bond, can be traded on one of the major stock exchanges or can be "exercised" to buy the stipulated number of shares of common stock. The latter course is practical only if the price of the common has exceeded the exercise price of the warrant. Warrants are usually attached to subordinated debentures in order to enhance their appeal and sometimes to provide a slightly lower yield. The risk of such a bond is about the same as that of a subordinated debenture. Warrants as a speculative medium are discussed under the "Options" section in the next chapter.

Bond Prices and Yields Figure 16.1 shows selected bond quotations from the NYSE. There are a number of ATT bonds on the list. ATT is the American Telephone and Telegraph Company, which is the largest corporate debt issuer. Notice that prices are a function of the interest rate as well as the maturity date. That is, the lowest-priced issue is the ATT 2 5/8s 86, which closed at 69 7/8. The highest-priced issue is the ATT 8.80s 05, which closed at 106 3/4. We shall call the first issue ATT_1 and the second issue ATT_2. The dollar price of each bond is calculated as follows:

$$Price = Bond \text{ quotation as percent} \times Par \text{ value}$$
$$Price \text{ of } ATT_1 = .69875 \times \$1,000 = \$698.75$$
$$Price \text{ of } ATT_2 = 1.06750 \times \$1,000 = \$1,067.50$$

The price can alternately be figured as follows:

$$Price = Bond \text{ quotation} \times 1,000\%$$
$$Price \text{ of } ATT_1 = 69 \ 7/8 \times 1,000\% = \$698.75$$
$$Price \text{ of } ATT_2 = 106 \ 3/4 \times 1,000\% = \$1,067.50$$

Current Yield. The formula for the current yield is:

$$Current \ yield = \frac{Annual \ coupon \ rate}{Closing \ price \ of \ bond}$$

$$ATT_1 = \frac{2.625}{69.875} = 3.7\%$$

$$ATT_2 = \frac{8.8}{106.75} = 8.2\%$$

The current yield is the investor's return if the bond was purchased and later resold at the same price. This assumes that all coupon interest payments are received on time during the holding period of the bond. The current yield is shown alongside the bond quotations in Figure 16.1.

The current yield may represent a poor measure of the rate of return expected from holding the bond. This is because the current yield ignores any potential capital gain or loss. If an investor holds the bond to maturity, he would receive either a capital gain or a capital loss. Thus, the current-yield figures reported in the financial press may be very misleading. For example, ATT_1 appears to have a much poorer yield than ATT_2, on a current-yield basis. A better measure of rate of return on a bond is the return over time.

FIGURE 16.1 Selected New York Stock Exchange Bond Quotations. (*Source: Wall Street Journal, February 7, 1977, p. 24.*)

CORPORATION BONDS

Volume, $20,440,000

Bonds	Cur Yld	Vol	High	Low	Close	Net Chg
ARA 4⅝s96	cv	5	68¼	68¼	68¼	− ⅛
AbbtL 6¼93	7.1	6	88⅛	88⅛	88⅛	+ ⅛
AddM 9⅜95	9.5	16	99⅞	99	99	−1
AlaBnc 8s99	7.9	5	101¼	101¼	101¼	+ ¼
AlaP 8½s01	8.9	10	95½	95½	95½	+1⅜
AlaP 8⅞s03	9.0	10	98¾	98¾	98¾	− ¼
AlaP 8¼s03	8.9	3	93	93	93	− ⅛
AlaP 9¾s04	9.3	22	105	105	105	.....
AlaP 10⅞05	9.9	1	110	110	110	− ⅜
AlaP 8⅞06	9.0	20	99	99	99	− ⅜
Alaska 6s96	cv	26	92½	90	90	−2½
AllnGp 11½94	cv	7	118¾	118¾	118¾	−3⅜
AlldC 3½78	3.6	8	98	98	98	.....
AlldC 5.2s91	6.4	45	81¾	81⅝	81⅝	+2⅛
AlldC 8⅜83	8.0	10	104¼	104¼	104¼	.....
AlldPd 7s84	8.6	5	81½	81½	81½	+1⅞
AldSu 5¾87	cv	3	57	56½	57	+1
Alcoa 4¼s82	4.8	8	89	89	89	.....
Alcoa 5¼s91	cv	8	101½	100½	100½	− ½
Alcoa 6s92	6.9	3	87⅛	87⅛	87⅛	+ ½
AluCa 9½95	9.2	9	102¾	102¾	102¾	+ ⅛
AMAX 7½78	7.5	2	100¼	100¼	100¼	.....
AMAX 8s86	8.0	25	100⅜	100	100⅛	− ⅛
Amerce 5s92	cv	13	72½	72½	72½	....
AHes 6¾96	8.0	5	84	84	84	.....
AForP 5s30	7.6	31	66	64½	66	+1¼
AAirl 4¼s92	cv	22	57½	57	57	−1
AAirl 11s88	10.	12	108¾	108	108	− ¾
AAirl 10⅞88	10.	2	108¾	108¾	108¾	.....
AAirl 10s89	9.6	6	104	104	104	.....
ABrnd 5⅞92	7.0	5	84⅜	84⅜	84⅜	−1
ABrnd 9⅝79	9.0	25	106¾	106¾	106¾	+ ¾
ABrnd 8⅛85	7.9	75	102⅞	101¾	102⅞	+1¼
ABdt 9.35s00	8.7	1	107½	107½	107½	−2¼
ACan 3¾s88	5.0	3	75	75	75	.....
ACan 4¾s90	6.0	30	79½	77	79½	+2½
ACan 7¾s01	8.2	10	95	95	95	−1¾
AGnIn 6½94	6.4	5	102	102	102	−1¾
AHoist 4¾92	cv	35	122	117½	122	+6
AHoist 5½93	cv	77	96	94	96	+3
→ AHosp 5¾99	cv	10	106¾	106¾	106¾	− ½
AMF 4¼s81	cv	16	88	88	88	.....
AMedcp 5s97	cv	3	67	67	67	+1
AmMot 6s88	cv	21	61	61	61	.....
AmStr 9⅞90	9.2	1	107	107	107	.....
ASug 5.3s93	7.1	12	75	75	75	.....
ATT 2¾s80	3.1	35	89	88¾	88¾	− ¼
ATT 2¾s82	3.3	10	82¼	82¼	82¼	− ½
ATT 3¼s84	4.2	7	78	78	78	− ½
ATT 4⅜s85	5.3	26	82½	81⅞	81⅞	− ⅛
→ ATT 2⅝s86	3.7	14	69⅞	69⅞	69⅞	+ ⅞
ATT 2⅞s87	4.0	5	71	71	71	.....
ATT 3⅞s90	5.5	10	70⅞	70⅞	70⅞	− ⅜
ATT 8¾2000	8.2	122	106⅞	106⅝	106⅝	− ¼
ATT 7s01	7.7	69	91⅜	91¼	91¼	+ ⅛
ATT 6½s79	6.5	10	100¼	100¼	100¼	.....
ATT 7⅛s03	7.7	45	92⅜	92⅛	92⅜	+ ⅜
→ ATT 8.80s05	8.2	249	107	106½	106¾	+ ½
ATT 7¾s82	7.5	15	103⅜	102⅝	103⅜	+ ⅝
ATT 8⅝s07	8.1	166	105⅞	105⅛	105⅞	+ ⅞
Ames 10s95	10.	5	99	99	99	+1⅜
Amfac 5¼94	cv	38	66	65⅝	65⅝	− ⅞
Ampx 5½94	cv	64	61	60	60	−1⅛
Anhr 4½89	5.8	1	77	77	77	−3½

New York Exchange Bonds

Friday, February 4, 1977

Total Volume, $20,720,000

	Domestic Fri	Domestic Thurs	All Issues Fri	All Issues Thurs
Issues traded	844	875	859	894
Advances	369	252	376	258
Declines	256	374	259	381
Unchanged	219	249	224	255
New highs, '76-'77	40	30	40	30
New lows, '76-'77	3	15	4	15

SALES SINCE JANUARY 1

1977	1976	1975
$580,986,000	$678,790,000	$581,337,500

Dow Jones Bond Averages

−1974− High	−1974− Low	−1975− High	−1975− Low	−1976-77− High	−1976-77− Low		−1977− (Friday)		−1976− (Friday)		−1975− (Friday)	
....	.....	....	.. .	93.37	85.68	20 Bonds	91.15	− .11	....	....	....	....
91.70	78.52	88.05	81.03	99.10	87.46	10 Utilities	96.81	+ .10	91.21	− .19	86.82	+ .45
80.82	70.81	79.05	74.51	87.91	78.58	10 Industrial	85.50	− .32	79.70	− .11	77.46	+ .05

Bonds	Cur Yld	Vol	High	Low	Close	Net Chg
DetEd 7⅜01	9.2	1	80⅜	80⅜	80⅜	.....
DetEd 7½03	9.2	1	81½	81½	81½	−2¼
DetEd 9⅞04	9.5	103	104⅛	103¼	103½	.....
DetEd 12¾82	11.	14	115⅞	115	115	− ⅝
DetEd 11⅞00	10.	35	116½	116	116½	+ ¼
DetEd 10⅝06	9.7	22	109⅜	109⅛	109⅜	.....
Dilling 9¾99	cv	25	110	110	110	.....
Divers 9⅞91	13.	6	76⅛	76⅛	76⅛	− ¼
DmBk 9½83	9.0	56	106⅛	106	106	.....
Dow 7.75s99	7.9	5	98	98	98	+1
Dow 8.92000	8.6	11	103½	103½	103½	− ⅞
duPnt 8s81	7.7	69	103½	102⅞	103½	+ ½
DukeP 6.85s78	6.8	40	100¾	100¼	100½	+ ⅝
DukeP 8⅛03	8.3	20	98⅛	98⅛	98⅛	+ ¼
DukeP 13s79	11.	21	113½	113	113½	+ ½
DuqL 2¾77	2.8	2	98 5-16	98 5-16	98 5-16	−3-16
EGG 3½s87	cv	7	72½	71½	72½	+1⅞
ESys 4½s92	cv	13	98½	98½	98½	.....
EasAir 5s92	cv	56	54½	53½	54½	+1
EasAir 4¾93	cv	60	55½	55¼	55½	.....
ElPas 6s93	cv	14	88	88	88	+2
ElPas 8½95	cv	4	111	111	111	+2¾
ElPas 6s93A	cv	47	99⅜	98	98¾	+ ¼
ElPas 8½95A	cv	106	126	125	125	− ¼
Englh 5¼97	cv	8	118	118	118	− ½
Ens 9¾s95	9.2	10	106½	106½	106½	.....
Ens 10⅝s00	9.7	22	110¼	110	110	.....
EqutG 9⅝95	9.1	2	106	106	106	.....
EqtLf 6¾90	cv	10	93¼	93¼	93¼	−1¾
Estrl 12½95	11.	2	112	112	112	+1
Evans 6¼94	cv	40	86	86	86	.....
Exxon 6½98	7.6	6	86	86	86	−1⅝
ExxnP 8.05s80	7.8	26	103½	103⅜	103⅜	+ ⅞

Bonds	Cur Yld	Vol	High	Low	Close	Net Chg
Marco 6½88	7.6	11	85½	85⅛	85½	....
Marcor 5s96	cv	35	102	101½	102	.....
MarMa 6s94	cv	105	98⅜	98	98	− ¼
MdCu 5⅛94	cv	5	78¼	78¼	78¼	− ⅛
McCror 5s81	7.2	4	69½	69	69	− ½
McCro 7½94	14.	29	53¾	53¾	53¾	+ ¼
McCr 10½85	13.	18	84	83	84	....
McDnld 9s85	8.6	10	105	105	105	.....
McDD 4¾91	cv	14	86	86	86	.....
Melln 7.8s82	7.7	25	100⅞	100⅞	100⅞	.....
Melln 5.95s89	5.9	10	100¼	100¼	100¼	.....
Melvl 4⅞s96	cv	10	91	91	91	....
Merck 7⅞85	7.6	15	103¼	103¼	103¼	+1
MGM 9s92	9.2	5	98	98	98	.....
MGM 10s93	10.	34	97	97	97	−1¼
MGM 10s94	10.	41	97⅝	97½	97½	− ⅜
MGM 10½s96	10.	10	104⅛	104⅛	104⅛	+ ⅛
MGM 9¾s86	9.6	44	102½	102	102	− ½
MichB 7¾11	8.2	39	95	94	95	+ ¼
MichB 7s12	8.0	2	87⅞	87⅞	87⅞	−1⅝
MichB 9.608	8.6	25	111½	110⅞	111½	+ ⅝
MidMt 8s80	13.	23	61½	61	61½	− ½
MMM 8.20s	7.9	1	104	104	104	.....
MPcCp 8s94	cv	17	158	156½	157¼	+1⅝
MPac 4¼90	6.2	1	68½	68½	68½	+ ⅜
MPac 4¼05	7.9	5	54	54	54	−1
MPac 4¾20f	..	2	53⅝	53⅝	53⅝	+ ¾
MPac 4¾30f	..	33	53⅛	53⅛	53⅛	+ ⅛
MoPac 5s45f	..	129	54⅞	54¼	54¼	− ¼
Mobil 8½01	8.3	19	102⅞	102⅜	102½	+ ½
MohD 5½94	cv	10	55½	55½	55½	+ ½
MohD 12s89	cv	8	112½	112	112½	+ ½
MntW 7⅜88	7.8	32	94½	93⅞	94½	.....
MontW 9s89	8.7	10	104	104	104	− ½

EXPLANATORY NOTES
(For New York and American Bonds)

Yield is current yield. cv – Convertible bond.

ct – Certificates. f – Dealt in flat. m – Matured bonds, negotiability impaired by maturity. st – Stamped. ww – With warrants. x – Ex-interest. xw – Without warrants.

vj – In bankruptcy or receivership or being reorganized under the Bankruptcy Act, or securities assumed by such companies.

Year's high and low range does not include changes in latest day's trading.

Yield to Maturity. The return overtime is an important concept and is usually called the yield to maturity. This involves the present-value concept, because we want to know how much we should pay today for a future stream of semi-annual interest payments plus a final receipt of $1,000 when the bond matures. Thus, the determination can be made in two ways. The yield to maturity can be approximated by the following formulation or it can be determined precisely by the prevailing market rate (yield to maturity) used to calculate the present value of a bond.

$$\text{Yield to maturity} \atop \text{(approximation)} = \frac{\text{Interest} + \dfrac{\text{Par value} - \text{Market value}}{\text{No. of years to maturity}}}{\dfrac{\text{Par value} + \text{Market value}}{2}}$$

$$\text{YTM of ATT}_1 = \frac{26.25 + \dfrac{1{,}000 - 698.75}{9}}{\dfrac{1{,}000 + 698.75}{2}}$$

$$= \frac{26.25 + 33.47}{855}$$

$$= 7.0\%$$

$$\text{YTM of ATT}_2 = \frac{88 + \dfrac{1{,}000 - 1{,}067.50}{28}}{\dfrac{1{,}000 + 1{,}067.50}{2}}$$

$$= \frac{88 - 2.41}{1{,}033.75}$$

$$= 8.3\%$$

Thus, ATT_1 has a yield to maturity almost as high as that of ATT_2. When time is considered (9 years to maturity for ATT_1 versus 28 years to maturity for ATT_2), ATT_1 is probably the best buy. This is true because interest rates are a function of risk, and risk is a function of time. So the investor would and should expect a higher yield to maturity on a long-term bond, *ceteris paribus*.

Present Value. The present value of a bond is determined by the prevailing market rate, not the coupon rate of the individual bond. Thus, if we assume that the prevailing market rate is 8 percent and interest is paid semiannually, the calculation of the present value of each bond is as follows:

$$\text{Present value of ATT}_1 = \text{Semiannual interest}(\text{IF}_{\text{PVA}} \text{ of \$1})$$
$$+ \text{Par value}(\text{IF}_{\text{PV}} \text{ of \$1})$$
$$= 13.13(12.660) + 1{,}000(.494)$$
$$= \$660.23$$
$$\text{Present value of ATT}_2 = 44\,(22.22) + 1{,}000(.1112)$$
$$= \$1088.88$$

Thus, at a market rate of 8 percent, the ATT_1 bond is selling a little too high and the ATT_2 bond is selling at a little less than its present value.

Corporate-Bond Risk   For a given corporation, secured bonds usually rank higher in quality and trade at lower yields than do unsecured bonds. However, debentures (unsecured bonds) of industrial firms may trade at lower yields than do many of the secured railroad issues. Corporate bonds are rated by Moody's and Standard & Poor's. Moody's ratings range from Aaa (highest grade) to D (lowest grade). Standard & Poor's ratings range from AAA (highest grade) to D (lowest grade). An explanation of Standard & Poor's ratings for corporate bonds is shown in Table 16.3.

TABLE 16.3 Standard & Poor's Ratings, Corporate Bonds

BANK QUALITY BONDS—Under present commercial bank regulations bonds rated in the top four categories (AAA, AA, A, BBB or their equivalent) generally are regarded as eligible for bank investment.

AAA—Bonds rated AAA are highest grade obligations. They possess the ultimate degree of protection as to principal and interest. Marketwise, they move with interest rates, and hence provide the maximum safety on all counts.

AA—Bonds rated AA also qualify as high grade obligations, and in the majority of instances differ from AAA issues only in small degree. Here, too, prices move with the long-term money market.

A—Bonds rated A are regarded as upper medium grade. They have considerable changes in economic and trade conditions. Interest and principal are regarded as safe. They predominantly reflect money rates in their market behavior, but to some extent, also economic conditions.

BBB—The BBB, or medium grade category, is borderline between definitely sound obligations and those where the speculative element begins to predominate. These bonds have adequate asset coverage and normally are protected by satisfactory earnings. Their susceptibility to changing conditions, particularly to depressions, necessitates constant watching. Marketwise, the bonds are more responsive to business and trade conditions than to interest rates. This group is the lowest which qualifies for commercial bank investment.

BB—Bonds given a BB rating are regarded as lower medium grade. They have only minor investment characteristics. In the case of utilities, interest is earned consistently but by narrow margins. In the case of other types of obligors, charges are earned on average by a fair margin, but in poor periods deficit operations are possible.

B—Bonds rated as low as B are speculative. Payment of interest cannot be assured under difficult economic conditions.

CCC–CC—Bonds rated CCC and CC are outright speculations, with the lower rating denoting the more speculative. Interest is paid, but continuation is questionable in periods of poor trade conditions. In the case of CC ratings, the bonds may be on an income basis and the payment may be small.

C—The rating of C is reserved for income bonds on which no interest is being paid.

DDD–D—All bonds rated DDD, DD and D are in default, with the rating indicating the relative salvage value.

Source: *Standard & Poor's* Bond Guide.

Of greater importance than the ratings is the financial strength of the issuer and his ability to service the debt (that is, to pay the interest and principal). In general, where the investor has the option of investing in two bonds of similar rating (or risk) with the exception that one is secured and one unsecured, the investor would normally prefer the secured bond.*

Bond-Market Cycles   Broad moves in the bond market appear to occur every 50 to 54 years. Nothing states that the cycle must be exactly so. However, bond yields peaked (and bond prices bottomed) in 1869, 1920, and 1974. The preparation period (period between peaks in bond yields) after the peak in yields may last from five to ten years. Patience is necessary on the part of the investor in bonds. Time is the essential ingredient for any investment program.

Thus, investors who bought corporate bonds when the corporate AAA bond average peaked above 9.3 percent in the second week of October 1974 are realizing some handsome capital gains. This is shown by a comparison between bond prices in mid-1974 and in February 1977, in Figure 16.2. After only two years, the yield on AAA corporate bonds had declined from 9.3 to 8.5 percent. This means that bond prices had risen considerably in two years, as is evidenced by the comparison of prices for 1974 and 1977.

Figure 16.3 portrays the bond-market cycle. It is rather persuasive in itself. When it is coupled with the Kondratieff long waves discussed in Chapter 5, one has to give some attention to long waves. The investor who respects the long waves and the broad moves in the bond market, and acts accordingly, will make money.

The bond cycle becomes even more important when one realizes that action in the stock market is preceded by action in the bond market. In other words, when bond prices firm and begin to rise, the same can be expected to occur in the stock market. The reverse also holds true. That is, a decline in bond prices is followed by a decline in stock prices.

PREFERRED STOCK

Ranked according to risk on the risk–return curve, preferred stock is located between subordinated debentures and high-grade common stock. Even though preferred stock is an ownership security, it is similar to a bond in that the dividend paid to preferred shareholders is usually a fixed dollar amount. The basic preference granted to preferred stock is (1) preference of its dividends over common-stock dividends, and (2) preference of its claim on assets over common-stock claims in event of liquidation. That is, dividends on preferred stock are paid after bond interest and income taxes, but

---

*A reason some investors prefer bonds is the small commission charge. Some brokerage charges per bond are as low as $10.

FIGURE 16.2 Comparison of 1974 and 1977 Selected Bond Prices. (*Source: Barron's, February 7, 1977, p. 78.*)

LISTED BOND QUOTATIONS

1974 High	Low		Sales $1,000	Weekly High	Low	Last	Net Chg.
26	14	vjAnnArb 4s95f	6	15	14	15	+ 1
103	97½	AppalPow 9s75	48	99¾	99	99¾	+ ¼
102⅞	96¾	AppalP 8⅝s76	15	97½	97	97	+ ¼
98½	90	Appal P 7¼s79	2	90⅛	90⅛	90⅛	+ ⅛
88½	70	ARASv cv4⅝96	105	77	74½	74½	− 1½
10[illegible]⅞	91	Aristar 9½s89	28	93	91	91	− 3½
103	98⅝	ArizPSv 8.50s	5	99¾	99¾	99¾	+ ¼
97	80½	ArizPSv 7.45s	10	82	82	82	+ 1½
103	92½	Armco 8.70s95	7	93¾	93½	93¾	− 4¾
101½	97	Armco 8.25s75	14	98⅜	97¾	98	.....
71¾	66⅛	Armour 5s84	10	68	67⅝	68	+ 1⅞
112⅛	87⅝	Armr cv4½s83	6	89½	89½	89½	− ½
.....	.....	Armr 4½83 reg	7	89	89	89	......
99	89¼	ArmstgCk 8s96	5	92	92	92	......
78½	65	AshlO cv4¾s93	57	65⅛	65	65	.....
104⅞	90⅛	AssoCp 9¼s90	9	94	93½	93½	+ ⅜
102¼	97⅞	AssoCp 8½s77	5	97⅞	97⅞	97⅞	− ¾
91⅝	73⅝	AssoInv 7⅜88	33	74⅛	73⅝	74⅛	+ ⅛
92¾	91¼	AssoInv 5¼77	30	91¾	91¼	91¼	− ½
91¾	86¾	AssoInv 4½76	36	89	86¾	86¾	− 1¾
60⅛	55⅛	AtchT&SF 4s95	8	57	57	57	......
59	45½	Atchison 4s95st	1	49⅝	49⅝	49⅝	......
75	59	AticoM 6¾s82	38	60⅝	60	60⅛	+ ⅛
68⅛	63	AtlCstL 4¾s88	4	63	63	63	− 5⅛
107½	98	AtRch 8⅝s2000	5	100	100	100	+ 1¾
93⅞	90	AtlRich 7¾s03	11	90	90	90	− 2
100½	94¼	AtlRich 7s76	120	96	95	95	− 1
81⅞	69	Atl Rich 5⅝s97	28	71½	71⅜	71½	− 2¾
51	47⅞	ATO cv4⅜s87	11	48½	47⅞	48	− ⅜
75⅝	75⅛	Aurora cv4⅝80	10	75⅝	75⅝	75⅝	......
113	104	Avco Fin 11s90	75	105⅞	104¾	105¼	+ ½
104¼	98	AvcoFin 9¼s89	58	99	98	98	− 2
76	60	Avco Cp 7½s93	53	60⅜	60	60⅜	+ ⅜
57	41	Avco cv5½s93	120	47	42⅞	47	+ 4½
104	97½	AvcoFin 9¼s90	32	98½	98½	98½	− ½
103	98	AvcoFin 8⅞s77	14	98½	99½	98½	.....
94	88	AvcoFin 7⅞s89	17	88	88	88	......
103⅞	98½	Balt GE 8¾s75	5	99	99	99	− ¾
61	57	BaltGE 4s93	4	57	57	57	......
110	102¼	B&O 11s77	5	106	104¼	106	+ 2
110	75½	B&O cv6¼s97	112	78	75½	76	− 2
56	46	B&O cv4½s10f	10	47	47	47	.....
48¾	40½	B&O cv4½s10A	115	42	40½	40½	− ½
51½	46	B&O 4¼s95	11	48	46¾	48	+ 1⅜
80⅜	75	B&O 4s80	10	75¾	75¾	75¾	− ⅛
75½	58⅞	BangP cv8¼94	5	61	61	61	+ 2
90	70⅛	Bk Cal cv6½96	3	75	70⅛	70⅛	− 4⅞
99	84½	Bk NY cv6¼94	35	85½	84⅝	84⅝	+ ⅛
98¾	93¼	Bankam 7⅞s03	6	93¼	93¼	93¼	− ⅝
100	84	Barnet cv8½98	21	84½	84	84	− 1¼
130	106½	Bax Lb cv4¾90	250	113½	111	111¾	− ¼
128	108	Bax Lb cv4⅜91	92	115	108	108	− 6½
62	50½	Beaunt cv4¼90	18	53½	51½	53	− ½
85½	76½	Becton cv5s89	38	78¼	78	78¼	+ ¼
92¾	85½	Becton cv4⅛88	70	88½	87	87	− 1¼
58½	50	Beech cv4¾s93	5	52⅛	52⅛	52⅛	− ⅞
63	55	Belco cv4¾s88	11	56½	56	56	......
102	89⅞	Beldn cv8s90	20	91½	89⅞	90	− 1½
105½	97	BellTPa 8⅝s	82	100	98	99½	+ ¼
94	80	BellTPa 7⅛s	5	81¼	81¼	81¼	+ ¼
100½	91	BellTPa 7s80	55	94	93	93	− 2

1976-77 High	Low		Sales $1,000	Weekly High	Low	Last	Net Chg.
114	100⅛	ArizPS 10⅝s00	10	112	111½	112	− ¾
56	44	ArlenRl cv5s86	20	56	55	56	+ 1
86	77½	Armco 4.35s84	14	84	84	84	− 1¼
87½	77⅜	Armco 5.90s92	25	87½	87⅛	87⅛	+ 2⅜
106½	95	Armco 8.70s95	8	101⅝	101⅝	101⅝	+ ⅛
106	100	Armco 9.20s00	5	103	103	103	− ½
105¼	100	ArmcoStl 8½01	5	101⅛	101⅛	101⅛	− 4⅛
106½	90⅝	Armour cv4½83	2	96⅝	96½	96½	+ 1¼
86⅛	75	Armour 5s84	25	85½	84¼	84⅜	+ ⅛
		Armour 5s84r	3	84⅛	84⅛	84⅛	......
106	101	ArmCk 8.45s84	5	103⅞	103⅞	103⅞	− 1¼
73¾	59¼	ArmR cv4½s87	23	73¾	72⅝	73¾	+ 1⅛
86	62	AshO cv4¾93	191	85½	82½	85	+ ⅜
104½	100¼	AsDGCr 8⅞s83	5	103	103	103	− ⅛
102	100	AssoCp 8½s77	41	100 23-32	100⅛	100⅛	...
104	92⅝	AssoCp 9¼s90	42	102½	102¼	102½	+ ¾
103½	99½	AssocCp 8⅝s81	25	103½	103½	103½	+ 1½
100¼	97¾	AssoInv 5¾77	14	100¼	100¼	100¼	+ ⅞
99¾	95	AssoInv 5¼77	35	99¾	99¾	99¾	+ ½
94½	86	AssoInv 5⅛79	2	94½	94½	94½	......
84	70¾	AssoInv 4½83	55	83½	83	83	− 1
80⅜	71	AssoInv 4⅜84	26	79	77⅝	77⅝	− 1⅝
77¾	65⅞	AssoInv 4⅝85	2	77¾	77¾	77¾	......
90½	77	AssoInv 7⅜88	20	90½	90½	90½	+ ½
58⅝	55	Atchison 4s95st	14	58	58	58	+ 1⅞
65½	56⅝	AtchT&SF 4s95	7	65½	62⅞	65½	+ 2½
60	42½	AticoM 6¾s82	69	59¼	57	57	+ ¼
80	65⅜	AtlCstL 4.95s88	12	74⅛	73⅜	74⅛	+ ¾
86¾	72⅜	AtlRch 5⅝97	10	81⅝	81⅝	81⅝	− ⅝
106⅛	94⅞	AtlRch 8⅝00	36	104	102	102	− 1½
100½	88	AtlRch 7.7s2000	33	95⅞	95½	95½	......
102	87¼	AtlRch 7¾03	30	95⅝	95⅝	95⅝	− 2⅜
64½	47	AvcoC cv5½93	297	63⅞	62½	62½	− 1⅜
78	58⅜	AvcoCp 7½93	74	78	77	78	+ ⅛
115	98	AvcoCp cv9⅝01	300	113½	109⅞	111½	− 2
86½	72⅛	AvcoFin 6⅛s87	4	84⅛	84⅛	84⅛	− 2⅜
104	85¾	AvcoFin 9¼s89	21	103	102⅛	103	......
112	100	AvcoFin 11s90	5	110½	110¼	110¼	− ¾
108½	103	AvcoF 10½s82	5	108	108	108	+ ⅜
107½	102½	AvcoFin 9¾s83	35	106⅞	106⅞	106⅞	......
102½	97¼	AvcoFin 8½s84	39	101⅞	100	101⅞	+ 3½
		—B—					
105	99⅜	BPNoAm 9s80	40	103¼	103¼	103¼	......
87⅝	79	B&O 4s80	3	87⅝	87⅝	87⅝	......
59	49¾	B&O 4¼s95	31	59	58¾	59	+ 1¼
60	50	B&O cv4½s10A	59	60	57	58	− ½
62⅜	52	B&O cv4½s10f	1	58¾	58¾	58¾	− 2¼
106½	97¾	B&O 11s77	52	102	101 31-32	102	......
110⅝	102¾	BaltGE 10s82	43	109	108	109	......
112	100¾	BaltGE 9⅞s05	23	109	108¾	108¾	− ¼
104	98¾	BaltGE 8⅜06	15	101	101	101	− ¼
77	60	BangP 5¾s92	2	77	77	77	+ 2
87	60	BangP cv8¼94	18	87	85	85	− ⅛
89	70	BkCal cv6½96	65	89	84	89	+ 4
100½	82¾	BkNY cv6¼94	66	99½	98½	98½	− 1
100½	87¾	Bankam 7⅞s03	15	96⅛	96⅛	96⅛	+ ⅜
108	98	Bankam 8⅞s05	50	106	104⅛	104⅛	− ⅞
107¼	99⅛	Bankam 8¾s01	40	105	103¾	104¾	− ¼
100½	95⅛	BankTr 6⅜s78	5	100¼	100¼	100¼	......
99⅞	82½	BankTr 8⅛s99	23	99½	98	99½	+ ¾
127	104	BaxLb cv4⅜91	42	106¾	104½	104½	− 3½
112¾	91	BaxLb cv4¾01	143	95½	94	95½	+ ½

FIGURE 16.3 Bond Market Cycles. (*Source: Board of Governors of the Federal Reserve System.*)

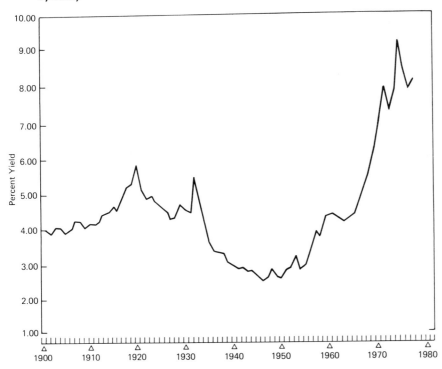

before payment of dividends on common stock. And in the event of liquidation, claims of debtors and bondholders are satisfied first, claims of preferred stockholders are paid next, and common stockholders receive the remaining assets, if any.

A Hybrid Security   Preferred stock is by nature a hybrid security. It is classed as debt or equity depending upon the point of view or the analysis being made. Preferred stock is considered debt if one requires equity shares to carry voting rights and to share in income. When analyzed as debt, preferred stock resembles bonds more than equity because preferred has (1) a prior claim feature, (2) a fixed dividend, and (3) dividends that usually accrue. Preferred stock is classed as equity if failure to pay preferred dividends does not cause default on the outstanding obligation. When analyzed as equity, preferred stock is similar in that equity requires no dividend payments when earnings are insufficient, and dividends on equity are not tax-deductible for the paying firm.

Characteristics of   Preferred stock has a stated or par value, and the dividend amount is
Preferred Stock   specified as a percentage of par in dollar amounts—for instance, $5 General Motors preferred stock. Most preferred issues are in denomi-

nations of $100, and the market price tends to fluctuate less than the price of common stock. Most preferreds are issued without a maturity date. Consequently, they are often known as "debt in perpetuity," since the issue may never be retired.

Preferred stock is normally nonparticipating with the common shares. Participating preferred, although very uncommon, has a special feature. In addition to the stated or contractual dividend, participating preferred is entitled to share in the earnings growth of the company.

Preferred stock is usually cumulative; this means that a preferred dividend that is bypassed is still owed to the shareholder. If the firm does not make a profit, dividends to both the common and preferred shareholders are not paid. However, the dividends that the cumulative preferred stockholders should have received will accumulate. When the firm earns a profit again, the cumulative preferred shareholders are entitled to the current year's dividend *and* those dividends accumulated from prior years. The common stockholders are not entitled to receive any dividend payments until all cumulative preferred dividends in arrears have been paid. The settlement of small arrearages is usually made in cash. Whenever large dividend arrearages occur, preferred shareholders are usually paid in common stock, or sometimes the issue is refinanced.

The Call Provision. In most instances, preferred stock is callable at the option of the issuing company. In such cases, the issuing company has the right to call and retire the stock at a specific price that is greater than par value. Such a price is known as the call premium. For example, a $100-par preferred may be callable at the option of the company at $105 per share. A preferred stockholder must be given two or three months notice prior to the call date. The absence of a call feature in a preferred-stock issue does not ensure that the investor can keep the stock indefinitely. In the 1960s, Bethlehem Steel, U.S. Steel, International Harvester, and Eastman Kodak eliminated their preferred stock outstanding through mergers and recapitalizations. Generally, such plans are quite generous, but they require the approval of the preferred shareholders.

Varieties of Preferred Besides convertible preferreds (to be discussed below), there are other varieties of preferred stocks. One is the preferred certificate with a common-stock purchase warrant attached. The warrants can be detached and submitted along with a check for the amount indicated to buy common stock. There are preferreds with sinking funds, either cash or reserve. And there are preferreds that have a maturity date, although such preferreds are the exception. Actually, the variety of characteristics of preferred stocks is limited only by the imagination and ingenuity of the makers of the preferred contract.

Quality and Ratings of Preferred Stocks   The amount of preferred stock issued reached its peak in 1929, at 19 percent of total corporate securities issued. Subsequently, the amount of preferred stock trended downward, reaching a low point of 2.62 percent of total securities issued in 1969. Since then, the use of preferred has increased significantly. This is shown in Table 16.4.

TABLE 16.4 The Dollar Value of Preferred Stock as a Percentage of Total Corporate Securities Issued

YEAR	PREFERRED STOCK TO TOTAL CORPORATE ISSUES (PERCENT)
1929	19.00
⋮	⋮
1965	4.53
1966	3.31
1967	3.62
1968	2.72
1969	2.62
1970	3.56
1971	8.22
1972	8.45
1973	10.34
1974	5.98
1975	6.56
1976	4.89

Source: Federal Reserve Bulletin.

There are several reasons to account for the recently increasing popularity of preferred stock with some investors. Chief among them is the fact that preferreds are usually slightly safer than common stock of the same company. Preferred-stock ratings are similar to those for bonds, with AAA, AA, and A being the highest-grade preferred ratings. The ratings are independent of the bond ratings, since they are not necessarily based on the issuing company's debt. They represent a considered judgment of the relative security of dividends and the prospective yield stability of the security. Standard & Poor's preferred-stock ratings are:

AAA	Prime	BBB	Medium Grade	C	Non-Paying
AA	High Grade	BB	Lower Grade		
A	Sound	B	Speculative		

CONVERTIBLES

Convertible securities consist of bonds and preferred stocks that are convertible at the option of the owner into common stock. Convertibles are attractive to the investor because they combine the stability of a fixed-income security with the growth potential of a common-stock investment. A convertible security, if chosen properly, can provide a limit on the amount of loss while giving an opportunity for a capital gain. In contrast, nonconvertible securities (straight bonds or preferreds) do not give the owner a direct method of participating in the growth of the firm through its common stock.

Terms of Conversion   *Preferred Stock.*   The rate at which a security is convertible into common stock is known as the *conversion rate*. The conversion rate for preferred stock is always expressed as a specific number of shares of common stock. For example, the convertible preferred of American Home Products (AHP) is shown in Figure 16.4. The *Stock Guide* shows that the AHP preferred is convertible into 4.5 shares of AHP common.

FIGURE 16.4   Common- and Preferred-Stock Quotations of American Home Products. (*Source: "NYSE–Composite Transactions," Barron's, January 3, 1977, p. 47.*)

1976 High Low	Stock (div.)	Sales 100s	Yield Pct.	P-E Ratio	Week's High	Low	Last	Net Chg.
37¾ 28½	AmHome 1	5042	3.1	19	32⅜	30⅝	32	+ 1⅜
167 130½	A Homepf 2	2	1.4 ...	143	143	143	+12½

The decision as to whether it is more profitable to convert or retain the convertible preferred stock rests with its owner. The convertibility feature conveys, potentially at least, a share of the income that accrues to common stockholders, the ability to share in any rise in the market price of the common stock, and voting rights. The conversion parity for preferred is:

$$\text{Conversion parity} = \text{Conversion ratio}$$
$$\times \text{ Market price of common stock}$$
$$\text{Conversion parity for AHP preferred} = 4.5 \times \$32 = \$144$$

Notice that the preferred stock of American Home Products closed at $143 on the same day the common closed at $32. Thus, the preferred stock moves proportionately to the common. If the common stock rises $10, the preferred will rise approximately $45 ($10 × 4.5 conversion ratio).

Bonds. The conversion rate of a convertible bond can be expressed either as a dollar amount or as a specific number of shares of common. If the rate is expressed as a dollar value, it must be translated into the number of shares. For example, convertible bonds of American Hospital Supply are listed in Figure 16.1. Notice that the American Hospital issue of 5 3/4s maturing in 1999 is convertible ("cv") into common stock. The *Bond Guide* indicates that this particular issue is convertible into common at $28 a share. The conversion ratio is:

$$\text{Conversion ratio} = \frac{\text{Par value of bond}}{\text{Conversion price}}$$

$$= \frac{\$1,000}{\$28}$$

$$= 35.71$$

Thus, one bond is convertible into 35.71 shares of common stock.

The Value of a Convertible Bond
A convertible bond has two values associated with it. The first is its value as a bond or straight security. If the price of the common stock declines, the price of the bond is eventually supported by its yield. If the yield is high, as is the current market yield on bonds, the price of the bond should stay near $1,000. In the case of American Hospital Supply, the yield on the bond is somewhat low. Therefore, one would expect the price of the bond to drop below $1,000 if it were not supported by the price of the common stock.

The second value of a convertible is the price based on *conversion parity*. Conversion parity is determined by the following:

$$\text{Conversion parity} = \text{Conversion ratio} \times \text{Market price of common}$$

$$= 35.71 \times \$28\tfrac{1}{8}$$

$$= \$1,004.34$$

Notice in Figure 16.1 that the American Hospital Supply convertible bond sold for $1,067.50. Thus the bond sells at a price higher than conversion parity.

Call Provisions of Convertible Bonds
Convertible bonds are almost always callable. The call feature is necessary, given the motivation behind the use of a convertible bond. A firm may not want to sell additional common stock at a low price. Instead, it sells a bond convertible into common stock in the future at a higher price. If the common reaches the higher price (conversion price), the firm may want to call the bond. Bonds are normally callable at $50 above par, or $1,050. Thus, the investor has a choice if the common is

selling above the conversion price. He is given 30 days' notice to decide whether to let the bond be called or to convert. In the case of the American Hospital bond, conversion would result in more profit per bond—$1,250 if converted into common, versus $1,050 if the bond is called.

Advantages and Disadvantages of Convertible Bonds

Theoretically, convertible bonds appear to be the best of both worlds, since they combine the safety of a good creditor obligation with the opportunity to share in the growth prospects and profits of a company. But they do have disadvantages: (1) They represent common stock and must be considered as such; (2) they are junior bonds and rank very low as bonds; and (3) they may be overpriced and purchased at too-high prices just like common stock. Convertibles are normally rated in the BB category and carry relatively low yields as bonds.

SUMMARY

Corporate bonds, preferred stock, and convertible issues round out the fixed-return securities issued by a corporation. Combined, these securities represent approximately 85 percent of all external corporate sources of financing. These securities provide good returns commensurate with risks if purchases are properly timed.

Bond yields appear to peak about every 50–54 years. Bond yields peaked in 1920, and it appears that they peaked again in 1974. If so, this means that a once-in-a-lifetime buying opportunity in fixed-return securities is occurring in the mid-1970s to the mid-1980s.

PROBLEMS

1. Calculate the present value of the following bonds, all of which pay interest semiannually:

BOND	PAR VALUE	COUPON RATE	MATURITY	MARKET RATE
A	$1,000	10%	20 years	12%
B	1,000	8%	10 years	10%
C	1,000	6%	15 years	6%

2. A company whose common stock is currently selling at a price of $40 a share plans to issue convertible bonds. The conversion price is set at $50

a share. Subsequently, the company's stock sells at $50 after a two-for-one stock split, and the issue is called by the firm.

a. How many shares of common will each bondholder receive at the split price of $50?

b. How much capital appreciation, if any, accrues to the bondholder? What is the annual rate of return?

c. How much capital appreciation would have accrued to a common stockholder over the same period? What is the annual rate of return?

3. If a person's marginal tax rate is 30%, which bond provides a higher effective yield:

a. a corporate bond issue at 9%

b. a municipal bond issue at 6.5%

4. Three bond portfolios have the following maturity schedules:

MATURITIES	BOND PORTFOLIO		
	A	B	C
Under 1 year	5%	30%	7%
Over 1 and under 3 years	0	30	9
Over 3 and under 5 years	0	30	9
Over 5 and under 10 years	0	10	15
Over 10 and under 15 years	30	0	15
Over 15 and under 20 years	30	0	15
Over 20 and under 25 years	30	0	15
Over 25 years	5	0	15
Total	100%	100%	100%

What outlook for changes in the level of interest rates is indicated by each portfolio? Why?

5. Consult a recent *Federal Reserve Bulletin* to determine the amount of external funds (bonds, preferred stocks, and common stocks) that were used by corporations last year. (Refer again to Table 16.1.)

a. What percentage was bonds?

b. What percentage was preferred stock?

c. What percentage was common stock?

6. Consult the *Wall Street Journal* to determine recent bond quotations for ATT 2 7/8s '87 and ATT 8.80s '05.

a. What is the quotation on each bond?

b. What is the dollar price of each bond?

c. Determine the current yield of each.

d. Determine approximate yield to maturity of each.

e. How do the yields compare with those used in the text for the same bonds? Why?

7. Consult Moody's or Standard & Poor's to determine yields on AAA corporate bonds for July 1974 and for the present.

a. List the yields.

b. What can be said about bond prices over the period from July 1974 to the present?

8. a. What is meant by "yield to maturity"?

b. Explain the derivation of the formula for approximating yield to maturity.

9. You have just purchased a newly issued $1,000, five-year Duke Power bond for $1,000. The bond pays $40 interest semiannually. You are now considering the purchase of a $1,000 Duke Power bond that pays $20 interest semiannually, was originally issued for ten years, and has five years remaining to maturity.

a. What is the "going rate" on Duke Power's bonds of similar risk and maturity?

b. What should you be willing to pay for the latter bond—that is, what is the present value?

10. The ABC Company is oriented toward growth. Its common stock earns $1 a share, pays only a 2% stock dividend, and sells at $25. The stock has been used with success in acquisitions.

a. Now the company offers a $100-par preferred stock with a $4 dividend rate (convertible into three shares of common) to be used in acquisitions. Why would the company plan to use such a stock rather than (1) cash, (2) common stock, (3) convertible debentures?

b. The common stock, soon after the preferred is issued, is priced in the market at $40. What is the conversion parity of the preferred stock?

c. Briefly, what are the qualities of this preferred stock that might make it attractive to a buyer?

17

Investment Securities: Common Stock and Securities Options

Stockholders are a varied lot—
Some look while others leap;
You can tell a lot about them
By the companies they keep.

George O. Ludcke

So far we have examined the fixed-return securities—government and municipal bonds in Chapter 15, and corporate bonds, preferreds, and convertibles in Chapter 16. Remember our frame of reference—the risk–return tradeoff curve. As we move along the curve, both expected return and risk are increasing.

In this chapter, we encounter the last group of security issues on the risk–return curve. This group has the highest degree of risk and the highest potential return for the investor of any corporate securities. These characteristics describe the ownership of the common stock of business firms. The ultimate risk and reward among financial investment securities is found at the top of the risk–return curve in securities options.

Over \$3.5 trillion worth of common stock is registered under the Securities Act of 1933. Approximately 25 million individual investors, and scores of institutional investors, own common stock. Common stockholders have a right to the earnings of the corporation and thus are the residual owners of the company. That is, common stockholders receive dividends only after the interest to bondholders and dividends to preferred stockholders are paid. Therefore, the residual owners are compensated only if the company is prosperous. In spite of this, investment to most people still means buying shares of common stock. A recent estimate shows that almost half the assets of Americans with a net worth of \$1 million or more is in corporate stocks. See Figure 17.1: The composition of wealth shown here is somewhat different from that shown for 1972 in Chapter 14, Table 14.1. Assuming that both studies are valid, money seems to be shifting from real estate to common stocks.

Par Value vs. Market Value   Ownership in a business is represented by certificates of common stock, which designate the number of shares owned by each stockholder. The stock may be issued with a par value or with no par value. Par value is the face value as stated on the stock certificate and is usually between \$1 and \$5. A stock with no par value is carried on the books at some stated value. In fact, the par value of par stock and the stated value of no-par stock are used only for accounting purposes. Par or stated value of the stock bears no systematic resemblance to the market value of the stock. It merely reflects the value of the stock as carried in the common-equity section of the position statement of the firm.

For example, the stock of Digital Equipment Corporation (DEC) has a par value of 33 1/3 cents per share, with 35,817,000 shares of common stock outstanding as of January 1977. Thus, the capital-stock value on the balance sheet of DEC was \$11,939,000 (\$0.33 1/3 × 35,817,000). The market price of DEC is shown in Figure 17.2 for January 3,1977, at 52 3/4*. Now multiply the market price per share by total shares outstanding. This gives the total

---

*Stocks are quoted in dollars and eighths of a dollar. Thus, 52 3/4 is \$52.75.

FIGURE 17.1 Boom in Millionaires. (*Source: U.S. News & World Report, July 26, 1976, p. 40.*)

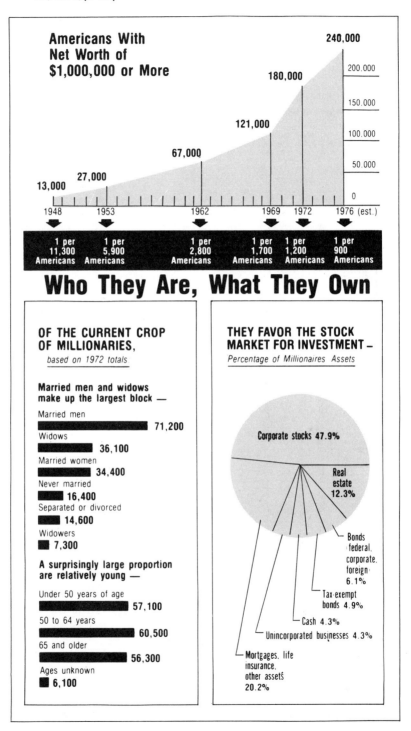

FIGURE 17.2 Selected Stock-Market Quotations. (*Source: Wall Street Journal, January 3 and January 4, 1977.*)

NYSE-Composite Transactions

Monday, January 3, 1977

Quotations include trades on the New York, Midwest, Pacific, Philadelphia, Boston and Cincinnati stock exchanges and reported by the National Association of Securities Dealers and Instinet.

−1976-77−				P-E	Sales				Net
High	Low	Stocks	Div.	Ratio	100s	High	Low	Close	Chg.
31⅞	21½	Cyprus	1.40	25	54	25½	25¼	25¼	+ ¼
		− D−D−D −							
8¼	4⅝	DPF Inc		11	72	7⅝	7¼	7¼	− ¼
11⅝	6⅝	Damon	.20	51	83	8⅛	8	8⅛	+ ⅛
11¼	7	DanRiv	.48	5	135	9⅜	9⅛	9⅜	− ⅛
29½	19¾	DanaCp	.92	10	63	29	28⅝	28⅞	− ⅛
41	27½	DartInd	.80b	8	92	35	34½	34⅞	+ ⅜
41½	32¼	DartIndpf	2	..	4	37¾	37	37¾	+ ¼
60¾	37⅜	Data Genl		23	139	45⅝	45⅛	45⅛	− ¼
17⅜	10⅝	Dayco	.50b	5	33	17⅛	16⅞	17⅛	......
68	50	Dayc pf	4.25	..	z10	67	67	67	− ¾
38¼	26¼	DaytnHud	1	10	189	38⅜	38	38⅛	− ⅛
20	17	DaytPL	1.66	11	88	19⅞	19½	19⅞	......
131	111½	DPL pf	12.50	..	z10	129	129	129	− ½
34½	29	Deere	1.10	8	341	31¾	31	31	− ⅝
29½	22⅜	DelMon	1.50	7	65	27⅞	27¼	27⅞	+ ⅝
14⅜	12¼	DelmaP	1.20	9	562	14¼	14⅛	14¼	+ ⅛
45⅞	34½	DeltaAir	.70	10	378	39¼	38⅜	39¼	+ ¾
7⅛	3¾	Deltec Intl		8	16	4⅜	4¼	4¼	......
7⅝	3¼	Deltona Crp		..	24	5	4⅞	5	......
24¾	19	DennisMfg	1a	8	27	23⅝	23¼	23¼	− ⅛
25¼	18⅛	Dennys'	.44	13	25	24⅞	24⅝	24⅞	......
34⅞	27½	Dentsply	.80	14	25	30⅜	30¼	30⅜	− ⅛
15	5¾	DeSotoIn	.60	9	20	14⅛	14	14	......
15⅝	13	DetEdis	1.45	10	478	15⅜	15⅛	15¼	+ ⅛
64¼	55	DetE pf	5.50	..	2	63¾	63½	63½	+ ½
98	82¼	DetE pf	9.32	..	z190	96	95¼	95¼	− ½
80¾	66	DetE pf	7.68	..	z650	79	78¼	79	+ ¼
78½	64	DetE pf	7.45	..	z1310	78	77¼	78	+ ⅛
77½	64	DetE pf	7.36	..	z300	77	75	75	− ½
28¾	24⅞	DetE pf	2.75	..	23	28⅛	28	28⅛	......
28¾	24¾	DeE pfB	2.75	..	6	28⅜	28	28	......
25	12⅛	Dexter	.80	10	14	24¾	24⅝	24⅝	+ ⅛
7⅜	4⅛	DiGiorg	.05e	10	151	7⅜	7⅛	7⅜	+ ¼
13½	10⅝	DiGior pf	.88	..	z100	14	14	14	+ ½
13¾	9	DialFinl	.70	7	8	13	13	13	+ ⅛
42½	33⅝	DiamInt	2	9	51	39⅞	39⅜	39⅜	− ⅝
22¾	14	DiamM	1.72t	4	14	17⅛	17	17	......
35⅜	32	DiamSh	1.10	9	182	34⅝	33¾	34⅝	+ ⅜
36¼	24½	Dia pfD	1.20	..	7	31	30⅝	31	......
11⅞	6⅞	DickAB	.20	15	19	8	7¾	7⅞	......
12	8¼	Dictaphn	.64	12	102	11¾	11⅜	11⅝	......
15	10½	Diebold	.44	10	57	14⅛	13¾	14	+ ¼
→ 57¼	46½	DigitalEq		25	669	54	52¾	52¾	− 1⅛
11½	7⅝	Dillingm	.48	5	52	9½	9¼	9⅜	......
37½	28⅞	Dillon	1.08b	12	45	30½	30¼	30¼	− ⅛
63	41⅛	Disney	.12b	20	651	47⅝	46¾	47	− ¼
2¾	1	Diversfd In		..	28	1½	1½	1½	+ ⅛
6¼	13-16	Diversd Mtg		..	73	1¾	1½	1½	......
17¾	11	DrPeppr	.44	18	199	14½	14¼	14½	+ ¼
46	32½	DomeM	.80a	15	18	44½	44	44½	+ ⅜

−1976-77−				P-E	Sales				Net
High	Low	Stocks	Div.	Ratio	100s	High	Low	Close	Chg.
35¾	31¼	GTIEl pf	2.50	..	3	34	34	34	+ ⅛
29	26½	GTIEl pf	2.48	..	30	28⅞	28⅝	28¾	+ ⅛
16½	14¼	GTFl pf	1.30	..	z500	16	16	16	+ ⅛
26⅞	18	GTire	1.10b	6	302	26⅛	25⅞	26	......
9	4⅞	Genesco Inc		8	242	5⅞	5½	5⅝	+ ⅛
24⅝	18⅜	Genstar	1.40	5	3	23⅜	23⅜	23⅜	......
41⅜	33¾	GenuPts	.76	18	24	37½	37	37¼	− ¼
38⅞	30	GaPacif	.80	18	377	38½	37⅜	37¾	− ⅝
28¼	26⅜	GaPw pf	2.52	..	24	28	27⅝	28	+ ½
29⅞	26	GaPw pf	2.75	..	29	29¾	29¼	29¾	+ ⅜
88⅞	69	GaPw pf	7.80	..	z7050	87⅛	87	87⅛	+ ⅞
26⅜	19½	Gerber	1.30	8	18	25⅛	25	25	− ¼
198¾	152	GettyO	2.50a	14	18	196⅛	194	194	− 2¼
18	16¼	GettO pf	1.20	..	16	18	18	18	+ ½
12⅞	8⅝	GiantPC	.60	9	6	10¼	10⅛	10¼	......
11⅜	7⅛	Gibr Fin		6	133	10¼	10	10¼	......
11½	5⅝	GiddLew	.40	11	46	9⅜	9	9⅜	+ ½
15¾	9⅛	GiffdHill	.64	7	10	15	14⅞	14⅞	+ ⅛
38⅞	24⅝	Gillette	1.50	10	309	28⅛	27⅝	27¾	− ⅛
18	7¾	Ginos Inc		7	177	9⅞	9⅝	9¾	− ⅛
14¾	6¼	GleasW	.18e	..	10	11⅜	11⅛	11⅛	− ⅛
11¼	6½	Global •Mar		..	65	8¼	7¾	7¾	− ¼
25¼	16¾	GlobeUn	1	7	66	25½	25	25⅛	− ⅛
20⅞	11½	GoldWt Fin		5	13	18¾	18⅝	18¾	+ ⅛
21	13⅛	GoldW pf	.78	..	6	19	19	19	+ ¼
29⅝	18	Goodrh	1.12	448	45	27	26¾	26⅞	......
25¼	20⅛	Goodyr	1.10	17	259	23⅞	23½	23¾	......
16¼	9⅝	GorJwlA	.40	6	104	12	11¾	11⅞	− ¼
31⅛	22	Gould	1	10	350	30¼	29⅞	30	......
30⅝	19¼	Gould pf	1.35	..	13	30½	30⅛	30⅛	− ¼
33⅞	24¼	Grace	1.70	9	197	29½	29	29¼	......
34⅛	24⅝	Grainger	.36	16	33	30¼	29½	29½	− ½
18⅜	12⅝	GrandUn	1	6	7	16⅞	16⅝	16¾	− ⅛
17⅜	12¼	Granitvl	.90	5	25	14⅞	14¾	14¾	− ⅛
19⅞	13¼	GrayDrg	.80	5	30	17⅝	17¼	17⅝	+ ¼
15⅝	10½	GtAtlPac		26	220	14⅜	14	14	− ¼
24½	18⅝	GtLkD	1.20a	5	7	23⅞	23½	23⅝	+ ⅜
20⅞	14⅛	GtNoIr	1.50e	15	41	20⅞	20⅜	20⅜	− ⅜
34¼	27½	GtNoNk	1.10	8	84	32¾	32	32	− ¾
24¾	13⅝	GtWnFin	.50	10	542	24	23⅜	23¾	+ ¼
31⅞	16½	GtWest Unit		6	19	20½	20	20⅜	+ ⅜
20¼	16⅝	GtWn pf	1.88	..	2	18¾	18¾	18¾	......
18½	15¼	GrGiant	1.08	22	35	18⅞	18⅜	18⅞	+ ⅜
27½	23⅛	GrGt pf	1.76	..	3	26¼	25½	26¼	+ 1½
17⅝	13	Greyh	1.04a	8	447	15⅝	15¼	15⅝	+ ⅝
3⅝	1¾	Greyhnd wt		..	108	2⅛	1⅞	2⅛	+ ⅛
3¼	1⅛	Grolier Inc		..	149	1¾	1½	1⅝	+ ⅛
18⅞	14	Grumm	.80	4	99	18	17¾	18	+ ⅛
17⅝	9⅜	GuardIn	.30	8	44	16⅞	16⅝	16¾	......
3½	1	Guard Mtg		..	28	1⅝	1⅜	1⅝	+ ¼
20⅞	14¾	GulfWstn	.60	4	392	18⅜	18	18¼	......

Monday's Volume
24,229,340 Shares; 126,000 Warrants

TRADING BY MARKETS

	Shares	Warrants
New York Exchange	21,280,000	125,900
American Exchange	4,100	....
Midwest Exchange	993,500	....
Pacific Exchange	693,400	....
Nat'l Assoc. of Securities Dealers	739,140	100
Philadelphia Exchange	253,100	....
Boston Exchange	94,500	....
Cincinnati Exchange	157,700	....
Instinet System	13,900	....

NYSE−Composite

Volume since Jan. 1:	1977	1976	1975
Total shares	24,229,340	12,378,500	....
Total warrants ..	126,000	....	....

New York Stock Exchange

Volume since Jan. 1:	1977	1976	1975
Total shares	21,280,000	10,300,820	14,797,450
Total warrants ..	125,900	36,900	195,800

MOST ACTIVE STOCKS

	Open	High	Low	Close	Chg.	Volume
Texaco Inc......	27¾	27⅞	27⅜	27½	− ¼	367,800
Philip Morr......	61⅜	61⅜	59⅜	59⅞	− 1⅞	323,600
Ramada In.......	4¼	4⅜	4⅛	4¼	− ⅛	214,000
Chrysler	20¾	21¼	20	21⅛	+ ¾	200,700
Occiden Pet.....	24⅛	24⅜	23⅞	24¼	+ ¼	184,200
Gen Motors......	78⅜	78½	77¾	78	− ½	157,100
Am Tel&Tel.......	63½	63¾	63	63⅜	− ⅛	154,700
Hughes Tool......	40¼	40⅜	39¼	39½	+ ¼	152,300
NCR Corp........	37½	38⅜	37¼	38⅛	+ ⅝	151,900
Southern Co.....	16½	16⅝	16⅜	16⅝	+ ¼	147,500

market value of DEC's common, $1,987,843,500. Summarizing, we have:

DIGITAL EQUIPMENT CORP.	VALUE PER SHARE ×	NUMBER OF SHARES OUTSTANDING	= TOTAL VALUE
Par value	$0.33⅓	35,817,000	$11,939,000
Market value	52.75	35,817,000	1,889,346,700

Thus, we see that market value bears little or no resemblance to par value.

Features of Common Stock   An analysis of common-stock issues reveals that they do possess a number of features that are similar. *First*, the owner of common stock has the right to transfer or sell his interest to another person. (The new owner should make certain that the issuing firm has changed its record of ownership. Otherwise, dividend payments, voting rights, and other rights will still accrue to the prior owner.) *Second*, the owners of common stock are entitled by law to the earnings of the firm. Since earnings tend to fluctuate, common stockholders' fortunes rise and fall with the earnings of the company. *Third*, the stockholder's liability is limited by the amount of his investment. But he does bear the most risk of any corporate-security holder, because other types of claims (bonds and preferred stock) rank ahead of the common-stockholder claims. *Last*, the degree of marketability of common stock depends on the number of shares of the issue outstanding. For this reason, stocks of small firms may be rather nonliquid and difficult to sell because there is a lack of buyers.

Preemptive Rights   New ownership securities may be issued via public offerings or preemptive-rights offerings. A public offering is simply sold to the public at large. A preemptive-rights offering, however, enables the existing stockholders to maintain their proportionate share of ownership of the firm. Such stock rights entitle the existing owners to the first right to buy a portion of any new common-stock issue. One right for each share of common ownership is *given* to the common stockholders. In general, a stock right is defined as a short-term option to buy a specified number of shares of common at a specified price, which is known as the subscription price.

For example, Polaroid (PRD) had a rights offering in early 1969 whereby each shareholder received as usual one stock right for each share owned. This entitled him to purchase one new share for every 30 stock rights at a subscription price of $95 per share. (See Figure 17.3.) The market price of PRD at that time was $110 per share and there were 31.7 million old shares outstanding.

Rights Needed to Purchase a New Share.   The number of rights needed to purchase one new share of common stock depends on the amount of new

FIGURE 17.3 A Rights Offering. (*Source: Barron's, March 10, 1969*).

This announcement is not an offer to sell or a solicitation of an offer to buy these securities. The offering is made only by the Prospectus.

New Issue

1,057,800 Shares

Polaroid Corporation

Common Stock

(Par Value $1 Per Share)

The Company is offering the holders of its Common Stock the right to subscribe for these Shares, subject to terms and conditions set forth in the Prospectus. The Subscription Offer will expire at 3:30 P.M., Eastern Standard Time, on March 19, 1969. The several underwriters have agreed, subject to certain conditions, to purchase any unsubscribed Shares and may offer the Shares, both during and after the subscription period, as set forth in the Prospectus.

Subscription Price $95 per Share

Copies of the Prospectus may be obtained in any State only from such of the several underwriters named in the Prospectus and others as may lawfully offer these securities in such State.

Kuhn, Loeb & Co.

Dillon, Read & Co. Inc. **The First Boston Corporation**

Blyth & Co., Inc. **Drexel Harriman Ripley** Incorporated **Eastman Dillon, Union Securities & Co.**

Glore Forgan, Wm. R. Staats Inc. **Goldman, Sachs & Co.** **Halsey, Stuart & Co. Inc.**

Hornblower & Weeks-Hemphill, Noyes **Kidder, Peabody & Co.** Incorporated **Lazard Frères & Co.**

Lehman Brothers **Loeb, Rhoades & Co.** **Merrill Lynch, Pierce, Fenner & Smith** Incorporated

Paine, Webber, Jackson & Curtis **Salomon Brothers & Hutzler** **Smith, Barney & Co.** Incorporated

Stone & Webster Securities Corporation **Wertheim & Co.**

White, Weld & Co. Incorporated **Dean Witter & Co.** Incorporated

March 6, 1969

financing needed by the firm. In the case of Polaroid, this was determined as follows:

$$\text{Number of new shares} = \frac{\text{New financing needed}}{\text{Subscription price}}$$

$$= \frac{\$100,491,000}{\$95} = 1,057,800 \text{ shares}$$

Next, the ratio of old shares outstanding to new shares is determined. The result is the number of rights (or old shares) to buy one new share.

$$\text{Rights needed to buy new shares} = \frac{\text{Old shares}}{\text{New shares}}$$

$$= \frac{31,734,000}{1,057,800} = 30 \text{ rights}$$

Value of a Right. Each right has a value, since the rights can be used collectively to buy a new share of common at a price less than the current market value. In the case of Polaroid, the new or subscription price was $95 per share, whereas the market price was $110. The value of each right is calculated as follows:

$$\text{Value of a right} = \frac{\text{Market price of old share} - \text{Subscription price of a new share}}{\text{Number of rights needed to buy one new share} + 1}$$

$$= \frac{M - S}{n + 1} = \frac{\$110 - \$95}{30 + 1} = \$.48$$

This is known as the *rights-on* value—that is, the value during the period when the rights cannot be separated from the stock if the stock is traded. The period when the stock can be traded separately from the rights is called the *ex-rights* period. See Figure 17.4 for a diagram of the process.

FIGURE 17.4   Life-span of a Preemptive Right.

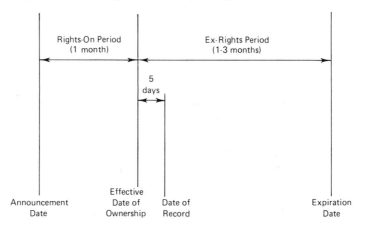

Advantages and Disadvantages of Rights. The firm is anxious for the common stockholders to exercise their rights—to subscribe to their share of the new financing needed. This is so because the firm has already planned to use the proposed financing. However, this method of financing may have disadvantages for the investor. Some advisors believe that the use of rights is a bull-market phenomenon and that it is unprofitable for the investor to exercise his rights. The evidence shows that in the majority of cases, after rights are issued, the market value of the common stock declines to a price lower than the subscription price of the stock, even though the new shares were offered to the stockholder at prices substantially below market value at the time.*

If rights are not used to subscribe to new shares of common, they can be traded in the organized exchange where the common is listed. Since the rights usually expire in three months, they should be used for subscription to new shares or sold at the going market price for each right. In the case of Polaroid, the rights sold for 50 cents each. However, the ex-rights price varied between $1.50 per right and zero when rights expired. For this reason, trading in rights is considered to be quite speculative.

Important Dates
There are certain dates that are important to the common stockholder. They are the announcement date, the effective date of ownership, the date of record, the ex-dividend date, and the actual date of payment of dividend.

The board of directors of the corporation declares a dividend and notifies the stockholders by public announcement. At the time of the announcement, the date of record is specified. This date is when the record of ownership is determined according to the name on the books of the corporation. Because of the time it takes to record transfers of ownership, the New York Stock Exchange and other exchanges specify that the effective date of ownership is really five full business days earlier than the date of record.

Dividends will be paid only to the stockholders of record—those on the books of the corporation. After the effective date of ownership, the stock sells ex-dividend. This means that the stock is sold without the dividend. In other words, prior to the effective date of ownership, the stock and the dividend are inseparable and must be sold as a unit. But after the effective date of ownership, the previous owner of the stock will receive the dividend, because he is the owner of record on the books of the firm. Therefore, if the owner sells after this date, the buyer of the stock will receive only the shares of common, not the dividend for the past period.

Preemptive rights have a similar dating process. There is one addition, since the rights will expire: An expiration date must be added to the other

---

*See *The Magazine of Wall Street,* October 3, 1958.

five dates. That gives an announcement date, an effective date of ownership, a date of record, an ex-rights date, and an expiration-of-rights date. These were shown in Figure 17.4.

Quality Classifications   Investors buy common stock because of the chance for capital appreciation over the long term. Stocks have tended to rise in price over the years, with the exception of temporary downturns in the business cycle. Since not all investors have the same investment goals, stocks can be divided into categories according to the risk taken. Stocks range in quality from high-grade investment stocks to highly speculative stocks. Common stocks are classed here by quality and in the next section by their investment characteristics.

Common stocks can be grouped in a number of ways. A very simple approach is the conservative versus the aggressive company. Another method of classifying stocks is by whether they are investment grade, good quality, or speculative. The latter method is more definitive and therefore more useful for investment purposes.

Investment Grade.   Common stocks of investment grade have the least risk and also the least potential reward. This classification is, therefore, the most conservative one for investors in common stocks. It includes the high-grade issues of companies that have strong financial records, sound capital structures, demonstrated earning ability, and long dividend-payment records. A person just beginning in the stock market should select some stocks in this category.

Investment-grade stocks include issues of companies such as Coca-Cola, International Business Machines, and Winn-Dixie Stores:

COMPANY	RATING	1976		CAPITAL STRUCTURE			DIVIDENDS PAID SINCE
		SALES (IN BIL-LIONS)	EARNINGS (IN MIL-LIONS)	DEBT (IN MIL-LIONS)	PRE-FERRED SHARES	COMMON SHARES	
Coca-Cola	A+	$ 3	$ 285	$ 8	—	60,126,000	1893
IBM	A+	16	2,398	275	—	148,535,000	1916
Winn-Dixie	A+	1	46	36	—	19,334,000	1934

Source: 1976 Annual Reports.

Good Quality.   Good-quality stocks are of somewhat lower quality than those of investment grade. As a result, prices of these issues may fluctuate over a wider range. Since there is more price volatility in this group, one would expect to encounter a little more risk. Likewise, one also can expect to receive a greater potential reward from good-quality stocks. For the beginning investor, the bulk of his common-stock investments should be in this category. Since common stocks offer the greatest potential for capital gain of all corporate securities, issues selected from this category represent the "pale" blue chips. These are companies that have a good track record and are participating heavily in the growth of the economy, such as Digital Equipment and McDonald's. Such investments are neither too conservative nor too aggressive. The two companies are shown below. Notice that they do not meet the dividend requirement of investment-grade securities.

| COMPANY | RATING | 1976 | | CAPITAL STRUCTURE | | | |
		SALES (IN MIL-LIONS)	EARNINGS (IN MIL-LIONS)	DEBT (IN MIL-LIONS)	PRE-FERRED SHARES	COMMON SHARES	DIVIDEND PAID SINCE
Digital Equipment	B+	$736	$ 73	$ 10	—	35,817,000	None paid
McDonald's Corp.	B+	700	108	459	—	40,380,000	1976

Source: 1976 Annual Reports.

Speculative Issues. This classification includes stocks of somewhat lower investment quality than issues in the other groups. Prices of such stocks fluctuate much more widely than do prices of higher-quality investments. The reasons for such price fluctuations involve business conditions as well as the capitalization of the firm. Quite often, business conditions center around some new concept or product. Data General and Intel Corporation are considered speculative because of relatively new products. If all goes well, the investor will reap handsome profits. But if the company suffers setbacks, the investor suffers accordingly. Notice that these companies are smaller and that they are relatively young firms.

| COMPANY | RATING | 1976 | | CAPITAL STRUCTURE | | | |
		SALES (IN MIL-LIONS)	EARNINGS (IN MIL-LIONS)	DEBT	PRE-FERRED SHARES	COMMON SHARES	DIVIDEND PAID SINCE
Data General	nr	$80	$15	—	—	7,973,000	None paid
Intel Corp.	nr	70	15	—	—	6,335,000	None paid

Source: 1976 Annual Reports.

Large amounts of debt or preferred stock, both of which have fixed and prior claims to the common, may cause unstable profits for the common-stock investor. Thus, the capitalization of these firms may result in potential gains or losses for the investor in speculative issues. Companies such as Lockheed Aircraft and Rapid-American have unusual amounts of debt and preferred in relation to the number of shares of common outstanding.

		1976		CAPITAL STRUCTURE			
COMPANY	RATING	SALES (IN BIL- LIONS)	EARNINGS (IN MIL- LIONS)	DEBT (IN MIL- LIONS)	PRE- FERRED SHARES	COMMON SHARES	DIVIDEND PAID SINCE
Lockheed	nr	$3	$39	$561	500,000	11,359,000	. . .
Rapid- American	C	2	12	834	380,000	7,853,000	. . .

Source: 1976 Annual Reports.

Investment Characteristics of Common Stock   In addition to the classification according to quality, stocks can also be classed according to investment characteristics. One characteristic, or type, of common may overlap with another. However, the following types do serve to give the investor greater insight in making investment choices.

Blue Chips. Blue-chip stocks* are high-grade investment issues of major corporations with long and unbroken records of earnings and dividend payments. Stocks of large and financially strong corporations are considered blue-chip. Issues of companies such as American Home Products, American Telephone & Telegraph, Coca-Cola, Eastman Kodak, Exxon, IBM, and Texas Utilities have the highest earnings and dividend ranking.

Growth Stocks. A growth stock is an issue of a company whose earnings and sales are growing at a faster rate than the economy as a whole, and faster than the average growth in its industry. Such companies are usually aggressive, plowing back earnings into the company to finance expansion. Many growth companies are also considered blue-chip. For example, IBM is a growth company as well as a blue chip. A number of companies have sustained growth records of 10, 20, even 30 percent per annum. Notice the companies in Table 17.1 that have high growth rates. All these are growth companies and should continue to outperform the average company. The prices of growth stocks rise (and fall) fast. For example, McDonald's Corporation fell from $77 to $23 in the 1973–74 business decline, and then rose to $66 per share in 1976.

---

*Blue chips, in poker, have the greatest monetary value (in contrast to red and white chips).

TABLE 17.1 Selected Common Stocks Listed on New York Stock Exchange

TICKER SYMBOL	COMPANY	EARNINGS AND DIVIDEND RANKING	DIVIDENDS PAID SINCE	PRICE PER SHARE (1962–77) (a = ADJUSTED FOR STOCK SPLITS)	RATE OF ANNUAL GROWTH (1962–77)	DIVIDEND YIELD (D/P)	EARNINGS YIELD (E/P)	PRICE–EARNINGS RATIO (P/E)	INVESTMENT CHARACTERISTICS[a]
AHP	American Home Products	A+	1919	7a– 32	10.5%	3.9%	6.9%	16	B, G
T	American Tel. & Tel.	A+	1881	40– 65	3.2	6.5	9.6	10	B, I, D
BAX	Baxter Laboratories	A+	1934	2a– 40	22.0	0.8	5.1	15	B, G
BGH	Burroughs Corp.	A+	1895	6a– 91	20.0	1.4	3.0	12	B, G
KO	Coca-Cola Co.	A+	1893	6a– 40	13.5	4.1	6.0	15	B, G
DEC	Digital Equip. Co.	B+	—	1⅝– 54	26.0	None paid	4.3	16	G
DD	du Pont (EI) de Nemours	A–	1904	92–135	2.5	3.9	7.2	14	B, C
EK	Eastman Kodak	A+	1902	20a– 86	10.5	2.6	5.0	16	B, G
XON	Exxon	A+	1882	19a– 55	7.5	5.7	10.4	9	B, I
FCI	Fairchild Camera/Inst.	B	1973	14– 41	7.5	2.7	4.0	11	G, C
GM	General Motors	A–	1915	40– 78	4.5	9.5	16.1	7	B, C
HWP	Hewlett-Packard	A	1965	7a– 87	18.2	0.6	4.2	20	G
HOU	Houston Ind.	A+	1922	22– 36	3.0	5.4	11.3	8	I, D
HT	Hughes Tool	NR	1973	30– 42	2.0	1.3	8.0	13	S
IBM	Int'l Business Machines	A+	1916	58a–286	10.5	3.9	5.3	16	B, G
KMG	Kerr-McGee	A–	1941	7a– 74	17.0	1.9	5.3	13	G, C
MCD	McDonald's Corp.	B+	1976	1⅛a– 52	29.0	0.2	5.0	14	G
PN	Pan Am World Airways	C	—	4– 4	0.0	Nil	Deficit	—	S
PRD	Polaroid Corp.	B+	1952	10a– 38	9.5	1.5	4.4	13	G
PON	Ponderosa System	NR	—	2a– 8	10.0	None Pd.	9.0	11	S

TABLE 17.1 (Cont.)

TICKER SYMBOL	COMPANY	EARNINGS AND DIVIDEND RANKING	DIVIDENDS PAID SINCE	PRICE PER SHARE (1962–77) (a = ADJUSTED FOR STOCK SPLITS)	RATE OF ANNUAL GROWTH (1962–77)	DIVIDEND YIELD (D/P)	EARNINGS YIELD (E/P)	PRICE-EARNINGS RATIO (P/E)	INVESTMENT CHARACTERISTICS[a]
TP	TelePrompTer Corp.	NR	—	1a– 9	16.0	None Pd.	31.0	250	S
TXU	Texas Utilities	A+	1917	18a– 22	1.0	7.1	10.5	8	I, D
UAL	UAL, Inc.	B	1974	9½a– 27	7.0	2.6	Deficit	13	C
X	U.S. Steel	B+	1940	25– 50	5.0	4.8	2.6	11	C
UTX	United Technologies	B+	1936	11a– 39	9.0	4.6	14.5	7	C
XRX	Xerox Corp.	A+	1930	2a– 58	25.0	2.7	7.9	10	G
DJIA	Dow Jones Industrial Average			520–999	5.0	4.6	10.0	10	

[a]B—Blue-chip; C—Cyclical; D—Defensive; G—Growth; I—Income; S—Speculative.

Source: *Standard & Poor's Stock Guide, April 1977, and Barron's, May 9, 1977.*

Income Stocks. Income stocks are issues that pay a higher-than-average dividend return (5 percent or greater). Many investors prefer such an issue because they are concerned with the need for current income more than for capital appreciation. There are pitfalls to guard against, however. Often a company is paying a high return because it is in a declining industry. Such a stock would not be a good candidate for investment because of the likelihood that its price will continue to fall. As a rule, young people should not be too concerned with income stocks. These are mainly bought by conservative trust funds, pension funds, and educational foundations. Notice that the rate of annual growth for income stocks is either very low or zero for the past fifteen years (see Table 17.1).

Cyclical Stocks. A cyclical stock is an issue of a company whose earnings fluctuate with and are magnified by the business cycle. For these issues, sales and earnings, and therefore stock prices, tend to vary more widely than the average with fluctuations in business conditions. When business is good, sales and earnings are up for cyclical companies. When business is bad, sales and earnings are down, resulting in profit losses at times. Cyclical industries include the automotive, building, chemical, metal, machinery, paper, steel, and transportation industries. Cyclical stocks should be bought at or near the bottom turning point of the business cycle.

Defensive Stocks. Defensive stocks are issues whose prices tend to be less affected by cyclical fluctuations than the average issue, because of more stable sales and earnings. Such stocks are considered to be relatively safe during periods of declining business activity. The issues of electric and gas utilities are usually thought to be the best defensive stocks. Other industries that suffer little from recessions are foods, drugs, beverages, and mining. Gold-mining stocks are also prime defensive issues.

Speculative Stocks. All common stocks are speculative in the sense that one is taking a risk that is higher than that for other securities. However, speculation in common stocks generally refers to the act of committing funds to securities of low quality and wide price movements. Speculative stocks range from high-priced glamour issues, to new issues, to penny mining stocks. The unusually high selling prices of glamour stocks cause them to be speculative in nature. Conversely, the low selling price of penny mining stocks is highly speculative because such stocks may actually be worthless. In the case of new companies, speculation is due to the lack of a track record for the company.

Quality and Ratings of Common Stock

The major advantage of owning common stock is the potential for profits, which is greater than for any other investment security. The major disadvantage is the risk associated with the unstable earnings and price of common stock. To aid the investor in selecting common stock, Standard & Poor's has developed earnings and dividend rankings for stocks. While these rankings are not absolute and are subject to change, they do serve as a rough guide for the investor. The Standard & Poor's rankings for common stock as to earnings and dividends are as follows:

A+	Highest	B+	Median	C	Marginal
A	High	B	Speculative	D	In Reorganization
A−	Good	B−	Highly Speculative		

Fortunes have been made and lost in the stock market, sometimes more than once by the same person. However, there is no substitute for common stocks as a way of achieving tremendous capital gains and having liquidity at the same time.

SECURITIES OPTIONS

The last area on the risk–return curve is that of trading in securities options. The market for options is unquestionably the most exciting and potentially rewarding speculation in the securities industry.

Call A call is a financial instrument that gives the owner the right to buy a specified number of shares of common stock from another investor at a specified price within a specified period of time. *Warrants* and *calls* are both options to buy common stock. The main difference is in the supplier of the stock for purchase. If a warrant is exercised, the stock is purchased from the issuing company. If a call is exercised, the stock is purchased from another investor. *Calls are financial claims on investors, not corporations.*

Warrants Like options, warrants give holders the right to buy stock at a certain price within a fixed time period, but the time period is longer. Moreover, the popularity of options has driven warrant prices down, making them at times more economical—and more profitable—to use than options. For example, Tenneco is a large producer of natural gas that could benefit from the government's decision to raise the ceiling on interstate gas prices. At the stock's August 1976 price of $33.75, 100 shares would have cost $3,375—or $1,687.50 using a margin account, through which you could borrow half the purchase price. An option to buy 100 shares of Tenneco at $30 a share before February 19, 1977, would have cost $450, while the price of April 1, 1979, warrants on 100 shares of stock would be $787.50, or $393.75 on margin. Say the stock goes to $40 a share. The option price would then be at least $10 and the warrant $13. The stockholder's profit would be $625, or 37 percent. For the option buyer, it would be $550, or 122 percent, but for the warrant owner it would be $512.50, or 130 percent. If the stock price falls, warrants give owners longer to await recovery.

CBOE Developments The Chicago Board Options Exchange (CBOE) was opened in April 1973 by the Chicago Board of Trade. The CBOE provides an exchange for the trading *put* and *call* options in certain securities. (CBOE began trading of calls in 1973 and puts in 1977.)

The recent rapid growth of the CBOE and option trading has changed the market for options. *First,* the option contract with respect to the number of shares under option has been standardized at 100 shares. *Second,* the expiration date of CBOE options is the Saturday after the third Friday of the option expiration month. Trading in an option begins approximately nine months prior to the expiration date. Thus, trading in three different expiration months usually occurs at any given time. Refer to Figure 17.5 and notice that some options have expiration dates of August, November, and February. Others have expiration dates of October, January, and April. *Third,* the exercise or *striking* price has been standardized. Notice the option and price in Figure 17.5. For example, five options are listed for Digital Equipment, with striking prices of 35, 40, 45, 50, and 60.

Option Trading There are two basic ways that the investor can trade in call options. They are option writing and option buying.

Option Writing. The most conservative approach to options is *writing an option* on 100 shares of a stock that you own. You are selling the right to someone to buy your 100 shares at a given price, the striking price, at any time the buyer chooses until the expiration date of the option. For such a right, the buyer pays you a premium based on the current price of the stock and the length of time until expiration. The longer the time, the more chance the stock has of going up during the option period, and thus the higher the price of the option.

The main reason an investor writes an option is to realize a return if the stock declines or remains unchanged in price. In such a case, the writer earns the premium paid to him for writing the option less a commission. The risk assumed by the writer of call options is that of an increase in the price of the common stock on which the option is written. When the market price of the common rises above the striking price, the writer begins to lose a portion of the premium. If the market price of the stock rises above the striking price and the premium, the writer incurs absolute losses. However, if the writer of

FIGURE 17.5 Selected Chicago Board Options Exchange (CBOE) Option Quotations. (*Source: Wall Street Journal, July 25, 1977.*)

Listed Options Quotations

Friday, July 22, 1977

Closing prices of all options. Sales unit usually is 100 shares. Security description includes exercise price. Stock close is New York Stock Exchange final price. p-Put option.

Chicago Exchange

		– Aug –		– Nov –		– Feb –		N.Y.
Option &	price	Vol.	Last	Vol.	Last	Vol.	Last	Close
A E P	19⅞	4	5⅜	1	5½	4	5⅜	25¼
A E P	24⅞	55	⅜	26	½	21	11-16	25¼
Am Hos	20	a	a	a	a	10	4⅝	23¾
Am Hos	25	a	a	125	1	5	1⅝	23¾
A M P	25	12	5	8	5½	a	a	29⅞
A M P	30	97	11-16	16	1 13-16	1	2⅛	29⅞
Bally	20	413	3	171	4¼	27	4⅞	23
Bally	25	541	7-16	280	1⅝	98	2½	23
Bally	30	3	1-16	67	½	b	b	23
Baxter	30	17	4½	a	a	2	5¾	34⅜
Baxter	35	15	¾	19	1 11-16	10	2⅜	34⅜
Baxter	40	a	a	2	⅜	b	b	34⅜
Blk Dk	15	32	1⅞	105	2¼	49	2⅝	16¾
Blk Dk	20	215	1-16	45	¼	90	⅝	16¾
Boeing	45	7	12½	16	12⅜	b	b	57¼
Boeing	50	41	7½	179	8¼	105	9¼	57¼
Boeing	60	178	¾	114	2½	81	3⅝	57¼
Bois C	25	22	3¼	a	a	a	a	28⅜
Bois C	30	29	¼	17	15-16	23	1⅝	28⅜
Bois C	35	a	a	1	¼	a	a	28⅜
C B S	60	74	1½	19	3	5	3¾	60⅞
Coke	35	14	5¼	50	5¼	5	5¾	40
Coke	40	135	⅞	186	1¾	14	2⅜	40
Colgat	25	379	1⅛	64	1 11-16	32	2⅛	26⅛
Colgat	30	a	a	22	¼	b	b	26⅛
Cmw Ed	30	a	a	18	1⅞	a	a	31⅝
C Data	20	110	2½	78	3¼	79	3⅝	22
C Data	25	299	⅛	127	11-16	88	1⅛	22
Gn Dyn	50	83	9	10	10	4	11¾	58¾
Gn Dyn	60	199	1⅛	55	3¼	16	4½	58¾
Gen Fd	30	8	5	2	5⅜	3	5⅜	35⅛
Gen Fd	35	110	½	101	1 1-16	13	1⅝	35⅛
Hewlet	70	62	12¼	8	14	a	a	81⅞
Hewlet	80	168	3⅛	95	5¾	2	7¾	81⅞
Hewlet	90	15	¼	b	b	b	b	81⅞
H Inns	10	29	4⅜	8	4⅝	1	4¾	14½
H Inns	15	66	5-16	135	¾	65	1 1-16	14½

		– Oct –		– Jan –		– Apr –		
Alcoa	50	11	5½	a	a	a	a	54½
Alcoa	60	67	¾	44	1 9-16	16	2	54½
Am Exp	35	71	5⅞	5	6½	a	a	40⅞
Am Exp	40	55	1⅞	5	2⅝	a	a	40⅞
Am Tel	60	26	4⅛	72	4¼	6	4½	63½
Am Tel	65	90	½	98	1	187	1½	63½
Atl R	50	39	8⅞	5	9¾	9	10¾	58
Atl R	60	293	2 3-16	279	3⅜	35	4⅜	58
Avon	45	81	5⅜	19	6⅛	a	a	50⅛
Avon p	45	50	½	37	1	a	a	50⅛
Avon	50	271	2⅛	190	2⅞	44	3⅝	50⅛
Avon p	50	169	2⅛	25	2⅞	10	3⅜	50⅛
BankAm	20	a	a	3	5⅜	a	a	24¾
BankAm	25	75	1	78	1 7-16	1	1⅞	24¾
Beth S	30	140	1 7-16	32	2	15	2⅜	30⅜
Beth S	35	87	3-16	67	½	a	a	30⅜
Beth S	40	3	1-16	a	a	b	b	30⅜
Bruns	10	10	3⅝	a	a	a	a	13⅝
Bruns	15	66	5-16	69	½	94	¾	13⅝
Bruns	20	2	1-16	a	a	b	b	13⅝
Burl N	40	4	12⅛	b	b	b	b	52¾
Burl N	45	9	7⅛	a	a	a	a	52¾
Burl N	50	78	3⅛	3	4⅛	2	5	52¾
Burrgh	50	100	19½	17	19⅝	b	b	69¼
Burrgh	60	214	10	81	11½	a	a	69¼
Burrgh	70	543	3⅛	186	5	20	6¼	69¼
Burrgh	80	50	⅜	b	b	b	b	69¼
Citicp	25	185	4¾	15	5⅛	20	5¼	29⅝
Citicp	30	342	¾	117	1 5-16	29	1⅞	29⅝
Citicp	35	15	1-16	b	b	b	b	29⅝
Delta	30	3	6½	a	7	a	a	36⅝
Delta	35	1	2½	3	3	1	4	36⅝
Delta	40	16	9-16	1	1 1-16	b	b	36⅝
Dig Eq	35	11	14¼	16	15	b	b	48¾
Dig Eq	40	156	9¾	46	10⅝	b	b	48¾
Dig Eq	45	385	5½	89	7⅛	15	8⅛	48¾
Dig Eq	50	[illegible]	2 11-16	118	4¼	18	5⅛	48¾
Dig Eq	60	35	5-16	b	b	b	b	48¾
Disney	30	10	7⅜	a	a	b	b	37¼
Disney	35	69	3⅜	a	a	9	5¼	37¼
Disney	40	60	1	52	1 15-16	3	2⅝	37¼
Dow Ch	30	139	3⅜	286	4	98	4⅝	32½
Dow Ch	35	278	11-16	555	1⅜	32	1⅞	32½
Dow Ch	40	52	⅛	25	5-16	b	b	32½
du Pnt	110	36	14¼	1	15	12	16	123⅛
du Pnt	120	108	6¼	36	8	51	9½	123⅛
du Pnt	130	189	1⅞	33	3½	b	b	123⅛
Eas Kd	50	121	10⅝	162	11½	14	12⅛	60⅝
Eas Kd p	50	119	3-16	217	⅝	57	1 1-16	60⅝
Eas Kd	60	1674	3⅜	285	5	303	6⅛	60⅝
Eas Kd p	60	379	2⅝	99	3⅝	138	4⅛	60⅝
Eas Kd	70	978	⅝	670	1 11-16	b	b	60⅝
Eas Kd	80	45	⅛	b	b	b	b	60⅝
Exxon	50	154	4⅞	18	5	35	5¼	54⅞

the option owns the stock, the risk is reduced, since losses on the option will be offset by a portion of the gains in the stock.*

For example, an investor owns 100 shares of Digital Equipment Cor-

---

*The writer (seller) of an option may write a covered option or a naked option. With a covered option, the writer owns the optioned securities. The writer of a naked option does not own the securities he has optioned (offered for sale at a predetermined price).

poration (DEC). Let us assume that he writes an option for DEC common stock with a striking price of $50 and an April expiration date. The premium is 5 1/8 and the closing price of the common is 48 3/4 as shown in Figure 17.5. When the transaction is completed, the writer gets the premium (less a small commission). Thus, the writer has earned $512.50. The profit or loss to the DEC option writer can be diagrammed as in Figure 17.6.

FIGURE 17.6 OPTION WRITER (SELLER)

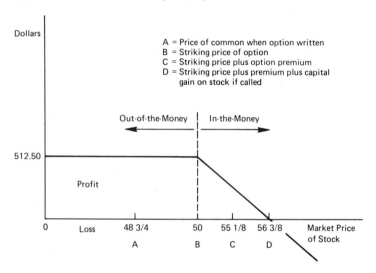

Option Buying. Buying an option is an inexpensive, leveraged way to make a profit if the stock price underlying the option rises. If not, the speculator can lose everything he puts in, but never more.

The price of an option is composed of two elements. One element is the theoretical value in the difference between the stock price and the striking price. If the value is positive, the option is said to be "in the money." If a negative theoretical value occurs, the option is said to be "out of the money." The second element is the speculative premium, which is the difference between the price of the call and its theoretical value, or zero if the theoretical value is negative.

For example, assume you buy the April 45 option on Digital Equipment Corporation for 8 1/8. Further assume that by the middle of April, the stock is selling for 61 1/4 and your option is now worth 16 1/4. You can sell for a clear profit of 100 percent (minus commissions). If the stock does not rise but falls to 20, you cannot lose more than the $812.50 you paid for the option. (Think of the loss if you had bought the stock at 48 3/4 and it fell to 20— $2,875.) The profit-and-loss position of the buyer of the April 45 option in DEC is shown in Figure 17.7.

FIGURE 17.7 OPTION BUYER

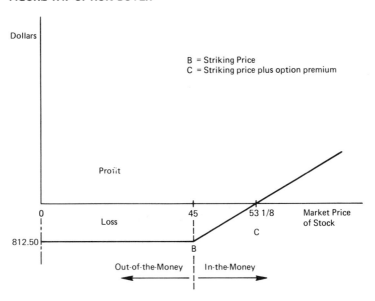

In the example above, the option is "in the money." The theoretical value is 3.75 (48.75 − 45). The speculation portion of the premium is the remainder, or 4 3/8(8 1/8 − 3 3/4).

Put A *put* is an option to sell 100 shares of a specific common stock at a specified price at any time during the life of the option, which can be for as long as approximately nine months. A put (the right to *sell* shares of stock) is the opposite of a call (the right to *buy* shares of stock). Thus, a put option and a call option involve totally separate transactions.

Believing that the market price of a stock will decrease at some time prior to expiration of the option, the buyer of a put hopes to either exercise the option or sell it to another investor at a profit. For example, assume you buy the Eastman Kodak April 60 put option for 4 1/8. (Notice in Figure 17.5 that put options are designated by p.) Further assume that by the middle of April, the stock is selling for $50 and your option is now worth $10. Your profit would be $587.50 ($1,000 − $412.50).

The seller (writer) of a put option writes the option because he wants to increase his cash flow or to own the stock at a price below the current market price. Thus, the writer of the April 60 put option on Eastman Kodak for 4 1/8 (Figure 17.5) may have to buy the stock at $60 per share if the price falls and the option buyer exercises the option. After taking into account the $4.125 premium received, the effective cost of owning the stock is $55.875 a share. Writing a put option produces an outcome similar to placing a limit order for the desired stock. However, the put has the advantage of producing the option premium in the event the stock is not acquired. In contrast, a limit order produces nothing unless the stock is acquired.

Spreads, Straddles, Straps, and Strips   A *spread* consists of both a put and a call contract. The option price at which the put or call is executed is specified in terms of a number of dollars away from the market price of the stock at the time the option is granted.

A *straddle* is similar to a spread except that the execution price of either the put or call option is at the market price of the stock at the time the straddle is granted. In essence, both the straddle and the spread accomplish the same thing.

There are at least two other combinations of put and call contracts. A *strap* is a combination of two calls and one put contract. A *strip* is a combination of one call and two put contracts. The strap is for the somewhat bullish* trader, the strip for the somewhat bearish† trader.

Quality and Risk of Securities Options   With the advent of the Chicago Board Options Exchange, some of the risks have been mitigated in options trading. The economic justification for trading in options is that of controlling risk. On the sell side, the investor is interested in preservation of capital and capital gains. On the buy side, the speculator is interested in "stepping up to the plate" and limiting his risk. However, this is an area for a professional investor or trader.

One should not attempt option trading without a good knowledge of the risks and rewards. Options differ from all other securities mentioned here in that they are not created by corporations, nor are they the obligations of corporations. Rather, they are obligations of one investor in corporate stock to another. Options are simply various combinations of hedging strategies that the investor or trader can use instead of buying and owning the stock outright. They are the epitome of speculation in securities for the investor or trader.

SUMMARY

Common stocks are the asset choice of most investors. They provide a chance for a high return but also entail a relatively high risk. The risks can be mitigated if investors buy at or near market bottoms. Techniques that enable the investor to buy at or near the bottom are discussed in the next chapter.

The opening of the CBOE has stimulated widespread public interest in the trading of options, securities once reserved for a small segment of the investment community. There are two basic ways an investor or speculator

---

*Describes one who believes that the market will rise.
†Describes one who believes that the market will fall.

can trade in options. The investor generally writes (sells) options against the stock he owns. The speculator, on the other hand, generally trades in options. He buys and sells short option contracts without owning the underlying security.

Two basic strategies should be employed by the investor and speculator in securities options. The investor should write (sell) options in stocks that have made their moves and are topping out. If the price of the security declines, the investor will not lose his stock because it will not be called. Instead he will keep his stock plus the option premium paid to him by the option buyer. The speculator should buy options in stocks that are getting ready to move to the upside. Thus, if the price of the stock rises above the striking price, the speculator can sell his option on the CBOE and pocket his profits.

PROBLEMS

1. a. From a current source of financial data such as *Moody's Handbook of Common Stocks*, determine three companies whose common stocks are yielding above 5%; three between 3 and 5%; and three below 2%. How would you explain the differences? Assuming that you had placed $1,000 in each of the nine issues ten years ago and did not reinvest the dividends, determine the present market value of the selected stocks. Determine the dividend income of each stock over the ten-year period. Determine the total increase or decrease in each stock (total dividends plus capital appreciation or depreciation).

    b. What is the value of your portfolio today? What is the value adjusted for price-level changes (that is, adjusting all ending values for the effects of inflation)?

2. Determine which stocks selected for Problem 1 are (a) blue-chip securities, (b) income securities, (c) speculative securities, (d) cyclical securities, (e) defensive securities, or (f) growth securities.

3. Identify the risks associated with each of the following (*Hint*: Risks were discussed in Chapter 15):

    a. Price of GM common stock falls from $70 to $50 per share.

    b. Price of Corvette goes from $8,000 to $12,000.

    c. GM bonds fall from $1,000 to $900 per bond.

    d. GM earnings fall from $8 to $5 per share.

4. The Jones Company, in its annual reports for the years ending December 31, reported earnings per share as follows: 1970—$3.00; 1971—$2.00; 1972—$2.50; 1973—$3.00; 1974—$1.80; 1975—$2.00; 1976—$2.50; and 1977—$2.50.

The following changes in capitalization took place in December of each of the years shown: 1971—100% stock dividend paid; 1974—2-for-1 split; 1977—20% stock dividend paid.

Adjust the reported EPS so that a comparison of changes in earnings on the common stock can be made.

5. ABC Corporation has decided to raise $10 million in new outside equity through a rights offering. Current market price of the common is $70, and it sells at 20 times earnings (P/E is 20). Current earnings are $35 million, and the subscription price is set at $50.

    a. What is the value of one right?

    b. How many rights will the holder of 100 shares receive?

    c. How many new shares can a stockholder of 100 old shares buy through the rights offering, assuming that everyone exercises their rights?

6. From the *Wall Street Journal*, determine five warrants that are currently being traded on the American Stock Exchange. Of these, which ones appear to have a greater buying advantage at the present time than a similar investment in common stocks? Explain your choices. In each case:

    a. What is the theoretical price of the warrant?

    b. Compute the speculative premium of the warrant.

7. The common stock of Coca-Cola is selling for $95 per share. Three-month 100 call options are selling for $2.

    a. If the price of common rises 25 points and the option rises 18 points, what are the returns (unadjusted) on the common and on the option?

    b. If the price of the common drops 50 points, what is the percent loss (unadjusted) on the common and on the option?

8. The common of Eastman Kodak is selling for $124 per share. You buy a three-month 120 call option for a premium of 8 1/2.

    a. What is the theoretical value of the option?

    b. What is the speculative portion of the premium?

    c. Is the option "in" or "out of the money"?

18

Approaches to Investment Analysis

There are two main approaches to investing. They are (1) the traditional approaches, and (2) the contemporary approaches. The traditional approaches consist of technical analysis and fundamental analysis. The former is a macro-oriented approach and the latter is micro-oriented. The contemporary approaches to investment are the portfolio approaches, through random selection and efficient diversification.

Investment analysis is defined as the process of determining the relative merits of investing in financial assets. Such an analysis may have a variety of objectives and an even greater number of techniques. Objectives can range all the way from a stock selection for making a short-term profit to a selection that will diversify asset holding in order to mitigate risk. The techniques we shall discuss will be confined to those covered by one of the four approaches to investment analysis.

Two of the schools of investment thought differ mainly in the methods by which they seek to gain information for purposes of forecasting common-stock prices. Fundamental analysis studies factors such as the economic outlook for a company, future earnings prospects of the company, and the capitalization* of projected earnings at some rate of return to arrive at intrinsic value,† which is compared with current market price. Technical analysis relies on the market itself to reflect and reveal the external factors, as well as the internal factors.‡ Technical analysts study the past history of stock-market action in an attempt to forecast future price movements. In view of the fact that the most valuable type of market information is that of timing, the technical analysis of the market is discussed first.

TECHNICAL ANALYSIS

The term *technical* as applied to the stock market has a deeper meaning than the usual dictionary definition of the word.§ Technical analysis involves the

---

Capitalization is the act of imputing a value for an investment asset based on certain benefits that accrue to the owner of the asset.

†*Intrinsic value* is the value justified by the facts—e.g., assets, earnings, dividends, and company prospects, which include its managerial talents.

‡External factors to the technician include such things as corporate sales and earnings. Internal factors include such things as the supply and demand for corporate securities.

§*Webster's New World Dictionary* defines technical (in a financial sense) as "designating . . . a market in which stock prices are sharply affected by short-run, speculative considerations (e.g., *technical rally*)." With permission. From *Webster's New World Dictionary*, Second College Edition. Copyright © 1976 by William Collins and World Publishing Company, Inc.

study of the market itself rather than a study of external factors such as corporate sales and earnings. Such analysis is often referred to as *internal analysis* or *market analysis*. Technical analysis is concerned with three things—supply of investment securities, demand for investment securities, and market psychology. According to technicians, supply, demand, and market psychology are the three factors that cause price changes.

Technical Analysis Defined

Technical analysis is defined as the art of studying the past market performance of securities prices and timing buy and sell decisions on the recognition of market indicators and price patterns that occur. It is based on the belief that market prices quickly reflect all available information, but that "inside" information is not reflected as quickly by the market, and that new information is not available to all investors at the same time. "Insiders" would be expected to receive certain types of information before the same information reaches the investing public.

For example, the common stock of Atlantic Richfield Company (ARC) was selling at around $100 per share early in 1968. When the officers and employees of the company learned of the probable Prudhoe Bay oil discovery, they began buying ARC common. The price rose to $125 per share. As friends and relatives learned that ARC and Exxon were partners in the venture, the price of ARC common rose to $140 per share. Finally, the institutions and general public learned of the news, and the price of ARC common reached $200 per share by July 1968.

The basic assumption underlying all technical analysis is that successive price changes are not independent. Stated positively, successive price changes are dependent on past market action. Technical analysis is then, in essence, the recording of the actual history of trading for an issue, an industry, or the aggregate market, and determining the future trend from such a historical analysis. Recordings include both price movements and the volume of transactions in a vertical bar chart. (Point-and-figure charts record only price changes.) Vertical bar and point-and-figure charts are shown for the DJIA in Figures 18.1 and 18.2. History does repeat itself in the marketplace, according to technical analysis.

Price Patterns

Almost all price patterns used in technical analysis are related to breakthroughs around resistance or support levels. A *resistance* level, such as the 1,000 level of the Dow Jones Industrial Average (DJIA), is where selling pressures are expected to appear; that is, the supply of securities exceeds the demand for them at a resistance level. For example, during the year 1976, the DJIA reached the 1,000 level twelve times and was unable to break through decisively. Once the DJIA moves above 1,000, this becomes a support level. A *support* level is one where buying pressures are expected to appear; that is, the demand for securities exceeds the supply at a support level.

Price patterns also apply to individual securities. Again, the patterns are mainly concerned with resistance and support levels. At resistance levels,

FIGURE 18.1 Vertical-Bar Chart of Dow Jones Industrial Average. (*Source: Wall Street Journal, February 3, 1977, p. 33.*)

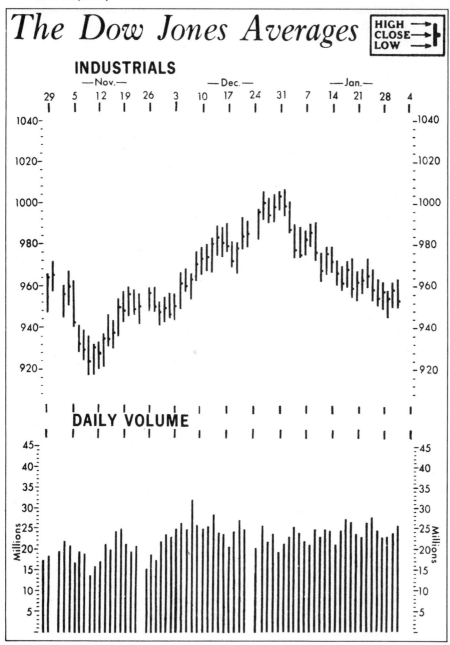

FIGURE 18.2 Point-and-Figure Chart of Dow Jones Industrial Average.

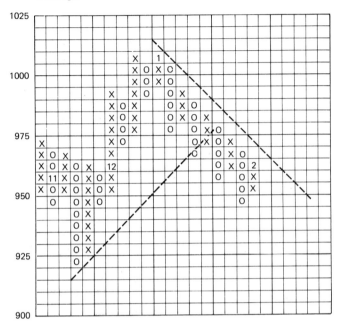

stocks are peaking in price. At support levels, prices are bottoming. Both can be detected by price patterns. Price (or chart) patterns are studied by the technician (or chartist) in order to permit him to predict future price movements. To make forecasts, it is necessary to commit past market action to a usable form. Bar charts present such a record. Prices, dates, volume, highs, lows, closes, and many more variables can be plotted arithmetically or logarithmically for the study of securities prices. Short interest, relative strength, and other measures can also be plotted on the chart. In addition to revealing trends and formations, price-chart patterns also indicate support and resistance areas. These areas are useful to the technician because he can expect a considerable increase or decrease in the demand for a security based on previous chart patterns.

In addition to price patterns, the technician relies heavily on technical indicators. Some of the more familiar indicators are discussed below.

Technical Indicators Numerous technical indicators are employed by the technician. Professionals are aware that the condition of the general stock market has a profound effect on individual stock price movements. For example, the common stock of McDonald's Corporation sold for $43 in May 1970, $77 in November 1973, $23 in October 1974, and $66 in March 1976. Even though the earnings of McDonald's increased substantially each year during this period, the price of the stock fluctuated with the market. That is, when stock prices rose, McDonald's rose, and vice versa.

Considerable effort has been spent developing indicators that attempt to broadly define underlying trends for the market as a whole. Technical indicators are used by many professionals and serious investors to interpret general market conditions. Basically, these indicators fall into three categories: (1) market price indicators, (2) market breadth indicators, and (3) market sentiment indicators.

Market Price Indicators. This group of indicators attempts to portray the market on the basis of general price fluctuations. By averaging the price movements of a number of stocks, the general direction of the group as a whole is derived. Probably the best known indicator, or index, is the Dow Jones Industrial Average (DJIA). The 30 stocks in the DJIA are all blue chips and account for nearly 25 percent of the roughly $600-billion market value of stocks listed on the New York Stock Exchange (NYSE). Yet the 30 stocks make up only 10 percent of the total shares listed on the NYSE.

Comparing different, variously composed averages often enables investors to learn something about the character of the market. For example, if the Dow Jones Industrial Average of 30 blue-chip companies is performing better than the more broadly based averages such as Standard & Poor's Index of 500 Composite Stocks, or the New York Stock Exchange Index, it is an indication that investors are cautious and placing more emphasis on the strong and financially sound stocks. If the broader averages are surpassing the stocks of the DJIA, it means that investors are acting more aggressively. A sharp divergence between the movements of the DJIA and S&P's 500 index is considered by technical analysts to be a clue to possibly forthcoming trend changes.

The American Stock Exchange Index, Value Line Average of 1600 Stocks, S&P's Index of 20 Low Priced Stocks on the New York Stock Exchange, Barron's Index of 20 Low Priced stocks, and the NASDAQ Index of over-the-counter stocks are all measures of more speculative aspects of the market. A comparison of the more speculative indexes with the more general market averages often reveals the current degree of enthusiasm for riskier securities.

The Dow Jones Utility Average (DJUA) often indicates the degree of defensiveness of the investor. The DJUA tends to lead the DJIA at turning points by about three to nine months.

The Dow Jones Transportation Average reflects the activity of stocks whose companies are in a vital area of the economy. If this indicator is not moving in the same direction as the more general averages, the trend of the market may be suspect.

Market Breadth Indicators. This group of indicators measures the market in terms of the number of stocks showing strength or weakness rather than of specific price movements. The Weekly Advance-Decline Line is a cumulative net total of the number of stocks that advanced during the week minus the number of stocks that declined. Technicians compare the A-D line with general price averages such as the DJIA and S&P's 500 index.

The High-Low Index also indicates market strength by measuring the number of stocks that have made new yearly highs or lows in any given week. This is charted by using separate lines for the highs and lows and smoothing each line with five-week moving averages of the data. When the average of new highs moves above the average of new lows, a bullish trend is considered to be confirmed. The reverse is true when the line of new lows exceeds the line of new highs.

Market Sentiment Indicators. This group of indicators enables the investor to study the psychology of the market by observing the activity of certain segments of the investing public. For example, odd-lot statistics provide a key to the attitudes of the small investor. Above-normal buying reflected in the Odd-Lot Index at a time when market averages are historically high has bearish implications. Conversely, below-normal buying, as reflected by the Odd-Lot Index, in the early phases of an advancing market is usually a bullish indicator. Unusually large odd-lot short sales pinpoint a market bottom.

The Mutual Fund Cash Position Ratio portrays the thinking of professional money managers by measuring the amount of cash and short-term government securities held by the funds in relation to their total investments. The amount of cash held usually reaches its peak (8-12 percent of total assets) at the bottom of the market and its low (two percent of total assets) at market tops.

The Short Interest Ratio measures the amount of stock sold short in relation to average daily trading volume for a 30-day period. Since every short sale must eventually be covered by a buy order, the index provides a clue to potential purchasing of stocks. A ratio above 1.5 is generally bullish and below 1.0 is bearish.

Some of the numerous other indicators used are the overbought–oversold index, credit and debit balances, 200-day moving average, speculative index, specialist short-sale index, and price–dividend ratio. Relative-strength analysis is a technique used by some to identify weak and strong industries.

Technical indicators as well as price patterns, then, are important in analyzing and forecasting the potential trend of the market. It is the overall trend of the market that will, over a period of time, dictate individual stock price movement. This means that, according to technical analysis, no matter how good the prospects for an individual company might be, the overall direction of the market will prevail in determining individual stock prices.

Tenets of Technical Analysis   The school of technical thought holds that it is futile in the short run to assign an intrinsic (or true) value to a security price. To illustrate, one share of General Electric common stock was worth $403 in August 1929 and only $8.25 in June 1932. By March 1937, it was selling at 64 7/8, and just one year later at 29 1/4. Such a wide divergence between presupposed value and actual price is not the exception to the rule; it is going on all the time in the stock market. More recently, Coca-Cola common stock sold for $63 in May 1970, $150 in March 1973, $42 in October 1974, $94 in March 1976, $73 in November 1976, and $80 in March 1977. The fact is that the real value of a share of common stock is determined at any given time solely by supply and demand. The interaction between supply and demand in the price of a security is reflected in the transaction consummated in the marketplace.

Technical analysis holds that there are many factors affecting supply and demand. The marketplace reflects not only the differing value judgments of many fundamental securities analysts, but also all the hopes and fears and guesses and moods, rational and irrational, of hundreds of potential buyers and sellers, as well as their needs and their resources. These factors defy analysis by orthodox securities appraisers. Such statistics are not available. Nonetheless, all are synthesized, weighed, and finally expressed in the one precise figure at which a buyer and seller get together and transact the sale. This is really the only figure that is reliable. In sum, the going price as established by the market itself comprehends all the fundamental information that the statistical analyst aspires to learn. In addition, some information is perhaps secret from him, known only to a few insiders; and much more information, of equal or even greater importance, is unknown to him.

The ability of stock prices to move along a straight line on a price chart is another underlying tenet of technical analysis. A mere glance at a price chart will reveal that prices have a prevailing tendency to move in a particular direction for sustained periods of time. Closer examination shows that this movement frequently assumes a definite pattern. In fact, it zigzags along an imaginary straight line until a definite trend is established. The ability of prices to cling extremely close to a straight line is one of the most extraordinary characteristics of chart movements.

Three points are necessary to establish a trend. More than three points confirm the trend. And the more times a trend is confirmed, the stronger the trend. This is shown in Figure 18.3, a chart of the DJIA from the late 1940s to the early 1970s. Notice that the uptrend was not reversed until 1968, which marked the end of the post–World War II bull market.*

Another basic tenet of technical analysis is that junctures occur. A juncture is a critical reversal, or change, in the trend of individual stock prices

---

*In 1968, a bear market began that lasted until the end of 1974. One casualty figure of the bear market is that the number of owners of common stock dropped from 30 million to 25 million.

FIGURE 18.3 Dow Jones Industrial Average from Late 1940s to Early 1970s. (*Source: Richard Russell, writer and editor of Dow Theory Letters.*)

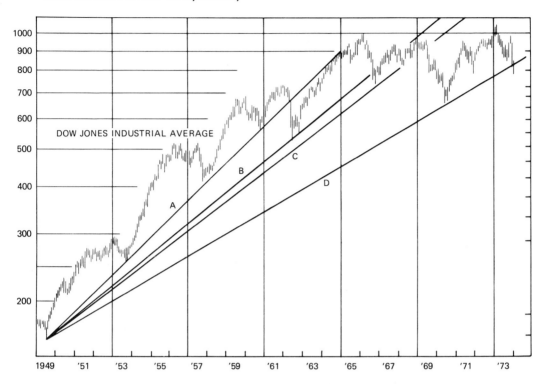

or in the aggregate market. Junctures aid the investor or trader in buying low and selling high. However, most people are unaware of a change in trend until it is well underway and at or near the end. There are a number of technical indicators that warn that a change of trend (or juncture) is imminent. Perhaps the best known indicator warning of a change in trend is the odd-lot index. Odd-lot trading (transactions involving less than 100 shares) is considered to be done primarily by the uninformed in the stock market. The uninformed, or general public, is considered to be naive when compared to the professional investor. The general public (or odd-lotter) is not always wrong; he follows the trend of the market fairly well. However, the odd-lotter is notoriously wrong at the critical junctures in the market. That is, he tends to become extremely bullish near market tops and too bearish near market bottoms. It is the odd-lotter's propensity to do the wrong thing (buy when he should be selling and sell when he should be buying), which causes him to incur severe losses in the market. Furthermore, the expectations of the odd-lotter become quite valuable to technical analysts, who consider his timing to be sufficiently wrong to have some predictive value.

The investment behavior of the general public may be summarized as follows:

At market tops:

1. Low short interest ratio (one or less)
2. Shift in odd-lot index from more selling to more buying
3. Very few odd-lot short sales

At market bottoms:

1. Very high short interest ratio (two or more)
2. Shift in odd-lot index from active buying to selling on balance
3. Very large number of odd-lot short sales (greater than 5 percent of total short sales)

Finally, the market is greatly affected by investor (or mass) psychology. Edson Gould,* one of the most accurate of the contemporary technical forecasters, sees the stock market as essentially nothing more nor less than a manifestation of mass or crowd psychology in action. In short, the stock market reflects the changing moods, emotions, and feelings of the mass of investors.

The theory of technical analysis is summarized as follows:

1. Market value is determined solely by the interaction of supply and demand.
2. Numerous factors, both rational and irrational, govern supply and demand. Such factors are composed of fundamentals, moods, guesses about the future, opinions, and blind necessities. The market automatically weighs all these factors.
3. Disregarding minor fluctuations in the market, stock prices tend to move in trends that persist for sustained periods of time.
4. Changes in trend are caused by a shift in supply–demand relationships. Such changes, however caused, can be detected sooner or later in the action of the market itself.
5. Finally, market psychology is best portrayed by technical indicators.

Critique of the Technical Approach There are five major criticisms of technical analysis. The first may be referred to as the "it-doesn't-work" argument. Skepticism of technical analysis is in the minds of many investors and analysts. Such feelings of disbelief are strengthened by technical forecasts that never materialize.

---

*Perhaps no one of the 1960s and 1970s is better known for a consistent ability to forecast stock-market movements correctly than is Edson Gould. Mr. Gould is one of Wall Street's pioneer technical analysts. For a profile of Edson Gould of Anametrics, Inc., refer to "Wall Street," *Business Week*, December 7, 1974, p. 90.

A second criticism of technical analysis is that it becomes a self-fulfilling prophecy. That is, if enough technicians act in unison in a relatively thin market, the possibility exists that the patterns the technicians claim have predictive value may actually be created by the action of other technicians and traders following their advice. In such a case, the self-fulfilling prophecy may even result in an efficient market.

A rebuttal to the idea of the self-fulfilling prophecy ultimately resulting in an efficient market is that only a few are convinced that technical analysis is the answer to forecasting stock prices. Fewer still, a handful maybe, actually act on technical factors.

A third criticism of technical analysis regards the subjective nature of this school of investment analysis. Claims for the efficacy of forecasting stock prices using technical factors are largely unproven. In dealing with subjectivity, the technician tends to dwell on the cases that support the tenets of technical analysis while disregarding the exceptions. This is a serious criticism of technical analysis and is not easily refuted. However, some successful scientific tests of the technical school of investment thought are beginning to appear.*

A fourth criticism is that much of the explanation for technical analysis remains unknown and therefore should be viewed as nonacademic. Even technicians admit that reasons why technical analysis works are not easy to deduce. For example, William X. Scheinman, one of Wall Street's most meticulous chartists, made the observation that the market may be forming a significant top. His rationale was as follows:

> The 958 level is important because, after peaking at 741.30 in 1961, the Dow plummeted 216.75 points—and if you add 216.75 to 741.30, you get 958.05. "The arcs of major declines often define major terminal points," Scheinman says cryptically. "Why? That's hard to say. . . ." But technical analysis is concerned more with patterns than with reasons . . . .†

Cohen, Zinbarg and Zeikel state:

> . . . the probability remains that many patterns and relationships will be unexplainable. Nevertheless, if the patterns are known to recur consistently, it seems sensible to take advantage of this knowledge even though the explanations remain unknown. After all, physicians do not know why aspirin works as well as it does, but they prescribe it nonetheless.‡

---

*See Robert A. Levy, "Conceptual Foundation of Technical Analysis," *Financial Analysts Journal*, July–August 1968, pp. 83–89.

†"A Divination by Charts," *Business Week*, April 15, 1972, p. 68.

‡Jerome B. Cohen, Edward D. Zinbarg, and Arthur Zeikel, *Investment Analysis and Portfolio Management*, 3rd. ed. (Homewood, Ill.: Richard D. Irwin, 1977), p. 546.

A rebuttal to the "unknown" aspects of technical analysis is that we need not know *why* one stock is stronger than another in order to act profitably upon that knowledge. The market itself is continually weighing and recording the effects of all the bullish information and all the bearish information about every stock. No one in possession of inside information can profit from it unless he buys or sells the stock. The moment he does, his buy or sell orders have their effect upon the price. That effect is revealed in the market action of the stock.

The most critical indictment of the technical school of investment analysis is the random-walk theory. The random-walk model, which has been tested sufficiently to convince many academicians of its validity, is discussed in the next chapter.

Conclusions Technical analysts attempt to predict stock price changes by observing patterns of stock prices. Such analysts argue that an objective study of stock prices without a subjective analysis of stock values or business conditions is the best way to time selections and forecast price movements.

The technician bases his forecast of market junctures on the average behavior of stock prices in the past (that is, the assumption is made that stock prices move in trends). Once an uptrend in price is underway, stock prices tend to continue to rise until a shift occurs in supply–demand relationships. Conversely, once a downtrend starts, stock prices tend to continue down until the supply–demand shift occurs.

A good summation of technical market analysis is given by Joseph Granville:

> ONLY SUPPLY AND DEMAND MOVES STOCK PRICES and that is measured in terms of money moving into stocks and out of stocks and it is this movement that is first detected by the *technical* market indicators.*

FUNDAMENTAL ANALYSIS

Fundamental analysis attempts to forecast securities prices by determining an intrinsic value (or investment value) for each security based on estimated earnings. A fundamental analysis of investment alternatives assumes that the market prices of individual issues fluctuate about investment value or tend to converge toward established intrinsic values. If such be the case, the determination of intrinsic value for a corporation's stock based on capitalization of future earnings has the same effect as predicting the common's future price.

---

*Joseph E. Granville, *A Strategy of Daily Stock Market Timing for Maximum Profit* (Englewood Cliffs, N.J.: Prentice-Hall, 1960), p. 9.

Fundamental analysis, then, is the traditional textbook approach to the selection and timing aspects of common stocks for investment purposes. Such an analysis is often referred to as *securities analysis* or *company analysis*. The primary task of the fundamentalist is to locate securities that are either over- or underpriced in relation to the actual value.

Fundamental Analysis Defined Fundamental analysis is defined as the art of studying characteristics, quality, prospects, and value of specific securities and interpreting the findings in order to form opinions about the securities. Implicit in a study of values is a comparison with other securities of comparable quality and risk. A good fundamental analysis of a security is the task of estimating and comparing the relative attractiveness of that security in the investor's portfolio. Such a task necessitates a review of one or more industries, firms, and individual securities in each analysis.

Numerous fundamental factors are considered in the valuation process. Such factors vary in importance among securities analysts. Important factors for fundamental analysis are (1) financial-statement data, (2) industry position, (3) economic outlook, (4) projections of earnings and dividends, and (5) qualitative factors such as management, product, sales potential, tax considerations, and government regulations.

Fundamental factors can be organized into demand and supply forces. Those factors affecting demand are (1) earnings; (2) dividends; (3) growth of the economy, industries, and firms; (4) competitive structure of industries; (5) tax patterns; (6) price-level movements; and (7) investor confidence. Factors on the supply side are (1) interest rates; (2) amount and distribution of savings; (3) capital spending by business, government, and individuals; (4) disposable income level and distribution, (5) the amount of stock-market credit, and (6) money-market conditions as related to the policies of the Federal Reserve and the U.S. Treasury.

From such secular determinants, there is a close relationship between gross national product (GNP) and sales, sales and profits, profits and dividends, and dividends and stock prices. A logical conclusion to be drawn from the relationships above is that as the GNP grows over the years, the total value of stock prices will grow in the same proportion. There is a basic criticism of such a macro-oriented approach to forecasting future stock prices. That is, the approach does not consider the differing capitalization rates between industries or between stocks of firms in the same industry.

Benjamin Graham favors the average future earning power as the most important single factor in determining value.* A central or intrinsic value is found by first estimating earning power and then multiplying the estimate

---

*Benjamin Graham, the late Professor Emeritus of Finance, University of California, Los Angeles, is the father of modern securities analysis. For a fascinating profile of Dr. Graham and securities analysis, the reader is referred to ''The Money Men,'' *Forbes,* June 15, 1975, p. 35.

by an appropriate capitalization factor. Therefore, the problem of determining intrinsic value is broken down into two distinct aspects—estimation of expected average earnings, and selection of a suitable capitalization factor.

Graham, Dodd, and Cottle limit the factors in the valuation of common stocks to four basic components. They are (1) the expected future earnings, (2) the expected future dividends, (3) the capitalization rates—or multipliers—of the dividends and earnings, and (4) the asset values. Graham et al. explain that a number of elements enter into these four factors:

> It should be pointed out that these four factors include, by implication, a number of elements which enter into both the quantitative and qualitative analysis of a common stock. Chief of these are the past and expected rates of profitability, stability, and growth; the abilities of the management; and the various underlying facts and hypotheses that will govern sales volume, costs, and profits after taxes.*

Expected Growth   An analysis of growth in the economy is an important fundamental to the investor. The expected growth of the economy has ramifications for both bond and stock investing. Common-stock prices are closely associated with the expected growth in the economy. It is necessary, of course, to relate the growth rate of the entire economy to specific indicators and companies. The significance of constant growth is shown by the following formulation:

$$P_0 = \frac{D_1}{k - g}$$

where:

P_0 = current price of the stock

D_1 = dividend expected at end of year 1

k = rate of return demanded by investor

g = expected rate of growth of dividends

For example, if a company has a constant growth rate of 6 percent and a dividend in year 1 of $4, and investors expect a 12 percent return, the price of the common is:

$$P_0 = \frac{D_1}{k - g}$$

$$= \frac{\$4}{.12 - .06}$$

$$= \$66.67$$

------

*Benjamin Graham, David L. Dodd, and Sidney Cottle, *Security Analysis*, 4th ed. (New York: McGraw-Hill, 1962), p. 443.

Earnings Multiples   At the heart of valuing stocks is the determination of the proper price–earnings ratio to use. Since stocks trade at different multiples of earnings, the process is not straightforward. Such multiples are influenced by a number of factors, including a company's growth rate, its stability of sales and earnings, and investor sentiment. A number of methods have been recommended for defining the range of multiples that may be appropriate for use in attempting to determine the intrinsic value of common stock. We shall examine two of the methods.

The earnings multiple may be estimated with the following formula:

$$\text{Earnings multiple} = 8.5 + 2G$$

where G is the annual forecast earnings growth rate. The formula assumes that investors will pay 8.5 times earnings for zero growth. For example, the earnings growth rate for the Coca-Cola Company is estimated at 10 percent for the next few years. Using the formula, the earnings multiple for Coke is:

$$\text{Earnings multiple} = 8.5 + 2(10)$$
$$= 8.5 + 20$$
$$= 28.5$$

Another approach to estimating the earnings multiple is the historical approach. Trendline's *Current Market Perspectives*, which is published monthly, contains the price–earnings ratios of 972 stocks. Trendline shows the historical high and low P/E ratio based on the trading in each stock over the last several years. The price of the stock tends to fluctuate between the high and the low P/E ratio lines. Thus, the stock is undervalued when the price is at or near the low P/E ratio line and overvalued when the price is at or near the high P/E ratio line. The high price-earnings line is shown for Coca Cola in Figure 18.4.

Dividend Payout   The market price of a share of common stock can be obtained by simply consulting quotations in the financial press, such as the *Wall Street Journal*. In contrast, the *intrinsic value* of the stock (its basic or underlying value) must be computed. The purpose of the computation is to attempt to determine whether the stock is underpriced or overpriced relative to its future values. To determine the intrinsic value of an individual security, the investor must view the general level of stock prices relative to corporate earnings. When the whole market appears to be depressed, he may be willing to invest a significant portion of his funds in common stocks. Conversely, if the general market appears overvalued, he may reduce his commitment of funds in common stocks. He should then analyze individual stocks for expected changes in earnings, dividends, and market value per share.

FIGURE 18.4 High and Low Price–Earnings Lines for Coca-Cola. (*Source: Trend-line's Current Market Perspectives.*)

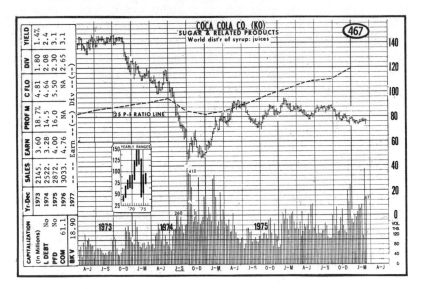

Graham, Dodd, and Cottle believe that the intrinsic value of a stock equals:

$$\text{Value} = M(D + \tfrac{1}{3} E)$$

where:

M = the earnings multiple at which similar issues trade

D = dividends per share

E = earnings per share

For example, if the expected dividend payout for Coca-Cola Company is 66 2/3 percent (that is, if the company earns $3 per share and pays a cash dividend of $2 per share), and if similar stocks are trading at an earnings multiple of 20, the intrinsic value of the stock is:

$$\text{Value} = 20[2 + \tfrac{1}{3}(3)]$$
$$= 20(2 + 1)$$
$$= \$60$$

If the earnings multiple of 28.5 calculated earlier is used, the expected price is:

$$\text{Value} = 28.5[2 + \tfrac{1}{3}(3)]$$
$$= 28.5(3)$$
$$= \$85.50$$

Based on 1978 earnings of $3 for Coca-Cola Company, the high and low P/E range for the stock is:

$$\text{High P/E} = 25(\$3) = \$75$$
$$\text{Low P/E} = 14(\$3) = \$42$$

Discounted Cash-Flow Method Regardless of the number and kind of factors used, fundamental analysis (or securities analysis) is concerned mainly with the problem of determining a true or intrinsic value of a security. Most modern-day stock-valuation methods are based on the present-value theory. That is, the present value of a share of stock is equivalent to the summation of all future dividends, discounted to the present at an appropriate rate of interest. Some claim that price changes in stocks discount both future dividends and earnings. Therefore, it does not matter whether future earnings or dividends are capitalized, because investors may elect to sell their stocks to others at capital gains or to retain their stocks in order to receive dividend income.

Valuation theories, therefore, are derived from two basic models—the dividend model and the capital gains model. The dividend model recognizes that the promised future rewards are the dividends that the shareowner expects to receive for an indefinite period, adjusted for the time value of money, as follows:

$$\text{PDV} = \frac{D_1}{(1+r)^1} + \frac{D_2}{(1+r)^2} + \cdots + \frac{D_n}{(1+r)^n}$$

where:

PDV = present discounted value

D = forecasted dividend per share at end of period t

r = annual rate of return

The capital gains model reflects the hope of the investor to sell at a higher price sometime in the future. Anticipated benefits are dividends received while stock is owned, plus selling price when stock is sold. The formula is:

$$\text{PDV} = \frac{D_1}{(1+r)^1} + \frac{D_2}{(1+r)^2} + \cdots + \frac{D_n}{(1+r)^n} + \frac{P_n}{(1+r)^n}$$

where:

D = forecasted dividend per share at end of period t

P_n = share price when sold

From such an intrinsic or central valuation, we notice the two basic factors that are involved in securities analysis. One is the rate and duration of growth, the other is the capitalization rate applied to the future stream of earnings or dividends.

Tenets of Fundamental Analysis

The school of fundamental analysis has the goal of appraising the intrinsic value of a security. Intrinsic value is the true economic worth of an asset. Although there are many factors (or variables) to appraise in order to make a fundamental analysis, an objective value that is independent of market price can indicate an overpriced or underpriced security. Once the intrinsic value has been determined, the securities analyst issues buy or sell recommendations based on his findings. If the true value is greater than the current market price, the analyst recommends buying the security because it is underpriced. If the true value is less than the actual price, the analyst recommends selling or avoiding the security because it is overpriced.

Fundamentalists hold that properly performed securities analysis is superior to technical analysis. There is justification in such a statement. This is because the "insiders" who are first aware of the underlying fundamental factors must act before the technical analyst is alerted. Even if the technical analyst acts before the information is made public, he is still later in his actions than are the "insiders." Therefore, the fundamental analyst who is perspicacious (or prescient) may detect such fundamental factors. In such a case, fundamental analysis is superior to technical analysis.

Fundamental analysis does not stress market timing. In fact, ways are found to avoid timing decisions, such as: (1) buy-and-hold policy, and (2) assuming the role of ownership of a business. In order to avoid the difficulties involved in timing market fluctuations, the investor can discharge his true functions as part owner of a business. In lieu of dealing in changes in market quotations, he can concentrate on evaluating individual issues as a stake in a property, with the purpose of securing preservation of his capital along with adequate income yield. He can further operate on the premise that continuing disparities between price and value offer recurring opportunities for advantageous purchases and sales.

Critique of Fundamental Analysis

Among the criticisms of fundamental analysis is the opinion that intrinsic value is not a panacea for the investor even though a fixed formula is used. Such a value can be computed from a number of fundamental factors and still prove to be somewhat meaningless. The concluding comment of Cohen et al. about central or intrinsic value is:

Although specific analytical procedures are presented . . . it would be a serious error for the reader to come away with the impression that the process of common stock evaluation is somewhat analogous to a recipe for baking a cake. One cannot simply mix together a number of statistical ingredients in accordance with a fixed formula and produce an acceptable result.*

However, Graham, Dodd, and Cottle argue that just the opposite is true. While recognizing that intrinsic value has difficulties and limitations, they state:

> The analyst could do a more dependable or professional job of passing judgment on a common stock if he were able to determine some objective value, independent of the market quotation, with which he could compare the current price. He could then advise the investor to buy when the price was at or below value—or, at least, when the current price lies within the indicated range of value—and to sell when the price was well above value.†

Another criticism involves the fact that securities analysis is a search for value—and this is a concept that has changed in meaning over the years. The actual definition of value as applied to corporate securities has always been elusive. At one time, valuation of assets (known as book value today) was the major consideration in determining if a stock was a buy or a sell candidate. However, the concept all but died (a few still cling to book value) with the collapse of railroad securities prices after World War I. Investors learned that there is a vast difference between position statement evaluations and actual liquidity value of fixed assets that are sold at greatly reduced prices, or are even unsalable.

Today, the securities analyst capitalizes earnings. However, the further into the future earnings growth is discounted, the greater the price decline, if the figure earnings picture becomes the least bit suspect. High-multiple stocks are especially hard hit, even when next year's earnings projections fail to materialize. The fall of 1971 saw the price of Wrigley's common stock drop more than $30 in one day because an analyst had overstated 1971 estimated earnings by only a few cents.‡

A serious challenge facing securities analysis is the lack of reliability of financial reporting. Studies by the American Institute of Certified Public Accountants show a lack of proper standards for annual corporate reports and inadequate disclosure of important information. A classic result of such procedures is what occurred with the Penn Central Transportation Company. Although a national firm of accountants gave a clean bill of health to Penn Central for 1969, the huge corporation filed bankruptcy proceedings in June

---

*Cohen, Zinbarg, and Zeikel, *Investment Analysis*, p. 381.
†Graham, Dodd, and Cottle, *Security Analysis*, p. 435.
‡"Heard on the Street," *Wall Street Journal*, Nov. 3, 1971, p. 32.

1970.* The raw data that the securities analyst must use to base his projections on is far from adequate. A question arises as to the paucity and veracity of corporate financial statements for use in determining securities prices.

At least three factors compound the problem of the securities analyst. First, various accounting practices have resulted in the mismatching of revenues and expenses. Second, net-income and earnings-per-share figures inevitably involve estimates and judgments. Finally, an audit is not a guarantee against loss for investors and creditors, because not every transaction is checked when financial statements are audited. This means that for years, stockholders and financial analysts have assumed certain things about accounting and auditing practices that were incorrect. For example, one erroneous assumption has been that the income statements of different companies are comparable—that earnings per share of one company could be compared with those of another. But neither corporate management nor the accounting profession had ever maintained that their objective was comparability. Until fairly recent times, the profession assumed that consistency in the accounting of an individual company was the important goal.

Another major criticism of fundamental analysis is that after all calculations are made, the securities analyst must assign an appropriate capitalization rate (or price–earnings multiple) to earnings projected for a number of years into the future. The difficulty in the selection of a proper capitalization rate is admitted by Graham, Dodd, and Cottle in commenting upon Value Line Investment Surveys' estimate of the 1956–58 DJIA prices:

> . . . the actual earnings estimate for the 29 stocks was very close to the actual. . . . By contrast, the aggregate market value estimate for 1956–1958 was significantly less accurate—missing by more than 22 percent the three-year mean price. . . . This tends to confirm our view that earnings can be predicted with more confidence than can the capitalization rate or multiplier, which to a major degree will reflect the market psychology existing at the time.†

Finally, even if the securities analyst does find an undervalued security, he must wait and hope that others will recognize this fact and begin to bid up the price of the security. Taking a long position in an undervalued security and waiting for the price to rise can be costly in terms of opportunity costs. This simply means that the money could be used to more advantage elsewhere until the undervalued security begins to increase in price. Technical analysts hold that their method can better detect price breakouts in such a case than can fundamental analysis.

---

*Another example is the Equity Funding Corporation of America, which declared bankruptcy with 62,000 fictitious customers on its books.

†Graham, Dodd, and Cottle, *Security Analysis*, p. 439.

Conclusions   We should not conclude that all is hopeless—that we should not attempt to analyze stocks fundamentally. However, we need to be aware that basic accounting data can vary widely, and that such variances can still be within generally accepted accounting principles. For example, a firm's earnings per share may be overstated, understated, or close to correct. And such disparities may be deliberate, accidental, or caused by ignorance. So we must first try to determine the accuracy of the financial data before making worthwhile fundamental analyses.

The intrinsic or central-value method is still based on certain assumptions that may not be easy to measure. When the intrinsic-value method indicates that a stock or the stock market is too high, the result can be hard to interpret and implement. For example, one must determine if the method is correct and the stock market *is* too high. Or is the market correct and the method used in error?

Perhaps market psychology has a greater influence on stock prices, and this is therefore a better gauge than any valuation formula or process.

RANDOM SELECTION

Studies have shown that a portfolio of securities selected strictly at random can provide a fair return. There are many ways to select such portfolios. Probably the best-known method is to select stocks by throwing darts at a listing of the stocks on the New York Stock Exchange. Ten to fifteen stocks are selected from as many throws.

In a test of random selection at our university, fifteen corporations were chosen. Two pages of the New York Stock Exchange in the *Wall Street Journal* were taped to two pieces of cardboard; then an air rifle was fired at the pages fifteen times from a distance of twenty feet. Each hole indicated a corporation to be used in the sample. The corporations randomly selected were: Ampex Corp., Eaton, Emery, Hanna, Hydrometals, Integon, Lenox, Marriot, NVF, Omark, Petrolane, RCA, Rucker, Tenneco, and Textron.

After selecting the corporations, a check was made to see if the corporations represented different geographical areas and different industries. It was found that they ranged from regional to international corporations. Their products or services also varied from insurance (Integon Corp.) to international air freight (Emery).

The data were collected every third weekday from the *Wall Street Journal* for one month. The monthly return on an annual basis for the randomly selected portfolio was 19.56 percent. The return for the DJIA for the same period was 16.8 percent.

While the results of the above study are impressive, we do not want to mislead the reader. Data from the returns on a number of randomly selected portfolios versus carefully chosen portfolios tend to favor the latter. We feel this is partially true because of the criteria for careful selection which included: (1) S & P stocks, (2) common stocks only, (3) stocks with an A rating or better, (4) dividend yield of at least 5 percent, and (5) a price earnings ratio of 10 or less.

Random selection works because there is a tendency for stocks to move together—up and down. Thus, when one selects a random portfolio of ten to fifteen stocks, the result is a diversified portfolio. This leads into the next section which deals with portfolio analysis through the efficient diversification of risk.

PORTFOLIO ANALYSIS

Whereas the fundamental and technical approaches focus on one or a few under- or overvalued securities, the portfolio approach looks at a bundle of assets. The portfolio approach is concerned with combinations of individual securities that meet portfolio requirements of risk and return. We can vary the amount of each security in the portfolio to provide the most satisfactory risk–return combination. Rationally, we should accept the portfolio that provides a higher return with a higher risk, or a portfolio that will provide a lower risk with a lower return. We will not accept a portfolio that will give the same return at a higher risk, nor a portfolio that provides a lower return for the same risk.

To illustrate, the efficient frontier of risky assets and combination of risky assets is shown in Figure 18.5. Point B represents a portfolio (or security)

FIGURE 18.5 Investment Portfolio Opportunities.

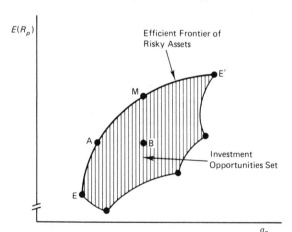

where risk could be reduced and return held constant by moving to point A. Alternatively, risk could be held constant and return increased by moving from point B to point M. The same is true for any portfolio (or security) that is not on the efficient boundary EE'.

The efficient frontier, which is represented by a heavy dark line in Figure 18.5, represents the real area of decision making for the investor. Here the investor can attain higher return only by accepting higher risks. Conversely, it is impossible to select a portfolio (or security) that will give a higher return at less risk on the efficient frontier.

The Riskless Asset Now consider a riskless asset such as Treasury bills. The investor is no longer limited to points along the efficient frontier of risky assets. He may now invest (lend) all his funds in Treasury bills, invest all funds in risky assets, or a combination of the two. This situation is shown in Figure 18.6. Since the typical investor is risk-averse and since he now has additional opportunities for combining portfolios of both risky and risk-free assets, the efficient frontier is now bounded by the straight line FM.

FIGURE 18.6 The Capital-Market Line.

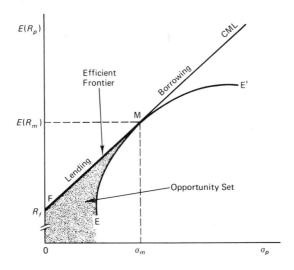

The Capital-Market Line The new efficient frontier of investment opportunities includes only one portfolio, M, of all risk securities. All other points along the line FM consist of combinations of risky and risk-free assets. Thus, every investor confronted with the new opportunity set, F E M, will seek to be tangent to FM. This is in keeping with the risk–return tradeoff principle. That is, on the new efficient frontier, every investor has the highest return commensurate with risk.

Furthermore, since FM represents the only efficient frontier of investments (portfolios), it is often known as the *capital-market line (CML)*. The return on an efficient portfolio of risk-free and risky assets is denoted by:

$$R(R_p) = R_f + \lambda^*(\sigma_p) \tag{11}$$

where:

$R(R_p)$ = required return on efficient portfolios

R_f = the risk-free interest rate

λ^* = the price of risk for efficient portfolios—i.e., the slope of CML, or $\dfrac{E(R_m) - E(R_f)}{\sigma_m}$

σ_p = the standard deviation of return on efficient portfolios

Thus, the capital-market line is the efficient frontier for portfolios composed of risk-free and risky assets. In keeping with our frame of reference, the CML deals with the tradeoff between risk and required return of efficient portfolios. An example of calculating the required return on an efficient portfolio stems from the data in Table 18.1. There the expected return and standard deviation of the market portfolio are computed. The $E(R_m)$ is .10, and σ_m is .2121. Thus, the return on an efficient portfolio can be calculated using the market parameters from Table 18.1, a risk-free return of 5 percent, and a portfolio standard deviation of .4. The required return is:

$$R(R_p) = .05 + \frac{.10 - .05}{.2121}(.4)$$

$$= .5 + .2357(.4)$$

$$= .5 + .0942$$

$$= .1442, \text{ or } 14.42\%$$

TABLE 18.1 Computation of Market Parameters

STATE	p	R_m	$p(R_m)$	$R_m - E(R_m)$	$[R_m - E(R_m)]^2$	$p[R_m - E(R_m)]^2$
Recession	.25	−.20	−.05	−.3	.09	.0225
Normal	.50	.10	.05	0	0	0
Boom	.25	.40	.10	.3	.09	.0225
			$E(R_m) = .10$			Var R_m = .0450
						σ_m = .2121

The Security-Market Line The security-market line (SML) shows the tradeoff between risk and required return for individual securities or single assets. Thus, the expected return for each security in relation to risk can be depicted as

FIGURE 18.7 Security-Market Line.

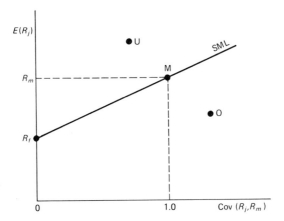

under- or overvalued relative to returns required by the market, as shown by the SML. The SML is depicted in Figure 18.7.

Notice that the market-line relationship for individual securities uses the covariance instead of the standard deviation as the independent variable. Thus, the price of risk for individual securities is the market price of risk normalized by (that is, divided by) the variance of market returns. The reason for using covariance instead of the standard deviation is that a portion of the risk as measured by standard deviation can be mitigated through diversification. Thus, the market is not willing to pay a premium for that portion of risk that can be diversified away in a portfolio of securities.* Calculation of individual securities parameters is shown in Table 18.2.

Restating equation (11) for individual securities gives:

$$R(R_j) = R_f + \lambda\, \text{Cov}(R_j, R_m) \tag{12}$$

where:

$R(R_j)$ = required return on an individual security

R_f = the risk-free interest rate

λ = the price of risk for individual securities—i.e., the slope of the SML, or $\dfrac{E(R_m) - E(R_f)}{\text{Var}_m}$

$\text{Cov}(R_j, R_m)$ = variance of security returns times variance of market returns, i.e., $(\text{Var } R_j)(\text{Var } R_m)$

---

*Diversifiable risks were discussed in Chapter 4.

TABLE 18.2 Calculation of Security Parameters

STATE	p	R_j	$p(R_j)$	$R_j - E(R_j)$	$[R_j - E(R_j)]^2$	$p[R_j - E(R_j)]^2$
Recession	.25	−.30	−.075	−.475	.2256	.0564
Normal	.50	.10	.050	−.075	.0056	.0028
Boom	.25	.80	.200	.625	.3906	.0976
			$E(R_j) = .175$		Var $R_j = .1567$	
					$\sigma_j = .4$ (rounded)	

TABLE 18.3 Calculation of Covariance for Market and Security Returns

p	$R_j - E(R_j)$	$R_m - E(R_m)$	$[R_j - E(R_j)][R_m - E(R_m)]$	$p[R_j - E(R_j)][R_m - E(R_m)]$
.25	−.475	−.3	.1425	.0356
.50	−.075	0	0	0
.25	.625	.3	.1875	.0562
			Cov $(R_j, R_m) =$	.0918
				or 9.18 percent

Using the covariance from Table 18.3 and a risk-free rate of 5 percent, the required return for the security can be calculated. First, the slope of the line is calculated:

$$\lambda = \frac{.10 - .05}{.045} = 1.11$$

Then the required return is calculated by using equation (12):

$$R(R_j) = R_f + \lambda \, \text{Cov} \, (R_j, R_m)$$
$$= .05 + 1.11 \, (.0918)$$
$$= .05 + .1018$$
$$= .1518, \text{ or } 15\%$$

Table 18.2 shows an expected return on the security of 17.5 percent. Since the expected return varies from the required return of 15 percent, market adjustments will occur. Since investors expect the return to be higher than the required return, they will purchase the stock. Such purchases cause the price of the security to increase. As the price increases, its yield or return decreases. When the price of the stock increases to the level where it yields a return of about 15 percent, the security will have reached its market equilibrium. That is, neither buying (demand) nor selling (supply) pressures prevail.

The market-line relationship for individual securities using covariance has been shown as:

$$R(R_j) = R_f + \lambda \, \text{Cov}\,(R_j, R_m) \tag{12}$$

where:

$$\lambda = \frac{R_j - R_m}{\sigma_m^2}$$

The market-line relationship for individual securities can also be expressed in terms of the "beta coefficient," namely:

$$R(R_j) = R_f + (R_m - R_f)\,\beta_j \tag{13}$$

where:

$$\beta_j = \frac{\text{Cov}\,(R_j, R_m)}{\text{Var}\,R_m}$$

Both the equations are the same.* Equation (13) multiplies the security's normalized risk index, the beta coefficient, by the market-risk premium to obtain the *risk-adjustment factor*. Equation (12) multiplies the security's covariance by the normalized market-risk premium to obtain the *risk-adjustment factor*. Thus, either method gives the same risk-adjustment factor, and the same required return once the risk-free return is added to the risk-adjustment factor.

The market return *always* has a risk of 1 on the SML. This is true because the relevant measure of risk is beta on the horizontal axis. Our use of beta is derived from a linear-regression model of the individual firm's return relative to market returns. Thus, it is a reliable estimate of the firm's risk. See the appendix to this chapter for the calculation of beta.

Point M on the SML is the symbol for the market portfolio of assets. If all assets were combined into one portfolio, they would be represented by point M. In practice, good representations of the market are the Dow Jones Industrial Average and Standard & Poor's Index of 500 Stocks. The return in the market is computed by the holding-period return discussed in Chapter 14. Again, the beta for the market return is *always* 1. Thus, all securities are measured relative to the market.

The returns for individual stocks can be computed on a ten-year basis using the holding-period formula. Betas for individual securities are estimated by determining the slope of the regression line of the returns. A high beta is greater than 1 (that is, a greater risk than the market). A low beta is less than 1 (less risk than the market). Securities with high betas are classed as aggressive issues, and low-beta securities are classed as defensive.

---

* $\quad\quad\quad\quad \lambda \, \text{Cov}\,(R_j, R_m) = (R_m - R_f)\beta_j$

since $\quad\quad\quad\quad \text{Var}\,R_m \equiv \sigma_m^2$

and $\quad\quad\quad\quad \lambda = (R_m - R_f)/\sigma_m^2$

and $\quad\quad\quad\quad \beta_j = \text{Cov}\,(R_j, R_m)/\,\text{Var}\,R_m$

Then $\quad \left[\dfrac{R_f - R_m}{\sigma_m^2}\right] \text{Cov}\,(R_j, R_m) = (R_m - R_f)\dfrac{\text{Cov}\,(R_j, R_m)}{\text{Var}\,R_m}$

Thus, by using betas, a shorthand for risk is established. In 1972, the firm of William O'Neil & Company calculated betas for the 1,354 common stocks then listed on the New York Stock Exchange. The result of those calculations is shown in Figure 18.8. The bar chart shows that there is a relatively even distribution of betas, with perhaps a slight skew to the right.

FIGURE 18.8 Distribution of Beta Coefficients for 1,354 Common Stocks. (*Source: William O'Neil & Co. Incorporated.*)

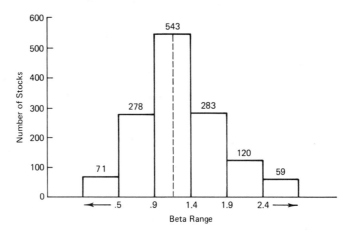

The line connecting the risk-free return and the market return is the SML. This is considered the equilibrium condition. That is, if an individual security's return is above the SML, the security is undervalued. Conversely, if a security's return lies below the SML, the security is overvalued, because its return is less than that of the market. As undervalued or overvalued assets are discovered, their returns are likely to change. Thus, it is reasonable to assume that asset returns tend to converge on the SML.

SUMMARY

The making of big money in the securities market is generally limited to a very small percentage of investors, who are known as big-money, or smart-money, investors. Such investors have substantial wealth plus a good working knowledge of companies in basic industries and how general business conditions affect stock prices of such companies. Smart-money investors often have first-hand information and take action based on such information. Theirs is a fundamental approach to investing—that the price of common is a result of many factors, such as newly developed products, innovations, management changes, sales, dividends, and earnings.

Professional traders seek to emulate or imitate the informed investors through the study of charts, volume, trends, and certain technical indicators. The rationale of the professional trader, and more specifically of the chartist or technician, is that only supply, demand, and market psychology are reflected in the movement of stock prices. This approach is called technical analysis, market analysis, or internal analysis.

Securities analysis, as distinct from market analysis, is a normative science that is concerned with what ought to be. In the process of determining value (what ought to be the value), the problem of assessing the true, intrinsic, or investment value of a security is paramount in securities analysis (that is, fundamental analysis).

Market analysis is a positive science. That is, it assumes that the action of the market as indicated by trends and relationships reveals what is currently happening. Based on such trends and relationships, future price movements are forecast.

Random walk refutes both technical and fundamental analysis. Many academicians have become convinced that it is futile to forecast securities prices. However, Wall Street practitioners are equally convinced that price movements are nonrandom. So the practitioners continue to use technical analysis for when-to-buy decisions and fundamental analysis for what-to-buy decisions. However, a random-selection method for building a portfolio has received some academic attention as an outgrowth of the random-walk hypothesis.

Diversification is not new. But the quantification of diversification is relatively new. Investors have known for some time that to diversify their holdings reduces their risk. But they also know that diversification may reduce their expected return. This is true because as some stocks in the portfolio rise in value, others decline.

Forecasting is not new. But forecasting the level of risk instead of return is a relatively new approach to investing. Conceptually, all the approaches attempt to do the same thing—to evaluate an asset's riskiness. The investment process can be viewed as finding under- or overvalued securities and acting on such information.

APPENDIX TO CHAPTER 18:
BETAS AND THE SML

Betas for individual securities can be calculated or obtained directly from a financial service such as the *Value Line Investment Survey*. Value Line lists the beta for each security based on weekly holding-period returns over a five-year period. Figure 18.9 shows a beta of 1.05 for General Motors Corporation, as of February 1977.

There are various methods of calculating beta. The holding-period return can be on a weekly, quarterly, or annual basis. Weekly and quarterly returns are usually for a five-year period. Annual returns are generally calculated over a ten-year period. Actually, betas can be calculated for any holding-period return that covers a period long enough to be significant. We will calculate beta for General Motors Corporation based on annual holding-period returns over a ten-year period, 1967 through 1976.

The data needed on stock prices and dividend yields are readily available in the financial press. Market parameters are based on the same holding period as individual stocks. In Table 18.4 we calculate the market parameters for the ten-year period, 1967 through 1976. There we find an expected market return on the DJIA of 5.9 percent, a variance of market return of 180—which translates into a standard deviation of 13.42 percent, and an average annual risk-free interest rate of 6.7 percent.

TABLE 18.4 Calculation of Market Parameters (1967–1976)

YEAR	DJIA	$\dfrac{P_t - P_{t-1}}{P_{t-1}}$	$\dfrac{D_t}{P_t}$	R_{m_t}	$R_{m_t} - E(R_m)$	$[R_{m_t} - E(R_m)]^2$	R_{f_t}
1966	871						
1967	864	(.01)	.04	.03	(.029)	.00084	.05
1968	905	.05	.03	.08	.021	.00044	.05
1969	870	(.04)	.04	.00	(.059)	.00348	.07
1970	730	(.16)	.04	(.12)	(.179)	.03204	.09
1971	875	.20	.04	.24	.181	.03276	.06
1972	962	.10	.03	.13	.071	.00504	.06
1973	920	(.04)	.04	.00	(.059)	.00348	.07
1974	732	(.20)	.05	(.15)	(.209)	.04368	.09
1975	757	.03	.05	.08	.021	.00044	.08
1976	955	.26	.04	.30	.241	.05808	.06
				.59/10		.18028/10	.67/10
			$E(R_m) = .059$		Var $(R_m) = .018$	$R_f = .067$	

Table 18.5 shows the calculation of beta for General Motors Corporation. The price (P_t) is the average price for the year (that is, the average of the yearly high and low). The return (R_j) on GM is an annual holding-period return. The return includes each year's percentage change in price plus the dividend yield. An expected return for GM is computed as 6.2 percent, a covariance of 189, and a beta of 1.05.

Next the security-market line (SML) is calculated and plotted as shown in Figure 18.10. The risk-free interest rate (R_f) is 6.7 percent (value comes from Table 18.4). The market-risk premium is a negative 0.8 percent ($E[R_m] - R_f = .059 - .067 = -.008$). The result is a negatively sloped

FIGURE 18.9 Beta for General Motors Corporation. (*Source: The Value Line Investment Survey, Arnold Bernhard & Co., Oct. 10, 1975.*)

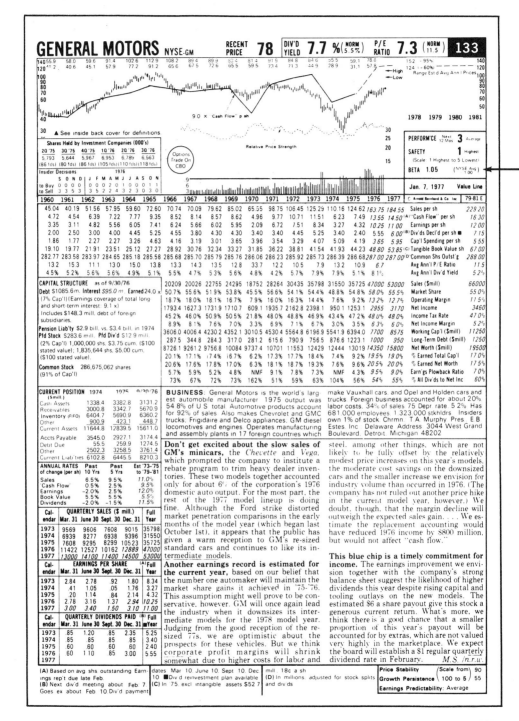

TABLE 18.5 Calculation of Beta for General Motors Corporation (1967–1976)

YEAR	P_t	$\dfrac{P_t - P_{t-1}}{P_{t-1}}$	$\dfrac{D_t}{P_t}$	R_{j_t}	$R_{j_t} - E(R_j)$	$R_m - E(R_m)$	$\dfrac{[R_j - E(R_j)]}{[R_m - E(R_m)]}$
1966	87						
1967	78	(.10)	.05	(.05)	(.112)	(.029)	.0032
1968	81	.04	.05	.09	.028	.021	.0005
1969	74	(.09)	.06	(.03)	(.092)	(.059)	.0054
1970	79	.07	.05	.12	.058	(.179)	(.0103)
1971	82	.04	.04	.08	.018	.181	.0032
1972	77	(.06)	.05	(.01)	(.072)	.071	(.0051)
1973	64	(.17)	.08	(.09)	(.152)	(.059)	.0089
1974	42	(.34)	.10	(.24)	(.302)	(.209)	.0631
1975	44	.05	.08	.13	.028	.021	.0005
1976	68	.55	.07	.62	.498	.241	.1200
				$\overline{.62/10}$			$\overline{.1894/10}$

$$E(R_j) = .062$$
$$\text{or } 6.2\%$$

$$\text{Cov } (R_j, R_m) = .0189$$

$$\beta_j = \frac{\text{Cov } (R_j, R_m)}{\text{Var } (R_m)} = \frac{.0189}{.018} = 1.05$$

FIGURE 18.10 Security-Market Line.

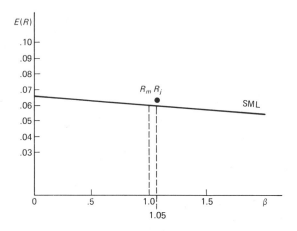

SML.* The beta for the market is always 1 ($\text{Var}_m/\text{Var}_m = .018/.018 = 1.0$). The expected return for GM is 6.2 percent and the GM beta is 1.05. Thus we see that GM has a slightly higher risk and return than the market. GM's

---

*A negatively sloped SML means that stock-market returns were not as good as the return on Treasury bills. This was true for the 1967–76 bear market. Consequently, many investors switched from common stocks to money-market instruments during that period. This situation has changed, however. Refer to Table 14.4 and find a 10 percent return on the DJIA for the 1971–76 period.

expected return is above the required-return line. So GM's common stock is undervalued relative to the return required by the market line.

The implication of the expected return of GM relative to the market is that the stock should be bought. According to capital asset pricing theory, as more investors recognize this fact, they *will* buy the stock. Such buying will cause the price of GM to rise and, conversely, the expected return on GM to fall until it reaches equilibrium at the return specified by the market line for the degree of risk (beta of 1.05) in GM.

One final note on the beta calculation. Besides the various holding-period-return calculations (weekly, quarterly, or yearly), the market return can be based on different indexes. The more commonly used indexes of the market are the Dow Jones Industrial Average, Standard & Poor's 500 Stock Index, and the New York Stock Exchange Composite Index. Value Line's beta of 1.05 for GM in Figure 18.9 is based on the NYSE composite average. Regardless of the market indicator used, the beta for the market will always be 1, because $\beta_m = \text{Var}_m/\text{Var}_m$. However, the beta for an individual security may range from .2 to over 3 as shown in Figure 18.8. It will vary slightly due to the holding period selected and the market index used.

PROBLEMS

1. Given the following figures, construct a market breadth index.

	ISSUES TRADED	ADVANCES	DECLINES	UNCHANGED
Monday	1,301	530	535	236
Tuesday	1,310	464	597	249
Wednesday	1,323	303	739	281
Thursday	1,295	607	453	235
Friday	1,308	807	241	260

2. How does the professional stock trader know a bottom is occurring in a bear market?

3. A stock has the following properties: Current "normal" dividend payout is expected to be 66 2/3% of $5 earnings per share at a growth rate of 9%.

    a. Calculate the earnings multiple.

    b. Calculate intrinsic value using $M(D + \frac{1}{3}E)$.

4. The Hudson Company's common stock paid a dividend of $1 last year. Dividends are expected to grow at a rate of 15% for each of the next five years, 10% for the second five years, and 6% thereafter. As long as the rate of growth is above average, the market demands a 10% per annum rate of return. When growth is average, the discount rate drops to 9%. How much should you pay for one share of Hudson's common stock?

5. The Barton Mint Company is expected to pay a cash dividend of $5 next year. Its dividends, which represent a fixed payout of earnings, are expected to grow at an annual rate of 6%. If you can earn 12% on similar-risk investments, what is the most you would pay per share for this firm? Why?

6. Avon's dividends and earnings are expected to grow at 14, 12, 10, and 8 percent, respectively, over the next four five-year periods, then 5 percent thereafter. The dividend for year zero is $1.40 1/3 per share and earnings are $2.50 per share. What is the value of a share of Avon today:

    a. If the discount rate is 14%?

    b. If the discount rate is 9%?

7. Go to the *Value Line Investment Survey* and find the beta for one of the 1,600 stocks listed. Secure the current Treasury-bill rate and use it as the R_f (risk-free) term. Next, consult the *Federal Reserve Bulletin* and calculate the market return on Standard & Poor's Index of 500 Stocks by use of the holding-period method (see Chapter 14). Plot the security-market line (SML) and return on your security. Is the stock you selected under- or overvalued relative to the market?

8. Assume that the risk-free rate is 6.5%. Calculate the expected return for security j for each of the following conditions:

    a. Market return of 15% and β_j of .75

    b. Market return of 15% and β_j of 2.00

    c. Market return of 15% and β_j of 1.00

    d. Market return of 5% and β_j of .75

    e. Market return of 5% and β_j of 2.00

    f. Market return of 5% and β_j of 1.00

Are the results what you would expect? Why?

9. Generalizing from the problem above:

    a. What will be the expected return if the market return is low and beta is high?

b. What will be the expected return if the market return is high and beta is low?

c. What will be the expected return if the market return is high and beta is high?

d. What will be the expected return if the market return is low and beta is low?

10. For the current period, Pan American's beta has been estimated to be 1.4, its expected return to be 13.5 %, the market return is estimated to be 12.8 %, the risk-free rate is 7.8%.

a. Calculate the required return.

b. Is Pan Am a buy or a sell candidate?

c. If the estimated market return is 6%, calculate the required return on Pan Am.

Financial
Markets

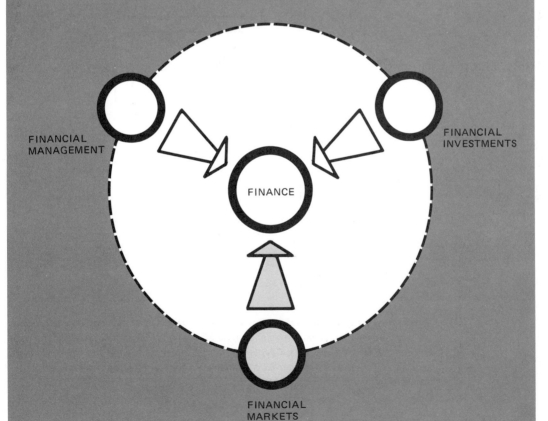

FINANCIAL
MANAGEMENT

FINANCIAL
INVESTMENTS

FINANCE

FINANCIAL
MARKETS

As indicated in the introduction to Part III, financial management in the firm and financial investments are different sides of the same coin. The link between financial management and financial investments is the financial market, the institutional and legal relationships designed to facilitate the distribution of financial claims from issuer to financial investor.

The model depicted in the figure below is an extension of the model presented in the introduction to Part III. The model shows, as previously, that households provide money to firms and receive goods and services in return. But there is a second set of relationships illustrated. In this second set of relationships, financial claims are sent by firms to financial markets where they are met by investment funds sent by households. This introduces the role of financial markets in the aggregate economic scheme.

Financial Markets in the Circular-Flow Model.

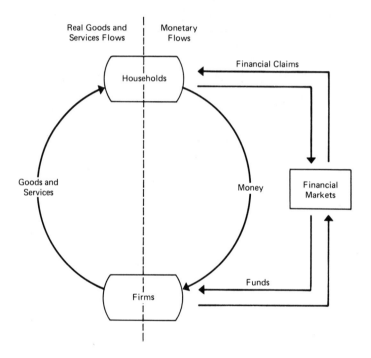

Part IV focuses upon financial markets. Chapter 19 defines financial markets and provides an overview of their economic role. Chapter 20 presents a treatment of prices and rates of return in financial markets. Chapters 21 and 22 treat the money and capital markets, respectively. Finally, in Chapter 23, the impact of economic stabilization policies, monetary and fiscal, on financial markets is discussed.

19

An Overview of Financial Markets

The activities conducted in financial markets represent a significant portion of the nation's economic activity. Financial markets are the institutional arrangements by which the financial claims of the firm get transmitted to the investor. Financial markets bridge the activities between the creation of financial claims in financial management and the purchase of financial claims in the investment arena. The discussion of markets here is divided generally into three parts: (1) definition of a market, (2) money markets, and (3) capital markets.

In this chapter, we shall first view generally the concept of the market. Then we shall construct an overview of the economic activity that gives rise to the production of financial claims, the savings-investment process. Finally, we shall set the stage for the following chapters, which analyze the activities of money markets and capital markets, respectively.

The concept of the market as an economic phenomenon is almost as old as recorded history itself. One dictionary defines a market as "a meeting together of people for the purpose of trade . . . and sale and usu. not by auction."*

There are several elements in this definition of a market. First, there is the meeting together of people for the purpose of sale. This introduces the participants in the financial markets, the transactors. It also implies that the goods or services traded in financial markets are financial claims—that is, claims upon those who accumulate economic capital ("productive stuff"), or claims upon financial intermediaries (commercial banks, savings and loans, and so on), which in turn buy *claims on* capital accumulators.

Note that the dictionary definition of the market *did not* specify it as a *place*. It is a common error to visualize a market as a spot on the surface of the earth. As long as the essential elements of a market are present— people to do the trading, and something to trade—there is a market present. It is a truism that a large part of the transactions in financial markets are conducted on the telephone, an idea that belies the image of buyers and sellers congregating at one location. Indeed, some financial markets appear superficially to be confined to one spot—the New York Stock Exchange, for example—but the purchases and sales that make up trading on the "Big Board" actually originate throughout the country.

What is the purpose of a market? Its basic purpose, whether it is the vegetable market on the corner or the market in U.S. Treasury bills, is to provide an outlet for the pressures of supply and demand for the good or service being traded in the market. Intuition indicates that price will rise or fall in response to supply and demand pressures. Prices produced in financial markets, interest rates, are used as a barometer of supply and demand pressures in any given financial market. More on this will be presented later in this chapter.

Where do financial claims come from? It has been stated that the objects traded in financial markets are claims either on those producing income-generating assets, or claims on financial intermediaries that in turn

---

Webster's New Collegiate Dictionary, 8th ed. (Springfield, Mass.: Merriam, 1975), p. 704. By permission. © 1975 by G. & C. Merriam Co., Publishers of the Merriam-Webster Dictionaries.

purchase claims on those who purchase income-generating assets. A glimpse into the process by which financial claims are created is in order.

THE SAVINGS-INVESTMENT PROCESS

We are going to construct a simple model of some economic relationships. Our model will perform the function of all models: It will allow us to see and understand the essential parts of our analysis.

Basic Definitions First, some definitions. There are only two things a person can do with his or her current income: consume it, or save it. These two concepts, because they are at the heart of objects traded in financial markets, bear further and careful examination.

Consumption is the act of using up one's income during the current income period. The purchase of food, clothing, fuel, and other such necessities of life is an example of consumption expenditure. One definition of *consume* is "to use up." It is clear we think that when one consumes, he uses up his current income.

Saving, on the other hand, is the act of *not* using current income to purchase consumption goods. We have become very accustomed to thinking of saving as an overt act such as going to the bank to make a deposit in one's savings account. But saving need not be an overt act. Taxes are a form of saving. Every dollar taxed away from you is not used to buy consumption goods. *It is therefore saving.** True, the savings funds generated through taxation do not belong to you, but that is not necessary to our definition of saving.

Many people erroneously regard taxation as a form of consumption, i.e., the consumption of the services of police, armed forces, legislators, and so forth. These services, however, are not savings; rather, they are investments (in the form of acquisition of social assets) made possible by savings. Of course, in this instance—that of taxation—the savings are involuntary. In order to understand the economic function of financial markets, it is necessary to understand clearly that saving and investment decisions are separate and independent of each other in a sophisticated economy.

One last definition is needed before we can complete the model. It is the definition of economic investment (as opposed to financial investment). Economic investment is the accumulation of capital goods, "productive

---

*Taxation is forced saving, in the sense that it is not a conscious, voluntary decision on the part of the saver. (Inflation, too, is a form of forced saving, for it forces one to moderate consumption.)

stuff," any goods that have an economic life greater than one income period.*
Machine tools, buildings, trucks—these are all examples of capital goods,
the accumulation of which is economic investment.

The Savings-
Investment Model

Now that we have these definitions firmly fixed in our minds, we can
start the construction of our simple model. But first, some basic sym-
bols we will be using:

$Y =$ level of income in dollars

$C =$ dollar expenditures on consumption goods

$I =$ dollar expenditures on investment goods

$S =$ dollar value of savings out of current income

There are only two ways we can dispose of current income, either individually, or collectively as a nation. We can either consume or not consume
(save) our income. Symbolically, we can state that relationship:

$$Y = C + S \quad \text{(Expenditure side)}$$

Given our simple two-sector model, there are only two activities upon
which national income is earned, the production of consumption goods and
the production of investment goods. Symbolically:

$$Y = C + I \quad \text{(Income side)}$$

Let's put the two sets of relationships together:

$$Y = C + S \quad \text{(Expenditure side)}$$
$$Y = C + I \quad \text{(Income side)}$$
$$S = I$$

One doesn't need a doctorate in mathematics to realize that, in
equilibrium, the dollar value of savings has to equal the dollar value of
investment. Algebraically, savings have to equal investment in the set of
relationships above. This statement, however, has significance far in excess
of its algebraic tautology. Economically, the statement says that the increase
in the nation's capital stock, the economic investment process, must be
financed out of the nation's savings from current income. In real economic
terms—that is, in terms of the allocation of resources—it means that the

---

*You are engaged at this very moment in accumulating perhaps the most
important capital good of your life, your education.

resources that we do not use up during an income period are available to be converted into capital goods.

So far, we have been using dollar values for savings and investment. But these dollar values represent control over real goods and services. You must condition yourself to believe that we must defer or deny ourselves consumption in order to release resources for capital goods. Stated a bit differently, the steel used for autos today is not available for use in machine tools to build the economy tomorrow.

Financial Claims   But where do financial claims fit in? Well, if we state savings and investment in real terms, in terms of economic resources, it is relatively easy to see that resources *not consumed* (*S*) are available for the production of capital goods (*I*). The theory would be airtight, flawless, and conceptually sound if only those people doing the "not consuming"—the saving—were the same people as the ones doing the capital accumulating—the investing. Such might be the case in a Robinson Crusoe or Swiss Family Robinson economy, where both saving and investing are in real terms, in terms of economic resources. The time Robinson Crusoe spends building a shelter is also time he does not spend consuming his hard-won berries and fruit. In this case, the savings *is* the investment, and because of this, $I = S$.

But what about a highly developed economy such as that of the United States? Here is a case where the production of a capital good (Robinson Crusoe's shelter) is not automatically financed by his saving (not consuming) at the same point in time. The assembly-line worker in Detroit does not automatically accumulate machine tools when he does not consume his income. (Remember that Robinson Crusoe does.)

The relationship among savings, investment, and national income is demonstrated by Figure 19.1. The level of national income is related to the rates of investment and saving. For example, if the economy saves at a rate greater than that at which it invests ($S > I$), the level of national income falls. Conversely, if the economy accumulates capital at a rate greater than that at which it saves ($I > S$), the level of national income rises. This is usually called an investment boom. Note that the savings decision is divorced from the investment decision in a large economy such as ours. (Again, the Detroit assembly-line worker does not accumulate machine tools.)

The Capital Gap   The channeling of savings into investment is a long-range process. Extrapolations of savings flows and competing uses of savings tend to conclude that the demand for savings will tend to outstrip the supply of savings. The figures for one such extrapolation are presented in Table 19.1. The estimate concludes that there will be a $506-billion shortfall of savings in the period 1975–84. This shortfall represents 13 percent of the savings projected for the period.

FIGURE 19.1 Savings, Investment, and the Circular Flow of Income.

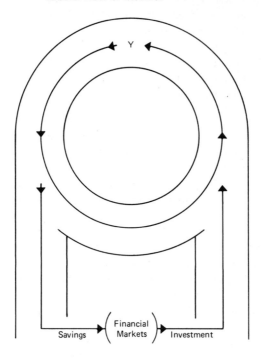

TABLE 19.1 Capital Needs, 1975–84
(trillions of dollars)

Demanders of capital:		
Government	.175	
Farms & others	.850	
Housing	1.005	
Plant & equipment	2.508	
		4.538
Suppliers of capital:		
Business saving	2.923	
Personal saving	1.109	
		4.032
Capital gap		.506

Source: New York Stock Exchange.

The basic problem is that of channeling savings into investment—that is, channeling the control ($) over real economic resources from those who do not want to use those resources (savers) to those who do want to use them (investors). The problem is greatly alleviated by the ability of the capital accumulators to sell claims upon their income streams in order to attract the savings needed. Thus, the auto manufacturer can sell stock, which is purchased by savers. The proceeds of the stock sale are used by the auto manufacturer to purchase machine tools and all the other capital required to produce cars. The saver, in turn, is promised a proportional share of the profits of the auto manufacturer in exchange for his savings. If you understand this uncomplicated example, you can readily understand why the payment of dividends and interest is sometimes referred to as the payment for abstaining from consumption. The saver transfers monetary control over resources to the investor, he does not transfer discrete "hunks" of capital goods.

This is all very relevant to the subject of financial markets. The claim that the capital accumulator issues on himself and his income stream is indeed the object that is traded in financial markets. We have discussed the nature of claims on corporate income when we discussed the job of the financial manager in trying to determine the cost of capital of his corporation. We should briefly describe these claims again, however, in order to understand what is being traded in financial markets.

CLAIMS ON CAPITAL ACCUMULATORS

Individuals and corporations wishing to accumulate productive stuff—capital—as we have said, tailor claims upon their asset structures and income streams in order to attract the savings needed. Schematically, the process is illustrated in Figure 19.2.

FIGURE 19.2 Financial Market Process.

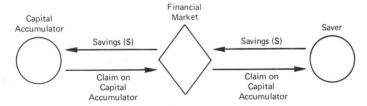

As we have said, the income earner engages in saving his idle income, which he wants to put to work. He is a candidate for a financial market transaction. Although he has the option of stuffing his savings in the proverbial mattress, he is a far wiser man than his counterpart in past times who did just that. There is a high probability that the saver of today recognizes the implicit cost in sterilizing his savings. The current saver is sophisticated enough to realize that he can earn a return on his savings until they are needed for future consumption. Therefore, the saver makes his savings available to a demander of funds in either the money or the capital market.

An Example   *The Saver.* Let's say, for example, that our hypothetical saver wants to invest in a security whose market value will tend to keep pace with price increases in the economy. This saver will not need his funds for another 25 years, at which time he plans to retire from his job and spend his golden years hiking the wild hills of the Appalachians. From this description of the saver's needs, it would appear that common stock of a large corporation would fit those needs perfectly. But how to buy common stock, and which one to buy, is a problem. The typical saver is not a sophisticated analyst of the stock market.

Our typical saver turns to expert advice. He goes to a stockbroker who has a sound and honorable reputation. After careful analysis of the saver's investment requirements, the broker recommends that he purchase shares of the A-Shoe Corporation. The past growth record of this firm as well as its policy of steady dividends is just the thing our investor is looking for.

Perhaps without realizing it, we are now deep in a financial market. Since a share is a perpetual claim on the income stream of a corporation, we are indeed in the capital market, the market for long-term funds.

Stop and take a look at what has transpired. The income earner has decided not to use all his current income for consumption purposes. He has therefore made a conscious decision to save. He wants to use his savings to prepare for life during his retirement. To do this, he in effect takes his savings to a financial market—the stock market, which is a component part of the capital market. We have explained the right side of the preceding diagram.

The Supplier of the Security. Turn now to the supplier of the security that is going to be purchased. The A-Shoe Corporation had to issue stock originally to start into business. Common stock, equity, is required in the founding of every corporation in the country. Some corporations have never sold additonal stock since they were founded. If their original stock is still being traded in the market, it is a part of the vast secondary market for corporate securities. The secondary market is the massive market for securities that are in the process of being traded between investors, and not between the original issuer and investors.

There is another secondary market with which we are all more familiar, although it is not usually known as a secondary market. The market that exists nationally for used cars is in effect a secondary market in cars. Using this analogy, we could say that the secondary market in securities is the market for "used" securities. And just as the used-car market provides support for the new-car market, the "used"-security market provides support for the new-issues market.

Let's assume that the A-Shoe Corporation's common stock is traded actively in the securities market, and that it is the original issue of the corporation. This active market provides a constant outlet for funds of people, such as our hypothetical investor, with savings to invest. The active market also provides a vehicle for people whose investment objectives change, and who want therefore to "roll out of" or sell their shares in A-Shoe Corporation.

In this case, the corporation originally—some time ago, to be sure—supplied securities to the market. At that time, the supply of common stock was sent to the market by A-Shoe. And at that time, the shares were met by savings of an income earner who did not consume. Thus, the corporation was able to sell claims upon itself and use the proceeds of that sale to purchase needed capital assets. And also at that time, the saver was able to put his idle income to work. This process is shown in Figure 19.2.

A Position-Statement Approach. The basic accounting statement, the position statement, can be used to illustrate the nature of financial claims and their role in financial markets. All financial claims appear as liabilities on someone's position statement. The claim also appears as an asset on the position statement of the financial investor who owns the claim. Tracing through the position statement locations of financial claims assists an understanding of the need for, and function of, financial markets.

In the transaction outlined above in which the A-Shoe Corporation issues stock, the position-statement version of the transaction would be:

A-SHOE CORPORATION		FINANCIAL INVESTOR	
+ Cash		− Cash	
	Common	+ Common	
	Stock +	Stock	

Note that the common-stock claim is on the liability side of the issuer's position statement, and on the asset side of the investor's position statement. In order to emphasize the importance of conceptualizing the position-statement approach to tracing financial claims, a further example is presented.

Consider the Treasury's issuance of bills, 13-week obligations. Conceptually (for the Treasury actually has no position statement), the bills appear as liabilities on the liability side of the Treasury's position statement, and as an asset on the position statement of the bill's owner. Thus:

TREASURY		FINANCIAL INVESTOR	
+ Cash	Bill +	− Cash	
		+ Bill	

The position-statement approach to conceptualizing the creation and flows of financial claims is a useful way of viewing the process.

Although we have used common stock as the instrument and the stock market as the centerpieces in the foregoing example, it is clear that the general principles outlined in the example are true regardless of the investment medium or the various submarkets of the money and capital markets through which it is traded.

FINANCIAL INTERMEDIARIES: A SPECIAL CASE

So far in this discussion, we have been dealing exclusively with those who save and those who accumulate capital goods. But although these are the two major participants in financial markets, there is another participant that neither saves nor accumulates capital goods. This participant channels savings between the saver and the capital accumulator. The financial intermediary, whom we are describing, acts as the conduit of savings in the economy, and makes the savings-investment process more efficient than it would otherwise be.

Capitalizing upon the previous schematic drawing, we represent the role of financial intermediaries in financial markets as in Figure 19.3.

FIGURE 19.3 Financial Intermediary.

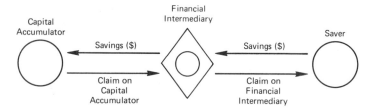

Let's define the financial intermediary as one who tailors financial claims upon himself to attract savings funds, and then uses these funds to purchase claims upon capital accumulators or other financial intermediaries. Perhaps one of the best-known intermediaries is the commercial bank. The banker accepts deposits, and uses these funds to buy IOUs of businessmen— that is, lends the funds to the businessmen.

But there are many other financial intermediaries. As long as one meets the criteria of our definition, it is a financial intermediary. Let's test the definition. Which of the following are financial intermediaries?

1. Savings and loan associations

2. Automobile manufacturers

3. Life insurance companies

4. Mutual savings banks

If you said that all except automobile manufacturers are financial intermediaries, you are correct. Savings and loan associations accept deposits (savings) and use the proceeds to purchase residential mortgages (investment). Life insurance companies sell policies for funds (savings) and use the proceeds to purchase mortgages, bonds, and a whole spectrum of other claims on capital accumulators (investment). And finally, mutual savings banks, found primarily in New England, accept deposits (savings) and use these funds to purchase claims on various capital accumulators (investment).

Automobile manufacturers are not financial intermediaries because they do not purchase claims on other capital accumulators. True, they do issue claims upon themselves (bonds, preferred stock, and common stock) to attract savings, but they use the proceeds to purchase capital goods for their own use rather than channeling the funds on for use by others. Because this is true, they do not qualify under our definition of financial intermediaries.

Position-Statement Approach to Financial Intermediaries Using the position statement to demonstrate the claims flowing into financial markets through financial intermediaries results in the following diagram:

HOMEOWNER		SAVINGS & LOAN		FINANCIAL INVESTOR	
+ House			Deposit +	− Cash	
	Mortgage +	+ Mortgage		+ Deposit	

In this case, the financial investor (saver) deposits his savings in a savings and loan, a financial intermediary. The savings and loan purchases the mortgage IOU of the homeowner, the ultimate capital accumulator.

The savings and loan association is an example of all intermediaries, and the mortgage represents all financial claims purchased by financial intermediaries.

The Impact of Financial Intermediaries Financial intermediaries make significant contributions to the economy. They do this in basically two ways: They increase the breadth of financial claims available to the investing public, and they increase the volume of savings available for the purchase of claims on economic investors.

By increasing the breadth of financial claims available, financial intermediaries perform two subservices. First, they provide an investment outlet for savers who do not desire to hold claims on capital accumulators; and second, by doing this, they tend to increase the volume of savings flowing into financial markets. Stated simply, the existence of financial intermediaries allows those people who want to own savings deposits and the like to invest in them instead of stocks and bonds. This permits them to become financial-market participants when otherwise they would not be.

The consolidation process performed by financial intermediaries permits larger volumes of funds to be channeled to capital accumulators. The consolidation process is the process of collecting the savings of many small savers into a large pool of savings available for use by capital accumulators. Financial intermediaries contribute to the existence of efficient financial markets, a market characteristic discussed in some detail later in this chapter.

LEGAL CHARACTERISTICS OF FINANCIAL CLAIMS

We turn now to a discussion of the legal characteristics of the objects traded in financial markets, the claims upon capital accumulators and upon financial institutions. Although there are short-term debt claims that are traded in money markets, we will confine our discussion here to the instruments of the capital market: bonds, preferred stock, and common stock.

All objects traded in financial markets are claims. This point has been emphasized throughout the discussion in this chapter. They are claims either upon capital accumulators or upon financial intermediaries that in turn purchase claims of capital accumulators. Since the legal characteristics of financial claims are primarily concerned with priority of claims on income and priority of claims on assets, the legal characteristics of financial claims will be discussed under these two broad headings.

Priority of Claims on Income   From precedents established first in Roman law, and later in British common law, it is traditional to consider that debt owners have priority over equity owners in claims on the income stream of the corporation. But many qualifications are in order.

Consider the options available to the financial investor, the income earner who has savings to invest in financial markets. He has the option of either buying debt—bonds, IOUs, and so on—or buying equity, here temporarily defined as common stock. What are his priorities under each option?

Bonds. If he buys debt, a bond, he establishes his primary claim on the income stream. The corporation issuing the bond promises to pay a stipulated rate of return on the bond. This return is normally lower than the return on common and preferred stock because of the fact that the corporation makes two concessions: It promises to pay a fixed and unchanging rate of return on the money it borrows, and it promises to pay the interest to the bondholder before all other financial claims on the income stream are paid. This says that if income available to pay financial claims to owners is limited, the bondholders are paid first.

Furthermore, failure to pay interest on bonds puts the corporation in jeopardy of bankruptcy, for the nonpayment of interest to bondholders is considered grounds for pursuit of this course of action. Because of these characteristics of interest payments on debt, they are considered "cost of doing business" by the Internal Revenue Service and are therefore tax-deductible. In summary, we say that the bondholder enjoys two positions superior to preferred and common stockholders. First, the rate of return is promised and fixed, and second, bondholders have the first claim on the income stream.

Preferred Stock. Then what would induce one to buy preferred stock? Perhaps the fact that the promised rate of return is higher on preferred stock than on bonds.

Although preferred stock is usually *legally* considered a part of the equity base of the corporation, it is *financially* usually considered with the debt. It has similar characteristics. For example, the preferred shareholder is promised a fixed rate of return. If earnings are generated, the preferred shareholder can always depend upon the promised rate of return. But if the corporation does not earn enough to pay both bondholders and preferred shareholders, bondholders get paid and preferred shareholders do not. Unlike bondholders, if preferred shareholders do not get paid, they usually have no legal recourse against the corporation. They are indeed paid a higher rate of return, but this higher rate of return is paid to compensate them for the risk that there might not be earnings. This risk they assume.

Common Stock. Common stockholders have a privilege—some would say that it is a responsibility—that the owners of other claims do not have. This is the right to vote for the directors of the corporation. The directors in turn set policy for the corporation and appoint the corporations' senior officers. Theoretically, the common shareholders can choose a board of directors that will manage the corporation in such a way as to provide large and positive values at the end of the income statement for the common shareholders. This implies, of course, that there are earnings available to pay all the other claims on the income stream, including the payments to bondholders and to preferred shareholders.

Debt vs. Equity. Both debt and preferred stock have contractually agreed upon, and distinctly stipulated, rates of return associated with them. The major characteristic of the return on common stock is that it is not fixed. The common shareholder has a claim on the residual income of the corporation. Whatever is left at the end of the income statement after *all* previous claims have been paid, including taxes, belongs to the common shareholders. As we have said previously and will say again in the future, this figure can be very large or it can be very small. There is even the possibility that it will be negative, meaning losses for the corporation. The common shareholder trades the possibility of very large returns for the possibility of very small returns or losses. There is, because of this, greater risk in investment in common stock.

Priority of Claims on Assets The only time that the owners of claims on the assets of the corporation would want to exercise their claims is when the corporation is in the position of being liquidated. This can come about in either of two basic ways. First, the shareholders can just decide to dissolve the corporation voluntarily. They have the right to do so. They own it. The other manner of liquidation is quite unpleasant. It is forced liquidation, usually through bankruptcy proceedings.

Liquidation literally means that the assets of the corporation are being liquidated—being turned into liquidity, cash. The cash is then used to pay the owners of the claims. Under these circumstances, the priority of claims becomes very important, for there is usually in bankruptcy proceedings not enough to pay all claimants. The priority established under law, and through contract, then becomes very important.

Generally, after short-term claims have been paid, the bondholders stand next in line for payment. This is true because of the debt nature of bonds. Part of the actual or implied contract that is a part of every debt issue is the agreement to pay bondholders before preferred shareholders and common shareholders. This is another reason why the return on debt is at the low end of the spectrum of rates in the capital market.

Last again we find the common shareholders. Part of the price common shareholders pay for the possibility of large returns is the possibility of not receiving anything in the liquidation of the corporation, should that come about. The last priority of the common shareholders in liquidation is a vivid testament to the risk position assumed by the owners of common stock.

MATURITY CHARACTERISTICS OF FINANCIAL CLAIMS

We define maturity as the date on which a financial claim has to be reclaimed, paid off, and canceled. As we shall see, only debt has maturity dates. Both preferred and common stock do not. The reasons for this we shall discover in the following discussion.

The Maturity of Debt Funds can be lent for any period of time, from less than a day to eternity. We normally refer to any debt of less than five years as *notes*.*

---

*In some parts of the United States, it is customary to refer to monthly payments made on installment-type loans as "notes." This usage should not be confused with the formal definition of a note given above.

Debts of over five years, and those that are sold in the marketplace—as opposed to face-to-face negotiations that result in loans—are called *bonds*.

A bond with an interesting maturity was issued in Great Britain in 1815. After having issued many bonds to finance the Napoleonic Wars, the British in 1815 issued a bond that had no maturity. It is a perpetual bond. This interesting bond is called a "consol" by the British, because its purpose was to consolidate the debt of the Napoleonic Wars. Although not extremely rare, perpetual bonds are not common. They really are preferred stock, because there is no promise ever to repay the principal to the lender. They are the classic income stream into perpetuity.

In the next chapter we shall see that, other things equal, the interest rates demanded by lenders in financial markets are directly related to maturity, in that money lent for long periods incurs greater risk than funds lent for shorter periods.

The Maturity of Stock, Preferred and Common
As we said above, both preferred and common stock have no maturity. Since the corporation issues no promise ever to return the principal—indeed, this is the wrong term, for we are not dealing in debt—there can be no date for return of the funds invested by the purchaser of the financial claim. Like consols, preferred and common stock are claims on income streams into perpetuity.

FINANCIAL MARKETS AND ECONOMIC EFFICIENCY

Efficient-Market Hypothesis
The efficient-market hypothesis (EMH) holds that the market is efficient and reflects market information. An efficient market is defined as one in which there are large numbers of equally informed, actively competing transactors maximizing profits. In such a market, price, at any moment in time, reflects information that is known and, according to some, those events expected to occur in the future. The degree of market information available differentiates the three forms of EMH. The three forms are:

1. Weak form, also known as the random-walk hypothesis.

2. Semi-strong form. This form contends that financial-market conditions reflect all publicly held information.

3. Strong form. This form contends that the market reflects all information, whether publicly available or not.

Since the weak form, the random-walk hypothesis, has received extensive empirical testing, we shall concentrate our discussion upon it.

Random-Walk Theory   *Random walk* is defined as a sequence of security price movements in which the direction of each successive price change is determined entirely at random. The random-walk hypothesis is also known as the weak-form test of the efficient-market hypothesis. The weak form of the EMH simply contends that security prices do not tend to follow patterns repetitively. Random-walk studies center on changes in security prices and associated trading volumes of securities to see if trends exist or if price changes stem from certain probability distributions.

Statisticians have demonstrated that the day-to-day (or week-to-week) changes in security prices are very much like a "random walk." This concept is shown in Figure 19.4. Such studies are conducted using rather sophisticated

FIGURE 19.4   Random-Walk Price Changes.

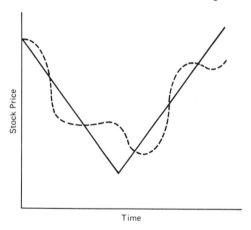

tests (serial correlation, analysis of runs, spectral analysis, and so on). Most of the studies confirm the belief that successive or lagged price changes are generally statistically independent.

Many academicians have wholeheartedly subscribed to the theory that short-term movements of security prices are random. The tests have convinced them that no amount of analysis of historical data on prices and volume can help forecast the movement of future security prices around their long-term trends. So academicians laugh at Wall Street because of its refusal to believe in the random-walk theory.

Critique of Random Walk.   There are at least five basic criticisms of the random-walk theory. The first is that random walk really proves nothing, because of the nature of the tests. The serial correlation studies "prove" that short-term price movements are random around their long-term trends. This will *always* be true. However, the long-term trend may be from $65 per share to $150 per share in two years.

Second, the fact that some academicians are overwhelmed by random walk may not be too significant.* More important, however, such scholars qualify their theory by admitting that security prices over a long period "drift" upward. Both fundamental and technical analysts point to the fact that security prices move in long- as well as short-term trends. So the academicians may be hedging their findings.

Third, random-walk theorists have not concentrated on the securities that act in a different, yet seemingly predictable, way. Such studies might be invaluable to the investor if forecasts could be made based on securities that perform in a different way from the majority of securities. However, the ones holding the random-walk view would probably not accept as valid a study that is based on securities that are considered nontypical.

Fourth, the veracity of the "efficient" market as defined by the random-walk hypothesis is open to question. The reason is that knowledge (or information) is invariably bestowed on just a few people. And of the ones holding superior knowledge, not all hold it with the same firmness. Therefore, from such a minute portion of market participants, only a few have the courage to act (or trade) on their convictions. Conviction increases as knowledge becomes public. As a result, security-price response to new information appears to be cumulative, not random. Knowledge, then, becomes valuable even if it is a function of recognition rather than of discovery.

And finally, the random-walk model defines the next move as the difference between the current price and the next one—that is, the lagged serial correlation between first differences of closing prices. Professional speculators earn their income by betting against the applicability of the random-walk hypothesis. But to define the next move in this way places a nonoperational constraint on the professional speculators. To infer from the lack of lagged serial correlation between first differences of closing prices that speculators have a low probability of profit is incorrect. The lack of lagged correlation means that security prices are overcorrecting in both directions in the first difference. Stated in another way, it simply means that speculators are efficiently smoothing price movements over time.

Conclusion. The random-walk model is a mathematical model in which a series of numbers are independent and identically distributed. The results of such studies are widely known and impressive. However, some studies are beginning to test the validity of the other approaches to investment analysis. More than one of these studies has proved successful. Although the model is statistically sound, the generic assumptions of the model are being questioned with more rigor. At a minimum, the random-walk model is

---

*Many academicians (especially economists) fully believed that the "new economics" in the 1960s would eliminate the business cycle by "fine-tuning" the economy. But the recession of 1969–70 weakened their case.

making all market participants assess and test their assumptions and theories of the stock market.

Aggregate Economic Activity   One consistent characteristic of a highly developed economy is the existence and widespread availability of capital markets to savers and investors. A consistent characteristic of less-developed economies is the absence of these same markets.

It would appear that the operation of financial markets has something to do with economic efficiency. And it does. The operation of financial markets provides for a smooth and efficient channeling of savings from consumers to those who want to use the savings for capital accumulation. Consider, for example, the relative ease with which a large industrial corporation "floats" new securities in the U.S. capital market. Contrast this with the absence of such activity in the newly developing nations of Africa, for example. Of course, part of the developing country's lack of capital-market activity is related to its relatively low income and, therefore, its low level of savings to be channeled into capital markets. But it should be clear that the lack of an efficient institutional framework, financial markets, for channeling savings into capital accumulation helps in turn to explain the low level of the nation's income in the first instance.

But all is not necessarily wonderful when financial markets do exist. It should be clear that financial markets, because they channel savings into investment, are directly involved in the production of real national income.* If financial markets break down, if the linkage between savings and investment is broken, national income can fall.

Sectoral Economic Activity   The relative efficiencies of financial markets can affect *sectors* of the economy as well as the level of national income. The residential construction industry in the United States has since World War II been cyclically unhealthy, not because of a lack of desire for housing, but because of discontinuities in the financial markets serving the housing industry.

And so it is with all sectors in the economy. If financial markets are not efficient, they cannot channel savings into investment at the lowest possible price. If, on the other hand, they are efficient, funds will be quickly channeled into economic investment, and the level of national income and well-being will increase.

With an understanding of the economic function of financial markets, and armed with some basic definitions, we turn in the next chapter to a discussion of the prices in financial markets, rates of return.

---

*Economists use the term "real" to indicate economic activity dealing with the production of goods and services, as opposed to financial activity.

SUMMARY

This chapter has presented the concept of the market with specific applications to financial markets. The basic function of financial markets is to channel savings from those who choose not to consume to those who choose to accumulate capital goods. In this process, financial claims are created and this gives rise to the institutional arrangements for their exchange—financial markets. The sophistication and efficiency of financial markets affect the flow of savings into investment goods and, in turn, the level of the nation's economic activity.

PROBLEMS

1. Analysis of less-developed economies reveals that they do not have highly developed financial markets, and the same analysis of highly developed economies reveals the existence of sophisticated financial markets. Is there a relationship between economic well-being and activities in financial markets? If so, what is the relationship?

2. Classify each of the following as either savings or investment:

   a. A deposit in a savings account.

   b. The acquisition of a typewriter by an attorney.

   c. The purchase of textbooks by a college student.

   d. The construction of a new classroom building by your school. (*Hint:* How is the building financed?)

3. Is there a relationship between real economic activity and activity in financial markets? If national income falls (rises) what happens to the volume of trading in financial markets? Why?

4. Assume there is a "capital gap" as suggested in Table 19.1. What can be done to alleviate the difference between the need for capital funds and their sources? Would the government become involved? Why?

20

Prices in
Financial Markets

The financial markets establish the interest rates—the prices—at which present funds are exchanged for future funds.

Charles N. Henning, William Pigott, and Robert Haney Scott, Financial Markets and the Economy, *1975*

Prices of securities are the result of market forces at work. Prices of securities represent the base upon which return to the investor is calculated, the base upon which the firm's cost of capital is determined. Security prices are important to the financial manager because they represent the proceeds of the sale of financial claims upon his assets. Prices are important to the investor because they represent the capital value of his investment wealth.

In this chapter, the determinants of prices in securities markets are analyzed and the pricing process of individual securities is examined. The capital asset pricing model is used to explain the relationship between return, risk, and price. Finally, rates of return on individual forms of securities are discussed.

The reader should keep in mind that the rates of return earned in financial markets, whether in the form of interest on debt or in the form of equity returns, are prices demanded for the use of funds. As prices, they perform the same function as all prices, and in order to clearly fix the role of prices in the reader's mind, we turn first to a brief discussion of the function of prices in markets.

It has been said—facetiously, we hope—that one could turn a parrot into an economist simply by training it to say "supply" when its left leg is pulled, and "demand" when its right leg is pulled. This homely observation unfortunately reveals many people's misunderstanding of market forces. The *forces* of supply and demand are important to the operation of all markets. They cannot be passed off in a crude joke.

The introductory course in economics will not be replicated here, but enough will be reviewed so the reader may clearly understand how the forces of supply and the forces of demand interact to create *prices* in financial markets.

Supply   A supply schedule is a listing of the number of units a supplier is willing to send to market at different unit prices. Supply schedules are positively correlated; that is, as the quantity supplied increases, so does the unit price. Why? A supplier is inseparably wed to his costs. More units cost more to produce, and for this reason, as the number of units offered to the market increases, so does the cost of producing them.* Hence, when the supply schedule is plotted, the following curve results:

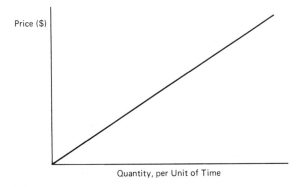

Price ($)

Quantity, per Unit of Time

---

*Microeconomic theorists tell us, in technical terms, that the firm's supply curve is the positively sloped portion of its marginal-cost curve.

Here, the vertical axis is the price axis, and the horizontal axis is the quantity axis. All supply-and-demand analysis is conducted for a given period of time—a day, a week, a month, or a year. It's a technicality, but a very important one, that the period in which the analysis takes place be specified. This will become apparent a bit later.

Demand   Now to the other side of the analysis, demand. A demand schedule is the listing of quantities demanded at alternative prices. The demand schedule reveals an inverse relationship; that is, the quantity demanded goes down as the price increases. Why? Because of the principle of diminishing marginal utility. It means that, *for a specified period of time*, the more of a product one consumes, the less enjoyment he derives from each succeeding unit. Consider consumption of ice cream. The first dish of ice cream is good. The second is good, but not as good as the first. The third is OK, but not quite as good as the second one. Somewhere during the fourth dish of ice cream *at one sitting*, one's marginal utility turns negative.* Note that all this ice cream is consumed at one sitting. Had it been spread over a longer period of time, there is a good chance that the ice cream eater would not get sick. The need for specifying the time period of the analysis is important. In analyzing financial markets, the time period will always be specified.

The inverse relationship between price and quantity demanded in the demand schedule is reflected in the negative slope of the demand curve. Repeating the preceding diagram, and adding the demand curve to it, we have:

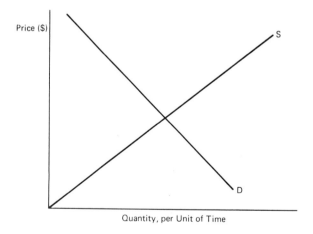

Quantity, per Unit of Time

---

*In plain English, the ice cream eater gets sick.

What is the significance of the intersection of the two curves? A mathematician would tell us that, at the point of intersection of the two curves, the quantity supplied is equal to the quantity demanded. In addition, he would indicate that the two values occupy the same spot on the graph, and therefore are equal in value. In terms of a transaction in a financial market, what does the intersection mean? It means that the desires of sellers (suppliers) are in perfect accordance with the desires of buyers (demanders) at this price. Stated just a bit differently, buyers are willing to take the quantity offered at this price and to pay the price consistent with this quantity. This is the market clearing price, so called because the quantity brought to market at this price (offered) is taken from the market (bought).

PRICES IN FINANCIAL MARKETS

Thus far, the discussion is in general terms. The market is cast in terms of no specific product or service. There is a reason for this: The principles of supply-and-demand analysis depend upon no product for their effectiveness. They are applicable across the entire range of goods and services. And this brings us back to financial markets.

The objects traded in financial markets are financial claims. Those needing to accumulate capital goods issue financial claims, which include bonds, preferred stock, and common stock.* Savers are the demanders of these securities. Those with funds saved out of current and previous income provide the funds moving into securities markets. Although savers are not normally thought of as "producers" of funds, they are. It takes higher and higher rates of return to induce the saver to increase the volume of his savings. Hence, an increasing cost function faces the saver, and this is as we have previously suggested.

On the other hand, who are the suppliers of securities? Those who desire to accumulate capital goods and need funds in order to do so. These supply the securities to the market, and this in turn results in the expression of demand for the savings being supplied to the market.

An Integration: All funds supplied to all financial markets, including debt markets and
Loanable Funds markets for preferred and common stock, can be accumulated into one category, loanable funds. All securities in these markets could be characterized as the demand for loanable funds. Integrating the two, we would have the relationships shown at the top of the next page.

---

*Financial intermediaries also issue such claims, as we have seen.

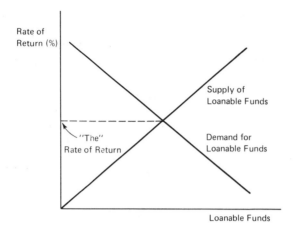

Since the term *loanable funds* includes *all* funds, the equilibrium rate of return represented in the graph is "the" rate of interest. "The" rate of interest, in this sense, is a market rate of return on securities that is an index of all market rates of return, including both debt and equity. The *structure* of rates comes about because of different risk factors inherent in each issuer of securities, and because of different maturity dates of the securities. Higher rates of return are associated with higher-risk issuers. Because of its size and lack of risk, the U.S. Treasury can borrow for a lower rate than an individual borrower can. A 30-year loan has a higher rate of return to the lender because a loan for 30 years is far more risky than one for 30 days.

Capital Asset Pricing There are three ways to view the value of an asset. One view is its selling price in the marketplace (the current market price). Another view is based on the future dollar value that accrues to the owner of the asset. A third view involves expressing the future dollar return as a percentage of the current market price. For example, an asset rises in price from $80 to $100 in one year. The annual return is $20 and the percentage return is 25 percent ([100 − 80]/80). Conversely, if an asset falls in price in one year from $125 to $100, the dollar loss is $25 and the annual percentage return is a negative 20 percent ([100 − 125]/125). This illustrates an important concept. If future dollar returns are the same, the percentage return varies inversely with the current market price. Table 20.1 illustrates this concept. Notice that the lower the current market price, the higher the percentage return, and vice versa.

The inverse relationship between current market price and return can also be illustrated by current market price and dividend yield. If the dividend yield rises, the market price falls, and vice versa.* For example, the common

---

*We assume that dividends per share remain unchanged.

TABLE 20.1 Inverse Relationship Between Current Market Price and Percentage Return for a Given Future Price

(1) CURRENT MARKET PRICE	(2) FUTURE PRICE	(3) DOLLAR RETURN (2 − 1)	(4) PERCENTAGE RETURN (2 − 1)/1
$ 50	$100	$50	100.0
60	100	40	66.7
70	100	30	42.9
80	100	20	25.0
90	100	10	11.1
100	100	0	0.0
125	100	(25)	−20.0
200	100	(100)	−50.0

stock of Amstar* sold for $30 a share in 1973 and paid a yearly dividend of $2.10. The resultant dividend yield was 7 percent (2.10/30). In 1974, the price dropped to $21 and the dividend yield rose to 10 percent (2.10/21). Note that the stock earned an excess return in 1974 and consequently was underpriced. This situation is usually followed by an increased demand for the security, which causes the price to rise and the yield to fall, and this is precisely what happened. In 1975, the price rose to $42 for a yield of 5 percent (2.10/42). Thus, we see that the market price varies inversely with the dividend yield.

Now we turn to the recognition of this process under capital asset pricing. Recall that the capital asset pricing model (equation 13 in Chapter 18) states that the expected return on a security (or asset) is equal to the risk-free rate of interest plus a risk premium. The risk premium is defined as the market risk premium (the difference between expected market return and the risk-free interest rate) weighted by the beta factor (the index of systematic risk of an asset or security). Thus, if the risk-free interest rate (the return on Treasury bills) is 5 percent, the market-risk premium is 6 percent, and the beta factor is 1.5, the required rate of return is computed as follows:

$$R(R_j) = R_f + (R_m - R_f)\beta_j$$
$$= .05 + .06(1.5)$$
$$= .14, \text{ or } 14\%$$

For financial-market decisions, the capital asset pricing model focuses on value instead of rate of return. We know from Chapter 18 that any statement about rate of return for a given series of future cash flows is actually a

*The figures above are actual prices for the 1973–75 period. A 2 for 1 stock split became effective November 1976. Thus, on an adjusted per share basis, all prior figures would be reduced one-half.

statement about value. For example, if an asset earns an excess return, this implies that its actual value is greater than its present cost. Conversely, for a low return, it follows that the asset's present cost is greater than its actual value. Therefore, we can restate the model for the security-market line in terms of value. This process is portrayed in Figure 20.1.

FIGURE 20.1

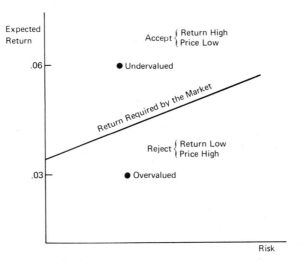

The market relationship between asset risk and return can be stated by defining the return in terms of the dollar return expressed as a percentage of the current market price and adjusting for risk. Thus, the market price is equal to the expected change in price divided by a risk-adjusted discount-rate factor. This factor is equal to the risk-free interest rate plus a risk premium. The risk premium is the market-risk premium weighted by the covariance between returns on a given asset and the market portfolio of assets. For example, assume an expected change in the price of an asset of $3, risk-free interest rate of 5 percent, market-risk premium of $1.25, and a covariance between asset return and return on market portfolio of assets of 8 percent. Then the price of the asset is figured as follows:

$$E(P_j) = \frac{3}{.05 + 1.25(.08)}$$

$$= \frac{3}{.05 + .1}$$

$$= \frac{3}{.15}$$

$$= \$20$$

In sum, the expected change in price is divided by a risk-adjusted discount-rate factor. Since we have now made full adjustment for the riskiness of the asset, the resultant price is based on the quantification of the risk–return tradeoff principle. The process is formulated in the appendix to this chapter.

The security-market line is the market-equilibrium relationship between asset risk and return. Since λ and R_f are market parameters, all assets have risk and return characteristics that fall along the security-market line in equilibrium. That is, the *required return* for an asset in equilibrium is on the SML. If an asset has an expected return that is greater than its required return, it is underpriced. The difference in returns will result in market adjustment. If some investors expect the asset's return to be greater than the required return for the risk level involved, they will purchase the asset. As purchases are made, the price of the asset increases until its return is equal to the required return. At this point, the asset has reached its market equilibrium. The process is shown in Figure 20.1. Asset A is above the SML and is therefore underpriced until its actual return equals required return as indicated by the SML for the asset's level of risk. When the return on the asset is in equilibrium, its risk–return will lie on the SML, as indicated by the arrow in Figure 20.2.

FIGURE 20.2 The Security-Market Line.

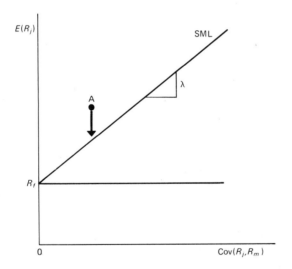

PRICES OF INDIVIDUAL SECURITIES

Bonds Bonds represent the long-term debt of the firm. By long-term we generally mean in excess of one year, and usually in excess of five years. Bonds are really IOUs of the corporation. A corporate bond is quite similar to the note that is signed when money is borrowed from the bank. The basic difference is that the corporate bond can usually be sold many times over by one financial investor to another before the borrower—the corporation—buys the bond back at maturity—redeems it.

Coupon Rate. Bonds are usually—but not always—issued in denominations of $1,000 and have a stipulated interest rate that the corporation agrees to pay the lender of the funds. This rate is called the "coupon" rate. The term comes from the method of payment of interest. For example, a 7 percent bond will pay $70 interest per year (.07 × $1,000). Since the bond may (and probably will) change hands many times between the time the corporation issues it and the time it is redeemed, the actual payment of the interest due becomes a problem. This problem is nearly solved by issuing bonds with coupons attached.

Interest on corporate bonds is usually paid semiannually—that is, every six months. Thus, the 7 percent bond will make two $35 payments each year through the use of sequentially numbered coupons. Every six months, the bondholder need only clip the current coupon and send it to the issuing corporation for payment of the $35 interest due.* With this system, the issuing corporation need not keep track of the owner of the bond.

Pricing a Bond. Clearly, a bond paying $35 semiannually is a 7 percent bond. If "the" market rate of interest were 7 percent currently—in other words, if other bonds in the same risk class were paying 7 percent—then the coupon rate would coincide with the market rate.

When the market rate of interest changes, the coupon rate on an already-issued bond cannot be changed. To price an already-issued bond when the market rate of interest changes, one need only convert the dollar interest flows and the maturity value of the bond to a present value, using the current rate of interest as the discount rate.

Assume that the market rate of interest rises from 7 percent to 10 percent. What is the value of the bond discussed above, which makes 20 periodic interest payments (semiannually for the ten years till maturity) and will have a maturity value of $1,000?

The problem involves finding the present value of an annuity of $35 for 20 periods, plus the present value of a payment of $1,000 20 periods from now, using in both cases 5 percent as the discount rate, since there are 20 periods at 5 percent (2 periods per year × 10 years). Using the time-line concept, the problem appears:

---

*This practice gave rise to an interesting slang term for a rich person, a "coupon clipper."

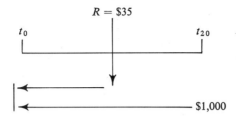

Solving first for the present value of interest payments, we have:

$$PVA = R(IF)$$
$$= \$35(12.462)$$
$$= \$436.17$$

where:

$35 = periodic interest payments

12.462 = interest factor for the present value of an annuity for 20 periods at 5%

Solving now for the present value of the terminal value of the bond, we find:

$$PV = FV(IF)$$
$$= \$1,000(.377)$$
$$= \$377$$

where:

$1,000 = terminal value of the bond

.377 = interest factor for the present value of a single payment for 20 periods at 5%

Adding the two present values together:

$436.17	Present value of the interest payments
377.00	Present value of the bond at maturity
$813.17	Present value of the bond at 10% (5% per period)

Thus, by using present-value techniques, the price of a bond may be found under varying interest rates.

Bondholders usually have prior claim to the income of the corporation, and for that reason, bonds are the senior capital source for the corporation.

Preferred Stock   As we have said, preferred stock is a hybrid. It has characteristics of both bonds and stock. Its major debt characteristic is the contractual nature of its dividends: The corporation usually contracts to pay specific dollar dividends periodically. These payments are very similar to interest payments on bonds. There is a major difference, however. Usually, if the corporation does not have the earnings to pay preferred dividends, they can be passed by with relatively little danger to the corporation. Such is not the case with periodic interest payments. If a corporation defaults on its interest payments, it is in some danger, for it has not met a legal obligation. Such is not the case with preferred stock.

Pricing of Preferred Stock.   The price of preferred stock is specified in dollars per share. The dollar price of a share of preferred stock is a function of the rate of return demanded by the preferred-stock investor.

The rate of return on preferred is specified as a percentage of the par value, which is usually $100 a share. If it is 8 percent preferred, the annual dollar dividend will be $8. Thus:

$$.08(\$100) = \$8$$

Let's assume that the rate of return on preferred stock of corporations in a similar risk class falls to 6 percent. What happens to the *price* of the preferred stock in question? The *dollar amount* of the dividend does not change. So the equation for finding the market value is:

$$\$8 = .06\,P_0$$

Transposing, and solving for x, the expression becomes:

$$P_0 = \frac{\$8}{.06}$$
$$= \$133.33$$

That is, the market value of a share of preferred went from $100 to $133.33 when the demanded return went from 8 percent to 6 percent. Paying $133.33 a share will yield a 6 percent return. That is:

$$.06(\$133.33) = \$8$$

The simple rule in determining preferred-stock price is to divide the market rate of return into the promised dollar dividend.

Because there is more risk attached to preferred stock, the return on preferred is usually higher than the return on debt. Additionally, preferred shareholders do not usually get to vote for the corporation's board of directors. This privilege is reserved for the common stockholders.

Common Stock   Common stock is the base upon which the corporation is built. A corporation may do without bonds and preferred stock, but it cannot do without common stock. Common stock is the base built by the residual owners of the corporation.

We know that residual profits belong to the common shareholders, and if the corporation chooses to retain them rather than distribute them as dividends, these funds then create a larger base for future profits.

Pricing of Common Stock.   As in the case of bonds and preferred stock, the price of common stock is a function of return. In Chapter 12, it was shown that *return on (cost of)* common stock is specified as:

$$k_j = \frac{D_1}{P_0} + g$$

where:

k_j = demanded rate of return
D_1 = dividend per share at the end of the current period
P_0 = current market price
g = growth rate of earnings

It can be seen in this expression that return is related to price, for return is on the left side of the equation, and price is on the right side.

Solving the expression above for price, P_0, reveals:

$$P_0 = \frac{D_1}{k_j - g}$$

In other words, the current price of a share of common stock is the capitalized value of the cash dividend into perpetuity.

Consider a common stock that has the following characteristics:

$$D_1 = \$2.50$$
$$k_j = .10$$
$$g = .05$$

That is, the coming dividend will be $2.50 a share, the common shareholder demands a 10 percent return on his investment, and the corporation's earnings are growing at 5 percent per year. What is the value of its stock? Substituting:

$$P_0 = \frac{\$2.50}{.10 - .05}$$
$$= \frac{2.50}{.05}$$
$$= \$50 \text{ per share}$$

As a check, we will substitute all values into the rate-of-return equation:

$$k_j = \frac{D_1}{P_0} + g$$

$$.10 = \frac{2.50}{\$50} + .05$$

$$.10 = .05 + .05$$

$$.10 = .10$$

The figure checks.

These relationships conclusively show that the price of common stock is related to its rate of return.

Summary All these claims—bonds, preferred stock, and common stock—are traded in financial markets. These claims are long-term in nature, and because this is true, they form the base of trading in the *capital market*. We shall define the capital market as trading in financial claims that have a maturity of greater than one year. The market for claims with maturities of one year or less are traded in the *money market*, which is defined as the market in short-term claims. We shall have far more to say about each of these in successive chapters where we discuss in some detail the operations of these markets.

RATES OF RETURN ON INDIVIDUAL SECURITIES

In this section, rates of return on specific financial instruments, including preferred stock, common stock, and debt, will be discussed. Because debt has a definite and certain maturity, there are several considerations attached to debt not found with equity. Among these are the term structure of interest rates and yield-curve analysis, each of which will be treated along with debt.

Dividends: The Return on Preferred Stock As we have said, preferred stock is a hybrid, with characteristics of both debt and equity. It is like debt in that a specific dollar return is promised, but the promise is made conditional upon the existence of earnings. The first characteristic, specific dollar return, recalls debt. The second, that the return is payable only if available, recalls equity. Hence the hybrid nature of preferred stock.

But what does the investor buy when he purchases preferred stock? He buys a specific dollar income forever.* The rate-of-return calculation is relatively simple. Since the investor purchases only the cash income stream into perpetuity, all that is needed is to relate that cash income to its purchase

*We ignore here the possibility of lack of earnings to pay the dividend.

price.* If the promised income stream is $6 per year and the preferred stock sells at par ($100), investors are satisfied with a 6 percent return on their investment, since DPS/PPS = $6/$100 = .06 or 6 percent. However, if the preferred stock later drops in price to $75, the return demanded by investors is calculated as follows:

$$k_p = DPS/PPS$$
$$= \$6/\$75$$
$$= .08 \text{ or } 8\%$$

Dividends and Growth: The Return on Common Stock

Common-stock owners are the owners of the corporation. They claim what is left of income after all expenses, including taxes, are paid. This residual income may be positive or negative. It is the greater risk that usually creates a larger rate of return to the common shareholder. As indicated previously, return is proportional to investment for a given level of risk.

Under common law, the common shareholder is not entitled to dividends. This is a deviation from the principle of dividends that is associated with preferred stock. No specific dollar dividend is promised or implied, whether the corporation has earnings or not. You are justified in asking just exactly what it is that the common shareholder is entitled to when he purchases common stock. The answer is earnings. The common shareholder accrues rights to *positive earnings*, regardless of whether they are paid out as dividends. A corporation's directors are not required to pay out earnings. Instead, they may retain the earnings to purchase additional assets for the purpose of earning additional income streams in the future.

The common shareholder pays for the privilege of receiving earnings either in the form of cash dividends or in the form of additional investment in the corporation that will increase the market value of the common stock. Conceptually, the increase in the market value of the common stock, if earnings are retained, should be equal to the value of cash dividends if they were paid.

The common shareholder conceptually purchases a cash income stream into perpetuity. This consists of the corporation's cash dividend, as well as the chance of increased dividends in the future. The return on the former is known as the dividend yield. The latter value is represented by the growth rate of the corporation, usually specified in growth of earnings.† Therefore, the capitalized value of the cash dividend (dividend yield) plus the growth rate of the corporation (earnings growth), represents the return to

---

*Keep in mind that the process of converting an income stream into a present-day asset value is called "capitalizing the income."

†One method of calculating earnings growth is to divide current earnings per share by a prior year's earnings per share. The resultant value is an interest factor (IF) that can be located in the Future Value of $1 Table. Find the IF in the appropriate year row. Then locate the interest percentage at the top of the column. This is used as the annual growth rate of the firm (that is, the growth rate of earnings compounded on an annual basis).

the shareholder. Symbolically:

$$k_j = \frac{D_1}{P_0} + g$$

where:

k_j = required return on common stock

D_1 = dividend per share at the end of the current period

P_0 = current market price per share

g = growth rate of the corporation

This formulation accounts for the flow of cash to the common shareholder as well as the retained earnings of the firm. Retained earnings are accounted for to the extent that growth is related to retained earnings.

In Chapter 12, the same formulation as above was presented to represent the cost of common capital to the firm. The return to the common shareholder is the cost of common capital to the firm. The following example uses figures from the cost-of-capital calculation in Chapter 12.

Assume that an investor is considering the purchase of a share of stock whose price is $50, that will pay a $2.50 cash dividend, and whose earnings grow at a compound annual rate of 5 percent. What is the rate of return? Substituting into the equation above:

$$k_j = \frac{\$2.50}{\$50.00} + .05$$
$$= .05 + .05$$
$$= .10$$

This calculation of return to the shareholder accounts for both dividend return and return on retained earnings.

Preferred and common stock have at least one characteristic in common: Their returns, be they dividends and/or earnings, are perpetual. That is, we conceive of returns to both preferred and common stock as being everlasting.

Interest: The Return on Debt When and if one borrows money at the bank, he promises to return the principal (the original amount borrowed) as well as an additional amount, the interest. The interest is computed as a percentage of the principal.* The same is true for the issuer of a bond. Unlike the return on stock, the payment for the use of the principal, as well as the return of the principal, is always scheduled for a specific date. This is a major differentiating characteristic.

---

*Installment loans complicate the calculation, but interest is still calculated as a percentage of the amount borrowed.

A borrower (bond issuer) also promises to pay a specific percentage of the principal as interest (the "coupon" rate). The coupon rate is the going rate at the time the loan is made, or the bond is issued. Regardless of what happens in financial markets, the borrower of the principal is obligated to pay the *dollar* amount of the interest. For example, if the coupon rate is 6 percent, and $1,000 is borrowed, the borrower will pay $60 a year in interest until the loan matures.

Now, what happens if the interest rate on similar obligations rises to 12 percent? The market has a way of making the 6 percent bonds salable in the current 12 percent market. The market asks this question: How much will be paid for a bond yielding $60 a year to make it yield 12 percent? If the bond paid interest forever—that is, if it were a perpetuity—the question could be posed algebraically, in the following way:

$$.12 \, PV = \$60$$

$$PV = \frac{\$60}{.12}$$

$$PV = \$500$$

The calculation above assumes the bond to be a perpetuity—that is, of a perpetual maturity or no maturity at all, which is not common, and thus has a 12 percent return. Assume the bond has a ten-year maturity. What is its value with interest rates at 6 percent? As before, it reduces to a present-value problem. The bond pays $30 every six months, and has 20 (2 per year $\times$ 10 years) interest periods to run. Interest factors for 3 percent, *not 6 percent*, are used, since there are two compounding periods in each year.

Present Value of Bond at 6 Percent per Year

PV of interest payments:	
PVA = R(IF)	
= $30(14.877)	
=	$446.31
PV of terminal value of bond ($1,000):	
PV = FV(IF)	
= $1,000(.554)	
=	$554.00
Total PV	$1,000.31

The bond is currently priced at its par value. (The .31 difference is due to rounding of interest factors.) This is a truism: When the market value coincides with the coupon rate, the bond price is its par value.

But what happens to the value of the bond when the market rate rises to 12 percent per year? The price will be adjusted downward to the point where the present value of $30 periodic payments plus the present value of the terminal value of the bond will represent a 12 percent return. This time 6 percent per period is used because there are 20 6-month periods remaining in the life of the bond. The calculation is the same except for the use of 6 percent interest factors:

Present Value of Bond at 12 Percent per Year

PV of interest payments:
$$PVA = R(IF)$$
$$= \$30(11.470)$$
$$= \qquad \$344.10$$
PV of terminal value ($1,000):
$$PV = FV(IF)$$
$$= \$1,000(.312)$$
$$= \qquad \$312.00$$

Total PV $656.10

The market value of the bond at 12 percent per year is $656.10. If one were to purchase the bond for $656.10, he would receive a 12 percent compound return on his investment.

Were the market rate of interest to fall below the coupon rate, the market value of the bond would rise above its par value. There is an inverse relationship between changes in market rates of interest and changes in market values of bonds. This is illustrated in Figure 20.3.

FIGURE 20.3 The Relationship Between Market Interest Rates and Market Values of Bonds.

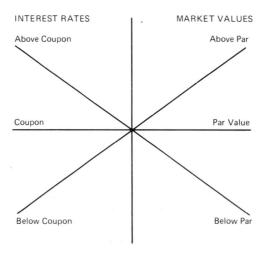

The basic principle is clear: A change in "the" interest rate changes capital values of existing debt securities. As interest rates rise, the value of existing financial assets drops, as in the example above. The opposite is also true: A fall in interest rates increases the value of all existing securities.

It should be easier now to see why a period of rising prices—inflation—which includes all interest rates, is feared and dreaded by those who own financial claims. Rising interest rates tend to erode existing capital values, and falling interest rates tend to enhance market values of existing securities.

THE TERM STRUCTURE OF INTEREST RATES

Debt is characterized by maturity dates, and in addition to the supply and demand for funds, one of the determinants of interest rates is the length of the loan period.

There are basically two maturity segments in debt markets. All maturities of a year or less are characterized as being part of the money market. In fact, that is how the money market is defined: It is the market for short-term debt claims. Among the instruments traded in the money market are notes, bills, and other short-term IOUs. Transactors in the money market use it to adjust their liquidity positions. If they have excess liquidity, they sell (lend) it for short periods of time to those who come to the money market to buy (borrow) liquidity. In the next chapter, borrowers, lenders, and other transactors in the money market are discussed.

The remaining maturities in debt markets, those greater than one year, are characterized as the capital market. The capital market is the locus of borrowing to get funds for fixed assets. These funds *will not* be used to bridge temporary gaps of funds inflows and outflows, but instead *will* be used to purchase long-term assets, which in turn will produce revenues for the repayment of the debt.

This division of the debt market into two distinct subdivisions may be a bit misleading, in that it may lead the reader to believe there are only two levels of rates, short- and long-term. Such is not the case. Interest rates in debt markets are actually a continuum, a spectrum of rates, which run from low to high, short- to long-term.

Interest rates are primarily the result of the forces of supply and demand. Funds are supplied (and demanded) within the term structure of rates; funds are demanded, for example, for short periods and also for long periods. The interest rate in each of these maturity sectors is then dependent upon the quantity of funds supplied in each of the maturity sectors. The realization that interest rates are dependent upon supply and demand forces in each maturity sector leads to an understanding of the *term structure of interest rates*. This expression refers to the alternative levels of interest rates that are associated with alternative debt maturities. A comprehensive understanding of the term structure of interest rates is greatly aided by the use of yield-curve analysis.

Yield-Curve Analysis   The yield curve is an extremely important tool for the student of debt markets. The yield curve relates yields on debt securities to their maturities. It is extremely important to remember that a yield curve does its job as of a certain moment in time. It is, in effect, a snapshot *right now* of all yields and their maturities. This point will continue to be emphasized in the following discussion.

Yield curves are constructed for debt issues of similar risk. We could, for example, construct a yield curve for U.S. government securities, and this would be proper, for if we have truly taken bonds of similar risk—and U.S. governments fit this description—the difference in yields (interest rates) shown on the yield curve is most probably due to differences in maturities, and that is what is attempted—to trace the relationship between yield (only) and maturity.

The important elements of the construction of the yield curve are (1) yield quotations all taken as of the same day, and (2) yield quotations all for debt of equal risk.

The Upward-Sloping Yield Curve.   The upward-sloping yield curve is frequently referred to as the "normal" yield curve, because it is the one most frequently found in debt markets. It appears as the positively-sloped curve in Figure 20.4.

FIGURE 20.4 Upward-Sloping Yield Curve.

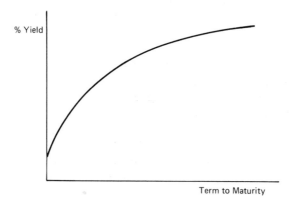

If indeed risk is equalized, the upward-sweeping yield curve portrays increasing interest rates as a function of time, and the higher rates are based upon the increased risk associated with longer maturity. The upward-sloping yield curve is intuitively appealing, because it is normal to think of long-term rates being higher than short-term rates.

Is there another explanation for the positive slope of the curve? One could argue that the forces of supply and demand create different yields in different maturity sectors. In the case of the upward-sweeping yield curve, the supply of short-term funds is greater than the demand, and therefore the yield is relatively low. The forces of supply are not as great in the longer maturities, and therefore yields are higher.

Remember that the yield curve exists at a certain date, and that it is a "photograph" of the rates existing on that date for securities of different maturities.

The upward-sweeping yield curve is usually associated with periods of economic prosperity.

The Downward-Sloping Yield Curve. This yield curve tells us that yields right now on short-term securities are higher than yields right now on long-term securities. This yield appears as the downward-sloping curve in Figure 20.5.

FIGURE 20.5 Downward-Sloping Yield Curve.

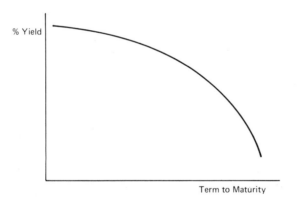

The downward-sloping yield curve is not intuitively appealing. It is more comforting to associate long-term rates with long maturities, but this is not the relationship the downward-sloping yield curve portrays. The downward-sloping yield curve suggests that not only is there less risk associated with long-term funds, there *may* be more risk associated with short-term funds. We must resort to supply-and-demand analysis to explain a more apparent than real controversy.

If, for any one of many reasons, the supply of *short-term* funds in markets is deficient relative to the demand for them, their price (rate) tends to rise. As the rate on short-term funds rises, funds suppliers shift to this segment of the market to take advantage of the rising rates. This activity halts the rise in short-term yields and the decline in long-term yields.

But recall that the yield curve is a snapshot of the term structure of interest rates at an instant of time. The relationship between maturity-sector yields portrayed in the snapshot above reveals short rates higher than long.

The downward-sloping yield curve is associated with uncertainty and reduced economic activity. For example, a recent period in which the negatively sloped yield curve prevailed was during the fall of 1974, a period of the most seriously depressed economic activity since the Great Depression of the 1930s.

Equality of Short and Long Rates: The Flat Yield Curve. There have been instances in the history of money and capital markets when short and long rates were the same. Such a condition results in the flat yield curve, as portrayed in Figure 20.6.

FIGURE 20.6 Flat Yield Curve.

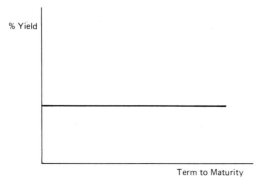

What market conditions result in the flat yield curve? Again, relying upon supply-and-demand analysis, the forces of supply and demand for funds in each maturity sector are balanced in such a way as to create equality of rates in all maturity sectors. Although they are not a common occurrence, we do find flat yield curves occasionally in financial markets.

The Yield Curve as a Tool. The yield curve is an extremely important tool of market analysis. Because of its "snapshot" nature, it clearly and accurately portrays current conditions in financial markets. Yield curves are also important because they are a distillation now of the market transactors' beliefs about rates in the future.

For example, the upward-sweeping yield curve reveals that, on net balance, "the market"—that is, all transactors in money and capital markets—feels that interest rates in the future will rise.

How is this conclusion drawn from the upward-sweeping yield curve? Simply: If securities *right now* are being traded at prices that create higher yields for longer-term securities, then, *at present*, investors on net balance must feel that rates in the future are going to rise. Were this not the case, security prices would not reflect a deep discount (higher yield). By supplying and/or demanding securities in the various maturity sectors, market transactors are expressing their collective views of *future* patterns of rates in money and capital markets.

Remember that the slope of the yield curve can change dramatically in a short period of time. "The market" can dramatically change its collective opinion of the future level of interest rates, and trade securities in such a way as to change the slope of the yield curve *right now*. Any number of factors can affect investor judgment about the future. But if a development affects investor *perceptions* of the future, this changed perception of the future will be acted upon currently by the investor in order to reflect his current perceptions of the future. For example, if investor perception of economic conditions for five years from now is shaken, this risk will be reflected in the yield curve by investors selling bonds of five-year maturities. This selloff will depress prices, and yields will rise. The yield curve, if it did not before, will now acquire a dramatic positive slope. Keep in mind that this change in degree of slope came about as a result of investors *acting now* upon their currently held perceptions of the *future*.

We can conclude our discussion of yield curves, therefore, by suggesting that they are a physical manifestation of current investor perceptions of the future.

SUMMARY

In this chapter, a close look has been taken at the prices paid for the use of funds in financial markets. The return on debt is interest. The return on preferred stock, since it represents the purchase of an income stream into perpetuity, is the cash dividend. The return on common stock is cash dividends and the expectation of growth in the future. Finally, the yield curve, a photo snapshot of the pattern of investor expectations of interest rates, is an extremely valuable financial-market tool.

APPENDIX TO CHAPTER 20: ASSET PRICING UNDER CAPM

A short proof of capital asset pricing follows under the capital asset pricing model. First, the equation for the security market line is stated from Chapter 18:

$$R(R_j) = R_f + \lambda(\text{Cov } R_j, R_m) \tag{12}$$

where:

$$\lambda = \left[\frac{E(R_m) - R_f}{\text{Var } R_m} \right]$$

Recall from Chapter 3 how present value (V_0) and future value (V_1) are related:

$$V_{j1} = V_{j0}(1 + R_j)$$

or

$$R_j = \frac{V_{j1} - V_{j0}}{V_{j0}} \tag{13}$$

Now substitute this into equation (12), and a formulation in terms of *value* is obtained:

$$V_{j0} = \frac{E(V_{j1}) - \lambda \text{ Cov}(V_{j1}, V_{m1})}{(1 + R_f)} \tag{14}$$

where:

$$\lambda = \frac{E(V_{m1}) - (1 + R_f)V_{m0}}{\text{Var } V_{m1}}$$

Alternatively, equation (12) can be restated by defining

$$R_j \equiv \tilde{P}_j / P_j$$

where:

P_j = the present price of asset j
$\tilde{P}_j$ (a random variable) = the change in price of asset j

Thus, the following equation for value or price is derived:

$$P_j = \frac{E(\tilde{P}_j)}{R_f + \lambda \text{ Cov}(R_j, R_m)} \tag{15}$$

where:

P_j = the present market price of asset
$\tilde{P}_j$ = the expected change in price of asset
R_f = the risk-free interest rate
λ = the market-risk premium
$\text{Cov}(R_j, R_m) = \sum (\text{Var } R_j)(\text{Var } R_m)/\text{Var } R_m$

Equation (15) is known as a risk-adjusted discount-rate formula. The primary difference between equations (14) and (15) is that the former expresses the total expected price in year 1 ($E[V_1]$) and discounts it at $(1 + R)$, whereas the latter discounts $E(\tilde{P})$ at R. For example, $\$63/1.05 = \$60$ or $\$3/.05 = \$60$. Both formulations are adjusted, of course, for risk.

PROBLEMS

1. You have a chance to buy one of two bonds. Both have five years till maturity, and both pay interest semiannually. Both are $1,000 par value. The other terms of the bonds are described below:

Bond A:
  Coupon 8%
  Price $1,085.20

Bond B:
  Coupon 12%
  Price $1,255.80

Which is the better buy? Why? (*Hint:* By trial and error, determine the discount rate that will result in each of the prices.)

2. If the preferred stock of the Acme Corporation is 9% and currently sells for $90, what rate of return is the investing public demanding on its investment?

3. Below are financial data of The Hermann Egeler Corporation:

EARNINGS

1972	$2.12
1973	2.24
1974	2.38
1975	2.52
1976	2.68
1977	2.84

The expected dividend for 1978 is $3 per share. The discount rate is ten percent. (*Caution:* The earnings for 1972 were announced at the *end* of the year. You are therefore dealing with only five years' growth.)

  a. What is the required return demanded by investors in Egeler common stock?
  b. At what price per share should the stock sell?

4. If "the" interest rate on corporate bonds were to double, what would happen to the market value of bonds already held in portfolios? Why?

5. From a recent issue of the *Wall Street Journal*, secure the listing of yields on U.S. government securities. From this listing, draw a yield curve. What is its slope? Why?

For Problem 6, assume that $E(R_m) = .10$, $E(R_j) = .20$, $R_f = .05$, Var $R_m = .04$, and Cov $(R_j, R_m) = .02$.

6. If the change in price in security j in the next period is expected to be an increase of $5:

    a. Find the slope of the security-market line.

    b. What is the present price of security j?

    c. What is the return required by investors on security j?

    d. Is the security over- or underpriced?

    e. Draw a graph with expected return on the vertical axis and Cov (R_j, R_m) on the horizontal axis. Plot the market portfolio at point M and security j at point B.

21

Financial Markets: Money Markets (Short-Term Obligations)

The money market has no specific place of operation; it consists simply of the total activity of all those who lend and borrow short-term funds.

Charles N. Henning, William Pigott, and Robert Haney Scott, Financial Markets and the Economy, 1975

The topic of the previous chapter, prices in financial markets, is an important one. The determination of the price of a security is as important to the issuer of the security, the financial manager, as it is to the purchaser, the investor. The perspective of the financial manager on "parking" his excess cash balances in short-term obligations is discussed in Chapter 8, "The Management of Cash." Prices are the stitches that sew issuer to investor.

The present chapter discusses the part of financial markets dealing with short-term maturities, the *money market.* Treatment of the money market permits the introduction of financial markets according to maturity of the financial claim being traded.

THE NEED FOR THE MONEY MARKET

Everyone has experienced the need for cash. The need to pay bills and other obligations of everyday life confronts us all. Similarly, we are confronted with the periodicity of income flows. Most working people receive their wages in cash, either biweekly or monthly. How many times have we been confronted with the planned or unplanned need for cash just prior to payday? The opportunity to buy something at a reduced price or the emergency requiring cash always seems to present itself when there is no convenient payday to fill the need.

The typical solution to this problem is borrowing to bridge the time gap between outgo and income. The loan might be an informal one from a friend or relative ("five till payday"), or it might be a formal short-term loan from the commercial banker ("sign on the dotted line"). In either case, the short-term loan from one who is not currently using the funds (the friend, relative, or banker) to one who needs the funds (you) erases the problem.

MONEY-MARKET TRANSACTORS

The Money Market Defined As homely as that simple example is, it is a manifestation of the typical money-market transaction. We formally define the *money market* as the market for short-term obligations, usually a year or less, existing throughout the nation, with its focal point in New York because the nation's largest banks are there. One could rather obviously define the money market as the market for money balances. Although this is an accurate definition of this market, it misses the essence of the typical money-market transaction.

Short-term obligations, which will be discussed and described in some detail in this chapter, are the expressions of demand for the temporary use of money balances.

Why Short-Term Funds Are Demanded We have suggested that those who demand short-term funds are those who experience outgo before planned income. Are these necessarily profligate businessmen who cannot manage their funds efficiently? Such is usually not the case. In fact, just the opposite is usually true. That is, not only are money-market demanders usually careful people, they are usually shrewd people, too.

Demanders of funds in money markets are those whose lines of business generally require payment for production inputs before the product can be sold. When one thinks about it, this tends to be the normal case in the business world. Doesn't the shoe manufacturer have to pay for leather, line, and labor before he sells his shoes and receives cash? Obviously, yes.

A typical borrower of funds in the money market is the sales finance company. These are large, well-known corporations (CIT, GMAC) whose primary function is to lend money to people to purchase consumer goods. Consider their basic problem: They need money now to lend to people who will pay it back later. Customers are constantly repaying loans on monthly installments. Normally, the inflows from loans will balance the outflow of funds made to lenders.* But what about a period in which the demand for consumer loans from the finance company increases—conditions, say, just prior to the Christmas season? The finance company knows that installment inflows, loan repayments, right after Christmas will start flowing back to the finance company.

It makes sense for the finance company to borrow money to bridge the gap over Christmas. Such borrowing would be done in the money market for the *required short period of time*.

Not all funds demanders are sales finance companies. Manufacturers needing funds to meet payrolls, commercial banks needing short-term funds to balance their reserve positions—these and many more constitute the demanders of funds in the money market.

Before moving over to the supply side, let us emphasize the two major characteristics of demanders of funds in money markets. They are in temporary need of funds to meet temporary obligations, and they have the size, the credit rating, and the overall ability to issue short-term securities in this important financial market in order to secure the funds they need.

Why Short-Term Funds Are Supplied

Suppliers of funds are those people and firms who find themselves in the enviable position of possessing money balances, albeit for a short period. Cash is sterile. It earns no income. It is rational that the financial manager or other person responsible for the funds desires to "put the funds to work" until they are needed for operations.

Take, for example, a college or university. Assume that the school has an enrollment of 8,000 and that tuition and fees are $500 per student per term. At the beginning of each term, the school takes in $4 million ($500 × 8,000), a healthy sum.

The financial manager of the school doesn't have to pay all the school's bills right now. For example, the faculty is probably paid monthly, and some portion of the revenue will be earmarked for paying faculty salaries a month from now, two months from now, three months from now, and four months

---

*This is called "keeping one's funds employed."

from now. For purposes of simplification, assume that faculty salaries are the only expense of the institution. A graph of our income–outflow relationship would appear as follows:

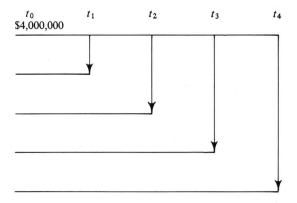

The time line assumes that there are four months (periods) in the school term. It also assumes (unrealistically, we know) that faculty salaries are the institution's only expense, so the monthly outflow from the $4 million will be $1 million ($4 million divided by four months).

Put upon this basis, perhaps it is clear that if the opportunity is available, the financial manager can "put to work" these funds for these periods of time:

$4 million for 1 month

$3 million for 1 month

$2 million for 1 month

$1 million for 1 month

Suppose the current interest rate is 6 percent, and the financial manager can find opportunities to place these funds at simple interest. Calculate the amount of income *in addition to income from tuition and fees* that will be earned if the funds are put to work:

$$
\begin{array}{ll}
1/12 \times .06 \times \$4 \text{ million} = \$20,000 \\
1/12 \times .06 \times \$3 \text{ million} = \$15,000 \\
1/12 \times .06 \times \$2 \text{ million} = \$10,000 \\
1/12 \times .06 \times \$1 \text{ million} = \$\ 5,000 \\
\hline
\qquad\quad \text{Total} \qquad\qquad\ \ \$50,000
\end{array}
$$

These funds, generated in addition to tuition and fees, provide income to the institution. It is frequently said that if a financial manager can earn an amount equal to his own salary in the money market, he is doing a good job. The financial manager in the example above probably is.

There are many such organizations in the economy, most of them business firms that have frequent periods of temporary surplus cash. These surplus funds, as above, can be put to work in the money market.

The job of balancing off surplus liquidity and deficit liquidity would be an efficient process if institutional relationships existed that permitted short-term lenders to purchase short-term claims quickly and efficiently while at the same time providing short-term borrowers the same speed and efficiency. There is such an institution, and it is the money market.

MONEY-MARKET INSTRUMENTS

By the term *money-market instruments*, we mean the various debt claims that can be used to soak up liquidity in the economy. These instruments range from the informal handshake between friends when money is lent for a short term on a personal basis, to the very formal printed instrument representing short-term debt of the U.S. Treasury, the Treasury bill.

Because, as we have said, any obligation that represents short-term debt is subject to being a money-market instrument, the range of instruments is wide indeed. We shall confine our discussion to six of the major money-market instruments: Treasury bills, negotiable certificates of deposit, commercial paper, federal funds, banker's acceptances, and Eurodollars.

The dollar volume outstanding of these instruments for the first six months of 1976 is given in Table 21.1. Clearly, the most prevalent instrument

TABLE 21.1 Dollar Volume of Selected Money-Market Instruments, First 6 Months of 1978 ($ billion)

MONTH	TREASURY BILLS	NEGOTIABLE CERT. DEP.[a,b]	COMMERCIAL PAPER	FEDERAL FUNDS[a,b]	BANK ACCEPTANCES
January	161.2	76.2	65.5	20.6	25.2
February	161.8	77.1	65.5	19.0	25.4
March	165.7	82.2	67.4	20.6	26.2
April	159.6	81.9	70.2	18.6	26.3
May	159.4	86.0	71.2	24.9	26.7
June	159.8	87.5	71.6	20.3	27.1

[a]Large banks according to Federal Reserve definition.
[b]Last Wednesday of month.

Source: Federal Reserve Bulletin.

is the Treasury bill. In June 1976, almost $161 billion worth were outstanding. Second in order of importance is the negotiable certificate of deposit. This is a relatively new instrument, which has become very important in recent years. Third in importance is commercial paper. As can be seen in the table, commercial paper is not growing as a money-market instrument. Fourth in importance is federal funds. This is an old money-market instrument that has enjoyed a resurgence of popularity in recent years. Banker's acceptances constitute an age-old money-market instrument, which remains a staple of the market.

Our discussions of these instruments will center on the origins of each instrument, its primary use, and its use in the money market. We start with the largest and most important, the Treasury bill.

Treasury Bills Treasury bills are short-term obligations, usually three-month, of the U.S. government. They are issued each week to assist the Treasury Department to bridge the gap between tax receipts and needed expenditures of the government. Treasury bills are important sources of funds for the Treasury. They are increasing in volume as sources of funds. In December 1968, there were $75 billion in bills outstanding. By March 1977, this figure had grown to $164.3 billion.*

It may be clear that the Treasury is a major demander of funds in the market, for the volume of Treasury bills in existence is physical testimony to the Treasury's demand for money balances. Once Treasury bills are issued, they are subject to trade in the secondary market—that is, the "used securities" market. The existence of secondary trading in Treasury bills permits liquidity adjustments to be made that otherwise would not be possible.

An example: Assume that an original purchaser of a Treasury bill finds he now needs cash for some reason. He can sell the bill for cash. Who would buy the bill? Obviously, someone with excess liquidity. Note that buyer and seller are both in better positions because of the existence of the money market and because of the existence of the Treasury bill as a money-market instrument.

Calculating Return on Treasury Bills. Assume that one wanted to purchase a Treasury bill off the shelf of a dealer. How would the price be determined? Price and yield are interrelated.

Let us say that the investment is to be made for 18 days, at which time the investor needs his cash back. Further assume that the price of a $1,000-par-value Treasury bill is quoted at $997, remembering that Treasury bills are sold on a discount basis.

Federal Reserve Bulletin.

The general form of determining the annual equivalent yield on a discounted Treasury is:

$$r = \frac{D}{CO} \times \frac{360}{M}$$

where:

r = annual equivalent rate of return; i.e., yield

D = dollar discount from par value

CO = cash outlay for the Treasury bill

M = days to maturity

Substituting the values into the formulation:

$$r = \frac{\$3}{\$997} \times \frac{360}{18}$$
$$= .0030 \times 20$$
$$= .06$$

An investment in this bill would yield a return equivalent to 6 percent per year. It is the equivalent of getting a discount of 3/10 of 1 percent twenty times per year, which in turn is equivalent to an annual return of 6 percent.

Commercial banks are the primary purchasers and holders of Treasury bills. The bill, because of its wide and deep market, permits commercial banks to make rapid and efficient changes in their liquidity positions. It also permits the bank to earn income on funds that might otherwise lie fallow.

Use of Treasury bills for money-market investments is not limited to commercial banks, however. Anyone with short-term liquidity to invest can use Treasury bills as an investment medium. For example, the financial manager to whom we alluded previously may use Treasury bills for the temporary investment medium he requires.

Negotiable Certificates of Deposit (NCDs) NCDs are relatively new money-market instruments that have grown rapidly, as evidenced by the fact that they are the second most important short-term investment medium.

Certificates of deposit originated in 1961 in a bid by banks to secure more funds to lend. They differ from savings accounts in the following ways: They promise a return of the principal on a specific date, usually in 30, 60, or 90 days, and they offer a slightly higher rate than does the passbook account.

The negotiable characteristic makes these instruments very important. Negotiability means that the instrument can be sold from party to party during its life, and ownership can be legally assigned to successive owners. This characteristic makes the use of the certificate of deposit as a money-market instrument very flexible. First, the certificate of deposit can be used as collateral for a loan.* But most important, the negotiable certificate can be legally bought and sold many times over before its maturity. This characteristic gives it the flexibility to be a temporary interest-bearing reservoir of funds.†

Calculating the Return on NCDs. As with Treasury bills, NCDs are sold on a discount basis. Assume that an institutional investor, such as a pension fund, has surplus cash to lend for 30 days. The pension fund negotiates with a securities dealer to purchase $1-million-par-value NCDs of a major bank for $994,000, the NCDs to mature in 30 days. What is the annual equivalent return on this money-market investment? Again, using the standard formulation:

$$r = \frac{D}{CO} \times \frac{360}{M}$$

with terms as defined as before, and substituting:

$$r = \frac{\$6,000}{\$994,000} \times \frac{360}{30}$$
$$= .006 \times 12$$
$$= .072$$

In this case, the pension fund receives a yield of 7.2 percent on an annual basis. It lent $994,000 for 30 days, and this is a 6/10 of 1 percent yield that it can effectively earn twelve times each year, for an annual yield of 7.2 percent.

NCDs came into their own as money-market instruments when several New York securities dealers started "making a market" in them. This means that a secondary market was created. Remember that a secondary market is a "used securities" market, and that it permits the purchase and sale of NCDs prior to their maturity. This feature of the secondary market permits investors to make portfolio adjustments flexibly and quickly.

Commercial Paper   Commercial paper consists usually of unsecured IOUs of large corporations that have periodic need for cash inflows for their operations. We have briefly alluded to the need of sales finance companies to bridge the

---

*This is true because the collateral can legally be transferred from the borrower to the lender in the event of default. Not all financial claims are negotiable. For example, U.S. savings bonds, Series E and H, are not negotiable.

†We should point out that NCDs are issued in denominations of $100,000 or more. They are not for the average household investor.

gap between funds outflows from loans they make and funds inflows from repayment of these loans.

Commercial paper is negotiable and, for this reason, serves as an excellent medium for the placement of short-term funds. It can be purchased from a dealer at any point during its period of life, and held till its maturity. This is possible only because dealers can hold commercial paper on their shelves for inventory—that is, because there is a secondary market in commercial paper. As we see by Table 21.1, commercial paper held its own during the period as a money-market instrument. It has a long and distinguished record in the money market, and will probably continue as a sound money-market investment.

Calculating the Return on Commercial Paper. As with Treasury bills and NCDs, commercial paper is sold on a discount basis. Assume that a major U.S. corporation receives $3 million in payment for the sale of one of its foreign plants, and that the funds will not be needed for 60 days. The corporation negotiates with a commercial dealer to purchase $3-million-face-value commercial paper for $2,970,000, the paper to mature in 60 days. What is the effective annual yield? As before, the formulation is:

$$r = \frac{D}{CO} \times \frac{360}{M}$$

with terms defined as before. Substituting:

$$r = \frac{\$30,000}{2,970,000} \times \frac{360}{60}$$
$$= .0101 \times 6$$
$$= .0606 \cong .06$$

In this case, the investing corporation receives an equivalent annual yield of approximately 6 percent.

Federal Funds   This is a deceptive term. It implies that we are speaking of federal tax revenues or expenditures. Such is not the case. The term *federal funds* is short for "funds on deposit at a Federal Reserve bank." How and why these funds get on deposit at Federal Reserve banks is the topic of the discussion following.

Banks chartered by the federal government are required to be a part of the Federal Reserve System and to maintain reserves against their deposits. These reserve accounts are maintained at Federal Reserve banks.

The reserve requirement is a ratio. For example, in February 1976, the reserve requirement on demand deposits of $0–$5 million in reserve cities was 17.0 percent. Whether or not a bank is complying with this ratio is determined in the following way: The bank's demand deposits for a week are averaged, and 17.0 percent of this average figure is the required reserve for the week. There are powerful inducements to have neither more nor less reserves than needed. If the bank has excess reserves in deposit at the "Fed," it is losing income from these fallow dollars. If it is deficient in reserves, it is penalized by the Federal Reserve authorities.*

Since all member banks in reserve cities† must calculate and settle their reserve positions by 3 P.M. each Wednesday afternoon, the conditions for a market in bank reserves are present. There are holders of excess reserves, those in need of these reserves, and a highly sophisticated means of transferring the funds between the two parties. A bank holding excess reserves can "sell"‡ them to a bank needing them simply by instructing the Federal Reserve to debit its own account and credit the borrower's reserve account.

Large banks are usually very sophisticated in the federal-funds market. They tend to act as wholesalers by buying (borrowing) from smaller banks, and reselling (lending) these funds in large blocks in the federal-funds market.

Funds traded in this market are not limited to funds currently on deposit at Federal Reserve banks. Anyone with liquidity to lend can enter this market by selling (lending) his liquidity.§ And anyone with the credit rating can purchase (borrow) funds for resale to a bank.

Calculating the Return on Federal Funds. Unlike the other money-market instruments discussed thus far, federal funds are not traded on a discount basis. They are quoted at simple annual-interest rates, but the loans are usually made for one or two days. The calculation of return is the calculation of simple interest:

$$R = Prt$$

where:

R = dollar return

P = principal

r = rate of interest

t = time, term of loan

---

*The penalty is in the form of a fine.

†This is a designation that includes the nation's largest cities.

‡Actually, these are loans rather than sales, usually for 24 hours, but the terms "selling" and "buying" have grown up in practice.

§An interesting development in the money market has been the entry of savings and loan associations as funds suppliers. They are, of course, lenders only, since they maintain no reserve position with the Federal Reserve.

Consider the case of the savings and loan association that has accumulated $10 million in anticipation of financing the construction of a shopping center, but the funds are not to be paid out for 24 hours. Rather than let the funds lie idle for that period, the managing officer of the savings and loan negotiates with a money-market bank for the "sale" (loan) of the funds for 24 hours at 6¼ percent. What is the dollar return to the savings and loan?

Substituting into the formulation above:

$$R = \$10,000,000 \times .0625 \times \tfrac{1}{360}$$
$$= \$1,736.11$$

It was prudent to place the funds in the federal-funds market, for the revenue of the firm rose by $1,736.11 with very little accompanying risk.

The federal-funds market, because of its very location in the bosom of the nation's banks, provides us with a very sensitive index of money-market conditions, the federal-funds rate.

Banker's Acceptances An acceptance represents the acceptance of legal responsibilities, principally the requirement to pay, of a debt by someone other than the original borrower. A bank acceptance is the acceptance of these responsibilities by a commercial bank.

Acceptances arise as a by-product of trade, both foreign and domestic. Perhaps a short example will help us understand how bank acceptances arise, and how they become money-market instruments.

Assume that an American dealer wants to purchase German automobiles for resale. He arranges with the German auto manufacturer to ship the autos with a 90-day draft and a negotiable bill of lading. The bill of lading, because it is negotiable, conveys title of the autos to its rightful and legal owner. The dealer also arranges simultaneously with his bank to borrow the money required to purchase the shipment of cars. The term of his loan is 90 days, the period in which he expects to sell the cars and repay the loan. Since the dealer is a good customer of the bank, the bank agrees to lend him the money to purchase the cars, and to accept the draft.

Note the net effect of this transaction. The bank has stipulated its willingness to substitute its credit and good name for that of its customer. The German manufacturer is perfectly willing to allow the substitution. He is probably happier to be dealing with a bank than with an individual.

The cars are shipped, and a 90-day draft and the negotiable bill of lading are sent to the bank. When the bank receives the draft and the bill of lading, it will do several things:

1. It will call the dealer and ask him to sign a note for the amount of the transaction.
2. It will then give the bill of lading to the dealer so he can get the cars and begin selling them.

3. It will stamp the word *ACCEPTED* across the face of the draft. The draft, now a bank acceptance, is returned to the German manufacturer. The bank now agrees to make payment at maturity in place of the purchaser of the cars.

Let's assume that it is the 67th day since the draft was drawn. Since it is not payable for 23 days (remember that it was originally drawn for 90 days), the German manufacturer may decide to sell it to get his money immediately. He can sell the acceptance to a dealer.* The price of the acceptance will be somewhat lower than the face value. The discount below the face value represents the return to the owner of the acceptance. The dealer now has two options. He can hold the acceptance till maturity. Most likely, however, he will sell the acceptance to someone seeking a short-term investment.

Calculating the Return on a Banker's Acceptance. Banker's acceptances are sold on a discount basis, and therefore the calculation of their return is similar to the calculation of return on any discount instrument.

In the example above, in which cars are shipped from Germany, giving rise to an acceptance, assume that the draft is for $360,000, and that it matures in 27 days. Further assume that the dealer purchasing it from the manufacturer pays $358,000 for it, and plans to hold the acceptance till maturity. What is the equivalent annual return on the investment? Using the discount formulation and substituting:

$$r = \frac{\$2,000}{\$358,000} \times \frac{360}{27}$$

$$= .0056 \times 13.3$$

$$= .074$$

By purchasing the banker's acceptance at a $2,000 discount, the dealer earns an annual-yield rate of 7.3 percent if he holds the acceptance till maturity.

This example contains all the necessary elements of a transaction that gives birth to a banker's acceptance. The banker's acceptance, as a by-product of both foreign and domestic commerce, has been and will continue to be a stable, reliable instrument of investment in the money market.

THE STRUCTURE OF MONEY-MARKET RATES

Eurodollars. An increasingly important money market medium is Eurodollars. Eurodollars are dollar-denominated deposits in banks outside the United States. These deposits are an attractive short-term investment medium

---

*Many dealers are commercial banks. There is nothing prohibiting the accepting bank from buying the acceptance for its own account.

because foreign banks generally pay interest on demand deposits, a practice which has been prohibited in the U.S. Not all Eurodollar deposits are demand however, many are time deposits.

Although a precise determination of the total volume of Eurodollars is impossible, it is variously estimated that the volume ranges between $60 and $150 billion. Eurodollar rates tend to be at the top of the structure of money market rates. In January 1978, for example, 3-month negotiable certificates of deposit were yielding 6.83 percent while 3-month Eurodollar deposits were yielding 7.32 per cent. Eurodollar rates are important money market indicators.* Changes in them tend to precede changes in domestic money market rates.

The structure of interest rates in the money market represents the cost of money, literally, in the economy. In this section, we shall discuss the structure of money-market rates and their interrelationships.

Since all money-market instruments tend to be good substitutes for each other, we would expect to, and do, find rates on major money-market instruments very close together, and furthermore, to find them moving together in the same direction.

Usually, but not always, we find the lowest rate in the structure to be the Treasury-bill rate. This is because Treasury bills do not have credit risk† associated with them.

The instances in Table 21.2 in which other rates exceeded the Treasury bill rate were caused by differences in the supply and demand factors associated with Treasury bills and their substitutes.

TABLE 21.2 Rates on Money-Market Instruments, First 6 Months of 1978 (percent per annum)

MONTH	TREASURY BILLS[a]	NEGOTIABLE CERT. DEP.	COMMERCIAL PAPER[b]	FEDERAL FUNDS	BANKER'S ACCEPTANCES[c]
January	6.44	6.71	6.75	6.70	6.86
February	6.45	6.89	7.76	6.78	6.82
March	6.29	6.85	6.75	6.79	6.79
April	6.29	7.04	6.82	6.89	6.92
May	6.41	7.42	7.06	7.36	7.32
June	6.93	7.82	7.59	7.60	7.75

[a]3-month Treasury-bill rate.
[b]90–119-day commercial paper.
[c]Banker's prime 90-day acceptances.

Source: Federal Reserve Bulletin, *except for Negotiable Certificate of Deposit Series, from Federal Reserve Bank of St. Louis.*

---

*Other money market instruments include federal agencies and maturing long-term U.S. Government securities. These are not discussed here since they comprise a minor portion of money-market transactions.

†See Chapter 15 for the definition of this term.

Next to the Treasury-bill rate is usually found the federal-funds rate. This rate on interbank borrowing is very sensitive to rapid changes in money-market conditions. On the average, however, we find the federal-funds rate very close to the Treasury-bill rate.

The next lowest rate is normally the rate on the negotiable certificate of deposit. NCDs are issued by commercial banks whose credit ratings are usually unquestioned. The rates on NCDs are usually a bit higher because, although NCDs are of very high quality, commercial banks do not enjoy the Treasury's freedom from credit risk. We are moving out in maturity also, and the higher rate is in part compensation for the higher risk associated with longer maturities.

Banker's-acceptance and commercial-paper rates are very close, because they are especially close substitutes for each other. They offer excellent short-term investment opportunities.

Figure 21.1 graphs the structure of three key money-market rates from January 1972 to January 1977. The three are the three-month Treasury-bill rate, the prime commercial-paper rate, and the banker's-acceptance rate.

FIGURE 21.1 Money-Market Rates. (*Source: Federal Reserve Bank of St. Louis.*)

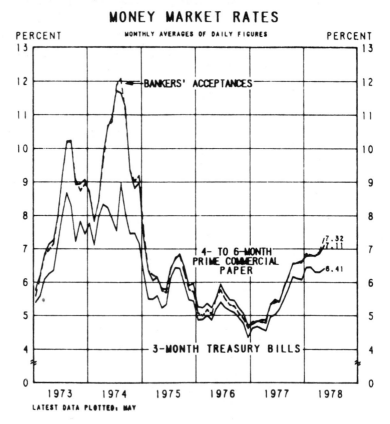

Several things should be noted about this graph. First, note that the three rates never range too far from each other. Again, this is due to their substitutability. Second, note that the rates move in the same direction simultaneously. For example, there was a sharp crack in the rates in the early months of 1972, and these three fell at approximately the same rate. And finally, note the volatility of the rates. The Treasury-bill rate went from a low of approximately 3.25 percent in early 1972 to a high of 9 percent in mid-1974. That is almost a threefold increase.

Those concerned with the economy in general, and financial economists in particular, are money-market-rate watchers. Since these rates reflect accurately and quickly the demand for money balances relative to their supply, money rates graphically portray developing economic trends.

THE ROLE OF THE FEDERAL RESERVE IN MONEY MARKETS

The Federal Reserve is charged with managing the nation's money supply in order to foster sound economic conditions. Since money is one of the commodities traded in the money market (the others being, of course, money-market debt instruments), it should be clear that the Federal Reserve has a large impact upon money-market conditions.*

There are three tools the Federal Reserve uses to affect economic conditions. They are changes in the reserve requirement, changes in the rate at which it lends money to member banks, and open-market operations. Each will be discussed for the purpose of tracing its impact on the money market.

Changes in Reserve Requirements Each member bank of the Federal Reserve System is required to maintain reserves on its deposits, both time (savings accounts) and demand (checking accounts). Assume that the reserve requirement is 10 percent. For every dollar's worth of deposits it takes in, a bank must deposit 10 cents in its reserve account at the Federal Reserve. The bank is then free to lend the remaining 90 cents. Now, assume that the Federal Reserve wants to "tighten up" and discourage demand for goods and services because of inflation in the economy. The Federal Reserve raises the reserve requirement to 20 percent. Each member bank can now lend only 80 cents out of each dollar's worth of deposits.

The impact of this change on money markets should be clear. Now banks must scramble for funds to meet the new reserve requirement. Money begins to get "tight." Short-term rates rise. Unnecessary spending is discouraged.

---

*The "money position manager" of a large bank—the officer who manages the bank's reserve position—recently told the authors that his job consists primarily of trying to outguess the Federal Reserve.

The Federal Reserve has accomplished its goal. Had it wanted to loosen the money supply, it could have lowered the reserve requirement from 10 percent to 5 percent and hoped that member banks would lend the additional loanable funds thus freed up.*

Changes in the Discount Rate   The discount rate is the rate at which Federal Reserve banks will lend to member banks. Federal Reserve banks will lend only for unforeseen difficulties in which a member bank finds itself. Therefore, the "discount window" is not a ready and reliable source of loanable funds. For this reason, one may not consider the discount rate a powerful tool of monetary control. It is not generally thought of as a major source of funds to the banking system, money markets, and the economy in general.

But some argue that the discount rate is a powerful psychological tool of the Federal Reserve. If the discount rate is lowered, they say, the Federal Reserve is "loosening up"—encouraging borrowing and economic expansion. Conversely, an increase in the discount rate signals the Federal Reserve's "tightening up." But outside of the disputed psychological impact, many monetary scholars conclude that changes in the discount rate are not powerful.

Open-Market Operations   Many people consider open-market operations to be totally incomprehensible. This, the most powerful control over money that the Federal Reserve has, is actually very easy to understand. It is the process by which the Federal Reserve exchanges money for U.S. government securities *in the hands of the public.*† If the Federal Reserve wants to encourage spending (economic growth), it will buy government securities from the public and replace them with money. This process encourages spending, for the public now has a spendable asset, money, in place of a nonspendable asset, government securities.

If the Federal Reserve wants to discourage spending, it will sell government securities to the public.‡ The public surrenders money and acquires government securities. This process leaves the public in a weakened position to spend, because it now has a nonspendable asset, government securities.

---

*Many monetary scholars argue that monetary policy is asymmetrical—easier to tighten up than to loosen up. The argument is that it is difficult to induce people to borrow when they don't want to.

†Open-market operations do not involve the Treasury directly. The only Treasury involvement is the trading of its securities between the Federal Reserve and the public.

‡How, and the conditions under which it does so, are outside the scope of this book. Any good money and banking text will give you a good description of the process.

Open-market operations have a tremendous impact upon money markets. The Federal Reserve's trading affects the supply of government securities in the hands of the public as well as the price of government securities, which in turn has an impact on all close substitutes for government securities—that is, other money-market instruments. Through control of the supply, at the margin, of Treasury securities, the Federal Reserve controls, within a range, the yields on money-market instruments.

THE ROLE OF THE U.S. TREASURY IN MONEY MARKETS

This section will be shorter than the preceding one, because the role of the Treasury in money markets is not a complicated one. Although the Treasury Department has economic stabilization responsibilities under the Employment Act of 1946, it does not discharge these responsibilities through the money market.

The basic role of the Treasury in money markets is that of the largest single demander of money-market funds. The federal government must make disbursements daily, but its receipts are sporadic, concentrated around scheduled income tax collections. Therefore, the federal government is a frequent and large demander of balances in the money market.

Its role is to space and time its borrowings and refundings in such a way as to attempt to minimize its impact on the money market. The Treasury must be cognizant of Federal Reserve goals and actions in its short-term financing schemes.

Overall, the major impact of Treasury action in money markets is the major by-product of its financing, the Treasury bill.

SUMMARY AND CONCLUSIONS

In this chapter, we have viewed the operation of the national market for money balances. We discovered that the function of the market is to bring together those with excess liquidity and those who have a need for such liquidity. The instruments of the money market, all short-term debt, are the investment media that bring them together.

An analysis of these debt instruments reveals that Treasury bills are the most important, closely followed by negotiable certificates of deposit, commercial paper, federal funds, and banker's acceptances.

The role of the Federal Reserve is to influence economic conditions, and to attempt to do this by influencing money-market conditions through purchases and sales of government securities. The role of the Treasury is primarily that of demander of funds.

PROBLEMS

1. Consult a recent edition of the *Federal Reserve Bulletin* and update Table 21.1 by placing the most recent figures in the table. Answer these questions:

   a. Which money-market instrument has grown the fastest?

   b. Which money-market instrument has grown the slowest?

   c. Write a short paragraph analyzing changes in money-market instruments and their relative importance.

2. Update the data in Table 21.2 for the most recent six months by consulting the *Federal Reserve Bulletin*. Answer these questions:

   a. Which money-market instrument has the highest rate now?

   b. Which money-market instrument has the lowest rate now?

   c. Write a short paragraph analyzing the differences between the rates quoted in Table 21.2 and those quoted in your update of that table.

3. You are responsible for the short-term investments of the XXI National Bank. The board of directors of the bank has specified that all short-term funds should be constantly employed, but in no case should funds be invested at less than 8%.

As short-term investment officer, you have the opportunity (and funds) to purchase $14,000,000-par-value Treasury bills that will mature in 45 days. They are offered to you at $13,850,000 for the package. Do you purchase them? Why, or why not?

4. You are investment counselor to a wealthy businessman. A securities dealer offers to sell him $8,000,000-par-value negotiable certificates of deposit (NCDs) that mature in 87 days, for $7,900,000. He is not good with figures, and asks you to tell him the annual equivalent yield on this investment. What do you tell him?

5. You manage the investment portfolio of Stammerford University, a major institution of higher learning in the United States. You must employ $6,000,000 in tuition receipts for 50 days. Dealer A offers you $6,000,000-face-value commercial paper, maturing in 40 days, for $5,950,000. Dealer B offers you $6,000,000 in banker's acceptances that mature in 50 days, for $5,950,000. Which money-market instrument do you purchase? Why?

6. As a result of your study of finance, you have become an expert financial consultant. One of your clients has heard about the federal-funds market and is all excited about his prospects for earning high returns for low risk. What do you tell him?

22

Financial Markets: Capital Markets (Long-Term Obligations)

> *Generally the total capital equipment of the economy is expanding over time, but this expansion occurs slowly.*
>
> *Richard Leftwich,*
> The Price System and
> Resource Allocation, *1955*

The preceding chapter discussed the money market, the market for short-term obligations. In this chapter, we move out in the maturity sector to discuss long-term obligations, the trading of which makes up the capital market. There are many similarities between the money market and the capital market, as well as many differences.

The capital makret is at once a source of investment opportunities for the saving public and a source of long-term funds for the capital-accumulating business sector of the economy. In demonstration of this very important point, the principles of the savings-investment process will be briefly reviewed and, once again, the differentiation clearly shown between financial investment and economic investment.

Recall our frequent references to the saver. He is the nonconsumer who decides not to consume a portion of his current income. What to do with this income that he does not use for current consumption becomes a problem. He can stuff it in a mattress or shoe box, but this would be "sterilizing" income, since it would produce no income for its owner. It would also be unavailable for use by those who require the funds to purchase capital goods.

Capital goods are those goods that have two characteristics: (1) They accrue income streams beyond the current income period—that is, they have relatively long lives; and (2) they are used in the production of consumer goods or other capital goods. We are speaking of such things as machine tools, buildings, transportation systems, typewriters, and indeed anything that is used in the further production of goods and services.

If there were no capital markets—that is, if there were no orderly, reliable means of smoothly transmitting funds from savers to capital accumulators—the level of economic activity would be significantly smaller. Why? It should be clear that if no conduit for the transfer of savings into economic investment existed, the business firm would be limited to only one source of funds for capital goods. That source would be savings out of its own current income. It could not borrow long-term funds from savers. It could not issue perpetual claims (common stock) on its own income in order to attract funds now. Conversely, savers who desired not to spend their entire current income would have no investment outlet for their savings.

Which brings us to our conceptualization of the capital market. The capital market is the series of institutional relationships that exist for the purpose of trading claims (bonds, common stock, preferred stock, and other claims) on those firms that want to accumulate capital goods. *Financial investment* is the purchase of claims on firms that accumulate goods. *Economic investment* is the purchase of newly-created capital goods by those firms issuing the claims. It is clear, we hope, that every dollar that is used to purchase a new claim in capital markets is channeled into capital goods. Even though the objects being traded in capital markets are financial claims, they represent real, tangible capital goods.

We shall, in the remainder of this chapter, outline and discuss the terms, conditions, rules, and constraints under which the long-term financial markets operate. Keep in mind that we are discussing the market for savings on the one hand, and the market for capital goods on the other.

THE GROUND RULES FOR CAPITAL MARKETS:
THE TWO BASIC ACTS

Probably no other area of finance has caught the attention of the general public as the capital market has. Most members of the reading public associate the trading of stocks and bonds with "high finance." It is in the trading of these securities that highly publicized excesses have taken place.

As a reaction to the excesses perpetrated in capital markets in the 1920s, Congress passed two acts that remain the bases of regulation of the capital markets today, and whose provisions help explain much activity in capital markets. The two laws are the Securities Act of 1933 and the Securities Exchange Act of 1934. We shall review the major provisions of each in order to provide a prelude to the following discussion.

The Securities Act of 1933   This act followed soon after the passage of several state "blue-sky laws." These laws were so named because it was once suggested that the basis of some speculative schemes was no more than "so many feet of the blue sky."

The thrust of the Securities Act of 1933 was the full disclosure of information about corporations issuing securities in interstate commerce. "Disclosure" is the key word. Congress in its wisdom set about, not to provide for government regulation and evaluation of securities issues and issuers, but to provide for the *dissemination of a maximum amount of information* to the financial investor so he could make a better evaluation of the securities and their issuers.

The major provision of the act is the requirement that new issues of securities entering into interstate commerce and involving a value of more than $300,000 must be registered. The period of registration is a minimum of 20 days. During this period, the securities may not be sold. The purpose of the registration statement is to allow the Securities and Exchange Commission to review the material in the registration statement to make sure that it contains full and faithful information required by the investor in making his purchase decision.

The act also requires that a prospectus be issued to each prospective purchaser before securities are sold. The prospectus contains basically the same information as the registration statement. Securities may not legally change hands until the customer has possession of the prospectus.

While there are many and more detailed provisions of the act,* they can be summarized by the one word, "disclosure."

---

*The law also provides for registration of secondary issues—issues already on the market, which are being sold by a principal stockholder or are being redistributed through an underwriter.

Securities Exchange What the Securities Act of 1933 did for the primary market (the issu-
Act of 1934 ance of new securities), the Securities Exchange Act of 1934 did for the
secondary market (trading of those securities already on the market).
Basically, the 1934 act contained the following major provisions:

1. It created the Securities and Exchange Commission to administer both
   the 1933 and 1934 acts.*

2. It provided for the registration and regulation of organized securities
   exchanges.

3. It provided for the disclosure of financial and other pertinent information by firms whose securities are listed on securities exchanges.†

4. It gave the Securities and Exchange Commission authority to regulate
   activities that might prove harmful to financial investors, such as manipulation of securities prices, proxy arrangements, and others.

The two laws complement each other in providing regulation of capital
markets: the act of 1933 providing for disclosure of information on primary
issues, and the act of 1934 requiring the same for secondary issues, as well as
providing the enforcement machinery, the Securities and Exchange Commission.

Given this treatment of the basic regulation of capital markets by the
federal government, we turn to a discussion of the market for new securities,
the primary market. In this section, we shall discuss the market for, and the
marketing of, new securities issues.

THE PRIMARY MARKET

Definition The *primary market* is defined simply as the market for new securities
issues. It can also be defined as the process by which new securities
are distributed from their issuer to the eventual financial investor. The process
is alternatively described as investment banking and underwriting. We shall
look at the process by viewing the participants in it as well as the process in
which they engage.

---

*Under the 1933 act, the Federal Trade Commission, established in 1914,
administered its provisions. The FTC was succeeded by the SEC in the 1934 act.

†A recent study of the effectiveness of the disclosure provisions of the 1934
act concludes, ". . . the disclosure requirements of the Securities Exchange Act of
1934 had no measurable positive effect on the securities traded on the NYSE."
See George J. Benston, "Required Disclosure of the Stock Market: An Evaluation
of the Securities Exchange Act of 1934," *American Economic Review*, Vol. 63, No. 1
(March 1973), 132–55.

The Participants   Conceptually, the distribution of new securities varies little from the distribution of any product. The typical manufactured product goes from the manufacturer to wholesalers and in turn to retailers and the consuming public. At each step along the conduit, bulk shipments are broken down into smaller lots for resale to the next level of transactions. The wholesaler, for example, breaks down the carload shipment of candies into cartons for sale and distribution to retailers. The retailer, in turn, breaks the cartons down into packages for sale to the consuming public. Although the titles of the transactors as well as the product line are different, there are many parallels between the distribution in securities markets and the distribution in retail markets.

The major institutions involved in the distribution of securities in capital markets are securities brokers and securities dealers. (The same individual, or firm, may function at different times as broker and as dealer.) They operate in both the primary and the secondary markets. However, we are concerned in this section with their role only in the primary market.

Broker.   The distinguishing characteristic of the broker is his function of bringing buyer and seller together. The broker is an agent. He never takes title, but can take possession of the commodity being traded. Therefore, he does not bear the risk of price change. The real estate broker, for example, is a well-known type of broker. His function is to bring the home buyer and seller together. He may, in the course of the transaction, take possession of the property of either the buyer or seller. He never, though, takes title to the property—in other words, he never trades for his own account. The securities broker is analogous to the real estate broker. The broker handles the public's orders to buy and sell securities or commodities. For this service, a commission is charged.

(Salesmen, or customers' representatives, as they are sometimes called, frequently refer to themselves as "stockbrokers," even though they may perform a variety of other functions for the securities firms for which they work.)

Dealer.   A securities dealer acts as a principal rather than an agent. Typically, a dealer buys for his own account and sells to a customer from his own inventory. The dealer's profit or loss is the difference between the price he pays and the price he receives for the same security—that is, the "spread" between the bid and the asked price of the security being traded. The dealer's confirmation must disclose to his customer that he has acted as principal.

The role of the dealer is contrasted sharply with that of the broker. The dealer buys and sells for his own account. In contrast to the broker, the dealer does not get paid a commission. As an entrepreneur, and as the principal in the transaction, he receives the difference between the purchase price and the sales price. In this respect, the securities dealer is no different from the car dealer, the shoe dealer, or indeed, any other merchant acting as principal in the sale of goods or services.

It was suggested previously that the real estate broker is the analogue of the securities broker. The real estate speculator* is the parallel of the securities dealer, then. The real estate speculator, or dealer, buys a real estate property at one price level and sells it at a different price level, a higher one. If the price drops after the purchase, the real estate dealer sustains the loss, in exactly the same way that a shoe merchant sustains the loss if his inventory of shoes must be "reduced for quick sale."

We find then that the firms operating in securities markets, both primary and secondary, even though called "brokerage houses," are actually operating as brokers and/or dealers. In the primary market, the securities market we are concerned with here, the role of these securities firms is that of dealer. It is necessary to understand the dealer role of securities houses in order to understand the underwriting process, the most frequently used method of distributing new issues.†

Securities Wholesaling: The Underwriting Process

In this section, we shall follow the process of distributing a new issue in capital markets from the inception of the issue to the final delivery into the hands of the ultimate financial investor.

The underwriting process starts with the need for new capital assets by a corporation. The need for the assets is recognized by the board of directors, which authorizes the officers of the corporation to enter into preliminary discussions with an investment banking firm for the purpose of determining the feasibility of a new securities issue to finance the needed asset expansion.

The Underwriting Function. The investment banking function is conducted by securities firms that wear many hats and perform many functions for the investing public. They are simultaneously investment bankers, securities brokers, and securities dealers. From now on, we shall use the term *securities dealer* to describe the investment banker, in order to continue to remind you of the other facets of the investment banking firm's activities.

At this point, the securities dealer is acting as agent of the issuing corporation. The corporation retains the dealer to examine all facets of the proposed new issue. Economic, marketing, engineering, legal, and accounting experts, and any other kind required, are consulted to try to predict the success of the proposed new productive activity as well as the current financial

---

*This term frequently has a negative aura about it. But one should remember that the speculator performs a valuable economic service: he prevents violent price fluctuations by constantly taking advantage of small price movements.

†The other method of distributing new issues is direct placement. In this case, the entire issue is sold to one or a few investors after negotiations have taken place.

health of the firm. The agent/securities dealer completes its study on the feasibility of the new project(s) and gives its estimate of the probability of success of such an issue at that time.

Let's assume the report is positive in all aspects, that it suggests that both the proposed project and its financing will be successful. The report is submitted to the corporation, and the securities firm is paid for its services. The agent-principal relationship between the corporation and the securities dealer is ended at this point. The report is read and digested by both the officers and the board of directors of the corporation, and the decision to undertake the new project and its financing is made.

Formation of the Syndicate. The officers of the corporation are authorized to invite a securities firm to form an underwriting syndicate for the issuance of the securities. A syndicate is a temporary organization put together to accomplish one specific function. In the case of an underwriting syndicate, the purpose is to wholesale the securities issue being proposed.

Although it is not required, there is a high probability that the securities firm that delivered the advisory opinion would be invited to form the underwriting syndicate. Such a step makes sense, because this firm knows a great deal about the issuing firm and its capital needs.

At this point, the role of the securities firm has changed. Whereas previously it performed the role of agent in the agent-principal relationship, it is no longer agent. As the firm organizing and managing the syndicate, it deals with the issuing corporation "at arm's length." From now until the issue is delivered to, and paid for by, the syndicate, the two will be bargaining on opposite sides of the table: the issuer to increase the total price of the issue, the syndicate to lower it as much as possible.

To form the syndicate, the syndicate manager invites other securities firms to participate in the underwriting, thus becoming part of the syndicate. Each firm joining the syndicate agrees to purchase a specified portion of the issue. The firm joining brings to the syndicate its credit rating, which will aid the syndicate in getting short-term bank credit to bridge the gap between the time the securities are purchased from the issuer and the time they are sold.

The syndicate organization is solidified. If the issue is very large and the syndicate requires assistance in its distribution, a selling group may be formed. A selling group is an organization of securities dealers who engage in the retailing of the issue. Members of the selling group purchase securities from the members of the syndicate. In this relationship, the syndicate acts as wholesaler and the selling group acts as retailers of the issue. If the issue is not large, or if it is thought it will be well received by the investing public, members of the syndicate may sell the issue directly to the investing public without the assistance of a selling group.

Figure 22.1 lists an underwriting group formed of dealers to underwrite a 400,000 issue of Surgicot, Inc. common stock.

This announcement is neither an offer to sell nor a solicitation of an offer to buy these securities. The offering is made only by the Prospectus.

January 14, 1977

400,000 SHARES

SURGICOT, INC.

COMMON STOCK
(Par Value $.01 Per Share)

PRICE $7.125 PER SHARE

Copies of the Prospectus may be obtained from such of the undersigned as may legally offer the securities in States in which the Prospectus may legally be distributed.

FURMAN SELZ MAGER DIETZ & BIRNEY
INCORPORATED

BEAR, STEARNS & CO.   OPPENHEIMER & CO., INC.   L. F. ROTHSCHILD & CO.

THOMSON MCKINNON SECURITIES INC.   WARBURG PARIBAS BECKER INC.

ALLEN & COMPANY   ARNHOLD AND S. BLEICHROEDER, INC.
INCORPORATED
A. G. EDWARDS & SONS, INC.   FAULKNER, DAWKINS & SULLIVAN, INC.

ROBERTSON, COLMAN, SIEBEL & WEISEL   C. E. UNTERBERG, TOWBIN CO.

DAIN, KALMAN & QUAIL   FOSTER & MARSHALL INC.
INCORPORATED
HAMBRECHT & QUIST   J. J. B. HILLIARD, W. L. LYONS, INC.

JOHNSON, LANE, SPACE, SMITH & CO., INC.   McDONALD & COMPANY

MOORE & SCHLEY, CAMERON & CO.   RAUSCHER PIERCE SECURITIES CORPORATION

RAYMOND, JAMES & ASSOCIATES INC.

KITCAT & AITKEN   PIERSON, HELDRING & PIERSON N.V.

SCHRÖDER, MÜNCHMEYER, HENGST & CO.   SINGER & FRIEDLANDER LTD.

The Selling Process   Now that we have all the transactors in their proper places, let's go back to the issuance of the securities by the corporation, and follow the transaction through its normal course.

At the agreed time, the corporation turns the securities issue over to the syndicate in exchange for a check paying for the entire issue. The corporation has accomplished its objective: It has issued the securities and received the proceeds without having to engage in the relatively expensive process of marketing them. It has turned that function over to a specialist.

The underwriting syndicate now has possession of as well as title to the securities. If a selling group is used, blocks of the issue are parceled out to firms that are members of the selling group. Members of the syndicate busily begin to sell the issue. If the issue is a desirable one, it "goes out the window"—that is, it is sold very quickly. Expenses are deducted from total revenues, profits are distributed, and the syndicate is disbanded. If, on the other hand, the issue moves slowly, the syndicate must make one of two decisions. It must intensify its selling efforts, thereby increasing costs, or it may decide to withdraw the issue from the market.

In either case, the risk must be assumed by the syndicate, since it has assumed all the risks of ownership. Although there have been instances of unsuccessful underwritings in which the issue did not sell, most are successful because of the planning and experience put into the underwriting effort.

Summary   The primary market is the market for new issues of securities. It is characterized by the underwriting process, in which investment banking firms, organized into syndicates, purchase entire issues and then either wholesale them to securities dealers in selling groups, or retail them themselves.

The underwriting of new issues by this method provides an efficient and readily available means of feeding new securities into the capital market.

THE SECONDARY MARKET

Definition   As we have suggested several times previously in this text, the secondary market is the national market for "used" securities. It is the market in common stock, preferred stock, and debt that have passed through the primary market, either through the underwriting process or through direct placements, and found their way into investor portfolios.

This national market in used securities is extremely important to financial investors. It permits them to make adjustments in their holdings quickly, efficiently, and economically.

The secondary market has two subdivisions. These two subdivisions involve trading on organized exchanges, and trading "over the counter"

(OTC). During the following discussion, we ask that you keep in mind that the commodity being traded is corporate securities, which include common, preferred, and debt.

The Over-the-Counter Market (OTC)   All securities that are not listed on one of the organized exchanges are traded in the over-the-counter market. The over-the-counter market is defined as the trading in securities between *dealers* and members of the investing public. This market is so named because dealers carrying inventories of securities stand willing and able to sell them "over the counter" to the financial investor.

Viewed in this light, the dealer in over-the-counter securities is no different from the dealer in over-the-counter shoes, or over-the-counter groceries, or over-the-counter anything. There should be no mystery attached to the over-the-counter market: The securities dealer, like any merchant, buys low and hopes to sell high. The spread is his margin and represents his income. Almost all corporate bonds and a very large volume of common stocks are traded over-the-counter.

Bid, Asked.   Over-the-counter securities are traded on a "bid-asked" basis. The "bid" quotation is the price the dealer is willing to *pay* for the security. The "asked" quotation is the price the dealer is willing to *take* for the security. Many people, when confronted with this observation, become confused and ask how there can be two prices for the same security.

If you think for a moment of the used-car market instead of the used-securities market, it might occur to you why there can be two prices. The used-car dealer who is trying to sell the 1974 Oldsmobile for $3,000 does not reveal to us that he paid $2,600 for it. The car dealer lives by selling cars for more than he pays for them.

The same is true of the securities dealer. One of the differences between the used-car market and the used-securities market is the fact that the securities dealer constantly advertises what he will pay for a security as well as what he will take for the same security; the used-car dealer usually does not reveal to his customers what he paid for the car he is trying to sell them.

Figure 22.2 shows OTC quotations for some stocks with a national market and being actively traded as of February 3, 1977. These quotations are collected from, and supplied by, dealers who are members of the National Association of Securities Dealers, and who therefore supply quotations for the NASDAQ computerized stock-quotation system.

Let's take a look at the listing for the American Express Company, a well-known corporation the world over. It is listed as "Am Express" for lack of space to write it out completely. Right next to the name is the figure "1". The 1 is the annual dividend of the company, $1. The next column is for "Sales in 100s." The figure for American Express is 692, which means that on this day of trading, 69, 200 shares changed hands. The next column tells us

FIGURE 22.2 Excerpt from Stock Quotations, National Over-the-Counter Market. (*Source: Wall Street Journal, February 3, 1977, p. 24.*)

Stock & Div.	Sales 100s	Bid	Asked	Net Chg.
--A A--				
AaronBro .20e	99	6¾	7¾	+ ¾
Acady Ins Grp	8	1⅜	1⅝	...
AccelratnC .80	18	14¼	15	...
AcetoChm 5.5l	16	14½	15¼	...
Acme Electric	1	13½	14	...
AddWesley .40	z96	7¼	7¾	...
Advance Ross	5	3⅜	3¾	...
Advan MicroD	137	25¼	26	− ¼
AEL Indust A	22	4	4⅜	...
AeroSystem 5i	178	15-16	1 5-16	+1-16
Aerosonc .06d	59	2¾	3⅛	...
Aerotron Incp	10	2½	2⅞	...
Air Florida Sy	26	3⅛	3⅜	− ⅛
Advent Corp	32	7⅝	8⅛	− ⅛
Affil Bnksh .84	17	15¾	16¾	+ ¼
AgMet Incorp	23	10¼	10¾	− ¼
Agnico Eagle	73	3⅜	3⅝	+1-16
AlaBncp 1.32g	1	23¾	24¾	− ¼
AlaTennN 1.40	18	18¾	19¾	+ ½
Alanthus C .25	26	4	4½	...
Alaska Gold	z2	3¼	4	...
Alaska Intl .24	5	6	7	...
Alberts Inc .20	10	7½	8¼	− ¼
AlexandA 1.06	175	37⅛	37⅝	− ⅛
Alex Bald 1.20	x80	15⅝	16⅛	+ ¼
AlicoIncp .17d	43	9	9½	...
Allegheny Bv	32	3⅞	4¼	− ⅛
Allergn Ph .10	76	22	22¾	+ 1
AlliedBncs .84	14	29⅜	29⅞	− ⅛
Allied Leisure	5	2¼	3	...
Allied Technlg	47	1¾	2	+1-16
Allied Tele .56	24	12¾	13¼	− ⅛
Allyn Bacn .45	28	8⅜	8⅞	...
AloeCrme Lab	5	3½	4	+ ⅛
AltonBoxBrd 1	11	17¼	18¼	+ ¾
Amarex Incor	258	18½	19	− ¼
Amco Energy	63	3⅜	3¾	...
Amdahl Corpn	189	34¼	35¼	− ¼
Am Aprsl .05b	6	4½	4⅞	...
AmBkr Ins .24	73	5	5⅜	...
AmBkTrPa 1g	6	17½	18½	...
AmBkrLf .20g	40	5¾	6¼	...
Am Biomedicl	150	3⅝	3⅞	...
AmBuildng .48	25	10⅞	11⅜	+ ¼
→ Am Express 1	692	36	36½	− ⅜
AmFidelLf .08	22	5½	6¼	...
AmFltrona .62	5	10	10½	...
Am Fncl .04g	302	13⅜	13¾	+ ⅜
AmFoundL .28	5	16¼	17¼	...
AmFletch 1.16	176	15½	16¼	+ ¼
Am Furniture	9	2⅝	2⅞	...

Stock & Div.	Sales 100s	Bid	Asked	Net Chg.
Am Greetg .34	163	9⅜	9¾	...
AmGuartF 10i	z6	4⅛	4⅝	...
Am Heritg .32	53	10	10½	− ⅜
Am Income Lf	50	11	11¾	...
AmIntlGrp .28	109	41½	42½	...
AmIntlRes .16	35	32	33½	...
Am Microsys	112	9	9½	+ ⅛
AmNatlFcl .44	44	10⅛	10½	− ⅛
AmNucler Cp	54	11½	11⅞	− ⅛
Am Pacif Intl	510	7	7½	− ¼
Am Quasr Pet	371	24½	25	− ¼
Am Reins .60	44	20⅝	21⅛	− ⅛
AmResrv .02b	190	5⅞	6¼	+ ¼
AmSLFla .19b	6	22½	23½	...
AmSL Utah 5i	12	11	11½	− ¼
Am SecTr 2.80	128	43½	44¼	...
AmStLife .30d	3	14⅛	14⅝	...
Am Telecomu	11	3¾	4¼	...
Am TeleC .05b	22	19¾	20½	...
Am Undrw .40	5	8	8¾	...
AmWeld M .80	17	10¾	11¾	− ¼
Amicor Incp	37	2¾	3⅛	...
Anacomp Inc	6	8½	9	+ ⅛
AnaditeInc .10	5	5⅞	6¼	...
AnalogDevc 5l	2	13	13¾	− ¼
Anaren Micro	10	1¼	1¾	...
Andrsn Jacob	5	3¼	3¾	...
AnheuserB .68	x475	22	22½	+ ⅜
Anta Corp .28	40	5⅛	5½	...
APF Electrnc	19	14½	15¼	...
API Trust .10b	17	4½	5¼	+ ¼
AppldDigit Da	3399	13⅞	14¼	+ ⅞
Applied Matrl	28	3½	4	...
Archon Inc	21	7¼	8¼	− ¼
ArgoPetrl .10b	72	10¼	10¾	+ ⅛
Argonaut Eng	65	7½	8¼	+ ½
Arizon Bk .60g	19	14¾	15½	− ¼
ArkWstGs 1.16	28	27	27¾	− ¼
Aspen Ski .40	25	12½	13¼	− ¼
AssoCocC .60a	4	14½	15¼	...
Assoc Host .10	46	6⅛	6⅝	− ¼
AsscFrtwy .80	15	21½	22½	...
Atl GasLt 1.24	54	16	16⅜	− ⅛
Atl Bncrp .68a	27	11¾	12½	...
Atl PepsiC .24	5	16¼	17¼	...
AtlantSteel .70	4	10	10½	...
ATO cv pf .40	8	5⅝	5⅞	...
Atwood Ocncs	45	7	7½	...
AutoMed Labs	7	7	7¾	...
Autotrol Corp	18	26	27½	− 1
AzconCorp .60	24	8⅝	9	...

the bid price, the amount dealers are willing to pay for the stock. The figure is 36, or $36.00 per share. The next column tells what dealers are willing to take, the asked price. The figure is 36 1/2, or $36.50. The spread, the difference between bid and asked, is 50 cents. It is for this spread that brokers are willing to trade the stock. The last column is the net-change column. This is the difference between today's closing asked price and yesterday's closing asked price. The figure here is −3/8, meaning that today's figure, 36.50, is 37 1/2 cents below yesterday's figure (36 7/8).

Although our example has used common stock, we hasten to point out the fact that most bonds, both corporate and government, are sold over the counter. Some are traded on the New York Stock Exchange and on the regional stock exchanges, but again, the greatest volume is traded over the counter.

Organized Exchanges: The New York Stock Exchange   Although most securities issues, stocks and bonds, are traded over the counter, it is the stock exchange that the general public tends to associate with trading in the secondary market. The organized exchanges do provide the focal point for securities trading, and because it is the largest and best known of them, we shall confine our discussion to the "Big Board," or the New York Stock Exchange.

The New York Stock Exchange is an association of securities traders and brokers organized together for the purpose of providing trading facilities for members of the association. The organization has been in existence since 1792, when a group of New York securities dealers agreed to band together to give each other preference in their trading.

The New York Stock Exchange has been reorganized several times in its history. It stands today as an organization that provides two principal services: (1) It provides the resources and space for a continuous auction market in corporate securities, and (2) it serves as the regulatory agency for policing its members' practices.

There are basically two groups making up the New York Stock Exchange: the members of the exchange, and the corporations whose securities are listed on it. We shall discuss each of these two groups.

Each member of the New York Stock Exchange is a securities trading firm and an individual trader. Membership permits the trader or his representative to enter the floor area where trading takes place. The exchange is governed by a 21-member board of governors, elected by the membership. The term of members is staggered. The basic function of the board of governors is to provide the rules of conduct for trading on the exchange.

Trading on the Floor.   Trading itself is conducted on the floor of the stock exchange between the hours of 10 A.M. and 4 P.M., Monday through Friday. Orders for both purchases and sales of listed securities are wired to the floor of the exchange. The sale and purchase orders are matched up by a constant bidding process. As agreements are made between the selling broker and the buying broker, the transaction is recorded and flashed to the world on the "ticker tape." Once a telegraphic paper tape that traditionally transmitted transactions, today the "ticker tape" is actually an electronic device that records and transmits transactions and their terms almost instantaneously. An illustration of the electronic video scanner is presented in Figure 22.3.

FIGURE 22.3   The Electronic Video Scanner ("Ticker Tape"). (*Note: Quotations as of September 1, 1976.*)

KO	MCD	IBM	DEC		ARCPr
3s87⅜	56	267⅞	1000	163⅜	63⅜

A round lot of 100 shares is portrayed on the tape at its price only, with no designation of quantity. For example, in Figure 22.3, McDonald's (MCD) is quoted at $56 a share for 100 shares. A round-lot transaction of between 200 and 900 shares (200, 300, 400, 500, 600, 700, 800, or 900) is quoted on the tape by one digit specifying the number of shares in hundreds, followed by a lowercase *s* and the price per share. Thus, in the figure, a 300-share transaction of Coca Cola (KO) at $87 3/8 is quoted. Transactions of 1,000 shares or more are quoted by the exact sales figure. Thus, a 1,000-share transaction for Digital Equipment Corporation (DEC) at $163 3/8 per share is shown in Figure 22.3.

The great majority of transactions on the floor of the exchange are broker transactions, in which a broker representing the seller of a security deals with a broker representing the buyer of the stock.* Although bonds, warrants, and rights are traded on the New York Stock Exchange, common stock is the largest-volume single type of security traded.

Listing Requirements. Not all corporations' stocks are traded on the Big Board. In fact, only a relatively few are. The number is constantly changing. As of April 1970, 1550 corporations were listed for trading.

How does a corporation get listed for trading on the exchange? Obviously, the New York Stock Exchange would desire that all corporations whose securities are listed for trading are large enough and have enough public interest shown in them to have an extensive market in their securities. In order to ensure this, only corporations that can meet certain requirements, primarily size, are permitted to have their securities traded on the Big Board. A corporation whose securities are to be listed must meet the following requirements, among others:

1. It must have earnings before taxes of $2.5 million for the current year. In addition to this, it must have earnings before taxes of at least $2.0 million for each of the two years preceding listing.

2. It must have net tangible assets of $16 million. This requirement can be waived if the investing public puts a high value on the corporation's common stock. If so, the market value of its publicly held common stock must be at least $16 million.

3. There must be 1 million shares outstanding, 800,000 of them in the hands of the public. This means that no more than 200,000 shares can be held by officers/directors of the corporation.

---

*There are also dealer transactions in the market, in the form of odd-lot (less than 100 shares) trading and specialist trading. The latter trading is between dealers on the floor of the exchange. These transactions do not, however, represent a significant amount of trading on the exchange.

4. The corporation must have 2,000 shareholders, with at least 1,800 owners of round lots (100 shares).

The basic purpose of these requirements is to ensure that the ownership, as well as the potential ownership, is wide enough to ensure volume trading of the listed corporation's common stock and other securities. In addition to meeting initial size requirements, the corporation, if accepted for listing, must agree to provide periodic financial statements, to be made available to the public.

Delisting. Once a corporation's securities are listed for trading, is the listing permanent? The answer is an emphatic *no*. There are two conditions under which a corporation's securities are no longer traded ("delisted"). The first is voluntary delisting, when, for some reason, the corporation no longer desires to have its securities traded on the exchange, or does not desire to continue to meet the requirements for listing. Frequently cited is the expense of providing frequent and detailed reports to the New York Stock Exchange for inspection by the investing public.

The second reason is involuntary delisting. There are criteria established for discontinuing permanently the trading of a corporation's stock. The delisting criteria are:

1. When the corporation has 900 or fewer round-lot owners

2. If there are 400,000 or fewer shares in public hands

3. If the market value of the publicly held shares is $4 million or less

4. If the corporation's net tangible assets falls to $7 million or less

It is apparent from an examination of these criteria that delisting requirements are approximately half those of the listing requirements. This means, of course, that the listed corporation is given some leeway before involuntary delisting takes place.

The Tracks of Exchange Trading: The Market Report. A useful and desirable by-product of trading on the organized exchanges is the volume of market information that issues forth. Since one of the purposes of an auction market is to provide the maximum amount of market information possible to buyers and sellers, all transactions in the major stock exchanges are reported publicly. Trading on the New York and American stock exchanges is reported the following day in the *Wall Street Journal.* City and regional stock-exchange trading is reported in the newspapers of those cities and regions.

Figure 22.4 portrays a few of the results of trading on February 3, 1977. Notice the listing for International Business Machines, listed as "IBM"

FIGURE 22.4 Excerpt from New York Stock Exchange-Composite Listing. (*Source: Wall Street Journal, February 4, 1977, p. 28.*)

NYSE-Composite Transactions

Thursday, February 3, 1977

Quotations include trades on the New York, Midwest, Pacific Philadelphia, Boston and Cincinnati stock exchanges and reported by the National Association of Securities Dealers and Instinet.

–1976-77– High	Low	Stocks	Div.	P-E Ratio	Sales 100s	High	Low	Close	Net Chg.
23 1/2	16 1/8	ICInds	1.40	7	137	23 1/4	23 1/8	23 1/8	– 1/8
45 5/8	33 5/8	ICInd	pf 3.50	..	16	44 7/8	44 1/4	44 7/8	+ 7/8
5 3/4	3	ICN	Pharm	8	112	5 1/2	5 1/8	5 3/8	.....
47 1/2	34 1/2	INACp	2.10	11	255	43 1/4	42 3/4	42 7/8	+ 1/8
20 7/8	16 3/4	INAIn	1.59a	..	12	20 1/2	20 3/8	20 3/8	– 1/8
13 1/4	9 5/8	IUIntl	.90	11	445	12 3/4	12 5/8	12 5/8	– 1/4
36 1/2	26 1/4	IUInt	A	..	3	35 7/8	35 1/2	35 1/2	– 3/8
31 1/4	26	IdahoP	2.16	9	69	28 1/2	28 1/4	28 1/2	.....
23 3/4	13 1/4	IdealBa	1.20	9	565	23	22 5/8	22 3/4	+ 1/8
9 5/8	6 1/8	IdeaToy	.32b	5	27	8 3/8	8 1/4	8 1/4	+ 1/8
28	22 1/2	IllPowr	2.20	10	110	25 7/8	25 3/4	25 7/8	.....
30	25 1/2	IIPow	pf2.35	..	z40	29	29	29	+ 1
54 3/4	50	IIPow	pf4.47	..	z1800	53	52 3/4	53	.....
30	21	ITW	.56	16	21	26 3/8	26 1/8	26 3/8	+ 1/4
18 1/8	10 1/4	ImplCpA	.24	5	91	15 3/4	15 1/2	15 1/2	– 3/8
37	25 1/8	INCO	1.40a	14	178	33	32 3/8	32 3/4	– 3/8
7 3/4	4 3/4	IncCap		..	24	7 1/8	7 1/8	7 1/8	– 1/4
10 1/8	8 7/8	IncCCu	.88e	..	9	9 1/2	9 1/2	9 1/2	+ 1/8
88 1/8	67 1/2	IndiM	pf7.76	..	z100	86 1/2	86 1/2	86 1/2	+ 1 1/8
98	76 1/2	IndiM	pf8.68	..	z10	96	96	96	+ 1/8
119 1/2	102	IndiM	pf 12	..	z1250	118	118	118	– 1/4
29	19 3/8	IndiGas	2.12	7	2	28 7/8	28 3/4	28 3/4	– 1/4
25 1/2	20	IndplPL	1.82	10	36	24 1/2	24 1/4	24 1/4	– 1/8
18	12 1/2	IndlNat	1.20	7	11	16 7/8	16 5/8	16 3/4	– 1/8
16 1/8	6 5/8	InexcoO		22	1364	16 3/8	14 3/4	15 7/8	+ 3/4
95 1/2	65	IngerR	2.68	12	143	67	66 3/8	66 1/2	.....
57 1/2	44 1/4	IngR	pf 2.35	..	5	46 1/2	46	46 3/8	– 1/8
34	24	InInd	Con 1	8	13	25 7/8	25 5/8	25 3/4	.....
58 5/8	41	InIndStl	2.60	9	120	47 3/4	47	47 1/4	– 1/2
17 3/4	7 3/4	Inmont	.80	7	215	17 1/4	16 3/4	16 7/8	– 1/4
15	8 3/8	Insilco	.80e	7	71	15	14 3/4	15	+ 1/4
19 1/2	12 3/4	Insil	pfA1.25	..	11	19	18 3/4	18 3/4	– 1/8
31 1/4	20 3/4	InspCop	.50e	..	4	28 3/4	28 3/4	28 3/4	– 1/4
2 1/2	1	InstInvTr		..	10	1 1/2	1 3/8	1 3/8	– 1/8

–1976-77– High	Low	Stocks	Div.	P-E Ratio	Sales 100s	High	Low	Close	Net Chg.
10 1/4	7	Integon	.36	7	20	9 3/4	9 1/2	9 1/2	– 1/4
48 3/8	38 5/8	Interco	1.66	8	19	40 3/4	40 1/2	40 1/2	.....
8 7/8	3 7/8	InterctDiv		..	14	7 5/8	7 3/8	7 5/8	+ 3/8
42 1/2	25 5/8	Interlak	2.20	6	42	36 7/8	36 1/2	36 7/8	+ 1/8
288 1/2	223 3/8	IBM	10	17	x814	271 3/4	269 3/4	271 1/8	– 5/8
28 3/8	19	IntFlavF	.44	20	745	19 1/4	18 7/8	19	– 1/8
33 1/8	22 3/8	IntHarv	1.85	5	282	32 1/8	31 5/8	31 3/4	– 1/8
42 1/4	32 3/4	IntMinC	2.40	6	212	39 3/4	39 3/8	39 3/4	+ 1/8
16 7/8	6 1/8	IntMng	.40e	7	16	16 3/4	16 1/2	16 5/8	.....
20 1/8	15 5/8	IntMulti	.85	7	21	19 3/4	19 1/2	19 1/2	.....
79 3/4	56 1/2	IntPaper	2	10	771	57 7/8	57	57 1/2	– 1/8
8	5 3/8	IntRectif	.20	..	19	6 1/4	6 1/8	6 1/8	– 1/8
34 7/8	22 1/4	IntTT	1.76	9	810	33 5/8	33 3/8	33 5/8	.....
102 1/4	71	IntTT	pfE 4	..	z20	101 1/2	101 1/2	101 1/2	.....
63 3/4	44	IntTT	pfH 4	..	10	63 1/4	62 1/2	63 1/4	+ 1/4
59 1/2	42 1/2	IntTT	pfJ 4	..	13	59	58 1/2	59	– 1/4
58 1/4	41 1/4	IntTT	pfK 4	..	54	57 3/8	57	57 1/4	– 3/8
65 1/4	47	IntTT	pfO 5	..	2	64 5/8	64 5/8	64 5/8	+ 1/8
41 1/2	27 7/8	ITT	pfN 2.25	..	31	40	39 3/4	40	– 1/4
63	45 3/8	ITT	pfI 4.50	..	3	62 1/4	62	62 1/4	+ 1/4
32	23 1/4	Intrpce	1.45	7	13	30 1/8	30	30 1/8	+ 1/8
32	16 3/8	IntrpGp	1.60	7	21	31 1/2	30 3/4	30 3/4	– 1
17 3/4	14 7/8	IntrsPw	1.45	10	20	17 7/8	17 3/4	17 3/4	.....
7	4 1/4	IntrstUn	.24	22	56	6 1/8	6	6 1/8	– 1/8
25 1/4	19 3/4	IowaBf		4	186	23 3/4	22 1/4	23 1/2	+ 1 1/4
17 7/8	13 1/4	IowaEl	1.40	9	39	17 1/4	17	17 1/4	+ 1/4
22 7/8	17 3/8	IowaIlG	1.84	11	99	23	22 7/8	23	+ 1/8
28 1/4	24 1/4	IowIll	pf2.31	..	z140	27	27	27	.....
26	21 7/8	IowaPL	2.10	8	34	25 1/2	25	25 3/8	+ 3/8
22 5/8	17 5/8	IowaPS	1.80	11	45	22	21 5/8	21 3/4	– 1/8
6 3/4	3 3/4	IpcoHsp	.05e	10	40	6 1/8	5 7/8	6	.....
18 5/8	8 7/8	ItekCp		33	482	17 3/4	16 5/8	17 1/4	+ 1/2
15 7/8	5 3/4	ItelCp	.30	6	181	14 7/8	14 5/8	14 3/4	– 1/8

because its name is too long to write out. Here is the entire line of data associated with IBM on this date:

1976–1977 HIGH	LOW	STOCK	DIV:	P-E RATIO	SALES 100S	HIGH	LOW	CLOSE	NET CHG.
$288\frac{1}{2}$	$223\frac{3}{8}$	IBM	10	17	x814*	$271\frac{3}{4}$	$269\frac{3}{4}$	$271\frac{1}{8}$	$-\frac{5}{8}$

The two left-hand columns are self-explanatory: The highest price of IBM during the years of 1976–77 was 288 1/2, and the lowest was 223 3/8. The column after the name lists the *annual* dividend in dollars; for IBM, it is $10 per share. The next column lists the price–earnings ratio, the number of

*The "x" in this figure means ex-dividend, that is, less the current dividend.

times annual earnings (*earnings*, not dividends) per share the investing public is willing to pay to get the earnings. As a general rule, the greater the price–earnings ratio, the less risky the corporation is as an investment. The reciprocal of the price–earnings ratio, the earnings–price ratio, is sometimes considered shareholder return on investment. In this case, the earnings–price ratio is 1/17, or 5.9 percent. This was not an exceedingly high rate of return on common-stock investments, given the capital-market conditions prevailing in February 1977.

The next column gives the sales in hundreds for the current day's trading. The number 814, translated into hundreds, is 81,400 shares. This is by no means a leading volume for the day. The most active stock for that day February 3 was Gulf & Western, with 705,900 shares traded. But 81,400 shares is a healthy number, and it indicates that the investing public was expressing interest in the stock.*

The next two columns, "High" and "Low," should be read together. The high price for IBM on this day was 271 3/4, and the low was 269 3/4. The difference between the two, the spread, is one measure of the demand–supply forces for the stock. Generally, the wider the spread, the more erratic are supply–demand forces for the stock. The absolute spread of $2.00 is small for IBM. It represents less than 1 percent of the high and low for the day.

The "Close" column tells us the price of the last transaction of the trading day. This figure has to be either the high, the low, or a figure between them, obviously. In this case, it is 271 1/8, a figure between the high and low. The figure of 271 1/8 tells us that the market for the stock had "evened out" during the trading day; that is, it was at neither its high nor its low for the day.

The last column tells us the difference between this day's closing price and the preceding trading day's closing price. Thus, we can tell not only the direction of trading in today's market, we can also tell whether the daily price level is up or down from the preceding day's trading.

There is a large amount of powerful and useful information contained in market listings. The stock investor, trading in this extermely important part of the secondary market, can secure up-to-date and extensive market information by consulting the newspaper.

NYSE-Composite Transactions. On January 26, 1976, the *Wall Street Journal* began reporting the results of trading on the New York Stock Exchange along with the results of trading in NYSE issues on regional

---

*Keep in mind that the 81,400 shares *sold* on this day were also *bought*. One frequent misstatement made in the press is, "Everyone is selling!" This is not possible. For each share of stock *sold*, one was *bought*. Recognition of this homely fact may prove useful to you.

markets as "NYSE-Composite Transactions." See Figure 22.4. This may be an intermediate step on the way to a national stock exchange system.

Membership in the NYSE.   As we suggested previously in this chapter, the New York Stock Exchange is a mutual association operated for the benefit of the owners. Its basic function is to provide physical facilities for trading and to provide the "rules of the game"—self-regulation.

As of May 1977, there were 1,366 members of the exchange, and the number of memberships ("seats") is limited. This limitation has created a market for trading privileges. They are treated (and traded) in exactly the same way as over-the-counter securities, on a bid-asked basis.

Prices for seats on the exchange in the halcyon days of 1968–69 went as high as $515,000. This is close to the high of $625,000 paid in 1929. The price dropped to $65,000 in 1974. The most recent trade, as of May 20, 1977, was for $60,000. The bid price was $54,000 and the asked price was $60,000.* The low of $17,000 for a seat was paid in 1942.

The "Third Market"   We have spoken of the primary market, the market for new issues, and the secondary market, the market for "used" securities traded over the counter and on the organized exchanges. These transactions are normally between the securities issuer and the investing public as in the case of the primary market, or between members of the investing public as in the case of the secondary market.

But in the 1950s and 1960s, institutional investors became important participants in the long-term-securities markets. Institutional investors are large-volume purchasers of securities, and are generally quasi-public institutions such as pension funds, insurance companies, mutual funds, commercial-bank trust departments, large universities, and so on. The one characteristic these investors have in common is the large size of their transactions, frequently in the range of 10,000 shares or more. Keep in mind that the standard unit of trading on the organized exchanges, the round lot, is 100 shares. Clearly, there was a need for trading facilities for large-unit transactions, and the normal facilities of the stock exchanges, designed primarily to handle 100-share transactions, were not suitable.

In order to accommodate the special trading needs of the large institutional investor, a special over-the-counter market was formed to provide for the interface of the large-block securities buyer and seller. This sector of the OTC market has been dubbed the "third market," in order to differentiate it from the trading characteristics of the primary and secondary markets.†

---

*New York Stock Exchange.

†Mention is also occasionally made of a "fourth market," the direct large-block trading between institutional investors.

Large-block trading has also been instituted on the New York Stock Exchange in response to the needs of the institutional trader. The NYSE defines a large block as 10,000 shares; commissions on large blocks are negotiated.

Third-market trading is increasing in importance in securities markets. As the size of public and quasi-public institutions grows, so will the importance of third-market trading. It is now estimated to be 25 percent of the NYSE dollar volume.

THE ISSUE OF EFFICIENT MARKETS

There is a strong relationship between the efficiency of an economy's securities markets and its gross national product. Efficient markets are necessary for the channeling of saved income into capital goods and equipment. The volume of capital goods is in turn strongly related to the economy's efficiency in turning resources into goods and services. Market efficiency has become the topic of research and discussion in the literature of finance, and deserves some discussion here. We summarize only the major points.

Operational Efficiency   There are two types of efficiency to be measured in securities markets: operational and allocational. Operational efficiency has to do with the relative efficiency of the institutions that conduct the flow of savings into investment goods. If two financial intermediaries—say, commercial banks—are lending in the same markets, and one bank is not well managed, it should and probably does occur that the latter bank will have to charge higher interest rates to finance its inefficiencies. Clearly, it further occurs that in a competitive market, and especially in a well and efficiently regulated market, there would be no room for inefficient firms, since no one would pay their higher interest rates when lower rates were available from a more efficient firm.

But what if *all* banks were inefficient? There would be no efficient one to reveal, through its lower rates, an inefficient operation. We cannot assume, and are not justified in doing so, that because all rates are the same, efficiency exists. Keep in mind that there are homogeneous prices in oligopolistic markets too, for that is one of the goals of the oligopoly. Operational efficiency, to sum up, deals with the efficiency in the institutions that make up financial markets. In the words of two nationally renowned financial scholars, "a low-friction financial machine is an efficient one."*

---

*Roland I. Robinson and Dwayne Wrightsman, *Financial Markets: The Accumulation and Allocation of Wealth* (New York: McGraw Hill, 1974), p. 398. This book is an excellent treatment of financial markets, and it is highly recommended.

Allocational Efficiency   Allocational efficiency, on the other hand, deals with the efficiency of moving funds to high-return and socially desirable uses. As the song says, this is "easier said than done." How is allocational efficiency to be measured?

A good example is the problem of financing residential housing in the United States. Congress, speaking for the people, has frequently stated that private home ownership is a highly desirable social goal. And yet, despite massive subsidy programs (such as FNMA and GNMA), the quantity supplied of housing has fallen dramatically behind the quantity demanded. And many financial economists argue that it is because of defective and inefficient mortgage markets that residential housing is not being built.*

Despite the discontinuities and relative inefficiencies found in U.S. securities markets, many financial scholars argue that they are, on net balance, relatively efficient.†

SUMMARY

This chapter has given an overview of the long-term financial markets. It has viewed the primary, secondary, and third markets as well as the institutional arrangements that go to make up these markets.

PROBLEMS

1. In Chapter 12, the formulation for the return to the investor (cost to the issuer) on common stock is given as $D_1/P_0 + g$. Assume that you require an 8% growth rate in all your investments; that is, $g = .08$. Using this and the data in Figure 22.4, calculate your rate of return on IBM.

2. The NYSE has a ruling that all buy and sell orders must go to the floor of the exchange. What is the purpose of this ruling?

---

*Consider the problem of "redlining." Officers of mortgage lending institutions draw a "red line" around a high-risk neighborhood and vow not to lend funds within the circle. They are criticized sharply by members of Congress for denying funds to areas in greatest need. They argue in response that the risk is too great, and they would violate depositors' trust by lending with such great risk. This is definitely a problem of allocational efficiency.

†For example, see Charles N. Henning et al., *Financial Markets and the Economy* (Englewood Cliffs, N.J.: Prentice-Hall, 1975), p. 227.

3. Below is described a series of financial-market transactions. Classify them as either primary- or secondary-market transactions:

a. You purchase 100 shares of common stock from a member of a selling group.

b. You buy a Treasury bill, which has 29 days to maturity, from a Treasury-bill dealer.

c. A direct placement of an entire issue of short-term notes is negotiated between a sales finance company (seller) and a pension fund (buyer).

d. You sell 100 shares of preferred stock, using the facilities of a member of the NYSE.

e. You borrow $10,000 for 90 days from your bank.

4. If an issue of new securities being underwritten by a syndicate is not purchased by the investing public, what happens to the issue? Who sustains the loss? Why?

5. Explain the difference between the bid and asked prices in OTC trading.

6. It has been suggested that trading on the NYSE is not truly economically competitive, since institutional investors with large-volume transactions can influence the price of securities. Evaluate this argument.

7. Refer to the footnote early in this chapter reporting a study that concludes that the disclosure provisions of the Securities Exchange Act of 1934 have had no effect on securities traded on the NYSE. If this is true, what function(s) does security-market regulation provide?

8. Secure a "tombstone prospectus" from a recent issue of the *Wall Street Journal*. Answer the following questions about it:

a. What security is being marketed?

b. How many members of the underwriting syndicate are there?

c. Which member of the syndicate is the managing partner? How did you determine this?

9. A major political issue of the 1970s is the philosophy of regulation of financial markets and financial intermediaries. The broad issue is greater regulation. Array arguments on each side. If you could make the policy decision, which would you decide upon? Why?

10. Explain why the greatest volume of trading in the secondary market is over-the-counter.

11. On Monday, September 21, 1976, the following transaction went over the tape:

$$\text{CBS}_{500s}58\tfrac{1}{2}$$

Interpret this transaction.

12. Given below are prices of two common stocks traded OTC. Analyze the changes between the two dates for the two stocks. What can be said about the market for each stock, based upon these observations?

	BID	ASKED
	July 26	
Sturm Ruger	13	14
Pabst Brewing	$26\tfrac{1}{8}$	$26\tfrac{5}{8}$
	August 23	
Sturm Ruger	13	14
Pabst Brewing	$22\tfrac{3}{8}$	$23\tfrac{7}{8}$

23

The Impact of Stabilization Policies on Securities Markets

The problems are caused by human actions, the solutions are devised by human minds, and the outcome affects people everywhere.

David P. Eastburn,
The Federal Reserve on
Record, *1965*

In our discussions of financial markets to this point, we have implicitly assumed that financial markets operate on their own, without influence from outside. Such is not the case. We turn now to a broadly based discussion of two major economic stabilization devices, monetary and fiscal policy, used to influence economic activity through changes in securities-market conditions.

This chapter treats the evolution of the two types of aggregate stabilization policies, as well as the important topic of the impact of monetary and fiscal policy on the two major dimensions of the securities markets, prices and rates of return.

The Great Depression had a major impact upon American life. Its effects were felt in politics, government, clothing fashions, and philosophical out- looks on life. Perhaps the major impact of the Great Depression, however, was the changed economic role of government. Advocates of the free market had a difficult time, in the bitter winter of 1933–34, explaining why the free- market system did not restore the economy to full-employment equilibrium.* Because the private sector of the economy wouldn't, or couldn't, regenerate itself, advocates of government intervention in or government management of the economy began successfully to impress their arguments upon the society and its Congress. The way was paved for President Franklin Delano Roosevelt's "New Deal," a program to regenerate economic activity through government leadership, persuasion, and legal force. Thus was changed the economic philosophy—and policy—from government "hands off" to active government participation in the economy, and acceptance of responsibility by government for the well-being of the economy.

The Great Depression was followed by World War II, which brought its own peculiar economic problems. The war forced acceptance of govern- ment influence in the private sector of the economy. The federal government became the major resource-allocation agent during the war in order to maxi- mize the production of the necessary material and munitions, and the sur- render of certain economic freedoms seemed a relatively small price to pay to win the war.

The conclusion of the war brought the fear of mass unemployment, what with the time lag for conversion from military to civilian production coupled with the massive infusion into labor markets of returning servicemen. In order to forestall the impending slowdown in economic activity,† Con-

---

*This is an observation, not a value judgment by the authors. The authors take no stand on the issue of intervention by government in the economy.

†The slowdown did not occur. In fact, the economy experienced the opposite problem, inflation. The inflation was brought on by a vast reservoir of pent-up demand for consumer goods at war's end. Very few consumer goods had been produced in the United States, and indeed in the western world, since the begin- ning of the war. People raced into consumer-goods markets at the end of the war with vast sums of liquidity to bid up the prices of goods.

gress passed the Employment Act of 1946, the primary purpose of which was to establish the policy of government action and responsibility for creation of economic well-being. Specifically, the act declared it was the responsibility of the federal government and its agencies to:

1. Foster full employment

2. Provide for stable prices

3. Foster economic growth

Two specific policies, monetary policy and fiscal policy, fall within the scope of the act. In this chapter, we will view the purpose and function of each of the two policy tools, and examine the means by which it is hypothesized they affect economic activity. We do this, not to evaluate their effectiveness, but to measure their impact upon securities markets.

Securities Markets and Stabilization Policies The impact of both monetary policy and fiscal policy is transmitted through the securities markets. In this respect, securities markets are the media that serve to transmit the policy. What the North Atlantic is to a modern ocean liner, the securities markets are to both monetary and fiscal policy. Our thrust is the securities markets and not the stabilization policy, but we shall have to view the stabilization policies in order to examine their imprint upon the market.

MONETARY POLICY

Monetary policy is the actions taken to control economic activity through changes in the money supply. It is also defined as the actions taken by the nation's central bank, the Federal Reserve, to change money balances in the hands of the public. A simple explanation of the impact of the policy would suggest that the Federal Reserve ("Fed") attempts to control spending (and aggregate demand) by controlling the major spendable asset, money. But it should be clear to you that changes in the nation's money supply change security-market conditions, principally the structure of interest rates.

Before we examine this important relationship, we should examine very briefly the Federal Reserve System and its monetary powers.

The Federal Reserve System The Federal Reserve System came about with the Federal Reserve Act in December 1913. Its primary function at that time was to provide for an elastic currency—one whose supply changed with changing needs—and to prevent periodic bank panics, which had become almost generic to the banking industry.

It is important to note that Congress *did not* commission the Federal Reserve System to attempt to control the nation's economy through changes in the money supply. The original purpose of the Federal Reserve System was backward-looking, to cure past ills. The story of the Fed's acquisition of its three tools of control over the nation's volume of demand deposits— its money supply—is in effect the story of the Federal Reserve's increasing influence over the economy as well as its banking system. We shall discuss, in turn, the three tools of control over the money supply, and the circumstances under which the Federal Reserve acquired them. Please keep in mind that all three affect directly and indirectly the volume of demand deposits— money—held by the spending public.*

Changes in the Discount Rate   The discount rate, actually the rediscount rate,† is the rate of interest charged by the Federal Reserve banks to their member-bank customers.

The discount window is a source of new funds to the banking system, and therefore a source of demand deposits for bank customers. If the Federal Reserve banks want to foster more bank credit, and therefore a larger volume of demand deposits, they will lower the discount rate. This action makes bank credit looser and money more available.‡ The framers of the Federal Reserve Act anticipated a symmetrical occurrence when the discount rate is raised—that bank lending, and therefore the creation and use of demand deposits, would be discouraged.

If indeed the change in the discount rate was intended to be a tool of monetary control—some argue that it was supposed to be a helping device rather than a regulatory one—it has not proved to be a powerful and efficient one. Some monetary scholars have suggested that the change in the discount rate is a public verification by the Federal Reserve of a change in monetary-policy direction made after the fact. Many Fed-watchers do rely upon this "announcement effect" of changes in the discount rate, but not many rely

---

*We shall not belabor the point, as some do, that demand deposits in commercial banks constitute the major portion of the nation's money supply. Demand deposits meet all the criteria of money. It is not necessary, as many believe, for a government authority to create money. The commercial banks of the nation, all in the private sector, create some 80 percent of the nation's money, demand deposits.

†The discount window, the mechanism for member bank borrowing, is sometimes called the rediscount window, because it was anticipated when the act was written that banks in dire need of funds would take their customers' paper, which had already been discounted once, and discount it again.

‡Actually, the Federal Reserve banks will discount paper for member banks only if member banks can prove dire need for the borrowed funds to meet a deposit drain from some *unanticipated* source. The discount window in effect makes it easier for banks to get out of trouble. But the process of helping member banks get out of trouble does increase the money supply.

upon the efficacy of the discount rate for sensitive control of the supply of money and spending rates by the general public.

Change in the discount rate was the only tool of monetary control contained in the original Federal Reserve Act, and since it is the weakest tool, some scholars use this as evidence that Congress intended that the Federal Reserve System only facilitate, not regulate, monetary activity.

Changes in Reserve Requirements   Banks that are members of the Federal Reserve System must maintain reserves against deposits. These reserves are kept on deposit at Federal Reserve banks. The reserves lessen the amount of loans that banks can make out of deposits, and therefore lessen the volume of demand deposits credited with loan proceeds. The money supply, and therefore potential spending, is below what it would be without the required setting aside of reserves. The principle is an inverse one: the greater the reserve requirement, the smaller the resulting loans and demand deposits.

The story of the Fed's acquisition of changes in the reserve requirement is an interesting one. Despite the advent of the Great Depression in the 1930s, gold continued to flow into the United States to escape the gathering war clouds of Europe. This massive gold inflow posed problems for the monetary authorities. They anticipated that these gold flows, deposited in U.S. banks, would set off a round of lending and spending that would turn economic depression into rampant inflation.

In order to sterilize the gold inflows—to prevent them from being lent to the U.S. economy and turned into demand deposits—the Board of Governors of the Federal Reserve System asked Congress for permission to raise the reserve requirements of member banks.

Congress responded by giving the Federal Reserve, in the Banking Act of 1935, the power to raise reserve requirements by 100 percent of what they were then. The Fed still has this power, and can change reserve requirements within the following ranges:

Demand deposits	10%–20%
Time deposits	5%–10%

Changing the reserve requirement, although powerful in impact, has not proved to be a flexible tool of control of bank loans and demand deposits. Its flexibility is limited by the fact that it cannot be used frequently enough to form the major tool of control. Bankers cannot physically keep track of, say, three reserve-requirement changes in one day. An indication of its ineffectiveness and inflexibility is the fact that reserve requirements were changed only once between 1969 and 1975. This powerful tool, then, is used infrequently by the Federal Reserve authorities to correct (or announce) a new and permanent level of operations.

Open-Market
Operations
If changes in the discount rate lack power, and changes in reserve requirements lack flexibility, *and if* these were the only tools the Fed had to control the money supply and aggregate spending, economic stability would indeed be a difficult mission to accomplish. But the Fed does possess a tool that has both the flexibility and the power to affect the stock of money and spending patterns. This tool is open-market operations. Its workings are perhaps the easiest to understand of the Fed's policies, and yet, for some reason, monetary authorities have compounded it beyond all reason.

In open-market operations, the Fed exchanges a monetary asset, claims upon itself, for U.S. government securities in the hands of the public. This is simple enough. The Fed replaces a nonspendable asset, U.S. government bonds, in the hands of the spending public with a spendable asset. The result in all probability is that the public will on net balance begin spending and indeed increase the level of national income.

The principle is symmetrical. If inflationary pressures exist—that is, if the spending public is trying to buy more than the economy can produce—the Fed can sterilize spending power, and thus take pressure off prices, by replacing spendable money in the hands of the public with nonspendable U.S. government bonds. If you grasp this principle, you now understand the principle of open-market operations. Admittedly, the process by which the Fed exchanges money for U.S. government bonds is a bit more complicated, but not much more.

Dealing through private securities dealers, the Federal Reserve buys U.S. government bonds (gives up money) when it wants to stimulate economic activity. The purchase of bonds is paid for with a check drawn on the Fed, a cashier's check. The securities dealer deposits the check in his bank. To this bank, the check represents a new lending capacity. This bank starts the lending process, providing the credit, and demand deposits as a by-product, to a depressed economy.

The opposite is true also. If the Fed desires to fight inflationary pressures, it sells U.S. government bonds to the public. The bonds are paid for with checks drawn on commercial-bank demand deposits. This process destroys money (checking accounts) and, along with money, it destroys aggregate demand. Hence, the principle is symmetrical, permitting the Fed to fight both recession and inflation.

Open-market operations are both flexible and powerful. The money supply can be changed by 1 cent or $1 billion *at the option of the Federal Reserve System*. This flexibility is not found in the other two tools of monetary policy. In addition, the Federal Reserve has the power to inflict its will upon the economy through open-market operations. Such is not the case with the other tools of monetary policy.

In summary of the three tools of monetary policy, we can say the following:

1. All three attempt to control the money supply and aggregate spending.
2. Changes in the discount rate are not powerful. Changes in the reserve requirement are not flexible.
3. Changes in open-market operations are both powerful and flexible.

THE IMPACT OF MONETARY POLICY ON SECURITIES MARKETS

The exercise of the tools of monetary policy by the Federal Reserve has powerful effects upon securities markets, and the trading in them.

The primary impact upon securities markets is through effects upon the *structure of interest rates*. The impact upon interest rates is through the supply of money (remembering that interest rates are the price for money) and the supply of fixed-return securities in the market.

Impact Upon Interest Rates
Changes in the Supply of Money. In a simple yet realistic way, we could argue that "the" interest rate is created by the demand for, and supply of, money balances. Any major shift in the supply of money will change the price of money, the interest rate, in exactly the same way that a major change in the supply of petroleum relative to given forces of demand will affect its price. If there are inflationary pressures in the economy, the Fed desires to "cool it off," so it will reduce the supply of money, driving up its price and, optimally, discouraging additional borrowing to buy and build. It is posited that the opposite is also true; that is, if there is unemployment of resources, then the Fed can increase the supply of money in the hands of the public and the banking system, hoping that at its new and lower price, the spending public will borrow the funds to buy and build, thus stimulating economic activity.

There are volumes written about the *degree of sensitivity* of changes in economic activity to changes in the interest rate.* But most agree, and indeed Federal Reserve monetary policy is predicated upon it, that the resulting spending (nonspending) that comes from a decrease (increase) in interest rates as a result of a change in the supply of money changes economic conditions.

Changes in the Supply of Securities. The second impact of monetary policy in the securities markets is through changes in the supply of government securities in the hands of the public. As the Federal Reserve System engages in the trading of U.S. government securities, it is constantly changing the quantity in the hands of the investing public.

---

*Economists use the term *elasticity* to indicate the degree of sensitivity between changes in two economic variables.

When the Fed is trying to stimulate economic activity, it purchases government bonds, replacing them with liquidity, and thereby presenting to the investing public, simultaneously, the need to purchase other securities for their portfolios and the liquidity with which to purchase them. This action, on net balance, encourages the channeling of savings into new capital goods and services.

Ultimate Effect of Monetary Policy At the margin, the Federal Reserve is the single largest force in securities markets. Participants in the market usually have their eyes on the Federal Reserve System, trying to anticipate its moves. The ability to anticipate Federal Reserve actions may mean large returns, for it results in successful prediction of the direction interest rates are going to take.

Consider Figure 23.1, which is a copy of a *Wall Street Journal* story detailing the surge in the money supply for the week ended January 5, 1977. Read the story carefully, and note how the reporter explores the possible implications of the increase in the money supply. In this particular set of circumstances, the reporter suggests that the surge in the money supply may actually result in a tightened stance by the Federal Reserve. This is what he means when he writes:

> As a result, short-term interest rates pressed upwards after the announcement on fears that continued steep growth in the money supply could prompt a tighter Federal Reserve credit policy.

Thus, the reporter speculates that the Fed is *selling* securities, adding to market supply, driving prices down and interest rates up. This is significant, for if the Fed continues its stance of driving short-term rates up, the impact will be transmitted to all maturity sectors, and with increasing interest rates across the board, spending will be discouraged.

The Federal Reserve, in trying to steer the nation's economy to full employment without inflationary pressures, has a major impact upon the nation's securities markets. Financial managers, investors, and securities dealers are constantly interested in the activities of the Federal Reserve for this reason.

FISCAL POLICY

Definition Fiscal policy* is defined as all actions taken with U.S. government *revenues and expenditures* to affect economic activity. We emphasize

---

*The term *fiscal* is frequently used as a synonym for *financial*, but its correct definition is the one given above. The term comes from the Latin word *fiscus*, which means "basket." Roman tax collectors carried baskets in which they gathered tax receipts. Hence, the term became associated with government finances.

FIGURE 23.1 A Report on the Implications of Changes in the Money Supply. (*Source: Wall Street Journal, January 14, 1977, p. 21.*)

Money Supply's M1 M2 Gauges Climb Sharply

Size of Boosts Is Surprising; Business Loans Drop at Major New York Banks

By a WALL STREET JOURNAL *Staff Reporter*

NEW YORK—The nation's basic money supply, known as M1, jumped $2 billion in the week ended Jan. 5. A broader measure of money, M2, rocketed $4.1 billion, according to figures released yesterday through the Federal Reserve Bank of New York.

Other figures showed that commercial and industrial loans on the books of leading New York banks tumbled more than $1.26 billion in the week ended Wednesday. About two-thirds of the decline, however, was due to a drop in holdings of brokers' acceptances, or trade bills.

The big increase in the money supply surprised dealers in the short-term money market. Most had expected increases but not of the size reported. As a result, short-term interest rates pressed upward after the announcement on fears that continued steep growth in the money supply could prompt a tighter Federal Reserve credit policy.

The Fed estimated that M1 averaged a seasonally adjusted $314.3 billion in the Jan. 5 week, up from $312.3 billion the previous week. M2 averaged $744.3 billion, up from $740.2 billion.

Key Indicator

M1 is the total of private demand, or checking account, deposits plus currency in circulation. M2 consists of currency plus all private deposits except those large ones represented by certificates.

Because the money supply represents funds readily available for buying goods and services, it is considered a key determinant of the economy. Too slow a growth in the supply could foster sluggish economic condi-

tions, economists say, while too fast a growth could renew inflationary fires.

The Fed had set an annual growth target of 3% to 7% for M1 for the last two months of 1976. The Fed set a 9½% to 13½% growth rate for M2 in the period.

Within Goals

Figures released yesterday indicated that the Fed actually achieved a 4.1% growth rate for M1 in the period and 11.3% for M2. Thus, the actual growth rates were within the specified target ranges.

The target figures for the December-through-January period aren't yet known, but analysts generally believe they weren't drastically changed from the November-to-December rates.

If that's the case, the Fed would have to slow the M1's recent fast upward move. The figures indicated that in December alone M1 grew at an 8.1% annual rate. M2 grew at a 12.3% rate in December, near the higher end of the two-month target.

Separately, the Fed reported that commercial and industrial loans at New York banks dropped $1.26 billion in the week ended Wednesday. That compared with a $101 million decline the previous week and with a $671 million drop in the like 1976 week.

According to preliminary estimates, about $800 million of the decline was caused by a reduction in bankers' acceptances which normally are considered market instruments but are counted as loans when held by banks.

Holdings Boosted

Banks had sharply increased their holdings of acceptances in the closing months of last year to dress up their financial sheets and to take advantage of certain tax benefits.

Other figures indicated that Citibank's prime rate formula today will call for a base lending fee of 6¼%, unchanged from the previous week. The formula is pegged to movements in short-term interest rates in the open market.

The money supply figures sparked a sharp price drop and rate rise late yesterday in money market securities.

For example, the latest 13-week Treasury bills closed at 4.54% bid on some quotation sheets, up from a low of 4.50% earlier in the day. The companion 26-week issue jumped to a bid of 4.81% from 4.70% earlier in the day.

483

both revenues and expenditures because changes in each can have powerful effects upon economic activity.

First we shall outline the impact of government revenues and expenditures on economic activity, in order to view the policy implications. Next, we shall treat the impact of each upon securities markets, our central interest.

Fiscal Policy as a Stabilization Tool

The focal point of fiscal policy is the control of the rate of spending by the public. Other things equal, if the economy is depressed—if all resources are not being employed*—one way to try to move the economy back to full employment is to stimulate spending.

Government Spending. There are two ways that fiscal policy can be used to stimulate spending. One obvious way is for the government to distribute money to people. Although not in highly obvious ways, this method has been used frequently. Examples are New Deal programs such as the Public Works Administration and the Works Projects Administration, which were thinly disguised income-distribution programs to get income into the hands of the unemployed in order to stave off poverty. More recent such programs include the Job Corps and the food-stamp program. Note that the common thread in all these programs is the distribution of income in the form of money or goods to those who are not employed or are underemployed. The use of this income would stimulate economic activity. Increases in Social Security benefits as well as the various veterans' programs, although not intended primarily as income-distribution programs, have the same effect.

Tax Remissions and Reductions. A second way for fiscal policy to stimulate spending is to reduce the tax burden and hope that the tax reduction (effectively an increase in personal income) will be spent and thereby add to effective demand.

An interesting example of tax reduction as a tool of stabilization policy was the tax cut proposed by President Kennedy in 1963. The president tried to sell the tax reduction on the basis of its self-financing nature. That is, Kennedy argued, the tax reduction would set off the following chain of events:

1. Reduce income taxes, run a deficit.

---

*We normally express unemployment in terms of the labor force, but the unemployment of any one of the factors of production (land, labor, capital, or entrepreneurship) results in economic waste.

2. People spend.

3. Spending causes incomes to rise.

4. Because of the progressive nature of the income tax, tax revenues will rise faster than incomes.

5. The "tax take" that results from rising incomes will more than offset the original deficit used to start the chain of events.

This was the first time that this argument was used for a tax-reduction program, and it took some time for the people and Congress to accept the argument.

Congress did accept the arguments put forth by the administration, and reduced income taxes. There was initial evidence that the tax cut did stimulate spending, but the final conclusion on its effectiveness was greatly clouded by the buildup for the Vietnam War in 1965 and 1966.

A recent example of a tax cut to stimulate economic activity was the tax cut of 1974, originated to counter the most serious economic turndown in the economy since the Great Depression.

THE IMPACT OF FISCAL POLICY ON THE ECONOMY

The program and desired thrust of fiscal policy, either increased spending or reduced taxes, is on spending patterns of consumers, although it does have a major impact on securities markets. Increased government spending and/or reduced taxes usually means that the federal budget will be unbalanced; that is, it will run a deficit. Deficits are financed by borrowing, and borrowing is represented by the issuance of bonds. Table 23.1 shows the dollar volume of gross public debt outstanding at the end of each year, 1973–1977, which ex-

TABLE 23.1 Gross Public Debt Outstanding, 1973–1977 Inclusive. (End of Year; Billions of Dollars)

	GROSS PUBLIC DEBT	ANNUAL CHANGE
1973	$469.9	
1974	$492.7	$22.8
1975	$576.6	$83.9
1976	$653.5	$76.9
1977	$718.9	$65.4

Source: Federal Reserve Bulletin

tended from July 1975 through June 1976. During these years, the volume of public debt securities increased annually on the average by 62.5 billion.

Table 23.2 is a highly simplified representation of the use of changes in government expenditures as a tool of fiscal policy. The table answers this question: Should increases (decreases) in government spending be used to change economic activity in recessionary (inflationary) periods? The federal government has been very active in financial markets during the period.

TABLE 23.2 Uses of Changes in Government Spending as a Tool of Fiscal Policy

	STATE OF THE ECONOMY	
TYPE OF POLICY	RECESSION	INFLATION
Expansion	Increase spending	Increase spending
Contraction	Decrease spending	Decrease spending

It is clear from Table 23.2 that prescribed policies in the two phases of the business cycle are mutually exclusive. That is, increases in government spending should be limited to the recession phase of the business cycle, and decreases should be limited to the inflation stage of the cycle.

Other things equal, increases in government spending tend to put upward pressure on the price level, and one important price is "the" interest rate.

Changes in Government Revenues The intake side of federal finances can also be manipulated to influence economic activity. In general, the economy can be stimulated in recessionary periods by reducing taxes, resulting in reduced government revenues. The government hopes that the income left—not taxed away—will be used to increase spending in the private sector, which increases aggregate demand.

The opposite is true during periods of inflation. One characteristic of inflation is inability of the economy to produce the goods and services effectively being demanded. The gap between scarcity of goods and services and demand for them is manifested in rising prices, the major characteristic of inflation. When these conditions prevail, prudent fiscal policy dictates that taxes be increased to "drain off" excess aggregate demand.

Table 23.3 attempts to show these points. It answers the question: Should changes in government revenues be used to change economic activity in inflationary (recessionary) periods?

TABLE 23.3 Uses of Changes in Government Revenue
as a Fiscal-Policy Tool

	STATE OF THE ECONOMY	
TYPE OF POLICY	RECESSION	INFLATION
Expansion	Decrease revenue	Decrease revenue
Contraction	Increase revenue	Increase revenue

Prudent fiscal policy dictates that revenues be manipulated to influence economic activity. There are only two sources of government revenues: taxes and borrowing. When Congress is unwilling or unable to increase taxes, then government operations must be financed through deficits, and deficits in turn are financed through the issuance of debt. Deficits have become more prevalent in recent years. Table 23.4 presents budget data for the 20-year period 1956–75.

TABLE 23.4 Federal Budget Data, Fiscal Years 1956–75
($ billion)

YEAR	RECEIPTS	OUTLAYS	SURPLUS OR DEFICIT (−)	PUBLIC DEBT (GROSS)[a]
1956	77.0	7.6	4.4	276.7
1957	84.5	83.3	1.1	270.6
1958	81.7	89.0	− 7.3	283.0
1959	87.5	95.5	− 8.0	290.9
1960	95.1	94.3	1.8	290.4
1961	97.2	99.5	− .7	296.5
1962	101.8	107.6	− 5.7	304.0
1963	109.7	113.7	− 4.0	310.1
1964	115.5	120.3	− 4.8	318.7
1965	119.7	122.4	− 2.7	317.3
1966	130.9	134.6	− 3.8	319.9
1967	149.5	158.2	− 8.7	326.2
1968	153.7	178.8	−25.1	347.6
1969	187.8	184.5	3.2	368.2
1970	193.7	196.6	− 2.8	389.2
1971	188.4	211.4	−23.0	424.1
1972	208.6	231.8	−23.2	449.3
1973	232.2	246.5	−14.3	469.9
1974	264.9	268.4	− 3.5	492.7
1975	281.0	324.6	−43.6	576.6

[a]Calendar years: totals may not sum due to rounding.

Source: Federal Reserve Bulletin.

THE IMPACT OF FISCAL POLICY ON SECURITIES MARKETS

The impact of fiscal policy on securities markets is manifested in two forms. These are (1) changes in the rate of government spending, and (2) changes in government demand for funds. We shall discuss both in turn in order to see that they have their confluence in their impact upon interest rates, and therefore upon securities markets.

It will greatly aid your understanding of these forces if you keep in mind that we are viewing these from the perspective of the government and the management of *its* financial affairs.

Changes in Government Expenditures The rate at which the federal government spends money greatly affects economic activity in the private sector. In periods of less-than-full employment of all available resources, increased government spending can quicken the pulse of private-sector spending. Increased Social Security and veterans' benefits are examples of ways new income can be injected into the economy. This newly injected income is spent in successive waves, and raises the aggregate level of national income.

The condition of the economy and the timing of the injections greatly affect the success of this form of fiscal policy. These same factors affect the impact on the structure of interest rates.

The federal government is the largest single transactor in the economy. Its operations on both its income and expenditure sides have primary and secondary effects. The primary effects are upon the level of national income, and are the principal purpose of fiscal policy. The secondary effects are upon securities markets.

Changes in Government Demand for Funds At the margin, the federal government is the largest single borrower in securities markets. If it increases its borrowings, there is the *threat* that it will "crowd out" other borrowers, corporate borrowers hoping to use bond-sale proceeds to build plant and equipment. There seems to be a strong correlation between federal deficits and high securities-markets interest rates.

As the nation's largest single borrower, the federal government dramatically influences the demand for loanable funds at the margin. As federal deficits increase, and the federal government borrows, interest rates reflect the increased demand for funds.

The management of the federal debt has a direct and powerful impact upon the entire structure of interest rates in securities markets. The line of causation runs thus:

Changes in supply of securities in the hands of the public	→	Changes in prices of securities	→	Changes in yields on government securities	→	Changes in yields on all securities	→	Changes in the structure of interest rates

The relationship between changes in the volume of government securities and interest rates is not highly complicated, but does bear some examination. Assume that the Treasury issues new bonds. The supply of government bonds in the hands of the public rises. Other things equal, the price of existing government bonds falls. This decrease in bond prices is a manifestation of increased interest rates.

Why? Assume a bond had been issued five years ago with a 5 percent coupon attached. This means that the government promised to pay the bearer of the bond $50 each year.* That is, the government borrowed $1,000, the face value of the bond, and agreed to pay 5 percent for the use of the money:

$$.05 \times \$1,000 = \$50$$

Now assume that the federal government borrows new sums of money. This new demand for funds causes their price to rise. The government issues additional bonds, but this time, it must promise to pay $60 to the bearer of each bond:

$$.06 \times \$1,000 = \$60$$

The 5 percent bond is still in the market. In fact, both the 5 percent and the 6 percent bonds are now in the market. But who would buy the 5 percent bond when he can get 6 percent for the same $1,000 investment? No one would, of course.

But there is a way of adjusting the price of the 5 percent bond to make it give a 6 percent return to its buyer. How much would the 5 percent bond sell for in order to make it give a 6 percent return? Keep in mind that the annual income stream remains $50 so the question is, $50 is 6 percent of what number?

$$.06x = \$50$$

$$x = \frac{\$50}{.06}$$

$$x = \$833.33$$

---

*For purposes of simplification, we are assuming that the bonds in this example are perpetuities; that is, they have no maturity.

In other words, you would be indifferent between purchasing a 5 percent bond for $833.33 or a 6 percent bond for $1,000. In either case, the return on your investment would be 6 percent.

From the example, we can see an inverse relationship between changes in market rates of interest and changes in market values of bonds. Note in the example above that increased demand for funds gave rise to increased interest rates, which in turn reduced the market value of existing bonds. Had the government moderated its demand for debt funds—had it been redeeming bonds—"the" interest rate would have fallen, and the market value of existing bonds would have risen. For example, assume that the market rate of interest has fallen to 3 percent, and you hold the 5 percent bond in our previous example. What is your bond worth?

$$.03x = \$50$$
$$x = \frac{\$50}{.03}$$
$$x = \$1,666.66$$

The bond at 3 percent is worth twice what it was worth at 6 percent.

Thus, the impact of deficit financing on securities markets is twofold. If the demand for funds to finance the deficit is great, interest rates will rise, and if interest rates rise, the market value of existing debt instruments will fall.

The change in market value of debt instruments in response to changing interest rates is limited by maturity of the debt. At maturity, bonds are redeemed for par value. The closer to maturity a bond is, the smaller the impact on its market value a change in interest rates will have. This is illustrated in Figure 23.2. From the diagram, it is clear that regardless of the degree of changes in interest rates in securities markets, these changes have smaller impacts upon the market prices of bonds as the bond approaches its maturity.

The timing of fiscal operations also has a large impact upon securities-market conditions. If federal expenditure requirements are concentrated into short periods of time, the federal government tends to bid the cost of funds upward.*

There can be little doubt that the large volume of U.S. government securities in existence is both a hindrance and a help for the economy. On the one hand, federal fiscal operations do tend to bid interest rates up, and to

---

*Federally regulated depository institutions—commercial banks and savings and loan associations—have ceilings on rates they can pay depositors. When rates on U.S. government securities exceed these ceiling rates, funds tend to flow from depository institutions into the government-securities markets. This development has caused great dissatisfaction among some bank and savings-association officers.

FIGURE 23.2 Relationship Between Changes in Market Values of Bonds and Market Rates of Interest.

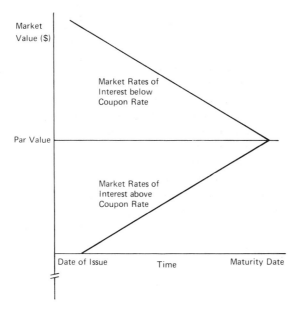

create pressures in securities markets that otherwise would not be there. But on the other hand, the large volume of U.S. government securities does provide a means of injecting into securities portfolios both liquidity and safety that, again, would not otherwise be there. We have discussed, for example, the role that government securities play in the transmission of policies of the Federal Open Market Committee in implementing monetary policy. With respect to the role that U.S. government securities play in the management of a financial portfolio, it has been said that if we did not have U.S. government securities, we would have to invent them.

SUMMARY

In this chapter, we have viewed the impact of national stabilization policies on financial markets. The purpose of the two types of stabilization policy is to influence economic activity to establish full-employment equilibrium in the economy. The two stabilization policies are monetary policy and fiscal policy.

Monetary policy is implemented by and through the Federal Reserve System. Its basic function is to influence economic activity through changes in the money supply. Monetary policy has important implications for financial markets, since the major tool of monetary policy is open-market operations. Open-market operations are transmitted to the economy by the purchase and sale of U.S. government securities, which in turn changes yields and interest rates.

Fiscal policy, the other stabilization policy, is concerned with manipulating federal government income and expenditures to influence economic activity. But again, these policy actions have impacts upon securities markets. Increased government spending financed by government borrowing tends to put stresses on the entire structure of interest rates. In general, interest rates and bond prices are inversely proportional. That is, when interest rates rise, old bond prices fall. When interest rates fall, old bond prices rise. And price action in the bond market is followed by price action in the stock markets.

Securities-market traders and participants keep a careful eye on formulation of the two types of stabilization policy. This surely attests to the important relationship between stabilization policy and securities-market conditions.

PROBLEMS

1. Consult the most recent *Federal Reserve Bulletin* and determine the discount rate currently in effect. Graph the discount rate for the most recent ten-year period, with the discount rate on the vertical axis and time on the horizontal. Interpret the graph in words.

2. The minutes of the Federal Open Market Committee (FOMC) are published periodically in the *Federal Reserve Bulletin*. Consult the most recent one, and read it carefully. Answer the following questions pertaining to the FOMC meeting:

a. What type of economic data were presented to document the overall condition of the economy?

b. The last paragraph of the minutes always contains the "consensus," the summary statement of the current condition of the economy, and the instructions to the manager of the System Open Market Account. What was the state of the economy during the period you have consulted? What were the instructions to the manager of the System Open Market Account?

c. How many members of the Federal Open Market Committee voted for the policy outlined in the consensus? How many voted against it?

3. Consult the Treasury Bulletin and list federal government expenditures monthly for the most recent year. Are they growing or diminishing? What is their net effect upon the liquidity of the economy?

4. Explain in your own words how, other things equal, deficit financing affects the level of rates in securities markets.

5. In your own words, explain the inverse relationship between the price of fixed-return securities (bonds) and their effective yield. Does this relationship have any impact on aggregate economic activity? Explain.

Emerging Areas
of Finance

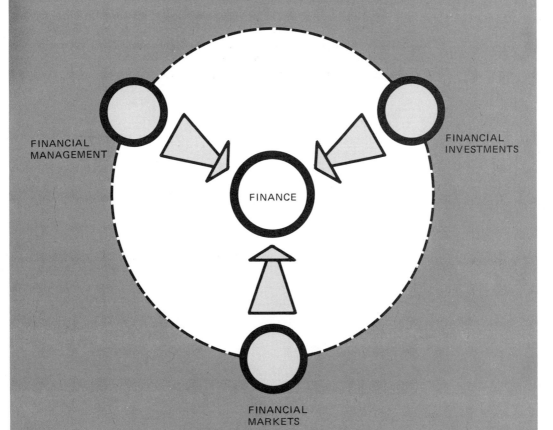

It is appropriate that the final part of this book be anticipative in nature. In Part V, we view areas of finance that are expected to be of increasing importance.

In Chapter 24, the treatment of financial issues germane to small business is undertaken. Although the United States is known as a nation of big business, small businesses are by far the most prevalent in the U.S. economy. Their financial problems bear consideration. In Chapter 25, issues emanating from international financial relationships are discussed. International finance is perhaps one of the most rapidly growing subareas of the discipline of finance.

The common denominator of Chapters 26 and 27 is that they treat the future development of issues that cut across the entire field of finance. The central theme of Chapter 26 is that, more and more, finance is becoming an integrated, homogeneous body of knowledge and skills that is less and less divisible into specialized areas. We attribute much of this development to the advent of the capital asset pricing model. The integration of finance also results partially from the increased usage of sophisticated financial analytic techniques in solving financial problems.

Finally, in Chapter 27, we present a series of developments in financial practice that we anticipate will come about. These are discussed under the headings of financial management, investments, and markets. The major theme of these future developments is the increased sophistication of financial techniques, practices, and institutions.

24

Small-Business Finance

Both the traditional and the contemporary approaches to finance virtually ignore small business. The traditional approach asserts that finance is concerned with either cash management or acquisition of funds, or both. It emphasizes the following areas: (1) "corporation" finance; (2) problems that arise only infrequently during a corporation's life cycle, such as consolidation, recapitalization, and reorganization; and (3) long-term financing. The biggest shortcoming of the traditional approach is that it provides only a descriptive treatment of procedures and of financial institutions with emphasis on large-scale business operations.

The contemporary or problem-centered approach to financial management involves a systematic analysis of the internal management of a firm, with emphasis on flow of funds in the corporate structure. The financial manager is viewed as making interrelated decisions about sources and uses of funds. Still, the thrust is toward large-scale business operations with tasks too numerous for any one person to handle.

Current textbooks in finance are a blend or combination of the traditional and the contemporary approaches. Descriptive and institutional material is used to provide content for both theory and financial decision models. However, such approaches to financing as found in general textbooks on financial management are oriented to the successful, well-established big business concern.

By comparison, there is a paucity of published material that is relevant to the small, fledgling firm. Such enterprises have some prevailing economic characteristics. This chapter is concerned with (1) small business in perspective, (2) characteristics of small business, (3) unique financial problems, and (4) sources of capital for small business.

SMALL BUSINESS IN PERSPECTIVE

It is estimated that there are approximately 10 million business firms in the United States. Of these, about 9.5 million are classified as small.* Thus, small businesses constitute 95 percent of all business enterprises in the nation. There are more small business firms than there are farms in the United States. Yet consider for a moment the vast amount of money the government has spent and is spending on agriculture, compared to the amount on small business. The Department of Agriculture has employees in practically every county in the nation. The Small Business Administration (SBA), by comparison, has less than 100 field officers in the country to serve small business.

Small-scale, local entrepreneurs are important to our economic development. First, they foster competition and aid in the restriction of monopolies. Second, small firms are more oriented to developing products to supply immediate consumer needs. Finally, our economic future depends upon the creation of "homegrown" enterprises, nearly all of which will be, initially at least, small.

The definition of small business depends upon its industry. Manufacturing firms are considered small if average employment in the preceding four calendar quarters did not exceed 250 persons, including employees of any affiliates. A manufacturing firm is defined as large if average employment was more than 1,500. Between 250 and 1,500 employees, there are varying standards for the particular industry. A wholesale firm is classed as small if yearly sales do not exceed $5 million. Retail and service firms are classed as

---

*Clifford M. Baumback, Kenneth Lawyer, and Pearce C. Kelley, *How To Organize and Operate a Small Business* (Englewood Cliffs, N.J.: Prentice-Hall, 1973), p. 3.

small if annual sales do not exceed $1 million. Finally, construction firms are classed as small if annual receipts are not more than $5 million.*

CHARACTERISTICS OF SMALL BUSINESS

Most small businesses rely on equity capital from savings and family sources. The "Mom and Pop" grocery store is a typical example. Such firms have high implicit labor costs and borrowing costs (unless borrowing from relatives at little or no interest). If such costs were recognized, they would become explicit costs and many small firms would go out of business.

Small businessmen tend to rely too much on their accountants, bankers, and lawyers. In fact, many small businessmen become captives of their accountants. In such a case, the accountant is "calling the shots." When the owner-operator relies too heavily on his banker, then the banker is managing the firm by giving advice to the businessman. Likewise, lawyers may also tend to operate the business by proxy. We are not saying that a businessman should not have an accountant, a banker, and a lawyer. We think he should. We are simply stating that the businessman should make his own decisions.

Because of the concentration upon production problems and day-to-day management problems, the small businessman tends to do very little long-range financial planning. Sometimes the larger firm is also guilty of not planning for the future. Risks are apparent when the business is allowed to take the course of least resistance. Since a business is a viable entity, it must be managed according to overall financial plans.

Risks in Small Business There are many risks inherent in beginning and operating a small business. Among the major risks are these:

1. No geographic diversification

2. No product diversification

3. The impact of business conditions

4. Smallness

5. Thin management, with little margin for error

6. New products and new service areas

7. Lack of records and ignorance of their use

---

*U.S. Small Business Administration, *SBA, What It Is . . . What It Does* (Washington, D.C.: U.S. Government Printing Office, 1973), p. 2.

UNIQUE FINANCING PROBLEMS

Certain small businesses have such advantages as easier entry into an industry, fewer government restrictions, and more flexibility in decision making. Although there are some advantages of being small, ease of financing is not one of them.

Financing is one of the first problems encountered in starting a small business. In fact, a traditional complaint of the small businessman is the financing problem. Undercapitalization (overtrading) and lack of adequate operating capital are typical. Every new firm, after organization of necessary productive resources, begins operations with what should be the worst cash-flow circumstances of its existence—that is, heavy expenses and little or no income for a period of up to three years.* The situation is even worse for the small business, which may experience negative cash flows during the initial period of operations.

Compounding the financing problem of small firms is the fact that many such firms are privately or family-owned and operated. An owner-operator of a firm is involved in several key areas of management, such as sales, production, and finance. As a result, financial management is often neglected because the owner-operator possesses neither the capabilities nor the time to administer properly the financial policies and procedures that are essential to a small business. Objective thinking and analysis are difficult when many other pressing duties must be done.

The small firm lacks access to the capital markets. Debt financing is difficult to obtain for new small-business ventures. Few institutional investors will lend money to new ventures because of the high number of past failures. Commercial banks may participate in short-term loans if they are adequately secured by assets such as real estate, collectible accounts receivable, or marketable raw materials. However, new small businesses seldom have access to term loans from commercial banks, life insurance companies, or other capital institutions. They are faced with the likelihood that intermediate- to long-term financing is unavailable to them.

SOURCES OF CAPITAL

A study of small manufacturers revealed that only two sources of financing were predominant in the financial structures of small firms.† This was true for both initial and growth financing. The two major sources of financing

---

*George W. Summers, *Financing and Initial Operations of New Firms* (Englewood Cliffs, N.J.: Prentice-Hall, 1962), pp. 1–2.

†Ray G. Jones, Jr., "Sources of Initial and Growth Financing for Small Manufacturers" (unpublished doctoral dissertation, Mississippi State University, December 1974), p. 112.

were equity and commercial banks. SBA and "other" debt financing were present to a much lesser degree. Major sources of risk capital financing (venture capitalists, investment companies, and Small Business Investment Companies) were practically nonexistent (less than 1 percent of total financing) in financial structures of the small manufacturer. Industrial aid bond financing provided a scant 1.5 percent of total initial and growth capital. The results of the survey are shown in Tables 24.1 and 24.2.

TABLE 24.1 Sources of Initial Financing for Small Firms

SOURCES OF FINANCING	PERCENTAGE OF FINANCIAL STRUCTURE	
Debt:		
Commercial banks	.251	
SBA	.044	
Industrial aid bonds	.008	
"Other" debt financing	.045	
Total debt		.348
Equity:		
Sole proprietorships	.154	
Partnerships	.101	
Stockholders	.397	
Total equity		.652
Total capital		1.000

Source: 1973 survey by the author of capital needs of small manufacturers.

TABLE 24.2 Sources of Growth Financing for Small Firms

SOURCES OF FINANCING	PERCENTAGE OF FINANCIAL STRUCTURE	
Debt:		
Commercial banks	.335	
SBA	.094	
Industrial aid bonds	.023	
Corporate bonds	.012	
Insurance company	.011	
"Other" debt financing	.042	
Total debt		.517
Equity:		
Sole proprietorship	.104	
Partnership	.095	
Stockholders	.217	
Retained earnings	.067	
Total equity		.483
Total capital		1.000

Source: 1973 survey by the author of capital needs of small manufacturers.

It should be noted that retained earnings provide less than 7 percent of growth financing. However, only 10 percent of the firms surveyed reported the use of retained earnings for growth. Although internally generated funds account for a large portion of all business financing in the United States, external sources of capital are particularly important to the small and expanding business.

Corporate Growth Through Going Public Virtually ignored by small-business management is the selling of corporate securities to the public. As a potential for capital funds, public financing is thought to be the sole province of big companies. Small businessmen give a variety of reasons for their avoidance of public financing. Robert Weaver, Jr., president of an international firm that is involved in the process of corporate growth through going public, sums up as follows the reluctance of small-business managers to use public financing:

1. They do not have a clear picture of the specific advantages;

2. They do not know how to go about getting such financing;

3. They fear that they will lose control of their businesses;

4. They do not want to account to outsiders;

5. They are reluctant to give up a "good thing" and allow others to share it;

6. They think that "now is not the time"; if they wait, they can get more;

7. They believe they are "too small";

8. They do not know where their appeal to the investor lies;

9. They misunderstand the role of the underwriter, and are distressed by the seemingly high fee;

10. They are unfamiliar with and unduly afraid of securities laws and SEC regulations.*

As a matter of fact, equity financing provides specific advantages to the small firm. Such financing furnishes funds in substantial amounts that are not as available from banks or similar sources. Capital may be acquired to finance operations for many years in one step. Equity financing enhances the credit standing of a firm and improves its stability because repayment is not required. All these advantages can be realized without loss of control of the company, which is of paramount concern to the small-business entrepreneur. A primary disadvantage of equity financing is the revelation of confidential data regarding operations. Another important disadvantage is

---

*Robert A. Weaver, Jr., *Initial Public Financing for the Small and Medium Sized Business* (Washington, D.C.: Investment Bankers Association of America, 1969), p. 7.

accountability for one's actions to stockholders, as well as to the Securities and Exchange Commission.

Other equity sources of capital for expanding firms are private backers, Small Business Investment Companies, and investment bankers. Although Small Business Investment Companies (SBIC) may accept greater risks than commercial banks or insurance companies, they charge up to 15 percent interest on some long-term loans.* In addition, SBICs may either purchase stock outright or by convertible debenture, or take debentures with warrants. Also, SBICs may use "put" and "call" options for possible exit from situations that might otherwise have been rejected.

The successful borrower may expect the SBIC to assume a substantial ownership position in the business, although not enough to gain control. Benefits accrue to the owner of the business, however. First, SBIC ownership enhances the credit standing of a small business, because SBIC furnishes managerial aid to operations in which it has invested money. Another benefit is that conversion of debentures by SBIC reduces the indebtedness of a small manufacturer. In some cases, SBICs may be a panacea to the small, growing business as well as the free, private-enterprise, capitalistic economy. After extensive studies, Congress concluded that the greatest threat to mature capitalism is a lack of risk capital financing.† SBICs are intended to fill a void in the financial structure of the United States.

Acquisitions and Mergers

Acquisitions and mergers are sometimes used by small-business entrepreneurs as alternative techniques of financing. Instead of going public, the firm can merge with another firm. By definition, the public has not put a value on the earnings stream of a private firm in the marketplace. Since this has not been done, there is a problem in valuation of the firm. Usually, such a valuation is a compromise among the book value of the firm, arbitrary rates of capitalization of income, and the liquidity value of the firm.

Financing Expansion by Borrowing

Private sources of capital are particularly available to the small businessman if his initial financing is conservative. James T. Cullen, Jr., an associate of the New York Securities Company, lists four general categories of sources of credit. They are, in order of quality:

1. Life insurance companies, trust departments of banks, and most pension funds;

---

*Bernard Greisman, ed., *J. K. Lasser's Business Management Handbook*, 3rd ed. (New York: McGraw-Hill, 1968), p. 60.

†Malcolm Monroe, "Risk Capital Financing: Financing by an SBIC," *Small Business Financing Library*, Vol. IV (Ann Arbor, Mich.: Institute of Continuing Legal Education, 1967), pp. 214–15.

2. Casualty insurance companies and some private pension funds and foundations;

3. Small Business Investment Companies; and

4. Various families, groups of executives, and the investment banker himself.*

Unless a small businessman is willing to offer at least $10 to $15 million in debt securities, he cannot finance via the public market.† Very few life insurance companies make term loans to small businessmen without some equity participation in the firm.‡ A little-known source of private financing, the Ford Foundation, prefers loans in excess of $1 million for a period of about ten years.§ Commercial banks and commercial finance companies then become choices for term loans.

A comprehensive listing of sources of debtor funds for small minority enterprises is found in a publication by the U.S. Department of Commerce. It lists such sources as:

1. Foundations

2. Churches

3. Insurance companies

4. Commercial banks

5. Savings and loan associations

6. Commercial finance or business finance companies¶

A long-term lease may be more economical than borrowing for a small business. A lease has the advantage of leaving limited equity capital for other uses. A distinct disadvantage of leasing is that less flexibility may result. The protective covenants attached to a lease are almost as binding as covenants of a long-term loan.

Some small businessmen resort to a lawyer's office when they cannot qualify for a bank loan or a loan from an insurance company, or from any institutional investor or foundation. Of course, these men cannot make use

---

*James T. Cullen, Jr., "The Role of the Investment Banker," *Small Business Financing Library*, Vol. IV (Ann Arbor, Mich.: Institute of Continuing Legal Education, 1967), pp. 66–67.

†Cullen, "Role of Investment Banker," p. 62.

‡Robinson, *Financing the Small Firm*, pp. 87–89, and the McDonald's case in Chapter 6.

§Gross, *Financing Small Businesses*, p. 153.

¶U.S. Department of Commerce, *The Local Economic Development Corporation* (Washington, D.C.: U.S. Government Printing Office, 1970), pp. 126–80.

of either underwriters or public stock issues. There are five specific sources of debt financing for such businessmen. They are:

1. The national commercial finance company (e.g., Walter Heller and Company, or James Talcott), which is structured for loans to small businesses
2. The local finance company of the same type
3. The Small Business Administration
4. The Small Business Investment Company
5. The local individual or private placement*

Advantages of commercial financial institutions are that (1) funds are readily available, (2) such institutions are more prone to refinance than to foreclose, and (3) no equity is sought. Two disadvantages are that all available assets are pledged as collateral, and high interest rates are charged.

Local commercial finance organizations have more flexibility than national finance companies. The disadvantages of local companies are that (1) less capital is available for loans, (2) additional loans are hard to get, and (3) a hard line is taken concerning minor defaults.

The Small Business Administration (SBA) was established to provide long-term financing to small businesses that are restricted mainly to short-term borrowings. Advantages of SBA loans are (1) no equity dilution, and (2) the lowest interest of the five sources named above. However, disadvantages of SBA financing are substantial (for instance, delay in closing and compliance with regulations) and result in a mass of paper work for the small businessman. Also, the SBA does not like to furnish additional capital if such a need arises. Finally, the SBA requires personal guarantees and attempts to place claims on personal assets of the borrowers.

The advantage of SBIC financing is a willingness to place money in an area of risk if good appreciation potential on the equity exists. Disadvantages of SBIC financing include probable dilution of equity and loss of control.

An advantage of private placement is the opportunity for negotiation between lender and borrower. However, the disadvantages are many. These include (1) no certainty as to amounts or closing times, (2) equity dilution and loss of control, (3) securities and "blue-sky" problems,† and (4) limitations on future funds; further, (5) the lender who is becoming a part of the business may know nothing about its area of operation.

---

*Stephen A. Bromberg, "Legal Problems of Risk Capital Financing," *Small Business Financing Library*, Vol. IV (Ann Arbor, Mich.: Institute of Continuing Legal Education, 1967), p. 239.

†See Chapter 22 for "blue sky" discussion.

In addition to private debt and equity capital, various quasi-public and public plans for financing land and buildings provide a source of funds for the small firm. Certain states have recognized that a need exists for financing the small business and have authorized state programs of financial assistance to manufacturing concerns.

Growth Financing of Small Businesses

After a new business venture is established, the business may level off or grow at a rate that requires raising additional capital. Growth of demand for a company's products is an indicator for expanding production. Although rising demand coupled with expansion of production does not guarantee profits, such factors provide an opportunity for a company to increase earnings. Rising demand may cover losses from managerial errors that occur as a new business grows. Without a rising demand, however, management may be reluctant to expand and take risks in order to increase profits.

Growth of a small business may attract outside investors with venture capital as well as improve economic welfare. In the United States, over 80 percent of manufacturing concerns employ less than 25 people each. For most of these, growth is a primary objective. Small, growth-oriented companies have often led technological advances, such as the shift from vacuum-tube to solid-state electronics. High price–earnings ratios of "growth" stocks, and the willingness of investors to supply venture capital, indicate the importance of corporate growth in the economy.*

Forbes estimates that at least $500 million was available for venture investments at the beginning of the 1970s. Since an initial venture investment rarely exceeds $1 million, such a sum is quite substantial. Venture capitalists prefer high-technology fields, such as computers and service and leisure-time companies.† *Barron's* states, "Venture capitalism is a tough business. . . . The first thing to look for is good people—which means they have to be honest, competent, and committed.‡

Every industry has a life cycle. In its early stage, demand expands rapidly. Opportunities for larger profits are numerous. Venture capital enters the field, and competition is normally, although not always, rife. As a rule, business mortality is high; surviving corporations lay the foundations for success. The needs for and sources of financing the small manufacturer vary as the firm moves from one stage in its development to another. Figure 24.1

---

*David W. Packer, *Resource Acquisition in Corporate Growth* (Cambridge, Mass.: M.I.T. Press, 1964), p. 1.

†"Has the Bear Market Killed Venture Capital?" *Forbes*, June 15, 1970, pp. 28–37.

‡"No Get-Rich-Quick Scheme," *Barron's*, February 12, 1973, p. 3.

FIGURE 24.1 Need vs. Availability of Long-Term Funds Related to Typical Growth Curve. (*Source: James F. Mahar and Dean C. Coddington, New Product Developing—Reducing the Risk, Denver: University of Denver Research Institute, 1961, p. 25.*)

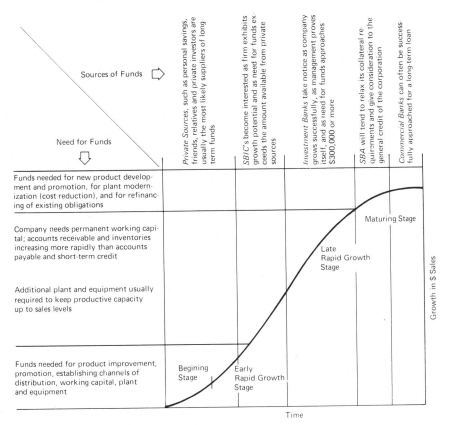

reveals the different types of private investors and financial institutions that tend to underwrite certain stages of small-manufacturer growth. The need for funds is the most critical in the beginning stage, and sources of funds for initial financing are the hardest to obtain in early stages of development.

The typical growth curve indicates that private investors provide long-term funds in the beginning stages of the firm. In the early rapid-growth stage, Small Business Investment Companies generally become interested as the demand exceeds funds supplied by private investors. Investment bankers typically provide funds in the late rapid-growth stage, as the firm continues to be successful. In the maturity stage, the Small Business Administration and commercial banks can be approached for funds.

A "financial gap" (that is, the lack of meshing of needs and resources) has been identified. The financial gap of small manufacturers consists of two parts—one real and one artificial. Firms in the beginning stages and in the early rapid-growth stage are sometimes affected by the real financial gap. New, untried firms are difficult for financial institutions to evaluate. Therefore, such institutions are often reluctant to supply long-term funds to small new firms. Newer firms must rely heavily upon private investors to supply their long-term financial needs. These investors are sometimes uninformed about the industry of the firm, the specific advantages or disadvantages of the firm's product, and the problem of marketing and distribution.

The artificial gap exists mainly in the rapid-growth stage. During this period when the need for funds is greatest, small manufacturers often lack experience in the fund-raising aspects of financial management. Likewise, financial institutions know little or nothing about the management of such firms. It is implied that a knowledge of the financial institutions removes the artificial gap.

SUMMARY

One of the gravest problems confronting a small business is a lack of cash flow (even a negative one) in the early years of its operation (1–3 years). This is usually caused by undercapitalization at the start. Few new businesses plan for adequate working capital in the formative stages. Quite often it is hoped that profits will alleviate this condition. However, unless the small business can get through the first few years when it usually experiences adverse cash flows, it is doomed to failure.

The lack of capital for beginning a business and for expanding has been one of the major obstacles facing the small business entrepreneur. Fortunately, many sources are readily available, provided the manufacturer has a well-prepared plan along with well-defined objectives. The commercial bank is the main source of much of small businesses' working capital not supplied by their shareholders. Banks, to an increasing extent, are a source of long-term funds as well. This basic method of financing is supplemented in many ways. The small business may also secure debtor funds from its suppliers, commercial finance companies, small business administrators, and various institutions.

A firm should not consider going public if adequate funds can be obtained more readily and economically from the sources named above. If adequate funds cannot be obtained, equity financing is a solution to a firm's need for funds. Acquisitions and mergers are sometimes used by small-business entrepreneurs as alternative techniques of financing.

PROBLEMS

1. What reasons can be given for a disproportionate amount of Federal aid to agriculture (compared with business)?

2. It has been said that only one-half of one percent of American businesses is large (i.e., over 500 employees). Does the percentage appear to be too small? Why?

3. If you were starting a small manufacturing firm (assuming you have a product and have done market research), briefly describe how you would select the kind and size of plant, equipment, inventory, and working capital. How would you finance these assets?

4. Which managerial decision is usually the most crucial to a new business? Why?

5. Given all the risks of small business and the high failure rate, why would anyone want to begin a small business? (Include at least five reasons in your answer.)

25

International Finance

International finance is an offspring of the international trade and international capital movements that give rise to it.

In this chapter, we shall view various facets of international finance and its source, international trade. The chapter is divided into three parts: (1) a brief overview of world economic conditions since World War II; (2) a consideration of the financing of foreign trade, and in its wake, the foreign exchange market; and (3) the topic of international capital flows, along with the most recent development in this area, the multinational corporation.

The disintegration of economic and financial conditions during and subsequent to World War II has been chronicled almost as many times as the
war itself. Suffice it here to say that the capital stock and therefore the productive capacity of Western Europe, victors and vanquished alike, was destroyed.
From London to Leningrad, war had left its mark in Europe. Contrast this
with the condition of the U.S. economy. Not only had the ravages of war not
been visited upon the United States, the war had actually increased economic
efficiency. Whereas the United States had entered the war with unemployed
labor and capital, it ended the war with a fully employed labor force and an
expanded capital base.

It became the policy of the United States to encourage reconstruction
and self-sufficiency among the war-torn nations. This was done by two basic
methods: the outright gift and distribution of capital goods, and grants of
funds in order to allow recipients to purchase needed services and equipment
from the United States. These activities required that the United States
purposely run a deficit in its balance of payments—that is, purposely extend
more claims on the economy than it redeemed. The deficit in the balance of
payments, it is emphasized, was policy-created and intentional, in order to
further the policy of encouraging the economic recovery of Europe and Japan.

The European Recovery Plan (the "Marshall Plan") was a manifestation of this policy. This program pumped some $2\frac{1}{2}$ billion in capital goods
into the economies of Western Europe. It has been credited by many as one
major milestone in the economic recovery of Europe.

The European Supported by the United States, the drive toward European unity gained
Community strength in the 1950s despite widespread doubts as to its ultimate success.

Its first notable success was the establishment of the European Coal and
Steel Community (ECSC) in 1952 to create a *common market** in coal, steel,
and iron ore covering the six nations of France, West Germany, Italy, Belgium,
the Netherlands, and Luxembourg. The next step toward economic unity was

---

*A common market is a customs union with removal of all restrictions on the
movement of production factors—labor, capital, and enterprise.

the negotiation and appraisal by the six countries of a treaty establishing the European Economic Community* (EEC) in 1957. The Treaty was signed in Rome on March 25, 1957, was ratified by the six countries, and was effective on January 1, 1958.

Great Britain, Denmark, and Ireland entered the European Community (EC) at the beginning of 1973. Other European countries are making various arrangements with the EC short of full membership. One country, Norway, voted (in 1972) not to enter the EC. In 1978, the EC countries decided to admit three new members—Spain, Portugal, and Greece.

The basic purpose of the European Community, is threefold. The main feature of the EC is the creation of a *customs union* for both industrial and agricultural goods. This involves the abolition of restrictions on trade among member countries and the erection of a common external tariff. A second objective is a full *economic union* with free movement of persons, services, and capital, and progressive harmonization of social, fiscal, and monetary policies. The ultimate objective is a *political union* of the member countries.

Today the customs union is nearing completion and many trade barriers have been reduced or eliminated within the European Community. In February 1971, the Council of Ministers agreed to a plan for a full economic union by 1980. The EC would, according to the resolution: (1) constitute a zone within which persons, goods, services, capital, and enterprise would move freely; (2) form an individual monetary unit within the international system, characterized by the "total and irreversible" convertibility of currencies, the elimination of exchange rates, and the irrevocable fixing of parity rates; and (3) hold the powers and responsibilities in the economic and monetary field.

Although a distant goal, the ultimate objective of the EC from the beginning has been a political union—the establishment of a United States of Europe. The EC is already a political union in specific areas of economic and social policy. Member nations have given up much of their sovereignty in international trade and agriculture. Yet, the national governments of the member nations still retain control. Thus, the real power remains with the national governments and the supranational power of the EC is limited.

The increased productive efficiency by pooling knowledge and resources among EC countries added a new force to world trade. As the 1960s began, the United States was feeling the pinch of increased competition from the EC countries. In the previous year, 1959, the United States had gone into a deficit balance of payments for the first time in the nation's history. The deficit came about as a result of increased imports (funds outflows) and increased competition from EC products in foreign markets (decreased funds inflows). These developments, along with continued capital outflows, caused the beginning of the U.S.

---

*More recently the union is known as the European Community (EC).

balance-of-payments problems. In fairness, it must be said that the massive funds and capital outflows associated with the Vietnam War also contributed to the U.S. deficit balance of payments in the 1960s.

The Dollar Glut In the years 1945 to 1955, the term "dollar deficit" was heard frequently. The term indicated that the dollar was in great demand, for the goods and services it purchased were also in great demand. But as the tide turned, and as the deficit in the U.S. balance of payments increased, the dollar became plentiful in the hands of foreigners. The "dollar deficit" turned into the "dollar glut." The position of the dollar as an international reserve currency became threatened. As the dollar increased in volume, its value in foreign exchange markets decreased. Fortunately, the dollar glut was checked, and the dollar's position as an international reserve currency was maintained. The severe U.S. recession of 1973–75 checked the decline of the international value of the dollar. As tragic as the recession was, it had one bright side.* The price of U.S. goods stabilized relative to the use of the other nations' prices, and U.S. goods and services became a "good deal" in world markets. This development checked the deficit in the U.S. balance of payments.† The value of the dollar bounced back with the surplus in the balance of payments.

A five-year profile of the U.S. balance of payments from 1970 to 1974 is presented in Table 25.1. Although all the figures show the U.S. in deficit, they illustrate that the recession of 1973 made U.S. goods cheaper to foreigners and helped reduce the deficit for that year.

TABLE 25.1 U.S. Balance-of-Payments Balance on Current Account and Long-Term Capital

YEAR	($ MILLION)
1970	(3,031)
1971	(9,550)
1972	(11,113)
1973	(977)
1974	(10,702)

Note: All figures are deficits.

Source: Federal Reserve Bulletin.

---

*It goes without saying that the authors do not prescribe recession as a policy of curing the nation's deficit on international account. The "classical medicine" for a BOP deficit is devaluation of a nation's currency.

†For example, the U.S. balance of payments went from a deficit of $11.1 billion in 1972 to a surplus of $1.6 billion in the third quarter of 1975.

The foregoing profile of the post–World War II history of international trade brings out two points related to international finance: (1) The international value of a nation's currency, its foreign exchange, is systematically related to its international trade position—that is, to its balance-of-payments position; and (2) a nation's balance-of-payments position is related to the efficiency of its economy relative to the economies of its trading competitors. In the pages that follow, we shall discuss first the financing of a typical foreign-trade transaction and see from this how the foreign exchange market is created.

FINANCING FOREIGN-TRADE TRANSACTIONS

It is not unusual for an American to eat a breakfast of Canadian bacon, look at his Japanese watch, and drive to work in his German car, all while wearing clothing made of Korean fabric. The expansion of the world availability of consumer and capital goods is part of the modern economic miracle.

Financing an Import   There are many ways that American importers can finance the importation of foreign goods. For example, the American importer can pay cash, or the foreign supplier can extend open-book credit to the American purchaser.* But since the foreign seller of goods usually wants payment in his own currency, the line of credit and drafting device are used.

Assume that an American dealer in German cars needs ten new cars for his inventory. He orders them from the German car manufacturer. The manufacturer can allow the American open-book credit till the cars are sold at retail in the United States. But chances are that the manufacturer wants his money, in West German marks, prior to the time the cars are sold at retail.

In the latter case, the American importing car dealer arranges ahead of time for a *line of credit* with his bank. This means that the car dealer may borrow at his option a specified amount of money during a specified period of time. Armed with this commitment from his bank, the American importer can instruct the German manufacturer to ship the cars and draw a draft in marks on the bank for payment. The German manufacturer does so, and attaches the negotiable bill of lading† to the draft. The draft with the attached negotiable bill of lading is sent to the bank of the American importer. When the bank receives the draft, it confirms that the importer has credit with it, and pays the draft by purchasing West German marks in the foreign exchange

---

*Open book credit is the extension of credit pending sale of the goods.
†The negotiable bill of lading conveys title to the shipment.

market.* The importer signs a note for the *dollar value* of the remitted marks, at which time the bank hands over the negotiable bill of lading to the importer, which permits him to claim the cars dockside. The entire transaction is consummated when the dealer sells the cars and pays off the bank loan with the proceeds.

Several observations about the transaction are in order. First, note that the net effect of the importer's line of credit with the bank is to permit the importer to substitute the bank's credit for his. Second, note that the manufacturer's draft was paid in marks that the bank purchased in the foreign exchange market. If the price of marks is high, this adds to the cost of the cars, obviously. Third, you may ask where the marks came from that were purchased by the bank. They were supplied to the foreign exchange market by an American firm that had accepted payment in marks from a German firm, or by tourists from Germany with marks, or by German tourists in the United States who purchased dollars to spend here and paid for them in marks. Thus, the foreign exchange market is a by-product of the international market for goods and services.

Financing an Export   In the case of an export, an American person or firm sells goods or services to a foreigner. Let's assume that an American machine manufacturer sells machinery to a British firm, and the American firm wants payment in dollars.† The American firm can extend open-book credit for later payment in dollars, but let's assume that it demands payment before the machinery is released to the British firm. The transaction then becomes a mirror image of the one described above. The British importer goes to *his* bank, arranges a line of credit, and instructs the American firm to draft upon his bank. The British bank must then purchase dollars in the London or New York money market for remittance to the American exporter. Thus, in this transaction, British pounds sterling are supplied to foreign exchange markets.

FOREIGN EXCHANGE

Foreign exchange is defined as the international cash claims against a nation's currency. This is an important definition, for it differentiates the international role of a national currency from its domestic role. For example, if a nation's products never enter into international trade, that nation never

---

*A discussion of this market follows shortly.

†The American firm could have accepted payment in British pounds sterling, and thereby would have assumed the risk of decline in value of the British pound sterling in the foreign exchange market.

earns claims on economies foreign to it; and if it never demands the products of foreign countries, it never has need for foreign exchange.

The demand for the currency of foreign nations, foreign exchange, is derived from the demand for that nation's products. The most realistic example is tourism. If the nation of Balavia becomes an extremely popular tourist spot—remember that tourism is really the export of a nation's beauty in the minds of its visitors—then tourists will demand Balavian currency to spend while they are in that country.* Other things equal, the demand for Balavian currency drives its price up relative to other currencies. Note that the demand for Balavian products (tourism) drives up the demand (and price) for its currency. So it is with all currencies that enter into the foreign exchange market. Over time, the relative value of a nation's currency in the international foreign exchange market is a mirror image of the international demand for the nation's goods and services.

The foreign exchange market, be it in London or New York, permits the firm dealing in international trade to distribute risk. If, for example, an American exporter shipping goods to Israel does not want to accept the risk of change in the value of the Israeli pound, he can demand payment in dollars. In this case, the Israeli importer must buy U.S. dollars (actually dollar bank balances) with his Israeli pound. The U.S. importer may have speculated, however, that the dollar value of the Israeli pound would rise. In this case, he would have accepted payment in Israeli pounds, and sold them later in the foreign exchange market. If he guessed correctly, he could have made two profits: one from the sale of his product, and one from the sale of the Israeli currency. Had he guessed wrong—that is, had the dollar value of the Israeli pound dropped—he could have wiped out the profit on the sale of his goods by the loss on the foreign exchange market. There is *risk* associated with the operation of this market.

Risk is reduced, however, by the impact of *arbitrage*. Arbitrage is defined as a simultaneous sale in one market and purchase in another. The purpose of arbitrage is to take advantage of price differences in two or more markets. Thus, the arbitrager buys in the low-price market and sells in the high-price one. Because arbitragers overhang every foreign exchange market, price spreads among markets are immediately perceived by them, and for this reason, price differences are kept to a minimum. Thus, the dollar price of, for example, the British pound sterling tends to be the same the world over. This tends to reduce the *locational* risk in foreign exchange markets, but it does not reduce the risk of price *changes* in foreign exchange markets.

---

*An interesting exception to this principle is the Soviet Union. The Soviet Union permits none of its currency to leave the country, and therefore Russian rubles do not enter into foreign exchange markets. Americans are encouraged by the Soviet government to spend *dollars* while in the Soviet Union. The Soviets thereby acquire claims on Western economies.

Foreign exchange prices are closely related to supply and demand factors, and because these can change at any time, there is an ever-present risk of price changes in foreign exchange markets.

Foreign Exchange Prices

Since the dollar is an international reserve currency—that is, since other nations hold *their* monetary reserves in dollars as well as gold—currency prices at any point in time are quoted in terms of dollars.*

For example, refer to Figure 25.1, which gives the dollar prices of foreign currencies (bank transfers of the currencies) as of February 4, 1977. The prices are listed in dollar values, but the dollar price listing can be used to convert one currency into the value of another. For example, suppose you wanted to determine the West German mark (DM) price (value) of the British pound sterling (£). From Figure 25.1, we know the following *dollar* values of the two currencies:

$$£1 = \quad \$1.7158$$
$$DM\ 1 = \quad \$\ .4131$$

Therefore:

$$£1 = DM\ 4.1535$$

That is, on the day of the exchange quotations, one British pound sterling would purchase 4.1535 West German marks. Test your intuition: What would happen if Britain's trade position should worsen (its products grow less attractive internationally), and this reduces the dollar value of the pound sterling to, say, $1.60? What does your intuition say now about the value of the West German mark relative to the pound sterling? Your intuition probably tells you that you can purchase *more* pounds sterling with your West German mark, and alternatively, you can purchase fewer marks with your pound sterling. First, support for the first point:

$$£1 = \$1.6000$$
$$DM\ 1 = \$\ .4131$$

The value of the pound *in terms of the mark* is now DM 3.8731.

Before the drop in the *dollar value* of the pound sterling, the mark value of the pound was DM 4.1535. A 6.7 percent ([1.7158 − 1.600]/1.7158) decrease in the *dollar value* of the pound sterling resulted in a 6.7 percent ([4.1535 − 3.8731]/4.1535) decrease in the *mark price* of the pound sterling.

---

*Since foreign exchange prices are *ratios* of the value of one currency to another, they can be quoted in terms of *any* currency as long as the exchange ratios are known. See the text below for a discussion of this point.

FIGURE 25.1 Foreign Exchange Quotations. (*Source: Wall Street Journal, February 7, 1977, p. 23.*)

Foreign Exchange

Friday, February 4, 1977

Selling prices for **bank transfers** in the U.S. for payment abroad, as quoted at 3 p.m. Eastern Time (in dollars).

Country	Friday	Thursday
Argentina (Peso) Finc'l	.0040	.0040
Australia (Dollar)	1.0889	1.0896
Austria (Schilling)	.0583	.0584
Belgium (Franc)		
Commercial rate	.026950	.026970
Financial rate	.026983	.026955
Brazil (Cruzeiro)	.0810	.0810
Britain (Pound)	1.7158	1.7139
30-Day Futures	1.7049	1.7030
90-Day Futures	1.6826	1.6811
180-Day Futures	1.6605	1.6597
Canada (Dollar)	.9784	.9798
China-Taiwan (Dollar)	.0265	.0265
Colombia (Peso)	.0280	.0280
Denmark (Krone)	.1686	.1687
Ecuador (Sucre)	.0375	.0375
Finland (Markka)	.2615	.2613
France (Franc)	.2011	.2011
Greece (Drachma)	.0285	.0285
Hong Kong (Dollar)	.2150	.2150
India (Rupee)	.1150	.1150
Iran (Rial)	.0143	.0143
Iraq (Dinar)	3.41	3.41
Israel (Pound)	.1150	.1150
Italy (Lira)	.001135	.001135
Japan (Yen)	.003472	.003472
30-Day Futures	.003470	.003470
90-Day Futures	.003464	.003465
180-Day Futures	.003461	.003461
Lebanon (Pound)	.3315	.3315
Mexico (Peso)	.0445	.0445
Netherlands (Guilder)	.3954	.3976
New Zealand (Dollar)	.9570	.9575
Norway (Krone)	.1882	.1884
Pakistan (Rupee)	.1025	.1025
Peru (Sol)	.01453	.01453
Philippines (Peso)	.1345	.1345
Portugal (Escudo)	.0310	.0310
Saudi Arabia (Riyal)	.2850	.2850
Singapore (Dollar)	.4068	.4068
South Africa (Rand)	1.1535	1.1535
Spain (Peseta)	.01450	.01451
Sweden (Krona)	.2345	.2346
Switzerland (Franc)	.3971	.3976
Thailand (Baht)	.05	.05
Uruguay (New Peso) Finc'l	.2500	.2500
Venezuela (Bolivar)	.2336	.2336
West Germany (Mark)	.4131	.4131
30-Day Futures	.4133	.4133
90-Day Futures	.4137	.4138
180-Day Futures	.4153	.4152

Supplied by Bankers Trust Co., New York.

These calculations support the fact that if the dollar (mark, pound sterling, yen, or whatever) prices of all currencies are known, the relative values of all currencies are known, and any one currency can be denominated in terms of any other as a result.

Foreign exchange rates—that is, the ratio of one currency to another—are in the long run indexes of the health of a nation's international-trade position, and in some cases, the index is of the nation's domestic economic conditions also. Generally, if a nation's currency consistently drops in value relative to all others, one can assume that its international competitiveness has been impaired. There is a strong chance that this in turn is related to dislocations and/or inefficiencies in that nation's domestic economic conditions. Italy and the United Kingdom are two recent examples. Conversely, when the value of a nation's currency is rising, it usually reflects economic strength. Examples of this are West Germany and Switzerland.

FINANCING INTERNATIONAL CAPITAL FLOWS

Capital, both economic and financial,* flows across international boundaries in increasing volumes. In this section, we shall discuss the two basic international capital markets, financial claims and economic capital.

The International Market for Financial Claims

Given the volume, efficiency, and sophistication of U.S. capital markets, the volume of foreign securities issues being floated and traded in U.S. financial markets, by both private-sector and government issuers, is increasing. For example, note the announcement that appears in Figure 25.2. The Kingdom of Norway placed $150 million in notes in U.S. capital markets. Listed below the details of the issue are the names of the securities houses that acted as intermediaries in the placement.

Some dealers regularly make markets in foreign securities traded in secondary markets. The bid and asked prices of some of these securities are regularly reported, such as in Figure 25.3. Among the better-known foreign corporations whose stock prices are listed are Cannon, Inc. (optical goods), Honda Motors, Nissan Motors (Datsun autos), and Toyota Motors. Many of the corporations listed in the South Africa section are gold-mining enterprises.

For each dollar of securities sold in the U.S. primary market, there is a dollar of monetary claims flowing out of the country. These claims are partially offset, of course, by a counterflow of funds from foreigners purchasing financial claims on U.S. firms. Nationals of other countries do invest in the U.S. economy, and to the extent that they do, they offset American purchases of foreign securities in the primary market.

Before leaving this form of international capital flows, we should make it very clear that financial claims on the U.S. economy by foreigners, and

---

*Keep in mind that *economic capital* is defined as goods and services used in production. *Financial capital* is defined as long-term financial claims.

FIGURE 25.2 Notice of the Placement of a Foreign Loan in the United States. (*Source: Wall Street Journal, February 4, 1977, p. 21.*)

New Issue

$150,000,000

Kingdom of Norway

7⅜% Notes Due February 1, 1982

———

Price 99.70%
and accrued interest

———

This announcement is not an offer to sell or a solicitation of an offer to buy these securities. The offering is made only by the Prospectus. Copies of the Prospectus may be obtained in any State only from such of the undersigned and others as may legally offer these securities in such State.

Kuhn Loeb & Co.
Incorporated

Goldman, Sachs & Co.

Merrill Lynch, Pierce, Fenner & Smith
Incorporated

Salomon Brothers

The First Boston Corporation	Bache Halsey Stuart Inc.	Blyth Eastman Dillon & Co. Incorporated	Dillon, Read & Co. Inc.
Drexel Burnham & Co. Incorporated	Hornblower & Weeks-Hemphill, Noyes Incorporated	E. F. Hutton & Company Inc.	Kidder, Peabody & Co. Incorporated
Lazard Frères & Co.	Lehman Brothers Incorporated	Loeb Rhoades & Co. Inc.	Paine, Webber, Jackson & Curtis Incorporated
Reynolds Securities Inc.	Smith Barney, Harris Upham & Co. Incorporated	UBS-DB Corporation	Warburg Paribas Becker Inc.

Wertheim & Co., Inc.

White, Weld & Co.
Incorporated

Dean Witter & Co.
Incorporated

Arnhold and S. Bleichroeder, Inc.

L. F. Rothschild & Co.

Shearson Hayden Stone Inc.

Shields Model Roland Securities
Incorporated

Weeden & Co.
Incorporated

Interstate Securities Corporation	Moore, Leonard & Lynch, Incorporated	Parker / Hunter Incorporated	Wheat, First Securities, Inc.

February 4, 1977

FIGURE 25.3 Bid and Asked Prices of Foreign Securities in Which a Market Is Made. (*Source: Wall Street Journal, February 7, 1977, p. 22.*)

Foreign Securities

Friday, February 4, 1977

Unless noted, all issues are American Depositary Receipts, or ADRs, representing ownership of securities physically deposited abroad. The quotes, in U.S. dollars, are valid only for securities supported by validation on certificates as proof of compliance with tax and ownership regulations. n-Not ADR.

AUSTRALIA					
Broken Hil	.80d	–	7⅞	8¼	...
GREAT BRITAIN					
Beechm Gr	.04d	–	6⅞	7¼	– ⅛
Burmah	Oil	3562	1 5-16	1 7-16	+1-16
Fisons Ltd	.07b	11	5½	5¾	...
RankOrgan	.10f	537	3	3⅛	...
HOLLAND					
nPhilps	Gloeil	19	10⅝	10⅞	+ ⅛
ISRAEL					
IDB Bkhld	.31d	–	6⅛	6⅝	...
IDB Hld pf	.50d	5	9⅝	10⅛	+ ⅛
JAPAN					
CanonIncrp	.35d	18	49⅜	49⅞	– ¼
DaiEiIncrp	.03d	–	7½	7⅞	+ ⅜
Fuji Photo	.20b	12	26⅝	26⅞	+ ⅛
Hitachi Ltd	.56d	–	31	31½	– ½
Honda	Motor	39	23⅝	24⅛	...
KyotoCerm	.05d	–	27½	28	– ¼
Mitsui Co	.59d	10	32	32½	...
Nippon El	.36d	–	24⅝	25⅛	– ⅜
NisanMotor	.20d	–	23⅞	24¼	– ⅛
TDK Electr	.20b	–	59¼	60¼	–1¾
Tokio M&F	.82b	–	83½	84½	...
TokyoShibr	.36d	–	21	21½	– ⅛
ToyotaMotor	5k	5	43¼	43¾	+1
MEXICO					
TelefnoMex	.13b	23	3⅝	3⅞	...
SOUTH AFRICA					
Anglo AGd	.86b	31	15¼	15¾	+ ⅛
Ang A SAfr	.30d	283	2½	2¾	+1-16
BlyvorGold	.71d	249	3¼	3½	...
Botswana	RST	1	7-16	9-16	...
Bufflsfontn	.38b	12	6⅜	6¾	+ ⅛
DeBeer Mn	.18d	1042	2⅝	2¾	+1-16
EastDriefG	.76d	151	5½	5¾	...
FS Geduld	1.92d	94	10½	11	...
Gold Field	1.49d	29	11¼	11¾	– ⅛
Kloof Gold	.43d	89	3¾	4	...
PalaboraM	.50d	25	11⅜	11⅞	– ⅛
PresBrGld	1.63d	60	9¼	9⅝	+ ⅛
Pres Steyn	.42d	70	6	6⅜	...
StHelenaG	1.63d	10	12⅜	12⅞	...
Union Corp	.39d	10	2⅛	2⅜	...
Vaal Reefs	.57b	68	10¼	10¾	– ⅛
WelkomGld	.11d	218	1½	1¾	...
WestDrief	3.23d	46	17⅞	18⅜	– ⅛
WstDeepLv	.43b	142	7¼	7⅝	– ⅛
West Hold	2.99d	57	13⅞	14⅜	+ ⅛

x-ex-dividend. r-ex-rights. c-ex-interest. (z) not available.

claims on foreign economies by Americans, range over the entire spectrum of claims by type (debt, equity) and by maturity. These financial flows consist of securities ranging from very short-term loans to preferred and common stock.

The International
Market for
Economic Capital</div> In the strictest sense of the word, the international market for economic capital, "productive stuff," is not really a financial market. Economic capital is defined as goods and services that are used in the production of other goods and services. But the increasing volume of real capital flows across international boundaries has real implications for international financial activities, and for this reason, economic capital flows are discussed.

Typically, an American firm will begin its international career as an exporter of its products to foreign countries. If the demand for its products is sustained and grows, the exporter starts thinking in terms of producing its product in the country that imports the greatest volume of its product. The reasons are understandable: lower shipping costs, no import duties, and indeed, all the benefits that accrue to being close to one's customers.

But moving production to one's foreign customers is not without risk. The risks of doing business in an alien environment are many. Among them are discriminatory taxes and nationalization. Nationalization is the process by which a foreign nation assumes ownership of American firms doing business within its borders. Nationalization may be accompanied by payment to the American owners of the firm, such as in the case of nationalization of American-owned oil companies by Saudi Arabia, or nationalization may be unilateral without payment, such as in the case of the Cuban nationalization of all American firms. Either way, the specter of nationalization presents risk to the firm that locates its facilities in a foreign country.

Those nations desiring direct economic investment by Americans and foreign governments will try, of course, to assure the potential investor that the risks are low indeed. Consider the advertisement by the Dominican Republic that appears in Figure 25.4. The Dominican Republic promises manufacturers that their money is safe (no nationalization?), and so are their persons (safety from kidnapping by terrorists?). There is no need to speculate, however, about what the Dominican Republic's tax policy for foreign firms is. Remission of taxes is apparently an inducement.

THE MULTINATIONAL CORPORATION

A fairly recent development in the area of direct investment has been the use of the *multinational corporation*. A multinational corporation is one that has substantial assets and/or markets in several nations. A multinational corporation, by its very nature, almost has to be a large firm. Multinational corporations are found in the petroleum and communications industries, as well as in others.

Because of their size and international orientation, multinational corporations tend to have powers and problems not germane to other

FIGURE 25.4 An Appeal for Direct Investment. (*Source: Wall Street Journal, March 9, 1976, p. 30. Note: Notice the promises of protection from the traditional risks of international direct investment.*)

Manufacturers!!
Look into The
DOMINICAN REPUBLIC
where your money is safe, and so are you

NO TAXES .... NO PROBLEMS
Full Government Cooperation!

INDUSTRIAL AND FREE ZONE

San Pedro de Macoris and Haina
5 minutes from seaports and
30 from major airport

Write or cable:
Secretary of State
Federico Antun
CORPORACION DE FOMENTO INDUSTRIAL,
P.O. Box 1472

Santo Domingo, Dominican Republic

corporations. For this reason, a subcommittee of the Senate Foreign Relations Committee has been formed to consider the affairs of multinational corporations.

As direct investment in foreign countries increases, the multinational corporation will increase in importance.

SUMMARY AND CONCLUSIONS

This chapter has presented a brief overview of world economic conditions since World War II to assist insight into current international financial relationships. The financing of international trade and its financial outgrowth, the foreign exchange market, were next viewed. From this was gained an understanding of world monetary relationships.

Finally, the process of international direct investment was examined. This process, the direct placement of capital goods and services, moves bilaterally from the United States to other countries, and from other countries to the United States. A development accompanying the increased volume of direct capital placement from the United States is the advent of the multinational corporation, a firm with substantial direct foreign investment in a number of foreign countries.

PROBLEMS

1. Consult a recent edition of the *Wall Street Journal* and determine:

    a. The U.S. dollar value of the Philippine peso

    b. The U.S. dollar value of the Finnish markka

    c. The value of the Philippine peso in terms of the Finnish markka.

2. Update Table 25.1 to the current period by consulting the *Federal Reserve Bulletin*. Has the balance of payments position of the United States "improved?" Why?

3. If the bank transfer price of the Danish krone is U.S. .1685 in London, and is U.S. .1700 in New York, how could you benefit from this difference? What is the process called?

4. Is the world suffering from a dollar surplus or a dollar shortage? Is there any relationship between your answer to this question, and your answer to Question 2? What?

5. It has been said that bills of exchange denominated in international currencies are by-products of international trade. Is this true? Why?

6. Foreign Exchange rates are given as:

    DM   1 = \$.4216
    Mexican peso 1 = \$.05
    Mexican peso 1 = DM .1055

    a. How can you take advantage of these rates?

    b. How much would you make if you began with \$1,000.00 (ignoring exchange charges)?

26

The Integration Trend in Finance

The more extensive a man's knowledge of what has been done, the greater will be his power of knowing what to do.

Benjamin Disraeli

A central theme of this book is that finance is an integrated, consistent body of knowledge concerned with the seeking and use of financial resources in the economy. Although the field of finance has been historically truncated and divided into components in the literature, the finance discipline, in order for its full significance to be understood, must be viewed as an integral whole. This chapter builds upon all that has gone before it. The basic purpose of this chapter is to demonstrate how the component parts of the discipline thus far discussed fit into an integrated whole. To demonstrate this point, the finance matrix model is presented to show the interrelationships among the component topics in finance. It is important to recognize that the component parts sum to the field of finance.

The important interrelationships within finance are illustrated in the model portrayed in Table 26.1. The purpose of this simple model is to show that the basic components of finance share common characteristics. The woof of the matrix is the three basic fields of finance, and the warp of the matrix consists of the common threads that bind finance together in an integrated whole. The circled ×s indicate the contribution of each area.

TABLE 26.1 The Financial Matrix Model

	FINANCIAL MANAGEMENT	INVESTMENTS	MARKETS
Analysis	⊗	×	×
Tools	⊗	×	×
Decision rules	⊗	×	×
Institutions	×	×	⊗
CAPM	×	⊗	×

The Woof: The Three Fields of Finance For convenience, finance has been divided into three basic fields: financial management, investments, and markets. It is important to recognize that these three perspectives are but different views of the same phenomenon, the field of finance, and the body of decision rules that accompany it.

Financial management, as is frequently indicated in this book, is all activities connected with the management of financial resources in the firm. These activities range from the acquisition of funds through the issuance of debt and equity claims, to the acquisition and management of assets, to management of the expenses involved in the acquisition of funds and asset management as well as production of the firm's product. This is the earnings-cycle model presented in Chapter 6.

Investments, the second perspective, is the set of decision rules and activities concerned with the purchase and holding of income streams, financial claims upon firms and government units. It is obvious, we hope, that the financial claims that are the by-product of the management of the financial resources of the firm are the focal point of investments. Thus, the considerations of the *sale* of these claims on income streams are also present in the considerations of their *purchase*. Chief among these is the consideration of the risk–return tradeoff as exemplified in the capital asset pricing model (CAPM).

Financial markets complete the triad. Financial markets are the institutional relationships, both tangible and intangible, that facilitate the exchange of claims on income streams, financial claims. As the facilitating agency that provides for the exchange of financial claims between saver and investor, financial markets serve as the mucilage cementing the field of finance together. Again, the capital asset pricing model (CAPM) serves as the unifying theme.

We have tried to show the commonality and integration of the fields of finance in the diagram which has begun each of this book's five parts. The three fields of finance are integrated, permanently inseparable components.

The Warp: Sinews that Bind   Contained in the rows of the matrix are five functional characteristics common to financial management, investments, and markets. All five are common to the three fields of finance, and all are important. But one, the capital asset pricing model (CAPM), is not only common to the three fields, it draws them together into one unified, integrated discipline. Therefore, we shall give it a section of its own, following this one.

Analysis.   The process of analysis is the process of breaking something into its components so that the structure and interrelationships may be more closely viewed and therefore better understood. Analysis is endemic to financial management. The financial manager must, as a minimum condition, engage in the process of applying analytical skills and insights. Minimization of costs and maximization of revenues, the conditions required by maximization of profit and shareholder wealth, require the application of analysis.

And so it is with investments and financial markets. The intelligent placement of funds into financial investments through the facilities of financial markets requires the application of analytical techniques. The adoption of investment goals and their implementation requires, at a minimum, the decomposition of the decision into its component parts for consideration. This is, of course, analysis.

Tools.   The process of analysis outlined above would be useless without the techniques of exploring the interrelationships among component parts. These techniques are the tools of financial analysis. Tools of financial analysis are usually of the mathematical variety. Chief among the analytical tools discussed in this book is ratio analysis, the primary topic of Chapter 7. Although ratios are the major analytical tool discussed, there are others. Among them are statistics, linear programming, and calculus. The body of tools usable in financial analysis is limited only by the imagination and ability of the analyst.

Decision Rules. Decision rules specify the normative aspects of finance. They specify the desired results of financial decision making, and as a result, they specify norms to be attained. Perhaps the most widely accepted decision rule in finance is the norm of the maximization of shareholder wealth. This norm states that a financial decision that contributes to the net wealth position of the firm's shareholders is good, and a decision that does not do so is not good. It provides for ordinal—as well as cardinal—applications. In this formulation, the wealth-maximization rule states that if two actions both contribute to shareholder wealth, the decision that results in greater shareholder wealth is the more desirable of the two.

There are other decision rules, of course. Consider the risk–return tradeoff decision rule. It states that if two options have the same risk, and one has a greater return, the latter should be chosen. Its basic formulation states that risk and return are related in positive fashion, and that additional return can be had at the expense of incurring additional risk. There are many corollaries to this basic decision rule, and they permeate the field of finance. The risk–return decision rule forms the basis of the capital asset pricing model used throughout this book, and reviewed briefly below.

Institutions. Institutions are the social, political, and legal *relationships* that provide for the issuance of debt and equity claims, their sale, and their trading subsequently among investors making portfolio adjustments.

Chief among financial institutions is the basic concept of the corporation as a legal entity. This permits it to issue financial claims, purchase others, and generally do anything financial that natural human beings can do. The advantage the corporation has over the natural human as a financial transactor is its size and scope. As a corporate entity, for example, General Motors can participate financially in the economy to a greater extent than any individual can do.

Institutions further include, for example, the concept of equity versus debt, the concept of saving and investment, securities markets such as the New York Stock Exchange and the over-the-counter market, and the legal principles that provide for enforcement of contracts. But the myriad of financial institutions is too great to discuss in its entirety. Financial institutions cut across the entire discipline of finance: financial management, investments, and markets.

THE CAPITAL ASSET PRICING MODEL (CAPM)

Although the general characteristics of finance discussed above (analysis, tools, decision rules, and institutions) are all common to the three basic divisions of finance (financial management, investments, and markets), they do not offer a common principle that will *explain* financial phenomena common to the three fields of finance. Fortunately, the capital asset pricing model is not only common to the three fields, it *explains* financial phenomena common to the three fields.

The capital asset pricing model is a rational, orderly analysis and explanation of a financial principle *common to all subdivisions of the fields of finance*, the risk–return tradeoff. The capital asset pricing model in its many forms and formulations is based upon the truism that the relationship between risk and return is linear and positive. This principle, in all its magnificent simplicity, suggests that the return on a financial claim is positively related to its risk, and it further specifies that the relationship is linear. Such a simple yet important recognition has vital implications and applications in the three fields of finance.

In the area of financial management, the principles of the model, for example, go a long way in helping us to understand and explain the firm's required return. The firm's required return (return to the investor) must rise as the firm issues incremental claims, because the element of risk is increasing. In other words, the firm is moving up and out on the risk–return curve.

But the cornerstone use of CAPM in financial management is the application to valuation in the firm. Consider the power of the model in bypassing the enigmas of going-concern values and capitalization rates to a practicable formulation of return to the firm's net assets under conditions of risk.

Since market price and return are differing dimensions of the same value, CAPM goes a long way in explaining rational investment activity in financial markets.

SUMMARY

The capital asset pricing model has gone further than any other development in showing that finance is an integrated whole, a body of knowledge that has closely related facets. This recognition is dispelling the view of finance as a field with separate, distinctly defined, and *loosely* related subdisciplines. Indeed, since all subdisciplines of finance are concerned with the relationship between risk and return (price), this fact demonstrates the integrated body of thought that makes up the discipline of finance, in contrast to the idea of a series of parts forced under an umbrella called finance.

Finance is an indivisible whole. Its parts cannot be separated; they are an integrated whole upon each of whose parts the spotlight temporarily shines before it moves on to the next.

PROBLEMS

1. The Capital Asset Pricing Model (CAPM) clearly illustrates the integration of the three fields of finance: financial management, investments, and markets.

    a. Briefly outline the basic points of CAPM.

    b. Explain how they assist in integrating the three fields of finance.

2. What norms guide the actions of the firm's financial manager? Are these norms different from the ones that guide the financial investor? Why?

3. The text suggests that the concept of the corporation is essential to the workings of financial institutions. Explain how the concept of the corporation is a key to financial management, investments, and markets.

4. How is the concept of risk important to the three fields of finance? Elaborate.

27

Changing
Financial World

Finance is a dynamic subject. Both the real world of finance and the academic study of it are constantly changing. There are many examples of the dynamic nature of finance. In the real world of finance, there are rapid changes in the way transactions are financed; witness the revolutionary advent of "plastic money," the credit card. In the scholarly world of finance, we have seen the integration of a broad spectrum of financial topics with the introduction of the capital asset pricing model (CAPM). (The implications of the Capital Asset Pricing Model were discussed in Chapters 1, 13, 18, 20, and 26.) There is no shortage of evidence of dramatic and rapid changes in the field of finance.

In this chapter, we attempt to *anticipate* future developments in finance. A disclaimer must be issued here that these prognostications are the educated guesses of the authors; but the guesses are educated in the sense that they are based upon study of financial phenomena.

The chapter treats anticipated developments in each of the three functional fields already used in this book: financial management, financial investments, and financial markets. In addition, several anticipated developments not strictly germane to any one of these topics are discussed under the heading of "Miscellaneous Trends."

Financial management is, of course, a key area of the field of finance. Significant developments in financial management are going to reverberate and be heard throughout the entire field.

A Change in Emphasis: We anticipate several developments, discussed below, that will be spun
Short-Term Accounts off from the trend of financial management to move toward emphasis
upon working-capital management and other activities involved in the management of the firm's current assets.

Short-term asset management is not as glamorous and exciting as long-term asset management. For example, capital budgeting, valuation theory, and financial structure have held court in the literature. Senior financial executives usually do not make it to the top as managers of cash accounts.

But there have been several developments that have changed the picture somewhat. First, there is the recognition of the time spent in current-asset management. Financial executives spend a preponderance of their time managing short-term assets.* Given the volume of time dedicated to short-term assets relative to their size, it would seem logical to assume that more efficient efforts will be dedicated to short-term asset management in the future in order to economize on time spent on it.

The computer has also affected the allocation of time from long-term to short-term assets greatly. The increasingly widespread use of the computer has increased the penalty for sluggish management of cash balances. This penalty, in the form of opportunity costs for the use of cash, may slice dramatically into revenue on the earnings statement. The result is, of course, lower earnings after taxes (EAT), and lower earnings after taxes is not a product of efficient financial management.

Finally, the rewards for efficient working-capital management are increasing. The more efficient the working-capital management of a firm, other things equal, the greater the continuity of the productive process in the firm. That is, raw materials, inventories, and other inputs will be ready when needed. The result is smoother production.

---

*See Chapter 8, Table 8.1.

A Growing Source of Funds: Increase in Factoring

Factoring is the process by which a firm liquidates (turns into cash) its accounts receivable by selling them to a firm that specializes in the purchase and collection of accounts receivable. Factoring is common in the textile industry, among others. Factoring can be on a notification or a nonnotification basis. On a notification basis, the debtor is told that his account has been sold to a factor and that future payments should be made to the factor. On a nonnotification basis, the debtor is not told, and he makes his payments to the firm that extended him open-book credit. The firm is then obligated, of course, to turn the funds over to the factor that bought the account.

The factor can provide valuable counsel and advice to the corporation extending short-term credit. For example, the authors know of one factor who prevented his clients from extending short-term credit to W.T. Grant. His advice held them in good stead. This type of service, one of many the factor extends, is one reason the factor is destined to grow.

We suspect very strongly that, given the coming emphasis upon working-capital management, factoring will become a more widespread practice in the industries in which it is now practiced as well as spreading to other industries. Look at it this way: A firm that "carries" its customers—extends open-book credit—is actually in the lending business. It has a portion of its working capital tied up in IOUs. It might be better for the firm to liquidate the IOUs and use the funds in its own line of business. As competition pressures increase, and financial managers get sharper pencils in the short-term area, factoring will become more widespread.

TRENDS IN FINANCIAL INVESTMENTS

Increased Use of the Beta Factor

The beta coefficient, discussed in some detail in the appendix to Chapter 18, is a measure of volatility of return (a dimension of risk) of an individual security relative to the market portfolio's rate of return.* As an index of volatility of a security's return, it is an index of, and a surrogate for, *risk*.

We anticipate that the beta factor (β) will in ten years, become as important as the price–earnings ratio in the retailing of securities. That is, the price–earnings ratio will be used as an index of the stock price's "reasonableness." The beta coefficient will be used to measure the riskiness of the

---

*For an excellent discussion of the beta coefficient as well as other dimensions of the measurement of risk, see Sharpe, William F., *Portfolio analysis and the Capital Markets* (New York: McGraw-Hill, 1970).

stock relative to other common-stock alternatives available to the investor. Investor services will include the stock's beta factor along with its P/E ratio, its dividend record, and other relevant criteria.

Increased Concern for Value and Return Measurements for Common Stock

What does the investor purchase when he buys a share of common stock? This question was discussed briefly in Chapter 13, under "Valuation." As frequently and in such volume as common stock is purchased in primary and secondary markets, there is still no unanimity of agreement about which values are most important in the investor's stock-purchase decision.

Some practitioners and scholars argue that earnings into perpetuity are being purchased without regard to the form the earnings take. Others say that the common-stock investor is purchasing cash dividends along with the opportunity for greater future dividends, owing to the growth of the firm. Still others, not many, argue that the common stockholder is purchasing a chance for an increase in his equity position, and he is indifferent to its form—cash, growth, prestige, and so on.

The argument is more than an academic one. The determination of what the common shareholder actually buys is important in determining the market value of the stock and measuring shareholders' required rate of return against actual rate of return.

No totally accepted determination has been made of what the shareholder buys. Until it is, stock values and shareholder rates of return will be compromises at best. We suspect that that important field of finance, investments, can no longer accept such compromises. For this reason, we feel that the capital asset pricing model, reproduced below, will become practicable. The formulation, used previously in Chapters 13, 18, and 20 attempts to measure the investor's *required* rate of return. The required rate of return on common stock is:

$$R_j = R_f + (R_m - R_f)\,\beta$$

where:

R_j = required rate of return on security j

R_f = risk-free interest rate

R_m = return on a market portfolio of securities

β = the systematic risk of the security relative to the portfolio

This will become a more widely used guide to investment behavior because of its practicability. The *actual* rate of return can be compared with the shareholders' required rate of return, and an investment decision can result.

Although CAPM was first applied to common stocks, the current practice is to use it for portfolios which consist of mixtures of common stocks and fixed-income securities. This treats stocks and bonds as if they are both a part of the same risk spectrum. There is increasing reason to believe that, in an inflationary world, this may not be the case. If so, a separate performance measurement for the stock and bond components of a portfolio is necessary. However, we believe that an accepted method will emerge that will make possible the treatment of stocks and bonds in a combined fashion. This may come about through a modified version of CAPM, as we know it now, or through a new technique.

Increased Importance of Municipal Finance The financing of state, county, and municipal governments is growing at an increasing rate. This is, of course, a reflection of the increased social and other services provided by local governments. Many times, these services outstrip the taxing ability of the jurisdiction to finance them, and the result is deficit financing, the issuance of debt.

The result is a mass of state, county, and municipal bonds coming into capital markets. The speed and volume at which these bonds come into the market creates significant problems. Although the bonds are usually analyzed and evaluated by the rating services, the bond ratings cannot always reflect the changing conditions of their issuers. Consider the recent problems of the city of New York, and the special financing arrangements undertaken to allow New York to avoid default on its debt obligations.

For these and other reasons, we feel that the field of municipal finance will bear special scrutiny in the years ahead.

TRENDS IN FINANCIAL MARKETS

An old adage suggests that "the propensity of the financial community to be ingenious is infinite." Although this is perhaps a bit overstated, it is in the area of financial markets that very innovative developments are taking and will take place. We identify here only the broad outlines of developments.

The Blurring of Financial Intermediaries Financial intermediaries developed historically because of the specialized services they offered. Consider the financial needs that gave rise to the savings and loan association. Basically, the first savings and loan associations (then known as building societies) provided a pool of funds that the members could draw upon to build housing. Thus, a very specialized financial service, home finance, gave rise to the savings and loan association as we know it.

Consider the commercial bank. It originated as a financial institution specializing in the financing of inventories for merchants through short-term loans.*

Thus, two highly specialized financial institutions were very different in origins and initial purpose. But the historical distinctions between them are now quite blurred. Commercial banks now make mortgage loans, and savings and loan associations make consumer loans. The historical monopoly of commercial banks, demand deposits (checking accounts), has been invaded by other financial institutions now making "third-party payments"—savings and loan associations now transferring their customers' funds electronically. In November 1975, Congress gave its approval for federally chartered associations to issue demand-deposit liabilities under certain circumstances. Thus, there is a further blurring of the lines between these two types of institutions.

We feel that the breaking down of unique characteristics of financial intermediaries, such as has happened with S&Ls and banks, will continue. The key to success of a financial institution is the conveying of financial services cheaply and at the convenience of the customer. Institutions that perform these functions will succeed, regardless of their historical derivations or of the currently specialized nature of their services. It's possible, for example, for the nation's fastest growing financial intermediary, the credit union, to evolve into an all-inclusive financial "department store," providing saving, checking, lending, insurance, and a whole spectrum of financial services.†

Regulation to Continue Primarily because of the excesses leading to the Great Depression, financial markets and financial institutions dealing in those markets are closely regulated. We have discussed in some detail in Chapter 22, for example, the two basic laws regulating trading in financial claims, the Securities Act of 1933 and the Securities Exchange Act of 1934. As the securities markets are regulated, so are financial institutions and financial transactions. Consider the agencies at the federal level that regulate financial institutions: the Federal Reserve System, the Comptroller of the Currency, the Administrator of National Banks, the Federal Deposit Insurance Corporation, the Federal Home Loan Bank Board, the Federal Savings and Loan Insurance Corporation, the Federal Credit Union Administration.‡ And these are only the agencies that regulate depository institutions at the federal

---

*Indeed, the very name for this financial institution indicates that, originally, a commercial bank financed only commerce, another term for the distribution of goods.

†Such a development would presume prior legislative authority, of course.

‡The list, of course, does not include the government financial institutions, such as the Federal Home Loan Mortgage Corporation, that were *created* by federal law.

level. It is fairly easy to document the existence of financial regulatory agencies.

Consider the regulation of lending activities. The "Truth-in-Lending Act," which specifies the notification to the borrower of *all* finance charges levied upon him, is one example of regulation of lending. Many states have usury laws that place a limit on the effective interest rate the lender can charge. These further regulate the lending process. It is not difficult to document the regulation of the lending process.

Space and time will not permit us to document all the federal, state, and local regulation of financial markets and the activities in them.

The authors feel that regulation will continue and increase in scope, intensity, and activity. There are several reasons. First, financial arrangements are increasing in scale and scope. Consider the national scope of the bank credit cards. Banks in the BankAmericard consortium do business across state lines, although banks may not legally branch across state lines.*

Another reason advanced for increased regulation is the increasing complexity of financial transactions. As just part of the array of *new* financial services available to the consumer, we now have Individual Retirement Accounts, automatic deposit of paychecks, and tax-sheltered annuity plans. The volume and complexity of new financial services will result in increased regulation of financial markets.

Broader and Deeper Financial Markets: Specialization

There is an accelerating trend toward increasing sophistication and speculation in financial markets.† Historically, the New York Stock Exchange and its regional counterparts have formed the prototype of financial markets in the minds of the "man on the street." As important as the NYSE is to the investing public, it represents perhaps the most obvious and archetypal form of financial market. The authors feel that new, specialized, and sophisticated financial markets will develop at an increasing rate.

Recent examples of the type of development that we foresee increases in are the NASDAQ variation of the over-the-counter market and organized options trading of the Chicago Board Options Exchange (CBOE).

The acronym NASDAQ (pronounced "nazdak") stands for National Association of Securities Dealers Automatic Quotation. It is basically a computerized market of over-the-counter market securities. Subscribers to the system making a market in various securities report their prices to a

---

*In 1977, the BankAmericard was changed to Visa.

†The perceptive reader may recognize that we are predicting trends in financial intermediaries that are opposite to those in financial markets generally. That is, *intermediaries* will become more generalized, and *financial markets* will become more specialized. Such is the case, we feel.

computer bank. Those using the service are given access by way of a cathode-ray tube to the bid and asked prices of various securities.

The system was begun only in 1971, but has proved successful because it gives the market participants a point of departure in their negotiations.* For example, one source has said:

> NASDAQ terminals have made the OTC market competitive with the organized exchanges—and might ultimately displace them by virtue of superior efficiency.†

Since its inception in 1971, NASDAQ has indeed become an important mechanism in financial markets of the type that we anticipate will increase in the future.

Another example of this trend is the Chicago Board Options Exchange. This exchange centralized and institutionalized the trading of put and call options to buy common stock. Prices for these options are quoted daily in the financial press. Previous to the inception of the Chicago Board Options Exchange, the market in "options" was a highly decentralized over-the-counter market.

We see a national stock exchange system emerging. The year 1977 may see an intermediate step in this direction if the New York Stock Exchange and the American Stock Exchange merge. The NYSE facilities would handle all stock transactions. Amex facility would trade bonds, put and call options, warrants, and other miscellanous instruments.

Physical Manifestation of Financial Claims to Change

We predict that the physical form of the financial claim will change, or disappear, in the near future. The stock certificate, the bond, the IOU have limited lives. In the future, we feel that owners of financial claims will not have certificates and other physical evidences of their financial assets.

The physical transfer of stock certificates among member firms of the New York Stock Exchange has given rise to the phenomenon called the "back-office mess," a condition in which transfers of funds among buyer-seller accounts and transfer of stock certificates and registration in new owner names have been severely delayed because of high-volume days on the floor

---

*There is a parallel computerized system for the secondary mortgage market. It is AMMINET (Automated Mortgage Market Information Network), a joint venture of the Federal Home Loan Bank Board, the U.S. League of Savings Associations, and the American Bankers Association. Subscribers list their mortgage "packages" for sale, and these are displayed to potential buyers by CRT. It is a computerized market analogous to NASDAQ.

†Roland I. Robinson and Dwayne Wrightsman, *Financial Markets: The Accumulation and Allocation of Wealth* (New York: McGraw-Hill, 1974), p. 403.

of the exchange. The delay caused by transfer of ownership of stock certificates in turn has caused some brokerage houses to go into default. The cause, we point out, was in many cases the failure to "move the paper"—to transfer stock certificates from one owner to another.

It would be more efficient, at least for volume traders, to be satisfied with a statement of ownership of securities from their brokers. Such is the case with the owners of demand-deposit claims against commercial banks, for example. The owner of each checking account is satisfied with a monthly statement listing all deposits and withdrawals (checks) on the account. Few feel it necessary to demand periodically that the bank show them their balances physically. But without physical manifestation, billions of dollars in claims change hands daily.

Why not, through an analogous system, avoid the gross inefficiencies and costs of the stock transfer system by adopting the banking system of accounting for claims? Instead of receiving and surrendering voluminous pieces of paper (certificates, bonds, and so on) when engaging in financial transactions, the financial investor would receive a monthly statement showing purchases (credits), sales (debits), and balances in account from brokerage houses. Of course, the customer who desires to get out of the market permanently could demand an accounting and receive the credit balance in his account in stock certificates, bonds, and other relevant financial claims, in exactly the same way that one wishing to close his checking account can demand his credit balance in currency and coin.

We feel that this development has to come about in order to avoid the gross inefficiencies of the current system used in stock- and bond-market transactions.

The Currencyless Society Much has been said and written about the cashless society. Generally, it is specified that within some time period, short-term credit arrangements will replace the use of currency and coin cash transactions that we know today.

We feel that this trend will continue and accelerate. Although we would prefer to see the term "currencyless society" applied to the phenomenon, we agree with it generally. It should be called the currencyless society because, technically, the short-term credit arrangements that serve to replace currency are a part of the definition of cash, so it is currency and coin that short-term credit is replacing.

The short-term credit arrangements of which we speak are primarily manifested in credit cards, both the type issued by merchants (oil companies and department stores) and the type issued by commercial banks.* The growth in availability and use of these credit cards has been rapid and wide-

---

*For obvious reasons, these are sometimes called "plastic credit."

spread. It is the substitution of seller credit or bank credit for the claims on the Federal Reserve or the federal government that the plastic credit replaced. The substitution of a direct credit claim on the buyer or his bank will grow at the expense of the use of claims on third parties, we feel.*

MISCELLANEOUS TRENDS

Growing Bridge Between Academic and Real-World Finance   There has developed within the last ten years a trend in which academia and its research efforts are becoming more pragmatic and useful in the everyday world of finance. One good example of this is the increasing use of beta (β) as an operational measure of risk of a security. As we suggested previously in this chapter, we feel beta will be reported regularly with the performance statistics of a financial security.

Another example is the body of guides to financial actions accruing to the body of literature generated about the capital asset pricing model (CAPM). The CAPM systematically treats the risk of the return accruing to an individual security, and the risk attendant upon the accumulation of securities into portfolios. Although it is now cast primarily in mathematical terms, we feel that the CAPM's internal rigor and beauty will be widely translated into operational guidelines in financial management, investments, and markets.

Growth of the Study of Finance   A recent Department of Commerce study reports that business administration is the most popular major for college students.† In October 1974, 16 percent of all college students in the United States were enrolled in this field.

We feel that finance as a major will increase in popularity. The study of finance has gone through several stages. It was at first of a highly descriptive nature in which the *characteristics* of financial phenomena were listed. Then it entered into a period of quantification and "mathematicalization."‡ This period coincided with the widespread availability of computer services on college and university campuses.

The most recent trend has been one of placing analytical techniques in the setting of finance in order to focus upon sharpened financial decision-making skills.

---

*It has been pointed out to the authors that credit cards allow the merchant to factor his accounts receivable *before* the transaction.

†Courtesy *Parade Magazine*, April 18, 1976, p. 17.

‡An example of this trend in finance is the advent of the *Journal of Financial and Quantitative Analysis*.

We feel the latter approach will appeal to the coming generation of business students, who will be able to use their greater sophistication in analytical skills in securing career satisfaction.

SUMMARY AND CONCLUSIONS

In this chapter, we have attempted to isolate and identify what we feel are coming trends in the field of finance. It is folly, perhaps, to put prognostications in print, for they are not easily repudiated should they prove inaccurate.

But the trends we have underscored we feel are probable and needed. They are all characterized by the application of increasingly sophisticated technology to problems in the field of finance.

"The times, they are a-changing."

Glossary

AAA or Aaa: Triple A bonds, the highest-quality rating given to corporate bonds by Standard and Poor's and Moody's, respectively.

Accelerated Depreciation: Methods of calculating depreciation charges that result in greater charges in earlier years, such as sum of the years' digits and double-declining balance.

Accounting Rate of Return: A capital budgeting technique. The mean of the capital project's revenues is divided by the project's cash outlay. Also called the average-rate-of-return method.

Accruals: The proportion of current liabilities that has accumulated at a given time since the last payment date. They include wages, rent, and taxes.

Annuity: A series of equal installments paid to or received by an annuitant at regularly spaced time periods.

Arbitrage: Act of buying an asset in one market and simultaneously selling in another at a higher price. By this process, undervalued assets are bought and overvalued assets are sold in related markets which are temporarily out of equilibrium. This tends to equalize prices of assets in different markets.

Asked Price: The lowest quoted price that any potential seller will accept for a security at a specific time.

Banker's Acceptances: Bill of exchange (for goods shipped, usually to an importer) drawn on or accepted by a bank.

Basis Point: One one-hundredth of 1 percent. Used for measuring small changes in interest rates.

Bear Market: A market in which most prices are falling, or are expected to fall.

Bearer Bonds: Bonds with the characteristic of negotiability. Whoever legally acquires them, legally owns them.

Beta (β): The ratio of the covariance of the returns of the individual security or asset with market returns (COV R_j, R_m), normalized (i.e., divided) by the variance of market returns, Var_m.

Bid Price: The highest quoted price that any prospective buyer will pay for a security at a specific time.

Big Board: The New York Stock Exchange. So called because of the board showing current stock prices on the wall of the trading floor.

Bond: Evidence of long-term debt of a firm or government unit.

Book Value: The value of an asset on the books of the firm.

Bull Market: A market in which most prices are rising, or are expected to rise.

Business Cycle: The periods of prosperity and recession that characterize economic activity.

Business Risk: The risk of default or variability of return.

Call: An option to buy a security at a specific price during a given period.

Callable Provision: A provision of securities that permits the issuer to purchase the security at a specified price during a specified period.

Capital Asset: An asset with an economic life of greater than one year.

Capital Asset Pricing Model: The expected return on a security or real investment is equal to a risk-free interest rate (R_f) plus a market-risk premium ($R_m - R_f$) that is multiplied by the beta (β) of the security or asset.

Capital Market Theory: A body of financial theory dealing with valuation of assets under conditions of risk.

Capital Budgeting: Long-term planning for proposed capital outlays and their financing.

Capital Gain: Positive difference between the purchase price and sale price of an asset held for longer than twelve months.

Capital Loss: Negative difference between the purchase price and the sale price of an asset held for longer than twelve months.

Capital Market: Financial markets for the trading of long-term securities—i.e., those of maturities greater than one year.

Capital Structure: The interrelationships among the long-term sources of financing represented by debt and owners'-equity accounts.

Capitalization Rate: The rate of discount used to convert the revenue streams of an asset to its present value.

Carry-Back, Carry-Forward: Operating losses that can be carried back and forward to reduce income tax liability.

Cash Budget: A schedule of expected cash receipts and disbursements.

Cash Flow: The net effect of cash receipts and disbursements for a specified period. Calculated as the earnings after taxes of a firm, plus charges for depreciation, depletion, and amortization.

CBOE: Chicago Board Options Exchange, an institution created to provide a market for put and call options.

Certificate of Deposit: Money-market instrument that is evidence of short-term debt issued by a commercial bank to a depositor of funds.

Cleanup: A provision in bank lines of credit that requires the borrower to be out of debt to the bank at least once a year.

Coefficient of Variation: The standard deviation of a distribution, divided by its mean.

Commercial Paper: Unsecured short-term notes of large, financially-strong corporations. Commercial paper is a money-market instrument.

Compounding: The process of adding the accrued value to the base for subsequent calculations. The result is an exponential function as opposed to a linear one.

Consol: A bond with no maturity; i.e., an income stream into perpetuity. So called because they were issued by the British government to consolidate its Napoleonic Wars debt.

Convertible preferred: Preferred stock that may be converted to common stock at the option of the owner.

Convertibles: Securities, usually bonds or preferred stock, that are convertible into other securities at the option of the holder.

Cost of Capital: An index rate of the firm's capital costs, usually calculated for use in the capital budgeting process (See *Required Rate* of *Return*).

Coupon Bonds: Bear bonds with coupons attached for payment of periodic interest.

Coupon Rate: The rate of return specified on a bond as a percentage of its par value.

Covariance: The variance of a security's returns multiplied by the variance of the market returns.

Current Ratio: Ratio of current assets to current liabilities.

Dealer: In the securities market, one who acts for his own account rather than as an agent for another.

Debentures: Bonds secured by the good credit of the issuer instead of by specific property; unsecured bond.

Debt Ratio: Total debt divided by total assets. This ratio is sometimes called the leverage ratio.

Debt Service: The interest and charges currently due on a debt, including principal payments.

Depreciation: The consumption of capital stock in the productive process.

Direct Placement: The placement of an entire new issue of securities into the hands of a single investor as the result of negotiations.

Discount Rate: The rate used in the discounting process or in other present-value calculations.

Discounting: The process of finding the value today (present value) from a sum in the future (single payment) or a series of sums (equal payments) in the future.

Dividend Yield: The dividend per share of a security divided by the current market price.

DuPont System: A method of calculating return on investment (ROI). It is calculated by multiplying asset turnover (Sales/Total Assets) by profit margin (Earnings after Taxes/Sales).

Earnings Multiple: The price–earnings ratio; i.e., price per share divided by earnings per share.

Earnings Per Share (EPS): Earnings after taxes divided by number of shares of common stock outstanding.

Earnings Statement: The accounting statement that nets all costs against revenues to arrive at net earnings, earnings after taxes.

EBIT: Earnings before interest and taxes; operating profit.

Economic Investment: Spending by business firms on new job-creating and income-producing goods.

Economic Order Quantity (EOQ): The optimum quantity of inventory to be held considering order costs and holding costs.

Efficient Frontier: The combination of securities that minimizes the variance of a portfolio of securities.

Efficient-Market Hypothesis (EMH): The body of financial theory that explores the relationship between market efficiency and market volume.

Ex Rights: Without *rights*. When a stock trades "ex-rights," it means that the rights have been retained or exercised by the seller.

Exercise Price: The price at which holders of warrants can purchase the number of shares on which they have an option.

Face Value: Nominal value of a security. Same as par value.

Factoring: The sale of accounts receivable to a financial institution (the factor) specializing in the practice.

Federal Funds: Reserves of member banks on deposit at Federal Reserve banks. Federal funds are the subject of money-market trading and the best day-to-day indication of interest rates.

Financial Investment: The purchase of financial claims on business firms and government units.

Financial Leverage: The magnification of returns to common shareholders through the use of debt. See *Debt Ratio.*

Flotation Costs: The costs of marketing new securities from the issuer to the ultimate investor.

Foreign Exchange Market: The market for foreign currencies and bank deposits denominated in foreign currencies.

Funds: Increases in asset values of the firm.

"Going Public": A term used to describe the first offering of a firm's common stock for purchase by the public.

Going-Concern Value: The value of a firm derived from the earning power of its assets.

Gordon Model: Valuation model that accounts for the value of the firm by discounting the net earnings into perpetuity.

Income Bonds: Corporate or municipal bonds whose interest is due and payable only if it is earned by the capital project that the proceeds of the bond financed.

Incremental Cost of Capital: The cost of the last unit of capital added.

Indenture: The formal agreement between bond issuers and bond purchasers.

Interest Factor: Value found in the body of compound interest and annuity tables.

Internal Rate of Return (IRR): The rate of discount that equates the cash outlay of a capital project with the present value of its net inflows.

Investment Banker: A securities dealer that engages in the process of distribution of new securities.

Investment Banking: The underwriting of new corporate securities and sale of them to individual buyers.

Investment Tax Credit: The provision that permits the reduction of a firm's taxes in an amount up to 10 percent of a newly acquired asset. Its purpose is to stimulate economic activity.

Lambda (λ): The slope of the market line (i.e., $E(R_m) - R_f/\text{Var}_m$) in the second version of the capital asset pricing model.

Listed Securities: Securities listed for trading on one of the organized exchanges.

Making a Market: The activities of securities dealers in standing by ready, willing, and able to buy or sell securities.

Margin: The amount of cash deposited by an investor with his broker to finance part of the cost of purchasing "listed" securities. The broker loans funds for the balance of the punchase.

Margin Requirement: The percentage of the purchase price of listed securities that must be paid for in cash.

Marginal Cost of Capital: The change in the total cost of capital as the result of adding one unit of capital.

Market Order: An order to a securities broker to buy (or sell) securities at the prevailing price in the marketplace.

Money Market: Financial markets for the trading of short-term debt instruments such as Treasury bills, commercial paper, and certificates of deposit.

NASD: National Association of Securities Dealers.

Net Present Value (*NPV*): A capital budgeting analytical technique. The net present value is the difference between the cash outlay of a project and the present value of the project's revenues, discounted at the cost of capital.

Net Worth: The difference between that which an individual owns or has due to him, and that which he owes others. Net worth is on a market-value basis.

NYSE: New York Stock Exchange.

Odd Lot: A number of shares that is less than the accepted trading unit (usually 100 shares).

Open Order: An order to buy or sell in the securities market at a stipulated price.

Option Writing: The process of selling call options against common stock owned.

Over-The-Counter Market: Securities markets in which trading is between dealers and members of the investing public.

Owners' Equity: The contributed capital (i.e., capital stock and capital surplus), retained earnings, and any reserves for capital expansion. Owners' equity is on a book-value basis.

Par Value: The face value of a security specified by its issuer.

Payback Period: A capital budgeting technique. The payback period is the period of time required to recover the cash outlay of a project.

Payout Ratio: Dividends per share divided by earnings per share; i.e., the percentage of earnings paid out in dividends.

Perpetuity: An income stream of equal payments (annuity) that continues forever.

Portfolio: A combination of assets (securities or real assets) held for income or depreciation purposes.

Present Value: The value at present of future payment(s) discounted at an appropriate rate.

Price-earnings Ratio (P/E): Ratio of market price per share of stock to earnings per share. The P/E is the cost of $1 of earnings.

Primary Market: The market in which new security issues are sold.

Prime Rate: The lowest rate of interest commercial banks charge large, financially-strong corporations.

Pro Forma Statement: A financial statement that is projected from a current statement to a future period based on a series of events (i.e., cash budget).

Profitability Index: The ratio of the present value of the returns on an asset to the cost of the asset.

Prospectus: A document issued to describe a new securities issue.

Proxy: A document that gives one party the authority or power to act for another.

Put: An option to sell a security at a specific price during a given period.

Quick Ratio: Current assets minus inventory and prepaid items, divided by current liabilities. It is a measure of liquidity.

Random-Walk Hypothesis (RWH): The hypothesis that the direction of successive price changes of securities is random (and therefore not predictable).

Refunding: The process of retiring one securities issue with the proceeds of another securities issue.

Required Rate of Return: Rate of return that suppliers of funds in the financial markets expect to receive for the use of their funds.

Retained Earnings: The residue of a firm's earnings after dividends have been paid.

Right: A short-term option to buy a specific number of shares of common stock at a specified "subscription" price.

Risk: The variability of expected returns.

Risk, Business: The risk that a firm's earnings may change, which will affect a company's ability to pay interest and dividends.

Risk, Interest-Rate: The risk that interest rates may change, which will affect the market value of securities.

Risk, Market: A change in "market psychology" that causes the price of a security to change regardless of any fundamental change in earnings.

Risk Premium: The difference between the expected return on a risky asset and the return on a risk-free asset.

Risk, Purchasing-Power: The risk that price levels may change, which will affect the market value of securities.

"Rule of 78": An approximate method for calculating the finance-charge refund due the borrower of a loan who elects to pay the loan before it is due. 78 is the sum of the months' digits in one year (i.e., $1/2(12)(12) + 1/2(12) = 78$).

"Rule of 72": An approximate method for determining when a principal will double, based on interest rate or number of years. If either the interest rate or number of years is known, divide into 72 to obtain the answer (i.e., $72/6$ percent $= 12$ years).

Saving: The process of not consuming income.

SBA: Small Business Administration.

Secondary Market: The market in which trading occurs in securities already issued.

Short sale: The sale of securities not owned. Delivery is made by borrowing securities from the broker.

Sinking fund: Periodic payments into a fund that will be used to liquidate an obligation.

Spread: The difference between the retail and wholesale interest rates, or prices of securities.

Statement of Financial Position: The accounting statement that lists the firm's assets and debt and equity claims against them; the balance sheet.

Striking Price: The price at which buyers of call options can purchase the number of shares on which they have an option; buyers of put options can sell the number of shares on which they have an option.

Subchapter S Corporations: Corporations that qualify under Subchapter S of the Internal Revenue Code to be taxed as groups of individuals rather than as corporations.

Subscription Price: The price at which securities in a rights offering may be purchased.

Times Interest Earned (TIE): A measure of financial leverage. It is calculated by adding the total-interest figure to earnings before interest and taxes (EBIT), and dividing the sum by the total-interest figure.

Treasury Bill: A 90 day obligation of the U.S. Treasury. It is a key instrument in the money market.

Underwriting: The process by which new issues of securities are marketed.

Underwriting Syndicate: The temporary partnership of securities dealers formed to market a new securities issue.

Valuation: The process of assigning dollar values to assets.

Variance: The square of the standard deviation.

Warrant: A long-term option to buy a specific number of shares of common stock at a specified "exercise" price.

Weighted Average Cost of Capital (WACC): The average cost of components of the capital structure, weighted by their relative importance in the capital structure.

Working capital: The difference between a firm's current assets and current liabilities. In other words, the portion of current assets that is funded with permanent financing.

Yield Curve: A graph of the relationship between yields and maturities of fixed-return securities at a particular point in time.

Yield to Maturity: The internal rate of return on long-term bonds.

Time-Value Tables
A1, A2, A3, A4

TABLE A.1 Future Value of $1 (Single Payment) : $(1 + i)^n$

PERIOD	1%	2%	3%	4%	5%	6%	7%
0	1.000	1.000	1.000	1.000	1.000	1.000	1.000
1	1.010	1.020	1.030	1.040	1.050	1.060	1.070
2	1.020	1.040	1.061	1.082	1.102	1.124	1.145
3	1.030	1.061	1.093	1.125	1.158	1.191	1.225
4	1.041	1.082	1.126	1.170	1.216	1.262	1.311
5	1.051	1.104	1.159	1.217	1.276	1.338	1.403
6	1.062	1.126	1.194	1.265	1.340	1.419	1.501
7	1.072	1.149	1.230	1.316	1.407	1.504	1.606
8	1.083	1.172	1.267	1.369	1.477	1.594	1.718
9	1.094	1.195	1.305	1.423	1.551	1.689	1.838
10	1.105	1.219	1.344	1.480	1.629	1.791	1.967
11	1.116	1.243	1.384	1.539	1.710	1.898	2.105
12	1.127	1.268	1.426	1.601	1.796	2.012	2.252
13	1.138	1.294	1.469	1.665	1.886	2.133	2.410
14	1.149	1.319	1.513	1.732	1.980	2.261	2.579
15	1.161	1.346	1.558	1.801	2.079	2.397	2.759
16	1.173	1.373	1.605	1.873	2.183	2.540	2.952
17	1.184	1.400	1.653	1.948	2.292	2.693	3.159
18	1.196	1.428	1.702	2.026	2.407	2.854	3.380
19	1.208	1.457	1.754	2.107	2.527	3.026	3.617
20	1.220	1.486	1.806	2.191	2.653	3.207	3.870
25	1.282	1.641	2.094	2.666	3.386	4.292	5.427
30	1.348	1.811	2.427	3.243	4.322	5.743	7.612

PERIOD	8%	9%	10%	12%	14%	15%	16%
0	1.000	1.000	1.000	1.000	1.000	1.000	1.000
1	1.080	1.090	1.100	1.120	1.140	1.150	1.160
2	1.166	1.188	1.210	1.254	1.300	1.322	1.346
3	1.260	1.295	1.331	1.405	1.482	1.521	1.561
4	1.360	1.412	1.464	1.574	1.689	1.749	1.811
5	1.469	1.539	1.611	1.762	1.925	2.011	2.100
6	1.587	1.677	1.772	1.974	2.195	2.313	2.436
7	1.714	1.828	1.949	2.211	2.502	2.660	2.826
8	1.851	1.993	2.144	2.476	2.853	3.059	3.278
9	1.999	2.172	2.358	2.773	3.252	3.518	3.803
10	2.159	2.367	2.594	3.106	3.707	4.046	4.411
11	2.332	2.580	2.853	3.479	4.226	4.652	5.117
12	2.518	2.813	3.138	3.896	4.818	5.350	5.936
13	2.720	3.066	3.452	4.363	5.492	6.153	6.886
14	2.937	3.342	3.797	4.887	6.261	7.076	7.988
15	3.172	3.642	4.177	5.474	7.138	8.137	9.266
16	3.426	3.970	4.595	6.130	8.137	9.358	10.748
17	3.700	4.328	5.054	6.866	9.276	10.761	12.468
18	3.996	4.717	5.560	7.690	10.575	12.375	14.463
19	4.316	5.142	6.116	8.613	12.056	14.232	16.777
20	4.661	5.604	6.728	9.646	13.743	16.367	19.461
25	6.843	8.623	10.835	17.000	26.462	32.919	40.874
30	10.063	13.268	17.449	29.960	50.950	66.212	85.850

TABLE A.1 (*Concluded*)

PERIOD	18%	20%	24%	28%	32%	36%
0	1.000	1.000	1.000	1.000	1.000	1.000
1	1.180	1.200	1.240	1.280	1.320	1.360
2	1.392	1.440	1.538	1.638	1.742	1.850
3	1.643	1.728	1.907	2.067	2.300	2.515
4	1.939	2.074	2.364	2.684	3.036	3.421
5	2.288	2.488	2.932	3.436	4.007	4.653
6	2.700	2.986	3.635	4.398	5.290	6.328
7	3.185	3.583	4.508	5.629	6.983	8.605
8	3.759	4.300	5.590	7.206	9.217	11.703
9	4.435	5.160	6.931	9.223	12.166	15.917
10	5.234	6.192	8.594	11.806	16.060	21.647
11	6.176	7.430	10.657	15.112	21.199	29.439
12	7.288	8.916	13.215	19.343	27.983	40.037
13	8.599	10.699	16.386	24.759	36.937	54.451
14	10.147	12.839	20.319	31.691	48.757	74.053
15	11.974	15.407	25.196	40.565	64.359	100.712
16	14.129	18.488	31.243	51.923	84.954	136.97
17	16.672	22.186	38.741	66.461	112.14	186.28
18	19.673	26.623	48.039	85.071	148.02	253.34
19	23.214	31.948	59.568	108.89	195.39	344.54
20	27.393	38.338	73.864	139.38	257.92	468.57
25	62.669	95.396	216.542	478.90	1033.6	2180.1
30	143.371	237.376	634.820	1645.5	4142.1	10143.

PERIOD	40%	50%	60%	70%	80%	90%
0	1.000	1.000	1.000	1.000	1.000	1.000
1	1.400	1.500	1.600	1.700	1.800	1.900
2	1.960	2.250	2.560	2.890	3.240	3.610
3	2.744	3.375	4.096	4.913	5.832	6.859
4	3.842	5.062	6.544	8.352	10.498	13.032
5	5.378	7.594	10.486	14.199	18.896	24.761
6	7.530	11.391	16.777	24.138	34.012	47.046
7	10.541	17.086	26.844	41.034	61.222	89.387
8	14.758	25.629	42.950	69.758	110.200	169.836
9	20.661	38.443	68.720	118.588	198.359	322.688
10	28.925	57.665	109.951	201.599	357.047	613.107
11	40.496	86.498	175.922	342.719	642.684	1164.902
12	56.694	129.746	281.475	582.622	1156.831	2213.314
13	79.372	194.619	450.360	990.457	2082.295	4205.297
14	111.120	291.929	720.576	1683.777	3748.131	7990.065
15	155.568	437.894	1152.921	2862.421	6746.636	15181.122
16	217.795	656.84	1844.7	4866.1	12144.	28844.0
17	304.914	985.26	2951.5	8272.4	21859.	54804.0
18	426.879	1477.9	4722.4	14083.0	39346.	104130.0
19	597.630	2216.8	7555.8	23907.0	70824.	197840.0
20	836.683	3325.3	12089.0	40642.0	127480.	375900.0
25	4499.880	25251.	126760.0	577060.0	2408900.	9307600.0
30	24201.432	191750.	1329200.	8193500.0	45517000.	230470000.0

TABLE A.2 Present Value of $1 (Single Payment): $\left[\dfrac{1}{(1+i)^n}\right]$

PERIOD	1%	2%	3%	4%	5%	6%	7%	8%	9%	10%	12%	14%	15%
1	.990	.980	.971	.962	.952	.943	.935	.926	.917	.909	.893	.877	.870
2	.980	.961	.943	.925	.907	.890	.873	.857	.842	.826	.797	.769	.756
3	.971	.942	.915	.889	.864	.840	.816	.794	.772	.751	.712	.675	.658
4	.961	.924	.889	.855	.823	.792	.763	.735	.708	.683	.636	.592	.572
5	.951	.906	.863	.822	.784	.747	.713	.681	.650	.621	.567	.519	.497
6	.942	.888	.838	.790	.746	.705	.666	.630	.596	.564	.507	.456	.432
7	.933	.871	.813	.760	.711	.665	.623	.583	.547	.513	.452	.400	.376
8	.923	.853	.789	.731	.677	.627	.582	.540	.502	.467	.404	.351	.327
9	.914	.837	.766	.703	.645	.592	.544	.500	.460	.424	.361	.308	.284
10	.905	.820	.744	.676	.614	.558	.508	.463	.422	.386	.322	.270	.247
11	.896	.804	.722	.650	.585	.527	.475	.429	.388	.350	.287	.237	.215
12	.887	.788	.701	.625	.557	.497	.444	.397	.356	.319	.257	.208	.187
13	.879	.773	.681	.601	.530	.469	.415	.368	.326	.290	.229	.182	.163
14	.870	.758	.661	.577	.505	.442	.388	.340	.299	.263	.205	.160	.141
15	.861	.743	.642	.555	.481	.417	.362	.315	.275	.239	.183	.140	.123
16	.853	.728	.623	.534	.458	.394	.339	.292	.252	.218	.163	.123	.107
17	.844	.714	.605	.513	.436	.371	.317	.270	.231	.198	.146	.108	.093
18	.836	.700	.587	.494	.416	.350	.296	.250	.212	.180	.130	.095	.081
19	.828	.686	.570	.475	.396	.331	.276	.232	.194	.164	.116	.083	.070
20	.820	.673	.554	.456	.377	.312	.258	.215	.178	.149	.104	.073	.061
25	.780	.610	.478	.375	.295	.233	.184	.146	.116	.092	.059	.038	.030
30	.742	.552	.412	.308	.231	.174	.131	.099	.075	.057	.033	.020	.015

PERIOD	16%	18%	20%	24%	28%	32%	36%	40%	50%	60%	70%	80%	90%
1	.862	.847	.833	.806	.781	.758	.735	.714	.667	.625	.588	.556	.526
2	.743	.718	.694	.650	.610	.574	.541	.510	.444	.391	.346	.309	.277
3	.641	.609	.579	.524	.477	.435	.398	.364	.296	.244	.204	.171	.146
4	.552	.516	.482	.423	.373	.329	.292	.260	.198	.153	.120	.095	.077
5	.476	.437	.402	.341	.291	.250	.215	.186	.132	.095	.070	.053	.040
6	.410	.370	.335	.275	.227	.189	.158	.133	.088	.060	.041	.029	.021
7	.354	.314	.279	.222	.178	.143	.116	.095	.059	.037	.024	.016	.011
8	.305	.266	.233	.179	.139	.108	.085	.068	.039	.023	.014	.009	.006
9	.263	.226	.194	.144	.108	.082	.063	.048	.026	.015	.008	.005	.003
10	.227	.191	.162	.116	.085	.062	.046	.035	.017	.009	.005	.003	.002
11	.195	.162	.135	.094	.066	.047	.034	.025	.012	.006	.003	.002	.001
12	.168	.137	.112	.076	.052	.036	.025	.018	.008	.004	.002	.001	.001
13	.145	.116	.093	.061	.040	.027	.018	.013	.005	.002	.001	.001	.000
14	.125	.099	.078	.049	.032	.021	.014	.009	.003	.001	.001	.000	.000
15	.108	.084	.065	.040	.025	.016	.010	.006	.002	.001	.000	.000	.000
16	.093	.071	.054	.032	.019	.012	.007	.005	.002	.001	.000	.000	
17	.080	.060	.045	.026	.015	.009	.005	.003	.001	.000	.000		
18	.069	.051	.038	.021	.012	.007	.004	.002	.001	.000	.000		
19	.060	.043	.031	.017	.009	.005	.003	.002	.000	.000			
20	.051	.037	.026	.014	.007	.004	.002	.001	.000	.000			
25	.024	.016	.010	.005	.002	.001	.000	.000					
30	.012	.007	.004	.002	.001	.000	.000						

can extend this table up to 60 yrs

TABLE A.3 Future Value of an Annuity of $1 for N Periods: $\left[\dfrac{(1 + i)^n - 1}{i}\right]$

PERIOD	1%	2%	3%	4%	5%	6%
1	1.000	1.000	1.000	1.000	1.000	1.000
2	2.010	2.020	2.030	2.040	2.050	2.060
3	3.030	3.060	3.091	3.122	3.152	3.184
4	4.060	4.122	4.184	4.246	4.310	4.375
5	5.101	5.204	5.309	5.416	5.526	5.637
6	6.152	6.308	6.468	6.633	6.802	6.975
7	7.214	7.434	7.662	7.898	8.142	8.394
8	8.286	8.583	8.892	9.214	9.549	9.897
9	9.369	9.755	10.159	10.583	11.027	11.491
10	10.462	10.950	11.464	12.006	12.578	13.181
11	11.567	12.169	12.808	13.486	14.207	14.972
12	12.683	13.412	14.192	15.026	15.917	16.870
13	13.809	14.680	15.618	16.627	17.713	18.882
14	14.947	15.974	17.086	18.292	19.599	21.051
15	16.097	17.293	18.599	20.024	21.579	23.276
16	17.258	18.639	20.157	21.825	23.657	25.673
17	18.430	20.012	21.762	23.698	25.840	28.213
18	19.615	21.412	23.414	25.645	28.132	30.906
19	20.811	22.841	25.117	27.671	30.539	33.760
20	22.019	24.297	26.870	29.778	33.066	36.786
25	23.243	32.030	36.459	41.646	47.727	54.865
30	34.785	40.568	47.575	56.085	66.439	79.058

PERIOD	7%	8%	9%	10%	12%	14%
1	1.000	1.000	1.000	1.000	1.000	1.000
2	2.070	2.080	2.090	2.100	2.120	2.140
3	3.215	3.246	3.278	3.310	3.374	3.440
4	4.440	4.506	4.573	4.641	4.770	4.921
5	5.751	5.867	5.985	6.105	6.353	6.610
6	7.153	7.336	7.523	7.716	8.115	8.536
7	8.654	8.923	9.200	9.487	10.089	10.730
8	10.260	10.637	11.028	11.436	12.300	13.233
9	11.978	12.488	13.021	13.579	14.776	16.085
10	13.816	14.487	15.193	15.937	17.549	19.337
11	15.784	16.645	17.560	18.531	20.655	23.044
12	17.888	18.977	20.141	21.384	24.133	27.271
13	20.141	21.495	22.953	24.523	28.029	32.089
14	22.550	24.215	26.019	27.975	32.393	37.581
15	25.129	27.152	29.361	31.772	37.280	43.842
16	27.888	30.324	33.003	35.950	42.753	50.980
17	30.840	33.750	36.974	40.545	48.884	59.118
18	33.999	37.450	41.301	45.599	55.750	68.394
19	37.379	41.446	48.018	51.159	63.440	78.969
20	40.995	45.762	51.160	57.275	72.052	91.025
25	63.249	73.106	84.701	98.347	133.334	181.871
30	94.461	113.283	136.308	164.494	241.333	356.787

40 $\dfrac{\Sigma R^2 - (ER)^2}{n}$ = variance

$\sqrt{\text{variance}}$ = SD

coefficient $\dfrac{SD}{ER}$

TABLE A.3 (*Concluded*)

PERIOD	16%	18%	20%	24%	28%	32%
1	1.000	1.000	1.000	1.000	1.000	1.000
2	2.160	2.180	2.200	2.240	2.280	2.320
3	3.506	3.572	3.640	3.778	3.918	4.062
4	5.066	5.215	5.368	5.684	6.016	6.362
5	6.877	7.154	7.442	8.048	8.700	9.398
6	8.977	9.442	9.930	10.980	12.136	13.406
7	11.414	12.142	12.916	14.615	16.534	18.696
8	14.240	15.327	16.499	19.123	22.163	25.678
9	17.518	19.086	20.799	24.712	29.369	34.895
10	21.321	23.521	25.959	31.643	38.592	47.062
11	25.733	28.755	32.150	40.238	50.399	63.122
12	30.850	34.931	39.580	50.985	65.510	84.320
13	36.786	42.219	48.497	64.110	84.853	112.303
14	43.672	50.818	59.196	80.496	109.612	149.240
15	51.660	60.965	72.035	100.815	141.303	197.997
16	60.925	72.939	87.442	126.011	181.87	262.36
17	71.673	87.068	105.931	157.253	233.79	347.31
18	84.141	103.740	128.117	195.994	300.25	459.45
19	98.603	123.414	154.740	244.033	385.32	607.47
20	115.380	146.628	186.688	303.601	494.21	802.86
25	249.214	342.603	471.981	898.092	1706.8	3226.8
30	530.312	790.948	1181.882	2640.916	5873.2	12941.0

PERIOD	36%	40%	50%	60%	70%	80%
1	1.000	1.000	1.000	1.000	1.000	1.000
2	2.360	2.400	2.500	2.600	2.700	2.800
3	4.210	4.360	4.750	5.160	5.590	6.040
4	6.725	7.104	8.125	9.256	10.503	11.872
5	10.146	10.846	13.188	15.810	18.855	22.370
6	14.799	16.324	20.781	26.295	33.054	41.265
7	21.126	23.853	32.172	43.073	57.191	75.278
8	29.732	34.395	49.258	69.916	98.225	136.500
9	41.435	49.153	74.887	112.866	167.983	246.699
10	57.352	69.814	113.330	181.585	286.570	445.058
11	78.998	98.739	170.995	291.536	488.170	802.105
12	108.437	139.235	257.493	467.458	830.888	1444.788
13	148.475	195.929	387.239	748.933	1413.510	2601.619
14	202.926	275.300	581.859	1199.293	2403.968	4683.914
15	276.979	386.420	873.788	1919.869	4087.745	8432.045
16	377.69	541.99	1311.7	3072.8	6950.2	15179.0
17	514.66	759.78	1968.5	4917.5	11816.0	27323.0
18	700.94	1064.7	2953.8	7868.9	20089.0	49182.0
19	954.28	1491.6	4431.7	12591.0	34152.0	88528.0
20	1298.8	2089.2	6648.5	20147.0	58059.0	159350.0
25	6053.0	11247.0	50500.0	211270.0	824370.0	3011100.0
30	28172.0	60501.0	383500.0	2215400.0	11705000.0	56896000.0

TABLE A.4 Present Value of an Annuity of \$1 : $\left[\dfrac{1 - \dfrac{1}{(1 + i)^n}}{i}\right]$

PERIOD	1%	2%	3%	4%	5%	6%	7%	8%	9%	10%
1	0.990	0.980	0.971	0.962	0.952	0.943	0.935	0.926	0.917	0.909
2	1.970	1.942	1.913	1.886	1.859	1.833	1.808	1.783	1.759	1.736
3	2.941	2.884	2.829	2.775	2.723	2.673	2.624	2.577	2.531	2.487
4	3.902	3.808	3.717	3.630	3.546	3.465	3.387	3.312	3.240	3.170
5	4.853	4.713	4.580	4.452	4.329	4.212	4.100	3.993	3.890	3.791
6	5.795	5.601	5.417	5.242	5.076	4.917	4.766	4.623	4.486	4.355
7	6.728	6.472	6.230	6.002	5.786	5.582	5.389	5.206	5.033	4.868
8	7.652	7.325	7.020	6.733	6.463	6.210	5.971	5.747	5.535	5.335
9	8.566	8.162	7.786	7.435	7.108	6.802	6.515	6.247	5.985	5.759
10	9.471	8.983	8.530	8.111	7.722	7.360	7.024	6.710	6.418	6.145
11	10.368	9.787	9.253	8.760	8.306	7.887	7.499	7.139	6.805	6.495
12	11.255	10.575	9.954	9.385	8.863	8.384	7.943	7.536	7.161	6.814
13	12.134	11.348	10.635	9.986	9.394	8.853	8.358	7.904	7.487	7.103
14	13.004	12.106	11.296	10.563	9.899	9.295	8.745	8.244	7.786	7.367
15	13.865	12.849	11.938	11.118	10.380	9.712	9.108	8.559	8.060	7.606
16	14.718	13.578	12.561	11.652	10.838	10.106	9.447	8.851	8.312	7.824
17	15.562	14.292	13.166	12.166	11.274	10.477	9.763	9.122	8.544	8.022
18	16.398	14.992	13.754	12.659	11.690	10.828	10.059	9.372	8.756	8.201
19	17.226	15.678	14.324	13.134	12.085	11.158	10.336	9.604	8.950	8.365
20	18.046	16.351	14.877	13.590	12.462	11.470	10.594	9.818	9.128	8.514
25	22.023	19.523	17.413	15.622	14.094	12.783	11.654	10.675	9.823	9.077
30	25.808	22.397	19.600	17.292	15.373	13.765	12.409	11.258	10.274	9.427

PERIOD	12%	14%	16%	18%	20%	24%	28%	32%	36%
1	0.893	0.877	0.862	0.847	0.833	0.806	0.781	0.758	0.735
2	1.690	1.647	1.605	1.566	1.528	1.457	1.392	1.332	1.276
3	2.402	2.322	2.246	2.174	2.106	1.981	1.868	1.766	1.674
4	3.037	2.914	2.798	2.690	2.589	2.404	2.241	2.096	1.966
5	3.605	3.433	3.274	3.127	2.991	2.745	2.532	2.345	2.181
6	4.111	3.889	3.685	3.498	3.326	3.020	2.759	2.534	2.339
7	4.564	4.288	4.039	3.812	3.605	3.242	2.937	2.678	2.455
8	4.968	4.639	4.344	4.078	3.837	3.421	3.076	2.786	2.540
9	5.328	4.946	4.607	4.303	4.031	3.566	3.184	2.868	2.603
10	5.650	5.216	4.833	4.494	4.193	3.682	3.269	2.930	2.650
11	5.988	5.453	5.029	4.656	4.327	3.776	3.335	2.978	2.683
12	6.194	5.660	5.197	4.793	4.439	3.851	3.387	3.013	2.708
13	6.424	5.842	5.342	4.910	4.533	3.912	3.427	3.040	2.727
14	6.628	6.002	5.468	5.008	4.611	3.962	3.459	3.061	2.740
15	6.811	6.142	5.575	5.092	4.675	4.001	3.483	3.076	2.750
16	6.974	6.265	5.669	5.162	4.730	4.033	3.503	3.088	2.758
17	7.120	6.373	5.749	5.222	4.775	4.059	3.518	3.097	2.763
18	7.250	6.467	5.818	5.273	4.812	4.080	3.529	3.104	2.767
19	7.366	6.550	5.877	5.316	4.844	4.097	3.539	3.109	2.770
20	7.469	6.623	5.929	5.353	4.870	4.110	3.546	3.113	2.772
25	7.843	6.873	6.097	5.467	4.948	4.147	3.564	3.122	2.776
30	8.055	7.003	6.177	5.517	4.979	4.160	3.569	3.124	2.778

$P/E = \dfrac{PPS}{EPS}$ $EPS = \dfrac{EAT}{shares}$ payout $= P/E \times$ yield

yield $= \dfrac{DPS}{PPS}$

$BP = \dfrac{CO}{CF} = IRR$ factor

B

Continuous-Compounding Table (e-value table)

TABLE B.1 Continuous Compounding of $1 ($e^x$) and Continuous Discounting of $1

$$(e^{-x}) : \lim_{m \to \infty} \left(1 + \frac{i}{m}\right)^{n(m)} \text{ or } e^{(i)(n)}$$

$V_n = Pe^{in}$

x	e^x VALUE	e^{-x} VALUE	x	e^x VALUE	e^{-x} VALUE	x	e^x VALUE	e^{-x} VALUE
0.00	1.0000	1.00000	0.45	1.5683	.63763	0.90	2.4596	.40657
0.01	1.0101	0.99005	0.46	1.5841	.63128	0.91	2.4843	.40252
0.02	1.0202	.98020	0.47	1.6000	.62500	0.92	2.5093	.39852
0.03	1.0305	.97045	0.48	1.6161	.61878	0.93	2.5345	.39455
0.04	1.0408	.96079	0.49	1.6323	.61263	0.94	2.5600	.39063
0.05	1.0513	.95123	0.50	1.6487	.60653	0.95	2.5857	.38674
0.06	1.0618	.94176	0.51	1.6653	.60050	0.96	2.6117	.38298
0.07	1.0725	.93239	0.52	1.6820	.59452	0.97	2.6379	.37908
0.08	1.0833	.92312	0.53	1.6989	.58860	0.98	2.6645	.37531
0.09	1.0942	.91393	0.54	1.7160	.58275	0.99	2.6912	.37158
0.10	1.1052	.90484	0.55	1.7333	.57695	1.00	2.7183	.36788
0.11	1.1163	.89583	0.56	1.7507	.57121	1.20	3.3201	.30119
0.12	1.1275	.88692	0.57	1.7683	.56553	1.30	3.6693	.27253
0.13	1.1388	.87809	0.58	1.7860	.55990	1.40	4.0552	.24660
0.14	1.1503	.86936	0.59	1.8040	.55433	1.50	4.4817	.22313
0.15	1.1618	.86071	0.60	1.8221	.54881	1.60	4.9530	.20190
0.16	1.1735	.85214	0.61	1.8404	.54335	1.70	5.4739	.18268
0.17	1.1853	.84366	0.62	1.8589	.53794	1.80	6.0496	.16530
0.18	1.1972	.83527	0.63	1.8776	.53259	1.90	6.6859	.14957
0.19	1.2092	.82696	0.64	1.8965	.52729	2.00	7.3891	.13534
0.20	1.2214	.81873	0.65	1.9155	.52205	3.00	20.086	.04979
0.21	1.2337	.81058	0.66	1.9348	.51685	4.00	54.598	.01832
0.22	1.2461	.80252	0.67	1.9542	.51171	5.00	148.41	.00674
0.23	1.2586	.79453	0.68	1.9739	.50662	6.00	403.43	.00248
0.24	1.2712	.78663	0.69	1.9937	.50158	7.00	1096.6	.00091
0.25	1.2840	.77880	0.70	2.0138	.49659	8.00	2981.0	.00034
0.26	1.2969	.77105	0.71	2.0340	.49164	9.00	8103.1	.00012
0.27	1.3100	.76338	0.72	2.0544	.48675	10.00	22026.5	.00005
0.28	1.3231	.75578	0.73	2.0751	.48191			
0.29	1.3364	.74826	0.74	2.0959	.47711			
0.30	1.3499	.74082	0.75	2.1170	.47237			
0.31	1.3634	.73345	0.76	2.1383	.46767			
0.32	1.3771	.72615	0.77	2.1598	.46301			
0.33	1.3910	.71892	0.78	2.1815	.45841			
0.34	1.4049	.71177	0.79	2.2034	.45384			
0.35	1.4191	.70469	0.80	2.2255	.44933			
0.36	1.4333	.69768	0.81	2.2479	.44486			
0.37	1.4477	.69073	0.82	2.2705	.44043			
0.38	1.4623	.68386	0.83	2.2933	.43605			
0.39	1.4770	.67707	0.84	2.3164	.43171			
0.40	1.4918	.67032	0.85	2.3396	.42741			
0.41	1.5068	.66365	0.86	2.3632	.42316			
0.42	1.5220	.65705	0.87	2.3869	.41895			
0.43	1.5373	.65051	0.88	2.4109	.41478			
0.44	1.5527	.64404	0.89	2.4351	.41066			

multiply factors to find intermediate values

Selected Solutions
to Problems

CHAPTER 2

1. $236,250 $217,100

2. a. $130,500, $82,500, $34,500,
      $82,500, $130,500, $82,500,
      $178,500, $418,500, $5,266,500,
      $82,500
   b. $0, $0, $0, $0, $0, $0, $0,
      418,500, $5,266,500, $82,500

3. a. First year's depreciation = $10,-
      000, $26,000, $16,650
   b. $32,100, $24,420, $28,908

4. Ordinary income method, $15,300
   Capital gains alternative, $14,400

5. $150,500

6. $1,436,13%

7. $765

8. $26,070, $20,620

9. $32,364

10. '72 $0, '73 $29,500, '74 $161,-
    500, '75   ($89,500)

CHAPTER 3

1. 12 years

2. a. 8%
   b. $2344.00

3. a. $2,300.19
   b. $15,000

4. a. $21,017.23
   b. $123,000

5. $20,097.14

6. 7.12%

7. $931.65

8. 7%

9. $20,944.60

10. a. $8,386.10
    b. $8,000

11. 17%

12. $5,355.47

13. $1,061.15

14. $1,498.75

15. $1,119.52

16. a. $29,220,20
    b. $190,400

17. 8,006

18. a. $40,275
    b. $74,690
    c. $50,000

19. a. $9,318.00

b. $9,621.00
c. $9,786.10
d. $9,901.06
e. $9,960.36

20. a. $849.53
   b. $875.48
   c. $1,000
   d. $1,226.25
   e. $1,000

21. a. 12%
   b. 7.5%
   c. 9%
   Alternative method:
   a. $9,168
   b. $4,158
   c. $8,310

22. a. 8.75 years
   b. $10,500

CHAPTER 4

1. a. $3,600, 1859, .516
      $70.60, 44.6, .632

2. a. $3,000, 379.47
      $1,000, 505.96

4. a. 2.78, .06

5. a. 9, 11.5
   b. 91.5 and 9.57, 445.25 and 21.1
   c. 1.06, 1.83

CHAPTER 7

1. a. 1.52
   b. .03
   c. 4.19
   d. 5.65
   e. .06
   f. 6.18
   g. .60
   h. $6.00
   i. .60

3. a. .07, .0175

5. $56,000
   64,000

CHAPTER 8

1. 10%

2. a. 8%
   b. 11.78%

3. a. $1,000,000
   b. $20,000

4. a. 2,000
   b. 1,000
   c. 1,200

5. 197,744

CHAPTER 9

1. a. 400

2. a. 1125
   b. 548

3. a. 37.9%
   b. 36.7%
   c. 50%

5. a. 489,898
   b. 12.24

CHAPTER 10

1. 7.3%

2. a. 14.8%
   b. 39.2%

3. a. 12.4%
   b. 29.1%

4. a. 11.1%
   b. 10%
   c. 18.5%

5. a. 18.4%
   b. 14.8%
   c. 13.6%

6. 14.2%

7. a. 1830
   b. $1310

8. 11.3%

9. a. 3,570
   b. $1177.76

10. a. 7,500
    b. 5,000

CHAPTER 11

1. $1,083.96

2. $914.60

3. a. $NPV_A = \$664.20$; $NPV_B = \$287.28$
   b. Project A
4. IRR $= 5\frac{3}{4}\%$ *11.73*
5. a.

	A	B	C
1. ARR	16.3%	23.3%	16.0%
2. PBP	6.1 yrs.	4.3 yrs.	6.2 yrs.
3. NPV	($453,538.40)	$193,097.60	($441,329.30)
4. IRR	10%	14%	8%

   b. Project B should be accepted
6. a. $15,000, $20,000
   b. $27,000
   c. ARR 27%
      PBP 3.7 yrs.
      NAV $65,915
      IRR 24%
8. Hot Dog Stand. Higher present value.

CHAPTER 12

1. 12.7%
2. b. optimum capital structure is 40/60
5. a. WACC alternative A $= 9.50\%$
      WACC alternative B $= 9.49\%$

CHAPTER 13

1. b.

	Before	After
Debt Ratio	.76	.83
TIE	6.00	4.17
ROE	.45	.59

2. Book Values, $8,000,000
   Capitalized Income at 9%, $19,-644,444
3. Total assets, $22,000,000
   Earnings after taxes, $2,378,727

CHAPTER 14

1. a. Retailer 9%; Gold miner 11.5%
   b. Retailer 91.5; Gold miner 445.25
   c. Retailer 9.56%; Gold miner 21.1%
   d. Retailer 1.06%; Gold miner 1.83%
3. a. $2,000
   b. $4,000
   c. $3,750
   d. $2,000
   e. $5,000
   f. $25,000
4. a. $10,000
   b. —0—
   c. $30,000
   d. $46.15
   e. $2,500
7. b. expected return .10; var. .0195; standard deviation .14

CHAPTER 15

1. a. 5%, 5 11/12 years
   b. $680
2. a. (1) $856.875
      (2) $1,011.875   (3) $1,065
      (4) $892.50
3. a. true
   b. (1) 14.3%   (2) 22.9%
4. a. 98.7125
   b. $9,871.25
5. "Flower" bond, $27,500
   Savings account, $13,520

CHAPTER 16

1. a. $849.54
   b. $875.37
   c. $1,000
2. a. 40
   b. $1,000 or 100%
   c. $30 or 150%
3. After-tax comparison:
   a. .063
   b. .065

Before-Tax comparison:
a. .09
b. .093

5. Probable range for each:
   a. 70-80%
   b. 2-6%
   c. 15-20%

9. a. 8% per annum
   b. $837.77

10. b. $120

CHAPTER 17

4. 1970—.60, 1971—.801, 1972—.60, 1973—1.20, 1974—1.44, 1975—1.60, 1976—2.00, 1977—2.50

5. a. .39
   b. 100
   c. 2

7. a. Return on common 26%
      Return on option 900%
   b. Low on common 52.6%
      Low on option 100%

8. a. $4
   b. $4.50

CHAPTER 18

1. Mon.—32, Tues.—165, Wed.—601, Thurs.—447, Fri. 119.

3. a. 26.5
   b. $132.50

4. $56.14

5. $83.33

6. a. $33.14
   b. $88.21

8. a. 12.9%
   b. 23.5%
   c. 15%
   d. 5.4%

e. 3.5%
f. 5%

10. a. 14.8%
    b. Sell
    c. 5.3%

CHAPTER 20

2. 10%

3. a. 10%
   b. $75

6. a. 1.25
   b. $66.67
   c. .075
   d. underpriced.

CHAPTER 21

3. .0864 or 8.64 per cent.

4. .0521 or 5.21 per cent.

5. The commercial paper option will be accepted since it has a return of 7.56 per cent versus the banker's acceptance return of only 6.05 per cent.

CHAPTER 25

3. a. Buy in London, sell in New York
   b. arbitrage

6. a. Exchange DM for pesos regardless of starting currency
   b. $124.13

Index